Conservative revolutionary

Manchester University Press

Conservative revolutionary

The lives of Lewis Namier

D. W. Hayton

Manchester University Press

Published by Manchester University Press
Altrincham Street, Manchester M1 7JA
www.manchesteruniversitypress.co.uk

British Library Cataloguing-in-Publication Data
A catalogue record for this book is available from the British Library

ISBN 978 0 7190 8603 8 hardback

First published 2019

Typeset by Servis Filmsetting Ltd, Stockport, Cheshire
Printed in Great Britain by Bell & Bain Ltd, Glasgow

In memory of
Keith John Jeffery (1952–2016)
and
John David Milner (1949–2016)

'Listen, Kolya, among other things, you are going to be very unhappy in life,' Alyosha said ... 'But even so, life on the whole you will bless.'

Dostoyevsky, *The Brothers Karamazov*

A man's fairest memorial is still his own portrait.

Goethe

Contents

Illustrations

Acknowledgements

I conceived the idea for this biography nearly twenty years ago while working through the archives of the History of Parliament Trust. I was engaged in writing the 'Introductory Survey' for the section of the History covering *The House of Commons 1690–1715* and was anxious to discover what the founding fathers envisaged as the purpose of the project, so that I could set my work along appropriate lines. What I found was a long and complicated story, at the root of which was the simple answer that there was no clear and agreed purpose. But in ploughing through the papers in the basement of the Trust's offices in Bloomsbury Square I came upon a treasure-trove of material relating to Namier, boxes of letters which had never been studied by anyone interested in his life and work. Since then I have examined scores of other manuscript collections, but have repeatedly returned to the *History*'s archive. It is only appropriate, therefore, that I begin this prolonged litany of thanks with an acknowledgment of the debt I owe to the History of Parliament Trust, its trustees and editorial board, and its current director, Dr Paul Seaward, not only for facilitating my research, but also for bearing with the publication of findings which may not always have been flattering to the public image of the *History*.

I owe an even greater debt to a previous editorial board, chaired by Dr Edward Miller, and including two close associates of Namier, Professor Ian Christie and Dame Lucy Sutherland, for giving me my first job, over forty years ago, and to Eddie Mullins, Paul Seaward's ultimate predecessor, for initiating me into what was in 1975 a decidedly peculiar organisation within the academic world. The shade of Namier presided over 34 Tavistock Square, where the *History* was then located, and a number of those with whom I worked had known Namier personally, some of them very well. Eveline Cruickshanks, who served as a research assistant on the section immediately preceding Namier's, has allowed me to interview her formally, as have three of Namier's surviving research students, Alan Hardy, Jean Spendlove and Peter Thomas, one of his last undergraduate pupils, Kenneth Hardman, and Stanley Katz, for whom Namier stood

Acknowledgements

as an informal supervisor in 1959–60 during Stanley's time in London as a Fulbright scholar. Joseph Fewster, who contributed to Namier's section of the *History*, and Vittorio Jucker, whose mother Ninetta was an early pupil and friend, also supplied me with their recollections. I very much regret that when I met the late John Brooke, who had been Namier's closest collaborator, I was very far from thinking I might write a biography of Sir Lewis. Professor John Cannon, who for a time worked alongside Namier and Brooke, had agreed to talk to me shortly before his sudden death in 2012 cut off the opportunity. However, I have since then interviewed Namier's secretary and research assistant, Mary Port (née Drummond), who worked with Namier, Brooke and Cannon, and whose memories are sharp and highly illuminating.

I have also enjoyed the privilege of corresponding with, and in some cases meeting, a number of Namier's surviving relations, notably his great-nephew Jarosław Kurski, and his first cousins once removed Andrzej Ehrlich (the son of his cousin Ludwik Ehrlich), Norman St Landau (grandson of his aunt Anka Landau), Hannah Selinger (daughter of his cousin Theo Frankel), and Jane Heyman (granddaughter of his aunt Stella Eliasberg). Jarosław and his wife Jolanta were splendidly hospitable hosts in Poland and, together with Andrzej, brought me to various locations connected with their family history.

Namier famously omitted to provide a bibliography to his books, explaining that 'There can be none for the life of a community.' Writing about an individual rather than a community, I have not been able to allow myself, or my publisher, that luxury, and thus I have an exceptionally large number of obligations to acknowledge.

The copyright in Namier's writings is vested in Balliol College, Oxford, and I must thank the Master and Fellows for permission to quote from them, as well as from material in the college archives. For permission to examine and to quote from other documentary sources, I am obliged to the marquess of Salisbury; the earl of Sandwich; Mr Adam Fergusson; Mrs Mary Port; Professor Peter Thomas; Miss Mary Clapinson (for the Sutherland and Kemp papers); Sir John Gilmour, Bt; Johnson and Alcock Ltd. (for the Rowse papers); Dr William Noblett (for the Plumb papers); the Lord Dacre of Granton Literary Estate (per Professor Blair Worden); the Trustees of the Sir Arthur Bryant Will Trust; Antrim and Newtownabbey Borough Council; the Board of Deputies of British Jews; the Board of Trustees, University of London; the British Broadcasting Corporation; the British Library Board; the Central Zionist Archives; the Clerk of the Records of Parliament; the Comptroller of Her Majesty's Stationery Office; the Deputy Keeper of the Records of Northern Ireland; the Director, Churchill Archives Centre; the Director of the Institute of Historical Research, London University; the Keeper of Manuscripts, Cambridge University Library; the Keeper of the Records of Scotland; the Keeper of Western Manuscripts,

Acknowledgements

Bodleian Library; the Lewis Walpole Library; the London School of Economics; Magdalen College, Oxford; Manuscripts and Archives, Yale University Library; the Mistress and Fellows, Girton College, Cambridge; the National Library of Wales; the Principal and Fellows, St Hugh's College, Oxford; Trinity College, Oxford; the Trustees of the History of Parliament Trust; the Trustees of the Liddell Hart Centre for Military Archives, King's College, London; the Trustees of the National Library of Scotland; Penguin Books Ltd (for the Hamish Hamilton archive); the Random House Group; the University Archivist, University of Reading; the University Librarian and Director, the John Rylands University Library, University of Manchester; the University of Toronto Library; and the Wiener Library.

Grateful thanks are also due to the earl of Sandwich and Mr Adam Fergusson, for their hospitality while I was consulting their family papers, and to the host of librarians and archivists who have made research for this book so much easier than I expected it to be: Brian Keough at Special Collections and Archives, University at Albany, SUNY; Penelope Bulloch and Anna Sander at Balliol College, Oxford; Matthew Chipping at the BBC Written Archives Centre; Ellen Doon, Moira Fitzgerald and Graham Sherriff at the Beinecke Library, Yale; Ilaria Della Monica at the Biblioteca Berenson, Villa I Tatti; Colin Harris at the Department of Western Manuscripts, Bodleian Library; Frank Bowles and Bill Noblett at Cambridge University Library; Rochelle Rubinstein at the Central Zionist Archives; Christine Colburn, Diana Harper and Amy Ridgeway at the Special Collections Research Center, University of Chicago Library; Judith Curthoys at Christ Church, Oxford; Sophie Bridges and Caroline Herbert at the Churchill Archive Centre, Churchill College, Cambridge; Sarah Wilcock at Culture Perth and Kinross; Andrew Lusted at East Sussex Record Office; Sue Inskip and Angela Mandrioli at Special Collections, Exeter University Library; Virginia Lewick at the Franklin D. Roosevelt Presidential Library; Lisette Matano at Georgetown University Library; Hannah Westall and Joan Bullock-Anderson at Girton College, Cambridge; Robin Harcourt-Williams at Hatfield House; Paul Seaward and Jenny Johnson at the History of Parliament; Carol Leadenham at the Hoover Institution Archives; Micah Hoggatt at the Houghton Library, Harvard University; Stephen Platt and Rebecca White at the House of St Gregory and St Macrina, Oxford; Ellen Parton at the Imperial War Museum; Lorraine Coughlan at the John Rylands University Library of Manchester; Margaret K. Powell, Mary Ellen Budney and Susan Walker at the Lewis Walpole Library; Sue Donnelly at the London School of Economics; Robin Darwall-Smith at Magdalen College, Oxford; James Peters at Manchester University archives; Sabina Beauchard at the Massachusetts Historical Society; Maria Castrillo at the National Library of Scotland; David Brown and Tristram Clarke at the National Records of Scotland; Alison Rosie

Acknowledgements

and Tessa Spencer at the National Register of Archives (Scotland); Simon Bailey at the Oxford University Archives; Jayne Hutchinson and Ian Montgomery at the Public Record Office of Northern Ireland; Ursula Mitchel at the McClay Library, Queen's University Belfast; Natalie Ford at the Random House Group Archive and Library; Adam Lines at Special Collections, Reading University Library; Wesley Bonar at Sentry Hill; Debbie Usher at the Middle East Centre Archive, St Antony's College, Oxford; Jonathan Smith at Trinity College, Cambridge; Clare Hopkins at Trinity College, Oxford; Loryl MacDonald at the University of Toronto Archives and Records Management Services; Nicole McCarvill at Special Collections, University of Victoria Libraries; Richard Childs at West Sussex Record Office; Katy Makin at Special Collections, University College, London; Lesley Pitman at University College, London School of East European and Slavonic Studies; Daniel Cesarani at the Wiener Library; Cynthia Ostroff at the Sterling Library, Yale University; and Gunnar Berg at the YIVO Archives, Center for Jewish History, New York. I owe particular debts of gratitude to Jennie De Protani at the Athenaeum, Aileen Ivory at Alexandra College, Dublin, Peter Brown at the British Academy, Tharik Hussain at the Khizra Foundation, and Anne Jensen at News UK Archives, each of whom provided me with specific archival information, and John Smith, who kindly kept an eye open on my behalf for Namier-related material in the Strutt papers at Terling Place.

Research of this kind, even in the age of digitised resources and electronically available catalogues, can still be a very expensive business, and I thank the Huntington Library and the Lewis Walpole Library for awards which enabled the consultation of material in the United States. Publication was facilitated by generous grants from the Marc Fitch Fund and the Jewish Historical Society of England. I am also greatly obliged to family and friends for providing accommodation: Neil and Ella Barclay in Oxford, Linda Clark in Islington, Nick and Sarah Hall in Devon, Thom and Anita Hayton in Warwickshire, Clyve Jones in Bedford Park, Robin and Joy Kempster in West Yorkshire, Conal and Danielle Hayton, Philip Mooney and the late John Milner in Manchester, Ravi and Lata Shenoy in Fife, the Dahlin-Nolan family in Toronto, and Kevin and Mary Ann Sexton in Washington, DC.

Various parts of the book have been delivered as seminar papers and lectures, at the universities of Aberystwyth, Cambridge, Maynooth, Oxford, Reading, St Andrews and Winchester, Queen's University Belfast, Trinity College Dublin, the Institute of Historical Research, and the Senior Historians' Conference. I am grateful to all those who listened patiently and offered comments. I would particularly like to thank the participants at the conference on 'Jewish conditions, theories of nationalism', held under the auspices of the Woolf Institute at Cambridge in May 2016, from whom I learned a very great deal, especially David Aberbach, Joshua Cherniss, Adi Gordon,

Acknowledgements

John Hall, Dominic Lieven and Jan Ruzicka. I have also depended on the kindness of others, who have discussed Namier's life with me, pointed me in new directions, helped with access to relevant documents, and posed or answered specific questions: Colin Armstrong, Toby Barnard, the late John Beattie, Eugenio Biagini, Richard Butterwick-Pawlikowski, Mary Clapinson, Linda Clark, Catherine Clinton, Sean Connolly, Paul Corthorn, Maciej Cybulski, Alan Downie, Marie Therese Flanagan, Christopher Godden, Aaron Graham, Peter Gray, Stephen Green, Carl Griffin, Andrew Hanham, Frances Harris, Colin Haydon, William Hayton, Dominic Henry, James Hickie, Boyd Hilton, Andrew Holmes, Julian Hoppit, Joanna Innes, Alvin Jackson, Jan Jedrzejewski, Clyve Jones, the late David Lewis Jones, the late Peter Jupp, Lucy Kidd, Mark Knights, Charles-Édouard Levillain, Pamela Linden, David Livingstone, Anthony Malcomson, Ryan McCloskey, James McKeown, George Misiewicz, John Morrill, Mahon Murphy, Michael Port, Martyn Powell, Nick Rogers, Avi Roshwald, Philippe Sands, Mark Seaman, Paul Seaward, Ian and Tony Selinger, Oliver Shanks, Richard Sharpe, Anthony Stanonis, George Steiner, Eliyahu Stern, Miles Taylor, Stephen Taylor, Peter Thomas, Roland Thorne, Alex Titov, William Waldegrave (Baron Waldegrave of North Hill), George Woodman, Blair Worden, Christopher Wright, Chris Wrigley and Andrzej Zięba. Three scholars who went before me in seeking to elucidate Namier's life, character and ideas, Linda Colley, Amy Ng and Norman Rose, have helped me in different ways. My findings have not always agreed with theirs, but I could have done very little had I not been able to build on their work.

I am particularly grateful of those who pushed the boundaries of friendship by reading and commenting on drafts. Colin Kidd and Alan Sharp brought their expertise to bear on particular chapters. Michael Bentley, Andrzej Ehrlich and Adam Sisman read the entire manuscript: extraordinary acts of generosity for which I am duly thankful. Each improved the text by his advice, but cannot be held in any way responsible for what remains.

My primary debt as a historian is to an inspiring schoolteacher, Bob Faithorn. I also owe an incalculable amount to my wife and family, for allowing Namier to intrude so much into their lives and conversation over the past decade. But I have chosen to dedicate this book to the memory of two people who died of cancer within a month of each other during the book's preparation: my close professional colleague Keith Jeffery and my old university friend John Milner. That I was able to bring my study of Namier to a conclusion was owing in great measure to the practical assistance they gave me (including, in John's case, a close reading of drafts) and to their constant encouragement and unfailing good humour, even during the last stages of torturous illness. I hope the outcome is something that both would have enjoyed, and bitterly regret that neither is here to see it.

Abbreviations

The following are used throughout the notes. In the citation of printed works, the place of publication is London unless otherwise stated.

1848 L. B. Namier, *1848: the revolution of the intellectuals* (1946)

Amer. rev. L. B. Namier, *England in the age of the American revolution* (2nd edn, 1966)

Avenues L. B. Namier, *Avenues of history* (1952)

Babington Smith House of St Gregory and St Macrina, Oxford, Constance Babington Smith papers

Baffy *Baffy: the diaries of Blanche Dugdale 1936–1947*, ed. Norman Rose (1973)

Balliol Balliol College, Oxford, archives

BL British Library

Bodl. Bodleian Library

Churchill The Churchill Archive Centre, Churchill College, Cambridge

Colley Linda Colley, *Lewis Namier* (1989)

Conflicts L. B. Namier, *Conflicts: studies in contemporary history* (1942)

Crossroads Sir Lewis Namier, *Crossroads of power: essays on eighteenth-century England* (1962)

CUL Cambridge University Library

CZA Central Zionist Archives, Jerusalem

Dacre Christ Church, Oxford, Dacre papers

Abbreviations

Dip. prelude	L. B. Namier, *Diplomatic prelude 1938–1939* (1948)
Dugdale diaries	Typescript copies of the original diaries of Blanche Dugdale (in private possession)
EHR	*English Historical Review*
Europe in decay	L. B. Namier, *Europe in decay* (1950)
Facing east	L. B. Namier, *Facing east* (1947)
FO	The National Archives, Foreign Office papers
Guardian arch.	The John Rylands Library (University of Manchester) *Manchester Guardian* archive
HPT	History of Parliament Trust archives, London
In the margin	L. B. Namier, *In the margin of history* (1939)
IHR	Institute of Historical Research, University of London
KCL	King's College London, Liddell Hart Centre for Military Archives
LH	King's College London, Liddell Hart Centre for Military Archives, Liddell Hart papers
LMA	London Metropolitan Archives
LWL	Lewis Walpole Library, Farmington, Conn.
Namier	Julia Namier, *Lewis Namier: a biography* (1971)
Ng, *Nationalism*	Amy Ng, *Nationalism and political liberty: Redlich, Namier and the crisis of empire* (Oxford, 2004)
NLS	National Library of Scotland
NLW	National Library of Wales
NRS	National Records of Scotland
Oxf. DNB	*The Oxford Dictionary of National Biography* (online edition: www.oxforddnb.com)
PA	Parliamentary Archives
Personalities and powers	L. B. Namier, *Personalities and powers* (1955)
PRONI	Public Record Office of Northern Ireland
RO	Record Office
Rose, *Zionism*	Norman Rose, *Lewis Namier and Zionism* (Oxford, 1989)
Rylands	John Rylands Library (University of Manchester)
Skyscrapers	L. B. Namier, *Skyscrapers and other essays* (1931)

Abbreviations

SSEES	University College, London, School of Slavonic and East European Studies
Structure	L. B. Namier, *The structure of politics at the accession of George III* (2nd edn, 1965)
TLS	*Times Literary Supplement*
TNA	The National Archives [of the UK] Kew
'Turbulent Zionist'	Julia Namier, 'A turbulent Zionist' (typescript in Babington Smith papers)
UCL	University College, London, Library, Special Collections
UL	University Library
Vanished supremacies	Sir Lewis Namier, *Vanished supremacies: essays on European history 1812–1918* (1958)
Weizmann A	*The letters and papers of Chaim Weizmann*, ser. A, ed. M. W. Weisgal et al. (23 vols, London, New Brunswick and Jerusalem, 1968–80)

Prologue: in search of Namier

Few historians in twentieth-century Britain were as well known in their own life-time as Sir Lewis Namier. Acclaimed in the decade after the Second World War as 'England's greatest historian', Namier produced books and essays that were genuinely original and highly influential – most famously on English politics in the 1760s, but also ranging across the history of Europe in the nineteenth and twentieth centuries. More than fifty years after his death in 1960 he can still be read for pleasure and profit. While works produced by his contemporaries often seem museum pieces, his writing retains sharpness and immediacy. Its epigrammatic style continues to draw admiration, sometimes from unlikely quarters.[1] He also gave a new word to the English language: to Namierise, usually defined as the study of institutions through the collective biography – or prosopography – of their members.

Today Namier is not only synonymous with a particular historical technique, but also with a way of understanding the world: a belief that the things that matter in society are the thoughts and actions of elites rather than the views of the population at large, and a view of politics in which issues are essentially unimportant, principles are a cloak for self-interest, and those who enter public life do so in pursuit of personal and material advantage. This is an exaggeration, if not entirely a distortion, of Namier's view of the nature of human psychology and human relations, but it has attained such a broad acceptance as to make him a hero to social and political conservatives, and almost a demonic figure to those on the left, like former Prime Minister Gordon Brown, who came close to ascribing the decline in the concept of public service in the Britain of Margaret Thatcher to the pernicious influence of the 'Namier school of history, which suggests that everything is less to do with ideas and popular concerns than with the manoeuvrings of elites'.[2]

Equally, Namier remains a controversial figure among academic historians, perhaps more often denigrated than praised, but still regarded as a Goliath who has to be toppled. In particular, to the practitioners of the history of political thought he stands

1

as an arch-enemy: the man who supposedly declared that in political discourse any reference to ideas was 'flapdoodle'.[3] For those who study politics in action, he is identified with an approach now generally regarded as rather too restrictive in scope. The emphasis in his work on Parliament and its membership is easy to characterise as elitist, and out of kilter with the political culture of modern mass democracy. Since Namier's death much greater attention has been paid by English historians to 'public opinion', even in those middle decades of the eighteenth century which constituted his own precisely mapped domain. Nevertheless, his technique is still productive: historians of political institutions continue to make use of collective biography, and not just in the ongoing History of Parliament project, which embodies the 'Namier method', and with which he was closely associated.

For all that Namier's published output, in books, essays and reviews, was vast and varied, his impact revolutionary and his influence long-lasting, his life encompassed a great deal more than research and writing about the past, and was lived vigorously in the world of 'public affairs', beyond libraries, record offices and country-house muniment rooms. His time in the Foreign Office during the First World War and the ensuing peace conference; his work, formal and informal, in the 1930s and 1940s for the Zionist Organisation and for Jewish refugees from Nazi tyranny; his role as a public intellectual in post-war Britain: all placed him at the heart of the great and terrible events of the first half of the twentieth century, events which were for him, as an East European Jew, especially terrible.

Despite the accolades, the social advancement, the official recognition marked by his knighthood, Namier remained an outsider. Born into a family of conforming Jews in late nineteenth-century Poland, he grew up with no religion and rejected the national identity his parents assumed. He was brought up to regard himself as neither Pole nor Jew; and although he became a naturalised British subject, idealised the British aristocracy and the British empire, and did his best to integrate into British society, he was always regarded as an exotic in his adopted land. There was good reason for this. For most of his life he seems almost deliberately to have put himself at odds with established authority in whatever form he encountered it, whether as a civil servant, a political activist or a historian. The outcome was not what he wanted, but it was not something he could help. One writer described him as 'English history's towering outsider'; another summarised his life as 'the waving of a rolled umbrella for taxis that did not stop. A scholar trying to be a gentleman, an expatriate trying to be English, a misfit rebel trying to be a Tory.'[4]

For over forty-five years no attempt has been made to write a biography of this formidable and extraordinary man. There have been detailed studies of certain aspects of his career,[5] but no comprehensive account of his life and work to supersede the

intimate account provided in his widow Julia's extended biography, written and published in the decade after his death. Even Professor Linda Colley's stimulating short
study of Namier the historian, which appeared in 1989, depended heavily on Julia
Namier's book for facts about Namier's life.

Julia provided a detailed portrait of the man whom she had come to know better
than anyone else, full of personal information, extending to the minutiae of daily life,
and written with considerable literary flair. But for all the praise lavished on the book
when it was published, not all Namier's friends were convinced by the picture presented in this official biography. Most obviously, there was no attempt to assess his
stature as a historian, a task for which Lady Namier felt unqualified and decided to
'leave to experts'.[6] Other equally important aspects of his life were elided, especially
in relation to his family background in Russian and Austrian Poland, while others
were given a particular spin, either Namier's own or Julia's. The devotional (almost
hagiographical) nature of the work made some readers uneasy, as well as the fact that
Namier himself had originated much of the detail about his personal history before
their marriage in 1947.[7] As Lady Namier acknowledged, the source material for his
childhood and adolescence was predominantly 'my notes of L[ewis]'s recollections'.[8]
In many important respects, her book was a ventriloquised autobiography.

It was Namier's choice that Julia should write the story of his life, and the decision can be dated precisely. In February 1955, Namier was sitting alongside his wife
in a shelter on the promenade at Bognor Regis, where they had gone for some sea air
in order to recover from persistent chest colds.[9] Each was susceptible to respiratory
infections, Namier because of botched nasal surgery as a child. The misery of ill health,
exacerbated by the weather, seems to have made him unusually morose. According
to Julia he 'began to elaborate his opinion on a biographer's moral obligations':

> If I survived him, I should let no self-important biographer get hold of those scraps of
> information about him that only I had. There could be no preventing an enthusiastic dis-
> torter or misinterpreter from saying what amused him or writing what he thought prof-
> itable. Against exploitation by that crew I should be on guard, bearing in mind that solid
> facts, when wrongly grouped, could bolster up untruth. A smear cleverly coiled round
> correct facts makes of the combination a heinous lie. An honest biographer should above
> all serve the truth hidden in his subject's unobtrusive self. Lacking empathic insight
> into it, a writer should keep his own impressions if any, to thumbnail sketches, and to a
> straight chronicling of verified activities.[10]

Reading these words, anyone contemplating writing Namier's life must feel a freezing breath not unlike the sea mists of Bognor in February.

Although his own approach to the study of the past was primarily through the
lives of individuals, Namier was always acerbic in his comments about biographers.

As early as the 1920s he observed that 'the heroes of biography are often approached in a sceptical, would-be humorous, depreciatory manner, and this is the main tangible expression of the doubt which besets the writers as to whether these men truly deserve the prominence they receive'.[11] But as Lady Namier noted, his seaside ruminations were the product of a particular cause célèbre, the acceptance by the London publisher Collins of Richard Aldington's hostile biography of T. E. Lawrence.[12] Namier had enjoyed a close friendship with Lawrence in the 1920s and, though not blind to Lawrence's faults, cherished his memory: one of the pictures adorning the flat in which the Namiers lived was a print of Eric Kennington's 'ghost portrait' of 'T.E.', the original of which was painted in 1920, when Namier's friendship with Lawrence was being rekindled.[13] Aldington's manuscript denounced the hero of Arabia as a liar and a charlatan, and for good measure scratched over the ashes of his private life.[14] Namier did not need convincing that Aldington had provided an object lesson in the perennial failings of the biographer. Namier himself had been approached by the family to write an authorised life of Lawrence but had been too busy to undertake it, and was also rather nervous about the task, for he had once been the unwilling recipient of a confession as to T. E.'s 'real predicament', the detail of which he never disclosed, but which would have made the task of writing the biography a delicate matter.[15]

Lawrence's youngest brother, Arnold, sought to mobilise friends to prevent Aldington's work from seeing the light of day. Namier did what he could in letters to the publisher, and managed to impose last-minute changes to the manuscript.[16] He was naturally concerned lest something similar happen to him. There were skeletons in his closet which might have been held up to the public's gaze: his father's gambling; his own disinheritance; his disastrous first marriage, which collapsed into a humiliating separation after his wife left him for another man; his protracted love affair with his sister's friend Marie Beer, who ended her days in a mental hospital; a long-term, and essentially casual, sexual liaison with a woman whose identity Julia hid under a pseudonym. All these a muck-raker could exploit in order to destroy Namier's reputation.

And so Namier spent long evenings in their flat in Shepherd's Bush regaling Julia with monologues about his early life. Later, when she had written her book, Julia suffered the disturbing experience of discovering that the husband who had been so rigorous in his determination to discover historical truth and expose error, and who seemed incapable of obfuscation or calculated mendacity in his daily life, had told her tales which were at odds with the recollections of those who had known him. Namier's friend and 'co-worker' in eighteenth-century history, Lucy Sutherland, informed Julia politely that her husband's account of a seminar in Oxford at which he said he had been the subject of 'harsh abuse' was overblown.[17] More worryingly, after the book appeared, a surviving cousin cast doubt on the depiction of Namier's parents. Far from being the dominant partner, as Lewis had always insisted, his father was deemed to be 'a useless waste' and 'a bore'.[18]

For all his prodigious intellectual gifts, Namier possessed a memory which was no less fallible than anyone else's. He told and re-told stories about his life, which acquired a patina in repetition. Many dealt with the process by which he came to realise the importance of his Jewish heritage. They usually involved memorable encounters with individuals, such as the Scotsman with whom he conversed on a train to Edinburgh and who, as the train was finally pulling into Waverley Station, observed, 'You are the first Jew I ever liked.' Namier was sufficiently pleased with his riposte – 'Would it interest you to know whether I like Scotsmen ... then why do you expect me to be interested in what you feel about Jews?' – to put it into print and repeat it verbatim a decade later in a letter to the military historian Basil Liddell Hart.[19] The effect of recalling events from his own past, again and again, was heightened by his experience of psychoanalysis, which began in the early 1920s in Vienna, was resumed in the mid-1930s and continued until about 1942, when he gave it up.[20] It is tempting to ascribe his fixation with his difficult relationship to his father to the influence of this constant self-scrutiny. As Julia herself wrote, 'L[ewis]'s active interest in psycho-analysis ... had not only pushed back his childhood memories to the age of about two; it had entwined all his memories with a caustic self-analysis.'[21] And perhaps invested certain events with an importance they may not have possessed at the time, or glossed them in a way that was as much constructed as remembered.

Julia also brought her own perspective to the evidence her husband bequeathed her. As Lucy Sutherland confided to a friend, everything Julia wrote was 'heightened by her sympathies'; 'the whole work ... is so clearly that of a devoted widow, and so many ... incidents are palpably the reverse of objective'.[22] Julia's own Christian beliefs informed her account of her husband's life, which she depicted as a slow and erratic journey towards God.[23] In order to make her case she leapt upon any element of religious experience to be found in an existence that appears generally devoid of it: she highlighted visits paid by Namier as a boy to local churches, in the company of a female servant, and, later, his occasional comments of sympathetic appreciation of the importance of his wife's religious observances.[24] The very last paragraph of the book reported an incident after his death in which she had found herself, as she thought, 'blindly doodling' on a writing pad while half-asleep, in a kind of 'automatic writing', only to discover what appeared to be a message from her husband from beyond the grave.[25] This was evidently one of several 'communications' that she received from Namier in the next world, reports of which made even her Orthodox spiritual adviser uneasy.[26] This aspect of her portrayal of her husband made no sense to old friends like Lucy Sutherland, who recalled a remark of Namier's to a mutual acquaintance that 'Julia is a mystic; I am not', or Isaiah Berlin, who remembered Namier as resolutely irreligious and 'a ferocious anticlerical', and implied that the picture Lady Namier had drawn was evidence of no more than an intensely uxorious man humouring his wife.[27]

Lady Namier's biography concentrated on the inner life of her subject: his character, his development as an individual, his struggles, and the complexity of his personal relationships. In doing so, she exposed all the lurking scandals that a prurient biographer would have seized upon, presumably to ensure that an authorised version of these events was established. In fact, she went further, and recounted highly sensitive episodes known only to herself – volcanic rages and melodramatic posturing – which Namier would have been mortally embarrassed to see in print. At the same time, she included relatively little about aspects of his life which outside observers would have thought important. Besides saying almost nothing about his writing, she made no attempt to assess his contribution to public affairs. His time in the civil service in 1915–20 was discussed only in relation to his state of mind, friendships with colleagues and conflicts with 'intriguers' (his favourite word for personal enemies). Although Julia did prepare a lengthy account of Namier's contribution to the Zionist movement, intending to publish it separately, this element of his story was also abbreviated in the biography.[28] What is particularly telling is that two-thirds of the volume have passed before she reaches the turning point in Namier's life, in 1929, when his first major book was published, and he was appointed political secretary of the Zionist Organisation, bringing him back into the corridors of power and marking the real beginning of his work for the Zionist cause.

Many of these problems were immediately visible on publication. Nonetheless, as one would-be biographer conceded, the grand scope of the work, its apparently comprehensive treatment of its subject's private life, and the privileged position from which it was written, effectively deterred others from travelling the same road.[29] It was feasible to tackle specific aspects of Namier's career and achievements to which Julia had herself paid scant attention, to do justice to his history, for example, or to his Zionist agitation, but not worthwhile to try to do the job again.

Perhaps the greatest inhibiting factor was that the surviving documentary record of Namier's life seemed to be relatively thin, and to offer no very attractive prospect: a matter of gleaning scattered references rather than harvesting an abundant crop. But in fact this turns out not to be the case. Despite the fact that some of the documents which Julia used have been destroyed or lost, enough remains to enable a biography to be written that does not – as indeed it cannot – depend on personal knowledge or on Namier's own recollections: his own archive, which, although dispersed is still very substantial, the memoranda he wrote for the Foreign Office and for the Zionists, and his published work, especially his journalism, which the wonders of digitisation enable us to recover with relative ease.

Namier's personal papers suffered periodic ravages. He himself burned some in 1940, when a Nazi invasion seemed imminent.[30] When he died in August 1960 he left a confused heap of documents in the bedroom which he used as a study. Things were 'incredibly jumbled'.[31] With the assistance of John Brooke, Namier's chief assistant on the History of Parliament, Julia managed to sort them.[32] Brooke, who was responsible for seeing through to publication Namier's section of the History, was then given papers relating to Namier's historical work, including notebooks and drafts. The rest, together with Lady Namier's own notes of conversations with Namier about his life, and additional items gathered from friends, relations and institutions, would serve as her source material.

When Julia finished her book she destroyed some papers, especially her own letters, which she felt were too intimate to be read by anyone else.[33] She entrusted the remainder to Brooke, with the exception of documents relating to work for the Zionist cause, which went to the Central Zionist Archives in Jerusalem. He gave some of the papers he had received to the Lewis Walpole Library in Farmington, Connecticut, which preserves the archive of Namier's friend Wilmarth ('Lefty') Lewis, the editor of Horace Walpole's correspondence. The notes Julia had made remained in her possession. They were consulted by Professor Norman Rose when he was preparing his study of *Namier and Zionism* (1980), and after Julia's death in 1977 they passed, with her other papers, to her literary executor, Constance Babington Smith, a journalist (and wartime aircraft intelligence analyst), who had become friendly with Julia after converting to the Orthodox Church, and eventually wrote her biography. Miss Babington Smith (who herself died in 2000) was able to make them available to Professor Colley. Subsequently, they passed through the Babington Smith family and eventually fetched up at the House of St Gregory and St Macrina, an Orthodox foundation in north Oxford, where I was given permission to consult them. While there is much in the collection that is of value for understanding Lewis and Julia Namier and their life together, Julia's notes for the biography seem to have disappeared along the way.

That was the state of play when Professor Colley published her book on Namier in 1989. Since then Brooke's collection has been purchased by the John Rylands Library at Manchester University, where it has been sorted and catalogued. There was also one more set of Namier papers, which Professor Colley was told could not be found, but which has since come to light: letters that were in his office in the History of

7

Parliament when he died. They remained with the History during the time that Julia was writing her biography, since she was uninterested in the practicalities of her husband's research. The archive has now been arranged and listed: there are twenty boxes, some letters from as far back as the 1930s. Taken together with the papers in Manchester, Oxford and Jerusalem they make up as extensive a collection as exists for any twentieth-century historian. And this can be supplemented by letters in a vast range of other locations: the archives of friends and enemies, associates in the Zionist Organisation, and fellow historians. The most important body of material is probably the mountain of memoranda, notes and commentaries Namier made on Polish, Czech and Austrian affairs while working for the British government during 1915–20, which are preserved in The National Archives at Kew. There are also good runs of Namier correspondence in 'Lefty' Lewis's collection at Farmington, in the papers of Basil Liddell Hart at King's College, London, and in the *Manchester Guardian* archive, also at Rylands.

Namier did not approach letter-writing as a literary exercise.[34] Although he corresponded at length with some close friends, discussing historical questions or public affairs, the majority of his letters were brief and businesslike, especially from the mid-1920s onwards, when he found it increasingly difficult to use his right hand and depended on a secretary to type for him. But even in his more expansive communications he tended to say little about himself, seldom divulged his inner feelings and hardly ever gossiped. He regarded his time as too important to waste on trivialities. On the other hand, Namier was also a person about whom others always had a great deal to say, whether for good or ill, and some of the most interesting survivals in the contemporary record are comments about him.

Namier's published writings, of which there is a huge corpus, also reveal his personality and feelings as well as his ideas. Throughout his adult life he was a prolific contributor to newspapers, magazines and journals. Some of his articles and book reviews were collected into volumes, published at first by Macmillan and subsequently by Hamish Hamilton. But this was only the visible part of the iceberg; numerous short pieces, especially his reviews, have never been reprinted and, indeed they were not known to Lady Namier, who made efforts to track down fugitive items in the *Manchester Guardian* and in *The Nation* but seems to have been discouraged by the difficulties posed by their incomplete files.[35] In the internet age, however, the construction and publication of digitised and machine-searchable editions has transformed newspaper and journal research, to the extent that even anonymous reviews in the *Times Literary Supplement* can be identified and retrieved without leaving one's desk.[36]

In print, Namier opened his mind to his reader: he did not disguise or dissemble. It was not in his nature to wrap things up, even to spare the feelings of friends, but always to tell the truth as he saw it. This could be a painful experience for those at the receiving end. Even if he were trying to write a favourable review, to 'puff' a book, he could not fail to point errors of fact or faults in construction, as at different times writers as diverse as J. H. Plumb, Alan (A. J. P.) Taylor and Rebecca West discovered. Nowadays this relentless candour might be considered as an indication of some minor psychological disorder, but it is extremely helpful as far as his biography is concerned. In his writing he made no effort to hide his prejudices, most notoriously his visceral Germanophobia, to which he not only gave full rein but also sought at different times to explain and justify. Nor did he omit reference to his own personal circumstances, where he considered that this would be relevant to understanding his arguments. As a result, and unlike some of those with whom he crossed swords in print, his published writings are direct, uncontrived and offer another window into his character and experiences.

What follows is an attempt to make sense of Namier's difficult and, in some respects, obsessive personality, and his long and complicated life in all its aspects, largely by means of surviving written sources. I have sought to explain his ideas about history and politics by setting their development in the context of his biography, without which their development cannot be properly understood. In pursuit of this aim, I have opted for a broadly chronological approach rather than the thematic analysis which would be more appropriate to an 'intellectual biography'. Inevitably, at some points what I have to say will supplement, modify, or contradict the account given by Lady Namier, and these points have been highlighted, but I have tried to avoid turning this book into a dialogue with its predecessor.

There is a final point. In planning the book, I adopted the conceit of giving each chapter the title of one of Namier's volumes of collected essays. I persisted with this scheme even after discovering that most of the titles of the collections published by Hamish Hamilton were not devised by Namier himself but by an office junior with a particular flair in that direction. 'Jamie' Hamilton, who ran the firm, had allowed Namier to choose the first title, *Avenues of history* (1952), but subsequently considered this to be a disaster and would not let the great man have his way again. He once declared that the next book might just as well be called 'Up the garden paths of history, with Namier'.[37] During occasional bouts of pessimism I have wondered whether Hamilton's jocular suggestion might not in the end turn out to be an appropriate title for the present book. Whether this has turned out to be the case, I leave to the reader to decide.

Notes

1 For example, Clive James, *Cultural amnesia* (paperback edn, 2007), 535–42.
2 Quoted in *Observer*, 30 Sept. 2007 (the original interview was given in 2003). See also Tom Bower, *Gordon Brown, Prime Minister* (rev. edn, 2007), 144. Brown read history at Edinburgh University in the late 1960s and early 1970s.
3 For the context of this quotation, see p. 177.
4 *TLS*, 21 May 1971; Dan Davin, *Brides of price* (1972), 105.
5 Ng, *Nationalism*; Rose, *Zionism*.
6 Julia Namier, *Namier*, xii.
7 E. H. Carr, *From Napoleon to Stalin and other essays* (1971), 184–5; J. A. Cannon, 'Lewis Bernstein Namier', J. A. Cannon (ed.), *The historian at work* (1980), 153.
8 *Namier*, xi.
9 Basil Liddell Hart to Namier, 25 Feb. 1955 (HPT, N–61); Namier to Mrs Elizabeth Fooks, 9 Mar. 1955 (ibid., N–60). Characteristically, Namier took work with him (Namier to Mary Drummond, 22 Feb. 1955 (papers in private possession)).
10 *Namier*, 305–6.
11 *Skyscrapers*, 45–6. See also Namier to Basil Liddell Hart, 19 Jan. 1952 (LH, 1/539/85); Namier, 'History: its subject-matter and tasks', *History Today*, ii (1952), 157–62.
12 *Namier*, 306. See also Namier to Basil Liddell Hart, 23 Feb. 1955 (written from Bognor) (LH, 1/539/132).
13 Julia Namier to Constance Babington Smith, 20 May 1972 (Babington Smith).
14 Richard Aldington, *Lawrence of Arabia: a biographical inquiry* (1955). On the controversy aroused by the book, see F. D. Crawford, *Richard Aldington and Lawrence of Arabia: a cautionary tale* (Carbondale, Ill., 1998), which takes a position more favourable to Aldington's work than most commentators have done.
15 Julia Namier to Basil Liddell Hart, 8, 14 Jan. 1963 (LH, 1/539/184, 186).
16 Namier to Basil Liddell Hart, 30 July, 18, 22 Sept. 1954 (LH, 1/539/131); Julia Namier to same, 14 Jan. 1963 (ibid., 1/539/186).
17 *Namier*, 299–300; Sutherland to Julia Namier, 30 Oct. 1970 (Bodl., Sutherland papers, box 9). See p. 329.
18 Colley, 9, quoting from a letter in the Babington Smith papers which appears to be no longer extant.
19 *Conflicts*, 126; Namier to Liddell Hart, 4 Apr. 1951 (LH, 1/539/61).
20 Lady Namier to F. G. Steiner, 6 Dec. 1964, 22 Feb. 1965, Dr Katherine Jones to Steiner, 7 Jan. 1965, Steiner to Lady Namier, 18 Feb. 1965 (Churchill, Steiner papers, 6/5/1).
21 *Namier*, xii.
22 Sutherland to J. S. Bromley, 13 Nov. 1970 (Bodl., Sutherland papers, box 9). Mana Sedgwick, the wife of Namier's long-time friend and collaborator Romney Sedgwick, found the book 'a work of striking imaginative reconstruction but the Lewis Namier I knew does not emerge from it' (to W. S. Lewis, 22 May 1971 (LWL, Lewis corresp., Sedgwick)).
23 Constance Babington Smith, *Iulia de Beausobre: a Russian Christian in the west* (1983), I have used the Anglicised spelling of Julia's name, since this was Namier's usage, and her own, when writing in English.
24 *Namier*, 21–2, 331–3.
25 *Namier*, 333.

26 Constance Babington Smith to Irina Prehn, 27 Jan. 1979 (Babington Smith); Irina Prehn to Constance Babington Smith, 23 May 1980 (ibid.).

27 Sutherland to Julia Namier, 17 May 1971 (Bodl., Sutherland papers, box 9); Isaiah Berlin, *Building: letters 1960–1975*, ed. Henry Hardy and Mark Pottle (2013), 479. See also Richard Cobb to Hugh Trevor-Roper, 16 Aug. 1971 (Dacre, 1/1/Cobb); A. J. P. Taylor, *Letters to Eva 1969–1983*, ed. Eva Haraszti Taylor (1991), 251–2.

28 'Turbulent Zionist'.

29 Rose, *Zionism*, [v].

30 Namier to Lucy Sutherland, 14 June 1940 (Bodl., Sutherland papers, box 9).

31 *Namier*, xi.

32 Julia Namier to Basil Liddell Hart, 1 Sept. 1960 (LH, 1/539/165–6).

33 John Brooke to W. S. Lewis, 27 Sept. 1972 (LWL, Lewis correspondence, Brooke (1)).

34 I have attempted a comprehensive listing in 'The writings of Lewis Namier: an annotated bibliography' in the *Bulletin of the John Rylands Library* (forthcoming).

35 In 1963 the deputy editor of the *Guardian*, Patrick Monkhouse, supplied Lady Namier with a list of her husband's contributions to the paper between 1919 and 1950, but with a large gap between 1925 and 1937. He was unable to make this good because 'relevant ledgers … are absent from the archives'. Details of the missing items can now be supplied through accessing 'The Guardian and Observer Digital Archive' (available at www.theguardian. com). See Lady Namier to P. J. Monkhouse, 19 Nov. 1963 (*Guardian* arch., D/977/11), Monkhouse to Lady Namier, 29 Nov. 1963 (ibid., D/977/14). For the failure of attempts to search for Namier's pieces for *The Nation* (in the archives of the *New Statesman*, into which *The Nation* had been subsumed), see Julia Namier to Lucy Sutherland, 14 Jan. 1964 (Bodl., Sutherland papers, box 9).

36 Via the 'TLS Historical Archive' (Cengage Learning).

37 Note by 'Jamie' Hamilton on a letter to him from R. V. Machell (Bristol UL, Hamish Hamilton archive, DM/352/Ii). Namier's alternative title for *Avenues of history* had been even worse: 'Treasure-chambers of history' ([Machell] to Namier, 31 Oct. 1951 (ibid.)).

1

Avenues of history:
the child and the man, 1888–1913

The Jewish cemetery in Warsaw is today an eerie relic of a community that has all but disappeared. Neglected and overgrown, it stands at the boundary of the ghetto whose inhabitants were cruelly and systematically destroyed by the Nazis during the Second World War. But it contains poignant reminders of very different times for Warsaw's Jewish community: elaborate funerary monuments to families and individuals who prospered in nineteenth-century Poland. Two such memorials are the imposing black marble columns, prominently situated near the main entrance, which mark the graves of Lewis Namier's paternal grandparents, Jakob and Balbina Bernstein (Bernsztajn). Jakob, the archetype of what the late nineteenth-century Polish novelist Bolesław Prus called 'top-hatted, frock-coated Jews', was a wealthy banker and businessman residing in a mansion in the same street as the reformed synagogue at which he worshipped. His portrait suggests a comfortable, even complacent, affluence, but this does not tell the whole story.[1]

Jakob was born in 1825 in Winnicy (Vinnytsia in Ukrainian), which was then in Russian Poland, some 250 kilometres south-west of Kiev, to a family which had probably made its money in the very lucrative business of army clothing contracts.[2] Their original surname, Niemirowski, which may indicate an origin in the nearby town of Nemirov (Nemyriv), had been replaced as part of the enforced Germanisation of Jewish surnames in the late eighteenth century.[3] While Jakob's son and grandson reverted to the family's ancestral name, partly to hide their Jewish ancestry, there is no indication that Jakob himself ever attempted to do so.[4] On the other hand, he did make every effort, short of abandoning his religious observance, to assimilate himself and his family into Polish society and culture. The gravestones erected for him and his wife display inscriptions in the Polish language as well as the obligatory Hebrew. He even took part in the nationalist insurrection of 1863, after which he spent a year in a Tsarist prison, a mild enough punishment compared to that of fellow rebels, who were summarily executed, but nonetheless an ordeal which permanently damaged his health.

Although Jakob died before his grandson was born, Balbina remained alive and influential for the first six years of Namier's existence. She was by all accounts a domineering woman who sought to control the lives of her many children. She also had a very strong sense of her own and her family's importance. In particular, she prided herself on being the great-great-granddaughter of the most important and revered Jewish intellectual of the modern era, Elijah ben Solomon (1720–97), the 'Gaon' (genius) of Vilna (Vilnius), a fact that was inscribed on her gravestone.[5] At that time it was a common conceit for east European Jews to claim a relationship to the Gaon, not just as an intellectual distinction, but almost as a special stamp of their Jewishness.[6] In Balbina's case it was true. And her pride in this remarkable lineage was passed on to her own descendants. Namier was said by friends to brandish at every opportunity his descent from the Gaon,[7] and occasionally inserted such references into his writings.[8]

Namier's mother came from an orthodox Jewish family living much further south in the Pale of Settlement, in the vicinity of Trembowla (in Ukrainian, Terebovlya), close to the city of Tarnopol (Ternopil) in what is now the western Ukraine but which at the time of Namier's birth was the Austrian province of Galicia. Following emancipation in 1867 Jews in Galicia were afforded many freedoms which the Bernsteins in Russian-controlled Warsaw were denied. Namier's maternal grandfather, Teodor Sommerstein (Sommersztajn),[9] was a self-made businessman, 'hard-headed' according to Lady Namier, as all self-made businessmen surely have to be.[10] Having gathered a fortune through industry and commerce, he bought a clutch of landed estates to the south and west of Trembowla, which he treated as business enterprises, ploughing up tracts of virgin steppe for arable crops.[11] Half a century later, Namier may well have had his grandfather's agricultural projects in mind when deprecating the inefficiency of peasant farming, as compared with that of 'the big capitalist estates'. The memory of his grandfather, in whose company he spent a good deal of time during his boyhood, may also have inspired Namier's scholarly interest in the upwardly mobile manufacturers and merchants who made their way into the eighteenth- and nineteenth-century British ruling elite.[12] More immediately, grandfather Teodor offered an alternative role model to Namier's father Józef, who was highly intelligent and sophisticated, but supposedly lacked Teodor's application and resilience. Throughout his adult life Namier was attracted by their contrasting qualities: on the one hand he admired and sought to join the cultivated society of intellectuals, especially those from an aristocratic background; on the other he prided himself on making his own way in the world, and on his toughness in matters of money.

As Jakob's second son, Józef Bernstein studied law at Warsaw University and was expected to follow the profession of advocate.[13] According to Namier's account of him, which has to be treated with caution, not least because it resembles a little too closely the self-destructive characters created by Namier's favourite novelist, Dostoyevsky, Józef was over-sensitive and lazy, and made little progress in the career he had chosen, or that had been chosen for him. He was, moreover, like Dostoyevsky himself and some of his creations, a compulsive gambler. A weak man, very much under his mother's thumb, Józef may have been attracted to gambling as a relief from the pressures of everyday life and as an expression of the self-assertion denied him within the family. Then in 1885 he married the 17-year-old Anna Sommerstein, ten years his junior. Anna was astute and spirited, and her dowry was large; she was also anxious to marry since her widowed father had taken a second wife and displaced her as chatelaine of their country house in Darachów (Darakhiv), a responsibility she had assumed after giving up her education in Germany. Although the Sommersteins were orthodox Jews (a distant relation, Emil Sommerstein, was a prominent Zionist leader in Galicia), neither bride nor groom had much time for religion.[14] Nonetheless, the wedding ceremony was conducted with 'meticulous traditional observances',[15] presumably to please Balbina and the Sommersteins, and the young couple set up home in Warsaw. In 1886 Józef's elder brother Ludwik died, making him the head of the family. This was not as happy a position as it might have been, for the presence of eight surviving sisters, who could all in due course require dowries, was potentially a very significant encumbrance on the estate. A year later Józef and Anna's first child was born, a daughter, Teodora, known within the family as Dziunia. But all was far from well with married life. Józef had resumed his bachelor habits, spending his nights at the gaming tables. Inevitably he was losing money. Nor had old Sommerstein paid more than half his daughter's dowry, having, we may imagine, taken the measure of his son-in-law. So, when Anna fell pregnant for the second time, Balbina decided that Józef should give up his legal practice and move his family out into the country, to the estate of Wola Okrzejska, over a 100 kilometres to the south-east of Warsaw, which the Bernsteins used for summer retreats, having purchased it from Bishop Ciechanowski, uncle of the Nobel-prize-winning author Henryk Sienkiewicz (author of *Quo Vadis?*).

Located in the Mazovian Plain, in a generally featureless terrain relieved only by extensive forests, Wola Okrzejska was a modest manor house, suitable for holidays rather than permanent residence, but set in a very large estate (comprising over 6000 acres), with rose gardens, orchards, and fishponds fed by a system of canals. It was there, on 27 June 1888, that Anna gave birth to her second child, prematurely and with difficulty, her labour having been brought on suddenly by a driving accident which could easily have proved fatal. Hoping for relief from the baking heat, she had consented to go out into the woods in a calèche with the agent for the estate, but the horses took fright and overturned the carriage, throwing Anna to the ground. When her baby son was born, he was presumed dead and put to one side, only for signs of life to be recognised belatedly, and almost accidentally, by one of the women in attendance. This, at least, is the tale told in Lady Namier's biography. It makes for a suitably dramatic entrance into the world, and it also bears an uncanny resemblance to the story of the birth of Thomas Hardy, who was also pronounced stillborn and only rescued by the sharp eyes of a midwife. But that of course does not mean that it is untrue.[16]

While Anna recovered from her ordeal Józef went back to Warsaw, unwilling to sever entirely his links with the law or the gaming tables. The child had been named Ludwik, after Józef's deceased elder brother.[17] That Józef registered his son as Jewish may have been a sop to Balbina's feelings, although he was to do the same with a third, stillborn, child nine years later, long after his mother had died.[18] Little Ludwik was not circumcised, however; nor was he brought up as a Jew. Anna was sufficiently determined on this point to be able to maintain it in the household of her father, to which she removed both children soon after Ludwik's birth. Józef and Anna called themselves Roman Catholics, though until their children were grown up they seem to have given little or no time to the practice of any religion. Why they identified themselves as Christians is nowhere explained, but it may be significant that they were not the only family members in their generation who abandoned their parents' faith. The most obvious explanation would be that this was a response to the hardship and persecution endured by Jews in the Pale of Settlement; but another factor may have been the increasing politicisation of the Jewish community in late nineteenth-century Galicia, which obliged Polonised Jews, especially those like the Bernsteins who by family tradition were Polish liberals, to make a choice between what they perceived as their ethnic and their national identities.

For two years mother and children remained with their grandfather, spending the summers in Darachów and the winters in Teodor's town house amid the provincial elegance of Tarnopol, with Józef an occasional visitor. Years later, Namier told what one friend called 'a characteristic story of his childhood', namely that before the age of two he had liked nothing better than to be 'put on top of a cupboard, and would sit there for hours, looking down on the people below, observing them'.[19] This suggests a picture of a busy and happy house, as well as (perhaps self-consciously) an early manifestation of the detached observer of human nature that Namier saw himself having become, as a historian.

Eventually, Teodor Sommerstein persuaded Józef to leave Warsaw and take over the management of one of the Sommerstein properties, Kobylowloki (Kobylovoloky), which lay about 50 kilometres south of Tarnopol, in the hillier steppe lands leading

1 The Bernstein family, *c.*1893

2 Koszylowce, at the funeral of Tadeusz Modzelewski, 1936

down to the valley of the Dniester. Wola Okrzejska eventually passed to Józef's younger brother Henryk, whose son Leon kept the estate going until the Second World War. After the defeat of the Polish army in 1939, Leon joined the Polish under-ground, was betrayed to the German authorities and, after a period of imprisonment in Lublin Castle, was despatched to Auschwitz. The house itself was destroyed during the Soviet advance in 1944, and the land subsequently redistributed.[20]

Childhood and adolescence

The family's removal to Kobylowloki in 1890 began a confused and uncertain period, which the adult Namier remembered as a mixture of idyllic rural scenes and inex-plicable domestic tensions. Compared with Wola Okrzejska, the single-storey house was cramped, and the estate sufficiently remote to induce social isolation. Suitable company was a long way off. The Bernsteins kept aloof from the local peasantry: Ludwik was not permitted to attend the village school, though he did spend time with household servants and workers on the estate.[21] Afflicted by poor health, he was a lonely child: one of his aunts remembered him as a 'sad, sick little boy'.[22] Relationships with his mother and elder sister seem to have been difficult; at least, what he remembered was a succession of misunderstandings, slights and rebuffs, and a desire to escape. Over half a century later, in a public lecture on the character of King George III, he included a passage which perhaps gives some insight into his own experience, as he remembered or had reconstructed it:

> Isolation by itself would be apt to suggest to a child that there was something wrong with those he had to shun … so the boy spent joyless years in a well-regulated nursery, the

nearest approach to a concentration camp: lonely but never alone, constantly watched and discussed, never safe from the wisdom and goodness of the grown-ups; never with anyone on terms of equality.[23]

One saving grace was provided by the maid, Ella (a Moravian German), who took him with her to church, and gave him an opportunity to observe a very different world than the one which he inhabited at home, or rather a series of worlds, since she attended different denominational services indiscriminately. Another relief came with riding lessons, which started a lifelong love of horses, and brought him on expeditions into the country.

Meanwhile, possibly to everyone's surprise, Józef seemed to take to agriculture, and did well enough to enable his father-in-law to re-sell the property and move the family to another newly acquired estate, at Nowosiólka (Novosilka), close to the town of Skalat, north-east of Trembowla. There Józef was to manage the estate and various commercial and manufacturing interests. The house was larger than Kobylowloki, with a comfortable and well-stocked library, and more extensive gardens. The surrounding landscape was also more varied. Tarnopol and the Sommerstein country house at Darachów were each a comfortable drive away, and there were occasional trips much further afield, to Vienna and to Merano in the Italian Tyrol. But domestic tensions remained, exacerbated for Ludwik by periods of serious illness, including a bout of diptheria. Again, he was not allowed to attend the local school, where he would have to mix with peasant children. Even though teaching was through Polish, the language that Józef insisted be spoken in the home, his schoolfellows would be conversing in Ukrainian, which the Bernstein children were forbidden to learn, but which they seem to have picked up naturally in talking to servants and farmhands.[24] Józef was himself a gifted linguist, and made sure that Teodora and Ludwik were instructed in French and German, but in the Habsburg empire nationality was defined by language, and for a Polonised Jew determined to maintain his Polish identity the language of the peasantry was to be shunned.

In later life Namier thought back to the landscape of his childhood with a heartbreaking nostalgia. Middle-aged and successful, and separated forever from a world that had disappeared, he reviewed a volume of reminiscences by a Ukrainian émigré, and gratuitously inserted a personal note:

> Which of us would not recognise that family coach, drawn by four, six, or eight horses, along a road which could hardly be called a road, in the mud of a late autumn, and grandmother inside, between furs, rugs, and children, consulting the thermometer to see whether we were warm enough? That road, that coach, and that thermometer, what symbols they were of our lives! But we outgrew the family coach … and after that who of us does not remember the rides in the open steppes, the light and colours, the burning

summer days, the music of the Ukrainian nights, 'the deep blue nights … with their bright moonlight', or the magic of the forests in winter? Who can forget the freedom which we enjoyed against a background of savagery and approaching destruction?[25]

As for the peasantry, who formed such an integral part of the landscape, Namier's published writings reveal the same kind of nostalgic idealisation, but also a considerable ambivalence. These were essentially Russian peasants, for Namier always thought of Galicia as part of Ukraine, and of Ukraine as 'Little Russia'. Its Slavs he considered to be ethnically the same as other Russians, despite differences in language and religion: the Ukrainian tongue was in any case closely related to Russian, and the Uniate churches to which ethnic Ukrainians belonged, self-governing Eastern Catholic churches in full communion with the papacy, shared the liturgical and theological traditions of Orthodoxy. The Russian peasant, he believed, embodied the essence of the nation: 'one needs to have lived in an East-European village … to understand the power of the peasant community; governments and masters pass away, but the village commune goes on, a close, self-conscious congregation'.[26] In the dark days of the Second World War he took comfort from a belief that, ultimately, the adamantine strength of the peasants of eastern Europe would ensure the defeat of Hitler.[27] Yet at the same time his opinion of the peasantry as a class could be condescending and even hostile. He regarded the peasant farmer as hopelessly inefficient, and the prosperous peasants as the worst exploiters of the poor.[28] Moreover, a successful peasant revolution inevitably meant the eradication of any kind of refinement in society: 'a radical in so far as the land question is concerned, [the peasant] is otherwise mediaeval in his thinking, egoist and exclusive in his class feeling, brutal and narrow'.[29]

The clue to this ambivalence may lie in the description of 'the village commune' as 'a close, self-conscious congregation'. For it was a 'congregation' (the religious connotation of the word is important) from which Ludwik and his family were excluded. Nor was it the only such community to which they obviously did not belong. The Bernsteins and Sommersteins had nothing in common with the Jews of the countryside, the *shtetl* Jews, some of whom were employed on their estate, nor with most of the Jewish population in Tarnopol and other neighbouring towns, who, unlike Namier's family, had refused to abandon their religion in pursuit of assimilation to another culture. These Jews attended synagogue and conversed in Yiddish – a language considered by Józef to be as far below his family as Ukrainian[30] – and their politics were oriented around Jewish rather than national issues. Moreover, Hasidic Jews, who were numerous in Galicia, had a hostile perception of Józef's distant but much prized ancestor, the Gaon of Vilna, who in his lifetime had been a strenuous opponent of Hasidic doctrines and practices.[31]

In their own self-image, Józef and his family were members of the landed class, and in Galicia this was essentially Polish. There are numerous passages in Namier's later writings which show a willingness to identify with a landowning aristocracy, and a profound appreciation of its virtues and value to society at large. In a piece written in 1922 he observed that before the First World War

> the manor-houses on the big landed estates were centres of high culture and mainstays of modern economic life in Eastern Europe. They resembled Roman villas in semi-barbaric lands. Their inhabitants read the works and thought the thoughts of the most advanced civilisation in the midst of an illiterate peasantry.[32]

At the same time, he was sensitive to the precarious, and indeed essentially artificial, position occupied by the proprietors of Galician manor houses, the 'Pans' who spoke a different language from the native peasantry, practised a different religion and nurtured a different sense of nationality.[33] They were 'over-civilised in some ways, cranky and peculiar in others, and fundamentally ill-adjusted to the world in which they lived'.[34] His family did not truly belong to this class either, a point hammered home by an incident in his adolescence, when he overheard a group of strangers in a railway carriage making fun of his father as a Jew trying to be more Polish than the Poles.[35]

We should of course be careful in searching the mature writings of Sir Lewis Namier for evidence of the childhood experiences of Ludwik Bernstein. Much happened in between that worked upon his understanding of the circumstances of his upbringing, not least his conversion to Zionism, and the political upheavals in eastern Europe after the First World War, which destroyed the genteel social world of the Galician squirearchy and impoverished the Bernstein estates. Nonetheless, his family's circumstances were sufficiently peculiar to explain the sense of restlessness that is highly visible in his own account of his early years and remained close to the surface throughout his life. Looking back, he felt that this was at the core of his problems with his immediate family, and his father in particular, remembering especially a quarrel on his tenth birthday in which Józef told young Ludwik that he was neither a Christian nor a Jew, but a 'nothing'.[36] Although time spent with extended family, on both sides, and especially with his grandfather, would have made Namier fully aware of his Jewish ancestry, he grew up as a classic example of the individual without roots looking desperately for somewhere to anchor himself.

In this respect he was far from unusual. Another notable Galician Jew, the novelist Joseph Roth, born six years after Namier in the predominantly Jewish town of Brody in the north-east of the province, was equally unsettled and to an extent deracinated, but in a way that was very different. Brought up in an orthodox Jewish household,

Roth rebelled against the provincial, Yiddish-speaking culture of his childhood and craved the cosmopolitanism of Vienna, whose sophisticated German-speaking Jews looked down on *Ostjuden*. While Roth idealised the Habsburg state for its liberal accommodation of a variety of splintered national and religious groups, and wrote its panegyric in his great novel *The Radetsky march*, Namier, who did not truly belong to any community, saw Austria-Hungary as a state disconnected from its peoples and by its very existence encouraging the continuance of ethnic rivalries by offering an external source of authority to which competing groups could appeal. In Namier's view the empire was an outdated political entity which needed to be broken up, and at the end of the First World War he found himself in an unexpectedly privileged position, in the British Foreign Office, where he could promote the dissolution over which Roth was to grieve.[37]

Namier's radical ideas developed early in life, partly through reading, thinking and arguing (of which a great deal went on at Nowosiólka), and partly through the private tuition provided for him. He briefly attended the Polish classical *gymnasium* at Tarnopol,[38] but most of his education took place at home. The explanation given for this contravention of the legal requirement that children be sent to public schools was his continuing ill-health. Although he was tall and would have appeared to a casual observer to be physically sturdy – able to enjoy long walks or rides in the countryside – his parents regarded him as an invalid, principally because of chronic respiratory problems, for which eventually, when he was 17, his father resorted to the ministrations of specialists in Vienna. The intervention proved disastrous: an operation to relieve a blockage in the nose did more harm than good, resulting in permanent damage, for which Namier always blamed his father. But since he had to be kept at home a private tutor was engaged. The choice is surprising, if we accept his son's testimony that Józef was a liberal of the old school, a devotee of the writings of John Stuart Mill, for the new member of the household turned out to be a brilliant young freelance journalist called Edmond Weissberg, a Polonised Jew with a dynamic personality and advanced socialist views.

While tutoring Ludwik, Weissberg was also organising a young socialist group in Lemberg, the capital of east Galicia, modern-day Lviv (Lwów in Polish), and running a socialist newspaper. His later career was the stuff of legend: after 1939 he carried out hair-raising acts of bravery in the Polish underground before being murdered by the Nazis.[39] As a young man, his irruption into the Bernstein household made an extraordinary impact. Weissberg was not only a vibrant character with strongly held principles which he was courageous enough to try to put into practice, but was also handsome and athletic. He captivated both Anna and Teodora, and seems to have aroused in Ludwik a kind of hero-worship. They went for long walks together, and Weissberg once brought his pupil on a climbing holiday in the Carpathians. Weissberg's socialist beliefs were meat and drink to a boy with a powerful and unfulfilled emotional side to his character, and Ludwik became a socialist too, joining Weissberg's group and involving himself in propaganda work.[40] When Weissberg had to move on he recommended a successor, Adam Heilpern, who was cut from the same cloth.

These were disturbed years for socialist and social democratic movements in Poland generally, and in Galicia in particular. The Polish Socialist Party (or PPS), the largest and most important socialist organisation in Poland, would break up in 1906 into the Polish Socialist Party-Left, which adhered to a strictly Marxist programme, and the Polish Socialist Party-Revolutionary Fraction, headed by Józef Piłsudski and others, which had a stronger nationalist bent and stressed the importance of striving for an independent Poland.[41] And in Galicia there were two other organisations that were equally important: the Polish Social-Democratic Party (PPS-D), which cooperated with the PPS, and included a strong representation of assimilationist Jews who had adopted Polish nationalism alongside socialism, and the Żydowska Partia Socjalno-Demokratyczna (ŻPPS–D), a more specifically Jewish party which had split from the PPS-D on the grounds that Galicia's Jews, as a separate nation, needed to be addressed in their own language (Yiddish) and on issues which mattered to them. Complicating matters further, both these parties were distinct from, and indeed opposed to, the Zionists.[42] How Weissberg's youth organisation fitted into this fragmented picture is unclear, but there are clues perhaps in the development of Namier's own ideas, which can be glimpsed, as it were, through a bead curtain, in Lady Namier's biography, and which would suggest a connection with the more nationalist PPS-Revolutionary Fraction. For a time Namier professed admiration for Piłsudski, and placed great store by national self-determination, a position which led him to become critical of orthodox Marxism.[43]

The mainspring of this sympathy was not the liberal nationalism of his father and grandfather, for which he never had much respect, but something altogether different: the ideas of the panSlavist movement. It seems most probable that Namier's panSlavism came from Weissberg, though there may have been some influence from his reading. We do not know when he first encountered, and became devoted to, Dostoyevsky, but certainly in later years admiration for the great novelist as representing the 'soul' of Russia was embedded in his own political writings. This new departure created difficulties with Polish socialist colleagues, for although Namier supported Piłsudski's call for an independent Poland, within Galicia he took up the cause of the Ukrainian majority.[44] It also put him further at odds with his family who, like other east European Jews, were hostile to Russia and looked instead to Germany for cultural leadership. A vocal commitment to panSlavism must have aggravated his difficulties with his father and made for heated discussions around the dinner table, or in the library during the evenings, which Józef liked to spend in formal disputations on subjects of their own devising.

Acquiring an education: false starts

In the family's last years at Nowosiólka, Ludwik took significant steps towards adulthood. Endless debates with his father, and time spent going over the estate accounts, made him painfully aware of Józef's weaknesses. At the same time, through Weissberg he was making acquaintances among the socialists of Lemberg. One of these, a philosophy student from the Jagiellonian University in Cracow called Stanisław Kot, came to coach him through the closing stages of preparation for his final school examinations. Kot would later become a renowned Polish historian, and during the Second World War a minister in the Polish government in exile. He and Namier would be lifelong friends.[45] But at this stage there was little Kot needed to do to help his young charge through his examinations and Ludwik was able to spend much of his time reading in Józef's library.

In other respects too, Namier was exerting his own personality. Unbeknown to the rest of the family, he learnt to shoot, and went off hunting boar. He also experienced the first stirrings of romantic passion. One of his sister's friends, Marie Beer, an Austrian from a Jewish family which had also converted to Roman Catholicism, paid a long visit to Nowosiólka in 1904, and the 16-year-old boy was immediately fascinated by her beauty and the air of intellectual and artistic sophistication with which she was wreathed. In the following year Teodora and Ludwik accompanied their father on a visit to Vienna, and brother and sister were again much in Marie's company. It was a painful experience, for Marie was significantly older than Ludwik, already in her 20s, and Teodora seemed to find the whole idea of her brother's infatuation humorous. But this would prove more than a childish passion, and reveals aspects of Namier's character that long outlasted adolescence and may seem at first glance surprising in someone who could often appear severe and 'hard-headed':[46] a capacity to generate within himself powerful emotional attachments, a romantic imagination – a side to his nature which as an old man he wryly described as 'sentimental'[47] – and acute sensitivity to anything that smacked of mockery.

In 1906, when Namier was in his eighteenth year, Józef was finally able to purchase an estate of his own, which meant another removal, this time even further south than Kobylowloki. The estate of Koszylowce (Koshylivtsi), a two-hour journey by horse and trap from the nearest railway station, sat on an area of high ground above the long valley of the Dzurin (Dzurhyn) river, a tributary of the Dniester.[48] The land round about, steppe punctuated by wooded river valleys, was exceptionally fertile, with great wheatfields spreading over the plains. An English visitor in the 1920s described the substantial house as 'standing on a large hillock, with a view down a long valley where we could see a small church with onion domes'.[49] Anna began work on transforming the garden into what became under her guiding hands a botanical treasury.[50] Ludwik was exhilarated by the prospect of a property which would one day be his own. His father was finally a landowner in his own right, instead of merely a manager, and this status, he assumed, would pass to him in due course. With his sister he explored the country, on foot and on horseback, perhaps their happiest time together, at least as he remembered it.

One particular source of interest was a prehistoric tumulus on the estate, in a small promontory carved out by the meandering of the Dzurin. In the first summer at Koszylowce Ludwik and Teodora spent a great deal of time on amateur excavations, perhaps inspired by the recent discovery at Nowosiólka of a warrior's tomb containing a skull which was said to resemble the Neanderthal type, a discovery which caused considerable fluttering among archaeologists and anthropologists.[51] Brother and sister came upon the Koszylowce site by accident, in the summer of 1906, when workers who had been brought in from the village to dig the foundations for their mother's new greenhouse unearthed a small clay figure. Surprised that Ludwik should be interested in such things, they told him where more might be found, and pointed him to an *oboz* (a camp), in the woods near the river. There he and Teodora dug up more female figurines and pottery fragments, amassing a large collection.

They were, however, literally scratching the surface of what was to prove a highly significant Neolithic hoard. Not long afterwards their aunt Therese's brother-in-law, Sigmund Herzberg-Frankel, happened to be visiting Koszylowce. A professor of history at Franz-Josef University in Czerniowce (Chernivitsi), he was sufficiently intrigued to inform a colleague, who undertook more formal excavations in 1908, after which the site quickly became widely known and its importance established.[52] Further work before the First World War revealed the remains of a small-scale industrial complex, while much later, in the 1920s and 1930s, Namier's friend, the English amateur archaeologist Denis Buxton, found wattle-and-daub houses, flint implements, arrowheads and axeheads, as well as more pottery and figurines.[53] The discoveries made by Ludwik and Teodora in the *oboz* fired in both brother and sister a long-lasting interest in the history of the countryside in which they lived, and in the movement and settlement of ancient peoples. In later life Teodora would become an ethnographer, studying Polish folk costume,[54] while her brother's historical thinking embodied a profound belief in the importance of ethnicity and the relationship of a people to territory.

Namier only had a single summer to explore and enjoy Koszylowce. It was enough to implant in him a love for the estate, and a belief that this was *his* personal territory. In the autumn he went to university to study law, as his father had done. The intention seems to have been that he would equip himself for a career in business or public affairs. His first experience of university life proved disastrous, however. He was sent to Lemberg, where, according to Lady Namier, he 'at once came up against nationalist students of the extreme type – resembling the Nazis of later days'.[55] These were members of the right-wing National Democratic Party, headed by Roman Dmowski, who later would become Namier's *bête noire*. The National Democrats certainly had an anti-Semitic element, which became more pronounced as time went by; nonetheless, Lady Namier's account does not ring true. Namier never talked to her of his experiences in Lemberg. Instead, her information came from his friend August Zaleski (president of the Polish government in exile after 1947). But since Zaleski was in London in 1906–7 he could not speak from personal knowledge. Furthermore, although the university recorded the religion of students at enrolment, and Namier would have been entered as Jewish because of his registration at birth, it is unlikely that he would have been picked out for ill-treatment on those grounds. Lemberg had a large and active population of Jewish undergraduates: two of Namier's cousins attended at about the same time, and both graduated successfully.

A much more important factor was the poisonous political atmosphere in the city and the university: the National Democrats were engaged in a bitter conflict with the socialists, and with the PPS in particular. It seems more likely that Namier's socialist views rather than his race were the cause of National Democrat hostility. There were additional complications, for the PPS was itself bitterly divided: it would soon split into hard-line Marxist and nationalist factions, at the party congress in Lemberg in November, when Namier was back in Koszylowce. And in a final twist, he found it difficult to navigate a path through the cross-currents of Jewish factionalism in the city and university. He had little sympathy for the assimilationist party, well-established but now increasingly on the defensive, while the Zionist students, who were highly organised and politically assertive, were quite alien to him.[56] Although much later he declared that he had been 'a strongly Jewish nationalist' or at least 'a theoretical Zionist' since about 1906, this seems to have meant no more than that he was curious about his Jewish heritage and identified with Jewish sufferings.[57] In political terms he had little in common with Zionists, whose insistence on using Yiddish would have left him cold. Nor can he have relished their criticism of Polonised Jews like his own family, and their characterisation of assimilationists as 'house Jews'.[58] It seems little wonder that, despite the charms of the city's wedding-cake architecture, cobbled streets and lively cafés, he found his situation insupportable: as Lady Namier put it, having 'no group to join or any congenial men to consort with ... he wrote to his father and returned home'.[59]

There may also be a more straightforward explanation for Namier's removal from Lemberg: another breakdown in his health. In November 1906 he was sent to Switzerland, to be placed in the care of the internationally renowned lung specialist, Professor Demiéville, and to enrol in the faculty of law in the University of Lausanne. At Lausanne students could choose their own programme of courses, and many treated the university as a preparation for study elsewhere, moving on after a short time. In the single term when Namier was a student until March 1907 he studied no law, but followed courses in sociology, political economy, statistics and 'sciences financières', general philosophy and the history of the French Revolution. He also worked on his Russian.[60]

Namier's choice of courses gives the first clue to the way in which his mind was developing. His history professor, the Swiss-French Edmond Rossier, was a distinguished man (indeed, he was nominated for the Nobel prize for literature), but a literary rather than a 'scientific' historian. More interesting, in the light of Namier's later development, was his lecturer in 'sociology', Vilfredo Pareto, an Italian polymath who, having begun as an engineer, was now professor of political economy. At the time he lectured to Namier, Pareto's most important published work was in economics, and he was developing a mathematically based theory about the inevitability of the unequal distribution of wealth in societies. This theory did not always work out in practice, and Pareto subsequently turned to sociology for a more satisfying explanation of human behaviour. His *Trattato di sociologia generale* (1916) would develop a theory of elite formation and decline, based on the understanding that human action is not always driven by the rational calculation of advantage but by deeper motivations, which he called 'residues' (a term derived from Durkheim, and ultimately from J. S. Mill) and their 'derivations', but which Freud would describe and define somewhat differently, as the working of the subconscious mind.[61]

Pareto impressed Namier, and it is tempting to detect echoes of his thought in Namier's approach to history.[62] But we should be careful not to overstate the connection. Namier certainly took from Pareto's lectures a keen interest in economics and sociology, and also perhaps the first inklings of dissatisfaction with socialist economic analysis, of which Pareto strongly disapproved. Namier also believed strongly in the importance of establishing detailed and accurate statistical information about social and political questions, but Pareto was only one of several influences pointing him in this direction. Any suggestion that he was directly influenced by Pareto's ideas must founder on the lack of direct evidence. Although, as a historian, Namier focused on the British eighteenth-century elite, he never subscribed to Pareto's cyclical theory of elite formation, while his emphasis on the importance of the irrational in human motivation almost certainly owed more to Freud and to his own early immersion in the novels of Dostoyevsky.

Socially, Lausanne was a success. There were some chilly encounters with German students, none of whom, he assumed, 'could have risked, even at that time, to be seen in company with a Jew'.[63] But Namier resided away from the city, at the Grand Hotel Eden in Montreux, overlooking Lake Geneva, and made friends with a French family staying there, whose son was also a student. Under their influence, Namier decided that the only place for him to complete his education was the Sorbonne. But on returning to Koszylowce after a holiday in Italy he found his father in no mood to indulge him. A bundle of letters had been delivered, from a married French actress who, while staying at Montreux, had engaged in an affair with Namier's new friend, and now sought Ludwik's advice as a matter of urgency on what she should do, caught between lover and husband. At least that is what he told his father. Józef, suspecting something worse, forbade further exposure to the wiles of French womanhood and vetoed Paris. Instead, taking advice from 'an Anglophile' cousin, and remembering some remarks from Pareto, Ludwik went off to the London School of Economics, confident in the belief – shared by many central and east European Jews – that England was 'the most civilised and humane society in the world'.[64]

In comparison with the elegance of the cities he knew in childhood, and the mountain scenery and crisp air of Switzerland, London was bound to be a disappointment in aesthetic terms. Namier took lodgings in Bedford Place, a late-Georgian terrace running between Russell Square and Bloomsbury Square. He found the ambience ugly and oppressive, and the 'urban wretchedness' of the English proletariat repellent.[65] His extraordinary aptitude for languages enabled him to acquire a fluency in spoken and written English. But his 'heavy' accent – which on occasion he may have been tempted to exaggerate for effect – could make it difficult for others to understand him, accentuating his social unease.[66] Nor did he particularly enjoy his classes.

Nevertheless, in helping to shape his ideas the time spent in London was not wasted: it pushed his thinking further along lines that were already becoming established. Later he picked out as particularly important the lectures given by the director of the School, the geographer Halford Mackinder, which had drawn attention to 'geographical factors in the shaping of history'. Mackinder's pioneering studies in geopolitics, and in particular his 'heartland theory', appealed strongly to Namier, since it identified Eurasia as the most important part of the global land mass, and focused on eastern Europe as the 'pivot area', the key to control of the 'heartland' and thus of the world's resources. This fitted with the development of Namier's under-standing of the dynamics of great-power politics.[67]

In a different way Namier may also have taken something from the teaching of the political scientist Graham Wallas, whose book *Human nature in politics* (1908), Namier used many years later as a peg on which to hang his own thoughts on the same subject.[68] Wallas argued strongly against the tendency of students of politics to 'exaggerate the intellectuality of mankind', and insisted that 'most of the political opinions of most men' – a careful qualification – were not the product of 'reasoning tested by experience' but 'half-conscious inference fixed by habit'. This was reminis-cent of Pareto's 'residues' and 'derivations', and although Namier wrote over forty years later that he considered Wallas's book 'naïve', it may still have left a trace.[69] The lectures and writings of Pareto and Wallas would have kept his attention on col-lective rather than individual behaviour, which was a feature of his historical work.

Another of his teachers was the Finn Edvard Westermarck, who gave an inau-gural lecture during Namier's time at the LSE on 'Sociology as a university study'.[70] Westermarck was a different kind of sociologist from Pareto; more of an anthropolo-gist, in fact. His exposition of *The origin and development of moral ideas* (1912), ana-lysed the ethical systems of non-European peoples to explore the origin of morality and to explain the fact that different societies operate under different moral frame-works.[71] Westermarck's denial of moral absolutes appalled the religious-minded. His conclusions also undermined the universalist Enlightenment belief in the supremacy of reason, and could well have reinforced notions which eventually took shape in Namier's mind, that in politics the individual was less important than the group, and that the collective will of the group had little to do with rationality.

Despite his general air of dissatisfaction, Namier made some enduring friendships at the LSE, where students and staff socialised on semi-equal terms.[72] He became close to August Zaleski, then working towards a master's degree, and enjoyed the company of two radical young women: Tegan Harris, whose husband Frank, a Foreign Office civil servant, was preparing a biography of the first earl of Sandwich (Cromwell's admiral and Charles II's ambassador to Spain), and Rachel Barrett, a vivacious Welsh suffragette, one of the few people prepared to tell Namier to shut up and listen.[73] The method of teaching by seminar also suited him, accustomed as he was to formal disputations with his father. Outside the school, he involved himself in the Fabian Society, which had a close association with the LSE. According to Lady Namier he joined the society in November 1907. In that month his name appeared in one of the lists of 'candidates for election' which appeared in *Fabian News*.[74] Oddly, it did not subsequently figure in the society's subscription list.[75] Namier almost cer-tainly attended meetings and, later on, joined the Oxford University branch of the

Fabians,[76] though we should perhaps be wary of Lady Namier's stories of his hobnob-bing with such luminaries as H. G. Wells and Bernard Shaw.[77]

Namier also attended several of the Fabian residential schools at Pen-yr-allt on the north Wales coast. 'Ludwik Bernstein', giving his address as the LSE, was among those present at an Easter 'education conference' in April 1908, an event organised by the society's education group.[78] It was there that he met Thomas Jones ('T. J.'), the future cabinet secretary who was then a lecturer in political economy at the University of Glasgow. The others were a very mixed bag, mostly schoolteachers but also a violinist, a 'teacher of Swedish gymnastics', a 'tabulator of digits in a savings bank' and a Scotsman who described himself as a 'vagabond, railway official in spare time'. The ingredients seem to be there for a comic novel. Not surprisingly, perhaps, Namier secured a room to himself. He enjoyed walks in the shadow of Cader Idris. But he did not return to another residential school until Easter 1910, by which time he had left the LSE.[79] The summer school in 1910 was directed by the Webbs, about whom he was later rather rude. Details are recorded in the log book, the days consist-ing principally of lectures, interspersed with sports and outdoor excursions, while evenings were passed with debates and concerts, and one 'fancy-dress ball'.[80]

Relief from the squalor of the London streets came in spring 1908. Namier had gone home to Koszylowce for Christmas, and was more depressed than ever on his return to Bloomsbury. Not even a move from Bedford Place to new lodgings near Kensington Gardens could raise his spirits. Tegan Harris's husband, who had been at New College, had already made several unsuccessful efforts to interest people in Oxford in this brilliant and unusual young man, thinking that he would be much better suited there than at the LSE. Then, out of the blue, Namier received a letter from A. L. Smith, a fellow of Balliol, asking him to lunch. The explanation, which he did not know, was that Westermarck had contacted Smith, recommending his pupil Bernstein as 'the ablest young man he had ever come across'.[81] Lunch went well, and Namier left Oxford with the assurance that he would return in the autumn to begin reading for a degree in modern history. In July he was invited again, to a more formal lunch with the Master of Balliol, the Scottish classicist J. L. Strachan-Davidson, a close friend and college ally of Smith, and formally offered a place.[82]

Balliol

Balliol, and its 'tranquil consciousness of effortless superiority', made an enormous and lasting impact on Namier.[83] The combination of intellectual and social distinc-tion was intoxicating. For the remainder of his life, the college remained a kind of lode-star to him. Balliol contemporaries, like the writer and Alpinist Arnold Lunn, alongside whom Namier received a knighthood in 1952, were invariably regarded as old and dear friends, whether or not their paths had regularly crossed with his in the meantime.[84] Here, as in much else, all may not have been quite as Namier remembered it: the widow of the historian Douglas Cole, whom Namier described as 'one of my best friends' in college, thought that their acquaintance had actually been 'comparatively slight'.[85] Nonetheless, almost half a century after his time as an undergraduate, when writing to owners of manuscripts whose collections he wished to inspect, he would introduce himself, if possible, through a Balliol connection: 'you will not know me, but I was up with your uncle', or some such phrase. And for his tutors, particularly F. F. ('Sligger') Urquhart and A. L. Smith, he retained an almost filial devotion. He was especially attached to Smith, to whose memory he paid a heartfelt tribute in the preface to his first major book.[86]

According to the reminiscences of those who knew him in college Ludwik Bernstein also made a great impact on Balliol. The contemporaries who answered Lady Namier's call for assistance with her biographical research remembered 'Berners' as a striking personality, a college 'character', around whom a mythology quickly grew up among his fellow undergraduates. Namier's imposing physique, heavy accent and outlandish personal history were enough to make him stand out, leaving aside his unusual keenness to learn (he was the only freshman in his year to take seriously the compulsory divinity course – 'divvers' – much to everyone's amusement)[87] and encyclopaedic knowledge of foreign countries about which most undergraduates had barely heard. He was also a social 'oddity' in a different way. One of Lady Namier's informants hinted at this in a letter which remembered him 'bursting with first-hand information about eastern Europe and', the tell-tale addition, 'eager to communicate it to us'.[88] His enthusiasm to expound, the origin of his reputation among the English as a frightful bore, was a warning sign to the smarter undergraduates, and even the more academically inclined could find it off-putting. Arnold Toynbee, genuinely a close friend, recalled that as a final-year undergraduate he had received an early morning visitation from the freshman Namier, announcing: 'I am Bernstein; I am coming to have breakfast with you.' This was in flagrant disregard of the convention that 'senior men' invited freshmen for breakfast, not vice versa. Moreover, once ensconced in Toynbee's rooms, Bernstein subjected him to a 'stream of talk'. Not everyone, Toynbee observed, took such *gaucherie* in good part.[89]

What Lady Namier's correspondents remembered most about Berners (or what they were willing to tell her) was his outstanding intellect, the fact that he was slightly older than his contemporaries and seemed to have more experience of the world, and of course that he was able and willing to 'hold forth' at every opportunity on his pet subjects: he was 'a mature foreign savant, with all that that implied, a man among boys'.[90] Unfortunately, there are few contemporary references to his undergraduate career against which we may check this retrospective evidence, or his own roseate memories of Oxford in general and Balliol in particular. However, an Australian, Allen Leeper, one of his exact contemporaries in college, did mention Namier several times in letters home. In later years Leeper would work with Namier at the Foreign Office. As freshmen they were much together. They played tennis regularly, Leeper invariably winning with embarrassing ease, for Namier was 'quite rotten' at the game, though, because of a desire to fit in, always keen to play.[91] Less than a month after the start of their first term, Leeper wrote that he had been on the college courts with 'Bernstein (a Galician Jew … *very* clever but I don't care for his strong Semitic characteristics)'.[92] A year later, his opinion had mellowed. Quoting Namier's opinion on a mutual friend, he added,

> I think I've talked about Bernstein before. He is a most curiously interesting man – one of the few Jews I take to – a Pole and a sceptic – but yet unlike most sceptics and most Jews, the reverse of aggressive. I didn't care for him much at first but I have got to see that he is much nicer than I thought. I was round to breakfast with him last Tuesday and met Toynbee.[93]

The fact that Leeper could think it perfectly natural to write: 'I don't care for his strong Semitic characteristics' or 'He is … one of the few Jews I take to' underlines what must seem to the modern observer the most obvious difficulty for Namier in adjusting to life in Oxford. So casual was the anti-Semitism of the social world into which he had dropped, that it was almost a reflex.[94] The historian does not have to work very hard to find examples – even A. L. Smith, in a reference he wrote for Namier, confessed that 'I started on him with the usual prejudice against Jews'.[95] But the picture was complex. A venomous strain of anti-Semitism was certainly rife among the young 'bloods', men like the classicist Patrick Shaw-Stewart: the 'golden generation' that perished on the battlefields of the First World War.[96] However, Shaw-Stewart and his friends, who formed a self-conscious social elite within the college, were at an extreme point on the spectrum.[97] Jewish undergraduates were by no means unusual in Edwardian Oxford, and were particularly attracted to Balliol, where they could and did thrive. Leonard Stein and Philip Guedalla, both undergraduates at Balliol, each held the presidency of the Union, while their friend Leonard Goldsmid Montefiore, also a Balliol man, was secretary and treasurer. Stein's diary suggests that their lives at Oxford were much the same as other undergraduates': evenings spent in clubs and debating societies, much drinking and 'ragging', followed by the inevitable disciplinary action from the college authorities.[98]

Stein, Goldsmid Montefiore and Guedalla represented different strands of Jewishness: Stein attended synagogue and in later life was a prominent Zionist; Goldsmid-Montefiore, the son of the founder of Liberal Judaism, belonged to the University Jewish Study Circle; Guedalla's family was utterly secularised. But all came from wealthy families and had been educated at public schools. In fact, the Stein and Guedalla families knew each other well. They were at ease in Edwardian Oxford, even if they still needed to be careful not to give offence by seeming to presume. In 1908 another Balliol contemporary, Gerald Rufus Isaacs, the son of Sir Rufus Isaacs, Liberal MP for Reading and a future viceroy of India, failed to secure election to the Arnold Society. According to Arnold Lunn (himself the son of a travel agent), it was Isaacs's 'affected manner, his unique conceit, and his blood hunting' which had offended the members. Instead of the 'very superior' Isaacs they chose a notorious drunkard, which Lunn thought a great joke.[99] Isaacs's punishment was short-lived, however, and by the following year he had been safely elected to the Brackenbury Club.[100] Things seem to have been different for Harry Sacher, the *Manchester Guardian* journalist, an undergraduate at New College a few years earlier. Sacher, the son of a tailor in the East End of London, did not enjoy his time at Oxford to anything like the same extent, and attributed his failure to secure election to a fellowship of All Souls to the twin handicaps of being a Jew and 'not a public schoolman'.[101]

Namier was neither an upper-middle-class public-school educated Jew like Stein, nor a working-class boy making good, like Sacher. His background and heavily accented manner of speaking – almost as if he had been a poor *shtetl* Jew – marked him out.[102] To the anti-Semites in college it made his racial identity appear even more obvious. At the same time, Jewish undergraduates also regarded him as a very different kind of creature from themselves. As reported by Lady Namier, his recollection was that 'English-Jewish undergraduates, who knew only their own kind and impoverished small-town immigrants from the Eastern Pale, could not make him out at all'.[103] He told her that, out of curiosity, he had once been to a meeting of the Adler Society, a discussion group which had been established a few years earlier by the University section of the Oxford Hebrew Congregation, and had come upon the members arguing whether 'there should or should not be organs in the synagogue. As I had never been to a synagogue and did not intend to go to one, I felt that a society which carefully engaged in such discussions was no fit place for me.'[104] Clearly, though, he was much interested in Jewish affairs, and was on relatively good terms with both Stein and Goldsmid Montefiore.

Many years later Stein later recalled that Namier had once presented himself 'at the door of my rooms in Balliol soon after his arrival there in 1908 with the brusque announcement, "I have come to discuss the Jewish question"'.[105] In 1911, while on a journey to south Wales, Namier paid a short and unsuccessful visit to Montefiore's father at the family seat in Hampshire, which must mean that he had been provided with an introduction by the son.[106] For Guedalla, on the other hand, he seems to have nurtured a lasting contempt.[107]

According to Lady Namier's biography her husband would have no truck with the idea that there was anti-Semitism in the Oxford of his day. If her statement is correct, he may simply have been unaware of prejudice, which is possible, given his undeveloped social antennae, and the gentlemanly discretion which Oxford manners dictated in the expression of such views. Alternatively, he may have wiped it from his memory in his idealisation of the university in general and Balliol in particular. In the first draft of her biography, however, Lady Namier alluded to some unpleasantness during Namier's time as an undergraduate. Before she was persuaded to change her text, she wrote that the undergraduates of the time were 'nice boys – plagued with a protracted adolescence that in the nastier ones could easily turn into unworthy per-siflage'.[108] And Namier himself once let slip a comment which suggests that he may have been aware at the time of a different attitude towards him on the part of some of those among whom he had come to live. In a short book on the origins of the First World War, published in 1915, he inserted an unnecessary paragraph discussing the psychological obstacles that lay in the path of German émigrés, which can be read as an indirect reflection on his own experience:

> It is a hardship for anyone to undergo a complete change of 'system' and of intellectual and social surroundings; it is all the harder, the higher the intellectual level and the social position attained by the emigrant in his old home. For a German belonging to their upper … caste, it is painful to find that the best among the Anglo-Saxons unconsciously apply to themselves an ancient Greek maxim, preserved to us in Aristotle's *Politics*: the Hellenes, he says, considered that their own nobility were nobles, wherever they went, but that barbarians could be nobles only at home … To any German, as to any other human being, it causes a good deal of pain to find himself a stranger within someone else's gates, to fall from the level of a citizen to that of a *metoikos*, to have to justify his existence, to be looked upon with childish, unreasoning contempt, or, at the best, with magnanimous, self-conscious toleration.[109]

Assuming that Namier was not subjected to manifestations of overt anti-Semitism – and it is a big assumption – the reason might have been that he was saved by his very foreign-ness; that he was simply too extraordinary to fit with the stereotypes that his fellow undergraduates had constructed. He was a Polish Jew, but, despite his accent, not at all like the poor Yiddish-speaking immigrants whom the English cus-tomarily despised. Possibly for this very reason he played up his family's landowning background. Allen Leeper thought he was a 'landowner's son', though technically this had only been the case since 1906.[110] Others were given the same impression: H. W. C. Davis, a Balliol history don, wrote that Namier was 'undeniably a Jew, but ... free from the ordinary faults of his race, and is a gentleman'.[111] Indeed, Namier himself went so far as to describe Niemirowski as his 'gentry name', ignoring the reality of his paternal family background in finance and trade.[112] So even 'Sligger' Urquhart, whose snobbery was sufficiently refined for him to favour Etonians above the products of any other public school, took Namier under his wing and admitted him to soirées in his rooms.[113] Namier cherished his status as an exotic specimen to the extent that he was quite put out when his cousin Ludwik Ehrlich, another physically imposing Galician Jew with a brilliant mind, a stiff accent and strong political views, followed him to Oxford, to Exeter College, in 1913: 'Berners' was no longer unique, and did not like it.[114]

Most of what we know of Namier's time at Balliol has been filtered through his own memory, and the memories of others. But the scraps of contemporary documentary evidence support the general picture drawn by Lady Namier, that for the most part he went his own way and concentrated on his studies and on other matters of great seriousness. He kept his distance from the more juvenile aspects of undergraduate life: the endless round of 'rags' and drunken escapades recorded in Lunn's Wodehousian diary, which brought frequent tussles with the 'progs' (proctors) and the police, arrests, gatings, rustications and worse.[115] Namier did not care for this kind of behaviour, sometimes showing his resentment openly; nor did he have any time for the kind of tuft-hunting that made Isaacs unpopular.[116] Indeed, he was not particularly gregarious: one of his friends thought him to be 'a rather lonely man'.[117] There was no chance that he would ever be prized as a social companion: despite his political views he was not elected to the Shaftesbury Club, a left-wing society which required conviviality as well as intellect. The societies he joined were the Arnold, where in a discussion of the unemployment problem he made an intervention which, whatever it was, 'created great comment';[118] the university branch of the Fabians; and the college History Club.[119] What excited him was 'his intellectual life',[120] and in his final year he organised a study group for his fellow undergraduates.[121] This increased his popularity: as Smith put it, 'he used to act as a sort of universal mental provider for his contemporaries'.[122]

Later in life Namier was to write, 'Balliol taught me to think. All I've done I owe to Balliol.' To some extent this must have been owing to the company he kept, in what was intellectually the most formidable college in the university. The current crop of undergraduate historians was particularly intimidating. Besides gifted individuals like Leeper and Stein, who would make their mark in politics or public service, the

History Club boasted a quiverful of young men who would go on to be leading figures in the discipline. Toynbee became a fellow of Balliol and later director of the Royal Institute of International Affairs (Chatham House). His controversial multi-volume *Study of History* made him for a time 'the most famous historian in the world'.[123] Others included Namier's fellow Fabian, Douglas Cole, a future star of the Left Book Club and eventually Chichele Professor of Social and Political Theory at Oxford, and two regius professors: G. N. Clark, who became Sir George Clark, regius professor of modern history at Cambridge and president of the British Academy; and Vivian Galbraith, director of London University's Institute of Historical Research and then regius professor at Oxford.

The history curriculum, however, was exceedingly old-fashioned, by the standards of more progressive universities on the continent, and even elsewhere in England. Oxford still taught constitutional history in the tradition of Bishop Stubbs. The innovations of the Manchester school, headed by T. F. Tout, with its emphasis on administrative history and on research training, had not been imitated. An Oxford history degree remained primarily a preparation for public service.[124] This is not to say that new currents did not touch the banks of the Isis. H. A. L. Fisher, a don at New College, who had studied at the École des Chartes in Paris and at Göttingen, gave a talk to the History Club in 1908 on the 'sociological view of history', but such an occurrence was unusual, to say the least.[125] Both Allen Leeper and Harry Sacher complained that 'research' was simply not a feature of Oxford teaching; indeed, Leeper told his father that everything was directed towards the final examinations (Schools): 'love of learning in the sense that the French and Germans feel it is non-existent'.[126] The atmosphere was very different from Namier's brief experiences of Lausanne and the LSE. And yet, despite his advanced views on some political and social questions, Namier seems to have taken to it. This must have been owing at least in part to the social elitism of Oxford, Balliol's ethos of patriotic service, and the sense that its undergraduates were the future rulers of empire, all of which appealed to Namier, and made up for a lack of intellectual novelty and excitement.

He had also fallen under the spell of his tutors. Urquhart was an uninspiring teacher, but solicitous for his students' welfare. Davis, too, even if concerned that Namier 'does not know when he has stayed too long in my rooms', liked and helped him.[127] But the most profound influence was Smith's. As Namier wrote much later, 'A. L.' was 'much more than a teacher to us old Balliol men'; 'he was our friend and teacher to whom we turned for help and advice, and who often helped us without our asking or even knowing'. He was also 'perhaps the best history teacher of our time'.[128]

At first glance Smith might seem an unlikely influence on Namier; certainly a very unlikely role model, for he was not a modern 'scientific' historian devoted to

35

documentary research, of which the mature Namier would become one of the greatest examplars. Smith excelled at cramming undergraduates for final examinations. As one of his pupils observed, 'I never thought of A. L. as a man who "led you on" to the original sources and to research.' While appreciating the importance of 'criticism, analysis, tabulation, [and] statistics' as the 'instruments of modern research', Smith always laid greatest stress on 'the faculty of imagination'.[129] When praising the work of the great legal historian F. W. Maitland, it was Maitland's prose style and 'constructive imagination' that he particularly admired.[130] Smith saw the purpose of history as 'instruction in moral and social obligations, and the meaning of nationalism'.[131] In his understanding of English constitutional development, and of the divine purpose that lay behind the rise of British empire to world leadership, he was an unreconstructed Stubbsian.

If Namier had been nothing more than a 'scientific' historian, Smith would have been his antithesis. But although Namier the undergraduate showed a particular interest in, and aptitude for, economic and statistical analysis, there was another side to his character, especially marked in youth and early manhood but present throughout his life – a tendency which broke out most often in his historical essays but was occasionally visible in his most detailed forensic work on eighteenth-century politics. He could see history in long sweeps, and make broad generalisations about peoples, which emphasised the power of religion in fashioning national culture. Above all, he argued the vital importance of a national territory. His early panSlavism, and his later Zionism, rested on these foundations, as indeed did his veneration of the British social and political system, not only as the product of historical evolution but as an expression of the essential English character.[132] And his writing itself was full of imaginative jumps and striking metaphors. He too believed that the truth about the past could not be attained simply by lining up 'facts'. Although undeniably of great value, statistics and tables could also prove to be tyrants which it was the historian's duty to resist. All this explains why he did not find Smith's approach to history uncongenial.

But it was above all Smith's personality that captivated his unusual protégé. As a tutor, Smith 'was … unequalled'.[133] He asked sharp questions of his students, and was fertile with suggestions of topics and reading matter. In Namier's case what seems to have been most important was that Smith took the young man seriously. He was, Namier said, 'the person who first tried to make a man of me'.[134] He challenged assumptions and opinions in a way that was neither hostile nor dismissive. Furthermore, discussions were not confined to the tutorial room. Namier joined in the long walks to which Smith was addicted, and was a frequent visitor to the large house in Mansfield Road, 'King's Mound', which had been built for Smith and his wife. Originally intended to provide accommodation for working-class aspirants to a Balliol education whom Smith took in to prepare for the Oxford entrance examination, it was filled with Smith's nine children, seven of whom were daughters.[135] Namier was such a frequent visitor to the house in later years that some members of the family devised a limerick about him:[136]

There was a young person called Namier
Who came 'ere and came 'ere and came 'ere …

But they also adopted him as one of their own: to Smith's granddaughter Rosalind Mitchison he was 'Uncle Lewis'.[137] The psychoanalysts who treated the older Namier would doubtless have had a ready explanation for Namier's attachment to the Smith family. For a young man (and Namier was only 20 when he came to Balliol for all that his manner made him seem much older), and one whose relationship with his own parents had been uneasy, Smith provided a more satisfactory father figure than Józef, and King's Mound an altogether happier household than Koszylowce.

The importance of Smith to the development of Namier's thinking was two-fold. First and foremost, Namier absorbed Smith's conviction of the moral purpose behind Britain's imperial mission. This became a fundamental principle to which he would adhere throughout his life. Although impressing those who met him in Balliol as a 'strong Jew' (whatever that meant), he was also 'a keen student of Anglo-Saxon institutions and ways and … enthusiastic for our civilisation, which he regards as the only genuinely liberal one'; genuinely liberal, that is, if one focused on the white dominions and chose to ignore the more unsavoury episodes of colonial exploitation, or compared the British empire only with the oppressive autocracy of Tsarist Russia and the 'hugger-mugger' of Habsburg Austria-Hungary.[138] This devotion to British imperialism owed much to Smith's personal example, but it was also reinforced by other influences. The ethos of Balliol, a production line for British statesmen, was one of service to empire. Among Namier's closest friends in college were Ronald Wingate, whose father Sir Reginald was governor-general of the Sudan; colonials like Allen Leeper and the Canadian Cuthbert Holmes, with whom he went once on a reading party to Brighton;[139] and the American Rhodes scholar Whitney Shepardson, a man with a marked interest in, and sympathy for, the British imperial tradition.[140] For Shepardson, Britain and the United States were the two great 'Anglo-Saxon' nations, and while at Oxford Shepardson won the Gladstone prize for an essay on the causes of 'the revolt of the American colonies'.[141]

Smith's particular influence can also be seen in the way that Namier understood the nature of empire in cultural terms. The Protestant radicalism that underpinned Smith's Christian socialism – something Namier had already encountered among the Fabians and which was a powerful element in Edwardian Oxford[142] – produced in him a strong attraction to the English Puritans who had made the 'Anglo-Saxon nation' in British north America. Although Namier only ever expressed any inclination towards religious faith in old age, in the company of Julia and her friends, he was always fascinated by religion as a social and cultural phenomenon. For him the nature of the Russian soul, especially that of the Russian peasantry, was defined by a patient devotion to Orthodox Christianity; and the society in which he now found himself, and the empire to which it had given rise, was likewise characterised by the Protestant tradition. His first choice as a possible subject for research was seventeenth-century English Puritanism, and in 1918, while at the Foreign Office, he gave a series of evening lectures at King's College, London, on Puritan writers.[143] For a time he was even drawn into an admiration for the theology of John Calvin, though probably more for the rigour of Calvin's thought than for any spiritual dimension.[144] He later bragged to a Zionist acquaintance that he was 'probably the only person alive' to have read all six volumes of Calvin's *Institutes* in the original Latin.[145]

In this flirtation with radical Protestantism he may also have been indulging a revulsion from the Counter-Reformation Catholicism synonymous with Austrian imperial hegemony. A decade later, in a paean to President Masaryk of Czechoslovakia, he placed Czechoslovak nationalism firmly in the tradition of John Hus, in opposition to 'that combination of theocracy and bureaucracy, of Roman Catholic clericalism and mental and moral unfreedom, which were the very foundation of the Habsburg regime'.[146]

Triumph and disappointment

Namier's hard work and devotion to his studies paid off handsomely, though in the long run he was to be disappointed of the clouds of glory that he had allowed himself to expect. In the 'Mods' examinations at the end of his second year he was unofficially 'proxime accessit',[147] and in the following March, having achieved a string of Alpha plus marks in college examinations, was awarded a special prize (of £10) by the Balliol history tutors.[148] Even before the results of his final examinations were known, Smith and others were touting him for an academic post at the University of Toronto. Such advancement would not have been unusually precocious: James Todd, a Balliol man who had graduated the previous year, was already lecturing at Edinburgh. Namier himself seems to have been eager to try his luck in north America.[149] The references were glowing: he was said to be exceptionally talented, 'the ablest man we have had in economics and history for some years'.[150]

38

Although reading modern history, he was taking the political economy special subject, under the statistician Francis Edgeworth, and demonstrating a remarkable capacity for abstract economic analysis. Unfortunately, some referees expressed a concern about his command of English; not written English, which although 'cumbrous' in style, according to H. W. C. Davis, was perfectly clear, but his speech, with its strong accent. Although Smith and others refused to recognise this as a problem, Godfrey Lloyd, the professor of political economy at Toronto, who was spending the summer in England and interviewed Namier, did not find his diction easy to follow.[151] Lloyd's colleagues, who were probably already uneasy at the prospect of appointing an east European Jew, however brilliant, preferred a safer candidate, a dull but reliable product of the English public school system, who had taken a second-class degree in economics from Cambridge.[152] One Toronto professor observed that Namier must have 'the misfortune to have the Jewish characteristic of indistinct articulation strongly developed'.[153]

That was not quite the end of the story, for Kenneth Bell, a Balliol product who had gone to Toronto two years previously as a history lecturer and was back in England for the summer, decided that he had better stay at home to help run his family's publishing firm, and recommended Namier as his successor. Bell also admitted to an initial prejudice against Jews, but said that when he met Namier he had been vastly impressed. Namier came to stay and the Bells grew to like him immensely.[154] But as far as Toronto was concerned, Namier was no better for history than he was for economics. They did not like 'the choice of a Polish Jew as an interpreter of history … who by his broken accent constantly proclaims it'.[155]

In the meantime, Namier took the expected outstanding first-class degree. This encouraged him to try for an All Souls fellowship, which would not only keep him in Oxford but, more important, would serve as proof – to himself, his family, and his friends – of his intellectual distinction. The adventure of the New World was put on hold. He spent part of the summer teaching for a residential school which Smith organised for the Workers' Educational Association.[156] Despite his diction, he seems to have been a great success. Smith considered him a born teacher, and his very exoticism may have helped him win over the 'working men'. They would also have appreciated his expertise in economics: much later he wrote that 'study-circles of working men, when asked what subject they would like to take, almost invariably answer with a request for "economic history"'.[157]

He was booked to attend the Fabian summer school in late August 1911, held that year in Switzerland, but in the meantime was both alarmed and intrigued by an outbreak of anti-Jewish rioting in south Wales, beginning in Tredegar and spreading to some other towns nearby, with mob attacks on Jewish-owned shops and other property.[158] Much later he described it as 'a small pogrom'.[159] He travelled to Wales to see for himself, with the intention of writing a newspaper article, but was 'asked by local Jews to let the matter die down'.[160] On his way he stopped at the home of his Balliol contemporary Leonard Goldsmid Montefiore, whose father Claude – no Zionist sympathiser – he proceeded to quiz about the state of European Jewry. He remembered his host's refusal to answer any of his questions as highly disconcerting.[161] It may have sown the seeds of his later contempt for those wealthy English Jews who denied their Jewishness.[162] The frigidity of Montefiore's response contrasted sharply with the warm welcome he received from an 'ultra-Orthodox rabbi' whom he met in south Wales. As Namier remembered it,

> he kept me for a meal, but before we sat down I realised that I was in for some elaborate prayers. I had to explain … that, not having been brought up in the Jewish religion, I did not know our religious customs. He looked at me with real feeling, and said: 'You have come to see what has happened to us. You have a good Jewish heart. That's all that matters.'[163]

After the Fabian summer school Namier returned to Koszylowce, where his Oxford triumphs cut little ice. According to Lady Namier's biography, his relationships with his parents and sister were more difficult than ever. At least in part, the fault lay with Namier himself. He was drifting away from his family. In the gathering crisis in the Austro-Hungarian empire his panSlavist radicalism was sharply at variance with the orthodox Polish liberalism espoused by Józef and Teodora. Loud and prolonged arguments broke out between them. The interest in his Jewish roots which had taken him to the Oxford branch of the Adler Society, and then to Tredegar, may also have disturbed his father. Probably even more distressing were his adaptations to Oxford life, which made it seem that he was in the process of becoming a different person. Some of Ludwik's pronouncements struck his family as absurd, such as his objection to his father's decision to take up Roman Catholic worship, on the grounds that he was himself strongly inclined towards Calvinism.[164]

Suspicions of a change of loyalties were confirmed by his decision to change his name in England. This he had done in December 1910, by deed poll, to Lewis Bernstein Naymier, just after Józef had himself reverted from Bernstein to Niemirowski. Perhaps Ludwik was falling in love with England and with the English upper classes that surrounded him in Balliol, and was ham-fistedly trying to make himself 'one of us'. But he may also have seen it as a defensive measure, being aware of the reaction that the name 'Bernstein' immediately evoked among some English gentlemen. If so, the ploy did not work. Having first chosen Naymier because, being so close in sound to Napier, it seemed to him to have a truly English character, he quickly realised that the inclusion of a 'y' had struck a false note, and removed this by another legal instrument. In fact, what was left, 'Namier', was just as unusual and un-English: he looked exactly what he was, an east European Jew trying to pass for an *echt* English gentleman. To his parents, it must have seemed a stark rejection of his background and upbringing; indeed, of all that they stood for.

Conflict came to a head over what Ludwik was to do now that he had completed his degree. Józef was of the opinion that he should take up some remunerative employment, and begin a career in business: according to Namier, the family's strait-ened financial circumstances required it, and he considered his spendthrift father to blame. As luck would have it, an excellent position had opened up in America. A Jew from the Darachów estate, whose father had been employed in one of Teodor Sommerstein's distilleries, had made good in New York. His name was Louis N. Hammerling (originally Eleazar Hammerling, or 'Leiser' for short),[165] and a few years previously he had founded an agency, the American Association of Foreign Language Newspapers, which controlled advertising in a myriad of local newspapers across the United States. Hammerling would take the young Ludwik as his princi-pal assistant and ultimate successor.[166] The prospects were excellent: the business was lucrative and because of Hammerling's influence with immigrant communities across the country he had contacts at the highest level of American politics. Józef may well have thought that his son would have greater opportunities than in England. But, despite his earlier enthusiasm for America, Ludwik had now set his heart on staying in Oxford, alongside college friends like Toynbee and Clark. After all, he had done as well in his examinations as they had, and his tutors had not only encouraged him to enter the competition for an All Souls fellowship but were actively coaching him. Following a family conclave, it was agreed that he could try for the fellowship first, and failing that, join Hammerling in New York.

Namier's failure to secure the 'All Sogger', as Allen Leeper called it, despite Smith's legendary skill at cramming and Urquhart's advice on social etiquette, was a blow which he never forgot. It was the first of many rejections at Oxford, and he was at a loss to explain it. Others understood only too well what had happened. Alfred Zimmern (who was himself Jewish), a classical scholar and later a colleague in the Foreign Office, had no doubt that Namier would have been elected if he had been an aristocratic Gentile.[167] The fact that All Souls did not knowingly elect a Jew as a fellow until Isaiah Berlin in 1931 speaks volumes.[168] However, Namier himself refused to believe this to be the reason, and invented various suppositions based on what he could remember having written in his examination answers.[169] Some modern histo-rians are of the same opinion.[170] But there is direct evidence. We know that Namier impressed the electors with his brilliance,[171] and that Patrick Shaw Stewart, who had been elected the previous year, confided to a close friend that: 'We elected three miserable specimens, but no one jolly was in, and anyhow by the strenuous efforts of me and one or two others, the election of a Polish Jew from Balliol, much the strongest candidate really, was prevented.'[172] Finally, no less an authority than the eminent Tudor historian A. F. Pollard, who had also been present, reported to his sister that

> The meeting on Friday morning for the election of fellows was lively … we had two [candidates] for history. The best man by far in sheer intellect was a Balliol man of Polish-Jewish origin and I did my best for him, but the warden and majority of fellows shied at his race, and eventually we elected the two next best.[173]

None of this was known to Namier and had he been aware of what had transpired, the consciousness that anti-Semitism was indeed a powerful force at Oxford, and not merely a casual pose adopted by undergraduates with whom he had little in common, might have changed his view of the university. His failure seemed incomprehensible. So he tried another route to becoming a don: a prize essay. Prize-winners were eligible for college fellowships, and almost every prize-winner before the First World War went on to an academic career.[174] Toynbee had won the Jenkins Prize the previous year, which enabled him to travel in Italy and Greece, and on his return to take up a fellowship. Namier chose as his target the Beit Prize, established in Oxford by the imperialist Alfred Beit in 1905 for an essay on 'some subject connected with the history of the British Empire or the British Commonwealth'. No doubt encouraged by the prospect that Lionel Curtis, arch-advocate of imperial federation and founder of the 'Round Table', would be the Beit Lecturer in the university in 1912–13, Namier took as his subject 'Proposals in the direction of a closer union of the Empire before the opening of the Colonial Conference of 1887'.[175] Though he did not know it, this essay was to set him on a path that he would follow for the rest of his life, seeking to understand the American revolution, whose impact on global history had been so profound.

The text of the essay did not survive Lady Namier's weeding of her husband's archive, so we must rely on her abstract of its contents.[176] It evidently foreshadowed Namier's later works in that it was based on systematic research into primary materials, collected in the Bodleian, the British Museum, and in the Royal Colonial Institute, of which he became a fellow in 1912.[177] This method of working came as much from his own character and mentality as from the influence of his teachers – certainly Smith had not trained him in research methods – and he seems to have found his materials in his own way. He transcribed passages from eighteenth-century pamphlets, calendars of contemporary documents, and edited works by American colonial specialists. There were very few original documents: his enthusiasm for manuscripts would come later.[178] The texts he used were also concentrated in the period leading up to the American revolution, and so heavy and unwieldy was his documentation, indicating a determination to leave no stone unturned, that the essay, having begun at the English Civil War, got no further than the 1770s before running out of time and space. It was impressive enough, however, to win a half-share of the prize.

A half-share was not quite good enough, however, and in 1912 Namier tried the All Souls competition again.[179] Again he failed. To make matters worse, G. N. Clark was one of the successful candidates. Not surprisingly, perhaps, Smith wrote that Namier 'has been a little embittered by what he thinks "failure" at Oxford'.[180] He then cast about for some employment which would enable him to stay in England. Journalism, of a serious kind, was the most obvious. Urquhart wrote on his behalf to the recently appointed editor of *The Times*, Geoffrey Robinson, asking whether the paper would 'consider any articles' written by Namier on eastern Europe. Robinson, a fellow of All Souls and a strong imperialist, had come across Namier already but felt obliged to consult his Vienna correspondent, Henry Wickham Steed. He noted that Urquhart had described Namier as 'rather a remarkable creature', and added,

> His name is either Naymier, or Bernstein – I forget which, he has changed it from one to the other. He is, as you might suspect, a Jew, with a real power of writing, and I am told very considerable knowledge of the politics of the south-east of Europe … You will shudder, I feel sure, at the thought of a Galician Jew corresponding with *The Times*, but I propose to say that he may submit articles from time to time, *through you*. I am rather anxious to test his worth in practical work.[181]

Even though Wickham Steed thought the proposal excellent and deprecated any thought of 'shuddering' – 'When has *The Times* been inhospitable towards the Chosen Race?' – there was no financial arrangement, and an article which Namier had prepared on Austro-Hungarian affairs was never published.[182] At the same time, he was also in touch with H. W. Massingham, the editor of the Liberal weekly *The Nation*, but had no luck there either. The only option was to join Hammerling in New York. In later life he saw himself as having been 'sold … as bondsman' by his family to pay his father's debts, but this seems unreasonable, even melodramatic. There was, after all much to be said for America, as he himself had recognised only a short while before: the drawback was that it was not Oxford.

Stepping forth

By 1913 Namier had acquired a new name, a new nationality (having become a naturalised British citizen in March of that year), and some new enthusiasms, most notably for Oxford, for England and the English ruling class and for the British empire. He had fallen in love with Edwardian Oxford for its intellectual cachet rather than for any shallow aristocratic glamour. What one historian has called his 'almost uncritical admiration for the country's ruling class'[183] was based firmly on the notion of an elite offering moral and cultural leadership, and a dedication to public service: despite some cavalier tendencies he remained very firmly with Smith in the Roundhead camp. He was also drawn to the English ruling class because it was unlike the 'narrow oligarchy' to be found in many European states, especially those in central and eastern Europe. As he argued in his later writings, the families of successful businessmen, English versions of the Bernsteins and Sommersteins, had been able to assimilate into the eighteenth-century English social and political elite.[184] It had even been possible for a converted Jew like Disraeli to become prime minister.[185] And Namier's veneration for the British empire stemmed from a profound trust in its liberal and civilising tendencies.

However, for all their manifold attractions, Oxford, the English aristocracy and the ideal of service to empire had not provided him with a means of self-definition which he could adopt unreservedly as a replacement for the confused and fragmented identity created by his upbringing. For one thing, Oxford had passed him over. For another, there were different, and competing, points of reference, not least his increasing consciousness of his Jewishness, which had grown ever since he had left Galicia, and may well have begun to crystallise during his conversation with the avuncular rabbi in south Wales.

Nor had Namier lost all trace of the young firebrand who had helped to organise the socialists of Lemberg and who had scorned his father's and his sister's outmoded liberalism. During a weekend with the Wingates, Ronald's father, the *sirdar* of Khartoum, an imperial servant 'straight out of Kipling', had formed the opinion that his guest 'had at times almost nihilistic tendencies'.[186] When he left Oxford Namier was still a radical in his politics, sympathetic to revolutionary movements in eastern Europe and exhibiting a general concern with social reform, but his background made him into a radical of a particular kind. His very first publication, an essay in the Oxford undergraduate magazine *The Blue Book*, published in 1912, was a prime expression of *de-haut-en-bas* aristocratic radicalism. Drawing on his experiences as a WEA tutor, and adapting for an industrialised society his recollections of the moral and cultural leadership supplied by the gentry in Galicia, he called for 'the proper education' of the English working classes in order to protect the values of the 'vieux monde', which were in danger of being fatally compromised in the age of mass democracy. In western Europe the threat came not from an ignorant and narrow-minded peasantry but from the rampant philistinism of the petty bourgeoisie, who had 'mastered the technicalities of education' but had not developed the power of critical thinking which was the essential safeguard against 'vulgarity'. The bulk of the article was a disdainful denunciation of the 'vulgarisation' of life in the capital, which 'the South London cockney has invaded'. He quoted Shaw, but then lambasted the social types he had encountered among the Fabians: 'sad un-Greek hypochondriacs' and 'ladies in reform dress' who 'go on preaching the gospel of progress and … plead eloquently in favour of … the necessity of reforming the old universities', which were of course the true nurseries of refinement.[187]

This article affords a glimpse into Namier's state of mind as he launched himself upon the world. Although at first sight it might appear conflicted, with aristocratic pretension and progressive values in direct opposition, a strong unifying thread runs through it: his deep contempt for bourgeois culture. This alone would mark out the young Namier as by temperament a 'modernist'; and despite his vaunted concern for the 'vieux monde', and his engagement with imperialism, he was to demonstrate in his historical writings other features often seen as typical of 'modernism': what Peter Gay has called 'the lure of heresy' – an overwhelming desire to produce something new and striking, and a bristling impatience with, not to say contempt for, established authorities – and 'a principled self-scrutiny'.[188] Namier's peculiar upbringing, which had left him uncertain of his loyalties and of his proper place in society, made him a perfect seed-bed for such attitudes, and over the next two decades a succession of disappointments would serve to magnify the 'modernist' in him. However, these developments were still to come. The Namier who emerged from his Oxford education in 1913 was a complex personality, coming to terms with a variety of influences and experiences. He was now to embark for the New World, and for a city whose startling appearance and bracing atmosphere sent a powerful message 'of a new life and its unbridled force'.[189]

Notes

1   It is reproduced in *Namier*, opposite p. 31, but wrongly identified as Namier's maternal grandfather, Teodor Sommerstein (I am grateful to Jarosław Kurski for clarification on this point).

2   I must thank Dr Andrzej Zięba of the Jagiellonian University, Cracow, for sharing with me the fruits of his researches into the Bernstein family, which form the basis for my own commentary.

3 In an article on Trotsky published in *The New Europe* in 1918, and reprinted in *Skyscrapers*, Namier wrote, 'Braunstein [Trotsky's original name] is one of those innumerable names, compounded of German, common to Jews in Eastern Europe. At the time when Poland was partitioned, most Polish Jews had no family names, but were simply known by their personal names and patronymics … The Prussian and Austrian officials, who in 1795 obtained dominion over what subsequently became Russian Poland, manufactured names by the thousand for the Jews, going through the whole gamut of flowers, animals, colours and stones, sometimes venturing, to the best of their German taste, upon attempts at humour' (*Skyscrapers*, 81–2).

4 In 1909–10 Namier's father successfully petitioned the government in Vienna for permission to resume his ancestral name of Niemirowski (*Namier*, 92), and when he was naturalised as a British subject three years later Namier gave his parents' names as Joseph and Anna Bernstein Naymier: certificate of naturalisation, 25 Mar. 1913 (TNA, HO 334/59/23240; HO 144/1250/233560).

5 'A descendant [or twig] from the stock [or trunk] of the Gra [the Gaon Eliyahu of Vilna].' I am grateful to Professor Eliyahu Stern for this translation from the Hebrew.

6 Eliyahu Stern, *Elijah of Vilna and the making of modern Judaism* (2013). Once again I must acknowledge a debt to Professor Stern, for enlightening me as to the Gaon's influence and reputation.

7 Arnold Toynbee remembered that, when he met Namier in Oxford in 1908, 'one of the first bits of information that he gave me about his world was that he was descended from Elijah ben Solomon, the Gaon of Wilno, the redoubtable enemy of the Chassidim' (A. J. Toynbee, *Acquaintances* (1967), 66). See, also Walter Elliot to Blanche Dugdale, 25 July 1940 (NLS, Elliot papers, Acc. 12198/10); Namier to Isaiah Berlin, 8 May 1956 (Bodl., MS Berlin 148, fo. 24). Even at the end of his life his 'team' of co-workers on the History of Parliament were frequently regaled with references to the Gaon (information from Mary Port).

8 See for example, *Conflicts*, 172, which relates that, 'when I was a boy, there was an old Jew on our estate in Eastern Europe who used to tell me stories about my ancestor Eliyahu ben-Solomon, the Gaon of Vilna'.

9 His full name was Maurice Teodor Sommerstein, but he was always known as Teodor.

10 *Namier*, 6.

11 Details of the estates owned by M. T. Sommerstein in 1902 and 1904 in the database 'Genealogia Polaków' (http://genealogia.okiem.pl). Nine separate properties are listed, with distilleries, breweries and other businesses.

12 *Facing east*, 123–8. See also *Skyscrapers*, 151.

13 Unless otherwise stated, the details in this account of Namier's family background and early life are taken from Lady Namier's account in *Namier*, chs 1–3, supplemented by information from Dr Zięba.

14 *Jewish Chronicle*, 14 Oct. 1960. When receiving a letter out of the blue in the 1950s from a Jewish historian who had been assured by Emil Sommerstein of a family relationship, Namier could only reply that being himself 'by now rather a poor expert in family genealogy', he would have to accept Sommerstein's word for the connection: Philip Friedman to Namier, 4 July 1954, Namier to Friedman, 7 July 1954 (Center for Jewish History, New York, YIVO Archives, Friedman papers: RG 1258, folder 164).

15 *Namier*, 7.

16 It also served to prefigure what the adult Namier would come to see as his rejection by his family, and for this reason alone the story is likely to have been at least embellished.

17 His sister, who as a small girl found the pronunciation of 'Ludwik' difficult, took to calling him 'Ulu', a family nickname which stuck.

18 *Namier*, 11.

19 Dugdale diaries, 1941, 132.

20 Information from Maciej Cybulski, director of the Museum Sienkiewicza, Wola Okrzejska.

21 John Brooke, 'Namier and Namierism', *History and Theory*, iii (1964), 333.

22 *Namier*, 175.

23 *Personalities and powers*, 50.

24 As did Anna, who spoke Polish, German and Ukrainian, but not French: [Emily Buxton,] 'A dig long ago in eastern Galicia', *The Times*, 21 Oct. 1963.

25 L. B. Namier, 'Ukraine remembered', *Observer*, 14 Feb. 1932.

26 *Facing east*, 123.

27 Walter Elliot to Blanche Dugdale, 17 Aug. 1940 (NLS, Elliot papers, Acc. 12198/10).

28 *Facing east*, 126–7.

29 *Skyscrapers*, 153. See also his description of the Polish peasantry in 1919, in the context of Polish democratic politics, as 'an extremely dangerous element, half-illiterate, open to cajolery and bribery, suspicious of anyone who is not a peasant' (memo by Namier on 'The Polish elections', 27 Feb. 1919 (FO 371/3897, file 30573)); and his criticism of the Polish Peasants' Party in 1920: though one 'watches with regret the disappearance of manor houses, houses of a higher civilisation and centres of a better agriculture than that of peasant huts, agrarian reform must not be weapon of aggressive jingoism whether of nobles or the now fashionable democracy': [Namier,] 'Russian land and Polish men', *New Europe*, 23 Sept. 1920.

30 Evidently some Viennese cousins were brought up to speak it (Eva Schutz, *My long journey to London* (privately printed, 1994), 1).

31 One of Isaac Babel's stories of the Polish-Soviet war depicts a bitter debate between Galician Jews, in which the Gaon was roundly denounced by the Hasidim (Isaac Babel, *Collected Stories*, trans. Walter Morison (Penguin edn, Harmondsworth, 1961), 126).

32 *Skyscrapers*, 151.

33 *Personalities and powers*, 106–7. 'Pan' (feminine Pani) is the Polish word for a lord or gentleman, often used as a form of address.

34 Namier, 'Ukraine remembered'.

35 *Namier*, 54–5; Tadeusz Pawlawicz, *Obraz pokolenia* (Cracow, 1999), 230. See also Toynbee, *Acquaintances*, 66.

36 *Namier*, 34–5.

37 Ng, *Nationalism*, ch. 2.

38 Godfrey Lloyd to Robert Falconer, 13 July [1911] (Toronto UL, university archives, A67.0007/021); Namier to James Headlam-Morley, 15 Mar. 1919 (Churchill, Headlam-Morley papers, box 2). Cf. *Namier*, 34.

39 *Namier*, 44.

40 Amy Ng, 'A portrait of Sir Lewis Namier as a young socialist', *Journal of Contemporary History*, xl (2005), 622.

41 Norman Davies, *God's playground: a history of Poland*, ii: *1795 to the present* (2nd edn, Oxford, 2005), ch. 17; Jerzy Lukowski and Herbert Zawadski, *A concise history of Poland* (Cambridge, 2001), 175–83.

42 Joshua Shanes, *Diaspora nationalism and Jewish identity in Habsburg Galicia* (Cambridge, 2012), 243–7.

43 *Namier*, 41–2, 137–8.

44 For Namier's lingering attachment to panSlavism, as late as 1919, see his comment, 30 Sept. 1919 (FO 371/3926, file 133586).

45 Namier to W. P. Crozier, 13 Jan. 1944 (*Guardian* arch. B/N8A/301): 'Professor Kot ... is one of my oldest friends – we have called each other by our Christian names for the last forty years.'

46 C. J. G. Montefiore to A. L. Smith, 27 June [1918] (Balliol, Smith papers, M 64).

47 Information from Alan Hardy.

48 [Emily Buxton,] 'A dig long ago in eastern Galicia'.

49 [Emily Buxton,] 'A dig long ago in eastern Galicia'.

50 *Katalog szkólek drzew owocow ych Anny Niemirowskiej, Koszyłowce* (Lwów, privately printed, n.d.).

51 William Wright, 'L'Europe préhistorique', *Nature*, lxxvii (1908), 577.

52 R. F. Kaindl, 'Neolithische Funde mit bemalter Keramik in Koszylowce (Ostgalizien)', *Jahrbuch für Altertumskunde*, ii (1908), 144; *American Journal of Archaeology*, xii (1908), 114. Namier's own account (*Namier*, 60–1) was that he himself contacted Kaindl, 'a friend of Heilpern's, a student of primitive cultures who lived and worked at Czerniowce'.

53 K. Hadaczek, *La colonie industrielle de Koszyłowce ... de l'époque énéolithique: album des fouilles* (Lèopol, 1914); *British Museum Quarterly*, iii (1928), 62; *Man*, xxxii (1932), 214; [Emily Buxton,] 'A dig long ago in eastern Galicia'.

54 Teodora Modzelewska, *Tkaniny i hafty ludowe z powiatów: zaleszczyckiego oraz okolicznych* (Lwów, 1930); Teodora Modzelewska, *Stroje ludowe Warmii i Mazur* (2 vols, Olsztyn, 1958); A. A. Zięba, 'Teodora Modzelewska', *Etnografowie i ludoznawcy polscy. Sylwetki, szkice biograficzn*, ii, ed. Eve Frys-Pietraszkowa and Anna Spiss (Wroclaw–Cracow, 2007), 210–12.

55 *Namier*, 60.

56 Wacław Wierzbieniec, 'The processes of Jewish emancipation and assimilation in the multiethnic city of Lviv during the nineteenth and twentieth centuries', John Czaplica (ed.), *Lviv: a city in the crosscurrents of culture* (Cambridge, Mass., 2005), 234–8.

57 'Turbulent Zionist', 1; Rose, *Zionism*, 8. In a paper which Lady Namier discovered after his death Namier stated that he became interested in Zionism while at the University of Lausanne in the winter of 1906–7, in other words when he had removed himself from Galicia, and could consider his situation more objectively: Lady Namier to Lucy Sutherland, 11 Sept. 1961 (Bodl., Sutherland papers, box 9); same to R. V. Machell, 19 Sept. 1961 (Bristol UL, Hamish Hamilton archive, DM/352/Ii).

58 Shanes, *Diaspora nationalism and Jewish identity*, 199–201.

59 *Namier*, 61. Lemberg's townscape, complete with a forest of baroque churches, embodied everything Namier came to detest about the Austro-Hungarian empire.

60 J. P. Chatelanat, secretary-general of the University of Lausanne, to Lady Namier, 10 May 1961 (Rylands, Namier papers, 1/1a/15).

61 J. V. Fernier and A. J. Marshall (eds), *Wilfred Pareto: beyond disciplinary boundaries* (Farnham, 2012).

62 *Namier*, 92; Colley, 24–5, 74, 102; Stefan Collini, *English pasts: essays in history and culture* (Oxford, 1999), 82; Ng, *Nationalism*, 64–5.

63 *Conflicts*, 37–8.

64 *Namier*, 67–8; Isaiah Berlin, *Personal impressions* (1980), 66; Colley, 9.

65 Ironically, in the 1920s and 1930s these very streets were to be his great stamping

ground. Close at hand were the British Museum, where he did so much research on the Newcastle papers, and the headquarters of the Zionist Organisation, at 77 Great Russell Street (which coincidentally is next door to offices presently occupied by the History of Parliament).

66 *Namier*, 69–70.

67 *Namier*, 72; H. J. Mackinder, 'The geographical pivot of history', *Geographical Journal*, xxiii (1904), 421–37.

68 *Personalities and powers*, 1–7.

69 In his early years as professor at Manchester, Namier read and criticised a chapter of the first book to be published by his younger colleague Edward Hughes, which in its final version makes reference to *Human nature in politics*, a text whose presence in a piece of dessicated administrative history otherwise seems incongruous: Edward Hughes, *Studies in administration and finance 1558–1825* (Manchester, 1934), 267.

70 E. A. Westermarck, *Memories of my life*, trans. Anna Barwell (1929), 230–1.

71 E. A. Westermarck, *The origin and development of the moral ideas* (2 vols, 1912). See Timothy Stroup (ed.), *Edward Westermarck: essays on his life and work* (Helsinki, 1982); and *Oxf. DNB*.

72 Westermarck, *Memories*, 201.

73 F. R. Harris, *The life of Edward Montagu, K.G., first earl of Sandwich (1625–1672)* (2 vols, 1912).

74 *Namier*, 68; *Fabian News*, Nov. 1907, 9.

75 List of members of Fabian Society, 1890–1919 (LSE, Fabian Society archives, C 55/4).

76 Programme of Oxford University Fabian Society, Hilary term 1910 (Southampton UL, Stein papers, MS 170/AJ244/44).

77 *Namier*, 68.

78 Summer school visitors' book, 1907–12 (LSE, Fabian Society archives, G 9); E. R. Pease, *The history of the Fabian Society* (New York, 1912), 199–200.

79 Summer school visitors' book, 1907–12 (LSE, Fabian Society archives, G 9); brochure for summer schools, 1907 (ibid., G 24/1). Namier attended in Easter and summer 1910, and again in Easter 1911, the last school to be held at Pen-yr-allt.

80 Summer school log book, 1907–12 (LSE, Fabian Society archives, G13).

81 A. L. Smith to the principal of Reading College, 25 June 1918 (Balliol, Smith papers, Letters, N1).

82 Allen Leeper to his father, 1 Nov. 1908 (Balliol, Leeper papers, IIA).

83 John Jones, *Balliol College: a history* (2nd edn, Oxford, 2005), ch. 16. The phrase was H. H. Asquith's.

84 *Namier*, 289.

85 Namier to Isaiah Berlin, 26 Jan. 1959 (Bodl., MS Berlin 156, fo. 57); *Namier*, 85, 107; Margaret Cole, *The life of G. D. H. Cole* (1971), 44.

86 *Structure*, xii–xiii.

87 *Namier*, 94.

88 *Namier*, 83. The identity of the writer is not supplied.

89 Toynbee, *Acquaintances*, 62–4.

90 Lucy Sutherland to Julia Namier, 5 Nov. 1963 (Bodl., Sutherland papers, box 9).

91 Leeper to his mother, 4 Nov. 1908, to ––, n.d. (Balliol, Leeper papers, IIA). Leeper was a formidable opponent, who played tennis and hockey for the college (*Balliol College register, 1900–1950*, ed. Sir Ivo Elliott (Oxford, 1953), 129), but in fact Namier seems to have lacked the physical coordination necessary for any ball game. He was equally hopeless

at golf, to the dubious delights of which Ronald Wingate once tried to introduce him (*Namier*, 95).

92 Leeper to his parents, 1 Nov. 1908 (Balliol, Leeper papers, IIA). Original emphasis.

93 Leeper to his father, 26 Nov. [1909] (Balliol, Leeper papers IIB).

94 M. G. Brock and M. C. Curthoys (eds), *The history of the university of Oxford*, vii: *Nineteenth-century Oxford, part 2* (Oxford, 2000), 802.

95 Smith to [?Godfrey Lloyd], 5 July 1911 (Toronto UL, A67.0007/021). Namier's friend Kenneth Bell began a similar recommendation with the words, 'There is a certain amount against Bernstein which I had better say at once: he is, as his name implies, a Jew and looks it too, and … speaks English with an accent though perfectly intelligibly. But he is really a most unusually able man' (Bell to G. M. Wrong, 15 July [1911] (ibid.)). For a discussion of anti-Semitism at pre-First World War Oxford, see Thomas Weber, *Our friend 'the enemy': elite education in Britain and Germany before World War I* (Stanford, Calif., 2007), ch. 6. On 201–2 Weber discusses the evidence in relation to Namier, as presented in Lady Namier's biography.

96 For examples, see Shaw-Stewart to Lady Diana Manners, 5, 17 May 1910 (BL, Add. MS 70712, fos 141, 143). An admiring depiction of Shaw-Stewart as a fallen hero of the First World War is provided in the biography by his school and college friend Ronald Knox: *Patrick Shaw-Stewart* (1920). A similar approach is taken in Miles Jebb (Lord Gladwyn), *Patrick Shaw-Stewart, an Edwardian meteor* (Wimborne Minster, 1910), which devotes only one paragraph to a consideration of his anti-Semitism, which for the most part is seen as no more than 'the robust parlance of the day' (133–4),

97 Shaw-Stewart to Viola Tree, n.d. (Viola Tree, *Castles in the air: the story of my singing days* (1926), 148; Shaw-Stewart to Lady Diana Manners, 5 May 1910 (BL, Add. MS 70712, fo. 141).

98 Leonard Stein, diaries 1909–10 (Southampton UL, Stein papers, MSS 170/D9–10). See also Jowett Society programme, Trinity 1910 (ibid., MS 170/AJ244/46); Shaftesbury Club programme, Trinity 1910 (ibid., MS 170/AJ244/49); Palmerston Club programmes, Trinity 1909–10 (ibid., MS 170/J244/53–4); Arnold Society, record of motions 1889–1906 (Balliol); Brackenbury Society minute book 1902–12 (Balliol).

99 Lunn diary, 1908 (Georgetown UL, Lunn papers, box 10, folder 4).

100 Brackenbury Society minute book 1902–12 (Balliol). Isaacs was also 'gated' for a fortnight in December 1909 for involvement in 'a disturbance' in New College, which suggests a full engagement with undergraduate life ('English register' 1908–24 (Balliol)).

101 Sacher, 'Palestine memories', fragment of typescript autobiography, 17 (Marks and Spencer Company Archive, Leeds, Sacher papers, Q2/2).

102 There is an intriguing possibility that Namier may have cultivated his accent for this very purpose: according to Stanley Katz, who first met him in 1959, Namier pronounced his words in the way a native Yiddish speaker might, rather than speaking English like a Pole, which was how the Bernstein children had been brought up.

103 *Namier*, 95.

104 'Lady Namier's notes', quoted in Rose, *Zionism*, 8.

105 Draft review by Stein of Lucy Sutherland's obituary of Namier in *Proceedings of the British Academy* (Bodl., Stein papers, box 121).

106 *Namier*, 96. See also C. J. G. Montefiore to A. L. Smith, 27 June [1918] (Balliol, Smith papers, M 64).

107 See Namier to Basil Liddell Hart, 19 Jan. 1952 (LH, 1/539/85), in which he called Guedalla 'a sad buffoon'. This seems an unduly harsh judgment, originating perhaps in some

strong personal dislike, feelings which may well have been reciprocated (see Guedalla to G. N. Clark, 6 Oct. [?1914] (Bodl., Clark papers, 216)). Guedalla's liberal politics and failure to identify himself fully with the Zionist cause would also have been anathema to Namier.

108 Sutherland to Julia Namier, 16 Mar. 1970 (Bodl., Sutherland papers, box 9). The same letter also advised her to omit a reference to Jewish undergraduates, which might give some indication of the nature of the 'unworthy persiflage'.

109 L. B. Namier, *Germany and Eastern Europe* (1915), 82–3.

110 Leeper to his parents, 1 Nov. 1908 (Balliol, Leeper papers, IIA). When marrying in 1917 Namier entered his father's occupation as 'landowner'.

111 Bell to G. M. Wrong, 15 July [1911] (Toronto UL, A67.0007/021); Davis to Bell, 6 Aug. 1911 (ibid.).

112 Godfrey Lloyd to Robert Falconer, 13 July [1911] (Toronto UL, A67.0007/021). Many years later, however, Namier would sharply deny any careless imputation that his family background was among the Polish gentry, wanting it made clear in any publication that 'I am of purely Jewish descent' (Namier to the editor of the *New Statesman*, 26 Oct. 1957 (LH, 1/539/140)).

113 Namier to E. S. Cohn, 25 Sept. 1951 (HPT, N–50); *Namier*, 89; Jones, *Balliol*, 233–5.

114 Toynbee, *Acquaintances*, 74. Ehrlich (1889–1968) did some history teaching in Oxford after graduating, then taught at Berkeley and at the universities of Lwów and Cracow, became a renowned jurist, and was a for a time a judge in the International Criminal Court in The Hague. He was a strong Polish nationalist and took a very different view from Namier of Polish national rights, and the future of Galicia: Ludwik Ehrlich, *Poland, Prussia and culture* (Oxford, 1914); Ludwik Ehrlich, *Modern Poland* (Berkeley, Calif. 1917).

115 Lunn, diaries, 1907–9 (Georgetown UL, Lunn papers, box 10, folders 2, 4). A similar story unfolds from the college's disciplinary records ('English register', 1908–24 (Balliol)); and *A freshman's diary, 1911–12: Willie Elmhirst*, ed. Sir John Masterman (Oxford, 1969), 29, 21–2, 57, 59, 60, 71, 83, 93.

116 *Namier*, 83.

117 *Namier*, 88.

118 Lunn, diary, 27 Oct. 1909 (Georgetown UL, Lunn papers, box 10, folder 4).

119 History Club papers 1907–9 (Balliol).

120 *Namier*, 83; Galbraith in *Balliol College Record*, 1961, 40.

121 Godfrey Lloyd to Robert Falconer, 13 July [1911] (Toronto UL, A67.0007/021).

122 Smith to [?Lloyd], 5 July 1911 (Toronto UL, A67.0007/021).

123 Peter Clarke, rev. of W. H. McNeill, *Arnold Toynbee: a life* (Oxford, 1989), *London Review of Books*, 17 Aug. 1989.

124 R. N. Soffer, 'Modern history', M. G. Brock and M. C. Curthoys (eds), *Nineteenth-century Oxford, part 2* (Oxford, 2000), 361–84.

125 History club papers 1907–9 (Balliol). Cf. Michael Bentley, *Modernizing England's past: English historiography in the age of modernism, 1870–1970* (Cambridge, 2005), 56.

126 Sacher, 'Palestine memories', fragment of typescript autobiography, 17 (Marks and Spencer Company Arch., Leeds, Sacher papers, Q2/2); Leeper to his father, 2 May [1911] (Balliol, Leeper papers, IID).

127 Davis to Kenneth Bell, 6 Aug. 1911 (Toronto UL, A67.0007/021).

128 *Structure*, xii. Smith's influence was said to stretch beyond Balliol and to predominate in the Oxford History school more generally: J. R. H. Weaver, *Henry William Carless Davis 1874–1928* (1933), 29.

129 H. W. C. Davis, *A history of Balliol College*, rev. R. H. C. Davis and Richard Hunt (Oxford, 1963), 240–3; Christopher Parker, *The English historical tradition since 1850* (Edinburgh, 1990), 72–4, 105–6.

130 A. L. Smith, *Frederic William Maitland: two lectures and a bibliography* (Oxford, 1908), esp. 6–7.

131 R. N. Soffer, *Discipline and power: the university, history, and the making of an English elite, 1870–1930* (Stanford, Calif., 1994), 140–1.

132 A. L. Smith had praised Maitland's achievement in relating 'a nation's system of government to that nation's character' (Smith, *Maitland*, 34).

133 Davis, *Balliol*, 240–1.

134 Davis, *Balliol*, 243.

135 *Namier*, 89; Jones, *Balliol*, 235–6; William Whyte, *Oxford Jackson: architecture, education, status and style, 1835–1924* (Oxford, 2006), 108.

136 *Namier*, 107. Alan Taylor reported this as 'There was a Jew called Namier/Who came here and came here and came here', which is not impossible (A. J. P. Taylor, *A personal history* (1983), 111–12).

137 *Namier*, x; Rosalind Mitchison to Namier, 3 Feb., 11, 15 Aug. 1954 (HPT, N–58). Mitchison thought that Namier had adopted 'the whole family' (recorded interview with Christopher Smout, available on DVD from London University).

138 Godfrey Lloyd to Robert Falconer, 13 July [1911] (Toronto UL, A67.0007/021); Bell to G. M. Wrong, 26 Aug. [1911] (ibid.); Ng, *Nationalism*, 72; *Namier*, 92 (for the term 'hugger-mugger').

139 For Holmes, see J. F. Bosher, *Imperial Vancouver Island: who was who, 1850–1950* ([Woodstock, Oxon.,] 2012), 365; for the Wingates, father and son, *Oxf. DNB*.

140 *Namier*, 87–8, 91–2; A. L. Smith to Namier, 30 Sept. 1913 (Rylands, Namier papers, 1/9/19).

141 Printed programme for Encaenia, 18 June 1913 (Franklin D. Roosevelt Presidential Library, Shepardson papers, box 1).

142 Eustace Percy, *Some memories* (1958), 11–12.

143 *Namier*, 130.

144 *Namier*, 90, 232–3, 255; Irina Prehn to Constance Babington Smith, 11 May 1980 (Babington Smith).

145 Columbia University, Butler Library, Columbia Centre for Oral History, 'Reminiscences of Dr Maurice Perlzweig' (transcript), 330, 382.

146 *Skyscrapers*, 116.

147 Allen Leeper to ——, n. d. (fragment) (Balliol, Leeper papers, IIB).

148 Kenneth Bell to G. M. Wrong, 15 July [1911] (Toronto UL, A67.0007/021); 'English register', 1908–24, 21 Mar. 1911 (Balliol).

149 Namier to [Godfrey Lloyd] 14 June 1911 (Toronto UL, A67.0007/021). Smith visited Toronto in 1910 and became well acquainted with members of the university staff ([Mary L. Smith,] *Arthur Lionel Smith, master of Balliol (1916–1924): a biography and some reminiscences* (1928), 177, 179).

150 Smith to [?Lloyd], 5 July 1911 (Toronto UL, A67.0007/021).

151 Lloyd to James Mavor, 12 July [1911] (Toronto UL, A67.0007/021).

152 Lloyd to Robert Falconer, 4 Aug. [1911] (Toronto UL, A67.0007/021). The successful candidate was G. E. Jackson, who was eventually promoted to professor of economics at Toronto, and in 1935 left the university to become adviser to the governors of the Bank of England.

153 Mavor to Falconer, 20 July 1911 (Toronto UL, A67.0007/021).

154 Bell to G. M. Wrong, 26 Aug. [1911] (Toronto UL, A67.0007/021).

155 M. L. Friedland, *The University of Toronto: a history* (2nd edn, Toronto, 2013), 234.

156 Bell to Wrong, 26 Aug. [1911] (Toronto UL, A67.0007/021). He taught a course on nineteenth-century European history ('Turbulent Zionist', 2).

157 *Skyscrapers*, 44.

158 Anthony Glaser, 'The Tredegar riots of August 1911', Ursula Henriques (ed.), *The Jews of south Wales: historical studies* (Cardiff, 1993), 151–76.

159 *Conflicts*, 172.

160 Rose, *Zionism*, 9.

161 The story runs that Namier sat down at breakfast and announced that there would be a discussion of the plight of Rumanian Jews, to which the elder Montefiore replied: 'Now Bernstein, you will eat your egg, and there will be no discussion either of Rumanian Jews or any other subject': J. L. Talmon, 'The ordeal of Sir Lewis Namier: the man, the historian, the Jew', *Commentary*, xxxiii (1962), 239. For Montefiore's opposition to Zionism, see *An English Jew: the life and writings of Claude Montefiore*, ed. Edward Kessler (2nd edn, 2002), 17.

162 *Conflicts*, 132–3, 154–5, 162, 165–6, 168–9; Rose, *Zionism*, 7.

163 *Conflicts*, 172.

164 *Namier*, 93.

165 Namier, 'Louis B. Hammerling' (typescript), 1 (CZA, Namier papers, A312\4).

166 For Hammerling, see M. B. B. Biskupski, *The most dangerous German agent in America: the many lives of Louis N. Hammerling* (DeKalb, Ill., 2015). Hammerling's own account of his early life differs significantly from the version provided by Namier, but Hammerling was prone to self-serving fabrications and his version of his Galician background cannot be trusted. There is no supporting evidence for the notion, purveyed by Arnold Toynbee (in *Acquaintances*, 71–2), that Hammerling was an orphan whom Namier's family had brought up, but it is possible that either Józef or his father-in-law had provided the young man with the funds which had enabled him to emigrate.

167 Zimmern to C. P. Scott, 13 June 1919 (*Guardian* arch., A/N2/4). The candidates elected were both historians: Charles Cruttwell, later principal of Hertford College (and a hate-figure to Evelyn Waugh), and Alwyn Williams, who became bishop of Winchester.

168 Leo Amery had been elected in 1897 but concealed his Jewish origins for fear that this fact would have weighed against him (W. R. Louis, 'Leo Amery and the post-war world, 1945–55', S. J. D. Green and Peregrine Horden (eds), *All Souls and the wider world: statesmen, scholars and adventurers, c.1850–1950* (Oxford, 2011), 266–7).

169 In a letter to the editor of the *New Statesman* in 1942 he claimed it was his extreme anti-Germanism (see p. 282); in conversation with his friend and fellow eighteenth-century historian Romney Sedgwick it was his failure to mention the Peninsular War in an essay about the downfall of Napoleon, a fatal blunder since one of the examiners was an expert on this subject (Romney Sedgwick, 'The Namier revolution: Sir Lewis Namier (1888–1960)', *History Today*, x (1960), 723).

170 W. D. Rubinstein, *A history of Jews in the English-speaking world: Great Britain* (Basingstoke, 1996), 895. Cf. Elisabeth Albanis, 'Jewish identity in the face of anti-Semitism', *Historical Journal*, xli (1998), 895–6.

171 Geoffrey Robinson to Henry Wickham Steed, 12 Dec. 1912 (Rylands, Namier papers, 1/9/7).

172 Shaw Stewart to Viola Tree [Nov. 1911] (Tree, *Castles in the air*, 149).

173 Quoted in *Namier*, 103. Lady Namier gives no source for the letter, but it is likely to have been one of those shown to G. N. Clark in the early 1950s by Pollard's daughter (Margaret Butler to Clark, 6 Jan. 1952 (Bodl., Clark papers, 175)).

174 Soffer, *Discipline and power*, 176.

175 For Curtis see Deborah Lavin, *From empire to international commonwealth: a biography of Lionel Curtis* (Oxford, 1995); and *Oxf. DNB*; and for his impact on Oxford, Lavin, *From empire to international commonwealth*, 119; and Michael Howard, 'All Souls and the Round Table', Green and Horden (eds), *All Souls and the wider world*, 155–66.

176 *Namier*, 104–5. The Namier papers at Rylands contain a single page that may have come from a draft of the Beit prize essay (1/1b/9).

177 *The Times*, 24 May 1912.

178 See his surviving notes, in Rylands, Namier papers, 1/6/7–8, 1/21/2. These are undated, but some at least must have been made at this time. The only manuscript sources which occur are BL, Add. MSS 5839, 5842, part of the collections of the eighteenth-century Cambridge antiquary William Cole, from which Namier took snippets. They seem an odd choice for his research into American politics, and may have been recommended to him.

179 Allen Leeper to his father, 26 July [1912] (Balliol, Leeper papers, IIE).

180 Smith to Sir Cecil Spring Rice, 6 Apr. 1913 (Churchill, Spring Rice papers, Ii/16). Nearly thirty years later Namier confessed to Isaiah Berlin that he had nursed a grudge against the historian Sir Charles Grant Robertson, one of the All Souls electors, for preferring another candidate (Berlin, *Personal impressions*, 64).

181 Robinson to Wickham Steed, 12 Dec. 1912 (Rylands, Namier papers, 1/9/7).

182 Wickham Steed to Robinson, 14 Dec. 1912 (Rylands, Namier papers, 1/9/7); *Namier*, 106.

183 Colley, 10.

184 See for example, his review of Esmé Wingfield-Stratford, *The history of British civilization*, *Nation and Athenaeum*, 22 Dec. 1928.

185 For Namier's fascination with Disraeli, see Colley, 12; Ng, *Nationalism*, 158.

186 Sir Reginald Wingate to Ld Kitchener, 28 Sept. 1914 (TNA, Kitchener papers, PRO 30/57/45); Michael Korda, *Hero: the life and legend of Lawrence of Arabia* (paperback edn, 2012), 46.

187 L. B. Naymier [*sic*], 'C'est à l'amour du vieux monde …', *Blue Book*, i, no. 1 (May 1912), 3–11.

188 Peter Gay, *Modernism: the lure of heresy from Baudelaire to Beckett and beyond* (2007).

189 *Skyscrapers*, 2.

2

Personalities and powers, 1913–17

New York and New England

Namier embarked for America in May 1913 on the RMS *Carmania*, one of the largest ocean liners in the Cunard fleet. By chance, one of his travelling companions was Sir Cecil Spring Rice, travelling out to replace James Bryce as British ambassador to Washington, and accompanied by Lord Eustace Percy, a younger son of the duke of Northumberland, whose acquaintance Namier had made at Oxford. Although only a year older than Namier, Percy was already in the diplomatic service and returning to Washington as an attaché. Since Spring Rice was an old Balliol man, A. L. Smith alerted him to the fact that Namier would be sailing, and wrote a letter of recommendation.[1] Although sure of his protégé's talents, Smith felt he had to explain Namier's peculiar character:

> Not every Englishman would be wide-minded enough to appreciate his really exceptional ability and originality, but most would only feel overpowered by his perennial flow of ideas and speech … Withal, he is full of fine aspirations – he is *certain* to be a great force in the USA.

As a further encouragement Smith reported a recent comment which exemplified Namier's naive self-confidence: 'Spring Rice will do better than Bryce, for he is a real diplomatist.'[2] In fact, there was no need to worry. As always, Namier was socially successful with those who shared his interests and were gripped by his enthusiasm and specialist knowledge. He made a strong impression on Spring Rice, and would keep in contact with the Washington embassy throughout his time in New York, where his employment afforded him access to valuable sources of information.[3]

During the voyage Namier passed his time in writing a review for Oxford's *Blue Book*. His subject was a piece of travel writing which James Bryce had published on South America. The book engaged Namier's interest for two reasons: first, as a foretaste of the exciting scenes he envisaged opening up in the New World; and second, because it provided a series of case studies of a political problem which fascinated him, how 'small white communities … when freed from the tyranny of the Spanish state and the Spanish church, had to start independent political life, although they had no pre-existing constitutional forms or ways and … were in addition burdened with the disadvantage of a large native population'.[4] There was an obvious lesson to be drawn, he felt, in the contrast between the bewildered Hispanic *colons*, deprived of any previous political education by an authoritarian Catholic empire, and the sturdy democrats of north America, who derived their constitutional principles from sound British example.

Namier's reaction to his first sight of New York was no different from any other passenger who made the transatlantic journey: astonishment. He described the experience in an essay published over a decade later:

> when in the early morning the weary ocean boat glides up the Hudson River, a mirage arises before the traveller's eyes, incongruous at first, wondrous when found to be real. He sees the long-drawn, even line of Manhattan Island with the rows of ordinary houses, but high above the grey gloom and the mist of the river-side there arise gigantic structures, a new world in different dimensions. The dim houses along the river recede, like an uncertain reminiscence, and the eye fastens on the city above the clouds, which in its splendid whiteness reflects the morning sun. The skyscrapers, superhuman, seemingly conscious of their own mystic symbolism, deliver America's message of a colossal reality.[5]

In this essay he would used the skyscraper as a symbol of what he called the 'mass individuality' of the modern age: man had 'in a thousand ways outgrown the day of the lonely individual; the direction of mass effort takes the place of solitary achievement'.[6] It was by no means an original observation, since all manner of intellectuals, including anthropologists, psychologists and avant-garde artists, were preoccupied with the effects of the submersion of the individual in the crowd, a process that modern technology was rapidly accelerating. In Namier's case, his appreciation of the significance of the skyscraper came from experience as well as reading and observation: when he settled down to work it was in an office on the ninth floor of the newest and tallest of them all, the recently completed Woolworth Building on Broadway in lower Manhattan, across from City Hall. Even though he disliked the particular aesthetics of the Woolworth Building,[7] he saw the powerful structure of these monumental edifices as representing something forward-looking and healthy. On a practical level, just as in his early childhood when perched on top of a cupboard, he could now peer down from his office on the teeming crowds in the streets below. The memory may even have played a part in prompting his later reference to the eighteenth-century British Parliament, and political society in general, as an 'ant-heap'.[8]

The nature of Namier's work for Louis Hammerling remains elusive: his own recollections differ sharply from those of Hammerling's son Max, as related nearly thirty years later to Isaiah Berlin, and both are at odds with the scraps of contemporary evidence which have come down to us. According to Namier himself, he was employed in starting up 'a mail order house for the foreign-language population' in the United States rather than, as he had been led to expect, to act as 'understudy for the President of the Foreign Languages Press'. A glorified clerk in a mail order house was scarcely appropriate to his aspirations, even if his relative poverty required him to knuckle under, and he fell into a 'resentful rage' that time was slow to dispel.[9] In reality, of course, money was not so tight as to prevent him from living in the style to which his upbringing had accustomed him, and he took up permanent residence in the highly fashionable Hotel Van Rensselaer on East 11th Street, less than a block from Fifth Avenue.[10]

Max Hammerling remembered things quite differently: he told Isaiah Berlin that his father had employed Namier to write leading articles that were syndicated through the hundreds of publications for which his agency was responsible.[11] Hammerling's own bi-monthly English-language news magazine, the *American Leader*, listed Namier as one of its three editors, and he contributed various articles under his own name, some of which he sent to A. L. Smith.[12] The term 'editor' was a loose one in the context of the *American Leader* but as a full-time employee Namier was much busier than the various luminaries who were styled 'contributing editors' on the basis of submitting one or two articles a month. In particular, Namier's linguistic skills were invaluable in translating articles from foreign-language newspapers, a staple of the magazine.[13]

As for Hammerling himself, Namier thought him stranger than anyone he had ever met. Brash, unscrupulous and sometimes frankly dishonest, Hammerling was the archetypal immigrant on the make. 'A brilliant ruffian', Namier called him; a '*condottiere*' in business, yet with an engaging personality and a touching regard for the family in Darachów whose patronage had set him on his way. Lady Namier's biography described how Namier became fascinated with his employer's extraordinary personality as a psycho-pathological study.

One point of tension was the fact that employer and employee held fundamentally opposing views on the gathering European crisis. According to Max Hammerling, his father disapproved of the fiercely anti-Austrian and anti-German tenor of Namier's articles, and especially disliked Namier's advocacy of an American intervention in European politics, since this might alienate Catholic readers and offend the prevailing isolationism of American opinion.[14] Hammerling and Namier differed sharply in their attitude towards Austria-Hungary. Hammerling was grateful for the Habsburgs' tolerationist policies, and did not understand the young man's sympathy for Slavic nationalism. He was convinced that Jews would get a better deal under Austria, and even Germany, than under Tsarist Russia, and for this very reason, once war came, took the part of the Central Powers.[15] But he and Namier do not seem to have fallen out until 1915, when Hammerling came into the open with his support for Germany, and Namier was back in England, in the service of his adopted king and country.[16]

Naturally, while working in New York, and for an organisation which numbered many Yiddish-language newspapers among its clients, Namier was in contact with representatives of American Jewry and with American Zionists. His own recollection was that

> I was much interested in Jewish affairs but not in touch with Jews. I studied in books and reviews problems of Jewish immigration and development in America. In fact I was not wildly excited about Zionism which in those days seemed to me an interesting but rather impracticable and unimportant side-show. The thing which really interested me was the mass migrations of Jews from eastern Europe to western Europe and to America.[17]

Nonetheless, he was sufficiently interested, and sufficiently well connected, to take a hand in arrangements for the translation and publication in 1913 of the Zionist Arthur Ruppin's *The Jews of today*, by Kenneth Bell's firm in London and Henry Holt and Co. in New York.[18]

Just as in Oxford, Namier's interest in Jewish affairs had to compete with other attractions. The great issue of the Anglo-American relationship was of more concern to him than the hostile reception given to immigrants from eastern Europe, with whom, at this point in his life, he did not identify himself. Hammerling did not set a helpful example, since his propensity to equivocation extended to race and religion. Like the Bernsteins, he had converted to Roman Catholicism, and according to Namier, in order to enable the two hundred Roman Catholics among his newspaper editors to continue to work for him, Hammerling went so far as to deny publicly that he was Jewish, even though the untruth of this statement must have been crashingly obvious to all those with whom he did business.[19] Yet he dragged Namier off to a synagogue on Yom Kippur, the day when many secular Jews attended, saying simply 'we had better go'.[20]

Hammerling had other, more influential, contacts in the highest reaches of American life. As a committed supporter of the Republican Party, as well as a man of influence through his newspapers, he was courted by President Taft's administration (1909–13), and was a frequent visitor to Taft's White House, something he naturally exploited for his own advantage, but which he also used to promote the interests of immigrant communities, including Jews.[21] This was another indication that the firm was closer to American Jewish interests than Namier was subsequently willing to concede. A particular friend was the lawyer Charles Nagel, Taft's Secretary of Commerce and Labor, and one of the so-called 'contributing editors' to the *American Leader*. Although the son of a German Jewish doctor, Nagel did not practise his religion, and in power did not always satisfy Jewish lobbyists, but he was certainly more flexible on immigrant issues than his predecessors and, moreover, had married the sister of the well-known Zionist Louis Brandeis. The fact that his employer was on intimate terms with Nagel was of great value to Namier in familiarising him with influential American opinion, reports of which he sent to Eustace Percy and Spring Rice.

New York City did not mark the geographical limit of Namier's American experience. Hammerling encouraged him to travel, and Namier also exploited his own Balliol contacts. Smith offered introductions, while admitting that his acquaintances were of a different order to the crowd with whom he assumed Namier was mixing: 'they are not wealthy people, or financiers, and perhaps you only go for such now, on your rapid road to bossdom'.[22] The American undergraduates Namier had known in Oxford offered more promising opportunities: Whitney Shepardson was at Harvard Law School, and another Rhodes scholar with whom he had become friendly, Frederic Schenck, had also come back to Harvard, to take up an academic career.[23] They were precisely the sort of Americans with whom he liked to socialise: privately educated offspring of wealthy, long-established Yankee families.[24] His most frequent visits were to Yale. Here doors were opened by another Balliol Rhodes scholar, who as luck would have it had also been a passenger on the *Carmania*: Alfred Biddle, scion of a prosperous Philadephia family which claimed an ancestor on the *Mayflower*.[25] Biddle was a Yale man and a footballer. His contacts in New Haven were very different from Smith's. And these friends welcomed Namier whole-heartedly, despite the newcomer's background and accent (which he was now making serious – but futile – efforts to alter by elocution lessons). Namier later told Julia that he had been 'voted into a select undergraduates' club' at Yale, even though he was a Jew. 'As one enthusiastic and outspoken' young man had explained to him, he was not like other Jews: 'he carried a clean hull, with no Jewish barnacles attached'.[26] Remarkably, Namier seems to have accepted this bald statement of prejudice with equanimity.

The White Anglo-Saxon Protestants at Yale fascinated him, and, just as at Oxford, the anti-Semitism to be found in this privileged elite was something he chose to ignore: they were the descendants of the Puritan settlers whom he had once intended to study, and were linked indissolubly to the mother country. Moreover, they personified the problem that had occupied his mind ever since he had embarked on the Beit prize essay. How had English (and Scottish) America come to separate from Britain? Finding the answer to this question might well enable the achievement of

3 Lewis Namier, 1915

4 A. L. Smith

one of the visions of Curtis and the Round Table: reconciliation between the two great powers and a more effective formulation of the means by which existing British imperial connections with the dominions could be reinforced.

Namier observed a stark contrast between the original settlers and other, more recent, immigrants into the United States. The readers of Hammerling's newspapers were 'hyphenated' Americans, who, according to Namier, suffered the 'tragedy' of forfeiting their own nationality without ever acquiring that sense of community which forms the basis of 'good citizenship'.[27] The descendants of English-speaking colonists did not see themselves as 'hyphenated'. Yet their American national identity required the renunciation of their British heritage, something Namier found perplexing, especially as his new friends seemed to regret it as well.[28] He celebrated the Fourth of July in 1913 in the Town Square of New Haven surrounded by a 'noisy, surging crowd':

> I heard Italian, French, Polish and Greek spoken around me. I saw hundreds of little American flags, and coupled with them flags of many nations. The one flag which was nowhere to be seen was that of Britain, the land which once had been loved as the mother country, which is now honoured by Americans as the centre of the great sister-commonwealth, but which on the 'Fourth of July' is dimly thought of by the multi-lingual crowd in the New Haven square as a brutal tyrant.

Later that evening, after he had dined in private with 'descendants of the founders of the state … Anglo-Saxons of the purest lineage', he walked among the crowd 'with a descendant of the first Puritan settlers', possibly Alfred Biddle. Eventually, when they had turned into a side-street, his companion

> remarked with a smile … 'We teach more foreigners English than does Great Britain, we compel them to adopt our language, laws and constitution in a way unknown to the British Empire.' The Englishman spoke in him; there was not a drop of blood in him which was not the best blood in England. I felt like asking him why he did not unfurl the flag of his own ancestors and make the strangers in the square and all their little foreign flags bow to it?[29]

Namier's visits to Yale, which sometimes extended to excursions into the surrounding countryside to trace the movements and settlements of 'the Puritan founders of the state', reinforced his determination to understand the cataclysmic events which had sundered 'Anglo-Saxondom'.[30] These pilgrimages not only provided inspiration but put him into contact with the work of American academics who were themselves engaged in rewriting the history of the revolutionary era. Smith had offered to introduce him to historians at Yale, in particular Wilbur Abbott, a scholar of seventeenth-century England,[31] but Namier was principally interested in making the acquaintance of another member of the faculty, Charles M. Andrews, the professor of American history. Andrews was a leading light in the so-called 'imperial school' of historians, which included Herbert L. Osgood at Columbia and George L. Beer, a self-consciously 'revisionist' movement intent on understanding the American revolution and the period leading up to it from the perspective of the imperial government.

The approach adopted by the 'imperial school' was one reflection of the increasing 'Anglo-Saxonism' which Namier had observed in the American academic community, a cast of mind which recognised that the evolution of the United States into a constitutional democracy was owing to the colonists' racial inheritance from England. As applied by Andrews and his friends, it resulted in a tendency for historians to sympathise with the mother country at the expense of the rebellious colonists. The 'imperial school' depicted the eighteenth-century British government as fair-minded and seeking above all to protect its American subjects, who had responded to generosity with manifest ingratitude and the manufacture of unjustified grievances.[32] It is easy to see how this picture would have appealed to Namier. In all probability it was already familiar to him, since his friend Shepardson's Gladstone Prize essay at Oxford had focused on the ways in which 'new research' was modifying understanding of the American crisis of the 1770s.[33]

Moreover, Andrews and his colleagues were producing a kind of history to which Namier himself now aspired: self-consciously professional, 'scientific' and 'objective', with a firm foundation in archival research.[34] This was something he probably encountered for the first time in America. It was not a style of history writing to which tutorials at Balliol had exposed him, despite the growing recognition among Smith and others of the limitations of Whig constitutional historians and the importance of detailed documentary research in constructing a credible picture of the past on its own terms.[35] Nor would Namier have been able to observe much trace of the new 'scientific history' in the prevailing English scholarship on the eighteenth-century British empire. The first inklings of a movement to revise the Whig interpretation of George III's reign were already visible, but as yet these efforts had resulted in either 'breezy' generalisations or tentative rearrangements of detail.[36]

According to Namier, it was a chance remark from Andrews which set him on the path that would lead, fifteen years later, to the publication of his first great book, *The structure of politics at the accession of George III*. Andrews told his visitor that 'while a great deal of work on the condition of the empire in the eighteenth century is being done in America, they received but little help from our side'.[37] In saying this, Andrews was offering constructive encouragement, rather than attempting to fence in his own territory. The previous year, in a short study of colonial America, Andrews had commented that 'on British policy very little has been written'.[38] He knew full well that ample materials existed. His first book, a study of the English administration of overseas colonies in the seventeenth century, had exploited sources in the British Museum, the Public Record Office and the Bodleian Library.[39] So too had Beer and Osgood in various publications.[40] Furthermore, Andrews had recently prepared calendars of manuscripts relating to American history in British repositories, the first two volumes listing substantial quantities of relevant documents in the Newcastle papers in the British Museum, a collection that Andrews had inspected personally.[41]

In due course, Namier's detailed explorations into the Newcastle papers would form the bedrock of his own reinterpretation of eighteenth-century English politics. For the moment, his ambition was confined to working up the Beit essay into a publishable form, but his encounters with American historians expanded his horizons. His research was snowballing, as it always tended to, and he was beginning to look systematically at collections of manuscripts as well as pamphlets and printed editions of primary sources.[42] As he later wrote, with more than a tinge of self-righteousness, recalling his time in New York, 'I had to enter business, but as this carried me across to America, where public libraries are open at night and on Sundays, I was not debarred from continuing my studies.'[43] The most important of these libraries was the New York Public Library, where he worked on the extensive transcripts of primary sources relating to the American revolution compiled by the nineteenth-century historian and diplomat George Bancroft.[44] On visits to New Haven Namier also consulted the manuscripts of Ezra Stiles, a congregationalist minister and Yale's seventh president, the contents of which were wide-ranging and informative about the politics of the pre-revolutionary decades.[45] His surviving notes show that his focus was still on the American side, and the development of constitutional ideas, but Andrews' advice had sown a seed.[46]

Probably the most important American influence on Namier was the great 'Progressive' historian Charles A. Beard, who in 1913 created a sensation with the publication of his major reinterpretation of the American revolution, *An economic interpretation of the constitution of the United States*.[47] Oddly enough, Namier seems not to have mentioned Beard in his conversations with Julia; at least, Beard's name does not appear in her biography. We know that Namier read Beard's work and was impressed, but this information comes indirectly from a younger historian who knew Namier much later in his life.[48] Why Lady Namier has nothing to say about Beard is a mystery. Namier must have known of Beard and his book while he was in New York, since it had created such a stir. Moreover, Beard had links with Balliol and the circles in which Namier had moved when at Oxford. Beard had studied at Balliol between 1899 and 1902, where he had been involved in the Fabian Society and in the movement for the education of working men.[49] In 1913 he was teaching at

Columbia, and Namier could easily have gone to see him, although he may have been deterred by the controversy engendered by the publication of Beard's book and the denunciation of its author by the conservative Republicans with whom Hammerling consorted, not least President Taft.[50]

Whether or not they met, Beard's intellectual influence on Namier is undeniable.[51] Beard's emphasis on the importance of economic factors in determining the course of political history in eighteenth-century America would have struck a very loud chord. Beard, like Namier, was at pains to deny that he was a Marxist, or that his work was in any way reductionist, but the radical thrust of the *Economic interpretation of the constitution* was to identify and prioritise the economic motivations of the leading actors in the struggle for American independence. Most important of all, perhaps, was his method. At the book's core was an exercise in prosopography: a long central chapter built around brief biographies of the 55 members of the Philadelphia convention of 1787. The concluding analysis which summarised the evidence considered only the members' income, but the biographies, based on documentary sources and the publications of local history societies, were broader in conception, providing details of family background and career.[52] This was precisely the method that Namier would use a decade later in his researches into the members of the Westminster Parliament.

The expanded version of Namier's Beit Prize essay on 'The imperial problem during the American revolution' was intended for Lionel Curtis and the Round Table, to form part of a major collaborative work on which Curtis and his friends were labouring, which Curtis called 'The Egg'. The intention was to produce a full and reasoned statement of Britain's imperial problem, setting out options for the governance of the empire, and Namier was to supply a piece on the American colonies. Curtis considered Namier's contribution to be so 'weighty' that it had to be included in full.[53] But the new vistas opened by American scholars and American libraries had expanded Namier's ambitions to an impracticable extent, while at the same time devilling for Hammerling deprived him of the time to carry through properly the research he now felt necessary.

Curtis and his co-editor, Edward Grigg, found Namier almost impossible to deal with. The sending of the essay was promised and postponed several times.[54] One letter from America, sent in August 1913, convinced Curtis that Namier was 'clearly on the edge of a nervous breakdown'.[55] Then in October Namier wrote to Curtis in a sharper tone:

> I don't think there is any point in my printing the thing in your 'Studies' at all. Why not better print it as a book straight away, if it will never be enlarged any more? Of course, even into this book I shall not be able to put some of the material which remains unused,

but which is not fit for use in its present state. But why print a thing for private, free circulation which I want to put into the book-market three or four months later?

Instead he proposed to send the essay first to Douglas Cole 'for stylistic corrections', and then to have it typed up and circulated to friends for advice.[56]

Curtis fell in with this plan in the hope of having the work set up for publication by whichever publisher Namier preferred.[57] It was important to get things moving; otherwise, Namier's 'tremendous standard of historical scholarship' would result in a process of rewriting that would have no end.[58] Curtis was also anxious that Namier not be obliged to pay a penny towards the cost of preparing the typescript for the press: 'some day he will be a multi-millionaire but at present he is not at all well off and I stipulated at the outset that he should be put to no expense'.[59] But Namier, whom Grigg described as 'an incalculable person', continued to plague the editorial staff. Letters rained down from New York with changes of mind and 'elaborate revisions'. 'He no sooner sends me the final copy', complained Grigg, 'than he follows it up with further additions and corrections, and I feel we shall never know when he will really get the work out.' It was now intended for the Clarendon Press and A. L. Smith was to take charge of it.[60] Needless to say, the much-promised final version never appeared, a foreshadowing of the fate of many of the unwritten works that Namier projected throughout his life.

By April 1914 Namier decided to seek a career that would be more rewarding, both intellectually and financially. First he would return to England and complete his book, which, with characteristic over-optimism, he expected to have ready by the autumn. Then he would take up the law. Hammerling, still wishing Namier well, wrote on his behalf to Charles Nagel, who had returned to legal practice in the Midwest following Taft's defeat in the presidential election of 1912. Nagel offered to take Namier under his wing while the young man read for a law degree at Washington University in St Louis, Nagel's alma mater: Nagel would write on his behalf to the dean of the law school.[61] Namier then set sail for Britain on the *Lusitania* on 21 April 1914. His departure made the columns of the *New York Times*, which listed among noteworthy passengers 'Professor Lewis B. Namier of Oxford University' – a revealing display of vanity and wishful thinking (assuming that he himself had supplied the information).[62] He was not to know it, but he would never return.

War

Leaving the ship at Glasgow, Namier went immediately 'on a short tour of central and eastern Europe', researching material for one last article for the *American Leader*, on 'the European situation'.[63] Close observation confirmed his pre-existing apprehensions of an impending disaster generated by the decline of Habsburg power, and the expansionist ambitions of Russia on Austria-Hungary's southern borders: 'Europe is proceeding with its preparations for the storm of our age, for the *détente* which seems to break over it in every second or third generation.'[64]

Much later, Toynbee remembered that Namier had been warning of a gathering storm in the Balkans during their time as undergraduates, when everyone else's attention was focused on Anglo-German rivalry in the west.[65] Long after the First World War had been fought, Namier plumed himself on having predicted the explosion that the tensions between Austria and Serbia would ignite. He argued that there was no essential antipathy between the Hohenzollern and Romanov empires; in fact, there was much that drew the two powers together. Both were both governed by 'Baltic gentry', the Tsarist government being dominated by German officials. Nevertheless, Germany would inevitably be dragged into a war with Russia by the collapse of her ally in Vienna. 'For purposes of foreign policy', he wrote, with some relish, 'Austria … is a dead body, without any inherent force or initiative of its own.'[66] The recent Balkan wars had fatally weakened the Austrians and strengthened Serbia; Austria had lost its former allies in the region; and at the same time Russia was 'arming on an enormous scale'.[67] Moreover, echoing the analysis of global geopolitics that Mackinder had preached at the LSE, he argued that Germany could not afford to see herself cut off from the Balkans, and reduced 'from a central European power into a merely north European power'.[68]

Having completed his article, Namier wrote to Nagel in early June from the Grand Hotel in Cracow (as usual, the best and most expensive he could find in the city). He had taken the opportunity to call in at Koszylowce, where his father agreed to support him financially while he finished his book, on the assumption that a successful and prosperous legal career would follow.[69] Namier asked Nagel to direct all future correspondence to Balliol, where he was going for six months in order to bring his 'historical work' to a conclusion before he returned to the United States.[70] He must have reached Oxford soon afterwards, where he took lodgings and engaged a secretary, and was apparently dining in All Souls, possibly as a guest of Lionel Curtis, when news came through of the assassinations in Sarajevo. To the assembled company Namier declared that a full-scale European war was now inevitable. His fellow diners, who included the editor of *The Times*, begged to differ.[71]

On his return to Oxford Namier resumed an unlikely friendship with T. E. Lawrence. The two men had originally become acquainted through a shared interest in archaeology and an association with the Ashmolean Museum. Lawrence had haunted the museum even as a schoolboy, and was a protégé of the keeper.

Namier, who had brought his finds from Koszylowce to Oxford in 1908, sold three lots to the Ashmolean the following year in order to raise money.[72] During the summer of 1914 he and Lawrence spent much time in each other's company. Though their personalities were very different, and Namier never quite came to terms with Lawrence's subversive sense of humour and adolescent fondness for pranks, they had much in common, not least difficult relationships with their families. Presumably to prepare for the war that both knew was coming, Lawrence took Namier with him to practise rifle shooting at a makeshift range in north Oxford that Lawrence's brother had set up.[73]

Two days after Britain declared war on Germany Namier enlisted in the Royal Fusiliers and in September was incorporated into the 18th Battalion, one of the several 'Public Schools Battalions', formed from volunteers from the universities and public schools (and for that reason known as 'the UPS'). Thoughts of the law were deferred, and in due course abandoned entirely (a decision for which generations of Midwestern attorneys would have had reason to be grateful, had they known what would otherwise have been in store for them). The official description of him was: 'six feet tall; clear complexion, blue-grey eyes, dark brown hair; no scars or marks'.[74] His determination to enlist is often illustrated by an apocryphal story that, having been rejected at first because he failed the compulsory eye test, he returned the following day and, using his photographic memory, studied the optician's card until he had memorised it and was able to pass the second time. Clearly the doctors concerned must themselves have had very poor memories.

With other new recruits he was sent for training to Woodcote Park, on Epsom Downs. Uniforms did not arrive until November, so at first the fusiliers paraded in civilian clothes.[75] Nor were there any huts, which meant being billeted with landladies in Epsom. Among his fellow volunteers Namier stood out like a sore thumb, but he seems to have managed the strangeness of it all, and there is no reason to suppose that he was unpopular: his peculiar, almost paradoxical, combination of *naïveté* and cosmopolitan cleverness lifted him out of the ordinary, and those who did not argue with him on politics or matters intellectual always found him generous and kind. Despite an intense concern for personal privacy, he even coped with the inconvenience of sharing a room with another fusilier, Frank Stott ('Stottie'), a hapless Lancastrian whose antics amused him.[76] But military life was not pleasant: he presumably enjoyed route marching, given his habit of taking long walks, but drill would not have been to his taste, and the days were full of routine duties, from six in the morning until at least eight o'clock at night, and frequently much later. While at Epsom the troops were confined to within five miles of the town, and weekend leave was rare.[77]

Nonetheless, Namier somehow found the time to prepare an article for the new journal *Political Quarterly*, edited by a former pupil of A. L. Smith. There was a strong Balliol link: Smith himself, A. D. Lindsay, G. N. Clark, Douglas Cole and Arnold Toynbee were regular contributors. The issue for December 1914 included an article by Namier on 'Germany and eastern Europe', which reprised some of the arguments from his recent piece in the *American Leader*.[78] Although Britain had entered the war 'on purely west-European grounds', the real causes were to be sought further east, in the challenges of Slavdom to the rotting Austro-Hungarian empire and the resultant shift in Germany's Balkan strategy. This time he was much more positive about Russia, emphasising its increasingly liberal policies and commitment to Slavic nationalism rather than, as previously, its militaristic bent. The article was heavily weighted with historical narrative, and at its heart was an analysis of panSlavism, in which he distinguished two strands, religious and linguistic, of which the former had traditionally been the province of churchmen, while the latter had been developed and espoused by the liberal intelligentsia in the nineteenth century. Now, however, linguistic nationalism was predominant among Slav peoples, joining Orthodox, Uniate and Roman Catholic in the same great cause. It was driven by the simple emotional understanding of the peasantry, in whose crude and unreasoning minds 'the spirit of Slavdom is alive'.

Prefiguring arguments that he would develop more fully in the years to come, Namier distinguished between the uncomplicated nationalism of the Czechs, 'the leaders and pioneers of linguistic panSlavism', and the more complex and compromised attitudes of the Poles, whose upper classes had been more thoroughly westernised in the early modern period and alienated from their Slavic heritage, and who were, in addition, inhibited from taking action against Austria by fear of Russia. There was some hope for the Poles, however, in the recent repudiation in St Petersburg of 'Prussian policies'. Namier also noted in passing that in east Galicia, where his family's estate lay, the Ukrainian majority was ruled by a Polish aristocracy owing allegiance to Vienna: the first hint of a deeply held view about the ultimate course of self-determination in that province.

Over the winter conditions of service deteriorated. When the makeshift barracks were completed, the battalion moved inside: there were forty-eight men to a hut, and a roster was established for the necessary duties: sweeping and scrubbing, preparing tables for food and clearing up afterwards.[79] The close proximity of so many men must have been torture to Namier. Household chores were also a new experience. And despite a generous provision of blankets, the huts were freezing cold. Lord Kitchener came to inspect the battalions at Epsom after a foot of snow had fallen. Once he departed there was tobogganing and a massive 'snow fight' which enraged the local constabulary, but one cannot imagine Namier taking part in either activity. The fusiliers were also given the task of digging trenches, to acclimatise themselves to conditions in Flanders. This meant *reveille* at 4 30.[80] It must therefore have been an enormous relief when Namier was rescued, and brought back in to civilian life. Anxious as he was to serve king and empire – and he was to attempt to return to his regiment several times during the war – he and the army were profoundly unsuited.

Propaganda and intelligence

In February 1915 Namier was discharged, on the basis of a letter from the War Office to his commanding officer, and sent to work at the War Propaganda Bureau. He assumed that his deliverance must have been owing to the efforts of his friends in Balliol, in particular C. G. Stone, the historian and philosopher, who had been an undergraduate contemporary and was now a fellow.[81] But there is no reason to suppose any involvement from Oxford. Namier's particular talents and expertise were already widely known. British universities had produced few enough experts in the affairs of central and eastern Europe, and Sir Reginald Wingate had already brought his name to Kitchener's notice as someone with valuable local knowledge and unrivalled linguistic skills. Kitchener had not acted on his letter as Wingate had also expressed concern about Namier's political opinions.[82] Since then Namier had not only published in the *Political Quarterly* but had also written a short pamphlet on Russia for a series that his old tutor H. W. C. Davis was editing for Oxford University Press. It was not published, as Davis considered that it assumed too great a degree of background knowledge in the reader, and required revisions that Namier had neither the time nor, one suspects, the inclination, to make.[83]

Namier was particularly well qualified for the work that was being undertaken at Wellington House, which at this stage of the war was still principally directed at public opinion in the United States. Lord Eustace Percy, who was back in London, saw an opportunity, and on 1 February 1915 called Namier to a meeting at the Foreign Office.[84] Within a fortnight a letter of request had been sent to his commanding officer, an initiative that for the War Office was remarkably prompt, and he returned his uniform and reported for duty at Wellington House, in Buckingham Gate.[85] There he found some old friends: Arnold Toynbee, Allen Leeper, who despite his sporting prowess at Balliol had been graded as unfit for active service, and Allen's younger brother Rex, who had also been at Oxford. The company was congenial, and the political views of his colleagues were aligned with Namier's: all were at least liberal in their leanings, while Toynbee was a Fabian social reformer. More specifically, they shared Namier's determination that after the war there should be a reshaping of central and eastern Europe in which the subject nationalities of the Austro-Hungarian empire should be granted autonomous statehood.

In the meantime Namier had expanded his article in the *Political Quarterly* into a book with the same title – really a glorified pamphlet, a little over 30,000 words in length – which was published by Duckworth in the spring of 1915. He wrote it during his time in the army, and when challenged over an inaccuracy admitted that 'during my short visits on leave to Oxford and London, I was unable to do more than verify the main points and quotations'.[86] All the acknowledgments were Oxford-orientated. The historian H. A. L. Fisher, formerly of New College and soon to be a Liberal MP, supplied an introduction. In addition, Namier specifically thanked the Russian-born professor of jurisprudence at Oxford, Paul Vinogradoff, the classicist Alfred Zimmern and the foreign editor of *The Times*, Robert Seton-Watson, also formerly of New College.[87] All three were enthusiasts for Slavic nationalist movements. Seton-Watson, who had met Namier in August 1914 at a WEA summer school in Oxford, shared his belief that the Austrian empire had failed in its duty to the various ethnic groups over which it ruled, and must now be destroyed.[88]

To have been able to write even a short book so quickly, and under such difficult circumstances, was a remarkable achievement, but unlike the projected work of imperial history on which Namier had laboured in New York, this was more akin to journalism. Although the structure was historical, surveying European history from the middle ages to the present, the tone was brisk and the purpose didactic. Namier argued that since the causes of the war were to be found in eastern Europe 'the future of the nationalities inhabiting Austria-Hungary remains its central and most important problem'. Talk of 'stamping out the spirit of German militarism' was futile, since militarism was engrained in the German character. Namier assumed that Germany would be financially ruined by defeat and should not be humiliated by being deprived of national territory, though 'non-German provinces' would have to go. Instead, the principal Allied war aim should be the dismemberment of the Habsburg empire. At this stage he was still prepared to make small allowances for the positive historical role played by Austria-Hungary: the empire had always been a 'prison' for three major national groups – Rumanians, Serbians and Italians – but for the remainder it had served for a time as a kind of boarding house providing much-needed shelter, and for that reason its passing could be marked with a 'sentimental, tolerant sadness'.[89] Nonetheless, the days of European empires were emphatically past, and the Habsburg lands would have to be reorganised on principles of nationality, however difficult that might prove. The future for empires, and for 'the white race', lay outside Europe, with Britain, Russia and the United States. 'Their mutual relations, their internal development, and their relations to the coloured races will in all probability form the chief contents of the history of the twentieth century.'[90]

Fisher's introduction was supportive, if a trifle patronising: he recalled that Namier's 'grasp of Slavonic affairs was made so familiar to his Oxford friends'. Leaving his aside the author's contentious insistence on the dissolution of the Austro-Hungarian empire, 'the value of Mr Namier's interesting pamphlet lies … in his first-hand knowledge of the Slavonic peoples of the middle east, coupled with a sound and independent grasp of modern historical literature'.[91]

The book possessed many of the characteristic features of Namier's mature writings: a command of recent European history that was both broad and detailed, a talent for short, sharp character sketches, often dismissive, and a propensity for apophthegms which carried the weight of an assumed maturity.[92] As always, *idées fixes* were to the fore. The Germanophobia which he had exhibited since his undergraduate days, and which was a function of his youthful attraction to panSlavism, rampaged through the book.[93] The imperialists of the Hohenzollern *Reich*, showed 'an insolent, typically German, disregard' for the feelings of the majority of the population in their colonies; while the German cultural organisation, the *Singerbund*, 'develops, on the social level of a suburban cycling-club, the discursive aggressiveness of a German professor'.[94] Although he quoted Goethe with approval, always an exception to his general aversion from German culture, he could not resist a swipe at Nietzsche and Wagner, both of whom were identified with the 'Prussianisation of Germany':

> The unpractical German 'thinker', the inhuman German sentimentalist, the neurasthenic individual who dreams of power, the complex mind which, tired of its own shallow complexity, yearns for the simplicity of force, but incapable of real strength overshoots its mark and glorifies brutality.[95]

In his early days at Wellington House Namier spent a good deal of time assessing transatlantic opinion, although he was always expected to look at European newspapers as well, focusing on those published in Austria-Hungary and its dependencies.[96] One of his first tasks was to prepare an analysis of the views of expatriate Polish groups in the United States, and the conclusions make interesting reading in the light of the way in which his views were to develop over the next few years: the majority of Polish immigrants, he observed, were both anti-Russian *and* anti-Austrian, but in respect of Russia their hatred was directed against government rather than people, and a movement to unify all Slavic national groups in America had the potential to check both pro-Austrian and pro-Russian factions.[97] Soon, however, he was concentrating on the places in Europe which he knew best, Galicia and the surrounding territories of the Austro-Hungarian empire.

Namier's reports bore the unmistakable stamp of his personality. His first efforts were rambling and discursive, but he soon settled into his stride and produced summaries and memoranda which he considered to be 'uncluttered and matter-of-fact', though in reality they were far from being purely factual.[98] Founded on his accustomed mastery of detail, some of it drawn from personal knowledge, they were expressed with brilliant clarity and supreme confidence, but often strayed into dogmatism and sometimes even into polemic. They were also written with a journalistic verve (despite the fact that he was using what was in effect his fifth language), and showed flashes of linguistic exuberance – striking metaphors and memorable aphorisms – which were far from common currency in Foreign Office reports. Namier's hand is recognisable even in composite papers circulated anonymously.

Joining the staff of Wellington House enabled Namier to make a full return to the social world which he had left to join the army. He spent more time in Oxford, where in June 1915 he entertained the Polish socialist lawyer, Stanisław Patek, a man who had courageously defended revolutionary socialists in 1905–7 and was to serve as Polish minister for foreign affairs in 1919–20. Namier met Patek through 'mutual friends' and found him 'kind-hearted' and well-intentioned but 'full of shallow, doctrinaire liberalism'.[99] Then in September Namier stayed for some time at Lionel Curtis's house in Herefordshire.[100] He is known to have contributed to the *Round Table* during the war, but articles there were unsigned, and sometimes the product of more than one author, so his handiwork cannot be identified with certainty. Certainly, the commentaries on events in central and eastern Europe reeked of Namier's panSlavist enthusiasm and desire to see the dissolution of Austria-Hungary, and some also showed characteristic traces of his prose style.[101]

He began to extend his journalistic contacts, mainly on the left, writing for liberal weeklies such as the *New Statesman* and *Westminster Gazette*, and even for newspapers, the popular *Daily Chronicle* as well as *The Times*.[102] This was an extension of his work in Wellington House, where, besides providing digests of news extracted from newspapers across Europe, he was involved in the preparation of propaganda materials. Some were distributed in the United States through outlets which he himself cultivated, including foreign-language newspapers, bringing him into direct conflict with his former employer, Hammerling, who was drumming up American support for Germany.[103] Namier's journalism served much the same function as his propaganda work. Inevitably, the focus was on central and eastern Europe and the thrust was on the rights of the peoples of the Habsburg empire to self-determination. With both European and American opinion in view, it was necessary for him to depict Russian promises to the Slav nations as credible, arguing that the Tsarist regime had now cast aside (at least to some degree) its repressive past, while correspondingly the

Germans were not to be trusted, because of their traditional enmity to the Slavs and territorial ambitions in the east.[104]

The most florid expression of his Slavic nationalism came in an essay published in April 1916 in Hilaire Belloc's *Land and Water*, a weekly devoted to articles on the progress of the war. In this piece Namier depicted the conflict in the east as the latest manifestation in a timeless struggle between Teutons and Slavs.[105] Russia's 'infinitely patient peasant folk' would endure the German advance as they endure 'the wind that straggles across the plains'; 'the Russian peasant can put up with much that is unpleasant, and Russia has put up with plenty of Germans'.[106] He contrasted the character of the two nations, and by extension their two nationalisms – the one linguistic, the other religious or rather spiritual – through their writers: Russia personified by Dostoyevsky, 'that simple human giant', the genius of whose books German critics failed to understand.[107] It was an extraordinary piece, unlike anything else in the journal. At times the tone became quite emotional: understandable given that at the time Namier must have been wracked by helpless anxiety over his family, who were perilously close to the fighting on the eastern front.

Questions of national self-determination: Czechs and Poles

As the war ground on, and the allies failed to achieve a decisive breakthrough in the west or the east, Namier's attitude to Austria-Hungary hardened. He took up the cause of the Czechs with particular fervency, and in December 1916 published an article in the *New Statesman* on 'The case of Bohemia', which the Czech National Alliance in Great Britain reprinted separately. Seton-Watson, who was also an enthusiast for Czech nationalism, and an intimate of the Czech nationalist leader Tomáš Masaryk, may well have facilitated the connection, though Namier had himself developed a friendship with Edvard Beneš, a minister in Masaryk's government in exile.[108] Namier's argument was that, because of its geographical position, Bohemia had historically been at the focal point of Slavic resistance to German expansionism. Conversely, for the Germans, the removal of the 'Czech wedge' was essential to the aim of reviving a 'universal monarchy' in *Mittel-Europa*, which was now their principal war aim, both in itself and as a foundation to attack British and Russian imperial interests further east. Securing the independence of Bohemia would therefore not only constitute a crucial test of the principles of the allies – commitment to the cause of Slav brotherhood, in the case of the Russians; national self-government in the case of Great Britain; liberty in the case of the French – but would also be vital to defending Russian and British imperial interests.

Namier had abandoned any respect for Austria-Hungary as a shabby but service-able 'boarding-house' for smaller nationalities, and now described its government in racial terms: a malignant alliance of Germans and Magyars formed in order to dominate the Slavic peoples.[109] His brief historical account of Czech nationalism reproduced familiar ideas, while prefiguring arguments that he would deploy many years later in academic work on nineteenth-century European history. After the sup-pression, first of Hussite and then of Protestant, resistance to German universalism, Bohemia had for centuries been 'a dead nation'. 'Execution and banishment swept away its upper classes, its wealth and education. Nothing remained but a peasant people as indestructible as the soil, and as passive.' Rebirth came with 'the … literary renaissance of the romantic age'. Czechs and Slovaks proved mature enough to resist the siren call of German revolutionaries in 1848, and refused to attend their Frankfurt Parliament, an assembly Namier regarded not as the embodiment of liberal values but as 'the heir of the Holy Roman Empire'. Instead, the Czechs summoned a panSlav congress in Prague. When this noble experiment failed, there ensued a 'nightmare'. Bohemia was 'buried alive' while the Slovaks 'were handed over to the mercies of the Magyars'.[110] The defeat of Germany in the present conflict must therefore be followed by a re-creation of Bohemia, which, 'by her very existence will destroy the nightmare of a German-Magyar hegemony of Europe'.[111]

Namier restated and expanded these arguments (with some outright repetition) in a longer pamphlet, published after the United States had entered the war in 1917. He took as his starting-point the statement of Allied war aims that included the lib-eration of 'Italians, Slavs, Roumanians and Czecho-Slovaks'. *The Czecho-slovaks: an oppressed nationality* was a straightforward piece of political propaganda, seeking, from the perspective of the British government, to persuade Czechs and Slovaks of the iniquity of Austrian rule and that their future lay instead with the Allied cause. Namier also pushed a more personal agenda, that an independent Czecho-slovak state was not only desirable but necessary.

Having explained that Czechs and Slovaks were not two nations but one, he rehearsed the historical narrative of Czecho-slovak oppression by the Germans and Magyars, which now began in the dark ages with the Hunnic irruption into Europe.[112] Modern Czecho-slovak nationalists were continuing a centuries-old resistance of Slavs against the German-Magyar axis. The revived national conscious-ness of the nineteenth century, at first 'limited to a narrow circle of philologists and writers', expanded by 1848 as 'millions of men reawakened to their Slav conscious-ness'.[113] In 1848 the Bohemian revolutionaries recognised 'the double-faced character of German-Magyar "liberalisms" – of liberalisms which claim rights for "master nations" (*Herrenvölker*) and forge chains for weaker nationalities', and optimistically put themselves under the protection of Austria.[114] But they were deluded. After Austria's defeat in 1867 the ruling clique in Vienna aligned itself with its Prussian conqueror, and the empire became 'a jail, with the Germans and Magyars for its jailers'.[115] In order to convince his British and American readers of the underlying loyalty of Czechs to the allied cause, he concluded with a long account of their cruel treatment at the hands of the Austrian government.

But while Namier was passionate about the Czech national cause, the same did not apply to Poland. He was not wholly antagonistic to Polish nationalism, but his residual sympathies were significantly diminished by the unfortunate complications of Polish nationalist politics; namely, that Piłsudski's socialists, the party to which he was still emotionally attached, had aligned themselves with the Central Powers,[116] while Dmowski's National Democrats, whom he had always detested, supported Russia. Moreover, neither the left nor the right in Poland was free from the taint of 'imperialist' ambitions for the acquisition by a restored Poland of its eastern 'borderlands', at the expense of Lithuanians, 'White Russians' (Belorussians) and 'Little Russians' or 'Ruthenes' (Ukrainians). Namier found it easy, therefore, to follow the official Foreign Office line that discouraged the aspirations of Polish nationalists for an autonomous state, since this stood in direct opposition to Russia's war-aim, the reunion of all Polish territory within the Tsarist empire: the so-called 'Russian solution'.[117] As Namier put it, to encourage notions of future Polish autonomy would 'go against the programme of Russia and therefore of the Entente'.[118]

In much of this early writing Namier viewed the Polish question through the prism of wartime contingencies. Some of his contributions to journals (signed and unsigned) were propagandist, designed to persuade Poles and Polish-Americans of the nefarious intentions of the Central Powers, but they also reflected his own beliefs.[119] In April 1915 he drafted an article (not published until two years later) arguing that Poland had to be given the port of Danzig, partly in order to provide the Poles with access to the Baltic, but principally to thwart Germany of her desire to control 'the Vistula basin'. In Namier's formulation a restored Poland, complete with a Baltic coastline, should be placed firmly within the Russian empire.[120] His pro-Czech pamphlets informed readers that, unlike the Czechs, mid-nineteenth-century Polish revolutionaries (including of course his own grandfather) had failed to uphold their Slavic heritage. Poland's problems had begun when the Poles had forgotten their community of interest with their eastern neighbours – not, admittedly, all their own fault, given the cruel and repressive nature of Tsarist autocracy. But they had allowed themselves to be used, first by the Austrians and then by Bismarck, for whom tension between Poles and Russians was a creative force in maintaining the stability of Prussia's eastern frontier, just as the Berlin government was now exploiting the gullibility of Polish nationalists to advance its own expansionist agenda.[121]

In practice, Namier felt uncomfortable with Polish politicians of all stripes, even those like August Zaleski, who were old friends. He steered clear of the Polish Information Committee (PIC), the organisation through which the British government was working to influence Polish opinion in Britain, and whose members included Zaleski as president and Seton-Watson as secretary. In general, Namier thought it safer for Wellington House to work with individuals, and to keep away from émigré organisations. Indeed, when his superiors ordered him to pay a visit to the offices of the PIC, he described it as the equivalent of the Holy Roman Emperor Henry IV's humiliation before Pope Gregory VII at Canossa.[122] His irritation increased with the arrival in London in November 1915 of Roman Dmowski, the leader of the National Democratic Party, a man determined to propagate his own vision of an independent Poland, and in the first instance to replace the left-leaning PIC with his own organisation, the Polish Exiles Protection (PEP).[123]

Whether Namier had met Dmowski personally before 1915 is unclear, but previous encounters with members of Dmowski's party had been unpleasant. Their leader in the flesh he detested. As an individual Dmowski was abrasive, uncompromising and relentless (not so different perhaps, in these respects, from Namier himself). Politically, he represented everything Namier loathed. He was very much a man of the right, who had always been prepared to work with the Tsarist regime and had accepted election to the Russian Duma in 1905 when Polish socialists boycotted the polls. Dmowski was committed to an independent Polish state that would include territories in which ethnic Poles were a minority, including east Galicia. Above all, he was notoriously anti-Semitic. Although Dmowski's devout Catholicism won him a few friends in high places, notably Sir Edward Grey's private secretary, the Catholic convert Sir Eric Drummond,[124] most British politicians and civil servants, even those who were well disposed to his party, found him a hard man to like. His belligerence and addiction to intrigue became wearisome, and his diatribes against Jews were too crude.[125]

Since one of Dmowski's earliest critics in the Foreign Office was none other than Lord Eustace Percy, some historians have inferred that Namier must already have been at work behind the scenes.[126] Certainly Dmowski soon became aware of his hostile presence. If he had not heard of Namier before he came to London, there were plenty of people able and willing to enlighten him. When both men were engaged in January 1916 to contribute lectures to a course on Polish history organised by Seton-Watson at King's College, London, one of Dmowski's English supporters, the writer Laurence Alma-Tadema, a daughter of the painter, protested to the permanent under-secretary at the Foreign Office, Sir Arthur Nicolson, against the inclusion of Namier and a Jewish professor from Lemberg. 'The Polish Jews and socialists', she wrote, 'are all anti-Russian and consequently anti-Ally.'[127] Reassured that Namier would 'carefully avoid any controversy with M. Dmowski' and that for his part Dmowski would make no attacks on Polish Jews', Nicolson allowed Namier to participate. Arnold Toynbee remembered seeing each attend the other's lectures, saying nothing but listening attentively and glowering.[128]

It was not long before Namier showed his colours. The occasion centred on Dmowski's behaviour at a conference of Polish political groupings in Lausanne in February 1916, in which the delegates agreed to try to persuade the Allies to postpone any discussion of Poland's future until after the war was won. In his report of the conference, which was meant to be based on press extracts, Namier included an assertion that Dmowski had performed a volte-face to advocate a proposed 'reinsurance plan with Austria'. His evidence came from private information and from an Austrian report which had been passed through 'secret channels' to Masaryk.[129] It was flatly contradicted by other Foreign Office sources, who suggested that the story may well have been a piece of 'black propaganda' concocted by the Central Powers, and that Namier had allowed prejudice to get the better of his judgment.[130] Since Namier's summaries enjoyed wide circulation in the Foreign Office and beyond, Dmowski was alerted by a sympathiser in the Press Department of Military Intelligence, and immediately lodged a formal complaint with Sir Arthur Nicolson. Flustered, Nicolson told Ernest Gowers, Namier's section head, that in future Namier's reports must be confined to extracts from the press, and that if he wished to make separate reports he should do so through Gowers, who would vet them before onward transmission.[131] It was not exactly a 'reprimand', as one historian has characterised it, for there was clearly a recognition that although Namier had been misled on this occasion he might still have useful things to say.[132] But it was personally embarrassing, especially as Dmowski's specific complaint had reached the ears of the foreign secretary himself.

Dmowski did not rest with this small triumph, however, and pushed his luck too far. His friend Count Jan Marie de Horodyski (who was also operating as a British agent) suggested to Drummond that Namier and others were 'perhaps unwittingly being used for pro-Austrian purposes' and should be 'closely watched'.[133] The security service was ordered to investigate, and returned with a clean bill of health. Namier had been to Balliol, had served in the Royal Fusiliers, and was a friend of Lord Eustace Percy: obviously, he was above suspicion.[134] But rumours based on Namier's report of the Lausanne conference were still circulating, as far afield as Russia. In July one of Dmowski's associates felt obliged to deny them in a Moscow newspaper: they were the work of 'Austro-German agents', one of whom, 'a certain Namier', had been 'unmasked by the English authorities'.[135] Namier was reassured that this attack had done him no harm, and so it proved. Even if Drummond still considered Dmowski to be 'entirely reliable', elsewhere in the Foreign Office a reaction in Namier's favour was gathering momentum.[136]

The last straw came in December, when the postal censors intercepted a letter in the diplomatic bag from Moscow. It was addressed to the editor of the *Quarterly Review* by Bernard Pares, professor of Russian at Liverpool University and official British correspondent on the Russian front, and was a paean of praise to Dmowski as a loyal supporter of the allied cause. Regrettably, Pares reported, a libel had been in circulation against Dmowski, falsely alleging that he had turned his coat at the Lausanne conference. It came 'with the authority of [the British] government, under the hand of a Mr Namier, an Austrian Jew with an English education'. Pares, who would later come to know Namier well, and whose son Richard would be one of Namier's closest friends among historians of eighteenth-century England, was at this time, as he admitted, unacquainted with 'Mr Namier', but had heard that 'he is a Jew, born in Budapest, named I think Bernstein'. Namier's Jewishness was presented as an explanation for his hatred of Dmowski: in fact, the entire letter had an anti-Semitic tone, alleging among other things that all Jews in Poland supported the Central Powers. It received short shrift in the Foreign Office and the ambassador in Petrograd was ordered to give Pares a stiff talking-to.[137]

Marriage

For the time being Namier could feel secure from Dmowski's 'intrigues'. The winter of 1916–17 found him working harder than ever, staying at his office until ten or eleven at night to plough through Polish newspapers from Austria and Russia before returning to lodgings in Great Ormond Street. Yet he still found time to write articles for the press, some of which he used to further the propaganda work of the department.[138] He even had time to improve his Russian, the weakest of his many languages because of its proximity to Ukrainian, and engaged a teacher on the recommendation of the Leeper brothers.[139]

This was a fateful decision. Clara Sophia Poniatowska, who was three years younger than Namier, and was then acting as a clerk in the office of the Russian government committee in Holborn, was a perfect *gamine*, with considerable charm, and a waif-like quality that immediately attracted Namier, who was drawn to women needing his protection, as they offered an opportunity for domination, and even perhaps a feeling of possession.[140] Clara's other, less attractive, characteristics, her secretiveness and nervous anxiety, were not immediately apparent. Teacher and pupil soon became lovers. If Namier's widow is to be believed, this may well have been Namier's first satisfactory sexual relationship in England, though not for want of trying. As a young man he sought and obtained casual sex with avidity. Lady Namier wrote that he had enjoyed 'easy, friendly, more or less fleeting relations with women' whom he had met on the continent, and presumably also in America. In England, she said, he had encountered nothing but failure. Acquiring from his father a morbid fear of venereal disease, a reflection of what became in due course a more general hypochondria, Namier avoided prostitutes (or at least said he did) and focused his attention on what Julia called 'amiable amateurs', a turn of phrase more evocative of the tennis club, perhaps, than the bedroom. However, the sexual partners he found were either frigid, or altogether too 'brash'.[141] Sex with Clara was a comfortable experience, which did not interfere with his hectic routine of work, writing and lectures.

Then Namier received an unpleasant surprise. He had assumed that Clara was married and estranged from her husband: she now told him that she was a widow, and wished to get married. Appalled, he consulted one of his colleagues in the Department of Information, Edwyn Bevan. A classical scholar, Bevan was nearly twenty years older than Namier, a man with a strong Christian faith, of the evangelical variety, and impeccable social credentials: he was the son of banker and the grandson of a bishop, and had married into the English aristocracy.[142] According to Lady Namier's biography (and in this instance the voice must be Namier himself) he was 'of rare distinction in appearance, manner, feelings and mind – a just man of the Anglo-Saxon stamp'.[143] One senses that Namier wanted Bevan's approval as much as his advice. Confessing to his highly moral friend that he had embarked on a casual sexual relationship, one which, moreover, he had no intention of abandoning, was a brave thing to do. Mercifully, Bevan expressed no moral judgment, while counselling Namier firmly in favour of marriage. And so, on 6 January 1917, he did marry Clara, in St Giles's registry office in London, with Bevan and Allen Leeper as witnesses, after which he went to live with her in a boarding house in Bloomsbury.

The account Namier gave Julia about Clara's background is confused. He said that Clara had led him to believe that her first husband was called Poniatowski, and that he discovered many years later, examining their marriage certificate, that she also went by the name Edeleff. The fact that she had a Russian passport and that her Russian was more fluent than her Polish, suggested that Edeleff was her maiden name. Namier, with his customary concern about race, deduced that this indicated 'Tartar' origins, and observed that she had 'some endearing Mongolian characteristics'.[144] But all this has a ring of artificiality. His rumination on the irony that he, of all people, should have been bamboozled over details, seems contrived. Clara signed herself in the marriage register as 'C. S. Edeleff' and on the marriage certificate her father appeared as 'Alexander Poniatowski, medical doctor, deceased.' This would be consistent with the conclusion that her family was Polish and her first husband Russian. A. L. Smith, to whom she was introduced, certainly thought she was Polish.[145]

At first Clara had a very positive influence on her husband. Before meeting her, and possibly as a consequence of overwork and the tension produced by his conflict with Dmowski, he had fallen prey to insomnia, something which in later life would plague and debilitate him. But this vanished with Clara's arrival. And to friends they appeared very happy.

A significant change also occurred in his pattern of work. In May 1917, he and several of his close friends, including Toynbee, Bevan and the two Leepers, were assigned to the new Intelligence Bureau established within the Department of Information. Another, more senior, colleague, James Headlam-Morley, the historian and educationalist, with whose family Namier had become friendly, was appointed assistant director.[146] The bureau had its offices around the corner from Wellington House, in Victoria Street. Its creator, the novelist John Buchan, envisaged its purpose as 'to study the internal conditions, feelings and tendencies in foreign countries … with a view to supplying the government with succinct memoranda'.[147] Instead of summarising press reports and preparing propaganda, Namier would provide analysis and commentary, and would do so on the basis not merely of foreign newspapers but of intelligence supplied by the Admiralty and War Office, among other official and unofficial sources.[148] Together with Seton-Watson, he was assigned to cover east and central Europe.[149] This would give full rein to his abilities, and also to his principles and prejudices. He was ideally placed to influence what would happen to Austria-Hungary and its territories. It is by no means certain that his family, struggling with life in war-torn Galicia, knew just how high he had risen, or realised how influential he would soon become. Had they been fully aware of his position, it is a moot point whether their principal reaction would have been pride in Ludwik's achievements or apprehension at what his involvement in the preparation of British policy might bring about.

Notes

1 Cf. *Namier*, 107–8. See also Smith to Spring Rice, 9 Mar. 1913 (*The letters and friendships of Sir Cecil Spring Rice: a record*, ed. Stephen Gwynn (2 vols, 1929), ii, 189–90).
2 Smith to Spring Rice, 6 Apr. 1913 (Churchill, Spring Rice papers, Ii/16). Original emphasis.
3 Spring Rice to Namier, 25, [?28] July 1913 (Churchill, Spring Rice papers, I/5/4).

4 Draft review (Rylands, Namier papers, 1/19/5).

5 *Skyscrapers*, 1–2.

6 *Skyscrapers*, 8.

7 *Skyscrapers*, 7.

8 *Structure*, xi.

9 Namier's notes on 'Zionism and Jews', quoted in *Namier*, 108.

10 Namier to Charles Nagel [Apr. 1914] (Yale UL, Nagel papers, 364/I/11/165).

11 Isaiah Berlin, *Personal impressions* (1980), 74.

12 Smith to Namier, 30 Sept. 1913 (Rylands, Namier papers, 1/9/19). Namier was described, or described himself, as an 'editor' in a New York trade directory (*Trow's general directory of the boroughs of Manhattan and Bronx, city of New York*, cxxvii (1913–14)).

13 Namier, 'Louis B. Hammerling' (typescript), 4–5 (CZA, Namier papers, A312\4).

14 Berlin, *Personal impressions*, 74.

15 Joseph Rappaport, 'The American Yiddish press and the European conflict in 1914', *Jewish Social Studies*, xix (1957), 118.

16 Even then, Namier still carried on business dealings with Hammerling into the 1920s, possibly on his father's account: Namier to 'Mr Lewis' [c.May 1921] (Rylands, Namier papers, 1/9/7).

17 Namier, 'Notes on Zionism', quoted in 'Turbulent Zionist', 10–11. See also Rose, *Zionism*, 11.

18 'Turbulent Zionist', 11.

19 *Namier*, 112; A. J. Toynbee, *Acquaintances* (1967), 72.

20 Toynbee, *Acquaintances*, 72.

21 M. B. B. Buskupski, *The most dangerous German agent in America: the many lives of Louis N. Hammerling* (DeKalb, Ill., 2015), chs 3–4; A. J. Ward, 'Immigrant minority "diplomacy": American Jews and Russia, 1901–12', *Bulletin of the British Association for American Studies*, new ser., no. 9 (1964), 14.

22 Smith to Namier, 30 Sept. 1913 (Rylands, Namier papers, 1/9/19).

23 For Schenck, who died young in 1919, see *The American Oxonian*, vi (1919), 109; and for his friendship with Namier, Namier to Liddell Hart, 27 Mar. 1951 (LH, 1/539/61).

24 He had, for example, managed to secure election to the socially exclusive New York Athletic Club, which he was still giving as his address in 1915 (*Royal Colonial Institute Yearbook* (1915), 180).

25 W. C. Greene to Lady Namier, 20 Mar. 1913 (Rylands, Namier papers, 1/19/5). Alfred A. Biddle (1885–1967), later of Newtown Square, Pennsylvania, made a career in banking.

26 *Namier*, 110–11.

27 *Skyscrapers*, 11–12.

28 L. B. Namier, 'The hyphenated', *New Statesman*, 4 Mar. 1916, repr. in *Skyscrapers*, 9–20. He returned to this theme in 'The disinheritance of America', *Nation and Athenaeum*, 26 Jan. 1929, repr. in *Skyscrapers*, 21–33.

29 *Skyscrapers*, 18–20.

30 *Skyscrapers*, 17–18, 19.

31 Smith to Namier, 30 Sept. 1913 (Rylands, Namier papers, 1/9/19).

32 Peter Novick, *That noble dream: the 'objectivity question' and the American historical profession* (Cambridge, 1988), 81–2.

33 Printed programme for Encaenia, 18 June 1913 (Franklin D. Roosevelt Presidential Library, Shepardson papers, box 1).

34 Novick, *Noble dream*, 46.

35 A. L. Smith, review of Hannis Taylor, *The origin and growth of the English constitution*, *EHR*, xiv (1899), 749; A. L. Smith, rev. of Sidney and Beatrice Webb, *English local government ...*, ibid., xxv (1910), 353–4. Nonetheless, Smith still found much to praise in the exposition of authors like Hallam and Macaulay.

36 Compare Herbert Butterfield, *George III and the historians* (1957), 176–89; P. B. M. Blaas, *Continuity and anachronism: parliamentary and constitutional development in Whig historiography and in the anti-Whig reaction between 1890 and 1930* (The Hague, 1978), 6–8; Michael Bentley, *Modernizing England's past: English historiography in the age of modernism 1870–1970* (Cambridge, 2005), 147–8.

37 Namier to P. H. Kerr, 11 Aug. 1926 (Rylands, Namier papers, 1/1a/1/4–6).

38 C. M. Andrews, *The colonial period* (New York, 1912), 254.

39 C. M. Andrews, *British committees, commissions and councils of trade and plantations, 1622–1675* (Baltimore, Md, 1908).

40 G. L. Beer, *The old colonial system, 1660–1754* (2 vols, New York, 1912); H. L. Osgood, *The American colonies in the seventeenth century* (3 vols, New York, 1904–7). Osgood was continuing his research into the eighteenth century, and a companion work was published posthumously: *The American colonies in the eighteenth century* (4 vols, New York, 1924–25).

41 C. M. Andrews and F. G. Davenport, *Guide to the MSS materials on the history of the United States to 1783, in the British Museum, in minor London archives, and in the libraries of Oxford and Cambridge* (Washington, DC, 1908); C. M. Andrews, *Guide to the materials for American history to 1783, in the Public Record Office of Great Britain* (2 vols, Washington, DC, 1912–14).

42 Originals (and later typed copies) of notes and transcripts which Namier made at this time can be found in Rylands, Namier papers, 1/6/7–8, and 1/21/2.

43 *Structure*, ix.

44 Namier to P. H. Kerr, 12 Aug. 1926 (Rylands, Namier papers, 1/1a/1/5); same to Whitney Shepardson, 4 Nov. 1926 (ibid., 1/1a/2); Namier transcripts (ibid., 6/7–8).

45 For Namier's use of the Stiles archive, see *American rev.*, 32, 39, 159, 241, 243, 259.

46 Rylands, Namier papers, 1/6/7–8, 1/21/2. In writing to Philip Kerr in 1926 (ibid., 1/1a/1/4–5), Namier implied that he had begun work on English politics even before going to America. This is inconsistent with other contemporary evidence. He may well have started his investigations into English MPs while in New York, though he had evidently made little headway on English parliamentary history before returning to Britain in 1914.

47 For Beard see Richard Hofstadter, *The Progressive historians: Turner, Beard, Partington* (New York, 1968); Forrest McDonald, 'Charles A. Beard', Marcus Cunliffe and R. W. Winks (eds), *Pastmasters: some essays on American historians* (New York, 1969), 110–41.

48 John Hawgood to Lady Namier, 8 July 1971, cited in Colley, 25, 112.

49 B. T. Wilkins, 'Charles A. Beard on the founding of Ruskin Hall', *Indiana Magazine of History*, lii (1956), 277–84.

50 Hofstadter, *Progressive historians*, 212; C. A. Beard, *An economic interpretation of the constitution of the United States* (2nd edn, New York, 1935), viii.

51 J. M. Price, 'Party, purpose and pattern: Sir Lewis Namier and his critics', *Journal of British Studies*, i, no. 1 (1961), 77.

52 C. A. Beard, *An economic interpretation of the constitution of the United States* (New York, 1913), ch. 5.

53 Curtis to E. W. M. Grigg, [*c*.1 Oct. 1913] (Bodl., Curtis papers, MS Eng. Hist. c. 786, fos 26–7).

54 [Grigg] to Curtis, 16 Oct. 1913 (Bodl., MS Eng. Hist. c. 786, fo. 28).

55 Curtis to Grigg [*c*.1 Oct. 1913] (Bodl., MS Eng. Hist. c. 786, fos 26–7).

56 Namier to Curtis [Oct. 1913] (Bodl., MS Eng. Hist. c. 807, fo. 45).

57 Curtis to Grigg, 17 Oct. 1913 (two letters) (Bodl., MS Eng. Hist. c. 786, fos 44, 47).

58 Curtis to Namier, 17 Oct. 1913 (Bodl., MS Eng. Hist. c. 786, fos 49b–50).

59 Curtis to Grigg, 22 Oct. 1913 (Bodl., MS Eng. Hist. c. 786, fo. 51).

60 Grigg to Curtis, 1, 5 Nov. 1913 (Bodl., MS Eng. Hist. c. 786, fos 70–71, 77).

61 Hammerling to Nagel, 17 Apr. 1914, Namier to Nagel, [Apr. 1914] (Yale UL, Nagel papers, 364/I/11/165); Nagel to Namier, 4 May 1914 (ibid., 364/I/11/166); Namier to Nagel, 24 May 1914 (ibid., 364/I/11/168); Nagel to Namier, 9 June 1914 (ibid., 364/I/11/169).

62 *New York Times*, 22 Apr. 1914.

63 Published on 9 July 1914, and reprinted in *Skyscrapers*, 62–72.

64 *Skyscrapers*, 63.

65 *Radio Times*, 4 June 1964.

66 *Skyscrapers*, 67.

67 *Skyscrapers*, 71.

68 *Skyscrapers*, 69.

69 *Namier*, 119.

70 Hammerling to Nagel, 5 May 1914 (Yale UL, Nagel papers, 364/I/11/166); Namier to Nagel, 3 June 1914 (ibid., 364/I/11/169).

71 Berlin, *Personal impressions*, 74.

72 *Namier*, 84–6. The sale consisted of figurines, pottery vessels and fragments, and an arrowhead (Arthur MacGregor, *Ashmolean Museum, Oxford: summary catalogue of the continental archaeological collections* … (Oxford, 1997), 233, 244–5), for which Namier received in total £19 (*Namier*, 86). Arnold Lawrence, T. E.'s brother, dated his first recollection of Namier to about 1909 (ibid., 116).

73 *In the margin*, 74.

74 Certificate of discharge no 5382 (Rylands, Namier papers, 1/9/7).

75 Photograph of Public Schools' Battalion, Royal Fusiliers, marching through Ashtead, Surrey, 1914 (National Army Museum, 2001–06–121–5).

76 *Namier*, 117–18.

77 Detailed accounts of camp life in letters written home in 1914–15 by a soldier in another of the Public Schools Battalions, Fusilier Thomas McKinney, are preserved in the family collection at Sentry Hill, Newtownabbey, Co. Antrim.

78 *Political Quarterly*, no. 4 (Dec. 1914), 70–93.

79 Thomas McKinney to Isabel Dundee, 14 Mar 1914 [*recte* 1915], to his aunt, n.d. (Sentry Hill collection).

80 Thomas McKinney to Meg McKinney, 24 Jan. [1915], to Janet Dundee, 24 Jan. [1915], to Elsie McKinney, n.d. (Sentry Hill collection).

81 *Namier*, 115, 119. Namier and Stone had been close friends in college, possibly because both were outsiders: in Stone's case it was deafness, stammer and a general air of eccentricity which set him apart from the normal run of undergraduates (Fay Anderson, *An historian's life: Max Crawford and the politics of academic freedom* (Melbourne, 2005), 26).

82 Sir Reginald Wingate to Ld Kitchener, 28 Sept. 1914 (TNA, Kitchener papers, PRO 30/57/45).

83 John Clarke, 'All Souls and the war of the professors', S. J. D. Green and Peregrine Horden (eds), *All Souls and the wider world: statesmen, scholars and adventurers, c.1850–1950* (Oxford, 2011), 171, 174.

84 Percy to Namier, 1 Feb. 1915 (Rylands, Namier papers, 1/9/19).

85 Certificate of discharge no. 5382 (Rylands, Namier papers, 1/9/7); Schuster to Percy, 13 Feb. 1915, Schuster to Namier, 13 Feb. 1915 (Rylands, Namier papers, 1/9/19).

86 Namier to Ld Cromer, 24 Sept. 1915 (Rylands, Namier papers, 1/9/7, a copy made by John Brooke of a letter in the Cromer papers in the Bank of England archives).

87 L. B. Namier, *Germany and eastern Europe* (1915), viii, 30. In 1918 Vinogradoff edited two volumes of medieval texts jointly with Namier's cousin Ludwik Ehrlich: *Year books of Edward II*, xii: *6 Edward II, A.D. 1312–1313* (Selden Soc., ser. 5, xxxiv, 1918); *Year books of Edward II*, xiv, pt. 1: *6 Edward II, A.D. 1312–1313* (Selden Soc., ser. 5, xxxviii, 1921).

88 Hugh Seton-Watson and Christopher Seton-Watson, *The making of a new Europe: R. W. Seton-Watson and the last years of Austria-Hungary* (1981), 158, 167.

89 Namier, *Germany and eastern Europe*, 126.

90 Namier, *Germany and eastern Europe*, 128.

91 Namier, *Germany and eastern Europe*, vii.

92 Namier, *Germany and eastern Europe*, 95, 109, 112–13.

93 This aspect of Namier's book received a mild reproof from A. L. Smith, who in an otherwise very favourable review suggested that the sentence 'German militarism will survive as long as there remains one German' was 'too strongly worded' (*Political Quarterly*, 6 May 1915). Smith was always alarmed by the virulence of Namier's animosity towards Germany (Smith to the principal, Reading College, 25 June 1918 (Balliol, Smith papers, N1)).

94 Namier, *Germany and eastern Europe*, 54, 86.

95 Namier, *Germany and eastern Europe*, 63.

96 Schuster to Namier, 13 Feb. 1915 (Rylands, Namier papers, 1/9/19); Sir Horace Plunkett's diary, 22 Apr. 1915 (National Library of Ireland, Plunkett papers, MS 42222/35). He continued for some time the practice of scanning American newspapers: Namier, 'Observations on Polish activities in America', 31 May 1916 (FO 395/10, file 106874); memo by Namier 16 June 1916 (FO 395/10, file 117776); Namier to Basil Thomson, 17 Aug. 1916 (FO 395/10, file 16242).

97 97 Preliminary report from Namier, 13 Mar. 1915 (FO 371/2450, fos 33–7); memo by Namier, 'Observations on Polish activities in America', 31 May 1915 (FO 395/101, file 106874).

98 *Namier*, 123.

99 Memo by Namier on 'The Polish cabinet' [Dec. 1919] (FO 371/4385, fos 145–6); memo by Namier, 23 Jan. 1920 (FO 371/4384, fo. 239).

100 Namier to Ld Cromer, 24 Sept. 1915 (Rylands, Namier papers, 1/9/7).

101 See for example, articles in no. 16 (Sept. 1914) on 'The war in Europe', 'Germany and the Prussian spirit' and 'The Austro-Servian dispute' (*Round Table*, iv (1913–14), 591–676) and in no. 17 (Dec. 1914) on 'The doctrine of ascendancy' and 'Russia and her ideals' (ibid., v (1914–15), 70–135).

102 FO 371/4366, fo. 212.

103 See for example, Namier to Ld Eustace Percy, 8 Dec. 1916 (FO 395/26, file 246560); memo by Namier on 'Forced labour in Poland' [Dec. 1916] (ibid.).

104 This is the theme of various anonymous contributions to the *New Statesman* in 1915–16, all of which bear strong similarities to Namier's style, both in their tone and their mastery

of detail, but which at present cannot be attributed unequivocally to his pen: 'The siege of Przemyśl' (27 Mar. 1915); rev. of Virginia Gaydo, *Modern Austria: her racial and social problems* (25 Sept. 1915); 'The smaller nationalities of Russia' (30 Oct. 1915); 'Germany and the Polish question' (12 Feb. 1916); and 'Germany and Poland' (15 Apr. 1916).

105 'The spirit of Russia', *Land and Water*, 13 Apr. 1916, repr. in *Skyscrapers*, 73–80.

106 *Skyscrapers*, 73–4.

107 *Skyscrapers*, 76.

108 Namier to Sir William Tyrrell, 26 Sept. 1918 (FO 371/4361, fos 215–17).

109 A series of anonymous articles in the summer of 1916 in the weekly *Everyman* (a magazine for which Namier is known to have written) developed similar arguments about central Europe in the context of Austrian 'pan-Germanism' (see the issues for 4, 11 and 18 Aug.).

110 L. B. Namier, *The case of Bohemia* (1917), 5–8.

111 Namier, *The case of Bohemia*, 10.

112 Namier, *The Czecho-slovaks*, 5.

113 Namier, *The Czecho-slovaks*, 8–9.

114 Namier, *The Czecho-slovaks*, 9.

115 Namier, *The Czecho-slovaks*, 13–14.

116 Preliminary report from Namier, 13 Mar. 1915 (FO 371/2450, fos 33–7).

117 Ng, *Nationalism*, 100–1.

118 Memo by Namier, 15 Dec. 1916 (FO 395/26, file 255781).

119 See, for example, an article in the *New Statesman*, 18 Nov. 1916 entitled 'Germany's Polish gamble' and signed 'E. E. A.', which was one of Namier's pen-names.

120 L. B. Namier, *Danzig: Poland's outlet to the sea* (1917).

121 Rev. of W. Alison Phillips, *Poland*, *TLS*, 17 Feb. 1916.

122 Memo by Namier, 15 Dec. 1916 (FO 395/26, file 255781); K. J. Calder, *Britain and the origins of the new Europe* (Cambridge, 1976), 56.

123 Norman Davies, 'The Poles in Great Britain, 1914–1919', *Slavonic and East European Review*, l (1972), 68–72; Christopher Seton-Watson, 'Czechs, Poles and Yugoslavs in London, 1914–1918', *L'émigration politique en Europe aux XIXe et XXe siècles; actes du colloque de Rome (3–5 Mars 1988)* (Rome, 1991), 278–83.

124 Paul Latawski, 'Roman Dmowski, the Polish question, and western opinion, 1915–18', Paul Latawski (ed.), *The reconstruction of Poland, 1914–23* (Basingstoke, 1992), 3.

125 J. D. Gregory, *On the edge of diplomacy: rambles and reflections, 1902–1928* ([1928]), 170. See also Margaret MacMillan, *Peacemakers: the Paris conference of 1919 and its attempt to end war* (2001), 219–20, 221–2.

126 Paul Latawski, 'The Dmowski–Namier feud, 1915–1918', *Polin: studies in Polish Jewry, ii* (Oxford, 1987), 40. The notion that Percy was Namier's 'spokesman' in the Foreign Office (Calder, *Britain and the new Europe*, 87) does seem an exaggeration, however.

127 Seton-Watson and Seton-Watson, *Making of a new Europe*, 158–9.

128 *Namier*, 124.

129 According to a memorandum composed by Namier in *c.*1925 on his relations with Dmowski, formerly in the possession of John Brooke, and now lost: Latawski, 'Dmowski-Namier feud', 48.

130 Memo by J. D. Gregory, 20 Mar. 1916 (TNA, CAB 37/144/51); Latawski, 'Dmowski-Namier feud', 40.

131 Nicolson to Sir Edward Grey, 6 May 1916 (FO 395/25, file 95630); note by Hubert Montgomery, 18 May 1916 (ibid.).

132 Latawski, 'Dmowski-Namier feud', 41.

133 Latawski, 'Dmowski-Namier feud', 41–2; Calder, *Britain and the new Europe*, 53, 85.

134 Report on August Zaleski, 20 Sept. 1917 (FO 371/3016, fo. 245).

135 *Namier*, 125 (Lady Namier's translation from the original Russian).

136 Latawski, 'Dmowski-Namier feud', 42.

137 Bernard Pares, *My Russian memoirs* (1931), 481; Hubert Montgomery to Sir George Buchanan, 9 Dec. 1916 (FO, 395/26, file 249249).

138 Namier to Geoffrey Butler, 22, 29 Jan., 8 Feb. 1917 (FO 395/108, files 19554, 23081, 3269); Ernest Gowers to Hubert Montgomery, 30 Jan. 1917 (FO 395/108, file 24953).

139 *Namier*, 130.

140 Compare the description of Clara in *Namier*, 130–4, with the more positive appreciation in A. J. P. Taylor, *A personal history* (1983), 167–8; and A. J. P. Taylor, *Letters to Eva 1969–1983*, ed. Eva Haraszti Taylor (1991), 251.

141 *Namier*, 131.

142 For Bevan, see *Oxf. DNB*.

143 *Namier*, 132.

144 *Namier*, 130–4.

145 Smith to the principal of Reading College, 25 June 1918 (Balliol, Smith papers, N1).

146 *Namier*, 133. According to Headlam-Morley, he was himself personally responsible for Namier's appointment (Headlam-Morley to Sir William Tyrrell, 9 Sept. 1918 (FO 371/4358, fo. 259)).

147 Seton-Watson and Seton-Watson, *Making of a new Europe*, 207, 218.

148 Alan Sharp, 'Some relevant historians – the Political Intelligence Department of the Foreign Office, 1918–1920', *Australian Journal of Politics and History*, xxxiv (1988–9), 358–9.

149 Seton-Watson and Seton-Watson, *Making of a new Europe*, 207.

3

Facing east, 1917–20

The February revolution in Russia and the abdication of the Tsar transformed the political landscape of eastern Europe. Among the immediate consequences was an improvement in the prospects for an independent Polish state, as the provisional government in Petrograd abandoned the 'Russian solution' to the Polish question. The puppet kingdom of Poland, established in German-controlled territory, was soon accorded a degree of autonomy under a council of regency. At the same time, in the south a Ukrainian People's Republic was set up in Kiev, under the umbrella of the provisional government in Russia. Then came the Bolshevik revolution in October, the ensuing peace between Russia and the Central Powers at Brest-Litovsk in March 1918, and an outbreak of hostilities in the Ukraine between pro-German and Bolshevik forces. The cumulative effect of these changes was to create a much more fluid situation, which political parties in Poland and exiles in the west each sought to exploit. Eventually, after the defeat of Germany, a Polish republic was established, with territorial ambitions that included east Galicia.

As events unfolded, Namier became more and more preoccupied with Polish and Ukrainian affairs. He was indignant at the possibility that the victorious Allies might countenance Polish nationalist claims to lands in which ethnic Poles formed only a minority of the population, especially in the east, and was also anxious at the treatment of Jewish communities by Polish troops. His duty, as he saw it, was to oppose Polish expansionism in every quarter, and especially in east Galicia, where he consistently espoused the interests of the Ukrainian peasantry against the Polish landowning elite, to which, of course, his family belonged.[1] Much of his animosity was focused on Dmowski and the National Democratic Party. It was probably in this context that Hamish Paton, a college contemporary working for naval intelligence, remembered Namier as so far from being a Polish patriot that 'he referred to the Poles as "Polacks" with a superior, if not a malicious, smirk'.[2] But Namier also came to take a harsher view of Poles whom he had formerly counted as friends. Piłsudski, who had already slipped from his hero's pedestal by cooperating with the Central Powers, made things worse by allying with right-wing nationalists when he became head of state in the Polish republic in October 1918. Namier's disgust at his former hero and hostility to the emergent republic would inevitably compromise his relationships with former allies on the Polish left like August Zaleski and Marian Kukiel (a soldier whom Namier had also known since his youth), who entered the service of the new state.

Eastern Europe in flux

In articles in the *New Statesman* in November and December 1916, published under a pseudonym, Namier appealed to Polish opinion to resist cynical attempts on the part of the German government to win over those groups not already committed to fight on their side.[3] By the following spring, the situation had improved from an Allied perspective, though adroit diplomacy was still required to take advantage of the opportunities. Piłsudski was looking for a rapprochement with the Entente powers, and was eventually given a pretext in July 1917 when the Polish legions under his command refused to swear allegiance to the Kaiser and were interned. On the other side the National Democrats left Russia en masse in the aftermath of the February revolution and reconstituted themselves as a political force in the west. The French promised to work for a genuinely independent Polish state, and Dmowski based his principal émigré organisation, 'the Polish National Committee', in Paris. His supporters were also active in Britain, whose government needed to be persuaded of the Polish claim. The National Democrats' propaganda emphasised Polish commitment to the Allied cause, and the advantages of gaining the assistance of a Polish army.[4]

Namier remained the sharpest thorn in the National Democrats' side, the man whom Dmowski called in his memoirs, 'that *żydek galicyjski*, a compatriot of the faith of Moses, a one-time Jew from Galicia called Bernstein, a foster-child of Oxford who in England uses the name Louis Namier'.[5] An anonymous article in the *New Statesman* in March 1917, which looks very like Namier's work, denounced the National Democrats and other right-wing elements as willing collaborators with the Germans in accepting the proposal of a regency council for the puppet kingdom, while centrists and those on the left had been more reluctant, distrusting the Central Powers and only prepared to accept a Polish state with guarantees.[6] The magazine published further anonymous articles across the summer and autumn, in which it is tempting to discern Namier's hand: they reiterated the possibility that the Poles could still be pushed into the arms of Germany, and stressed the continuing importance of Russia as a counterweight to German imperialism. Revolutionary Russia was 'the natural guardian of freedom and the champion of progress and social reform in Eastern Europe'.[7]

For the British government Namier drew up a private memorandum in April 1917, at the request of Philip Kerr, private secretary to the new prime minister, Lloyd George. In this way Namier was able to make his voice heard in the highest echelons of government. His personal knowledge of eastern Europe – so far in advance of most British public servants – and his reputation as 'a very intelligent fellow' ensured that he would be taken seriously.[8] Namier and Kerr had become acquainted through the Round Table: Kerr later confessed that although he did not find Namier 'congenial company' he was 'overawed by his leonine personality and felt him to be a man of unusual intellectual power'.[9] In these terms it made practical, if not entirely ethical, sense for Kerr to consult Namier privately.

The document that Kerr received, marked 'confidential', provided a blueprint for a Polish policy.[10] After years of ignoring Poland's national aspirations for fear of antagonising Russia the British government would now have to do something quickly to 'rehabilitate' itself with the Poles, who were 'becoming a nation'. Namier recommended announcing that a Polish representative would be admitted to the peace conference on the same footing as other powers. The burden of Namier's argument, however, was that the government must steer clear of the National Democrats. This was not a personal matter:

> You know me well enough to believe me that I am not actuated here by personal resentment against Dmowski and his whole Polish black hundred crew … I have never known any of them personally and merely distrusted them as one disliked and distrusted their Russian reactionary confreres. But as all Poles have the appearance of being 'persecuted', Englishmen have often gone wrong and may yet go wrong with regard to the Polish reactionaries.

Dmowski and his cronies had already been 'swept off the surface' in Russia, where liberals could not easily forget their support for autocracy.

> There is no getting away from the fact that the Russian revolution, which at last has straightened out the issue of this war, has also changed the grouping of forces. The main division through Europe will run as between the old regimes and the new forces.

Needless to say, when this document was passed to Sir Eric Drummond, it was held at arm's length. 'Of course I know Mr Namier', he wrote, 'and Eustace Percy vouches for his absolute honesty. At the same time I regard him with considerable suspicion.'[11]

This was the first in a series of incidents in which Namier was perceived as having overstepped the mark. Drummond regarded attacks on Dmowski as the betrayal of a loyal ally. Particular objection was taken to Namier's repeated argument that alienation from the new Russian government would inevitably result in Dmowski turning to Germany, which made it necessary for Britain to cultivate left-wing opinion in Poland instead.[12] Namier did not help himself by the frequency with which he denounced the National Democrats. From May 1917 onwards he submitted a series of memoranda on the 'crisis in Poland', some of which were sent directly to cabinet over his name or initials, without any redaction.[13] They warned that Russia and Germany might orchestrate a compromise agreement which would be welcomed by Polish conservatives, 'ultra conservative landowners' and 'ultra-clericals' as well as the National Democrats.[14] Within Poland the political balance was swinging to the right, and Polish exiles were increasingly under Dmowski's influence. Even though 'the anti-German feeling which prevails in Poland among all classes alike must revolt against this idea of fighting on the side of Germany against a Russia which renounces all aggressive ambitions' there was a plausible – or at least a popular – battle-cry which Dmowski could use to mobilise support. Namier called it 'Polish imperialism'. Polish nationalists were demanding territory to which they were not entitled by the principle of national self-determination: in Lithuania, Volhynia, White Russia and east Galicia. Such eastward expansion would inevitably produce a conflict with Russia, and therefore 'it is quite likely that the Central Powers will now take some definite step in the direction of furthering the Polish imperialist claims in order to create a new ground for discord between the Poles and the Russians'.[15]

While many in the Foreign Office, including the Foreign Secretary Arthur Balfour, preferred for the time being to listen to other voices on the 'Polish question', notably the Oxford historian Sir Charles Oman, who submitted reports of a very different bent,[16] Namier was supported by colleagues in the intelligence bureau, who also believed in the necessity for the post-war reconstruction of central and eastern Europe on a basis of nationality.[17] The bureau staff contributed articles to the *New Europe*, the periodical founded by Seton-Watson that embodied this ideal.[18] Although Seton-Watson had undertaken to renounce his editorship, he had not done so. Headlam-Morley always argued that writing for the press served a useful purpose, provided nothing was published without official approval and the articles were 'carefully written … serious, responsible statements by men who are thoroughly qualified to deal with the special subject'.[19] He told his superiors that he thought Namier particularly well suited to this task, since he was 'one of the very few people on whom we can fully depend, and who has personal knowledge', and listed a host of newspapers and magazines to which Namier contributed.[20] The catholic nature of the list was important, since Headlam-Morley was anxious that there should be 'no special favouring of certain papers or of papers with one political complexion'. It would be dangerous if, for example, the *New Europe* were to get a reputation as 'the organ of this department'. However, his rules were honoured in the breach.[21] The department's staff used the *New Europe* just as Headlam-Morley had feared. The only concession was that articles were published under pseudonyms.

Drummond and others remained vigilant for instances in which staff exceeded their brief. In May 1917 Namier produced a paper on 'Austria-Hungary's inner and foreign policy', which argued passionately for Britain to pursue as a principal war aim the right to self-determination of all the peoples in the empire. There were characteristic flourishes: the portrayal of Austro-Hungarian rule as a 'German and Magyar dominion', emphasis on the common Slavic identity of subject peoples and condemnation of Polish imperialist ambitions.[22] Namier's memorandum was sent to the Foreign Office, where at least one official considered that the author had 'strayed from the collection of news' to the giving of advice.[23] Very soon, and on the foot of another memorandum, a joint effort on Russia, the staff of the bureau received explicit instructions to 'confine themselves to facts'.[24] This was partly a matter of civil service politics: fear that the cabinet would be receiving information and advice from sources outside the Foreign Office. In this respect concern was justified: Namier's reputation was such that in July 1917 he was summoned to brief a committee appointed by the Committee of Imperial Defence on the situation in Austria-Hungary.[25]

Further commotions over Poland were inevitable. In July 1917 Dmowski submitted a paper to the British government, urging the establishment of an independent Poland large enough to act as a buffer between Germany and Russia. He warned of the danger posed by an independent Ukraine, which might look to Germany for support, and proposed that Ukrainian territory, including Galicia, be given to Poland.[26] Namier immediately subjected Dmowski's geopolitical arguments, and their basis in demography, to a devastating scrutiny.[27] Having observed that Dmowski's solution presupposed the unlikely event of 'a crushing and simultaneous defeat of both the Central Powers and Russia', he focused on the impracticability, as well as the injustice, of the unchecked growth of an independent Poland. The majority of the populations affected, Lithuanian, White Russian and Ukrainian, all 'hate the Poles with a truly fanatical hatred', the 'hatred of a land-hungry peasantry against alien landlords'. The notion that these peoples had 'no clear consciousness of their nationality' was nonsensical. A state formed along the lines that Dmowski prescribed would be chronically unstable and would quickly fall prey to German domination. Interestingly, Namier had no scruples about allowing Poland to incorporate ethnically German populations within its western borders: 'even an extension of Poland to the sea at Danzig might be reconciled to some extent with ethnographic justice'.[28]

Namier's comments were forwarded by Sir Eric Drummond to the Foreign Secretary Arthur Balfour, with a health warning.[29] Drummond's Catholic susceptibilities were already inflamed by reports from Namier drawing attention to the involvement of the Vatican in the 'intrigues' of 'Polish imperialists'.[30] (It was a recurrent theme of Namier's memoranda that ultramontane Catholics, including the Polish Superior-General of the Jesuits, wished to see 'another great Roman Catholic state like Austria-Hungary arise in eastern Europe under Polish leadership').[31] Drummond dismissed Namier's allegation that Dmowski wanted huge tracts of Russian and Ukrainian territory given to Poland:

> Mr Namier is an American – half-Pole, half-Jew – and is therefore torn by different emotions. His sincerity and patriotism cannot I think be questioned – they are proved by the fact that when the war broke out he left America to fight for the Allies. I do not, however, believe in his judgment. He is a violent opponent of Dmowski and much of what he writes and says is coloured by this dislike.[32]

Balfour, too, was unconvinced by the factual assertions in Namier's paper, which was passed to Oman for a second opinion. He was not impressed:

> I know Mr Namier well, having examined him when he was an Oxford undergraduate, and seen him a good many times in later years. He is quite sincere, but very self-centred and disputatious: he used to consider himself as the only authority in England on the Ruthenian question, and to resent anyone else having independent views upon it … In my opinion Mr Namier's criticism … is written in a spirit of exaggerated hostility, making the worst of the Polish case wherever it is possible to do so.[33]

In October Namier repeated his message in another lengthy report, which analysed German intrigues in the 'occupied Russian provinces', Latvia, Lithuania and the White Russian districts. He made some sidelong comments on Polish imperialists and their intrigues to detach Lithuanian and White Russian territory from Russia in order to be able to annexe it themselves.[34] Drummond protested again:

> I am sorry to be so persistent, but it is clear that whoever writes these Polish reports cannot refrain from expressing in a very marked way his own personal views. I understand he has already been warned on the subject, but the warning seems to have had little effect … If the writer cannot confine himself to a record of facts I do not think he ought to be allowed to write official papers.[35]

Although Namier's fears were exaggerated, and occasionally bordered on paranoia (as when he convinced himself that the National Democrats were plotting his assassination)[36] his suspicions about Foreign Office mandarins were well founded. Senior officials had come to accept that Dmowski's party constituted Britain's principal 'friends' among the Poles,[37] and in October 1917 the Foreign Office recognised

Dmowski's man, Count Sobanski, as the official representative in London of the Polish National Committee, much to the disgust of the British liberal press.[38]

The Political Intelligence Department

Frustration got the better of Namier in the winter of 1917–18, and once more he tried and failed to rejoin the army.[39] But there was a sudden turn for the better in February when it was announced that the Intelligence Bureau was to be transferred to the Foreign Office, to become its 'Political Intelligence Department'. Namier and his colleagues could have been alarmed at the prospect of losing their independence, and being placed directly under the authority of conservative-minded officials who were predisposed to be sceptical of their advice. But to a man they embraced the change. When Lord Beaverbrook, the newly appointed Minister of Information, attempted to keep the bureau within his own domain, a mass resignation was threatened.[40] According to Beaverbrook the staff had fallen victim to the glamour and prestige of the Foreign Office.[41] They were certainly excited to be closer to the centre of power. There was also a welcome increase in salary.[42]

Namier was pleased with the leadership of the new department. The deputy head was James Headlam-Morley, and above Headlam-Morley stood Sir William Tyrrell, an old Foreign Office hand. Tyrrell had warned of the threat from Germany long before 1914, which put him on Namier's wavelength. Moreover, despite his apparently casual attitude to business, Tyrrell had a sharp mind and a fierce loyalty to his staff. He was also Sligger Urquhart's brother-in-law, and an old friend of Sir Cecil Spring Rice, which gave Namier two points of contact.[43] For his part Tyrrell trusted Namier's judgment, and was prepared to ask his opinion in areas in which Namier did not usually take the lead, as for example in May 1918, when the Czech National Committee asked for official recognition. Namier was not the first port of call on Czech matters, but on this occasion Tyrrell 'came to my room, carrying a pack of files … and asked me to prepare … a short minute of our previous dealings with the Czechs, and a memorandum on further action'. Namier, a great supporter of the Czech cause, naturally urged recognition, and was gratified when his recommendation was adopted.[44]

The two years that Namier spent in the Political Intelligence Department (PID), had a formative effect on his personality and his political attitudes. Although the role of the PID was supposed to be limited to the evaluation of information,[45] reports inevitably ventured beyond, into the making of recommendations. This was certainly the case with Namier, who never shrank from offering an opinion. In later years, references to his time in the Foreign Office became as frequent in his conversation as 'when I was at Balliol', or references to his descent from the Gaon of Vilna. In reminiscing to captive audiences he may well have exaggerated for effect, most notoriously in claiming personal credit for the downfall of the Austro-Hungarian empire. A favourite story was that at a crucial stage in negotiations at the end of the war he advised Headlam-Morley that Britain should wait before coming to terms with the Habsburg emperor. This advice was supposedly passed upwards until it reached the foreign secretary, then the prime minister, and even the American president, Woodrow Wilson. 'I said "Wait," and while they waited the Austro-Hungarian Empire disintegrated.' This afforded him a particular pleasure: 'I may say that I pulled it to pieces with my own hands.'[46] But while his hearers might privately have questioned whether his influence was really so profound, there is no doubt that his views did penetrate to the highest levels, both formally, through the endorsement of his reports by Headlam-Morley and Tyrrell, and informally, through private communications with Eustace Percy and Philip Kerr.

At a very basic level, it was during his time in the PID that Namier became accustomed to using his initials instead of his surname, to indicate that he had seen a circulating document. After he left the department he routinely signed letters and notes 'LBN'. The documents preserved in the files of the PID are peppered with his initials; usually attached to memoranda on Austrian and Polish affairs, with the occasional observation on Czech politics.[47] But like all his colleagues he was given a sight of a wide range of material, from every part of the world, including the Middle East, the Far East and the Americas – digests of foreign newspapers, diplomatic and military despatches, reports from postal censors, intelligence information, secret cables and intercepts.[48] He was also expected to contribute to collective memoranda on areas outside his particular expertise. One can trace Namier's presence in a wide range of papers, in the views expressed and the language employed – pellucid and assertive, with the occasional imaginative flight, parading a personal knowledge of the people and places being discussed, and an authoritative (and often gratuitous) historical background.

The torrent of privileged information coming his way, which had to be assessed analysed and deployed at great speed, make his time in the PID a wonderful traing for someone with the ambition to write history. It was always Namier's view that the best training in prose writing was practice. In the process he also developed ideas about European history that he would reuse in books and essays. These memoranda prefigured his history writing in another way, in the acute character sketches of individuals, whose beliefs and motives were often traced back to family connections and material interests. But the work was hard and the pressure unrelenting. In May 1918 he wrote to A. L. Smith to canvass the possibility of Smith's historian son-in-law, the

Canadian Murray Wrong, coming to the department as his assistant. Namier told Smith that he was already doing 'what would practically be enough to keep three men busy – Poland, Lithuania, Austria, Hungary, and occasionally the Ukraine'. It was hard to find help. 'All I need is an intelligent person who knows German perfectly and is prepared to be coached (and occasionally bullied) by me.'[49] Perhaps wisely, Wrong did not take up the offer.

Equally important to Namier were the friendships he made, men like the career Foreign Office bureaucrat Walford Selby and the future historian E. H. ('Ted') Carr. In the long run the most important of all proved to be Arthur Balfour's niece, Mrs Edgar Dugdale, who was not herself attached to the Foreign Office but came into regular contact with Namier through her work in naval intelligence and in 1919 was briefly seconded to the PID. Blanche Dugdale, known universally to friends by her childhood nickname of 'Baffy', was a remarkable person, highly intelligent, forceful and tenacious, and formidably well connected, both through her father's family, the Balfours, and through her mother, a daughter of the eighth duke of Argyll.[50] These qualities by themselves would have attracted Namier, but her political sympathies also intersected with his at crucial points. She was an enthusiastic Zionist, and quickly came to share Namier's views on east Galicia, activated by concern for the fate of the large Jewish population there, and persuaded by Namier's authoritative account of the situation, in contrast to the ignorance of Foreign Office ministers like her cousin Lord Robert Cecil.[51] For Baffy the obvious anti-Semitism of right-wing Polish nationalists like Dmowski, manifested in their personal attacks on her friend Lewis, automatically damned their claim to sovereignty over Galician Jewry, no matter how deplorable the alternative might be. That she was nearly ten years older than Namier, and already married with a family, put their friendship on safe ground emotionally. There was never any question that they would be anything more than friends, however intimately they worked together.

The end of the war: the collapse of Austria-Hungary and conflict over Poland

The armistice agreed between the Central Powers and Bolshevik Russia in December 1917, leading to peace negotiations, meant that for the Allies 1918 began badly, despite the arrival of American troops; 'I would say badly beyond expression', Namier wrote in a letter to A. L. Smith, 'were it not for my historical training, which teaches the force of things. They survive in spite of human stupidity.'[52] The outlook did not improve for some time: the treaty of Brest-Litovsk, and German offensives on the Western Front, seemed to be bringing events to a crisis. In the Ukraine the situation was also fraught: fighting between the nationalist Ukrainian People's Republic and Bolshevik insurgents was followed after Brest-Litovsk by a German invasion and the establishment of a puppet government. This did not bring stability, and the information Namier received presented a picture of the countryside in a condition close to revolution, with acute shortages of food.[53] Elsewhere, he took comfort from news of strikes and army mutinies in Austria. Although these were quickly put down, the public statements of the Austrian socialist party seemed encouraging, calling for independence for 'the Slav and Latin races' of the empire, and the establishment of social and political democracy within Austria itself.[54] It was not until the tide turned on the western front, in the summer of 1918, that Namier could breathe more easily, and the Foreign Office as a whole could think in terms of preparing for peace.[55]

The prospect of an end to the war made the pressure of work even more intense, against a background of anxiety about his family's fate in war-torn east Galicia. Clara was becoming another cause for concern. Air raids in London unnerved her, and her employment at the Russian agency had ended with the Bolshevik seizure of power; so Namier agreed that she should move to Oxford.[56] He kept a base for himself in London during the week, moving his lodgings frequently, though always in the same general area: during 1918 and 1919 he rented rooms in several houses in Longridge Road, near Earl's Court; then in Powis Square, Notting Hill; and finally Cheyne Row in Chelsea.[57] As for Clara, she did not care for his Oxford friends, and lived a forlorn existence without him.[58] In desperation, she expressed a desire to study agriculture at University College, Reading, and Namier persuaded A. L. Smith to send a letter of recommendation to the principal. Thanking Smith, Namier wrote, 'Your reward will be some day the sight of a well managed farm in Kent, Herefordshire, or on the Lebanon'.[59] Nothing came of it. Lady Namier, taking her cue from her husband, dismissed the project as one of Clara's fantasies, and perhaps it was.

Unlike the more conservative elements in the British establishment, Namier had not instinctively recoiled from the October revolution in Russia. So deep was his hostility to the old dynastic empires of central and eastern Europe – Austrian, Russian and Ottoman – that he was prepared to accept even the Bolshevik regime as a step towards the liberation of subject nationalities. Looking back in his 60s, by which time he had moved much further to the right, he rationalised his earlier views in such a way as to make himself appear consistent.[60] He had been

> Pro-Russian and anti-German, a conservative by instinct, predilections, and doubts, but not from material interests or from fear – in short, a Tory radical – I carefully watched the Russian Revolution without being affected by the hysterics which drove certain types of conservatives into the dangerous absurdities of a home and foreign policy dominated by the fear of Soviet Russia.

In the aftermath of the Bolshevik seizure of power Namier wrote, in the same manner as Wordsworth in 1789, that 'the Russian Revolution came like a current of fresh air through a stifling heavy atmosphere, like the promise of a new, better world'.[61] Alongside others in the PID he supported the idea of coming to an understanding with the Bolsheviks, in the hope of preventing the consummation of Russian peace negotiations with Germany. In January 1918, as part of a campaign to persuade public opinion – and more importantly Foreign Office opinion – that such an understanding was practicable, he published in the *New Europe* an article on Trotsky, with which he was evidently pleased, and which made quite a stir. Despite reports sympathetic to Trotsky which were coming from the British envoy in Moscow, Namier's friend Robert Bruce Lockhart,[62] Lord Robert Cecil was known to be hostile to any understanding with the Bolshevik leaders, and with Trotsky in particular. Cecil considered Trotsky to be a dupe of the Germans, if not a German agent. Namier's account backed up Bruce Lockhart: Trotsky was a man with a love of pleasure, a relish for power and a sense of humour, someone with whom the Allies could do business. At the same time, Namier was careful not to countenance Bolshevism as a political movement: he contrasted Trotsky's evident humanity with the very different personality of Lenin, 'a calm, iron ascetic with … an inhuman mind', who was a much more typical example of his kind. Revolutionary socialism of the Bolshevik variety embodied 'the logic of ideas'. This produced political leaders who were fanatics, intent on imposing their visions against the grain of history and the realities of economic and social organisation, human motivation and behaviour. 'Conservatism', by contrast, was 'the philosophy of reality'.[63] It was an analysis which the unfolding events in Russia in 1918 would emphatically confirm. In January Namier composed an internal memorandum which branded socialism – the creed of his youth – as 'catastrophic', and while this may have been pandering to his superiors' prejudices, such finesse was not something for which he was renowned.[64]

Nevertheless, he recognised that the realities of central and eastern Europe meant that social revolution was inevitable. In Russia, where 'the immense, almost inconceivable suffering inflicted … by the criminal callousness and corruption of the *ancien régime* has resulted in a psychological catastrophe … a collapse of framework and tradition', the elemental force of the Russian masses had swept away the Tsarist reactionaries and the 'educated bourgeoisie'.[65] The same fate threatened Austria, and the whole of eastern Europe, from the Baltic to the Ukraine.[66] It would be a grave mistake for the western powers to support counter-revolutionary forces, since the indigenous populations would inevitably 'range themselves on the revolutionary side'.[67] Where Namier went wrong, of course, was in assuming that the Bolsheviks could not control the tidal wave which had swept them to power. He thought that such 'blind

elemental forces' as peasant hunger for land, or the demand from repressed nationalities for self-determination, could not be coerced by 'the intellectual revolutionaries
who sail in the storm'.[68] Lenin and Stalin would prove him to be very mistaken.

Namier's analysis was unusual in that he saw two causes for the revolutionary dynamic: national hostilities and class hostilities. His colleagues were ready to
allow the importance of nationalist sentiment among the submerged peoples of
the Austrian and Russian empires – this was, after all, a principal tenet of the *New
Europe* group – but were much less comfortable with the idea of class warfare.
The Cambridge historian Harold Temperley, on secondment at the War Office,
thought that in this respect Namier's PID memoranda exaggerated out of all proportion. For Temperley, the problem was 'the oppressed nationalities rather than
the oppressed proletariats', and he regarded Namier's conclusions about military
strategy as 'incredibly crude'.[69] But for Namier the history of eastern Europe meant
that national and social issues were intertwined, and it was not the proletariat with
whom he was chiefly concerned.[70] Territorial aggrandisement in the middle ages and
early modern period had resulted in a form of colonialism across central and eastern
Europe. This had happened with Prussian intrusion into the Baltic lands, Magyar
rule in Hungary and the establishment of a dominant Polish aristocracy in Lithuania,
Belarus and the Ukraine. The best way for Namier to explain the situation to English
readers was by analogy with Ireland before the nineteenth-century Land Acts, and he
was quick to observe that 'there is no other nation of which the conservative upper
classes are capable of the sacrifice made by those Acts': Germans, Magyars and Poles
would never show such self-denial. The subject races in central and eastern Europe
were peasants, not by nature 'socially radical'; indeed, some had been bamboozled by
the Habsburgs into helping to defeat the bourgeois radicals of 1848.[71] But while they
were not radical they could be revolutionary, for the social revolutions that Namier
saw coming would not mean a triumph for the ideal of democracy, but would instead
bring '"a turn of the wheel" – the rule of the downtrodden'.[72]

Namier's belief in the inexorability of peasant revolutionary movements determined his analysis of central and eastern European politics. During 1918 he wrote
numerous papers on Austrian affairs. Many were unsigned, but Namier always
headed the circulation lists, and the texts reflect his preoccupations and bear the
hallmarks of his style. Occasionally he would even slip into using the personal pronoun. Although his reports dealt with a succession of different crises, he saw these
as 'merely the symptoms of the one permanent, incurable crisis which has its root in
the nature of the Austrian state and which now saps its government organisation', a
state of affairs in which he took satisfaction.[73] The tendentious nature of some of the
arguments and the blunt language – dismissing contradictory evidence as 'absurd' or

'eyewash', and insisting that the Austrian aim was to 'extort dominion' over 'subject races' – set senior officials' teeth on edge. But it was impossible to gainsay the depth of knowledge, and hard to construct cogent counter-arguments; indeed, Namier's analysis of the collapse of the Austro-Hungarian empire would eventually be enshrined in the official history of the peace conference (edited by Temperley, of all people).

As early as May 1918 Namier gave his categorical opinion that the Austrian empire was doomed.[74] What he called 'the Habsburg *Staatsidee*', which had always been 'merely dynastic', was only supported by 'feudal aristocrats, princely bishops, high government officials, a small group of professional army families, and lastly a part of the Vienna populace which, as so often occurs in the case of capitals, conceives itself associated with the dynasty in the ownership of subject lands and peoples'. Centrifugal forces were tearing the empire apart. Subject nationalities could not be given independence within the empire, since this would frustrate the territorial claims of the dominant ethnic groups – Germans and Magyars in Yugoslavia, Poles in Galicia – or, in the case of Czechoslovakia, would result in the interposition of 'an alien Slav state' between the kindred peoples of Germany and Austria.[75] Nor was it possible for the Habsburgs to reverse their policy and enlist the support of Slavic nationalities, since this would spark a series of social revolutions which would spread back to Austria itself. By October 1918 Namier was happy to announce that the empire's death throes had begun: as soon as Czech, Yugoslav, Polish and Ukrainian representatives withdrew from the *Reichsrat*, the game was up. 'A German-Austrian republic had arisen in fact, though not yet in name', and with the rout of the Austrian army only the Socialist party could hold the country together. Conflict would inevitably break out between the various national groups, which would turn into a war between classes, since national questions were 'bound up with social contrasts'. The class struggle would be violent even in the dominant nations and Austria itself would become another Russia.[76]

These views were not confined to internal Foreign Office memoranda and anonymous articles for the press. Through Toynbee, the PID became involved with the Labour Party's advisory committee on international questions, coordinated by Douglas Cole. In the late summer of 1918 that committee decided to publish a series of pamphlets on foreign affairs and requested the help of PID staff. According to Headlam-Morley, Namier

> put forward a paper on the Habsburg policy which was practically identical in doctrine with … [a] memorandum issued by this department, the substance of which, also with permission, was printed in *The Times*; he also attended a meeting of the committee at which he discussed and supported his thesis that the complete overthrow of the Habsburg monarchy was necessary and feasible, against Mr [Goldsworthy] Lowes Dickinson and Mr [Henry] Brailsford, who contended that this would take years of warfare.[77]

Namier's expertise stretched beyond Austria-Hungary. Inevitably he came to be acknowledged as the PID's pre-eminent expert on Poland. This was not the case at first: others, notably Rex Leeper, who occupied the Russian desk, had a claim to be heard.[78] More to the point, Tyrrell and Headlam-Morley were cautious about encouraging Namier's advice on Polish affairs after he had been targeted by the National Democrats. Nonetheless, Namier elbowed his way to the front and by late spring was examining all Polish papers received and drafting every memorandum from the department relating to Poland.[79] In the same way, his intimate knowledge of, and consuming interest in, events in Galicia meant that he also became the first port of call on developments in the Ukraine.[80]

For all his customary determination to ride hobby horses with spur and whip, even Namier's fiercest detractors would have conceded that he provided a flow of informed reports on Poland, embodying an acute analysis of political developments and the development of German policy. This was especially true in the spring and summer of 1918, when the principal concern of the western powers was with German ambitions to annex Polish territory.[81] Namier regularly used the formidable forensic skills which would be so evident in his historical writing to distinguish between reports providing information that was genuinely useful and documents which were intended to mislead, such as the text of a supposed treaty between Germany and Russia over the future of Poland.[82]

Nevertheless, opinion constantly intruded into his analysis. He dismissed any reliance on conservative politicians in Poland. The great landowners, supported by the church, would naturally look to the Central Powers to protect their interests. Moreover, they would be a political liability when the region was reshaped into independent nation-states, for everywhere the masses – peasantry and proletariat – were demanding social reform.[83] In the Ukraine the Slavic majority was bitterly anti-Polish, and linked to Russia through political sympathy as well as ethnicity, since they knew that the Russians would take their side against the Polish landowners.[84] Socialism was also popular, especially in Galicia.[85] In the last resort the 'Polish upper classes' in Galicia would rather live in an Austrian or German province than a Ukrainian peasant republic.[86] In August 1918 he warned of the possibility of an arrangement between Germany and Poland, whose 'reactionary, imperialist' upper class would embrace dependence on the Germans, as they had previously sought their advantage in the arms of Russia and Austria.[87]

Namier denounced the ambition of Polish nationalists to extend the boundaries of their state beyond Poland's 'demographic borders' as not only 'fanciful' but fraught with dangerous complications. Provoking conflict between Poland and Russia would only benefit Germany.[88] Russia, even under Bolshevik rule, had to be seen as the 'pivot for British policy in eastern Europe'. The arguments of Polish émigrés that a revived Poland represented the best chance of combating Bolshevism were, in his view, nonsense. While the war raged, aggression against Russia could never 'square with our anti-German policy'. The weapons to defeat the Bolsheviks were 'the national idea against class warfare' and 'moderate reform', in particular agrarian reform, which could never be accomplished by Polish interests in the borderlands. To make Poland the basis for anti-Bolshevik action would obscure these issues, and strengthen the Bolsheviks by allowing them to appear as champions of national integrity.[89] He was even prepared to argue that Poland could never be a genuinely independent power: it had to fall within either the Russian or the German orbit.[90] For Britain and France to build up the strength of an independent Polish state would provide a cause – the reduction of Poland – in which Germany and Russia could cooperate, a fatal consequence that would destroy the natural balance of power in Europe.

It is easy to see why Namier enraged the National Democrats and their English friends. The stream of acerbic commentary in official documents and articles in the press which obviously came from his pen, even if they were unsigned, seemed designed to sap government and public support for the Polish cause, and for Dmowski's Polish National Committee in particular.[91] Not only was Namier intent on demolishing the case for Polish expansion in the east, by subverting and contradicting any demographic data brought forward to demonstrate Polish claims to territory, he was always sneering at National Democrat pledges of loyalty to Britain, triumphing at the discovery of inconsistencies in their public statements and drawing attention to unsavoury elements in the lives and activities of their leaders.[92] This made things particularly difficult for Dmowski, whose supporters were having to fight off an attempt in the spring of 1918 by Polish socialists, headed by Zaleski, to challenge the British government's recognition of the Polish National Committee.[93] Namier himself remained to some degree emotionally bound to the 'the Polish parties of the left', who, he said, were the people to whom the British government should be listening.[94]

The final straw for the National Democrats and the Polish National Committee arrived during the course of one of Namier's articles in the *New Europe*, on the consequences of the Treaty of Brest-Litovsk for Polish politics.[95] There he argued that the terms of the treaty proved that Germany would never be prepared to relinquish its 'Polish' lands. Poles would have to accept 'the utter bankruptcy of the *Realpolitik* of the Polish upper classes'. Dmowski's first response was to denounce his tormentor as an agent of the Central Powers. He passed to a contact in Military Intelligence a dossier on Namier, which Sir William Tyrrell thought 'perfect rubbish'.[96] Dmowski's friends then turned to the press. An article appeared in the *New Witness*, a weekly edited by G. K. Chesterton which was strongly committed to the Polish cause.[97] This took as its starting point Namier's article in the *New Europe* on Trotsky, and drew a comparison between these two east European Jews, Bernstein (Namier) and Braunstein (Trotsky), both of whom had changed their names to disguise their origins, and were committed to the destruction of a particular country: in Trotsky's case Russia; in Namier's Poland. The writer attributed Namier's hatred of Poland to the natural fear of the 'east European Hebrew' that a resurgent Polish nation-state would supplant those Jewish interests which had hitherto controlled the country's economy. 'Hating all nationalism, the Jew has a peculiar hatred of Polish nationalism, for he has long considered Poland as his own peculiar possession.' Namier was not openly accused of being pro-German, but it was noted that 'Jews have been the chief agents of German influence in Poland', and the article concluded:

> We have no quarrel with Bernstein. But we think it is not fitting that an east European Jew should conduct an anonymous propaganda campaign in the British press against Poland and the Polish National Committee, a body recognised by our own and by all Allied governments: above all, this should not be done while he is employed in a government department, with access to special information and the prestige which such employment gives him.

The article was unsigned, but Namier knew it to have been by the journalist Robert Ussher, a Catholic convert and friend of Laurence Alma-Tadema. Ussher gloried in having tackled 'the worst enemy of Poland in England'.[98] He also wrote a leader for the ultra-conservative *Morning Post* on the same lines, entitled 'Bernstein on Braunstein'.[99]

While Namier regarded these attacks as beneath contempt, it was a different matter when they were repeated in a Polish journal. *Tygodnik Polski*, the organ of the Polish National Committee, welcomed Ussher's article and identified Bernstein as coming 'from a Jewish family resident in the village of Koszylowce in east Galicia'. Namier told his superiors that he expected the article to be reprinted in National Democrat papers in Cracow and Lemberg (renamed Lwów by the Poles), to the detriment of the British government, and also perhaps to the detriment of his own family, who would thereby be brought to the attention of the Austrian police.[100] He was now able to trace the campaign against him back to the National Democrats.[101] The permanent under-secretary at the Foreign Office, Sir Charles Hardinge, was furious, and told Drummond that personal attacks on Namier 'must be stopped or our subvention must cease'.[102]

With the staunch support of Tyrrell and Headlam-Morley, Namier could feel secure. In April 1918 he composed a minute questioning the wisdom of acceding to a proposal from the Polish National Committee to establish a commercial agency. This, he argued, would only serve party political interests and enable the National Democrats to conduct an anti-Semitic trading policy in Poland.[103] Tyrrell passed the minute to Hardinge, with a strong endorsement, and when Lord Robert Cecil sounded a hesitant note of disagreement, suggesting that 'a very impartial and intelligent observer' like Sir Charles Oman might be consulted, the Foreign Secretary Balfour brushed the reservations aside.[104] In another example, after further tentative criticism of a memorandum from Namier on east Galicia, refuting National Democrat claims about its essentially Polish character, Headlam-Morley charged to his protégé's defence. Given his extraordinary familiarity with his subject, Namier would never have blundered over details. However, in an off-the-cuff remark Headlam-Morley revealed exactly why he and others trusted Namier implicitly, namely that they were themselves ignorant of what he was writing about: 'Of course I have no knowledge as to the actual facts.'[105]

The peace conference and the struggle against Polish 'imperialism'

On the day that the armistice was declared in November 1918 Namier was in London, and according to Lady Namier celebrated in the streets. He 'danced ... through Horse Guards Parade to Trafalgar Square with a throng of men and women he never saw before or after'.[106] What he was going to do now that the war was over was not immediately clear. He wrote to A. L. Smith in January 1919, proposing to come up to Oxford to discuss 'my "demobilisation plans". They are not yet altogether settled as this office cannot give me any definite reply as to when they will not need me any longer.' The PID was only to remain in operation for the duration of the peace conference, and the staff had no claim to permanent employment.[107] College friends and contemporaries were returning from war and some were settling into academic life. Namier hoped to do likewise. But three days after asking for an appointment he had to write again to say that he could not, after all, come that weekend: 'I have work with which I have to go on at top speed.'[108]

In fact, the PID had more to do than ever, preparing reports for the British delegation to the peace conference in Paris. Technically, Namier's responsibilities still ranged widely, but he came to be utterly preoccupied with what he called 'the Polish question'.[109] The establishment of a Polish republic in November 1918, with Piłsudski as head of state, changed the political situation across eastern Europe as profoundly as the Russian revolution had done. The few green shoots of the socialist revolution that Namier had once considered inevitable in Poland withered. Piłsudski threw in his lot with conservative nationalists and by January 1919 Poland's socialist prime minister had been replaced by the pianist (and national hero) Ignacy Paderewski, whose first concern was to engineer an alliance between Piłsudski and Dmowski.[110] For a time Namier pinned his hopes on the radical Peasants' Party, which made significant gains in the elections; it represented a class interest and he detected in the visceral hostility to landlords a kind of Bolshevism.[111] But the Peasants' Party proved to be committed to expansion, since the peasants themselves stood to gain lands from conquest.[112] The end result was a stable government bent on establishing Poland as a powerful independent state, extending as far east as its 'natural' borders.

Namier denounced Piłsudski in forthright terms. The general was an able conspirator and guerrilla leader, but no politician, and had 'never shown any real understanding of popular mass-movements … that was how he lost control of the Socialist Party about 1904 and wrecked it in 1906'. He was also a hopeless administrator, and if not 'exactly a monomaniac' had a mind that was possessed by particular ideas: 'First it was "Polish independence", which made him carry on a simply mad policy in 1904–6 and in 1914. Now it is Vilna and Lithuania.'[113] The depth of Namier's anger was such that he wrote in terms which would surprise those who know only his later disparagement of the importance of political ideas:

Men matter little in politics, systems and ideas are everything … In the realm of politics a man cannot act efficiently except through one faith – in a leading idea. He who simultaneously harbours two conflicting ideas is like a photographic plate with two photographs, the one superimposed on the other. That is what Pilsudski turned out to be. And now he is a political wreck.[114]

Armed conflict ensued in all corners of the new republic. In November 1918 troops of the Ukrainian People's Republic entered east Galicia, and Lwów came under siege, with Polish volunteers holding out against the Ukrainians. Then in January 1919 the Czechs invaded Silesia. After a brief struggle the western powers managed to broker a truce between Poland and Czechoslovakia, leaving the disputed lands to be apportioned at the peace conference. Namier's advice, naturally, was strongly in support of Czech claims.[115] At the same time Lithuania's preoccupation with resisting a Soviet invasion enabled the Poles to open another front in the north, capturing Vilnius in the spring of 1919 and driving deep into Lithuanian territory.

From the outbreak of hostilities Namier argued that the Poles were to blame. His greatest anxiety was that the Polish government, with the active assistance of France, would persuade Britain and the United States that Poland was the only bastion against Bolshevism and manoeuvre the 'Anglo-Saxon' powers into a position where they would have to act against 'their principles and designs'. He had always asserted that Polish imperialist expansion would imperil European security by pushing Germany and Russia together.[116] 'And should Poland, with the help of the French and the Jesuits, obtain any part of White Russia or east Galicia, there will be … a war, and Poland will perish in it once more and forever.'[117] He ignored the obvious fact that there was a genuine Soviet threat to the integrity of Poland. So when Paderewski sent a secret telegram to the Admiralty urgently requesting help to resist 'Bolshevist invasion of former Polish territories' and 'the establishment of barbarism throughout Europe', Namier made his customary case, adding what he considered to be an indisputable point: that any Polish annexation would violate the principle of nationality that the great powers had accepted.[118] Britain should send no more arms to the Poles without a guarantee that these would not be used to subvert the demands of British policy, which included an armistice with Ukrainians.[119]

He had already warned that although the Poles would probably overrun east Galicia they would not be able to hold on to it: 'All that it will mean is that they will break down the moderate Ukrainian organisation', leaving the field clear for 'extremists'.[120] He was even prepared with a further option should the western governments reject the idea of incorporating east Galicia into the Ukrainian republic, or setting up 'an isolated Rutheno-Galician state'. It could become a League of Nations protectorate, under a high commissioner, or even come under Czech protection: conversations with Masaryk and other Czech politicians had convinced him that Czechoslovakia would willingly take on the role, and that this was a solution which the majority of Galicians would accept in preference to domination by Poles.[121]

With Piłsudski's about-turn, and the apparent ascendancy of Dmowski's party in the Polish republic, Namier's hostility to Polish nationalism became even more strident.[122] He lost no opportunity to contradict the Polish government and its officials, to draw attention to the excesses of its politicians and press, and to put the worst possible construction on any news report. This relentless denigration worried many in the Foreign Office, even those not naturally well disposed towards the Poles,[123] and taxed even the sympathy of his friends, who felt that it was playing into the hands of his enemies within the service.[124] He did not help himself by allowing his panSlavism to break out occasionally in ways that seemed to contradict the official line on Bolshevik Russia.[125] Headlam-Morley, stationed in Paris, counselled patience, pragmatism and moderation. He too would have preferred a different Polish government, but was prepared to keep an open mind. In February 1919 he obviously felt he had to read Namier a lesson:

> I am not going to attempt to discuss the justice of your reading of the Polish character, but I am quite sure that we ought not to let ourselves be too much influenced in our policy by this kind of thing. Most of us, I suppose, are quite prepared to dislike and distrust many of the nations with whom we have to deal; none the less, the only practical

policy is to make the best of the situation and to enable each of them to establish a firm government. If you will not mind my saying so, I know that nothing interferes so much with the value of your work as the feeling which you allow to appear that you have no sympathy with Poland at all. After all, you are charged with Polish affairs and what people look to you for is not merely criticisms of Poland, but sympathetic advice as to how the Poles can best be helped.[126]

What particularly agitated Namier was the possibility that the gains being made by Poland's armies might become permanent. Despite a statement by Arthur Balfour at the Supreme War Council that 'eastern Galicia, according to all the information at his disposal, did not desire to be Polish',[127] the issue was far from settled, and information coming to London in February and March concerning the likely 'provisional boundary' between Poland and the Ukraine was disconcerting.[128] The issue had been handed over to a commission, whose impartiality could not be trusted. Headlam-Morley's efforts to reassure his testy subordinate made little headway, especially as Headlam-Morley himself had to admit that the British officials on the spot tended to be unduly influenced by Polish opinion, having become 'pure Poles'.[129]

This was something of which Namier was already well aware. He expended rivers of ink in correcting what he regarded as the misleading reports of the British envoy-extraordinary to Poland, Sir Horace Rumbold, the commissioner Colonel Wade, and other army officers.[130] Namier was particularly concerned at Wade's insistence that the Poles had a legitimate right to east Galicia.[131] Even more worrying were the despatches of Sir Esmé Howard, the member of the British delegation in Paris primarily responsible for Polish affairs, who disagreed fundamentally with Namier's analysis, having 'fallen entirely under Polish influence'.[132] In April Namier devoted a lengthy memorandum to rebutting, point by point, a despatch from Howard which senior officials had considered to be 'very moderate' in tone, and which had recommended maintaining a balance between different political forces in Poland. By turns dismissive and sarcastic, Namier accused the Polish government of persecuting political dissidents and its army of behaving like bandits. He focused on the treatment of Jews, of which, he said, Howard had given a partial and wholly inaccurate account. In this he was going too far, and the acting permanent under-secretary, Sir Ronald Graham, did not bother to send on his memorandum.[133]

In other respects Namier was indulged, even cosseted: on the central question of Poland's claims to non-Polish territory he could count on the support of colleagues in the PID and his immediate superiors, Headlam-Morley and Tyrrell.[134] Encouraged to correspond 'quite freely' with Headlam-Morley in a private capacity, he stinted nothing in the violence of his denunciations of Polish politicians and

British ministers: Paderewski was 'a fantastic liar', Sir Esmé Howard was a 'dear old gentleman' whose despatches departed so far from the truth as to be merely amusing.[135] Namier was also permitted to write articles for the press which made a forceful case for the limitation of Polish territorial gains in the east, and in Silesia, while allowing the acquisition of Danzig as necessary to the country's economic development.[136] These were specifically sanctioned by the Foreign Office, on Tyrrell's recommendation.[137] Nothing, however, could lift Namier's deepening gloom, which, at its worst, prompted him to confess that 'I feel utterly desperate'.[138] He took to heart Headlam-Morley's complaint that there was no one on the British side in Paris 'with actual knowledge of the Galician question', and bitterly regretted that he was not present to talk to Philip Kerr in person, relying on private letters to Kerr to get his views across to Lloyd George.[139] When he heard that the deficiency was to be remedied by sending Hamish Paton to France he was even more dispirited: 'the fact that Paton has been summoned and I have been passed over will be exploited by my enemies' (who did indeed assume that a combination of French and Polish pressure had achieved this desired result).[140]

In his desperation Namier went to Oxford again to talk to Smith and Lindsay. Both were 'very keen that I should go back to Balliol for some kind of lectureship', though there were currently no openings available. Namier was even prepared to entertain a bizarre request from Hammerling to return to New York and 'join him in his business'; despite Hammerling's pro-German activities during the war, rumours that he had been an Austrian agent, and his current closeness to Paderewski. 'I certainly shall not reject the offer in an off-hand manner', Namier told Headlam-Morley. He intended to discuss things with Hammerling in person. 'I should like to write my book before I go out, but I am now in the position in which one cannot be a chooser.' In the event, Hammerling found another gullible partner before taking a boat for Europe, to begin a new and colourful career as a Polish senator.[141]

The Jewish question

An additional and very powerful reason for Namier's low spirits was the incessant flow of news from eastern Europe of the sufferings of Jews at Polish hands. Reports of pogroms had begun to surface as early as November 1918, arising from the actions of Polish troops at Lwów, but soon extending across Poland's eastern front.[142] Many came from Zionist sources, and all passed across Namier's desk. Starting from the belief that 'barring Germans, there are no worse anti-Semites in the world than the Poles'[143] – and this applied to socialists as much as Dmowskian nationalists – he accepted every allegation as genuine.[144] His reading of the anti-Semitic outpourings of the right-wing Polish press and the self-serving statements of Polish politicians and military officers did nothing to modify this opinion.[145] He therefore devoted a great deal of time and energy to picking apart what he saw as the sophistry of the Polish authorities (their 'more than Talmudic skill') in denying or justifying outrages; for example by alleging Jewish sympathy for the Bolshevik cause.[146]

In the face of systematic persecution from an aggressively nationalist Poland, he saw the only solution for Jews as emigration, and preferably emigration to Palestine. It is likely that Namier's sympathy with Zionism had been solidifying for some time, but the first direct evidence we have dates from December 1917, a month after the Balfour Declaration, when he and Arnold Toynbee submitted a joint report criticising a memorandum on 'the Zionist movement' from Samuel Edelman, the American consul in Geneva. Edelman had insisted that Zionism in the United States was the creed of poverty-stricken immigrants headed by a few demagogues, and warned against giving Jews exclusive political rights in Palestine, which would be undemocratic, discriminatory against indigenous Arabs and Christians, and politically disastrous, since Jews in Palestine would act in the interests of Germany. Toynbee and Namier dismissed these assertions, observing in passing, in a phrase that must have been Namier's, that Edelman must be 'an Assimilationist Jew' from an anti-Zionist faction.[147]

By 1919, when Namier met Chaim Weizmann for the first time, having already got to know other prominent Zionists,[148] he was moving rapidly in the direction of 'Jewish nationalism'. Indeed, in April 1919 he wrote that he had 'advanced even during the last few months'.[149] He understood that across the Pale of Settlement 'the Jews speak a language of their own, and form a distinct, separate nationality'.[150] This might still have been compatible with loyalty to a Polish commonwealth prepared to tolerate a variety of nationalities and allow a degree of autonomy. But it was impossible for Jews to remain in a Poland which embodied an exclusive nationalism. Not even assimilated Jews could

> partake of the Polish tradition of that *Volkstum* which is bound up with Poland's history, and its villages and fields, and its church and the graves of its ancestors and the altars of their saints. Equally undesirable is it that we should drop our own ancient traditions which are second to those of no community in the world, which are strongly and markedly national and which start with the prophets and will not end until the last of their prophecies come true. Assimilation ... [which] no Pole really desires, means crippling both sides.

Here, in a private letter to Headlam-Morley,[151] we find in embryo the ideas about nationalism which Namier would develop in his later writings and which seem to have been driven by his absorption in the politics of eastern Europe, his attraction to

Zionism, and his idealisation of the British political system and the British empire. Already, by implication, we can see the distinction on which he would later insist, between 'territorial' and 'linguistic' nationalisms: on the one hand the kind of 'nationalism' found in Britain or Switzerland, which arose from a historical attachment to territory, and on the other the Germanic and east European variety, which emphasised ties of blood, language and culture.[152] He told Headlam-Morley – who was sympathetic to Jewish settlement in Palestine but did not approve of the idea of a Jewish national state – that a nation was 'an organic entity, each part of [which] can profitably develop in its own setting alone, and it can be of no use … to cut off an arm from one body and try to graft it artificially as a third limb on the other'.[153] Britain's 'territorial nationalism' could accommodate such transplants; Polish nationalism by its nature could not.

This way of thinking had also turned Namier finally and decisively against Bolshevism, the polar opposite of nationalism in that it did not take account of tradition or of the common understanding that a nation was 'an entity, and not merely a collection of individuals'.[154] Residual sympathy evaporated with the realisation that the lot of Jews in Soviet Russia was no better than it had been under the tsars.[155] For Jews, true assimilation was impossible. Thinking no doubt of his father, but citing the case of the eminent Polish bacteriologist Ludwik Rajchman, 'a man … for whom … I have the greatest admiration', who had returned to work for his fellow countrymen, Namier observed:

> He has lost all trace of Jewish feeling and considers himself a Pole, but there is not in him, and indeed could not be, even a trace of Polish national tradition and *Volkstum*. The effect is that extraordinary clear-sighted, almost prophetic objectivism and that extreme logical radicalism. And if you carefully analyse where in that really splendid man the defects come from, you will agree with me that it is from the absence of roots and from the fact that he neither knows nor feels the words of the prophets which constitutionally ought to be his national inheritance.

Namier's anguish over the plight of east European Jewry was exacerbated by the frustrations he was experiencing in persuading the Foreign Office to accept his contention that 'a new anti-Semitic ferment' was arising in Poland,[156] and this in turn may have complicated his loyalties and pushed him further towards identifying himself as a Zionist. He was already having to struggle against the propaganda effect of planted stories in the English press which exonerated Polish forces or branded Jews as Bolsheviks,[157] without the additional provocation of reading British despatches which either denied or simply ignored allegations of the degrading treatment meted out by the Polish soldiery to Lithuanian or Ukrainian Jews, including evidence of 'simply beastly murders'.[158] When a Major H. G. Paris berated Galician Jews for welcoming Bolsheviks and Ukrainians, Namier commented that this was scarcely surprising: 'the Jews would welcome the Martians if these merely freed them from the Polish insults and oppression'.[159] The pro-Polish bias which he complained of in senior British representatives – Howard, Rumbold and Sir Percy Wyndham, the British commissioner in Poland, extended to their taking Polish self-justification on trust in the matter of alleged pogroms.[160]

Increasingly, Namier's minutes and memoranda were ignored. When stories of pogroms were raised in the House of Commons in April 1919, first by J. D. Kiley, Liberal MP for Whitechapel, and then by the more formidable Colonel Josiah Wedgwood, an independent Liberal soon to take the Labour whip, the under-secretary of state for foreign affairs batted them away with a reiteration of official Polish explanations. Namier, who may well have given Wedgwood his ammunition, urged on his superiors a further protest to the Polish government and the release of information to the press, but was told that the Foreign Office view was that continued parliamentary agitation was the best way forward.[161] A further written answer in the Commons in May included demographic statistics, presumably supplied by Namier, which hinted at a sudden and unexplained decrease in the Jewish population in Polish occupied territory, but a memorandum composed by Namier on pogroms in Lithuania was minuted 'No immediate action is called for'.[162]

In the meantime, Namier had at last been summoned to Paris. His old friend Zaleski had let it be known that Paderewski wished to meet him, and it was therefore agreed at the highest level that he should go, but for only three nights.[163] Paderewski's motives for requesting an interview are unclear, and it may be that he just wished to come face to face with the man whom many of his colleagues regarded as the main-spring of anti-Polish influence in Britain.[164] The official reason was that Namier had been 'so often mentioned in Polish circles … particularly about the Jewish question' that Paderewski thought an interview would be helpful.[165] Namier stayed a little longer than intended, as the question of further arrangements to be made for Jews in Poland came up unexpectedly and it was not thought desirable that members of the committee dealing with the matter should meet the interested parties. Headlam-Morley reported that Namier was 'doing really useful work buzzing about between Poles and Jews'.[166]

His discussions with Jewish leaders, especially Weizmann, were productive.[167] By contrast, the meeting with Paderewski went badly, though it did pander to Namier's egotism. His reports of these conversations focused on his own sharp replies to Paderewski's efforts to justify the Polish government and its army.[168] Predictably, there was no meeting of minds. Nor did he get on much better with Polish socialists. He recalled meeting one of the leaders of the Polish Left, a fine and fair-minded man. 'With us', he said, 'one hardly ever mentions the Jews now without cursing.' Still, he and his friends were prepared to stand up for Jewish rights – 'but', he added, 'then you must go with us.' 'Do what your conscience bids you', I replied, 'but don't on that basis, claim to mortgage our existence.'[169]

On the positive side, Namier was able to link up again with old friends who were attending the peace conference, notably Arnold Toynbee, Lionel Curtis and Whitney Shepardson. He was also able to renew his friendship with T. E. Lawrence, whom he ran into one day by chance 'in the lounge of the Hôtel Majestic'. It is a sign of Namier's total immersion in his own work that 'only when I met him ... in a colonel's uniform did I realise that he was "Lawrence of Arabia"'.[170]

A losing battle

Returning from Paris Namier continued to pursue vigorously his two personal campaigns, to forestall Allied recognition of Polish territorial expansion, and to persuade the British government to make the Poles (and to a lesser extent the Austrians)[171] abandon the persecution of the Jews. But he was aware that he was fighting a rearguard action and became increasingly bitter, as is clear from his letters to Headlam-Morley and Kerr, and to Brigadier Frederick Kisch, a member of the British delegation who had a special interest in Polish affairs and was not only a Jew but a future Zionist.[172] In one letter to Kerr Namier noted that a document submitted by the Polish government was 'a ludicrous forgery', adding, with heavy sarcasm, 'The Poles are a glorious nation and no one can deny it.'[173] The root of the problem was not, however, in the Foreign Office, where he still found some receptive listeners, so much as in the realities of international politics, where the French and Americans regarded Poland as a bulwark against Bolshevism.

A decision of the Supreme Council on 18 May 1919 to recognise Polish authority over the whole of east Galicia, pending a resolution of borders in the final peace treaty, was confirmed on 25 June despite a last-ditch British counter-proposal. Equally unsuccessful were subsequent British efforts to render the commission to investigate 'atrocities' in Galicia less obviously weighted in favour of Poland.[174] Incandescent at this turn of events, Namier sent Headlam-Morley possibly the most intemperate letter of the many he had written since the end of the war. The Poles were now 'winning all along the line'. He had been proved correct in warning that the Poles would exploit 'the Bolshevik bogey' to screw out of the Allies the military means to 'flout our decisions', and in consequence 'we have been arming bandits and helping them to pilfer helpless nations and defenceless peoples'.[175]

The clause relating to Jews in the minorities treaty, which was to be part of the general peace, had also been watered down. Headlam-Morley went into the conference chamber to 'fight the battle of the Jews', having been 'well coached' by Namier, but found himself 'more or less alone' and could not achieve all he had hoped for, though he did secure some autonomy for Jewish education.[176] This was particularly disappointing for Namier, who denounced assimilationist Jews and moderate Zionists prepared to accept the thin gruel offered. He was not surprised that 'the assimilants' were against encouraging the use of Yiddish or Hebrew; 'so probably would … every leaf which has fallen off the Jewish tree and which thinks it is time for the tree to perish because its own important entity has fallen off.'

> For the convenience of the small group of rich and educated people the great masses of Jews in eastern Europe have been refused the only conditions under which they could reasonably develop intellectually. The Polish language and Polish culture is strange to us and hostile. It is permeated by a spirit of Roman Catholicism and by the most rampant, intolerant anti-Semitism. To make the Jews feed on it is the same as to make men eat straw or wood.[177]

It was at this point that Namier received news that he must have dreaded since 1914. The eastern front had never been far from Koszylowce and Teodora had been involved in the war as a nurse. The onset of fighting between Polish and Ukrainian forces in 1919 left the Niemirowskis in even greater peril. In July 1919 an Englishman recently released from internment in Vienna brought a message from family friends that the estate had been attacked by Ukrainian forces, Namier's mother and sister had been carried off, and his father was 'seriously ill'. Namier immediately sent a letter to Seton-Watson's brother-in-law, Frederic Luttman-Johnson, a British military attaché in Bucharest, asking for help, and requested Headlam-Morley to intercede if possible with the Ukrainian delegation in Paris.[178] What had actually happened, though Namier did not discover the details for some time, was that a raiding Ukrainian detachment had looted and burned down the house. The bailiff, Mazurek, had been shot dead. The family, together with a Miss Jalowiecka, whose identity and position remains obscure, had found a brief refuge in the hut of a friendly peasant, only to be dragged out and physically assaulted. Namier's mother had been struck in the face so hard that on falling she had suffered an injury to her leg. They were then marched to the town of Zaleszczyki, where they were held until the approach of Polish troops, whereupon the Ukrainians had fled.[179]

When, after several weeks of anxiety, Namier finally heard that his parents and sister were safe, he wrote to thank Headlam-Morley, Seton-Watson and Kisch for their help.[180] Embarrassingly, it turned out that he owed more to Sir Percy Wyndham and the Polish government than to his own friends. The British Foreign Office had been greatly concerned with the fate of the Bernstein family.[181] Evidently Piłsudski had also taken a personal interest, and had despatched one of his aides-de-camp to scour east Galicia. Preparations had been made to exchange Ukrainian prisoners for the Bernsteins should the need arise.[182] General Ivaszkiewicz had also sent a special courier from Warsaw to ensure that the family were placed under the protection of the Polish army when they were recovered.[183] Even more disconcerting for Namier were the comments of the family themselves, as relayed by Wyndham. Józef, keeping to character, had decided to recuperate at the Bohemian spa town of Carlsbad while his wife and daughter guarded what remained of their property, and broke his journey at Lwów in order to thank the Polish general staff personally. He made sure to tell them that the Ukrainian forces – whom he considered 'worse than Zulus' – had included former officers in the German and Austrian armies.[184] The information which came from Namier's mother was even less welcome. Only a month after Namier had poured scorn on claims by the Polish prime minister of attacks on manor houses in Galicia by 'Jewish Bolsheviks', Anna testified that she recognised among her attackers a Jewish soldier called Epstein.[185]

Not only was this experience traumatic for Namier's parents and sister, it must also have made them more perplexed than ever by Ludwik's determination to uphold the Ukrainian cause, something that was public knowledge in Poland.[186] His opinions were not altered a jot by the events at Koszyłowce. On the contrary, he found the behaviour of the Ukrainian troops, and even Jews like Epstein, perfectly understandable. The Ukrainians, he told Seton-Watson, were 'a peasant nation exasperated by an oppression of centuries and fighting for its life against the big landowners and the foreign dominion for which these stand'. They could scarcely be expected to exercise

> super-human self-control. This is not merely war in east Galicia but also revolution. My father always took the Polish side and was closely associated with the Polish nobility, and now, pushed against the wall, the Ukrainians are simply taking reprisals, even cruel reprisals, against the big landowning class.[187]

Even while waiting for news he had been able to consider the situation objectively. He told Philip Kerr that he was 'flabbergasted' by decision to allow the Poles to take temporary control of east Galicia in order to protect the civilian population from 'Bolshevik bands', pending a final decision on the future of the province.[188] This would not solve the problem but perpetuate it: Poland did not have enough troops to occupy east Galicia; all that would be achieved would be to provoke 'the fiercest possible jacquerie'. And he still blamed the Poles for the violence. 'The Poles are hanging and shooting right and left, and deporting the Ukrainian intelligentsia simply *en bloc*. The Ukrainians retaliate wherever they can', and with predictable savagery, for 'a peasant in revolt and driven to utter despair is not soft-handed to his oppressor.'[189] This response does not seem entirely natural, and Lady Namier clearly had difficulties with it. She quoted a memorandum written by her husband at the time, in which he self-consciously justified his continued support for the Ukrainian cause: 'for all my personal loss and anxieties, I do insist that a grievous wrong has been done to the Ukrainians'. The responsibility for Ukrainian reprisals lay with 'the Polish jingoes and those Allied statesmen who, lacking adequate energy, bungled'. At one point it almost seemed as if he was blaming his father for provoking the raid by having been 'always on the Polish side'.[190]

In the summer of 1919 Namier grew increasingly desperate at the course of events in Paris and in the east.[191] He was finding it hard to convince even Headlam-Morley,[192] and was exasperated at the British government's failure to protest against Polish encroachments across the ceasefire line in Galicia.[193] Matters came to a head in August when the Allied commission on Polish affairs presented a proposed constitution for east Galicia under a Polish mandate, arrangements which Namier regarded as hopelessly weak, permitting the Poles to make land grants which would release an inundation of Polish settlers in advance of any plebiscite. He had in any case always expressed a dim view of plebiscites held in the presence of occupying forces.[194] His detailed, and unsolicited, critique of the treaty went directly to Paris by 'a private letter', and impressed many readers, including Kisch and E. H. Carr.[195] Subsequently, when petitions came in from the inhabitants of east Galician towns calling for integration into Poland, he produced another formidable demolition job, showing that these so-called expressions of popular opinion were an organised mobilisation of the minority population.[196] But the Polish government had the support of the French and Americans. Piłsudski threatened resignation unless his demands were met; then Paderewski announced that if the mandate scheme were not adopted the government would fall. Namier thought this an 'intolerable' form of blackmail: unavailingly, he revived his scheme for making east Galicia a Czech protectorate, which would allow the Czechs to 'remain in touch with Russia ... [and] hold their front against Germany'.[197]

While Namier lamented his own ineffectiveness, his political enemies took quite the contrary view, and continued to complain about him. In May 1919 the chairman of the Polish Relief Fund, Lord Treowen, put a coded question in the Lords in which he referred to 'sinister forces' undermining the admirable work of Sir Esmé Howard.[198] In November a Conservative MP, Alfred Raper, asked 'whether a Mr Namier has been in the employ of the Foreign Office; if so, in what capacity; whether his father is an Austrian (Galician), named Bernstein (Namierowski); and whether Mr Namier has been consulted in any way whatsoever regarding our Polish policy?'

The government chief whip replied politely by outlining Namier's background, identifying his father as a Polish citizen and adding that 'Mr Namier, whose knowledge of Poland and of Eastern Europe in general is remarkable, has frequently written papers or memoranda which have been of the greatest value.' Two Liberal MPs then stepped in to support Namier, as a former soldier in the British army who had, moreover, been educated at Oxford.[199] The matter dropped. But Dmowski's party did not give up. Raper's question was reported in the Polish press and in December 'Dmowski's organ', the *Gazeta Warszawska*, publicly identified the *éminence grise* lurking behind the circle of private advisers who were pulling Lloyd George's strings:

> the egregious Lewis B. Namier, or Ludwik Bernstein, the son of a big landowner from Koszylowce, near Brody. The activity of this gentleman has done great harm to the Polish cause during the whole of the war. The position of Namier in London is so strong that when in January in 1918 he published … a defence of Bolshevism and an apology of Trotsky, this act, which would have killed ten other people, has done no harm to him or his influence.[200]

This article might well have exposed Namier's father and family to reprisals, had another Warsaw newspaper not corrected the misapprehension, describing Józef as 'a universally respected landed proprietor in east Galicia' who 'considers himself as a Pole and is valued for his intense patriotism, which has brought down upon his head various repressive measures from the side of the Ukrainians'.[201]

The immediate effect of being made the subject of parliamentary questions and vilified in the Polish right-wing press was to confirm Namier in his convictions and drive these deeper into the fabric of his personality: he became even more pro-Zionist, and anti-Polish.[202] Poland was now for Jews a 'house of bondage', a 'torture-chamber', where life was a daily round of insult and oppression.[203] By September 1919 Weizmann was sending him information to be relayed to Balfour.[204] Weizmann was even moved to offer him a job.[205] For his part, Namier was openly pressing the Zionist cause: in a private letter to Philip Kerr he proposed that the government begin to train cadres of Jewish settlers in advance of the expected British mandate for Palestine.[206] It contained the germ of the idea of Palestine as an imperial dominion, for which he would subsequently be a strong advocate, combining his emotional ties to Zionism and to the British empire. The new colonists, whose arrival Britain should naturally support because of the commitment implicit in the Balfour declaration, would have to be 'a disciplined force composed of well-trained men, and not an unorganised mob of unskilled refugees'. The training had to be military as well as technical, so that Jews could defend themselves and not rely on a British army of occupation: 'the New Jerusalem has to be reclaimed by us … New England would never have become the moral force which it has, had Negro slaves done the work for the first Puritan settlers.' Jewish recruits should be taught Hebrew and English, their own mother tongue and the language of the empire with which they would be intimately connected. 'The policy as laid down in the Balfour declaration is a step which cannot be retraced, *ce sont des mots sur lesquels on ne revient pas*.'

In October 1919 the Namiers were temporarily homeless when the lease on their Oxford property expired, and they went to Folkestone for a 'half-vacation'. Namier felt that he deserved a break, having taken no more than ten days' holiday since the beginning of the year. His rest was soon interrupted, however, by the arrival of Henryk Loewenherz, a Jewish member of the Polish Committee for the Defence of Lwów, who had been in Paris supporting the efforts of the Polish government at the peace conference. A lawyer and a socialist, Loewenherz hoped to persuade Namier to help the Poles win the support of the British over east Galicia.

Namier described the ensuing conversations to his father, who probably passed the letter on to Polish officials, since a copy survives in the archives of the Polish foreign ministry.[207] It is more than likely, in fact, that Loewenherz had already been in contact with Józef before embarking on his mission. In the letter Namier explained why he could not acquiesce, and in doing so was clearly continuing a dispute that he had been having for some time with the rest of his family. He denied that he had 'pro-Ukrainian leanings', because his real interest was still in 'a single Russia' rather a separate Ukrainian state; not an argument which would have made much sense to Józef. Namier was also quite categorical in his dismissal of Polish claims to east Galicia.

> All your argumentation and stories on this matter do not convince me at all. Twenty per cent of the population (since counting Jews is ridiculous) has no right to impose its will on a mass of people three times the size. When it comes to civilisation, I have no doubt that Germans are more civilised than Poles, and still this does not deprive the Poles of their right to Poznań or upper Silesia, where the proportion of Germans is higher than that of Poles in eastern Galicia … What can we expect from a nation attacked by Poles from the west, especially if a national case goes hand in hand with social revolution? … And what did Polish troops do, unprovoked, in Lwów, in Pinsk, Lida, Vilnius? … It is worse than what was happening in German camps! And in spite of that, Poles are not denied their right to self-determination. And if the Ruthenians are louts, what would you call the majority in the Warsaw sejm?

Namier stated firmly that he would abide only by the dictates of his own conscience and what he considered 'best for my government'. Warnings of the harm he might do to Galician Jews, and even to his own family, made little impression, though he did tell Józef that 'if any Poles try to exert pressure on you, you can tell them that I am ready to step down from my office at any time upon my father's request'. There was no need to worry that he might come to Poland 'for propaganda purposes': 'as long as the decision is mine, I will never come to Poland'. But 'if you … were to suffer from any trouble because of me, please let me know. I am sorry if it is so, but the only thing I can do is to ask you to leave Poland and to help you to do that, should you fall hostage or victim to anyone.'

The Curzon line

In the winter and spring of 1919–20 the conflict between Poland and Soviet Russia intensified, and with all-out war across a wide front, including the Ukraine, any prospect of self-determination for the 'Ruthenian' majority in east Galicia vanished. The options were now incorporation into one or other of the competing powers. Successes against the White Russian counter-revolutionaries, and the conclusion of peace with Estonia and Latvia enabled the Soviets to concentrate their forces against the Poles, while Piłsudski came to an agreement with the Ukrainian People's Republic, and was able to launch a Polish offensive towards Kiev. The western leaders agreed on the urgent need to bolster eastern defences against Bolshevism. But despite the collapse of the Ukrainians, Namier refused to shift from his entrenched position. When representatives of the Ukrainian population of east Galicia arrived in London in January 1920, complaining that they had been unable to get a hearing at the peace conference, he pleaded their cause with the Foreign Office.[208]

Namier felt that he was engaged in an uphill struggle, and blamed the French government. Early in January 1920 he travelled to Nice for a few days to meet his parents, who were convalescing there.[209] On both outward and return journeys he stopped in Paris to talk to the Polish Minister for Foreign Affairs, the socialist Stanisław Patek, whom he had met in Oxford in 1915. At their first meeting Patek appeared conciliatory over Galicia, but a few days later his resolve had stiffened, presumably because French ministers had advised the Poles to maintain 'their excellent position of military conquerors'.[210] The course of the war was dictating political strategies. Once peace proposals emerged, Namier made what was in effect a last stand. A memorandum from him dated 25 March 1920 came before Lord Curzon (who had taken over from Balfour as foreign secretary in October 1919), protesting at what appeared to be the cessation to Poland of lands that were not 'ethnically Polish', in Lithuania, Belarus and Galicia. Sir Horace Rumbold, with whom Namier was crossing swords regularly,[211] was sufficiently exercised to reply in detail, in a despatch described in the Foreign Office as 'a strong anti-Namier memorandum if nothing else'. Rumbold answered Namier point by point. The decision of the Supreme Council in September had not 'fixed' Poland's eastern frontier, but had established a minimum eastward boundary, subject to a later agreement between Poland and Russia, which implied the possibility of further extension beyond 'the undisputed ethnographic line'. Namier's statements about the direction of Polish land policy were mere supposition, and the allegations of 'atrocious' behaviour in occupied territories were prejudiced and unfounded. The comments of the officials who saw both documents betray a deep unease at such a conflict of opinions, both of which were obviously *ex parte*. Namier still had his supporters but it was agreed that Rumbold's despatch should also be printed for circulation.[212] Such a public and very direct contradiction of Namier's expert opinion must have been hard to stomach.

Namier now felt that things were going so badly that he must resign his position, even with its salary of £400 a year. As Lady Namier put it, to his 'sense of corporate guilt was added the dismay of personal failure'.[213] This was still a bold step. The disastrous effects of prolonged warfare on east Galicia, culminating in the destruction at Koszylowce, made him more than usually worried about money. Although not poor by the standards of most working people, his comfortable upbringing rendered him acutely sensitive to the prospect of any level of impoverishment. And he had a wife to support. Even though Lady Namier's biography would have the reader believe that her husband's estrangement from Clara had already begun, some scraps of evidence that she preserved in her book suggest that there was still a depth of mutual affection, which on Namier's part would have translated into a powerful sense of responsibility.[214]

As for what he might do, he had made frequent visits to Oxford in the months before his resignation and seems to have assumed that his university friends would be willing and able to help him. But there was no possibility of a fellowship for Namier at Balliol, where Kenneth Bell, back from the trenches with a Military Cross, covered the teaching of modern history. Namier would have to make do with occasional tutorial work. Outside university teaching, his options were banking, which he briefly considered, and journalism, in which he had already dabbled.[215]

Back in the summer of 1919, Alfred Zimmern, who had connections with the *Manchester Guardian*, had recommended him for a position, and Namier had contributed a couple of articles.[216] Writing to C. P. Scott, the paper's legendary editor, Zimmern cited A. L. Smith and Lionel Curtis as referees, and added that Scott would find Namier 'easy to work with, provided you are interested in his subject, which you would be. He is a bit fond of talking, but since he has got a wife to expatiate to, this is much less marked.'[217] Namier had followed this up with a letter of application stating his keenness to 'take up journalistic work', and more particularly for a newspaper like Scott's: 'being myself a radical in politics, [I] should certainly be very glad of the opportunity of doing so in connection with a paper standing for the views which the *Manchester Guardian* represents'.[218] Negotiations dragged on until the winter of 1919–20, when Scott's son Edward interviewed Namier in Oxford.

Namier made it clear that he regarded any venture into journalism as 'a sideline' and that his main concern was his historical work. He had saved about £1,600, which he thought would see him through to finishing his book on the American revolution, but did not want to be left entirely without capital afterwards. So he proposed an arrangement at £500 a year to work through all the foreign news coming into the paper's London office – he did not propose coming to Manchester at all – which he felt would require 'drastic handling' by someone such as himself, who 'knew so much more of the domestic situation in foreign countries than the resident British correspondents'. Then, every ten days or so, he would contribute 'a general foreign article of a rather more detailed and factual kind'. He did not wish to write leaders because of his chronic insomnia – the first time it is mentioned in any contemporary document – which made work late at night unsuitable. Once his book was written, he would probably try his luck in finance. As outlined, Namier's idea of what he might do for the newspaper was not a particularly attractive proposition, but both Scotts still felt that they could use him for occasional articles. Edward, for one, was drawn to his personality:

> He seemed to me … extraordinarily able, and I am very glad to have met him, if only to hear him talk about the economies of central Europe. In a naïve and not displeasing way he was rather anxious to show how exceptional a person he was … he struck me as being tremendously public spirited and principled, fully conscious of his abilities but anxious that the public should have first call on them. I liked him … though his appearance is far from prepossessing, but, from his friends, I should judge that liking grows with friendship.[219]

In the short term Namier's long struggle to prevent Poland from taking over east Galicia came to nothing. In August 1920 Polish victories in the battle of Warsaw and in Galicia drove the Soviets back and eventually forced them to the negotiating table. By the Treaty of Riga in 1921 the entire province was absorbed into the Polish state. But Namier's efforts to persuade the British and Allied governments to accept his interpretation of the ethnic geography of Galicia would have long-term consequences. The so-called 'Curzon line', which the British government had put forward in 1919 as a boundary between Polish and Soviet forces was adopted by Stalin after the Second World War as the basis for the border between Poland and the Soviet Union, leaving many Poles on the Soviet side. The dividing line originally proposed by Lord Curzon passed east of Lwów, which had a substantial Polish majority. An alternative line had also been prepared, which veered to the west in Galicia, and left Lwów, and the Galician oilfields, on the Soviet side. Although Lloyd George reiterated Curzon's proposal in the international conference held at Spa on 11 July 1920, and pressed it on an unwilling Polish government, the supposedly agreed boundary which was communicated subsequently by the British to the Soviet commissar Chicherin followed the alternative line, giving Lwów and the Galician oilfields to the Soviets. The subsequent course of the Polish–Soviet war rendered this whole negotiation obsolete, as the Poles pushed much further east and were able to secure their territorial acquisitions in the peace treaty. But the note remained in Soviet hands, and was exploited twenty-five years later to Poland's disadvantage.

Namier is routinely execrated by extreme Polish nationalists as the man who 'forged' the Curzon line.[220] Some Polish historians have gone as far as to suggest that he delivered the note to Chicherin himself.[221] Plainly, this is impossible, since he had ceased to be an employee of the Foreign Office more than two months previously. However, there is a strong connection between Namier and the delineation of the boundary incorporated into the Chicherin note. For one thing, it corresponded almost exactly to his understanding of the 'ethnic limitation' of Polish territory. He recognised that there was a Polish majority in the city of Lwów, but did not consider this a valid argument for placing the city and its hinterland under Polish control. In January 1919 he had helped draft a proposed division of land between Poland and Ukraine which would have given Ukraine the whole of east Galicia on ethnic grounds.[222] A few months later he hand-sketched a boundary line on a map appended to a PID memorandum, which also took Lwów and most of east Galicia away from Poland.[223]

Moreover, Namier also had Lloyd George's ear through Philip Kerr. There is in Lloyd George's papers a memorandum on east Galicia, unsigned but with emendations in Namier's handwriting. Its description of 'the straight ethnographic divide between east and west Galicia' coincides so closely with the line given to the Soviets that, as Professor Norman Davies has observed, 'a detective would have good grounds at least for suggesting a connection between the two'.[224] The memorandum has no date, and could have been created at any time since January 1919. Nor was it explicitly a private or confidential document; indeed, it was no different from many other texts that Namier had produced for the Foreign Office. Finally, it did not contain a map, so officials would have had to draw the line themselves on the basis of the description. However, there can be little doubt that Namier's prolonged campaign to persuade ministers of the illegitimacy of Polish claims in east Galicia played a considerable part in shaping prime ministerial decisions. Namier himself wrote in the *Manchester Guardian* after the Spa conference applauding Lloyd George's decision to order the Poles back to their 'approximate ethnic border', which he saw as doing what had to be done to try to 'save Poland from herself'.[225]

Namier's resignation had come just before the fortunes of the war shifted in Poland's favour. Now entirely free of official constraints (not that he had ever allowed himself to be seriously constrained), he published articles in the *New Europe* denouncing the conduct of Poles in east Galicia and pressing the case for the independence of the region.[226] He continued for some time to write about Polish affairs for the *Manchester Guardian*, always commenting sourly on the antics of the Polish right, and criticising Piłsudski in particular.[227] And occasionally, like the hapless Mr Dick in David Copperfield, his King Charles's head reappeared: in July 1922, for example he expressed the forlorn hope that

> The general election in east Galicia, though illegal, might still give the Ukrainians a chance to prove the non-Polish character of east Galicia, and then, by refusing to enter the Polish diet, to show their determination not to submit to Polish annexation.

Poland's acquisition of the whole of Galicia had been a very bitter blow, rounding off Namier's disillusionment with the Foreign Office. Worse was to follow. With no contract from the *Manchester Guardian* his only choice was to return to Oxford and take up an offer of tutorial work at Balliol. He was now destined for further disappointments, which would presage the greatest crisis in his life.

Notes

1 A. M. Cienciala and Titus Komarnicki, *From Versailles to Locarno: keys to Polish foreign policy, 1919–25* (Lawrence, Kans., 1984), 121.

2 Paton to Arnold Toynbee, 11 June 1962 (Bodl., Toynbee papers, box 84). Much later in his life Namier used the term 'Polaks' in a letter to Blanche Dugdale, 30 Aug. 1940 (CZA, 3121\44).

3 [Namier,] Germany's Polish gamble', *New Statesman*, 18 Nov. 1916; [Namier,] 'The bargaining with Poland', ibid., 16 Dec. 1916.

4 Norman Davies, 'The Poles in Great Britain, 1914–1919', *Slavonic and East European Review*, l (1972), 73–4.

5 Davies, 'Poles in Great Britain', 74, quoting and translating from Roman Dmowski, *Polityka polska, i odbudowanie państwa* (2nd edn, 2 vols, Częstochowa, 1937), i, 280–2. The phrase *żydek galicyjski* may be rendered in English as 'Galician Yid'.

6 The socialists, the author added, were 'the best among them' and the 'spiritual heirs of the old Polish revolutionaries', inheriting both their virtues and their 'absurdities' ('A summary of recent developments in Poland', *New Statesman*, 24 Mar. 1917). Namier's authorship is strongly suggested by the argument and tone of the article, and the quotation from Goethe.

7 'Austria-Hungary: a summary of the position', *New Statesman*, 19 May 1917; 'Poland and the Russian Revolution', ibid., 30 June 1917; 'The crisis in Poland', ibid., 18 Aug. 1917; 'German peace manoeuvres', ibid., 29 Sept. 1917; 'The change in the government of Poland', ibid., 24 Nov. 1917.

8 Philip Kerr to Sir Eric Drummond, 5 Apr. 1917 (NRS, Lothian papers, GD 40/17/872/1).

9   Isaiah Berlin, *Personal impressions* (1980), 75.

10   Namier to Kerr, 2 Apr. 1917 (NRS, GD 40/17/872/2).

11   Drummond to Kerr, 6 Apr. 1917 (NRS, GD 40/17/872/3).

12   Ng, *Nationalism*, 112–13.

13   TNA, CAB 24/143/16 (17 May 1917), CAB 24/17/42 (22 June 1917), CAB 24/21/9 (24 July 1917), CAB 24/22/69 (10 Aug. 1917), CAB 24/24/44 (24 Aug. 1917), CAB 24/25/8 (4 Sept. 1917), CAB 24/26/89 (20 Sept. 1917), CAB 24/27/99 (4 Oct. 1917), CAB 24/29/45 (19 Oct. 1917).

14   See, for example, Namier, 'Memo on Poland, No. 1', 3 May 1917 (FO 371/3001, fos 13–22); Namier, 'Memo on Polish conference at Stockholm', 15 May 1917 (FO 371/3001, fos 40–1); Namier, 'Special memo on crisis in Poland', 24 May 1917 (FO 371/3001, fos 54–6); memo by Namier, 11 June 1917 (FO 371/3001, fos 103–5).

15   Namier, 'Memo on Poland, No. 1', 3 May 1917 (FO 371/3001, fos 16–17).

16   Memo by Oman, 3 Apr. 1917, with a comment by Balfour (FO 371/3016, fos 154–209).

17   See, for example, the comment by Rex Leeper on Namier's memo of 9 May 1917 (FO 395/108, file 104074).

18   Hugh Seton-Watson and Christopher Seton-Watson, *The making of a new Europe: R. W. Seton-Watson and the last years of Austria-Hungary* (1981), 207.

19   Headlam-Morley to Tyrrell, 26 Sept. 1918 (FO 371/4366, fos 200–11).

20   The *Round Table, Quarterly Review, Nineteenth Century, Times Financial Supplement, New Statesman, Land and Water, New Europe, The Nation, Everyman, The Times*, the *Daily Chronicle* and *Westminster Gazette*.

21   Seton-Watson and Seton-Watson, *Making of a new Europe*, 209.

22   Namier, 'Memo on Austria-Hungary's inner and foreign policy', 11 May 1917 (FO 371/2862, fos 249–55); Seton-Watson and Seton-Watson, *Making of a new Europe*, 210–11. See also Namier, 'Weekly report on Austria … the Austrian crisis', 5 May 1917 (FO 371/2862, fos 478–81).

23   Comments on memo by Namier, of 11 May 1917 (FO 371/2862, fos 249–55).

24   Seton-Watson and Seton-Watson, *Making of a new Europe*, 211.

25   Claud Schuster to Namier, 18 July 1917 (SSEES, Seton-Watson papers, 3/3/3).

26   Mark Baker, 'Lewis Namier and the problem of eastern Galicia', *Journal of Ukrainian Studies*, xxiii, no. 2 (1998), 63–4.

27   Namier, 'Remarks on "The problems of central and eastern Europe"', 14 Sept. 1917 (FO 371/3016, fos 212–27). See also Namier, 'Report on the occupied Russian provinces', 25 Oct. 1917 (ibid., fos 548–51).

28   Baker, 'Namier and the problem of eastern Galicia', 67. In February 1917 he published in *The Nineteenth Century and After* the article drafted two years earlier on Danzig. It was then printed separately as *Danzig: Poland's outlet to the sea* (1917).

29   Paul Latawski, 'The Dmowski–Namier feud, 1915–1918', *Polin: studies in Polish Jewry*, ii (Oxford, 1987), 44.

30   Weekly reports on Poland, 24 Aug., 4 Oct. 1917 (TNA, CAB 24/24/44; CAB 22/27/99).

31   Namier to Sir William Tyrrell, 25 Apr. 1918 (FO 371/4357, fo. 171).

32   Drummond to Balfour, 19 Sept. 1917 (FO 371/3016, fo. 210).

33   Oman to Drummond, 26 Sept. 1917 (FO 371/3016, fo. 229).

34   Namier, 'Report on the occupied Russian provinces', 25 Oct. 1917 (FO 371/3016, fos 548–51).

35   Drummond to John Buchan, 28 Oct. 1917 (FO 371/3016, fo. 547).

36   Berlin, *Personal impressions*, 75.

37 Minutes in relation to a letter from Lucien Wolff to Ld Robert Cecil, 28 Nov. 1917 (FO 371/3019, fos 126–7).

38 Davies, 'Poles in Great Britain', 77.

39 Jan Pisuliński, 'Nieznany list brytyjskiego historyka', *Zeszyty Historyczna*, 141 (2002), 225–32.

40 Alan Sharp, 'Some relevant historians – the Political Intelligence Department of the Foreign Office, 1918–1920', *Australian Journal of Politics and History*, xxxiv (1988–9), 360; Harold Temperley, *An historian in peace and war: the diaries of Harold Temperley*, ed. T. G. Otte (Farnham, 2014), 253–4.

41 Sharp, 'Some relevant historians', 360.

42 He was eventually accorded the position of temporary clerk in the Foreign Office at a salary of £400 p.a. (J. A. C. Tilley to Namier, 5 July 1918 (Rylands, Namier papers, 1/9/7)).

43 See Namier's appreciation of Tyrrell in *Vanished supremacies*, 107–11.

44 Memo by Namier, 23 May 1918 (FO 371/3135, fos 102–4); *Vanished supremacies*, 110–11.

45 Sharp, 'Some relevant historians', 361.

46 Berlin, *Personal impressions*, 75.

47 For examples in which Namier corrected office translations from Polish, see FO 371/3280, files 9716, 9743). See also his own translations from press extracts (e.g. FO 371/3908, fos 187–92).

48 See PID files, 1918–19 (FO 371/4357–69, 4371–82, 4384–7, 4399).

49 Namier to Smith, 28 May 1918 (Balliol, Smith papers, Letters, N1). Another Foreign Office official remembered that 'we worked under great pressure, and probably dealt with twenty or thirty papers every day' (E. H. Carr to Brian Pearce, 26 Nov. 1973 (Birmingham UL, Carr papers, box 26)).

50 For Blanche Dugdale, see *Baffy*, xi–xv; *Oxf. DNB*; and her autobiography, B. E. C. Dugdale, *Family homespun* ([1940]).

51 Arnold Toynbee, *Acquaintances* (1967), 65–6.

52 Namier to Smith, 12 Jan. 1917 [*recte* 1918] (Balliol, Smith papers, N1). He comforted himself by quoting lines from Goethe's 'Siegmund': '*Mußt mir meine Erde doch lassen stehen/Und meine Hütte, die du nicht gebaut,/Und meinen Herd, um dessen Glut du mich beneidest* [Still you must leave my earth intact and my small hovel, which you did not build, and this my hearth whose glowing heat you envy me].'

53 Note by Namier, 8 May 1918 (FO 371/3278, file 77920).

54 *Skyscrapers*, 107.

55 Eustace Percy, *Some memories* (1958), 58.

56 *Namier*, 133–4.

57 Information from electoral registers; Namier to C. P. Scott, 23 June 1919 (*Guardian* arch., A/N2/2); index card entry for Namier (ibid., A/N2/13).

58 *Namier*, 134.

59 Smith to the principal, Reading College, 25 June 1918 (Balliol, Smith papers, NI); Namier to Smith, 24 June 1918 (ibid.).

60 *Conflicts*, 94.

61 *Vanished supremacies*, 128.

62 R. H. Bruce Lockhart, *Memoirs of a British agent* (1932), 197, 200, 206, 226–8, 230–2, 243, 253–4; Namier, 'Notes on Zionism', 5 (CZA, Namier papers, A312\2).

63 Namier to A. L. Smith, 12 Jan. 1917 [*recte* 1918] (Balliol, Smith papers, N1); *Skyscrapers*, 85.

64 Memo by Namier [Jan. 1919] (FO 608/68, fos 36–40).

65 *Skyscrapers*, 90, 92; *Conflicts*, 99.

66 N[amier], 'Revolutionary forces in Austria', *New Europe*, 18 Apr. 1918; PID memo on 'The present situation in Austria', 15 Oct. 1918 (FO 371/4358, fos 211–13).

67 Namier to Sir William Tyrrell, 26 Mar. 1918 (FO 371/4357, fos 2–3).

68 *Skyscrapers*, 92, 153.

69 Temperley, *An historian in peace and war*, 287.

70 For the arguments which follow, see [Namier], 'The Habsburg policy', 6 May 1918 (FO 371/4358, fos 160–9). It was almost certainly this memorandum which had so offended Temperley.

71 The Czechs were an exception.

72 *Skyscrapers*, 84.

73 [Namier,] 'Parliament and government in Austria', 15 Aug. 1918 (FO 371/4358, fos 194–202).

74 [Namier,] 'The Habsburg policy', 6 May 1918 (FO 371/4358, fos 160–9).

75 On this point, see also [Namier,] 'Tisza and Burian', 22 Apr. 1918 (FO 371/4358, fos 139–42); memo by Namier, 24 June 1918 (FO 371/3135, fos 330–3).

76 [Namier,] 'The present situation in Austria', 15 Oct. 1918 (FO 371/4358, fos 211–13); *Skyscrapers*, 108.

77 Headlam-Morley to Sir John Tilley, 26 Nov. 1919 (FO 371/4384, fo. 186); *Namier*, 130; Sharp, 'Some relevant historians', 362; H. R. Winkler, 'The emergence of a Labor foreign policy in Great Britain, 1918–1929', *Journal of Modern History*, xxviii (1956), 247–58; Casper Sylvest, '"A commanding group"? Labour's advisory committee on international questions 1918–31', P. D. Corthorn and Jonathan Shaw (eds), *The British Labour Party and the wider world: domestic politics, internationalism and foreign policy* (2008), 48–63. The redaction in *The Times* is impossible to identify with certainty, but the most likely candidate is a short article published on 19 October 1918 under the by-line 'A tragi-comedy', which makes various points familiar from Namier's PID memoranda, and includes a typical historical reference (to the reign of the emperor Joseph II).

78 See, for example, FO 371/3912, files 131930, 145344. In 1919 Leeper was entrusted with writing the monthly reports for the dominion parliaments on both Russian and Polish affairs (FO 371/4382, fo. 207).

79 From 27 April his name was first on the departmental circulating list for reports on Polish affairs from MI9 (FO 371/4362, fos 132–60).

80 Between 9 and 25 May his name had jumped to first on the circulating list: FO 371/4357, fos 62, 76. Apart from occasional relegations, it remained there.

81 Memoranda by Namier, 13, [24], 31 May, 17, 28 June, 29 Aug. 1918 (FO 371/3278, files 82883, 92310, 92299, 92313, 105359, 113817, 148264).

82 Comment by Namier, 3 May 1918, on report from Petrograd (FO 371/3281, file 74578); memoranda by Namier, 1, 10 July, 6, 20 Aug. 1918 (ibid., files 92306, 116413, 150870).

83 PID memo, 'Czernin and the Czechs', 22 Apr. 1918 (FO 371/4358, fos 143–6); PID memo, 'Unrest in Austria-Hungary', 24 Apr. 1918 (FO 371/4358, fos 147–50).

84 Memo by Namier, 24 Sept. 1918 (FO 371/4368, fos 2–5); comment by Namier, 23 May 1918, on a paper concerning the congress at Rome (FO 371/3135, fo. 119); comment by Namier, 18 Jan. 1919 (FO 371/3894, file 2293).

85 Comment by Namier, 25 Nov. 1918 (FO, 371/3278, file 156564).

86 N[amier], 'Poland and Brest-Litovsk', *New Europe*, 21 Feb. 1918; PID memo, *The political situation in Poland*, 25 Apr. 1918 (FO 371/4363, 117–117A); memo by Namier, 3 May 1918 (FO 371/3278, file 74361).

87 N[amier], 'Revolutionary forces in Austria', *New Europe*, 18 Apr. 1918; PID memo, 'The

resignation of the Austrian cabinet', 27 June 1918 (FO 371/4358, fos 178–85); memo by Namier, 29 Aug. 1918 (FO 371/3278, file 148264).

88 Memo by Namier, 3 May 1918 (FO 371/3278, file 74361).

89 PID memo, *The political situation in Poland*, 25 Apr. 1918 (FO 371/4363, fo. 117A); memo by Namier, 20 Jan. 1919 (FO 608/68, fos 36–40).

90 N[amier], 'Poland and Brest-Litovsk'.

91 Davies, 'Poles in Great Britain', 77.

92 Memos by Namier, 26 Apr., 24 Sept. 1918 (FO 371/4359, fos 45–8; FO 371/4368, fos 2–5); comment by Namier, 3 Dec. 1918 (FO 371/32812, file 196225). See also FO 371/3278, files 154242, 153716, 200422.

93 Davies, 'Poles in Great Britain', 77–8.

94 Comment by Namier, 23 May 1918 (FO 371/3135, fo. 125); comment by Namier, 16 Sept. 1918 (FO 371/3278, file 154236); comment by Namier, 2 Oct. 1918 (ibid., file 162324); memo by Namier, 24 Sept. 1918 (FO 371/4368, fos 2–5).

95 N[amier], 'Poland and Brest-Litovsk'.

96 Latawski, 'Dmowski–Namier feud', 46.

97 *New Witness*, 26 Apr. 1918.

98 Ussher to Alma-Tadema, 6, 21 May 1918 (Bodl., Alma-Tadema papers, MS Eng. lett. c. 528, fos 76–7, 74–5).

99 Arnold Toynbee, 'Lewis Namier, historian', *Encounter*, no. 16 (Jan. 1961), 41.

100 *Namier*, 129.

101 Memo by Namier, 15 May 1918 (FO 371/4363, fos 302–3). See also *Namier*, 129; Baker, 'Namier and the problem of eastern Galicia', 72–4.

102 Hardinge to Drummond, 16 May [1918] (FO 371/4363, fo. 315).

103 Memo by Namier, 12 Apr. 1918 (FO 371/4359, fos 41–2).

104 Comments on Namier's memo of 12 Apr. 1918 (FO 371/4359, fo. 40).

105 Comment by Headlam-Morley, 26 Sept. 1918 (FO 371/4368, fo. 7).

106 *Namier*, 135.

107 J. A. C. Tilley to Namier, 5 July 1918 (Rylands, Namier papers, 1/9/7)).

108 Namier to Smith, 21, 24 Jan. 1919 (Balliol, Smith papers, N1).

109 See, for example, the circulation lists in PID papers, Feb.–Apr. 1919 (FO 371/4376, 4378).

110 Namier to James Headlam-Morley, 13 Feb. 1919 (Churchill, Headlam-Morley papers, 688/2).

111 Memo by Namier, 27 Feb. 1919 (FO 371/3897, file 30573); comment by Namier, 28 Feb. 1919 (ibid., file 31929).

112 Memo by Namier [Dec. 1918] (FO 371/4385, fo. 148).

113 Comment by Namier, 30 Sept. 1919 (FO 371/3909, file 109222).

114 *Namier*, 138–9.

115 Memo by Namier, 16 Feb. 1919 (FO 371/3897, file 20977).

116 Memo by Namier, [Jan. 1919] (FO 608/68, fos 36–40); memo by Namier, 16 Feb. 1919 (FO 371/3897, file 20977); comment by Namier, 26 Feb. 1919 (FO371/3897, file 30570).

117 Namier to James Headlam-Morley, 13 Feb. 1919 (Churchill, Headlam-Morley papers, 688/2).

118 Telegram, 31 Dec. 1918 (FO 371/3896, file 162); comment by Namier, 4 Mar. 1919 (FO 371/3897, file 32983).

119 Memo by Namier, 7 Jan. 1919 (FO 371/3896, file 8921)

120 Memo by Namier, 1 Mar. 1919 (FO 371/3906, file 340572); Namier to P. H. Kerr, 10 July 1919 (NRS, GD 40/17/216/454–6).

121 Memo by Namier, 20 Jan. 1919 (FO 371/3896, file 5255); comment by Namier, 10 May 1919 (FO 371/3907, fo. 1).

122 See for example memo by Namier, 8 Jan. 1919 (FO 371/3896, file 9163); 'Note on Teschen' and 'Note on Lithuania and White Russia', attached to memo by Namier on Poland, 11 Mar. 1919 (FO 371/3898, file 42554).

123 See, for example, comment on message from Namier to Headlam-Morley, 21 Jan. 1919 (TNA, FO 371/3897, file 11899).

124 Such as J. D. Gregory, counsellor in the British embassy to the Holy See, who confessed that he and Namier were 'unspeakable enemies': 'I think on the whole it has been a great pity that Mr Namier was ever introduced into the F.O. ... it has created very bad impression abroad and is generally believed in Poland that he is the head of the F.O. department which deals with Polish affairs and that the anti-Polish policy with which we are credited is to be attributed to his malign influence' (quoted in Sharp, 'Some relevant historians', 363–4).

125 Comment by Namier, 30 May 1919 (FO 371/3909, file 79212).

126 Sir James Headlam-Morley, *A memoir of the Paris Peace Conference 1919*, ed. Agnes Headlam–Morley et al. (1972).

127 Memo by Namier, 16 Feb. 1919 (FO 371/3897, file 20977).

128 Baker, 'Namier and the problem of eastern Galicia', 80–4.

129 Headlam-Morley, *Memoir*, 12, 25, 52–3.

130 See, for example, comments by Namier, 27, 31 Jan., 15 Apr. 1919 (FO 371/3896, file 11744; FO 371/3897, file 14244; 371/3898, file 55033); memo by Namier, 28 Feb. 1919 (ibid., FO 371/3910, file 30574).

131 Comment by Namier, 3 Feb. 1919 (FO 371/3897, file 17228); memo by Namier, 1 Mar. 1919 (FO 371/3906, file 30592); Namier to Headlam-Morley, 15 Mar. 1919 (Churchill, Headlam-Morley papers, 688/2).

132 Memo by Namier, with note by Howard, 20 Jan. 1919 (FO 608/68/35–40); Namier to Headlam-Morley, 13 Feb. 1919 (Churchill, Headlam-Morley papers, 688/2).

133 Memo by Namier, 15 Apr. 1919 (FO 371/3898, file 55014).

134 Comment by Leeper, 14 Jan. 1919, on memo by Namier (FO 608/68, fo. 40).

135 Headlam-Morley, *Memoir*, 2; Namier to Headlam-Morley 11, 14 Apr. 1919 (Churchill, Headlam-Morley papers, 688/2).

136 [Namier,] 'Polish ambitions: some untenable claims', *Manchester Guardian*, 21 Apr. 1919; [Namier,] 'A plain issue', *New Statesman*, 26 Apr. 1919.

137 J. C. Bailey to Sir John Tilley, 31 Mar. 1919, Tilley to Ld Curzon, 8 Apr. 1919, [G.M.C.] to Ld Curzon, 22 Apr. 1919 (Rylands, Namier papers, 1/9/7).

138 Headlam-Morley, *Memoir*, 24, 35–6; Namier to Headlam-Morley, 22 Jan. 1919 (Churchill, Headlam-Morley papers, 688/2).

139 See, for example, Namier to Kerr, 19 Apr. 1919 (NRS, GD 40/17/892/1).

140 Headlam-Morley, *Memoir*, 21, 29; Namier to Headlam-Morley, 13 Feb. 1919 (Churchill, Headlam-Morley papers, 688/2); Norman Davies, 'Great Britain and the Polish Jews, 1918–20', *Journal of Contemporary History*, viii (1973), 128.

141 Namier to Headlam-Morley, 31 Jan. 1919 (Churchill, Headlam-Morley papers, 688/2); M. B. B. Biskupski, *'The most dangerous German agent in America': the many lives of Louis N. Hammerling* (DeKalb, Ill., 2015), 88–92.

142 Comments by Namier, 14, 19 Dec. 1918 (FO 371/3281, files 201807, 205846).

143 Memo by Namier, 8 Feb. 1919 (FO 371/4377, fos 252–3). See also comment by Namier, 12 Dec. 1918 (FO 371/3281, file 200938); N[amier], 'Poland and Brest-Litovsk', *New Europe*, 21 Feb. 1918.

144 Modern historians sympathetic to the Polish cause are sceptical of this evidence: see especially Norman Davies, *White eagle, red star: the Polish-Soviet war, 1919–1920* (1972), 47–8, 54; Norman Davies, 'Great Britain and the Polish Jews, 1918–20', *Journal of Contemporary History*, viii (1973), 126–42.

145 Memo by Namier, 20 Nov. 1919 (FO 371/3904, file 154182).

146 Memo by Namier, 20 Jan. 1919 (FO 371/3896, file 5255); comment by Namier, 4 Nov. 1919 (ibid., 371/3899, file 138496).

147 Report, 19 Dec. 1917 (FO 371/3054, fos 251–3).

148 *Namier*, 163 states that they met in Paris, presumably when Namier briefly attended the peace conference. In 'Turbulent Zionist', 12, Julia quotes her husband as writing that he and Weizmann met 'some time towards the end or possibly after the end of World War I', and that they were introduced by the Russian Zionist Shmaryahu Levin, a man whom Namier certainly knew well (*Namier*, x; Namier to Malcolm MacDonald, 21 Jan. 1931 (CZA, A312\12); *Observer*, 2 Apr. 1933; *Conflicts*, 166, 168). Information included in a memo by Namier, dated 14 Mar. 1919 came from a nephew of Weizmann living in Poland, and may well have been transmitted by Weizmann himself: FO 371/3903, file 38028.

149 By September 1919 Weizmann was writing to Namier to clarify a previous discussion between the two men on the boundaries proposed for the new Jewish state: *Weizmann A*, ix, 215–16.

150 Memo by Namier, 8 Feb. 1919 (FO 371/4377, fos 252–3).

151 Namier to Headlam-Morley, 16 Apr. 1919 (Churchill, Headlam-Morley papers, 688/2), quoted extensively in David Vital, *A people apart: the Jews in Europe 1789–1939* (Oxford, 1999), 749–51.

152 *Vanished supremacies*, 32–3.

153 Vital, *A people apart*, 749–51, 756.

154 On this point see 'Turbulent Zionist', 16; cf. Ng, *Nationalism*, 124.

155 An unsigned review in the *New Statesman*, 21 Aug. 1920, possibly by Namier, dwelt on the ill-treatment of Jews in both Poland and Bolshevik Russia.

156 Memo by Namier, 22 May 1919 (FO 371/3903, file 80643).

157 Comments by Namier, 23, 25 Aug. 1919 (FO 371/3904, files 117913, 119487).

158 Memos by Namier, 13 June, 1 Aug. 1919 (FO 371/3907, files 86258, 109280).

159 Memo by Namier, 1 Aug. 1919 (FO 371/3907, file 109280).

160 FO 371/3903, file 763565; comment by Namier, 11 Dec. 1918 (FO 371/3281, file 202162).

161 *Hansard, H.C. Deb.*, cxvi, col. 165; memo by Namier, 30 June 1919 and endorsements (FO 371/3903, file 88314).

162 *Hansard, H.C. Deb.*, cxvi, col. 722; memo by Namier, 25 June 1919 (FO 371/3903, file 91277).

163 Note by Headlam-Morley, 22 Apr. 1919 (FO 608/68/477); Zaleski to Headlam-Morley, 23 Apr. 1919 (FO 371/4379, fo. 195); [Ld Curzon?] to Headlam-Morley, 26 Apr. 1919 (FO 608/68/474); telegram from Balfour to Curzon, 30 Apr. 1919 (FO 608/68/480); Balfour to Curzon, 25 Apr. 1919 (FO 371/4329, fo. 193).

164 For a glimpse of Polish governmental paranoia about Namier, see an unsigned note, 5 Apr. 1919, found in Paderewski's papers and cited in Davies, 'Britain and the Polish Jews', 128.

165 Headlam-Morley to Sir Ronald Graham, 30 Apr. 1919 (telegram) (FO 371/4379, fo. 192; memo by Headlam-Morley, 22 Apr. 1919 (ibid., fo. 194).

166 Note by Headlam-Morley [May 1919] (FO 608/68/474); Headlam-Morley, *Memoir*, 99.

167 *Namier*, 142.

168 Memo by Namier, 22 May 1919 (FO 371/3903, file 80643); and his later retelling in *Conflicts*, 166–7.

169 *Conflicts*, 167–8.

170 *In the margin*, 274.

171 See memo by Namier, 16 Sept. 1919 (FO 371/3544), quoted in F. L. Carsten, *The first Austrian republic 1918–1938: a study based on British and Austrian documents* (Aldershot, 1986), 29–30.

172 Headlam-Morley, *Memoir*, 53; Namier to Kisch, 16 May 1919 (NRS, GD 40/17/897/2); same to same, 12 June 1919 (FO 608/68, fo. 279).

173 Namier to Kerr, 26 June 1919 (NRS, GD 40/17/904).

174 Baker, 'Namier and the problem of eastern Galicia', 91–4; comment by Namier, 27 June 1919 (FO 371/3907, file 89887). See also FO 371/3907, file 94173.

175 Namier to Headlam-Morley, 26 June 1919 (Churchill, Headlam-Morley papers, 688/2).

176 Headlam-Morley, *Memoir*, 111–17. See Alan Sharp, 'Britain and the protection of minorities at the Paris peace conference, 1919', A. C. Hepburn (ed.), *Minorities in history: Historical Studies, xii* (1978), 170–88; Carole M. Fink, *Defending the rights of others: the great powers, the Jews, and international minority protection, 1878–1938* (Cambridge, 2006), 193–202.

177 Namier to Headlam-Morley, 2 July 1919 (Churchill, Headlam-Morley papers, 688/2).

178 Namier to Headlam-Morley, 4 July 1919 (Churchill, Headlam-Morley papers, 688/2).

179 Sir Percy Wyndham to Ld Curzon, 21 July, 9 Aug 1919 (FO 371/3923, files 107648, 114763). On this episode, see Baker, 'Namier and the problem of eastern Galicia', 94–6.

180 Telegram from Wyndham, 22 July 1919 (FO 3471/3923, file 106761); Namier to Headlam-Morley, 29 July 1919 (Churchill, Headlam-Morley papers, 688/2); Namier to Seton-Watson, 14 Aug. 1919 (SSEES, Seton-Watson papers, 17/18).

181 Wyndham made his reports directly to Lord Curzon, who had been left in charge of the FO while Balfour attended the Peace Conference.

182 Telegrams from Wyndham, 15, 16 July 1919 (FO 371/3923, files 103668, 104157); Wyndham to Curzon, 17, 21 July 1919 (FO 371/3923, files 105826, 107648).

183 Wyndham to Curzon, 4 Aug. 1919 (FO 371/3923, file 113659).

184 Wyndham to Curzon, 21 July, 4, 9 Aug. 1919 (FO 371/3923, files 107648, 113659, 114673); telegram from Wyndham, 2 Aug. 1919 (FO 371/3923, file 111561); note by W. H. S., 21 July 1919 (371/3923, file 104157).

185 Comment by Namier, 15 July 1919 (FO 371/3923, file 102492); Wyndham to Curzon, 9 Aug. 1919 (FO 371/3923, file 114763).

186 The account in *Namier*, 143–4, which implies that the episode affected Józef far more than his wife and daughter strikes a false note: in particular, the story that Teodora charmed their Ukrainian captors into taking her and her mother home does not tally with the evidence provided to the British.

187 Namier to Seton-Watson, 14 Aug. 1919 (SSEES, Seton-Watson papers, 17/18). See also Namier to Headlam-Morley, 4 July 1919 (Churchill, Headlam-Morley papers, 688/2).

188 Baker, 'Namier and the problem of eastern Galicia', 92.

189 Namier to Kerr, 10 July 1919 (NRS, GD 40/17/216/454–6); comment by Namier, 3 Sept. 1919 (FO 371/3907, fo. 245).

190 *Namier*, 144.

191 Note the tone of his letter to A. L. Smith, 18 Sept. 1919 (Balliol, Smith papers, N1): 'no rest in this mess'.

192 Headlam-Morley, *Memoir*, 175.

193 Memo by Namier, 8 Oct. 1919 (FO 371/3904, file 115716); comment by Namier, 11 Sept. 1919 (ibid., file 12334); memo by Namier, 25 Sept. 1919 (FO 371/3908, fo. 12); comment by Namier, 27 Sept. 1919 (FO 371/3909, file 133523).

194 Memo by Namier, 28 May 1919 (FO 371/3907, fo. 123); comments by Namier, 14, 16 Aug., 6, 12, 13, 23 Sept., 21 Nov. 1919 (FO 371/3909, files 113660, 116534; FO 371/3980, fos 139, 51, 48; FO 371/3899, file 103944; FO 371/3980, fo. 66); memos by Namier, 25, 28 Nov. 1919 (FO 371/3908, fos 52–3; FO 371/3900, file 154600); Taras Hunczak, 'Sir Lewis Namier and the struggle for eastern Galicia, 1918–1920', *Harvard Ukrainian Studies*, i (1977), 207–8.

195 Baker, 'Namier and the problem of eastern Galicia', 101–2; *Namier*, 146.

196 Baker, 'Namier and the problem of eastern Galicia', 102.

197 Comment by Namier, 30 Sept. 1919 (FO 371/3909, file 109222); memo by Namier, 25 Nov. 1919 (FO 371/4384, fos 174–7).

198 *Hansard*, H.L. deb., xxxiv, col. 959.

199 *Hansard*, H.C. deb., cxx, cols 1648–9.

200 Translation by Namier (FO 371/3908, fos 190–1). Kerr's backstairs influence was a favourite topic of the National Democrat press: Namier to Kerr, 19 Apr. 1919 (NRS, GD 40/17/892/1). It is impossible to say how much truth there was in these allegations, but the glimpses we have of Lloyd George's thinking on the 'Polish question' do show a remarkable similarity to Namier's (*Lord Riddell's intimate diary of the peace conference and after, 1918–1923* (1933), 191).

201 Translation of an article in *Przeglad Wieczorny*, 19 Nov. 1919 (FO 371/3929, file 156764).

202 Memos by Namier, 9, 25 Dec. 1919, 28 Jan., 12 Feb., 11 Mar. 1920 (FO 371/4384, fos 210–11, 224–33; FO 371/4385, fos 32–3, 8–13, 36–9); comments by Namier, 21 Jan., 18 Feb. 1920 (FO 371/3908, fo. 198; FO 371/3913, file 176646).

203 Vital, *A people apart*, 751.

204 Weizmann to Namier, 18 Sept. 1919 (CZA, A312\47).

205 'Turbulent Zionist', 22.

206 Namier to Kerr, 6 Sept. 1919 (NRS, GD 40/17/216/465–7).

207 The letter is printed and contextualised in Pisuliński, 'Nieznany list brytyjskiego historyka', 225–32. I am grateful to Anna Jedrzejewska for providing the English translation which I quote here.

208 Memo by Namier and Rex Leeper, 1 Jan. 1920 (FO 371/4384, fos 234–7).

209 *Namier*, 160.

210 Memo by Namier, 23 Jan. 1920 (FO 371/4384, fos 239–45); see p. 73.

211 Comment by Namier, 1 Apr. 1920 (FO 371/3908, fo. 215).

212 FO 371/3914, file 195113.

213 Ld Hardinge to Namier, 13 May 1920 (Rylands, Namier papers, 1/9/7); *Namier*, 151.

214 *Namier*, 150–1.

215 E. T. Scott to C. P. Scott, 31 Dec. 1919 (*Guardian* arch., A/N2/1a).

216 Zimmern to C. P. Scott, 5 Oct. 1918 (BL, Scott papers, Add. MS 50909, fo. 115).

217 Zimmern to C. P. Scott, 13 June 1919 (*Guardian* arch., A/N2/4).

218 Namier to Scott, 23 June 1919 (*Guardian* arch., A/N2/1a).

219 E. T. Scott to C. P. Scott, 31 Dec. 1919 (*Guardian* arch., A/N2/1a).

220 He is, however, exculpated in Bartłomiej Rusin, 'Lewis Namier a kwestia "linii Curzona" i kształtowania się polskiej granicy wschodniej po I wojnie światowej', *Studia z Dziejów Rosji i Europy Srodkowo-Wschodniej*, xlviii (2010), 95–116.

221 Piotr Eberhardt, 'The Curzon Line as the eastern boundary of Poland: the origins and the political background', *Geographica Polonica*, lxxxv (2012), 13.

222 Memo by Namier, 17 Jan. 1919 (FO 371/3897, file 12361).

223 FO 371/4379, fo. 71.

224 Davies, *White eagle, red star*, 167–70. The memorandum is at P.A., Lloyd George papers, LG/F/201/1/14.

225 *Manchester Guardian*, 27 Aug. 1920.

226 [Namier,] 'The new Polish government', *New Europe*, 5 Aug. 1920; [Namier,] 'Russian land and Polish men', ibid., 23 Sept. 1920. Another unsigned article on 'The international status of east Galicia', on 26 Aug. could well have been by Namier.

227 *Manchester Guardian*, 19 June 1922, 29 Mar., 8 June 1923.

4

In the margin of history, 1920–28

Oxford

Back in Oxford, Namier threw himself into the life of a tutor, and seems to have greatly enjoyed himself in the company of the young. The college authorities, who in the immediate aftermath of the war had been inundated by a record number of freshmen, were glad to send him undergraduates, for a fee of £5 each, and more came from Magdalen through the agency of Smith's son-in-law Murray Wrong, who was a fellow there. Namier also gave a course of formal lectures, at his own volition, for which at first he was not paid.[1] He may well have been imitating Smith in the manner of his relations with his pupils. He was also reliving his own undergraduate experiences at Balliol, when he had helped others with their studies.

He had always seemed more mature than his contemporaries. Now, fortified by his experiences in the Foreign Office, he was not only literally but temperamentally of a quite different generation from those he taught. Nonetheless, he treated them as equals. They never forgot the experience, and several wrote to Lady Namier with reminiscences when she was preparing her biography. Most said that they had counted Namier as a friend rather than a teacher, and several remained close to him throughout their lives, notably the diplomats Gladwyn Jebb and Ivo Mallet, and the maverick Conservative politician Robert Boothby. If accurate, Boothby's memory of how he acquired Namier as a tutor is particularly revealing, for it provides evidence not only of Namier's reputation in Oxford, but of his involvement with students socially. Although Namier's position was insecure, and he was overworking to a point where insomnia was again taking hold, he seems to have radiated self-confidence. Boothby, an undergraduate at Magdalen, was visiting Balliol when he ran across Namier in the front quad.

> He waved to me, and … when I reached his side, he said, 'You have been wasting your time by living a life of pure enjoyment. I am not against that. But you have done no real work, and if you want to get your degree, it is too late for reading or writing.' He gave a

deep sigh and then added, 'There is now only one hope. Talking.' 'To whom?' I asked. 'To me', he answered. I consulted the president of my own college about this, and he said: 'It is fortunate for you that your grandfather, and I myself, were at Balliol. Go to Namier.' I did. It was by far the wisest thing I have ever done in my life.'[2]

All Lady Namier's correspondents remembered Namier's 'passionate interest in his subject, the range of his knowledge, his wit and his talk', his love of argument, and abhorrence of vacuous generalisations unsupported by facts. There were occasional hints that the flow of conversation in his tutorials was one-sided, but few under-graduates object to a tutor doing most (if not all) of the talking, and Namier's ability to make the past come alive entranced his listeners. He was quite unlike anyone else they had encountered. One of his pupils commented, admittedly with the benefit of hindsight, 'we all knew he was a man of destiny and of a quite different mould from the other dons'.[3] It has to be said that they also found him outlandish and even a little alarming. When Boothby agreed to be best man at Gladwyn Jebb's wedding in 1929 he wondered whether Jebb had asked Namier to come. 'Appalling as the sight of that strange countenance must be upon any crucial occasion, it would delight him so much that I can find it in my heart to hope that you will take the risk of catching sight of him.'[4] This comment hints at what may have been the origin of the testimony of one former undergraduate that Namier had been 'somewhat cold-shouldered' in college, though on the other side of the argument it should be noted that Namier's lasting friendships from this period were not wholly confined to pupils.[5] The archae-ologist Denis Buxton, then secretary of the Balliol Junior Common Room, told Lady Namier: 'I don't remember how we became friends; it just happened.'[6]

Whether Namier was an effective teacher in terms of examination results is another matter: he may have made his students think about European history from a different perspective – Vienna rather than London – which transformed their understanding of the subject, but this preparation was not what was required.[7] He certainly did not emulate Smith's success as a crammer. Not all his pupils were as successful as Gladwyn Jebb. One of the brightest of Namier's Magdalen pupils, Peter Warren, a nephew of the college president, Sir Herbert Warren (and also of Lady Ottoline Morrell), was bit-terly disappointed not to have achieved his expected first, telling Jebb that he had not been properly prepared for the final examinations, and that in particular 'the second foreign [paper] did not give me or anyone who [had] been to Namier a chance'.[8] In Boothby's case, listening to Namier talk did not help him to anything better than a pass degree, though he was generous enough to say that in his own opinion he would have failed altogether without the benefit of these impromptu lectures.

Namier and Clara had decamped from London to an Oxford flat, 'across the bridge from Magdalen, above a choice and fancy grocer's shop'.[9] Namier resumed his intimacy with the Smiths, and found another surrogate family in the household of Kenneth and Esther Bell, whose children also called him 'Uncle Lewis'.[10] He also saw a great deal of T. E. Lawrence, who was living an unfulfilled and unsettled life as a fellow of All Souls. Through Lawrence he met, among others, the poet Robert Graves.[11] And when he could find the time he was busy with journalism, for the *New Europe* and the *Manchester Guardian*. These articles provide evidence of an abatement of his previous radical fervour. There was clearly a conflict in his mind between, on the one hand, a personal sorrow at the dissolution of aristocratic estates like Koszylowce, exacerbated by a profound distrust of revolutionary populism, and on the other, a commitment to justice for the oppressed Ukrainian peasantry, with all their faults:

> One naturally watches with regret the disappearance of manor house, homes of a higher civilisation and centres of better agriculture than that of peasant huts. But agrarian reform must not be made the weapon of an aggressive jingoism, whether of the nobles or of the new fashionable democracy.[12]

He was also working at history. The book about the American crisis, whose completion he had declared for the best part of a decade to be his prime ambition, and with which he intended to 'revolutionise our conceptions of eighteenth-century English history', was still under way.[13] This much is clear from a correspondence in March 1921 with the editor of the *Spectator*, John St Loe Strachey, whose son was one of Namier's pupils at Balliol. Namier had been using his college contacts to search for material on individual MPs, and had posed several 'conundrums' to Strachey relating to his ancestors. He was especially interested in members with strong commercial connections, such as East Indiamen.[14] But the parliamentarians of eighteenth-century England had to compete for his attention with the great questions of European history. When still at the Foreign Office he had developed an idea for another grand project: a history of Europe from 1812 to 1918. This appears to have temporarily supplanted his concern to elucidate the problem of the American revolution. The ambition to write a history of nineteenth-century Europe would remain with him until almost the end of his days. He spent some of his time at Balliol researching the revolutions of 1848, an interest which would eventually issue two decades later in a short and still famous work: *1848: the revolution of the intellectuals.*[15]

Namier was also writing on the recent past, in particular the post-war dissolution of the Austro-Hungarian empire. He had already drafted an extended chapter on 'The downfall of the Habsburg monarchy' which had been commissioned in 1919 for the massive, six-volume *History of the peace conference of Paris*, edited by Harold Temperley.[16] This was the first significant venture produced by Lionel

Curtis's recently established Institute for the Study of International Relations, and many of Namier's colleagues in the PID contributed to it, their participation specifically sanctioned by the foreign secretary.[17] Namier saw his chapter as something that would further enhance his reputation, and spent a great deal of time in polishing the text. It represented his last word on the defunct Habsburg state, and repeated ideas that he had already advanced in articles and unpublished memoranda.

He began by setting out the structural weaknesses of the Austro-Hungarian polity after 1848, its dependence on privileging larger national groups against minorities, and the consequences of the defeat by Prussia in 1867, which had tied Austria to Prussia's coat-tails and turned its focus away from Germany and towards its eastern territories. The Poles had then become the third of the 'superior nationalities' within the empire – alongside the Germans and Magyars – linked to the Austrians by their Roman Catholic religion, and privileged in particular against the Ukrainians in Galicia. The core of the chapter was a heavily structured narrative of political changes during the Great War and its aftermath with, inevitably, a strong emphasis on the Polish question. He argued that, despite its early promise, the Russian revolution had not produced a widespread social revolution across central and eastern Europe, for 'the socialist intelligentsia' had 'all alike been educated in nationalist ideologies', and 'cultivated nationality with a radicalism peculiar to their nature and ideas … based upon the living popular masses'.[18] The final outcome, the dissolution of the Austrian empire into independent states based on the constituent nationalities, was inevitable and not something over which tears should be shed.[19]

In December 1920 Balliol extended its financial arrangement with Namier by agreeing to add to his remuneration a further £10, 'in recognition of the value of lectures given voluntarily by him'.[20] But the colleges for whom he taught were slow to pay, and five years later he was still waiting for the balance of his money.[21] He did not do enough journalism to make up the deficiency, and his income from other sources, including shares, was insufficient for a married man with a wife at home.[22] So in the winter of 1920–21 he found himself trying to teach as many as forty-five tutorial pupils, an excessive workload that he may also have undertaken in a vain effort to impress college and university authorities. He spent all day at tutorials, beginning at nine o'clock in the morning, and seeing pupils at intervals of three quarters of an hour, which naturally exhausted him.[23]

There was still no prospect of a permanent post in Oxford despite Namier's appetite for work, his well-nigh unique knowledge of nineteenth- and early twentieth-century European history, and the brilliance of his writing, as evinced in his chapter in the *History of the peace conference*, which some considered the best in the book.[24] Senior common rooms were wary of him. Beyond the undeniable fact that he had acquired a reputation as a bore, and a particularly relentless and aggressive one, it is possible that a form of anti-Semitism was again involved, engendered by Namier's pro-Zionist views. Radical opinions were not in themselves a problem, particularly in Balliol, and in any case he had now retreated far from his initial enthusiasm for the Russian revolution, though he still told his pupils that 'if Britain wished to influence policy or events east of the Rhine, she must co-operate either with Germany or with Russia'.[25] The extent of his commitment to Zionism was a different matter, and was becoming increasingly obvious. His main point of contact was Leonard Stein, now political secretary of the Zionist Organisation, to whom Namier sent advice based on his intimate knowledge of the Foreign Office mind.[26] On one occasion he arranged for Stein to come back to Balliol to talk to the 'young men'.[27] Zionism attracted the sympathy of many in British public life, but did not appeal to everyone, and some in Oxford may have felt uncomfortable with Namier's involvement in the cause. Even A. L. Smith, although broadly sympathetic to the plight of eastern European Jewry, rejected the Zionist ambition for a Jewish homeland in Palestine if this meant the expropriation of Arabs.[28]

Namier was certainly the target of anti-Semites on the extreme right who, following the Balfour declaration and the emergence of Zionism as a significant political movement in Britain, had become even more vocal and venomous. When John St Loe Strachey casually informed his friend Lord Sydenham, the reactionary head of the British Empire League, that his son's tutor at Balliol was 'a very clever Zionist Jew called Namier ... who during the war did work at the War Office [sic]' his remarks uncorked a foam of apoplectic fury:

> Your letter is very interesting. A clever Zionist Jew don teaching history at Balliol! And employed in the War Office during the war! The 'Protocols' exactly. I am sure you know that there is now a strong corrupting influence at poor old Oxford ... *Cherchez le Juif.*[29]

Sydenham's fulminations remained private, but Namier was also cited publicly in *Plain English*, the extreme right-wing magazine founded by Lord Alfred Douglas, whose world-view was also centred on a belief in the authenticity of the notorious 'Protocols of Zion'. In May 1921 *Plain English* drew attention to the involvement of 'Namier, formerly Bernstein' in determining the Foreign Office's view on 'the so-called pogroms in Poland'. The following November, in a preposterous article, Namier was blamed for having led astray Oxford undergraduates to follow a path of Bolshevism and free love. According to Douglas's successor as editor of *Plain English*, the university had gone to pot 'since Russian Jews have been permitted to run and froth at large': 'Why the master of Balliol ever let Namier – a masquerading Jew – into his house and his confidence we shall probably never know'.[30]

In some quarters in Oxford such vituperation may even have produced a reaction in Namier's favour, though not a sufficiently strong reaction to persuade a college to employ him. His own response would have been robust. He had not been intimidated by similar attacks while at the Foreign Office, and it is easy to see him treating these latest outbursts with scorn. In fact it is likely that the experience of being denounced in the gutter press propelled him into a clearer sense of his own self-determination and an even stronger identification with the Zionist movement.

What did upset Namier was an increasing realisation that his ambition to re-establish himself in Oxford would not be fulfilled. It was a second refusal, not as direct as the first, when All Souls had rejected him, but equally painful; possibly more so, since this time it carried an air of permanence. And the distress was compounded by failures in his personal life. His marriage was unhappy, partly because a punishing work schedule kept him away from home for long periods. It was obvious that, despite the physical attraction between them, he and Clara were incompatible. All this was made worse by Namier's fractured relations with his family. The difficult political situation in Galicia, and in Poland more generally, even after the conclusion of hostilities with Soviet Russia in March 1921, heaped hardships on the Niemirowski household. Namier suggested that his parents partly blamed him for their difficulties, because of the notoriety he had gained in the Viennese and Polish press. He had certainly moved far from them in terms of his politics. It is easy to understand how perplexed Józef, Anna and Teodora would have been by Ludwik's pronouncements on Galicia, after they themselves had suffered physical injury and seen their property pillaged by the very Ukrainians whose cause he espoused.

A visit by Teodora to London in 1920 brought these tensions to a crisis. To say that she and Clara did not get on would be an understatement. According to Lady Namier, 'they loathed each other on sight'.[31] Namier's marriage thus became another source of grievance for his family: he had thrown himself away on a frivolous woman who may have been fit to be a mistress but should never have been taken as a wife by a 'man of standing'. At least this was his own recollection of what must have been some very difficult conversations. We have to tread carefully, however, since Namier's memories may well have been tainted by subsequent events. Moreover, while Lady Namier depicted Teodora as 'haughty' and cold, Namier's friends remembered her as vivacious and amusing; suggestive, although not by itself any kind of proof, that Namier's version was a partial one.

Whatever Teodora's opinion of his marriage and the effect this might have had on Namier's frame of mind, she also brought news about the family which disturbed him. While mother and daughter were struggling to keep afloat at Koszylowce, Józef had settled in Vienna, where he ought to have been raising funds for the restoration of his house and estate but was frittering away time and money. Teodora persuaded Namier to leave England, and Clara, during the summer of 1920, and travel to Vienna to keep an eye on his father. There he found the city and the country on the verge of political, economic and social collapse: 'a state of acute and infectious disorientation which reminded him of a war-weary person vulnerable to the Spanish influenza'.[32] Revolution was daily expected. As the value of the Austrian krone spiralled downwards, food became prohibitively expensive and obtainable only through the black market. The writer Stefan Zweig, another who had returned to Austria from Switzerland after the end of the war, vividly remembered 'my first sight of the yellow and dangerous eyes of famine'.[33]

For a few weeks Namier kept his father company in this decaying and dangerous city. Two of Józef's siblings resided in the Viennese suburbs: his sister Anna (Anka), a piano teacher, and his youngest brother, the biochemist Salomon Bernstein, who in a strange arrangement had married his own niece, Rachel (Szela) Parnas. Rachel's sister Maria was also living there with her husband, a cloth manufacturer of Bohemian origin named Alfred Hirsch.[34] Namier resumed his acquaintance with Teodora's glamorous friend Marie Beer, and through Salomon and Szela Bernstein got to know the psychologist Theodor Reik, a protégé of Freud, who first suggested to Namier that his debilitating insomnia might be curable by psychoanalysis. Namier would subsequently become a patient of Reik's, but for the time being he was too busy shadowing Józef. Inevitably father and son quarrelled: about money, about the politics of east Galicia, and possibly also about Zionism. When Józef forbade his son from accompanying him back to Koszylowce, where as a prominent Ukrainian sympathiser his presence was bound to cause problems for the family, their estrangement seemed complete.

This time, a return to Oxford failed to restore Namier's equilibrium. His marriage was in terminal decline: Clara was becoming more distant and distrait, and he sought solace away from home, in the company of friends like the Bells and T. E. Lawrence. Hopes of a future in university teaching were also disintegrating in front of his eyes. A. L. Smith, his great patron and supporter, was in poor health (he died in 1924) and could do little to help him. Eventually, alternative avenues of employment opened up which he felt he could not refuse. First he was offered the opportunity to submit articles as a foreign correspondent for the *Manchester Guardian*, and then Smith introduced him to a man called Noel Rawnsley, who was engaged in shipping raw cotton from England to be worked up in mills in Bohemia, and needed someone on the spot to take charge of his interests. The link came through Rawnsley's deceased father, Canon Hardwicke Rawnsley (a friend of Beatrix Potter), who had been at Balliol. Noel turned out to have a poor head for business. He quickly ran through the fortune he had inherited, and was declared bankrupt in December 1922. But in April 1921, when he offered Namier a three-year contract to manage the cotton exporting business, plus a share of the profits, he must have been plausible: his Czech venture had made £3,500 over the preceding three years.[35] It seemed too good an opportunity to refuse. With the fees for newspaper articles added in, Namier calculated that he would soon make enough money to finance his historical work. As Rawnsley's agent in Prague he would be within easy reach of Vienna, where he could turn to Alfred Hirsch for advice on the cotton trade, and where the presence of Marie Beer exerted a powerful attraction. He signed the contract, and when Trinity (summer) term was over took the boat train for the continent, leaving Clara to her own devices.

Prague and Vienna

While it had a lively intellectual and cultural life, Prague in 1921 was not yet the capital of modernism that it would shortly become, and while he stayed there Namier does not seem to have imbibed the atmosphere of the avant-garde. Instead, the milieu in which he moved was quintessentially bourgeois, the world of politicians, bureaucrats and businessmen, in their baroque palaces and art nouveau office-blocks. It was a period of rapid change that must have fascinated the apprentice historian: Prague was recovering from the traumatic collapse of Habsburg rule and witnessing the establishment of a Czechoslovak republic. Namier's previous acquaintance with Masaryk, the president of the new state, and the strong support he had himself given the Czech cause, ensured that he was welcome in the halls of government. Even though anti-Semitism was rife, and there was a recent history of violent attacks on the large Jewish community in the old town, Masaryk, who was himself sympathetic to Jewish grievances, had ensured that the constitution recognised the rights of Jews as a national minority. Namier must have sensed the tension felt by Prague's Jewish community, but – quite unlike his attitude to developments in Polish politics – his admiration for Masaryk overrode any inclination to question the ethos of this particular version of Slavic nationalism.[36] His principal memories were of lengthy conversations with the president, in Prague and at Masaryk's official country residence, the seventeenth-century chateau at Lány, 35 kilometres outside the city. This was exalted company for a young man who was at this point in his career no more than a part-time journalist without permanent employment.

Through Masaryk and Edvard Beneš, who was now prime minister, Namier met other members of the government, including the finance minister, Alois Rašin. According to Lady Namier, Rašin 'initiated L[ewis] into the financial subtleties of nation-wide industries, international concerns, and inter-state monetary operations'.[37] A lawyer by training, Rašin had achieved the remarkable feat of creating a stable Czechoslovak currency, the krone, out of the financial morass caused by the dissolution of the Austro-Hungarian empire, while at the same time avoiding rampant inflation. These policies came at a great cost to the ordinary people of Czechoslovakia, and in 1923 Rašin was assassinated by a communist bank clerk, but his successes made a great impact on Namier, who was much exercised by the contrasting situation in the new Polish state in which his family's fortunes were deteriorating. He was also impressed by Rašin's sophisticated understanding of the workings of currency markets, and of the ways in which movements might be anticipated to advantage. The articles that he sent to the *Manchester Guardian Commercial* (as 'a special correspondent'), were fixated on the currency question.[38] It was only later that he grasped how the rising value of the krone was making business impossible for Czech manufacturers, including Rawnsley's customers, whose orders were falling away.[39] At first he was more interested in opportunities than potential hardships and, fortified by inside information on the Czechoslovak government's future fiscal policy, began to shift his money between currencies, making windfall profits.[40] This was just as well, considering that his principal source of income, the cotton importing business, was about to collapse.

While Czechoslovakia exuded a sense of 'easy, comfortable, well-being', life was very different in Austria, which Namier visited frequently; indeed, for a time he shuttled between Prague and Vienna, and even on occasion ventured further afield, into the Balkans.[41] The primary object of these trips was to prepare his newspaper articles, but they also served a social purpose, since not only were several of his relations living in Vienna; friends and some former pupils from Oxford had also congregated there.[42] Namier made family visits, bringing money (in sterling) to give to his young cousins. For accommodation he preferred the creature comforts of the Hotel Sacher.[43] It was, he reassured his readers in the *Manchester Guardian Commercial*, 'one of the very best hotels' in the city.[44]

While Namier had been unaffected by the prevailing popular anti-Semitism in Prague, he reacted strongly in Vienna against what he saw as the timorous self-denial of assimilationist Jews.[45] The fact that many of them still hankered after the imperial past was an additional provocation. The Austrian capital was an extreme example of what he later described as 'the discoloured and discolouring surroundings of central European town life, where comparatively small communities of educated Jews, no longer rooted in the faith and no more in touch with the Jewish masses, tended to succumb to the nondescript, standardised average which is typical of Germany and her intellectual satellites'.[46] Viennese Jews controlled the industry and trade of the city, and were among the leaders of its intellectual and cultural elite, but, as Namier

became more aware of his own Jewishness, their cosmopolitanism and sophistication, which had briefly impressed him as a boy, appeared less admirable. 'In 1921, on
my first visit to Vienna after the war', he wrote, some twenty years later,

> I happened to engage in a discussion about Jewish nationalism and Zionism with one of
> those high-minded, broad-minded, open-minded, shallow-minded Jews who prefer to
> call themselves anything rather than Jews. 'First and foremost', he declared in a pompous
> manner, 'I am a human being.' I replied … 'I, too, once thought so; but I have discovered
> since that all are agreed that I am a Jew, and not all that I am a human being. I have there-
> fore come to consider myself first a Jew, and only in the second place a human being.'[47]

While in Vienna Namier took up Reik's suggestion of psychoanalysis, with mixed
results: Lady Namier reported that her husband detested Reik personally and soon
abandoned any hope of receiving real assistance from his ministrations. But Namier
did not give up the couch for many years, and his supposed disavowal of 'trick-
cyclists' fits in rather too neatly with his widow's prejudices to be entirely credible. At
about this time he also began an affair with Marie Beer, which he kept a secret from
everyone except Reik. The lovers met regularly in Vienna, and Namier arranged that
they could spend time together in clandestine assignations in Venice while he was
ostensibly on his way to see his father in Italy. Marie was no longer the beauty she had
been when she had captured the young Ludwik's heart nearly two decades before,
but retained much of her charm despite the reduced circumstances in which she was
forced to live; indeed, for Namier her financial dependence may have heightened her
attractiveness. Doubtless Reik would have made much of the fact that she had first
been his sister's friend and that their first encounters had occurred in a family context.

Despite these diversions, the situation in Vienna in 1921–22 was dire, at least for
the Viennese. 'Some indescribable catastrophe was expected to set in any day.'[48]
Desperation did not attend anyone from England with sterling in his pocket, for
whom it was 'dog-cheap to live', but the atmosphere was still oppressive: as one visitor put it, 'hot, dusty, dirty, unsafe'.[49] Namier was particularly concerned at the fate
of what he called 'the submerged middle class', those engaged in 'commerce, finance,
administration, literature etc.', many of whom were Jewish, including members of
his own family. These *nouveaux pauvres* had no one to speak for them, and in the
years after the Great War had been 'subjected to a long strain of poverty', which had
lain waste the dazzling city of his childhood. Paradoxically, while he held no brief for
the empire and its institutions, and expressed contempt for the assimilationist Jews
who had flourished in pre-war society, part of him regretted the dissolution of the
old Vienna: 'here one of the finest cultures in Europe is dying a slow death'.[50] This
was not unlike his love–hate relationship with the Galician aristocracy, who were
simultaneously an alien ruling class and a bastion of civilised values.

Namier's newspaper articles diagnosed Austria's troubles not only in economic but also in political terms. In contrast to the successful coalition of 1918–19, in which the Social Democrats had in Namier's view saved Austria from revolution,[51] the present, more conservative, government was incompetent. More generally, Austrians were the victims of nostalgia for a lost imperial past. Rehearsing his prejudices, he noted the unwillingness of the Roman Catholic church to part with its riches to help the poor, and the baleful intrusion of bureaucracy into all aspects of Austrian life. Distaste for the Austrian political system, and a belief that Germany's present weakness was only an 'artificial eclipse', persuaded him that union with Germany, which most Austrians wanted and the Allies had forbidden, was the only means by which Austria could recover.[52] His justification for *Anschluss* was an appreciation that the Austrian national identity was essentially German. This was an interesting exception to his general disapproval of German 'linguistic nationalism', and seems to have been driven by an immediate, practical concern for the beleaguered Viennese bourgeoisie.

In 1922 Namier predicted that the Austrians would not be able put their economy in order, but he was wrong. When he returned to Vienna in the spring of 1923 he found that Chancellor Seipel – a priest and exactly the kind of clerical politician Namier despised – had stabilised the krone. Namier remained suspicious. Clerical conservatives were not people to embrace the ideas of 'modern trade and finance': thorough reform required cooperation with the socialists. Instead, what had been produced was a temporary boom fuelled by inflation. Characteristically, the Viennese were again falling prey to 'mass delusions', this time a mania for speculation, afflicting all ranks of society, down to 'the waiter from the restaurant … the flapper typist and the shop assistant'.[53] This was creating a minor social revolution, with the old 'leisured class' replaced by a rabble of *nouveaux riches*, a development which reawakened Namier's distaste for petit bourgeois culture. 'Opinions may differ', he wrote,

> as to whether there should be at all a vast class of people living in opulence on unearned income. Still, whatever view is held, no one would wish the place of those cultured, though perhaps unduly expensive, heirs of the 'unbought grace of life' to be taken by inflation profiteers. These people, thrown up in great numbers by the financial revolutions of inflation, can now be seen, heard and admired in every luxury hotel or restaurant in Vienna and Berlin, or driving through their streets in gaudy motor-cars, with hooters enough to destroy the ears, nerves and patience of their fellow men.[54]

Namier himself continued to live comfortably: he stayed either at the Hotel Sacher or with wealthy friends (one letter gave his address as 'c/o Countess Königsegg', in a handsome apartment block well inside the Ringstrasse).[55] But his income was precarious: he relied on journalism for the left-leaning Viennese *Neue Freie Presse* and the *Manchester Guardian*, for which he was paid per article, and the returns on his investments on the London stock exchange.[56]

Although Namier's letters do not betray any sense of grievance, he cannot have failed to compare his own circumstances with the leisure and security enjoyed by those with academic posts in Oxford. He had not given up his ambition to write history: he was reviewing works on European affairs for English newspapers and periodicals, including memoirs and official publications relating to the Great War, and in March 1923 offered the *Manchester Guardian* a series of articles based on the material in the newly published volumes of German Foreign Office documents from the era of Bismarck, which he was 'working through slowly and systematically, with a view to my general work on recent European politics'.[57] Nor had he abandoned his great plans for an Anglo-American history. Back in England briefly during the winter of 1923–24 (to cover the general election for the *Neue Freie Presse*), he spent time reading in the Newcastle papers in the British Museum, and arranged to have the notes he had previously made in New York, London and Oxford brought together and sorted by a secretary, something he was never very good at doing himself.[58]

Intellectually, Vienna in the early 1920s was, like Prague, an exciting place to be, and here Namier does seem to have interested himself in the circulation of new ideas. Although we have no explicit evidence, it would be surprising if his commitment to 'scientific' history was not influenced – or at least confirmed – by exposure to the logical positivism of the Vienna Circle of philosophers. And certainly, through Theodor Reik, he came into contact with the latest developments in Freudian psychology. However jaundiced his opinion of Reik, Namier was both intrigued and influenced by Freud. The argument that the subconscious mind shaped conscious thought fitted with notions that Namier had imbibed from his university teachers in Lausanne and the LSE, and, indeed, had worked out for himself. Given the constant friction with Józef, Freud's particular concern with the conflict between fathers and sons also provided Namier with a key to understanding his own disturbed mental state. He may not have adopted Freud's theories lock, stock and barrel, but was keen to use the potential insights offered by Freudian psychology to understand the eighteenth- and nineteenth-century politicians whom he studied, usually focusing on their family relationships and childhood experiences.

Namier must have been aware of other currents agitating the Viennese intelligentsia. His aunt Anka was not only an assistant to the renowned piano teacher Richard Robert, but was also a neighbour of Arnold Schoenberg. However, Namier was not musically inclined, and the revolutionary impact of the Second Viennese School meant little to him. Expressionism in art was a different matter. Lady Namier recalled that 'though L[ewis] never understood modern art, he continued to find it stimulating'.[59] This fascination did not extend to abstract painting, which he considered pointless: in his view, while music could express emotions directly, art had always to take as its basis some kind of representation of the visual form.[60] At the same time, he was convinced that the purpose of art had to be more than a mere naturalistic rendition of the appearance of the subject. In a reflection on history as a discipline, he once wrote that: 'The function of the historian is akin to that of the painter and not of the photographic camera: to discover and set forth, to single out and stress that which is of the nature of the thing, and not to reproduce indiscriminately all that meets the eye.'[61] Modern artists could do this as well, if not better, than the painters of the past. He noted that his friend T. E. Lawrence 'was fond of Cubist paintings, and his statements sometimes partook of a Cubist character. It was easy to arraign them on formal grounds, but if probed they would often be found to express the truth better than would a formally correct account.'[62]

Among the pictures that Namier himself owned was a print by Picasso.[63] We have no direct evidence of his views on painting in the early 1920s, but in one of his articles on the Austrian economy there is a hint that his contempt for bourgeois taste extended to the visual arts. Seeing the poverty and hunger on the streets of Vienna in 1922, he suggested that the city fathers sell some of their treasures for the benefit of the poor: 'Without suggestion of cannibalism, could not Rubens' fat men and women, who crowd the walls of the late imperial museum, be used to provide food?'[64]

Estrangements

Namier's experiences in Prague and Vienna may have sharpened the edges of his intellect, but the really important events, which were to have cataclysmic effects on his personality, were taking place elsewhere. The first was the ruination of his marriage. He was living apart from Clara before he took up his position in Czechoslovakia. At some point in 1922 she told him that she had found someone else who suited her much better. This man had asked her to go with him to north America, where he had been offered a job. Lady Namier's version naturally shows Namier in a positive light: the put-upon husband, seeking to accommodate his errant wife, and doing whatever was reasonable in order to make life easy for her. All we know for certain is that Namier agreed to a legal separation from Clara in November 1922. According to her solicitors, the couple were at one point 'considering the question of divorce', but interest in this may have come solely from Clara. At any rate, a deed of separation was all that was agreed.[65] And eventually, after a rigmarole about her travel plans, Clara embarked at Southampton on 31 March 1923 as a second-class passenger on the *Aquitania* en route for New York.

As for her supposed paramour, Namier identified him as John Davenport, a married man with children, though he said he knew nothing more than this, and because Clara always referred to her lover as 'Davenport', he thought (not entirely seriously) that the man's name could have been Davenport John. Neither name appears on the *Aquitania* passenger list. A. J. P. Taylor, in whose house in Oxford Clara spent her last days, and who went through her possessions after her death, firmly believed that there was no 'other man' at all and that Clara had made him up as an excuse to leave her husband.[66] Assuming Davenport did exist, he may not have been, as Namier (through his wife) has led us to believe, entirely an intruder into the marriage, someone Clara had met on her own and with whom she had begun a relationship of which her husband remained ignorant until she announced her intention to leave. It is possible that he was known to both partners, for there is a teasing reference in Namier's correspondence in 1913, when A. L. Smith wrote to him about 'your man Davenport', whom Namier seems to have recommended to Smith and to Lionel Curtis.[67] If Davenport had been known to Namier, his appearance as Clara's lover would have been even more humiliating.

The separation, and Clara's departure for America, was not in itself a personal disaster: to all intents and purposes husband and wife were already separated, and, although by nature uxorious, Namier had some compensation for the loss of Clara in his deepening affair with Marie Beer. But the formal end of the marriage proved his sister's judgment correct, and the painful recognition of this fact doubtless aggravated his conflicted feelings towards his family. His aunt Anka remembered the awkwardness that attended a visit made by Józef, Anna and Teodora to Vienna in the autumn of 1921. Hearing that Ludwik would soon be in the city and had arranged to meet his parents there, 'I … asked them to say I would be happy to see him. But his mother, gone very hard, said "Better not!" When I said "Yes!" she strongly opposed me without explaining. But Dziunia honoured my request, and he came the day after he saw them.'[68] This episode does not in itself prove that Namier's mother had 'broken with' him, as Lady Namier's book alleged. It is just as likely that she, as well as her husband, regarded Ludwik as impossible, largely because of his unaccountable political views and the vehemence with which he expressed them.[69]

Matters worsened dramatically in April 1922, when Józef died suddenly on holiday at Merano in the Italian Tyrol. Namier was in Genoa, attending a conference on behalf of the *Manchester Guardian*, and did not hear the news until too late (and then only from Marie Beer, who sent him a note of condolence). He missed the funeral, and blamed his sister, who had not wired to him at the Hotel Sacher; instead she had sent the telegram to his business address in Prague. His reaction only increased the distance between them. An even greater blow was to fall the following year, when

Teodora married a Polish Catholic landowner from Galicia, Tadeusz Modzelewski, a man some years her senior. Namier was invited to the wedding, which took place in a convent in Lwów, but having by then discovered that his father had left the Galician property to Teodora, refused to attend.

A further invitation to visit Koszylowce, the estate he had imagined would one day be his, provoked him beyond endurance: he declared that he would never go there as a guest. In consequence, he never saw his mother or his sister again, though he evidently kept in touch with them. Eventually, he found it possible to forgive his father. Years later, when in Merano, he made a point of visiting Józef's grave, a pilgrimage which affected him deeply; he made arrangements for its upkeep and to replace the black wooden cross which had been the only marker of his father's final resting place.[70]

Within three years Namier had become disillusioned by the Foreign Office and disappointed at Oxford; he had endured the failure of his marriage; his father had died and he had become distanced from his immediate family; and he had been robbed of his dream of acting the part of the country gentleman (if only occasionally) in a restored Koszylowce. It was no wonder that he turned to psychoanalysis to understand his troubles. By all accounts he suffered a kind of nervous breakdown: insomnia became a permanent affliction, and he may have begun to experience the creeping paralysis in his right hand which in later years would make writing almost impossible.[71] The effects were described as a kind of writer's cramp, and at least one of his analysts considered it to be psychosomatic (though this would not necessarily be the view of medical science today).[72] His deterioration was obvious. In October 1923 one of 'Baffy' Dugdale's friends commiserated with her on hearing that 'Namier's nerves have gone again, in spite of his mumbo-jumbo'.[73]

London

The only real cure was work, and more particularly, 'history work'. Namier came back to England for good in February 1925, but rather than embarking on his history of nineteenth-century Europe, threw himself into research on eighteenth-century England. This could be interpreted as symbolically shaking off the dust of his own past. Indeed, he wrote nothing on European history for the next seven years, other than the occasional book review. His first port of call was Oxford, to which he had always presumed that he would return, having kept his bank account there ever since he had been an undergraduate.[74] But he soon decided 'to settle permanently in London',[75] where he would be close to the British Museum and his most important sources, and also close to influential friends. At first he rented two rooms 'on the top floor of a tiny house' at 21 Glebe Place, off the King's Road in Chelsea, with a temperamental Irish landlady, Mrs O'Grady.[76] From there he eventually moved back to familiar haunts in Kensington, and to a room in a Regency terrace at 15 Gloucester Walk, off Church Street, where he was to stay for two decades.

How was Namier to support himself while he carried out his research? He still had his shares, but the income from dividends was scarcely enough to support the life of an independent scholar, especially one who felt it imperative to employ a full-time secretary (at £4 a week). Inevitably, Namier would quickly run through the capital he had accumulated on the continent.[77] His first hope was to secure an arrangement with the *Manchester Guardian* of the kind that he had mooted to the editor, C. P. Scott, in 1919, to write regularly for a retainer. Unfortunately, he was obliged to inform Scott that it would be impossible for him to write anything 'of an editorial character', since the paper's opinions on foreign policy – especially in relation to Poland – were now diametrically opposed to his own. In particular, Namier deplored Scott's support for a French guarantee of Poland's western borders against Germany. He had already written trenchantly on this subject in the columns of the *Guardian* only five days before asking for a job, which cannot have put Scott in a receptive mood.[78] Namier added, however, rather grandly, that if articles 'on foreign politics … of a purely matter-of-fact, informative character' were required, he would 'consider how I could fit it in with my own historical work'.[79] It was an offer Scott found easy to refuse.[80] Namier contributed a short piece on Polish affairs to the columns of the *Guardian* in the following June, and in August a lengthy obituary of Conrad von Hötzendorf, the Austrian chief of staff at the outbreak of the Great War; but nothing more.[81] He did not even review again for the paper until he came to Manchester as professor of modern history in 1931, by which time Scott was no longer editor.

There were other newspapers and weekly magazines, of course. But short articles and book reviews, mainly for the *Times Literary Supplement* and the *Spectator*, were not lucrative: Namier himself calculated that he made £60 a year from this kind of work, the equivalent of about £3,200 today.[82] Things were already becoming desperate in August 1925 when he returned to Vienna in order to attend his first Zionist Congress. He was coming round to a firm engagement with the Zionist position, though as late as 1923 admitted that he still found 'strange' the idea of a Jewish homeland in Palestine. His ticket for the congress arrived courtesy of Walter Layton, the editor of the *Economist*, and he attended 'nominally as a correspondent' for the magazine, though nothing by him on the subject appeared in print.[83] In general he was unimpressed by the delegates and the debates, but spent a good deal of time with Chaim Weizmann, and was enthralled: Weizmann became his ideal of the charismatic leader of a nation 'in bondage', and although he never glossed over

Weizmann's failings as a politician he became a devoted follower.[84] Their relationship was so close that it is tempting to infer that Weizmann became a substitute for the father Namier had lost. Just as he had been with Józef, Namier was by turns idolatrous and exasperated, and occasionally struck with jealousy of any rival for Weizmann's favour.[85]

For his part, Weizmann quickly clutched at this second chance to recruit someone of Namier's obvious ability. The Zionist Organisation was about to lose the services of its political secretary, Leonard Stein, and Weizmann offered Namier the position, to start in October 1926. Here at last was a secure income, but it came at a cost, and so Namier's acceptance was strictly conditional. He agreed, 'provided they advance me the money I require in the meantime so that I could concentrate entirely on my history work without having to earn my livelihood'.[86] In the event, Stein's departure was delayed, but it was not a case of Namier pricing himself out of the market again, for, despite a chronic lack of funds, the Zionist Organisation was still prepared to lend him money in expectation that he would eventually come to work for them.[87] On reflection he was unhappy with this outcome, seeing it as an inappropriate use of the organisation's resources in view of 'the situation which we now have to cope with in Palestine' (the use of the personal pronoun is significant), and also perhaps because deep down he did not want to abandon his research for full-time employment, however worthy the cause.[88] He had come to accept the inevitable, that his book would take longer to complete than he had imagined (an experience to be repeated throughout his life). So it was with the greatest reluctance that he accepted a loan of £100 from the Zionists. At the same time he inquired about raising a further £350 (nearly £20,000 in present-day terms) on his several life insurance policies.[89] In desperation he also asked G. N. Clark, happily ensconced at Oriel College, whether there might be any opportunity to give lectures in Oxford, which would afford security for a bank loan: sadly, but predictably, there was none.[90]

Other friends came to his rescue. John Wheeler-Bennett, who had worked with Blanche Dugdale in the League of Nations Union, and who was independently wealthy, lent £500, to be paid in equal quarterly instalments, and repaid whenever Namier should be 'in a position to do so'.[91] Then there was the Rhodes Trust, which was intimately connected with Lionel Curtis's circle and the Round Table. Its secretary was none other than Philip Kerr, and in August 1926 Namier approached Kerr to see whether the trustees would make him a grant of £600 for the completion of his book, given its importance to imperial history and Anglo-American relations in general. He thought that he could publish the first part within a year if he had a free run, and the means to pay a secretary.[92] Determined to do his best for Namier, Kerr sought testimonials from H. A. L. Fisher and the imperial historian H. E. Egerton, who had been at All Souls ever since 1906 and had thus witnessed Namier's repeated rejection by the college. Kerr also alerted Curtis, in order that he might assist Fisher and Egerton to a proper appreciation of Namier's abilities.[93] The tactics worked: both referees supported the application, though Egerton managed to include one negative observation, to the effect that Namier, while 'a very conscientious and zealous worker', had 'one weak point … being that he has possibly an exaggerated view of himself'.[94]

The trustees awarded a grant, albeit only half of what Namier had asked for.[95] In conversation with Whitney Shepardson, yet another of Namier's old friends involved in Rhodes Trust business, Kerr had been led to believe that some money might be forthcoming from the Commonwealth Fund, so Namier promptly wrote to Shepardson, and followed this up with a further inquiry about the Carnegie Fund: neither produced any result.[96] The Rhodes grant and Wheeler-Bennett's loan proved enough to maintain employment for Namier's 'devoted, untiring' secretary, Miss Le Marinel.[97] It also paved the way for Namier to move from the attic in Glebe Place to Gloucester Walk. Baffy was, however, determined to shore up her friend's finances further. Through her own Zionist contacts she contacted the millionaire American philanthropist Julius Rosenwald, who, with his son William (known to friends as 'Rufus'), made Namier a further advance of £1,200, in two yearly instalments in 1927 and 1928, paid through Baffy as if 'from an anonymous friend'.[98]

This hand-to-mouth existence, in rented rooms, and the twin embarrassments of having to go cap in hand to institutions and having to accept substantial personal loans, did nothing to make Namier sit any easier in his view of the world and the way his life was going. To an Oxford friend he dramatised his plight as equivalent to 'starving in a garret', and he subsequently resolved never to endure the same uncertainties again.[99] 'In desperate cases', he wrote in 1929, 'one may undertake a thing and damn the consequences, or trust the future to take care of itself; in other words, enter on mad adventures … I let myself in for my own history work without sufficient financial cover, and I can say I really have paid the price for it.'[100] He was deeply impressed by individuals who showed him any generosity, such as the elderly Captain William Godsal, who not only allowed Namier to consult manuscripts in his house at Haines Hill in Berkshire, but also invited him to stay the weekend and pressed on him offers of service: 'Before I left, old Godsal (who knows that I am poor) shook me warmly by the hand and whispered to me, "If you ever want anything, old man, tell me."' Namier, overwhelmed, thought him 'the kindest man I have ever met'.[101] Conversely, his attitude to those who ignored or obstructed him had become, if anything, fiercer. In a letter to Clark in 1925 he expressed the hope that he might be able to add, through his own efforts, a piece of 'profound, though unauthorised, research to the vast work of the Oxford professors', which would show these 'distinguished' men that 'they have neither swallowed up nor are excr–m–nting all knowledge'; and recalled with some bitterness that 'when I, a few years ago, told the distinguished present regius professor [Sir Charles Firth] about the work I had started, he replied, in his omniscient manner, that Lecky had done all there was to be done about it'.[102]

Fretfulness over money and a simmering resentment at his lot made Namier work all the harder. Besides his research, he was continuing to write and review for newspapers and magazines, on a variety of subjects ranging from eighteenth-century Britain to the contemporary European scene, and he was also drawn increasingly into involvement with the Zionist cause. It may well be that he came to identify more and more with his Jewish heritage precisely because of the personal trials he was obliged to undergo; and even in some way because of his unhappiness, seeing it as the characteristic fate of his race, in the way that Stefan Zweig wrote of the German Jewish politician Walter Rathenau, 'rarely have I seen the tragedy of the Jew more strongly than in his personality, which, with all its apparent superiority, was full of deep unrest and uncertainty'.[103] Zweig might have been writing about Namier.

Whatever the reason, the talk with Weizmann in Vienna lit a fuse. Later in 1925 Namier determined to introduce the great man to Baffy Dugdale and in order to bring them together arranged a dinner party for Weizmann at Glebe Place. At one point the proceedings threatened to descend into farce when Mrs O'Grady suffered an attack of the vapours at the prospect of catering for socially exalted guests (who included the wife of the Prince of Wales's secretary, 'Tommy' Lascelles) and announced herself unable to cook. The party eventually sat down, in full evening dress, to a cold collation, most of it brought over by Baffy in a taxi.[104] Nevertheless, as Namier recalled, 'it was a good party, and after it Baffy and I saw much of the Weizmanns and became closely involved with the Zionist Organisation'.[105]

Namier now began to write journalistic articles on Zionism, which demonstrated how completely he had ingested its doctrines. An unsigned article in *The Times* in April 1926 was, in essence, an appeal to wealthy Jews in England to donate funds to the Zionist Organisation to assist in the settlement of Jewish refugees in Palestine.[106] The problem was acute, Namier argued, because the United States, the principal destination of those fleeing persecution before the Great War, was restricting Jewish immigration by a quota system. But it was not simply a matter of flight from intolerable conditions in Europe:

> Among the Jews themselves a spiritual counterpart to the immigration prohibitions is arising. No doubt, were the prohibitions lifted, hundreds of thousands would still cross the Atlantic to escape the economic misery and political degradation of eastern Europe;

but fundamentally they are tired of the thousands of years of wanderings which merely lead to further wanderings and being everywhere regarded as a 'problem', and yearn for a final resting-place in a national home, where they would form a complete, self-contained nation and live like other people, without having to make polite or embarrassed excuses for their very existence.

In another anonymous piece, a review for the *Times Literary Supplement* endorsing the Zionist Arthur Ruppin's analysis of the nature of Jewish settlement in Palestine, and the difficulties of bringing urban, and often highly educated, Jews into a relatively primitive agricultural economy, he repeated a previous analogy with the founders of America, who were still much on his mind:

> The Jewish immigrants cannot and must not be reduced to the incredibly low standard of living of the fellaheen [sic]; nor are these idealists in search of a new freer life willing permanently to assume the status of hired labourers; just as the pilgrims or puritans could not have been settled as labourers on the Virginia plantations in competition with coloured labour.[107]

These were short, and essentially occasional pieces. But he also put together two longer and more considered essays on the subject. They offer a clear statement of his own understanding of the meaning and purpose of Zionism. The first was published under his name in the *New Statesman* in November 1927 and had a 'profound effect' on the young Isaiah Berlin when he read it.[108] Having begun with an affirmation of his own identity –'we Jews' – Namier examined the two possible responses to the crisis faced by Jews in Europe: assimilation, which would amount to 'dissolution and ultimate disappearance', and Zionism. Jewry was 'a melting glacier', the waters of which were either evaporating (assimilation), or running off in a river (Zionism). Most Jews in western and central Europe had chosen assimilation, which did not mean renouncing the Jewish faith so much as abandoning a world-view which saw 'religion and nationality' as identical. Things were different in eastern Europe where the survival of a strong religious orthodoxy, abetted by cultural and linguistic markers, bound Jewish people together. Here was the real 'Jewish question': the largest concentration of Jews on the globe, and subjected to economic and political persecution.[109] Given America's quota system, the provision of a national home in Palestine was essential, and it was up to the British empire to honour its obligations under the Balfour Declaration.

The second essay, which he did not publish, proposed the means by which the British could guarantee the success of the Zionist experiment, by granting its Palestinian protectorate dominion status.[110] This was the argument he had put forward in 1919, and was at the heart of his understanding of what Zionism should mean: a partnership between the Jews and the great liberal empire which he idealised.

But there was a subtle change. Whereas previously Namier had been examining the Jewish problem as a concerned (indeed, a passionately concerned) outsider, he was now writing from a position firmly within the Zionist fold.

Despite the demonic pace he was setting himself Namier was able to resume a busy social life in London.[111] During his travels in Europe he had maintained contact with his friends and now lived within easy reach of them all, including T. E. Lawrence, of whom he continued to see a great deal: Namier's enthusiasm for the Zionist cause made no difference to their relationship, and indeed may have intensified it, since the desire for a lasting and satisfactory settlement in the Middle East was something they could share.[112] Through Baffy, Namier got to know one of her intimates, the Conservative MP Walter Elliot.[113] He also developed a friendship with Leonard Woolf, husband of Virginia, without making much impression on Mrs Woolf, to whom he was merely a Jew who came to call on Leonard.[114] More useful was the intellectual comradeship resumed with Romney Sedgwick, a former fellow of Trinity College, Cambridge, who had gone into the civil service but retained a strong interest in eighteenth-century history. He and Namier had first met at the London house of the diplomat Oliver Harvey, probably before 1922.[115] Since Sedgwick had already made use of the early sections of the Newcastle papers in his published work, he has been credited with pointing Namier in their direction (though Charles Andrews at Yale may already have done so long before Namier and Sedgwick ever met).[116]

These friends did what they could to sustain Namier and keep him from suffering the kind of mental 'disturbance' about which he constantly worried and for which he sought explanations from both professional and amateur psychologists.[117] But his equilibrium and capacity for concentration were not helped by unsettling developments in his personal life. Marie Beer had visited him several times in London and in 1927 Namier agreed that she should come to England to live. Through the Buxtons, Denis and his wife Emily, Marie found a home in Oxford and work tutoring undergraduates in German and French. She later moved to London and had a permanent address there when she obtained naturalisation in 1930.[118] But the sheen of her youth had gone: she was sometimes physically incapacitated and already showing symptoms of the mental illness which would ultimately lead to her confinement in a psychiatric ward. Lady Namier wrote coldly of her husband's ex-lover, and even with a flicker of cruelty that 'L[ewis]'s horror of insanity snapped his physical infatuation though his devotion to the unfortunate woman even increased'.[119] He certainly spent a good deal of time with Marie, helping her translate foreign novels into English, which was another call on his energies.

Even more disturbing was Clara's unexpected reappearance. In 1927 she wrote from America to inform Namier that she was once again a free agent. Davenport had died, having succumbed to alcoholism: he had been admitted to hospital with an attack of delirium tremens from which he did not recover. She was now able to move around, finding work in hotels. This had all happened suspiciously quickly, which lends credence to the idea that Davenport was a figment. Unsurprisingly, Marie Beer was alarmed. Worse was to follow. In April 1928 Clara arrived back in London and made contact. She offered to divorce Namier, first on grounds of desertion and then of adultery, with a man whom she said she had recently met, and who was possibly yet another fiction. Namier did not pursue the prospect of divorce, even though his solicitors advised him that they had enough evidence. Instead he reserved the right to institute proceedings at a later date, and meanwhile made Clara an allowance of £120 a year. This decision does not make much sense, unless he was still drawn to Clara and unwilling to renounce her, preferring to keep her in some degree dependent. She promptly decamped for the midlands, but Marie, the other dependent woman in his life, would have been right to worry.[120]

The eighteenth century

All this turmoil in his private life made it much more difficult for Namier to concentrate on historical research and writing at the hectic pace he had set himself. Nonetheless, ever since his return to England he had been making great strides. In June 1928, when he composed the preface to his first book, *The structure of politics at the accession of George III*, he described its construction in terms which suggested that the work of preparation had been compressed into the four years since 'the beginning of 1924', though he had in fact been based on the continent until early in 1925.[121] Given his circumstances, it was a truly remarkable effort; even more so when we remember that most of the research for the sequel, *England in the age of the American revolution*, which appeared in 1930, was completed at the same time. He had of course begun gathering material over a decade before, while at Oxford, had continued the work in American libraries and archives before the Great War, and had been busy in the British Museum at intervals ever since leaving the Foreign Office in 1920. But his early research had been focused on Anglo-American constitutional relations rather than the workings of the British parliamentary system. As well as the Newcastle papers – five hundred bound volumes in all – he was now ploughing through as many private collections as he could, and a mass of printed material. This included local histories and family histories, which were far from being the usual fare of historians of eighteenth-century politics, though Sidney and Beatrice Webb had made particular use of local sources in their standard work on *English local government*, published while Namier was an undergraduate and reviewed favourably by A. L. Smith.[122]

In a long letter to Whitney Shepardson, written on the foot of the award of the Rhodes grant, Namier set out in detail his plan for 'my book', of which he already had a clear picture in his mind.[123] It would 'fall into three parts (like everything since the days of Caesar)'. The first volume would be a 'static' survey of the parliament (actually the House of Commons) elected in 1761. It would correspond to the first, panoramic, volume of the French historian Élie Halévy's *Histoire du Peuple Anglais au XIXe Siècle* (begun in 1913 and still in progress) whose avowed purpose, to explain how England had avoided violent revolution, chimed with Namier's own beliefs about the relative health of evolutionary as opposed to revolutionary polities. To follow Halévy's example, Namier would have to set out 'the social and political structure of Great Britain at that time'. He would then explore 'the nature of government as developed under George II, in which I shall try to rectify various current misconceptions concerning the mutual relations between the king, the ministers, and parliament'. The remainder of the first volume would be taken up with a description of the electoral system and an analysis of the results of the 1761 general election. Then in two further volumes he would give 'a running account of the British parliaments of 1761–83', focusing on 'the attitude of the parliament and country to 'the American problem'.

At the core of Namier's research was a prosopography of the House of Commons, the method he is popularly considered to have pioneered; indeed, it is the essence of the dictionary definition of 'Namierism'. Originally the word conveyed no more than the identification of individuals by a description of their form or appearance, but the work of classical scholars in Germany in the late nineteenth century had extended its meaning to the accumulation of information relating to lives and careers.[124] In this limited sense, prosopography already existed in Britain. The most obvious example was the *Dictionary of National Biography* (*DNB*), published between 1895 and 1900 (itself a conscious effort to emulate the *Allgemeine Deutsche Biographie*). Local antiquarians, including Namier's friend Josiah Wedgwood, were also compiling annotated lists of Members of Parliament for particular counties and boroughs. In essence, however, all of this amounted to an accumulation of biographical data for its own sake. The key to the development of the prosopographical approach to history was the exploitation of the biographies of individuals in order to understand the group or institution that they composed. The first scholar to do so was Charles Beard, whose *Economic interpretation of the constitution of the United States* had appeared when Namier was in New York.[125] Within a few years Beard's footsteps were followed by two historians whose work Namier would also have come across: A. P. Newton, an English student of colonial America, in a study of the Puritan element in the early membership of the Providence Island Company; and the medievalist Gaillard

Lapsley, who, like Romney Sedgwick, was a fellow of Trinity College, Cambridge, and who used the method of collective biography to study the knights of the shire in Edward II's parliaments in an article published in 1919.[126]

Namier organised at least some, possibly the bulk, of his research on prosopographical lines. According to Lady Namier, he began by demarcating the chronological limits of his period of study, beginning in about 1740 and ending in 1783, since he recognised the impracticability of carrying out successfully the kind of detailed research he had in mind over a longer time-span.[127] In fact, he worked within an even narrower compass, for he informed an American friend in 1933 that he had 'a card-index covering all the Members who sat in Parliament between 1761 and 1784, besides dozens of note-books with biographical information about them'.[128] His original purpose was to use this data to attempt a calculation of the size of parties within the House of Commons, a subject on which his predecessors had happily pronounced from a position of ignorance. By contrast, he would be able to state with confidence the result of a general election, and thus understand better the process by which ministries were constructed and demolished. This compulsion to establish and demonstrate his own factual accuracy recalls the style of his Foreign Office memoranda and contributions to newspapers; it was as much the mark of Namier the political and economic analyst as of Namier the 'scientific historian'.

In fact, as he told Shepardson, his ambitions were much broader than this and his use of biographical material went beyond what other historians expected to achieve by prosopographical analysis. Namier's aim was to understand the political culture of the English governing class in the age of American revolution, or, as he called it (in an original phrase which has since become a term of art) the 'political nation'.[129] And to do so he naturally needed to understand its social basis. The membership of the House of Commons provided the raw material, since, unlike status-ridden representative institutions elsewhere in eighteenth-century Europe, it was open to the upwardly mobile, and thus presented a 'microcosmos' of the political nation. 'The social history of England could be written in terms of membership of the House of Commons, that peculiar club, election to which has at all times required some expression of consent on the part of the public.'[130] Thus, as he saw it, his work took on a 'sociological' character.[131] At a distance of time, such assumptions are easy to dispute, even to ridicule, as is Namier's confident assertion that 'public opinion' in the modern sense – the opinion of the masses – was unimportant.[132] But in the 1920s they were neither obviously reactionary nor potentially risible. In fact, there was a bracing freshness to them. As early as 1925, in reviewing a biography of the duke of Cumberland, Namier complained that the author, though writing a book that was perfectly satisfactory by its own lights, 'remains throughout in the sphere of the upper, not ten thousand, but one hundred, who in the eighteenth century recorded their ideas and activities with such ability and profusion that few historians have tried to go beyond them'.

> We possess full information about cabinet and court intrigues, about Whig dukes who rested on their powerful electoral influence, and the few real statesmen who stood 'on their heads' etc. But what has hardly been fathomed is the calm depths unknown to those who safely navigate the surface without having to explore them, without the deeper life of society which every generation in its own time knows subconsciously, takes for granted, but feels no need to sound or describe.[133]

This 'sociological' analysis required more than the accumulation and interrogation of basic biographical data. Namier was not attempting in some programmatic way to find answers to a set of predetermined questions, such as Beard or Newton had posed, and which could be answered by a recitation of abbreviated biographies: the relationship between economic interests and political behaviour among American revolutionaries, or between religious belief and colonial enterprise in early seventeenth-century England. Nor was he constructing a taxonomy of his MPs which could be presented, as Lapsley had done, in tabular form.[134] His intention, as he always said, was to find out 'who the chaps were';[135] in other words to come to a full understanding of the life of every Member, their circumstances, and if possible their psychology and motivations. Much later in life he read for the first time, and at his wife's recommendation, *Moby Dick*, recognising in its pages, or so Julia asserted, many truths about himself, one of which must surely have been Melville's rejection of systems of classification by details: 'What ... remains? Nothing but to take hold of the whales bodily, in their entire liberal volume, and boldly sort them that way.'[136]

Namier wanted 'to find out all I could about every single Member who sat in the House between 1761 and 1784'.[137] The first published fruits of his labours were biographical articles, focusing on relatively obscure Members: John Roberts, Henry Pelham's private secretary and the man who administered the 'secret service money' under the duke of Newcastle; the cloth merchant and colonial proprietor Brice Fisher; and two members for the Wiltshire pocket borough of Calne, one of whom, Thomas Duckett, was again a merchant.[138] These were much longer than the factual entries in standard continental prosopographies, and longer than the abbreviated notices provided by Beard or Newton. As scholarly papers they did no more than elucidate details of the lives and careers of their subjects, in much the same way as the *Bulletin* of London University's Institute of Historical Research routinely published revisions to entries in the *DNB*. Namier made no attempt to extrapolate conclusions. However, these articles still represented something novel: none of Namier's MPs had been thought to merit an entry in the *DNB*, and moreover, he based his commentaries heavily on manuscript sources, particularly the Newcastle papers.

More than anything else, it was the depth and apparently inexhaustible variety of his archival research that distinguished Namier's work from that of his contemporaries. It was not that other historians ignored manuscripts, but Namier dug more deeply and in places where others had not ventured, including 'examining wills with a view to discovering the things which remain hidden in a man's lifetime'.[139] It was not a matter of snapping up unconsidered trifles but of hauling in material by the sackful. No historian had explored the 500 volumes of Newcastle papers so thoroughly, a deposit he described as 'one of the most valuable collections of political manuscripts in existence'.[140] This rich harvest was complemented by other valuable returns from private archives, such as the Lansdowne papers at Bowood and the Sandwich papers at Hinchingbrooke. In an essay in 1925 he proclaimed that 'though English history in the eighteenth century is well known in its superficial outlines, very much more material is required for a deeper study, and masses of unused or even unknown correspondence rest (or rot) in country houses'.[141]

In hunting for these buried treasures, Namier always began by trying to establish some personal connection with the family. His first contact with Lansdowne was through a third party, but he followed this up himself with offers to help with family history.[142] Lord and Lady Sandwich were easier company, since they evidently shared Namier's political views, including an interest in Palestine, and he was soon on terms of close familiarity, becoming a regular visitor to their house at Hinchingbrooke, whose archive he claimed to know better than anyone.[143] Discoveries in muniment rooms intoxicated him: he seemed to have found a secret key to answering all the questions he had set himself. He was particularly excited by his visit to Captain Godsal at Haines Hill, where he made a great discovery: a typed transcript of the complete letter-books of the English colonial agent Charles Garth, which contained copies of many letters to correspondents in South Carolina, Georgia and Maryland that had not survived in American repositories.[144]

The process of tracking down manuscripts involved mobilising all possible contacts. Friends (especially Balliol men) were badgered for access to their family records or for introductions to other descendants of eighteenth-century politicians. Even a brief acquaintance would be enough to justify a letter from Namier asking for help.[145] John Jacob Astor (later 1st Baron Astor), the proprietor of *The Times*, a contemporary at Oxford (though not at Balliol), gave Namier an introduction to his brother-in-law the earl of Minto, who was 'most kind and hospitable' and allowed Namier to spend a week at Minto House.[146] Baffy Dugdale presumably interceded with her cousin, Lord Rayleigh, for Namier to see the Strutt papers at Terling Place in Essex, and also with various Scottish landowners,[147] though another close friend, Flora Macleod (who in 1929 inherited her family's castle of Dunvegan on Skye), may also have offered assistance north of the border. Namier was particularly proud of his enterprising efforts over the Bute papers: he began by mobilising the assistance of John Buchan's wife, a distant cousin of the marquess of Bute, then moved on to Bute's younger brother, the Conservative MP Lord Colum Crichton-Stuart, and eventually, in 1929, found that a part of the collection had been deposited in the British Museum.[148] Even so, he was not always admitted to houses which he suspected to contain archival riches. On receiving news of the grant from the Rhodes Trust, almost his first thought was to use his position as a sponsored researcher to seek access to the archive of Lord Harrowby at Sandon Hall, who had once owned Bute papers and whose door had hitherto been closed.[149] It remained impregnable.[150] To some of his friends this devotion to manuscripts appeared idolatrous to the point of absurdity. When Baffy was engaged in preparing her uncle's biography and allowed Namier a glimpse of the former prime minister's papers, Walter Elliot, who did not always take Namier as seriously as he might have done, could not resist writing to her, 'I'm amused at Namier and the papers. Of course it must be most thrilling to him to think that a lot of things which will be known as the Balfour Papers a hundred years hence, being actually handled by him now.'[151]

Making a reputation

Despite his lack of regular employment and financially straitened circumstances Namier was not exactly a ragged figure crying in the wilderness. His range of influential acquaintances, and frequent contributions to newspapers and periodicals, ensured that he was well known in social and literary circles.[152] And from the time of his resettlement in London he began to publish on the eighteenth century in literary magazines; mostly book reviews, but reviews which, rather self-consciously, advertised the unusual depth of his knowledge, and began to make him a reputation as an authority on the period. J. E. Neale, the Elizabethan historian who in the 1950s was to work alongside Namier on the editorial board of the History of Parliament recalled how at about this time 'We used to see reviews in the weeklies signed "L. B. Namier"... We pitied the *littérateur* and the weaker brethren who strayed into his field. We also enjoyed the reviews.'[153]

These reviews also show Namier parading the virtues of modern, 'scientific' history. Thus A. S. Turberville's *House of Lords in the eighteenth century* received faint praise, as 'readable, scholarly, and free from bias', but was chided for regurgitating hackneyed stories about the Commons without bothering to find out whether there was any foundation for them, and for endorsing 'the traditional view of eighteenth-century politics even though this is repeatedly contradicted by his own remarks'. It was regrettable, wrote Namier, that the author had relied on printed records and ignored manuscripts: 'one could wish Mr Turberville had more extensively abandoned the easy run of narrative for the tunnelling labour of analysis'.[154]

As Neale implied, Namier did not pull his punches; indeed, he seemed almost to delight in hitting as hard as he could. C. W. Everett's misconceived attempt to identify Lord Shelburne as the anonymous author of the letters of 'Junius' was comprehensively rubbished in the columns of *The Nation*, with a further jab in the *Observer* the very next day, and when Everett took up his cause in *The Nation*'s letters column Namier, who never shrank from combat, dealt him another heavy blow, closing with a demand that Everett 'now … withdraw his "main hypothesis"'.[155] Nearly two decades later he could still congratulate himself on driving Everett from the field: 'I hardly think I ever destroyed a book so thoroughly as I did that egregious performance.'[156] Well-meaning but ignorant amateurs were swept away in a personal crusade to rid the eighteenth century of the taint of the picturesque, the kind of attitude, for example, that had prompted Lytton Strachey to welcome the third volume of Mrs Paget Toynbee's edition of the letters of Horace Walpole with the statement that 'the aroma of a wonderful age comes wafting from these hundred pages, and enchants our senses'.[157] The Honourable Mrs Stuart Wortley, who had published a collection of letters from the Bute papers, and was complimented in the *American Historical Review* for her 'modest, restrained and intelligent' editing, found her work excoriated by Namier.

> Mrs Stuart Wortley says nothing about the MSS from which these letters are extracted, e.g. whether she has reproduced most of them, or whether this is a mere selection. Nor has she collated them with the rich extant literature on the events about which they treat, and even the explanatory notes are quite insufficient. Still, one hardly regrets this, seeing her unfortunate gift for getting even the most common facts wrong.[158]

Academic historians could also feel the lash. The young Cambridge historian George Kitson Clark, whose biographer has described him as someone whose 'bluff exterior' cloaked a 'sensitive temperament, easily hurt',[159] was flayed by Namier's review of his first book, on *Sir Robert Peel and the Conservative Party*. While Clark had made much of the work he had done on the Peel papers in the British Museum, in truth, Namier wrote, these documents 'do not add anything startlingly new to our knowledge of the period, and certainly do not change our view of it'. Furthermore,

> no fundamental questions are asked by Mr Clark, and his narrative takes its weary, meandering course through interminable debates and ephemeral political manoeuvrings. Brevity alone could have saved this book on the literary side, while Mr Clark's efforts to relieve its narrative by sententious reasonings, melancholy wise forecasts, and worst of all by elaborate imagery, fail completely.[160]

In some of these reviews Namier was clearly working out his own frustrations: against family historians lacking the rudiments of their craft, whose efforts queered the pitch for the professional;[161] against popularisers like Turberville or Namier's own college acquaintance Philip Guedalla, who in his view were too lazy to get to the heart of the matter and say anything new or important;[162] and against complacent university academics who had the job security and the stipends which should have enabled them to produce good 'scientific' history. Like any modernist, he seems to have held a particular animus against the 'old guard', establishment figures whose books were routinely praised without ever being subject to rigorous critical analysis. His *bête noire* was the elderly military historian and former royal librarian Sir John Fortescue, who in 1927–28 published a six-volume edition of the correspondence of George III.[163] While others greeted the appearance of volumes from Fortescue's pen with a conventional cornucopia of congratulation, Namier tore into his prey, remorselessly cataloguing errors in the scholarly apparatus. Of the index to the first two volumes, he wrote, 'its blunders defy all description'.[164] This was not language customarily used in the scholarly community towards such a venerable figure and was clearly intended to shock polite sensibilities.[165]

It was one thing for Namier to make a name for himself as a terrifying reviewer; but he still had to get his own books into print. He himself had no anxieties on this score, reassuring Philip Kerr in 1926, when applying for a Rhodes grant, 'As to publishers, I am under no apprehension; for many years of my life I have had to keep myself by literary work.'[166] Later that year Baffy introduced him to Harold Macmillan, the future prime minister, who was still only a junior partner in the family firm but was taking the initiative to recruit authors and further enlarge Macmillans' already prestigious list. The two men had Balliol in common (Macmillan had matriculated in 1912) and Douglas Cole had already signed for the firm. Bob Boothby was another mutual friend. Namier found Macmillan's politics congenial (a version of what came to be called 'one-nation' Conservatism, shared by, among others, Walter Elliot) and he appreciated the potential of Macmillan's aristocratic connections as son-in-law of the duke of Devonshire.[167] It was a happy conjunction. Macmillans not only took Namier's first book, but would remain his principal publisher throughout his life, and Harold Macmillan would become a close friend.

The early stages of the relationship were not entirely smooth. There was an agreement in principle to take Namier as an author as early as January 1927, when Baffy wrote to tell him 'how delighted I am about Macmillans'. Namier's first offering was a gathering of journalistic pieces, mainly on European politics and economics.[168] Some, though not all, would find their way into his first published collection of essays, *Skyscrapers*, in 1931. But that was after he had made his name. In 1927 articles on European finance from the *Manchester Guardian Commercial* had little appeal for Macmillan and the proposal foundered. Namier then offered essays based on his research on the eighteenth century. The reports he sent to the Rhodes Trustees suggest that what followed was plain sailing: he told them he had submitted a manuscript which Macmillan promptly agreed to publish, albeit with 'modifications'.[169] In fact the negotiations were prolonged, and the story still agitated him two decades later, when 'his debates with Macmillan on the format of *The structure of politics*' constituted the subject of one of the monologues which he inflicted on junior lecturers in the Manchester History department.[170]

Namier submitted at least two manuscripts in November 1927, one of which, entitled 'The British parliament in 1761' (an unexciting title even by his standards), and almost certainly the forerunner to *England in the age of the American revolution*, was sent to a reader and promptly rejected.[171] This must have been a nasty shock to Namier; nor was it really what the publisher had expected. However, the second manuscript, entitled 'Mid-eighteenth-century politics', was accepted by Harold Macmillan in January 1928, this time without a reader's report, although still subject to 'certain modifications'. One of these was the removal of an essay on Charles Garth (based on the papers at Haines Hill) which Namier thought might appeal to the American market, but which the publishers 'prefer me to hold … over for a special volume on colonial agents and merchants'. This news was enough to persuade the Rhodes Trustees to release £150 as the second instalment of their award, and in January Namier's revised manuscript, now called 'The structure of politics', was received by Macmillan and sent to be set.[172] The process of seeing the book through the press became a team effort for Namier's circle: Baffy Dugdale and Charles Stone helped with proofreading (Baffy even sent a set of proofs to her uncle, Lord Balfour, who made some suggestions which Namier took up), while Marie Beer and Emily Buxton checked the references.[173] By the summer of 1928 everything was done.

Namier had never for one moment doubted his own abilities, or that his work, when completed, would fundamentally alter accepted wisdom about his subject. After nearly ten years of struggle, with his livelihood always uncertain, he had completed the work conceived in America before the Great War. Given his recent personal history, we might assume that his state of mind in 1928 would be a mixture of euphoria and personal pride, peppered with a residue of bitterness against the historical establishment. And just such a picture does emerge from the only first-hand testimony to have survived, a letter sent by Baffy to Arthur Balfour in October 1928, recounting a dinner party she had given in London for Namier and the author Evan Charteris. The evening, she said, had been a great success: Charteris had stayed till half-past eleven ('Namier never goes till ejected, so is no criterion!') and the conversation had flowed.

For most of the time Namier held the floor: he 'told us, rather amusingly, of the faults and errors in recent history books (notably those of Sir John Fortescue) which he, Namier, has poured over vitriol upon [sic], in his reviews'. At the same time he 'gave the highest praise to three American historians, now alive, who were writing about America'. They were 'much superior to any living English historian'. Namier displayed a particular animus towards G. M. Trevelyan, regius professor of history at Cambridge and the doyen of 'Liberal-Whig' historians. According to Baffy, 'Lewis always takes a low view of George Trevelyan – says he has "no period sense"'.[174] It was only when Namier began to pronounce on Margot Asquith's past, a subject he knew nothing about, that Baffy decided she had better step in. Although 'it was usually easier to stop a charging elephant' than to divert Namier once he had set off, she felt she had to prevent him making a fool of himself, and 'so I just said, "Shut up Lewis, you know nothing of what you are talking of".' He 'took this nicely and apologised'. At this exciting stage in his life, now that he felt he had justified himself to the world, probably only someone like Baffy, an old and dear friend to whom he owed so much, could have succeeded in halting the rampaging pachyderm in his tracks.[175]

Notes

1 [Mary L. Smith,], *Arthur Lionel Smith, master of Balliol (1916–1924): a biography and some reminiscences* (1928), 289; 'English register', 1908–24, *s.v.* 19 May 1920 (Balliol).

2 Robert, Lord Boothby, *My yesterday, your tomorrow* (1962), 251–2. Gladwyn Jebb was also at Magdalen.

3 *Namier*, 156–9, 193. Jebb attributed the credit for his own first-class degree to Namier's 'patient and indefatigable coaching' (*The memoirs of Lord Gladwyn* (1972), 15).

4 [Boothby] to Jebb, 15 Jan. 1929 (Churchill, Gladwyn papers, 7/14). To judge by the lists of guests and of wedding presents in Jebb's papers (ibid.), Namier was not invited.

5 Cecil Roth, letter to the editor, *Commentary*, 1 Aug. 1962.

6 JCR minute book 1903–32 (Balliol); *Namier*, 193. Victor Cazalet, the future Conservative MP and pro-Zionist, may have been another: Lady Namier claims him as her husband's pupil (ibid., 159), but Cazalet's biographer only noted that Namier was a friend (Robert Rhodes James, *Victor Cazalet: a portrait* (1976), 72). Cazalet was at Christ Church, where his tutors were John Masterman and Keith Feiling (ibid., 69), though he was not a particularly assiduous student and may have taken himself to Namier for unofficial cramming in his final year.

7 Note by Lady Namier of a reminiscence by Edwin Samuel (2nd Viscount Samuel), a pupil of Namier's at Balliol (CZA, Namier papers, A312\1).

8 Warren to Jebb, 30 June 1921 (Churchill, Gladwyn papers, 8/3).

9 Julia Namier to Basil Liddell Hart, 30 June 1962 (LH, 1/539/170).

10 *Namier*, 153; Julia Namier to Constance Babington Smith, 4 Dec. 1961 (Babington Smith); Richard ('Dykah') Bell to Namier, 21 Sept. 1950 (Reading UL, G. D. Bell and Sons archive, MS 1640/389); Namier to I. L. B. Aitkens, 28 Nov. 1955 (HPT, N–60).

11 Basil Liddell Hart to Julia Namier, 9 July 1962 (LH, 1/539/179).

12 'Spectator' [Namier], 'Russian land and Polish men', *New Europe*, 23 Sept. 1920.

13 This is what he told Cecil Roth at the time (*Commentary*, 1 Aug. 1962).

14 Strachey to Namier, 8 Mar. 1921 (Bodl., Sutherland papers, box 9).

15 *Vanished supremacies*, v.

16 Namier, 'The downfall of the Habsburg monarchy '[ch. 1, pt III], H. W. V. Temperley (ed.), *A history of the peace conference of Paris* (6 vols, 1920–24), iv, 58–119 (repr. in *Vanished supremacies*, 112–65).

17 Alan Sharp, 'Some relevant historians – the Political Intelligence Department of the Foreign Office, 1918–1920', *Australian Journal of Politics and History*, xxxiv (1988–9), 362–3.

18 *Vanished supremacies*, 128–9.

19 This he maintained for ever afterwards, despite the popular argument from hindsight that the Austro-Hungarian empire, for all its faults, was better than what came after it (Namier to Hugh Seton-Watson, 10 July 1957 (HPT, N–66)).

20 'English register', 1908–24, *s.v.* 6 Dec. 1920 (Balliol).

21 Namier to HM Inspector of Taxes, 11 Jan. 1927 (Rylands, Namier papers, 1/1a/2).

22 Certificate of income from shares in Anglo-Persian Oil Company, 9 May 1921 (Rylands, Namier papers, 1/9/7).

23 *Namier*, 156, quoting a letter from Blanche Dugdale, who urged Namier not to lose 'the savour of life' in the drudgery of teaching.

24 See the review by Sir James Headlam-Morley, *TLS*, 13 Oct. 1921; and Philip Kerr's report to the Rhodes Trust, 8 Oct. 1926 (Rylands, Namier papers, 1/1a/1/10).

25 Robert, Lord Boothby, *Boothby: recollections of a rebel* (1978), 101.

26 Namier to Stein, 15 Feb. 1921 (CZA, A312\9).

27 'Lewis's notes on his early connections with Zionism' (Bodl., Sutherland papers, box 9).

28 Chaim Weizmann to Smith, Mar. 1919, Smith to Weizmann, 17 Mar. 1919 (Balliol, Smith papers, Z3).

29 Strachey to Sydenham, 14 June 1921 (PA, Strachey papers, 13/18/15); Sydenham to Strachey, 15 June 1921 (ibid., 13/18/16). Strachey's attitude is hard to fathom, given the friendly manner in which he was corresponding with Namier at this time. In 1918 he told Sydenham that he agreed 'with all you say about the Jews', adding: 'I used to be very proud as a young man of not being anti-Semitic, but these illusions have gone' (Strachey to Sydenham, 29 Aug. 1918 (ibid., 13/18/14)). If he was trying to humour Sydenham, this seems to be going beyond what was necessary.

30 *Plain English*, 7, 28 May, 5, 26 Nov., 3 Dec. 1921. See Colin Holmes, *Anti-Semitism in British society 1876–1936* (1979), 150, 156. *Free Oxford*, the left-wing undergraduate newspaper which was supposedly at the heart of this conspiracy, replied in its issue of 26 Nov. 1921.

31 *Namier*, 160.

32 *Namier*, 162.

33 Stefan Zweig, *The world of yesterday: an autobiography* ... (1943), 220.

34 Karl Johns, 'Maria Hirsch in the *Kunstwissenschaftliche Forschungen*', *Journal of Art Historiography*, 13 (Dec. 2015), [2]. Maria died in 1932; Alfred was murdered at Auschwitz.

35 *The Times*, 20 Dec. 1922.

36 For Namier's near-adulation of Masaryk, see his review of Masaryk's memoirs, *TLS*, 12 Nov. 1925 (repr. in *Skyscrapers*, 113–21): 'he is now the uncontested leader of the nation and the keeper of its conscience' (113).

37 *Namier*, 173; [Namier,], 'Czecho-Slovakia and Karl's defiance: Dr Benes's indictment of

Hungary', *Manchester Guardian*, 31 Oct. 1921; [Namier,] 'Czecho-Slovakia's new Cabinet: forecast of its policy', ibid., 26 Sept. 1922.

38 In a piece entitled, 'The art and science of currency stabilisation in Europe', *Manchester Guardian Commercial* on 9 Nov. 1922, he praised the Czech government's record, adding, by way of explanation, and even self-justification, 'For some time past I have been in close contact with directing circles in this country.' Unsigned articles and reviews appearing in the *Manchester Guardian* and *Manchester Guardian Commercial* have been identified from the lists supplied by the deputy editor to Lady Namier in 1963 (Rylands, *Manchester Guardian* arch., D/977/2/1, D/977/4).

39 [Namier,] 'The problem of east-central Europe', *Round Table*, June 1923 (xiii (1922–23), 581).

40 Namier to Sir Walford Selby, 14 Feb. 1951 (Bodl., Selby papers, MS Eng. 6600, fo. 175).

41 [Namier,] 'Inner meaning of central Europe's depreciated currencies', *Manchester Guardian Commercial*, 12 Jan. 1922; *Facing east*, 75–6.

42 Frederick Steiner to Lady Namier, 18 Feb. 1965 (Churchill, Steiner papers, 6/5/1); [?Christopher Harvey] to Gladwyn Jebb, 20 May 1922 (ibid., Gladwyn papers, 8/3).

43 Eva Schutz, *My long journey to London* (privately printed, 1994), 5–6; *Namier*, 170–1.

44 *Namier*, 170–1; [Namier,] 'Inner meaning of central Europe's depreciated currencies'.

45 'Turbulent Zionist', 26; Namier to Basil Liddell Hart, 8 Mar. 1951 (LH, 1/539/56).

46 *Skyscrapers*, 140–1.

47 *Conflicts*, 163. See also 'Vienna Jewry', *In the margin*, 78–83.

48 [Namier,] 'Property values in Europe', *Manchester Guardian Commercial*, 3 May 1923. See also *Nation and Athenaeum*, 31 Dec. 1921.

49 Milvrad Vanlitch to Alfred Zimmern, 30 Mar. 1921 (Bodl., Zimmern papers, box 17, fo. 82).

50 Namier, 'The economic situation in Austria', *Nation & Athenaeum*, 3 Oct. 1925.

51 *Skyscrapers*, 110–11; see also memo by Namier, 2 Aug. 1919 (FO 371/3530, quoted in F. L. Carsten, *The first Austrian republic 1918–1938: a study based on British and Austrian documents* (Aldershot, 1986), 7–8): 'Austria in the days of her greatness has never had such a decent government and such able statesmen as she has got now.'

52 [Namier,] 'The problem of east-central Europe', 572; [Namier,] 'Economic decay and the flight of capital: present plight and ultimate fate of Austria', *Manchester Guardian Commercial*, 24 Aug. 1922. He had advocated a closer union between Austria and Germany ever since 1919 (Carsten, *First Austrian republic*, 7–8).

53 [Namier,] 'Property values in Europe'; [Namier,] 'Currency problems in Austria; the "stabilisation" of the krone', *Manchester Guardian Commercial*, 14 June 1923; Namier, 'How Austria passed through her financial crisis: present-day openings for foreign capital', ibid., 20 Nov. 1924.

54 Namier, 'Inflation at close quarters: a study of its effects in central Europe', *Manchester Guardian Commercial*, 31 Jan. 1924.

55 Namier to R. W. Seton-Watson, 2 Jan. 1925 (SSEES, Seton-Watson papers, 7/18). Lucia, née von Wilczek (1895–1977), was the wife of Joseph Erwin, graf von Königsegg-Aulendorf.

56 *Namier*, 181; Namier to Seton-Watson, 17 Dec. 1923 (SSEES, Seton-Watson papers, 7/18).

57 Namier to C. P. Scott, 9 Mar. 1923 (*Guardian* arch., A/N2/7).

58 *Namier*, 181.

59 *Namier*, 165.

60 *Skyscrapers*, 2.

61 *Avenues*, 8.

62 *In the margin*, 278.

63 Irena Prehn to Constance Babington Smith, 19 Aug. 1980 (Babington Smith).

64 [Namier,] 'Economic decay and the flight of capital: present plight and ultimate fate of Austria', *Manchester Guardian Commercial*, 24 Aug. 1922.

65 Notes of business undertaken for Mrs Namier by her solicitors, Lee and Pemberton, 2 Nov.–21 Dec. 1922 (LMA, Lee and Pemberton papers, Acc/1887/002/04); Lee and Pemberton to Wontner and Sons, 17 Nov. 1922 (ibid.).

66 A. J. P. Taylor, *A personal history* (1983), 167.

67 Smith to Namier, 30 Sept. 1913 (Rylands, Namier papers, 1/9/19).

68 *Namier*, 173.

69 *Namier*, 339.

70 *Weizmann A*, xv, 198; *Namier*, 217.

71 But as late as 1931 he was still able to write a long personal letter rather than having it typed (Namier to Lady Sandwich, 7 Sept. 1931 (Mapperton, Sandwich papers, GH/PERS/3)).

72 *Namier*, 182; Namier to Ld Moyne, 24 Mar. 1941 (CZA, A312\16). Namier's condition is likely to have been a form of task-specific focal dystonia, which may have neurological causes but is also seen as arising from a combination of environmental and genetic factors. I am grateful to my son Thomas, a consultant neurologist at Queen Elizabeth Hospital, Birmingham, for advice on this point.

73 Elliot to Dugdale, 9 Oct. 1923 (NLS, Elliot papers, Acc. 12267/11).

74 Namier to R. W. Seton-Watson, 17 Dec. 1923 (SSEES, Seton-Watson papers, 7/18).

75 Namier to C. P. Scott, 24 Mar. 1925 (*Guardian* arch., A/N2/9a).

76 'Turbulent Zionist', 27–8.

77 Namier to HM Inspector of Taxes, 11 Jan. 1927 (Rylands, Namier papers, 1/1a/2). *Namier*, 181, 185, implies that Namier employed a secretary continuously from December 1923.

78 'Germany's eastern frontiers', *Manchester Guardian*, 20 Mar. 1925.

79 Namier to Scott, 24 Mar. 1925 (*Guardian* arch., A/N2/9a).

80 Scott to Namier, 26 Mar. 1925 (*Guardian* arch., A/N2/10).

81 *Manchester Guardian*, 11 June, 27 Aug. 1925.

82 Namier to HM Inspector of Taxes, 11 Jan. 1927 (Rylands, Namier papers, 1/1a/2).

83 'Turbulent Zionist', 26.

84 Rose, *Zionism*, 27–8. See also Namier's 'Leadership in Israel: Chaim Weizmann', *Facing east*, 151–9.

85 *Weizmann A*, xiv, 376.

86 Namier to G. N. Clark, 22 Dec. 1925 (Bodl., Clark papers, 268).

87 Norman Rose, *Chaim Weizmann: a biography* (1986), 241.

88 Namier to P. H. Kerr, 11 Aug. 1926 (Rylands, Namier papers, 1/1a/1/4–6).

89 'Lewis's notes on his early connections with Zionism' (Bodl., Sutherland papers, box 9).

90 Namier to Clark, 22 Dec. 1925 (Bodl., Clark papers, 268).

91 Namier to Wheeler-Bennett, 13 Oct. 1926 (Rylands, Namier papers, 1/1a/2); *Structure*, xiii. Wheeler-Bennett subsequently offered to cancel the debt, but Namier would not let him (*Namier*, 207).

92 Namier to P. H. Kerr, 11 Aug. 1926 (Rylands, Namier papers, 1/1a/1/4–6).

93 Kerr to Fisher, 11 Aug. 1926 (Rylands, Namier papers, 1/1a/1/1); same to Egerton, 11 Aug. 1926 (ibid., 1/1a/1/2); same to Curtis, 11 Aug. 1926 (ibid., 1/1a/1/3).

94 Egerton to Kerr, 12 Aug. 1926 (Rylands, Namier papers, 1/1a/1/7); Kerr's report to trustees, 8 Oct. 1926 (ibid., 1/1a/1/10).

95 Extract from minutes of Rhodes Trust, 14 Oct. 1926 (Rylands, Namier papers, 1/1a/1/11).

96 Kerr to Shepardson, 21 Oct. 1926 (Rylands, Namier papers, 1/1a/1/15); Namier to Shepardson, 4 Nov., 2 Dec. 1926 (ibid., 1/1a/2). See also Namier to Kerr, 15 Nov. 1927 (NRS, Lothian papers, GD40/17/230/421).

97 *Structure*, xii. She can be tentatively identified as Constance Le Marinel (*c*.1886–1937), the unmarried younger sister of a London clergyman, Matthew Le Marinel, who later returned to his native Channel Islands as dean of Jersey. Miss Le Marinel may well have been the secretary who told Namier that 'if she ever married and had twins she would call one op. cit. and the other loc. cit.' (memo by John Brooke, July 1968 (LWL, Lewis corresp., Brooke (1)).

98 Blanche Dugdale to Arthur Balfour, 5 Sept. 1927 (NRS, Balfour papers, GD 433/2/277/35); *Namier*, 191, 207.

99 V. H. Galbraith, memoir of Namier, *Balliol College Record*, 1961, 40.

100 Namier to J. C. Wedgwood, 19 June 1929 (LWL, Namier papers, folder 3).

101 Namier to ——, 7 Feb. 1927 (Rylands, Namier papers, 1/9/7).

102 Namier to G. N. Clark, 20 Dec. 1925 (Bodl., Clark papers, 268). H. W. C. Davis, one of Namier's tutors at Balliol, also told the young Lucy Sutherland in 1927 that there was 'no need for further work' on eighteenth-century England (Anne Whiteman, 'Lucy Stuart Sutherland, 1903–1980', *Proceedings of the British Academy*, lxix (1983), 616).

103 Zweig, *The world of yesterday*, 143.

104 'Turbulent Zionist', 27–9; 'Lewis's notes on his early connections with Zionism' (Bodl., Sutherland papers, box 9); Rose, *Zionism*, 29–30.

105 *Namier*, 204.

106 [Namier,] 'Jews in eastern Europe', *The Times*, 6 Apr. 1926; 'Lewis's notes on his early connections with Zionism' (Bodl., Sutherland papers, box 9).

107 *TLS*, 18 Mar. 1926.

108 Namier, 'Zionism', *New Statesman*, 5 Nov. 1927 (repr. in *Skyscrapers*, 128–37). See Rose, *Zionism*, 30–2.

109 *Skyscrapers*, 128–9, 132.

110 CZA, Namier papers, A312\6, quoted and discussed in Rose, *Zionism*, 32–4.

111 Baffy called him 'a born host' ('Turbulent Zionist', 27).

112 Julia Namier to Basil Liddell Hart, 14 Jan. 1963 (LH, 1/539/186).

113 See, for example, Walter Elliot to Blanche Dugdale, 27 Sept. 1925, [Jan. 1926], 18 Oct. 1926 (NLS, Elliot papers, Acc. 12198/3).

114 Leonard Woolf, *The journey not the arrival matters: an autobiography of the years 1939–1969* (1970), 185; Virginia Woolf, *The letters of Virginia Woolf*, ed. Nigel Nicolson (6 vols, 1975–80), iii, 485.

115 Mana Sedgwick to W. S. Lewis, 9 May 1962 (LWL, Lewis corresp., Sedgwick).

116 R. R. Sedgwick, 'The inner cabinet from 1739 to 1741', *EHR*, xxxiv (1919), 290–302; Ved Mehta, *Fly and the fly-bottle: encounters with British intellectuals* (1963), 233.

117 'Turbulent Zionist', 45–6; *Namier*, 146.

118 Certificate of naturalisation, 15 July 1930 (TNA, HO 334/112/18475). She described herself as stateless.

119 *Namier*, 195.

120 *Namier*, 196–8.

121 *Structure*, ix–x; Namier to P. H. Kerr, 11 Aug. 1926 (Rylands, Namier papers, 1/1a/1/4–6).

122 Sidney and Beatrice Webb, *English local government from the Revolution to the Municipal Corporations Act* (2 vols, 1907–8); rev. by A. L. Smith, *EHR*, xxv 1910), 353–64.

123 Namier to Shepardson, 4 Nov. 1926 (Rylands, Namier papers, 1/1a/2).

124 August Pauly et al. (eds), *Realencyclopädie der Classischen Altertumswissenschaft* (6 vols, 1839–52; a 2nd edn, by Georg Wissowa, had begun to appear in 1894 and had reached 21 vols by 1924); Elimar Klebs et al. (eds), *Prosopographia Imperii Romani Saec I. II. III* (3 vols, 1897–98). See T. G. Barnes, 'Prosopography, modern and ancient', K. S. B. Keats-Rohan (ed.), *Prosopography approaches and applications: a handbook* (*Prosopographica et Genealogica*, xiii, Oxford, 2007), 72–82.

125 A point made in J. E. Neale, *The age of Catherine de Medici and essays in Elizabethan history* (paperback edn, 1963), 241–2.

126 A. P. Newton, *The colonising activities of the English Puritans* (New Haven, 1914), 59–79; Gaillard Lapsley, 'Knights of the shire in the parliaments of Edward II', *EHR*, xxxiv (1919), 25–42, 152–71; Lawrence Stone, 'Prosopography', *Daedalus*, c (1971), 48–9.

127 *Namier*, 187.

128 Namier to Lewis, 23 May 1933 (LWL, Lewis corresp, Namier (1)). See also Namier to J. C. Wedgwood, 9 June 1928 (Rylands, Namier papers, 1/9/1).

129 See *Namier*, 199, for a report of Arthur Balfour's astonished reaction to reading it for the first time: 'Where did the fellow get the power of writing English? … political nation – is that his phrase? Or did he find it somewhere? Anyhow it's a most useful one.'

130 *Amer. rev.*, 3.

131 Namier to Wedgwood, 9 June 1928 (Rylands, Namier papers, 1/9/1).

132 *Structure*, ix.

133 *Spectator*, 3 Oct. 1925.

134 For Namier's lifelong aversion to 'statistical tables' in the context of biographical research, see p. 326.

135 Information from the late E. L. C. Mullins.

136 *Namier*, 310.

137 John Brooke, 'Namier and Namierism', *History and Theory*, iii (1964), 335.

138 Namier, 'Three eighteenth-century politicians', *EHR*, lxii (1927), 408–13; Namier, 'Brice Fisher, MP: a mid-eighteenth-century merchant and his connections', ibid., lxii (1927), 514–32; Namier, 'Thomas Duckett and Daniel Bull, Members for Calne', *Wiltshire Archaeological and Natural History Magazine*, xliv (1927–9), 106–10.

139 Namier to Lady Sandwich, 16 May 1934 (HPT, N–51).

140 *Structure*, xii.

141 *Spectator*, 3 Oct. 1925.

142 Namier to Macmillan, 18 Apr. 1928 (Reading UL, Macmillan archive, MAC/NAM); Namier to Ld Lansdowne, 19 Apr. 1929 (BL, Petty papers., Add MS 72907).

143 Namier to Dorothy May, 14 Oct. 1932 (CZA, A312\12); Ld Sandwich to Namier, 9 Mar. 1930 (HPT, N–70); Blanche Dugdale to A. J. Balfour, 24 Oct. 1928 (NRS, GD 433/2/277/82–5).

144 Namier to ——, 7 Feb. 1927 (Rylands, Namier papers, 1/9/7).

145 For example, Evan Charteris to Namier, [Feb. 1929] (Rylands, Namier papers, 1/9/7).

146 Namier to Walter Elliot, 27 Jan. 1953 (HPT, N–54).

147 Rose, *Zionism*, 42.

148 Namier to W. S. Lewis, 23 May 1933 (LWL, Lewis corresp., Namier (1)); Namier to Visct Sandon, 24 Apr. 1951 (HPT, N–56).

149 Philip Kerr duly wrote on behalf of the trust to reinforce Namier's application: Kerr to Ld Harrowby, 21 Oct. 1926 (Rylands, Namier papers, 1/1a/1/16); Namier to Kerr, 22 Oct. 1926 (ibid., 1/1a/1/18).

150 Harrowby to Kerr, 30 Oct 1926 (Rylands, Namier papers, 1/1a/1/21).

151 Walter Elliot to Blanche Dugdale [Jan. 1926] (NLS, Elliot papers, Acc. 12198/3).

152 Well enough at any rate that his presence was to be looked for among the party guests of the socialite Lady Colefax (Blanche Dugdale to Arthur Balfour, 17 May 1928 (NRS, GD 433/2/227/67)).

153 J. E. Neale, The *age of Catherine de Medici and essays in Elizabethan history* (1963), 242.

154 *Observer*, 29 Jan. 1928.

155 *Nation & Athenaeum*, 4 Feb., 24 Mar. 1928; *Observer*, 5 Feb. 1928; Alvar Ellegård, *Who was Junius?* (Stockholm, 1962), 89.

156 Namier to C. R. Fay, 29 Jan. 1954 (HPT, N–57). According to Richard Pares, 'Namier was generally held to have shown him [Everett] up' (Pares to A. L. Rowse, n.d. (Exeter UL, Rowse papers, MS 113/3/1/P)).

157 *Nation & Athenaeum*, 29 May 1926.

158 *American Historical Review*, xxxi (1926), 519; *Spectator*, 1 Aug. 1925.

159 Norman Gash in *Oxf. DNB*.

160 *Observer*, 25 Aug. 1929.

161 See his essay on 'Family history', *Morning Post*, 8 Sept. 1926 (repr. in *Skyscrapers*, 181–3), a tetchy outburst, even for him. He told Baffy's son-in-law, James Fergusson, that it was prompted by reading Maud Wyndham's *Chronicles of the eighteenth century, founded on the correspondence of Sir Thomas Lyttelton and his family* ... (2 vols, 1924), 'a most miserable production': 'I met her at dinner at your mother's, and sat next to her, and had to be polite to her about her book; and then I went home, and, like the slave of King Midas, had to whisper to the earth all I could not say to her at dinner' (Namier to Fergusson, 10 Aug. 1933 (HPT, N–54)).

162 See also his review of Lewis Melville's edition of *The Huskisson papers, Week-end Review*, 28 Mar. 1931: 'bookmaking of this kind is apt to cut the ground under more scholarly publication'. For Guedalla, see pp. 32–3.

163 For Fortescue, see *Oxf. DNB*. Namier told Lucy Sutherland in 1951 that in sorting the letters of George III in the royal archives before binding, Fortescue had removed supposedly blank pages on which there were endorsements or even postscripts. Fortunately, the 'simple artisan who did the mounting' had 'kept the pages which the great Fortescue (Honorary Fellow of Trinity College, Cambridge) had thrown away' (Namier to Sutherland, 30 Apr. 1951 (HPT, N–71)).

164 *Nation and Athenaeum*, 3 Dec. 1927, 7 Apr. 1928.

165 To his credit, Fortescue did not seem to take this badly: witness his graceful acceptance of a complimentary copy of *The structure of politics* (Fortescue to Harold Macmillan, 13 Feb. 1929 (BL, Macmillan archive, Add. MS 55065)).

166 Namier to Kerr, 11 Aug. 1926 (Rylands, Namier papers, 1/1a/1/4–6).

167 For Macmillan, see Alastair Horne, *Macmillan* (2 vols, 1988–89), and *Oxf. DNB*. For Namier's developing political views, and his shift to a position of support for what he called 'the left wing of the Conservative party', see p. 255.

168 Namier to C. P. Scott, 29 Aug. 1927 (*Guardian* arch., A/N2/11); Scott to Namier, 30 Aug. 1927 (ibid., A/N2/12).

169 Namier to H. A. L. Fisher, 6 Jan. 1928 (Rylands, Namier papers, 1/1a/1/ 22 (i)); Harold Macmillan to Namier, 22 Dec. 1927 (ibid., 1/12a/1/22(ii)).

170 J. P. Cooper to K. B. McFarlane, 10 Feb. 1948 (Trinity College, Oxford, Cooper papers, DD279/I).

171 'Record of manuscripts' (BL, Macmillan archive, Add. MS 56023, *s.v.* 30 Nov. 1927). The reader, identified in the publisher's ledger as 'Professor F. J. C. H.', was F. J. C. Hearnshaw,

of King's College, London, who, although primarily a medieval historian, had published a textbook on nineteenth-century Europe with Macmillan in 1918. Hearnshaw may have taken exception to Namier's arguments about the unreality of parties, given that, in an essay soon to be published in *The nineteenth century and after* (in February 1930), he praised the virtues of a two-party system such as had existed in England from the seventeenth century 'until the present day'.

172 Macmillan to Namier, 22 Dec. 1927 (Rylands, Namier papers, 1/1a/1/ 22 (ii)); Namier to Fisher, 6 Jan. 1928 (ibid., 1/1a/1/ 22 (i)); Kerr to Fisher, 11, 18 Jan. 1928 (ibid., 1/1a/1/23–4); 'Record of manuscripts' (BL, Macmillan archive, Add. MS 56023, *s.v.* 5, 11 Jan. 1928).

173 *Structure*, xiii; Blanche Dugdale to Ld Balfour, 17 May 1928 (NRS, GD 433/2/277/67).

174 See also the press cutting of a review by Namier of the third volume of Trevelyan's trilogy, *England under Queen Anne*, which had been published in 1934 (Rylands, Namier papers, 1/8/3). In an otherwise positive response, Namier wrote that 'if any criticism may be ventured upon this important work, it is that the reader seldom feels himself translated into the atmosphere of its time, and never meets its people at close quarters', a consequence of the author having opted for an 'extensive survey' rather than 'intensive research'. Much later, and privately, he described Trevelyan's work as 'poor in scholarship and muddled in thought' (Namier to Mrs Michael West, 27 Nov. 1956 (HPT, N–64)). For his part Trevelyan thought that Namier had 'no sense of the past' (David Cannadine, *G. M. Trevelyan: a life in history* (1992), 207).

175 Blanche Dugdale to Ld Balfour, 24 Oct. 1928 (NRS, GD 433/2/277/82–5).

5

Skyscrapers, 1928–32

'A new factor in the historical world'

The structure of politics at the accession of George III appeared in print in two volumes in January 1929. Early sales were slow, or at least slower than the author had expected: not quite four hundred copies in the first two months, though Namier was reassured by his publisher that 'for a book of that character the sales are very satisfactory'.[1] In many respects it was a curious production, lacking an obvious commercial market. The text was heavily burdened with detail about obscure individuals and their relationships, often quoting at length from original sources. The book had neither an overarching narrative nor an emphatic interpretive structure. It did not address directly those aspects of the subject which might have been expected to interest non-academic readers, such as the character and ambitions of George III and the nature of Britain's government of its colonies. Instead, it offered a series of essays on connected themes, beginning *in medias res* with an extended taxonomy of parliamentary types, under the heading 'why men went into parliament'; following this with a short survey of the membership elected in 1761, then a discussion of the payments made to indigent MPs and others from the 'secret service' fund (the accounts being printed as an appendix), case-studies of elections in Shropshire, Cornwall and two 'Treasury boroughs', and finally four character sketches of 'parliamentary beggars'. The pieces on individuals and elections were similar to those that Namier had already been publishing in academic journals, narrative in form and austerely factual.

There were no general conclusions. Presumably these were to come much later, at the end of Namier's great project. It was only in a few paragraphs in the preface that he explained his intention: to show that the truth of 'political transactions' could not be understood through declamatory narratives in a handful of 'classical texts' but by a process of painstaking re-creation using the fullest possible range of surviving contemporary documents. Indeed, the memorable phrases in the preface have been quoted more often than anything else in the book, notably Namier's likening of parliament to 'an ant-heap, with the human ants hurrying in long files along their various paths'.

Apart from the occasional authorial aside, Namier embedded his main arguments in the detail of his exposition, which exposed the three principal elements of what would come to be recognised as the 'Namier thesis'. First, the inherited party labels of 'Whig' and 'Tory' meant nothing when applied to the practicalities of parliamentary life in the 1760s. The Whigs had dissolved into a myriad of smaller factions, centred on individual magnates, while a rump of 'old Tory' squires, now reconciled to the Hanoverian regime, preserved their traditional identity in a different form, no longer sharing a common ideology beyond the ethos of 'independent country gentlemen'.[2] Second, political principle was not a factor in the 'personal reshufflings' which formed the basis of ministerial reconstructions. And third, the accepted narrative of the early years of George III's reign was a delusion: the notion that the young king, encouraged by his mother and his tutor Lord Bute, came to the throne determined to restore power to the crown, through massive corruption and the assistance of subservient politicians known as 'king's friends'. The origin of this 'black legend' Namier traced to Edmund Burke's pamphlet *Thoughts on the cause of the present discontents* (1770), which he saw as a piece of propaganda intended to advance the interests of the Rockingham faction by promoting their spurious claim to be the tribunes of true whiggism. From time to time in *The structure of politics* Namier took casual pot-shots at Burke, in order to fix in the reader's mind that Burke had been the instrument of the Rockinghams, but as with much else, he did not directly address the issue of Burke's portrait of George III. Instead, the refutation of the idea of the king as a would-be absolutist remained implicit, depending on the weight of evidence concerning the social profile of the Commons, the nature of the electoral system, and the politically inconsequential nature of the 'secret service' expenditure which was supposed to have underpinned 'the party of the crown'.

It was the quality of Namier's evidence and the way it was deployed that most impressed reviewers: the dense texture of the detail; the extraordinary mastery of a whole range of new, or at least unfamiliar, sources, especially the private correspondence of politicians which he had recovered from manuscripts in the British Museum and in country houses; the authority of his judgments; his evident familiarity with the characters and scenes described; and the way in which he seemed able to conjure up the reality of the past. To a reading public fascinated by the eighteenth century – then 'very much in vogue' in popular literature[3] – Namier seemed to have painted a picture from life. The anonymous reviewer in *The Times* welcomed a 'masterly piece of research': Namier clearly knew as much about the eighteenth-century House of Commons as the best-informed contemporary, and 'seems to regard every Member of Parliament as a personal friend'.[4] The *Listener*, which described the book as 'the most penetrating and substantial study of the political life of the days of the elder Pitt and the duke of Newcastle that has yet been made', considered that the author 'knows the political world of 1760 with an intimacy which even Lecky did not attain'.[5] Even more gushing was the review in the *Manchester Guardian*, by the Oxford historian Keith Feiling, which opened with the statement that: 'This is the most important book on the politics of eighteenth-century England published since Lecky', and, because of its methodological innovation, 'a more important book than that'. In particular, Feiling admired the unprecedented depth of the research, and Namier's determination to understand the eighteenth century on its own terms.[6]

The ovation continued, with universally excellent notices in heavyweight periodicals and regional newspapers, one of which compared Namier to Maitland.[7] There was even a generous commendation from G. M. Trevelyan, who in a letter to the author – which Namier had no compunction in showing around – described the work as a 'feat of a really novel character'.[8] While it is difficult to imagine such a book making an impact on public consciousness nowadays, in 1929 Namier created a literary sensation. The *Observer* even recommended the two volumes for summer holiday reading, 'if history is a passion and big books do not daunt'.[9] Such was the currency of Namier's work that an article for the *Times Literary Supplement* on the forthcoming general election used Namier's description of the working of the eighteenth-century electoral system as a framework for its own reflections.[10] Such universal acclaim would have turned anyone's head, and Namier was no exception.[11] The most gratifying compliments were probably Feiling's, who was himself a former prize fellow of All Souls, and could well have been present at one, if not both, of the college meetings in 1911–12 at which Namier was rejected.

At last everything seemed to be going Namier's way: he told Lady Sandwich in February 1929 that he had been unable to carry out research for her in the Public Record Office because of

> the great number of social engagements I have at present; one must not go to the Record Office in anything better than a navvy's suit, for the work on books and manuscripts there is as dirty as that of a house-breaking, and London distances being what they are, if on a day I have to go anywhere to a meal or a meeting, I cannot possibly go the same day to the Record Office.[12]

Life was a whirl of activity. He was preparing his second book, the first instalment of the narrative of *England in the age of the American revolution*, which would cover the period of the Bute-Newcastle ministry of 1761–63. He hoped to have it completed by September, and was sending it to Macmillan in sections, as soon as Miss Le Marinel finished typing each batch of text.[13] He was also continuing to review for newspapers and magazines, though his pace had dropped. And in March 1929 he was invited to join the Treasury committee established under the chairmanship of Josiah Wedgwood to investigate the possibility of preparing an officially sponsored history of parliament, a particular honour since 'the commission [sic] will be very small, and only two or three historians on it', but another call on his time, and his best clothes.[14] Weighing even more heavily on his mind was what he conceived of as his duty to his people. With his first book published, and the second on the way, Namier could no longer justify postponing acceptance of the Zionist Organisation's offer of employment. He found it impossible to resist Weizmann's blandishments and the call of his own conscience.

Alarmed by rumours of Namier's imminent appointment to the Zionist Organisation, Rufus Rosenwald wrote from Chicago in February 1929 to urge him not to abandon his study of the American revolution now that he had done the 'spadework' (Namier's own turn of phrase), but to 'complete what would be as fine a monument to you as any man could possibly desire'. He added that 'no less a man than Professor Felix Frankfurter, of the Harvard University Law School, is of the same opinion'.[15] Namier had only just discovered that the Rosenwalds were his anonymous benefactors. His response had therefore to be framed carefully. He was able to reassure Rufus that he had already done a great deal and that more was in hand:

> My next book, covering the period 1760–1764, and containing a good many of the fundamental points I have to make about the 'Imperial problem during the American revolution' will be ready in a month or two (it must not surprise you that these fundamental points should come in so early, but I find them in the political structure of the period rather than in mere incidents of the later years). If I possibly can, I should still like to write the history of the Rockingham government of 1765–6, for which I have a considerable mass of material in hand.

The question was, whether he should attempt this work now, before joining the Zionists. The answer he gave showed the complex pressures with which his mind was wrestling, and also the limit of his egotism:

> My primary aim was not to build a monument for myself (*aere perennius*)[16] nor to write a history of that period: but rather to acquire a position which would enable me to work effectively for the Jewish cause, and to make certain experiments in history-writing which would be interesting and important, quite apart from the specific subject of my book ... Once, in 1914, I broke off my history work for ten years because of a British war. Our own race is now in an infinitely more dangerous and difficult position than Great Britain was in 1914; for on a very moderate estimate half the world makes war on them, and they are practically helpless. I know, working for them is neither enjoyable nor remunerative ... Still I do consider that for a Jew who sees our position as I do, it is an absolute duty.[17]

He replied in similar vein to another of the many friends who wrote to congratulate him: the American lawyer and politician Charles Nagel, with whom he had not been in contact since 1914. 'I am a good Jew and a strong Zionist … I feel it my duty to break off once more my history work, and do whatever I can for the Zionist cause.'[18]

For the time being he could bathe in the warm waters of adulation. He ignored, or perhaps had not noticed, the fact that some reviewers, while recognising his originality, had expressed cautious reservations, which would eventually find echoes in the endeavours of later generations to subvert Namier's dominance over eighteenth-century political history. An otherwise highly favourable review in the *Times Literary Supplement*, which Namier considered 'a great honour to me',[19] questioned whether such a 'long catalogue of self-seeking' as Namier had related was really representative of public life and public morality in the eighteenth century. The author's 'cynical humour' had perhaps got the better of his sense of proportion.[20] Even Feiling had allowed himself to wonder whether Namier's conclusions about the irrelevance of party labels would have to be modified as the narrative of the 1760s and 1770s unfolded, observing that the term Tory still meant something to contemporaries like Horace Walpole, and also that 'one case at least, in the present work suggests that the old apple between Church and dissent still had life within it'.[21]

Reviews in English learned journals, which were slower to come in, struck the same note of mild scepticism, though it is worth noting that American historians, by contrast, thoroughly approved of Namier's methods and accepted his interpretations without reserve.[22] Sir Richard Lodge, formerly of Edinburgh University and a historian whom Namier admired, while impressed by the 'almost incredible industry' with which Namier had rescued important details about parliamentary representation from the Newcastle papers – 'the rubbish basket of the eighteenth century' – was not exactly profligate with his praise: 'Within its limits, which are much narrower than the title suggests, Mr Namier's work has great interest.'[23] Another important English reviewer was the Cambridge historian Denys Winstanley, whose own studies of the 1760s, published before the Great War, had covered much of the same ground. Winstanley is sometimes thought to have anticipated Namier in his emphasis on patronage and family connection, but he had at the same time been very clear in asserting that George III had ascended the throne anxious to recover the power his predecessors had lost.[24] In the course of a generally positive notice for the *English Historical Review*, Winstanley observed that, on the question of the unreality of party divisions, 'some of us may not be prepared to accept without further question all of Mr Namier's conclusions and implications'.[25]

Namier seized upon the warm reception of his first book to apply to the Rhodes trustees for a grant towards the production of the next. He was adamant that he would have to take up employment with the Zionist Organisation in the autumn. In part this was his 'duty', but there was also a powerful financial imperative:

> Work on the scale on which I have been doing it, can hardly be combined with teaching, whereby most historians, with no private means of their own, secure their livelihood. I gratefully acknowledge the help which the Rhodes Trustees gave me at a critical moment two and a half years ago. Still, the £300, though they were invaluable to me at a time of exceptional stringency, did not even pay for the work which my secretary has done on the book now published ... I cannot go on piling up debts indefinitely, and there seems to be no public endowments for history research, at least I have never been able to obtain a share in any except what I have received from the Rhodes Trustees. Therefore, if I did not take the post offered me by the Zionist Organisation, I should probably have to go into business to repay my debts and secure funds for my history work.[26]

The secretary, Philip Kerr, consulted the trustee best qualified to give an opinion, H. A. L. Fisher, noting that *The structure* ... 'has had a resounding success'. 'Few historical works of this nature have received such good notices.'[27] Fisher was equally impressed, in his way. His comments, however, were restrained; the book was 'a very substantial contribution', although 'in the later part of it the material is somewhat unorganised'.[28] He observed in passing that Namier 'clearly ought to have a fellow-ship at a college'. But, as always, it would have to be another college: his own, New College, 'can probably do little'. He would see 'whether I can move All Souls'.[29] He could not. But the trust did give Namier another £300, which enabled him to get the new book ready for the press in the autumn, and publication a year later.[30]

Namier was never good at devising titles, and for some time employed for this second book the working title 'England during the American revolution, volume I', reflecting the fact that he intended it to be the first in a series of chronological narratives. He also experimented with 'Government and parliament under the duke of Newcastle', but when the book appeared it was called *England in the age of the American revolution*, which gave a hostage to fortune in not adequately conveying the nature of the contents.[31] In essence, the book was to provide a detailed account of George III's first ministry, the uneasy and short-lived partnership between Newcastle and Bute, which lasted until Newcastle's resignation in May 1762. But despite the fact that Namier had already published what purported to be a scene-setting work for his great enterprise, it was still necessary to include a good deal of introductory matter. This was a reflection of the way the production of the two books had been rushed.

Namier began *England in the age of the American revolution* with a lengthy chapter on the 'social foundations' of politics, with reflections on social organisation and mobility, on the nature of the British state and of the 'imperial problem' (the latter probably incorporating material from his Beit essay, and including the occasional passage betraying the origins of his project in his interest in ideas of imperial federation).[32] The style was discursive, including personal reminiscences,[33] and replete with the *obiter dicta* with which Namier often dusted his shorter essays and book reviews: 'England knows not democracy as a doctrine, but has always practised it as a fine art'; 'the English are not a methodical or logical nation'. This wide-ranging prologue was followed by a discussion of the nature of constitutional monarchy under George II, and the character, education and aspirations of his grandson and successor. And after a narrative of the events leading up to the general election of 1761, Namier proceeded to analyse the new House of Commons, with specific reference to the Members' American connections and interests, before taking up his story with the circumstances surrounding Newcastle's resignation.

The book interspersed analysis of the composition of the House of Commons – what Namier called 'structural analysis' – with close descriptions of ministerial intrigues. The two narrative sections focused on dealings between the king, Bute, Newcastle and other leading figures like the duke of Cumberland, rather than events in parliament. Where MPs figured in the text they were described and counted, but Namier said little about how they spoke or voted. In part this reflected his method of working: research into individual MPs issuing in calculations of the strength of parliamentary connections and analyses of economic interests – he talked about 'compiling my list of the House of Commons'.[34] But, as with any empiricist, it also arose from the sources he had used, not the Commons' journals or reports of parliamentary debates, but the correspondence between the principals, especially in the Newcastle papers, from which he quoted extensively. Thus, despite serving a different purpose, in style and flavour *England in the age of the American revolution* strongly resembled its predecessor.

This time, however, Namier did engage directly with elements of the narrative of aspiring monarchical absolutism which had become a staple of vulgar Whig history writing, though without mentioning its creator, Burke, or the faction he served. He refuted the notion that 'responsible parliamentary government' had been established under the first two Georges, whose relations with parliament, especially in their choice of ministers, had been determined instead by the nature of parties and factions in the House of Commons. The gradual dissolution of the two-party system after 1714 fundamentally changed the environment in which monarchs operated. While George II lived the transformation of the political landscape had been disguised by the continuing existence of a 'reversionary interest' centred on the heir apparent, and by the king's personal commitment to the 'old corps' of Whigs headed by Newcastle. But 'the moment the king ceased to deem himself restricted to one group … the reality of "personal government" was bound to appear'.[35] Even so, 'the accession of George

III did not in itself mark the advent of any new ideas, nor, except for the disturbing and ineffective person of Lord Bute, did it immediately bring forth new men'.[36]
Namier was clear that 'the practice of George II's earlier years was no real innovation';
moreover, 'the Whigs', as he slipped into calling the Rockinghams, did not 'consider
the king's interference in the least unconstitutional, while it worked in their favour'.[37]

In a passage which has acquired notoriety, Namier considered the intentions of
the king himself. Elsewhere he attempted a 'mental diagnosis' of a young man 'yearn-
ing after great achievements' which was both sensitive and sympathetic,[38] but in
discussing George's notions of government he was abruptly dismissive: rather than
having been 'brought up in "aristocratic notions"', the prince had been 'nurtured on
constitutional platitudes which he duly copied, adorning them with the current verbiage about virtue and liberty'. Namier quoted examples of George's repetition of the
nostrums of the day, about the 'beauty, excellence and perfection of the British constitution' and its 'ancient liberty'. 'In short', he concluded, the king 'talked flapdoodle
of the most innocent kind – and the danger was only in what a man might do who
talked such flapdoodle'.[39] Half a century later, historians would pick up this phrase as
proof of Namier's contempt for doctrine or 'social theories' in general.[40] It is true that
he had an undisguised contempt for some theories and theorisers, but his intention
in writing about George III was very specific: to explore motivation, and whether the
king was really the would-be absolutist that Whig historians made him out to be. In
order to discover the mainsprings of action he felt it necessary to penetrate beneath
political slogans.

Present-day objections to Namier's dismissal of 'verbiage about virtue and liberty' are a product of the intellectual climate of post-war Britain. Such criticism
scarcely surfaced when his books first appeared, even in America, where one might
have expected a strong attachment to the conviction that eighteenth-century politics
was fundamentally about principles, at least on the revolutionary side. Only one
American scholar, William T. Laprade, ventured to suggest that 'a serious weakness' in Namier's work, 'so carefully done in many respects', was the failure to take
cognisance of 'public opinion', as expressed in 'the newspapers, periodicals and pamphlets which the rival politicians and their lieutenants used in their struggles with
each other'.[41] Laprade had himself investigated the part played by 'public opinion'
in the general election of 1784, and had emphasised its importance in large 'open'
constituencies like Westminster or Yorkshire, while recognising that these were
exceptional cases.[42] He did not dispute Namier's view that 'parliamentary elections
seldom decided anything of importance in the eighteenth century' but believed that
'the actions of politicians were in a considerable degree determined by the emotional
atmosphere of the time'.[43]

Namier had already written at some length about 'public opinion' in a magazine article, pointing out the folly of deducing from orchestrated press campaigns the actual views of the populace. He did not deny that something of the sort existed, and could influence the working of politics even at the highest level. 'Public opinion', as he constructed it, was neither sophisticated nor specific, a reading of evidence which reflected the pervasive presence in his thought of contemporary notions of crowd psychology. After questioning whether any election had ever been influenced by 'public opinion' on questions of policy, he concluded, perhaps thinking more of the peasantry of eastern Europe than of the people of his adopted country:

> And still – after all is said that can be said in ridicule of the conception of a 'public opinion' and of the methods employed with a view to ascertaining it, the fact remains that it exists … There is such a thing as a logic of ideas, and ideas, when looked at from a distance, seem to have an independent life and existence of their own; their 'logic' is the outcome of the slow, hardly conscious thinking of the masses, very primitive, simplified in the process of accumulation, and in its mass advance deprived of all individual features, like the pebbles in a river-bed. And there is such a thing as a mental atmosphere, which at times becomes so all-pervading that hardly anyone can withdraw himself from its influence.[44]

The first reviews of *England in the age of the American revolution*, in newspapers and weeklies, were complimentary but not as gushing as before. While some newspaper reviewers carried over their admiration from the first book and adopted a reverential tone, others felt able to criticise. *The Times* reviewer was firmly in the first camp, commenting, 'as one is now bound to expect, this book is illuminated by the author's almost uncanny familiarity, not only with all conceivable manuscript authorities but also with even more remote references in long-forgotten books and pamphlets of the period'.[45] Feiling, in the *Observer*, remained enthusiastic, even if his opening metaphor, likening Namier's scholarship to an '*Unterseeboot* … more heavily armed than ever, and formidable in all scientific equipment', would not have gone down well with the author.[46] Included in Feiling's review, however, was a phrase about Namier's 'bland aphorisms', and a repetition of Feiling's previous suggestion that 'a diagnosis of the Church and Dissent' might modify Namier's negation of the importance of party at Westminster. Other reviewers, while acknowledging Namier's scholarship, and his pre-eminence as a guide to the 'backwaters' of the period, felt a sense of déjà vu: this was more of the same.[47] In *The Bookman*, F. E. Whitton lamented that, despite his title, Namier had not done much to explain the American revolution, and in particular had said virtually nothing about British attitudes to the colonists: the book's 'limited, specialist scope' meant that it would prove to be a useful companion to existing studies, but no more.[48]

In some respects the least satisfactory review was by G. M. Trevelyan, in the *Nation and Athenaeum*.[49] Trevelyan had recently published the first volume of his own trilogy on *England under Queen Anne*, telling a story that unfolded against a backdrop of fierce party rivalries, and a political scene lit by conflict over constitutional principles. It was a very different work from Namier's both in its approach and in the thrust of its narrative. One can see why Trevelyan should modestly have begun his review of Namier by pleading incompetence. He said he had taken on the job solely in order to pay a public tribute to Namier's work and to encourage him to return to his research: 'It is rumoured that he is deserting history for practical affairs, and perhaps if he knows how much old stagers appreciate his irruption into their historical business, he may be the more likely to return some day.'

But Trevelyan, for all his honourable intentions, was at bottom unsympathetic to Namier's kind of history, and did not find it easy to countenance the repudiation of the traditional Whig interpretation of George III's reign, more obvious in Namier's second book than in its predecessor. In an essay published in 1913 – essentially an anti-modernist manifesto – Trevelyan had spoken up for the idea of history as literature, and for the value of a grand narrative, especially the Whig grand narrative, against those who treated the subject as a 'science'. In his view 'scientific historians' had lost the art of story-telling: 'There is no "flow" in their events, which stand like pools instead of running in streams.'[50] Namier's analytical style put him on his mettle, and it may not be a coincidence that Trevelyan republished his ruminations on 'scientific history' in a new edition in 1930. Thus his review, while praising the early chapters in particular, carefully distanced itself from Namier's arguments. Namier's work had 'a touch of something unique'; he was 'a new factor in the historical world'; but his ideas were 'not as novel as he thinks', and not entirely convincing.

Trevelyan did not accept the idea that royal policy was unaffected by George III's accession, and suggested that when Namier had finished his projected series and taken the story beyond 1770, he might well think differently. And while Trevelyan accepted that party distinctions had little or no significance in the Commons in 1760, this was not, he said, the whole picture: there was still an underlying struggle between Whig and Tory in the constituencies, based on religious differences. Developing the hint dropped by Feiling, he suggested that the explanation for the survival of the parties into the nineteenth century lay in the continuing importance of the animosity between church and dissent. Here in a nutshell were the Whig objections to Namier's revisionism. Trevelyan concluded with an even more irksome suggestion, that there were various means of arriving at historical truth and Namier's was only 'one of the truths'.

Reviews in scholarly journals took a similar line, highly respectful of Namier's extraordinary industry and intimacy with the period, its personalities and archives, but now inclined to salt their praise with scepticism. Again, the relative generosity of American scholars stands out.[51] English authorities on the eighteenth century were more inclined to carp. Hugh Hale Bellot, who held a chair in American history at London University, began his notice by hailing 'the workings of so powerful and original a mind' and 'so signal an exhibition of learning and technical skill', before confessing that he found the chapter on 'The House of Commons and America' less than satisfying, the author not going 'to the root of the matter quite as he is accustomed to do'.[52] The LSE sociologist T. H. Marshall, an interesting choice for a reviewer, predictably enjoyed the analytical chapters but thought the narrative section gave an impression of 'aimlessness'.[53] And Sir Richard Lodge was more open than before in challenging Namier's conclusions, in relation to George III himself, and the question of party. While accepting that party names meant little in 1760 – a 'notorious' fact of which Namier actually had no need to remind readers – Lodge was adamant that they came back into use after 1763, as any historian would discover who paid proper attention to foreign affairs.[54]

For Namier *England in the age of the American revolution* was a more important book than *The structure of politics*, for, having fitted out his vessel, he was now launching out on his great enterprise. Its reception was thus of even greater consequence. That he was unhappy is clear from a letter written by Walter Elliot to Blanche Dugdale in October, even before Trevelyan's judgment had appeared.[55] Elliot felt that Namier should learn to balance things out: reviews of *The structure* had been 'over-good'; these were 'over-bad'. Elliot himself was unsure that reviewers had actually read the first book, 'but seeing this mass of learning and being overawed by the extracts they happened to pick out they played for safety. Now, having done reverence to the Unknown God once they feel that he is a known God and he falls into the ruck of "The Literature"'. Part of the problem, he felt, was Namier's style, which was becoming 'very pontifical and unreadably intricate, and idea-loaded'. Elliot observed cannily (and perhaps a trifle maliciously, with Namier's Freudianism in mind) that 'an overloaded style is a manifestation of the inferiority complex'. Namier should go back to writing popular essays, to which he was better suited. It seems unlikely that Mrs Dugdale passed on this advice. Namier's mood almost certainly worsened with the Trevelyan review, especially since it followed closely on the warm welcome given to Trevelyan's own very old-fashioned work on Queen Anne's reign, and, worse still, a gushing notice in *The Nation* by Philip Guedalla of the concluding volume in Sir John Fortescue's history of the British army.[56] Guedalla was precisely the kind of popular historian Namier despised, while Fortescue's scholarship Namier regarded as feeble to the point of inanity.[57] Here was the old guard once again patting itself on the back.

Was Namier's achievement in these two books as 'revolutionary' as early reviewers thought, and his admirers claimed? Later commentators have warned against assuming that he was wholly innovative.[58] He did not invent prosopography; nor was he the first historian to use the Newcastle papers, either for the elucidation of high-political intrigues or to expose local power-broking at parliamentary elections.[59] More important, perhaps, Namier was by no means the first to observe that in the 1760s the old two-party system had given way to a more fragmentary pattern. As far back as 1907 the Prussian historian Albert von Ruville, whose biography of the earl of Chatham appeared in English translation in that year, not only anticipated Namier in his close analysis of the ministerial changes of 1760–62 (though paying more attention to policy issues), but also assumed a parliamentary context of factional rather than two-party conflict.[60] Winstanley too, had written of 'the Bedford party', 'the Grenville party' or 'the Rockingham party', rather than Whigs and Tories;[61] and the American Clarence Walworth Alvord, whose two-volume study of *The Mississippi valley in British politics* (1917) Namier cited as an exemplar of research on the American side of the problem,[62] explicitly denied the existence of Whig and Tory in the England of George III, and depicted the parliamentary conflicts of the reign as 'a struggle for the fleshpots of Egypt' between factions 'lacking any kind of principle'.[63]

Nevertheless, Namier went much further than his predecessors in separating out the membership of the House of Commons into small groups, a process which in his second book occasionally resembled atomisation,[64] and provided names and numbers where others offered vague allusions. He also drew different conclusions about the consequences of the decline of toryism after 1745. He recognised that some form of 'party' politics was to reappear during the later 1760s, but unlike Feiling, Trevelyan and Lodge, did not see continuity. On the one side the Rockinghams, about whom he actually said little, were presented as just another faction, masquerading as the custodians of traditional Whig principles; on the other, the old Tories had transmogrified into 'independent country gentlemen'. And of course his representation of the character and intentions of George III broke the existing consensus: von Ruville, for all his views on party, had subscribed to the notion that George III was guilty of 'autocratic tendencies',[65] while Namier's praise of Alvord's work passed over politely Alvord's belief that one of the factions in the Commons was 'led by the king who entered the lists in the hope of saving his prerogative'.[66] In any case, the intensity of the research, the novelty of the detail and the precise observation in Namier's books, did together constitute something altogether new: an exact picture of a political world with which scholars had thought themselves familiar but had now to reacquaint themselves as strangers.

For some reason, the appearance of this 'new force' in history writing did not issue in a flood of imitators, which has prompted the observation that Namier's impact on his contemporaries has been overrated.[67] A possible explanation might be that the absence from his books of any serious engagement with political ideas was at odds with the temper of the times, given that the 1930s was a decade so obviously dominated by ideologies;[68] and some support for this argument may be located in the way that English historians in the 1930s seem to have refocused their attention on the seventeenth century. But academic historians' neglect of the eighteenth century cannot simply be ascribed to the non-ideological, apparently cynical, nature of Namier's history. In the 1930s work was still being done on the period c.1720–c.1785. Diplomatic historians like Lodge continued to ply their trade, and there was a trickle of books and articles on colonial or imperial history. But with rare exceptions, the research students working on eighteenth-century politics were those Namier himself supervised when he was eventually given an academic job. Apart from his friend Romney Sedgwick, who was, in his spare time, editing the correspondence of George III and Bute,[69] hardly any established scholar ventured into Namier's territory. A naval historian, Brian Tunstall, published a new biography of Lord Chatham in 1938, which made copious and fulsome acknowledgments to Namier's 'brilliant' and 'revolutionary' contributions to scholarship; but it was a disappointing book, which quickly sank beneath the waves.[70] Possibly many were simply frightened off. Before the appearance of *The structure of politics* William Laprade had written an article which attempted to reconstruct the political background to the passage and repeal of the Stamp Act of 1765 by making use of newspapers and pamphlets as well as published correspondence. Once Namier's work was in print he turned back to the early decades of the century: his next book, about 'public opinion' and politics, stopped at the fall of Walpole in 1742.[71]

Namier did, however, make a powerful impact on a handful of younger scholars, beyond those whom he himself taught. Lucy Sutherland, a lecturer at Oxford, had been preparing an article on the first Rockingham administration of 1765–66 when *The structure of politics* appeared. 'She could always remember the sudden flash of illumination on how eighteenth-century politics worked, and how she had torn up what she had written.'[72] She sent Namier a letter, to which he replied with encouragement and firm but constructive criticism, treating her very much as an equal.[73] Others of the rising Oxford generation also sought him out, including Richard Pares, a Balliol protégé of Charles Stone and Kenneth Bell, who was breaking new ground in the history of the eighteenth-century Caribbean plantations, and Michael Roberts, who went from Oxford to Liverpool to work for his PhD and was anxious to apply 'the Namier method' to early nineteenth-century politics.[74] As might have been expected, historians in America were also drawn to Namier's flame. Robert Walcott, a doctoral student at Harvard interested in the very early eighteenth century, was recommended by his supervisor, the Cromwellian scholar Wilbur Abbott, to make 'an examination of parliamentary parties in Queen Anne's reign by means of a detailed study of individual Members of Parliament'.[75] When Walcott came to England in pursuit of manuscripts he made a beeline for Namier.[76] Another of Abbott's pupils, Jack Hexter, took a similar approach to studying the Long Parliament of Charles I, and, in his first published article, went out of his way to cite Namier's achievement in overthrowing 'the Whig interpretation of eighteenth-century politics'.[77]

The History of Parliament

While Namier had used the prosopographical method in the research for *The structure of politics* and *England in the age of the American revolution* neither book was explicitly an exercise in prosopography as such. Its conclusions were based on the close study of individuals or particular groups, and in analysing the 1761 general election Namier categorised and counted MPs. He did not attempt any aggregation of biographical details for the entire House of Commons, as Beard had done for the Philadelphia convention. That would have been impossible given the time and resources at his disposal. His card index was of limited value in constructing his books; instead, his structural analysis focused on members, constituencies and episodes which caught his eye.

Driven by a need to discover everything about everything, Namier was drawn to the idea of extending his researches systematically to encompass every MP and every constituency. He also saw the possibility of doing far more with his material than explaining the workings of the House of Commons: parliamentary prosopography would enable historians to understand the evolution of English society. But no single researcher, even one as energetic and determined as Namier, and blessed as he was with a photographic memory and prodigious powers of concentration, could accomplish such a task alone. As Namier himself wrote, with recent personal experience at the forefront of his mind, 'what can one expect from the lonely student, not given even the most elementary help (e.g., of a secretary or an assistant to do for him some of the more mechanical work) or the necessary leisure for his researches'.[78]

A month after completing the manuscript of his first book Namier published an article in the *Nation and Athenaeum* which was a manifesto for a truly prosopographical enterprise; a comprehensive history of the Westminster Parliament, accomplished through collective effort.[79] Although the article was called 'The biography of ordinary men', Namier did not mean 'ordinary men' in the sense of 'working men' or 'the lower orders' (phrases used in the article); rather, his concern was with those insufficiently famous to be written about by authors catering to popular taste. They formed 'the dark, dumb, nameless crowd', whose actions and interactions gave rise to the great changes in modern society. In relation to political developments, such as those at Westminster which paved the way for the American revolution, they would be 'individual Members of Parliament … civil servants, etc.'; for a major economic change like the industrial revolution, 'the merchants who turned manufacturers or bankers, the landowners who became mining adventurers, etc.'. As Namier elaborated his argument the focus narrowed down to parliament, and the attempts already made, by antiquarians and local historians, to unearth biographical information about 'ordinary' MPs. How much more useful would such work be if undertaken 'horizontally' rather than 'vertically'; if, instead of studying a county or borough over a long period, an attempt was made to build up a picture of representation across the country at a given time, or rather at various times, since 'only by comparison can we gauge movement and correctly define its nature'. Naturally, such a mammoth undertaking would have to be 'organised on a national scale, given national standing, and financed from national resources'.

Namier's thoughts had probably been tending for some time towards the notion of a grand and properly funded collaborative history. Traces of the idea can be read into the essay on the cultural significance of the skyscraper, published in 1927. 'For good and evil', he had written, 'we have in a thousand ways outgrown the day of the lonely individual; the direction of mass effort takes the place of solitary achievement'.[80] But of course a skyscraper requires an architect, and collaborative history would require someone to plan and direct.

If Namier's article had been an isolated call to action it might have seemed quixotic, for, however well connected, he was at this time no more than a freelance historical researcher, eking out an existence on savings, borrowed money and occasional grants. But he was not alone. Moves were already afoot to try to establish just such a publicly funded dictionary of parliamentary biography, and Namier's article was an attempt not merely to support the venture, but to turn it in what he considered to be the right direction. The originator of the scheme was the Liberal-turned-Labour MP Josiah ('Jos') Wedgwood, a descendant of the great Staffordshire porcelain manufacturer of the eighteenth century and a larger-than-life character – the archetypal independent-minded backbencher – who shared with Namier both a passion for history and a strong attachment to Zionism.[81] Wedgwood's manner of arguing the Zionist case, by observing a natural affinity between 'the Anglo-Saxon race' and the

Jews, and a more specific similarity between the Puritan defenders of English liberty and the Jewish rebels of ancient times, also harmonised with Namier's ideas about race and religion.[82] Namier first met him at a meeting of a study group on Palestine at Chatham House in April 1926.[83] The two men were in close contact by early 1928: at the same time as Wedgwood was launching the scheme for a parliamentary history he was also promoting Namier's idea that Palestine be accorded dominion status within the empire.[84]

Wedgwood's approach to the History of Parliament was very different from Namier's.[85] He was himself one of the local antiquarians doing their biographical research vertically, in his case compiling a series of annotated biographical lists of the MPs for his own county.[86] His first inclination had been to set up a scheme with government funding to collate the work of local amateurs and publish the results as a supplement to the government 'blue book', the *Official returns of Members ...*, a set of volumes to stand alongside the *Dictionary of National Biography*, from which many MPs had been excluded as insufficiently distinguished. After he had consulted A. F. Pollard, director of London University's Institute of Historical Research, Wedgwood became fired by a different vision. Pollard's conviction that 'parliamentary institutions are the greatest contribution that England has made to the civilisation of the world' struck a chord, and henceforth Wedgwood viewed his project less as an exercise in scholarship than as a celebratory and educational enterprise: a history of parliament for a world increasingly in need of lessons in democracy.[87]

To begin with, Wedgwood proceeded carefully and with evangelical enthusiasm in check. In May 1928 he organised a petition to the Prime Minister Stanley Baldwin, signed by over two hundred MPs, calling for a select committee to prepare 'a complete record of the personnel and politics' of the parliaments from 1264 (the date of the first surviving lists of members of the Commons) until the Great Reform Act.[88] One of the reasons for stopping at the Reform Act was practical, since information for the nineteenth and twentieth centuries was rich and easily obtainable; another was ideological, based on the belief that by 1832 the modern parliamentary system was already formed. Similar reasons account for the exclusion of the Lords: the *Complete Peerage* (a second edition of which was under way) already provided biographical details of peers (though not bishops), and in any case, as most parliamentarians and constitutional historians were agreed, the real story of the development of parliament was the rise of the lower house.

There was no indication at this early stage that Wedgwood was considering the participation of academic historians, apart from Pollard, but others began to push their way in, scenting the prospect of public money to support their research. First to step forward was the Elizabethan historian, J. E. Neale, who had recently moved

from Manchester to University College, London. Neale was already interested in parliamentary prosopography, to the extent of supervising research students working on
particular parliaments, but had gone no further, on his own account, than a few articles on individuals.[89] Then came Namier. His conception of the project was broader
than Wedgwood's, broader even than Neale's, who focused on the contribution that
a multi-biographical approach could make to understanding English constitutional
history. Namier met Wedgwood to put his ideas across personally, and after a prolonged discussion, summarised his views in a letter.[90]

Much of what Namier had to say was to do with the practicalities of the work to
be done, of which he could speak from experience; this underlined the need for a
'national organisation' and proper financial support. Two general points stand out.
First, Namier saw that the work could and should be used as a means of understanding social as well as political and constitutional change. The House of Commons was
'a microcosmos' of the British 'political nation'.[91] 'A careful analysis of its personnel
throughout the centuries will show the rise and decline of classes and interests'; 'one
could write an economic history of England in terms of membership of the House of
Commons'. Second, he was insistent that the chronological sweep be broken up into
distinct periods, which should then be subjected to structural analysis. This seems
to have been his first explicit attempt to address the problem of how to reconcile his
own method with the need to understand change over time. 'The survey of one single
period must needs be more or less static, movements are shown by comparison
only.' Obviously the whole idea begged crucial questions, not least that its validity
depended on finding periods that were 'static' in terms of their social and political
foundations. This was something to which Namier himself, and to a greater extent
his critics, would return. For the moment, however, he marched ahead, citing the era
of the American revolution, 1761–84, as one such period, on which he had already
'done the work'.

Namier's articulation of the project's rationale was just what Wedgwood needed
to impress politicians and public. When Arthur Balfour was sent a file of papers concerning the prospective history, Baffy wrote excitedly to Namier about her uncle's
reaction:

> It was your letter to Jos. that did it. He kept exclaiming, 'This is a brilliant letter! What
> phrases! ... Look at this bit about *Alumni Cantabrigienses*:[92] here am I, chancellor of
> Cambridge, but I never heard of this work. I am grateful to him for that ... What an
> amazing race the Jews are!'[93]

In the summer of 1928 Wedgwood waited on Baldwin with academic historians in
attendance. Namier was not one of them,[94] probably because he had no academic

position, and also because he was hard to muzzle, and might well have made the history seem a different prospect than Wedgwood intended. Baldwin was naturally concerned about committing to expenditure, so Wedgwood trimmed his sails. His petition had asked for a committee to prepare a history, and privately Wedgwood set out a vision of the work with thematic essays as well as biographical entries.[95] But in the Commons he only asked for a committee 'to take evidence and report on what material is available', giving Baldwin the opportunity to offer a treasury committee (which could embrace non-parliamentarians) with a strict remit to report on the feasibility of a history, and no promises of public funding at the end of it.[96]

When appointed in 1929, the committee included six MPs and six historians. Namier was the only historian without an academic post. His nomination was suggested to the prime minister by one of the MPs on the committee, John Buchan, an old acquaintance from Wellington House, and also a Zionist sympathiser. Buchan wrote to Baldwin soon after the publication of *The structure of politics* to propose that Namier be added: 'His new book shows the most amazing knowledge of eighteenth-century parliamentary life, and he is one of the most learned men and hard workers I have ever known.'[97]

The committee began its deliberations in April 1929, with Wedgwood in the chair. Sub-committees were established, one for the medieval period, one for 1485–1707, and one for 1707–1832, comprising Namier, Buchan and another MP. Apart from one letter of Namier's to Wedgwood, all that survives is the bare record of meetings, which makes it hard to distinguish Namier's contribution.[98] Lady Namier's book is also unhelpful, since her account of the committee postulates a constant vigorous disagreement between her husband and Wedgwood on the direction the history should take, with 'long arguments ... often in private, late into the night'. This is just as likely to refer to their bitter conflicts over the later management of the history, once it was under way.[99]

Namier's sub-committee was the first to report, in June 1929.[100] The ensuing discussion provoked him to write privately to Wedgwood, complaining about the slow rate of progress.[101] The letter shows Namier bursting with vigour and, boosted by the reception of his first book, self-confident to the point of arrogance. He had a clear vision of what should be done, but was wildly over-optimistic, ignoring difficulties and rejecting counter-arguments out of hand. Above all, he was fiercely impatient with the older generation of historians. Whatever the committee's official remit, he assumed that its purpose was produce a history, and was anxious that it should be ready to start work as soon as possible. He told Wedgwood that he had 'tried to push these things through the third sub-committee as much as I could, but now I can do nothing more, unless you ... take action'.

The problem was the attitude of others on the committee. The medievalists (with good reason) were 'horrified at the greatness of the task which would confront them'. The only people who took an 'active' interest were Pollard, Wedgwood and Neale, and even they seemed 'chiefly interested in the search for materials and the missing returns' rather than 'the drafting of the biographical notes', which was where real historical expertise was needed, rather than antiquarian industry. Namier ascribed prime responsibility for this restrictive approach to the influence of the conservative-minded Pollard. After much talk about possible sources of money, Namier ended by re-emphasising the need for urgency, since he himself would soon begin work for the Zionist Organisation, after which all he would be able to offer would be 'supervision and advice'. The only thing to be done was for Wedgwood, Neale and Namier to get together to sort out 'ends and means'.

The following day Wedgwood received a letter from Pollard, warning against going beyond the committee's remit.[102] Events were 'reaching a crisis': their business should be 'the search for materials', not the writing of a history. The root of the problem lay with the 'third sub-committee', which was galloping off in the wrong direction. At first Pollard's view prevailed, but Wedgwood did not find the minimalist approach attractive.[103] In October, chairing a public lecture by Neale on Elizabethan parliaments, Wedgwood pressed the case for the preparation of a history of parliament in terms that combined his and Neale's concern for 'the real understanding of parliament and the growth of its powers', with Namier's broader ambitions, noting that such a history would show 'a slice of England under the microscope'.[104] At the same time Wedgwood drafted on his own initiative an 'interim report', which went far beyond the objective of merely adding names to the *Official return*; what was needed was 'to discover the politics of the members, both party and personal; and to provide such identification of the persons as may make the standing, profession and connections of the individual member clear'.[105] Here in a nutshell was Namier's conception of the history, and the phrase 'both party and personal', as well as the reference to the microscope, constituted a nod towards the historical approach of *The structure of politics*. The next step should be to begin the task, with paid editors and 'research workers', to produce volumes of biographies and explanatory material 'written by experts in the period'. The committee's terms of reference should be expanded, and it should be authorised to raise funds. In April 1930, at a meeting which Namier was unable to attend, another sub-committee was appointed comprising Wedgwood, Neale, and the MP Sir William Bull, to prepare 'a scheme for the editing and publication of the record of the personnel of past parliaments'.[106] Its report, accepted by the full committee in the following June (this time with Namier present), was prepared by Neale,[107] and proposed a History of Parliament divided into chronological sections, each containing a biographical dictionary of members. An interpretive introduction would 'analyse and correlate the facts'.[108] This set the pattern the History would follow throughout its first iteration during the 1930s, and again when it was revived in 1951, with Neale and Namier once more closely involved.

By the time the committee reconvened in the spring of 1931, Namier's circumstances had changed dramatically. He had not only resigned as political secretary to the Zionist Organisation, but had accepted a university chair. In that respect all appeared to bode well for the History of Parliament project and his participation in it. The committee submitted its 'interim report' to the treasury in October 1931, making the case for a collaborative history on grounds of 'public policy'. Wedgwood's voice could be heard in the argument that the truest means of gauging the strengths and weaknesses of an institution was by studying its past.[109] Across the world representative institutions were at risk, and a proper understanding of the development of this 'peculiarly English' institution would help to halt the march of totalitarianism. The report also cited 'historical and sociological reasons' for compiling a history, some of which reflected Neale's whiggish concern with explaining 'the evolution of parliament',[110] especially the rise of the Commons in the sixteenth and early seventeenth centuries. The 'sociological' reasons came directly from Namier:

> We shall be able to examine the connection of class with government … We shall know what economic interests were represented in parliament, and in what proportions, and how they … affected the work of parliament … We shall be able to say whether political principle explains the division between Cavalier and Parliamentarian, between Whig and Tory, etc., or whether family rivalry or county faction or some similar cause is not often a sounder explanation. In other words, we shall see legislators in groups and classes and discover – or approach nearer to discovering – from what motives or mixture of motives men's political theories and actions may be thought to have sprung.[111]

The Zionist Organisation

In 1930, when Namier was included for the first time in *Who's who*, he described himself as 'a Russian subject by birth, naturalised British, a Jew by race', publicly emphasising his Jewish identity.[112] And although he was still uncomfortable with the institutions of British Jewry, he managed to get himself elected to the board of deputies of British Jews, as deputy for Surbiton and Kingston Hebrew Congregation (with which he had no personal connection), since membership was necessary for his employment.[113] Afterwards, he played little or no part in the affairs of the board, and continued to keep away from rabbis and synagogues. But he had no qualms about including in the first chapter of *England in the age of the American revolution* a lengthy and perfectly gratuitous justification of the Zionist position, which he there acknowledged as his own, and a political appeal which was entirely out of character with the rest of the book:

> The relations of groups of men to plots of land, of organised communities to units of territory, form the basic content of political history ... to every man, as to Brutus, the native land is his life-giving mother, and the state raised upon the land his law-giving father; and the day cannot be long of a nation which fails to honour either. Only one nation has survived for two thousand years, though an orphan – my own people, the Jews. But then in the God-given law we have enshrined the authority of a state, and in the God-promised land the idea of a mother-country; through the centuries from Mount Sinai we have faced Arets Israel [sic], our land. Take away either, and we cease to be a nation; let both live again, and we shall be ourselves once more.[114]

Namier's duties were to start in October 1929, and, to prepare, he attended the Zionist congress at Zurich in July, to meet people and 'get acquainted with our affairs in the debates which took place over the problems of the agency'.[115] The Jewish Agency for Palestine had been established by the Zionist Organisation in 1921 to meet the provision in the League of Nations mandate 'for the purpose of advising and co-operating with the administration of Palestine in such ... matters as may affect the establishment of the Jewish national home and the interests of the Jewish population of Palestine'. The Zurich congress restructured the governance of the Zionist movement and replaced the existing Zionist executive by an expanded Jewish Agency which would include moneyed, non-Zionist Jews, interested in encouraging Jewish settlement in Palestine but not in establishing a Jewish state. There would still be close ties with the Zionist Organisation, which would select half of the representation on the agency's governing bodies, the president of the organisation serving as chair of the executive council. This restructuring served to perpetuate divisions within the movement, since there had already been strong opposition to the admission of non-Jews to the governing body of the Jewish Agency. Moreover, the 'revisionist' movement, headed by Ze'ev Jabotinsky, which insisted upon the establishment of a Jewish state across all the mandated territories and was bitterly critical of Weizmann's pragmatism and perceived pro-Britishness, now had another focus for discontent. In retrospect, Namier saw the Zurich congress as 'the beginning of the trail of our misfortunes'.[116]

Simultaneously, the situation in Palestine had deteriorated badly, and the attitude of British authorities was a prime cause of concern to Weizmann, Namier, and all those who felt that cooperation with the imperial power should be the keystone of Zionist policy. Tensions between Jews and Arabs in Jerusalem over access to the Western Wall erupted in August in mass demonstrations which degenerated into rioting, with violence on both sides, and finally into orchestrated attacks on Jewish communities. British forces, taken by surprise, restored order at pistol point. The Labour government under Ramsay MacDonald, equally wrong-footed, decided to set up a commission of inquiry to investigate the causes of the disturbances, headed by a retired colonial judge, Sir Walter Shaw.

With Leonard Stein taking a rest-cure at a continental spa, it fell to Namier in London to co-ordinate the agency's response, and to try and prevent the British government from taking action detrimental to the Jewish cause. This occupied him to such an extent that for a time he was obliged to stop 'history work' altogether.[117] His responsibilities gave him access to the powerful, and a sense of being at the heart of events, but the road he had to climb proved steep and stony. He felt himself to be hampered rather than assisted by his colleagues. Namier never suffered gladly those whom he regarded as self-important ninnies, and when innocent Jewish lives were at stake would not suffer them at all. He described Victor Jacobson, the agency's representative to the League of Nations as 'a giggling, chattering little fool' and Weizmann's deputy, Nahum Sokolow, as 'a little Jewish "factor" now raised to the level of pseudo-statesmanship'.[118] Nor was it easy to deal with government: MacDonald's private secretary Herbert Usher was a 'swollen-headed upstart'.[119] Unfortunately, such sentiments were not kept to himself, with the consequence that the enmity became mutual.[120]

Namier had other contacts, and in August 1929 visited the cabinet secretary Tom Jones, whom he had known since before the Great War, to press the urgency of the situation in Palestine and the difficulty of restraining American Jewish opinion.[121] 'We are doing all we can', he told Jones, 'to prevent the movement among them from assuming an anti-British character', adding that 'I myself ... having spent many years of my life in history work designed to improve Anglo-American relations, certainly feel strongly about it.' Namier did his best to persuade Jones of the socialist ethos of the Zionist cause.[122] But his cabinet masters stonewalled. Namier thought that they had been cowed by their civil servants, especially the officials in the Colonial Office, whom he never trusted.[123]

It had been an unhappy beginning, and things did not improve. Moreover, Namier's health was suffering. During the hectic months of August and September 1929, insomnia established a firm hold: 'the great excitement and strain was not conducive to good sleep. I had frequently to take drugs and work under extreme pressure.'[124] Even after Weizmann returned to London, it was impossible to arrange a meeting with Ramsay MacDonald, or to raise the agency's concerns with ministers. Disappointment got the better of Namier. Not even Weizmann escaped his anger. Although he still 'loved' his leader, and willingly acted as his adviser, spokesman, courier and comforter – his 'Figaro' – he was exasperated by Weizmann's capacity to be both unnecessarily secretive with close colleagues and at the same time hideously indiscreet.[125] Namier's frustration was made all the greater by the fact that he was himself on terms of close personal friendship not just with Tom Jones, but also with the under-secretary for dominion affairs, Ramsay MacDonald's son Malcolm, whom he had known at Oxford, and yet was still unable to make progress. Twice he travelled to Geneva, where talks were taking place at the League of Nations, an organisation in which he put no faith whatsoever, in order to try and arrange a meeting between Weizmann and the prime minister. Twice he failed.[126] Talking to junior ministers on his second visit, he gave vent to his feelings:

> The Arabs said that there would be no peace unless the Jews were disarmed. They were disarmed by the British authorities. They were massacred by the Arabs. They died wrapped in their prayer shawls and the warm sympathy of His Majesty's government.[127]

With the Colonial Secretary, Lord Passfield, the former Sidney Webb, relations were particularly frosty. Privately Namier referred to Webb contemptuously as 'Lord Passover', and the letters he wrote on Weizmann's behalf were stiffly formal. He would have had even more cause for concern had he known that Passfield was in communication with the noted Arabist St John Philby, from whom the government had received settlement proposals agreed between the Grand Mufti of Jerusalem (suspected by Zionists of having orchestrated the Arab disturbances), and the chancellor of the Hebrew University, J. L. Magnes, who favoured conciliation with the Arabs and opposed the idea of a specifically Jewish state. Their joint scheme was that Palestine should be ruled (under the British high commissioner) by a constitutional republican government, elected by Jews and Arabs in proportion to their numbers, with the power to restrict further Jewish immigration in accordance with the 'absorptive capacity' of the country.[128]

Namier's anger at what he saw as the 'disgraceful' pro-Arab stance of the British administration in Palestine, combined with the spinelessness of cabinet ministers, meant that the autumn and winter months of 1929–30 were especially trying for him, the more so since he would not abandon his belief in the importance of the British connection to the fledgling Jewish state. Again he made the comparison between the chaos in Palestine and Britain's loss of the American colonies:

> We have gone through the typical stages of a Russian pogrom. Jews were massacred; those who tried to defend themselves and their families were disarmed; it was argued that it was the Jews who had started the trouble; and lastly we are left to raise a relief fund … The years of work I have spent on the history of the American revolution have led me to one important conclusion: that America was lost not through the stamp duties or the

Townshend duties, but through the folly and insolence of ill-chosen officials sent out to the colonies, and upheld by the government at home on the wrong-headed pedagogic theory of never admitting that the 'children' may be right ... As far as we ourselves are concerned, we shall not give in. We shall fight to the last man and the last shilling, and we shall not let down those who have gone out already on the basis of our programme and of the pledges given by the British government... The time for polite phrases and diplomacy is gone, and we can no longer deceive ourselves with the hope that, if merely we proceed gently, things will gradually improve, and bitter enemies will turn into impartial administrators.[129]

Work for the agency became a treadmill; there were constant demands for him to draft letters, memoranda, and briefing documents, while in such free time as he could muster he read the proofs of *England in the age of American revolution*. In February 1930 he wrote to Lady Sandwich to thank her for the gift of a book on the eighteenth century:

I shall read it with much interest, but so far I have not had a moment to do so, as the work in the Zionist office is now most strenuous. In fact, I go on with this work at home, usually till about midnight and re-start at eleven in the morning (not even for the Zionist cause can I change my habit of late rising).[130]

When Shaw's commission reported in March 1930 the conclusions were as bad as Namier feared: while acknowledging that there had been unprovoked attacks by Arabs on Jews, the commission exonerated both the Palestine administration and Arab leaders and instead blamed the measures taken by the Jewish Agency. The scale of recent Jewish immigration had been 'excessive'. Careful consideration must be given to the issues of future immigration and the ownership of land.[131] Namier considered it 'a most unsatisfactory document of plainly anti-Jewish character'.[132] At last Weizmann managed to put the Zionist case directly to the prime minister, who was sufficiently embarrassed to promise a supplementary investigation, to be undertaken by someone more sympathetic to the Jewish cause.[133] But when a name was announced it proved desperately disappointing. Sir John Hope Simpson, a former Indian civil servant, was Passfield's choice, and the Zionists had little hope that he would withstand pro-Arab influences in the Colonial Office and the Palestine administration.[134] Namier never liked him, feeling that Simpson was 'not frank'.[135] Tom Jones recorded in his diary a visit from Weizmann and Namier, in which Weizmann confessed that his patience was 'broken'. He feared being 'crucified by my own people' and could 'bear the burden no longer'.[136] In any case, even before Hope Simpson had boarded ship the government 'suspended' the validity of over two thousand Jewish immigration certificates pending his report, in a move designed to placate the Arabs.

In Palestine Hope Simpson quickly concluded that both Jewish immigration and acquisition of land should be restricted, in order to safeguard the interests of the Arab community, and while his investigations were proceeding draft legislation was sent out to Palestine on the land question. In response, Namier mobilised all his contacts. An impassioned letter to Malcolm MacDonald argued that the 'suspension' of immigration was the 'violation of a vital right of ours'.[137] In defiance of instructions he went with Baffy to see her cousin Viscount Cecil, lord privy seal and British delegate to the League of Nations, the former Lord Robert Cecil whom Namier had known at the Foreign Office, hoping to secure Zionist participation in discussions between the British government and the Mandates Commission.[138] Namier even dragged T. E. Lawrence up from Plymouth for a meeting in the agency office in Bloomsbury, though to what purpose is unclear.[139]

The storm broke on 17 October 1930, when Hope Simpson's report, accompanied by a government white paper embodying proposals by Passfield, was delivered to the agency. Taking as a starting point the oft-repeated principles of British policy that the mandate entrusted Britain with a responsibility for interests of both Arab and Jewish communities, and that immigration could not be allowed to exceed Palestine's economic capacity, the white paper stated the government's determination to impose restrictions on the numbers of Jewish immigrants and on Jewish acquisition of land. Ministers also intended to proceed with setting up a legislative council to provide a measure of self-government. Weizmann, who had repeatedly threatened resignation, promptly carried out his threat. Others within the agency followed suit. Namier, who considered that 'we have reached rock bottom', determined to resign as well whenever Weizmann decided the time was right.[140]

Meanwhile, there was work to be done. He set about drafting a rebuttal of the detailed findings in Hope Simpson's report, vitally necessary since it was by Hope Simpson's statistics that Passfield justified himself.[141] This was the kind of exercise at which Namier excelled, and was reminiscent of similar demolition work carried out in the Foreign Office in 1918–20 on the claims of Polish nationalists. But the main thrust of the Zionist response had to be political. Outraged Jews were taking their cause to the court of 'public opinion', through newspaper campaigns and demonstrations, especially in the United States. This was a phenomenon about which Namier the historian had no illusions; he felt that he knew the real nature of 'public opinion' and the way in which it could be manipulated.[142] So he sent Baffy to see the former Conservative colonial secretary, Leo Amery, whose Jewish ancestry made him a Zionist sympathiser, with a proposal that Conservative Party leaders dissociate themselves from government policy by means of a public letter. Amery brought in Baldwin, and the former foreign secretary, Austen Chamberlain, and between them they did as

Baffy (prompted by Namier) had proposed. The letter, drafted by Namier, appeared in *The Times*. It was cunningly contrived, emphasising the valuable cooperation the British had enjoyed from Weizmann, suggesting that the government had unilaterally departed from the existing consensus, and implying that parliament should be consulted.[143] On 17 November a Commons debate took place, opened by Amery for the opposition and closed by Walter Elliot. Ramsay MacDonald found himself on the ropes, unable to respond to Elliot's inquiry as to 'what, if the government had made no change in policy regarding Palestine ... was the masterpiece of ineptitude on their part that had raised turmoil against them in the old world and the new?'[144]

Even before the Commons debate the prime minister had given ground: he set up a cabinet subcommittee headed by the Foreign Secretary Arthur Henderson, with a remit to discuss the white paper with the Zionists at a mini-conference. While MacDonald was careful to say at the outset that there was no question of the government changing its mind, it soon became clear that what was happening was a negotiation to modify significantly the operation of the policy outlined by Passfield. Weizmann, despite having resigned his position with the Jewish Agency, was one of the seven Jewish representatives at the conference. Namier was another, and a key figure at that, given his friendship with Malcolm MacDonald, who had been brought in as Henderson's personal assistant.[145] Between mid-November and February the conference met six times. The Zionists' unwillingness to meet 'Lord Passover' in the early sessions occasionally produced scenes of 'French farce', with the delegation shuttled between rooms in order to avoid accidental confrontations.[146] Otherwise there was a great deal of hard talking and attention to the detail of memoranda, notes verbale and draft ordinances. It was the kind of close forensic work at which Namier excelled, and, with help from Leonard Stein, he proved a match for a whole battery of Colonial Office civil servants. He also had the advantage of being able to communicate privately with Malcolm MacDonald, and thereby undermine Passfield and his officials.[147]

It had been an exciting few months for Namier. He was working under 'terrific pressure', which disrupted his sleeping habits and thus his health, but was playing a crucial role in matters of vital importance for his people and was rubbing shoulders with cabinet ministers, even the prime minister, whom he visited with Weizmann.[148] Friends received letters marked 'Confidential' which for once contained political gossip from the 'inside'. Namier wrote about the parliamentary world in a familiar vein, as if he belonged to it himself: Henderson was 'Uncle Arthur' (Henderson's nickname among colleagues); Herbert Morrison was ''Erbert'; Philip Snowden's wife was 'poor Ethel'.[149] Namier was also aware that this would be the last great service he would do the Zionist cause, for in the midst of the turmoil over the white paper he had at last received an offer of academic employment which he was resolved to take up. This not only concentrated his mind for one huge effort over Palestine but provided the prospect of relief in the near future from the petty quarrels and frustrations of the agency and gave yet another, and probably by this time quite unnecessary, boost to his self-confidence.

He revelled in the atmosphere of the negotiations. But at the same time they did not show him at his best. His naturally combative nature was too much in evidence. At one meeting with Sir John Shuckburgh, the permanent head of the Colonial Office, and some of his staff, Namier's aggressive questioning reduced Shuckburgh and his Old Etonian colleagues to 'piping' and 'wriggling' with outrage or embarrassment.[150] Harold Laski, the political scientist, who was one of the Jewish representatives, and a man not himself known for an emollient manner, thought Namier 'clever of course but an intolerable egoist'.[151] Nor was it only his Colonial Office adversaries whom Namier provoked. He was aware, for example, that Stein harboured some hostility to him, though, typically, professed himself unable to understand its cause.[152] Even Baffy sometimes found his behaviour a trial.[153]

The outcome of this long-drawn out process was a letter from Ramsay MacDonald to Weizmann on 13 February 1931 to explain the statements in the white paper, which removed the putative restrictions on immigration and land purchase. It was followed by the appointment of a new commissioner to Palestine, whom the Jews regarded as more sympathetic. From Namier's point of view this was a triumph, but it was not necessarily viewed as such by other Zionists. Throughout the negotiations he had been irritated by the attitude of some colleagues within the agency, who had been overly critical of any concessions and had obliged him to engage with government demands that he considered 'silly'. He suspected them of intriguing to replace Weizmann, who had gone off to Europe for a well-earned holiday.[154] Namier, left in London, found himself isolated. Taking violent exception to a meeting organised by the Zionist executive without his knowledge, to discuss 'outstanding problems' in their negotiations with the British, he announced his intention to resign. When asked to reconsider he replied with a sneering denunciation of the deficiencies of Zionist strategy and a lengthy list of conditions. There was some justice on his side, but even those sympathetic to his arguments thought his reaction disproportionate.[155] So he was left to his own devices, and spent his time in compiling a detailed record of the events leading up to the prime minister's letter. This 'historical summary' was a justification of his and Weizmann's conduct, possibly to be used at the next Zionist congress, and may also have been intended as a statement to posterity along the lines of the eighteenth-century manuscripts he had examined. Several carbon copies survive.[156]

The congress, at Basle in July 1931, was a disaster from Namier's point of view. Before the opening a message was received that Ramsay MacDonald wished to see Jewish representatives to discuss the issue of parity between Jews and Arabs as 'national entities' in Palestine. Despite Namier's unpopularity with fellow Zionists, he was deputed to fly back to Britain with David Ben-Gurion. They met the prime minister at Chequers, and persuaded him to sign a telegram to Weizmann in Basle to confirm that no alteration had been made to the policy set out in his letter to Weizmann.[157] But Weizmann could not convince the congress that his strategy or his leadership was the right one. Namier's presence at his side may well have fuelled his unpopularity.[158] Weizmann was told to his face that 'You have sat too long at English feasts', and a vote of censure was passed against him.[159] He walked out of the congress and into the political wilderness, followed by Namier. There was some consolation for Weizmann in the fact that Jabotinsky and the revisionists also seceded from the congress in a pique at not getting their way. Namier, however, drew no comfort. His anger was at boiling point, and he wrote to one of his former agency colleagues to condole with him for having to continue in post to work with 'those frogs born of the slime of the seventeenth congress'.[160] To Weizmann he gave a decalogue of strategic commandments, based on his own close observations of politics in both the eighteenth and twentieth centuries, but his advice fell on deaf ears: he was sure that he would be proved right, even if, as he told Baffy, his words 'seemed merely an expression of my bitter and violent nature'.[161] He turned back to history, and an opportunity that had suddenly and surprisingly opened up for him.

Professor

No sooner had *The structure of politics* appeared than Namier's friends began to think that he might at last be found a university post. In the winter of 1928–29 there were moves to push his qualifications for a newly endowed chair in modern history at Harvard. A. D. Lindsay, now master of Balliol, persuaded the Harvard historian R. B. Merriman, who had been at the college in the late 1890s, to recommend Namier. The chair of the appointing committee, Edwin Gay, then interviewed Namier on a visit to England. The arrangements for the interview had been made by Whitney Shepardson and Philip Kerr, with Namier kept in ignorance, convinced that Gay was keen to find out about his 'plan of work' because of its possible relation to his own.[162] Gay himself was evidently very impressed by Namier's first book, especially its strong quantitative basis,[163] but nothing came of Lindsay's scheme, possibly owing to the somewhat rarefied anti-Semitism that pervaded Ivy League universities.[164]

Namier had much better luck the following year, when to his astonishment there fell in to his lap a professorship at Manchester; the most prestigious history department in any English provincial university, still enjoying the reputation as a centre for research established under the leadership of the medievalist T. F. Tout. The canonical version of Namier's appointment derives from Lady Namier's biography, which is in turn partly based on Namier's own recollections, but more directly on an account Julia obtained while researching her book. It came to her in a letter from Ernest Jacob, who was head of department at Manchester in 1930, and is the person always credited with giving Namier, at long last, the opportunity of a university career.[165] Jacob, who was eight years younger than Namier, had been appointed from Oxford to the chair in medieval history at Manchester the year before.

Under Tout, Manchester had pioneered a 'scientific' approach to history in research and teaching, and had produced a string of outstanding and influential medievalists. Jacob's immediate predecessor, Maurice Powicke, himself a Manchester graduate, had gone to Oxford as regius professor. But, as Jacob discovered when he took up his position, the department was weak at the modern end. Following the departure of J. E. Neale to University College, London, the chair of modern history had been left vacant. In the spring of 1930 Jacob had been forced into a spur-of-the-moment appointment of an assistant lecturer to take on the teaching of nineteenth-century Europe, someone who had been recommended to him over dinner and to whom he immediately sent a telegram with a job offer, sight unseen. This was Alan Taylor, a brilliant young historian from a Lancashire background, who since graduating from Oxford had been studying in Austria and whose Viennese supervisor just happened to be in England in 1930, where he met Jacob.[166] But Taylor's arrival did not solve Manchester's problem, and for the remainder of that academic year the professor of modern history at Liverpool travelled over to help on a temporary basis. And so, the story goes, one afternoon in November 1930, when Jacob was taking his tea in the staff common room and pondering his difficulties, he alighted upon Trevelyan's review of *England in the age of the American revolution*, with its expression of regret that Namier should be 'lost to historical studies' by his appointment to the Zionist Organisation. According to Jacob,

> I thought of our Manchester situation … I ran downstairs, got a telegram form and wired Lewis. I had no warrant or any authority for doing this. But I told the vice-chancellor … that it was a unique opportunity to lift the whole teaching of modern history in Manchester on to another plane, and he … immediately consented to the summoning of a senate to interview Lewis and report.[167]

The university's archives tell a different tale. For some time Jacob had hoped to revive the chair of modern history, though he faced hostility from those in the university who resented the disproportionate influence wielded by Tout, and were determined 'to keep the History department in its place'.[168] On 7 November 1930, a full week before Trevelyan's review appeared, Jacob reported to the senate committee that 'the professors of history were of opinion that it would be desirable to make an appointment of a professor of modern history if it were possible to make an appointment of a scholar of the highest distinction'. The committee then drew up a short list of six, all Oxford historians by training, and some of them fellows of Oxford colleges.[169] Namier's was not the first name on the list; that honour went to Humphrey Sumner, a diplomatic historian and fellow of Balliol. Nor was Namier even in second place; that was Keith Feiling. Both Sumner and Feiling were All Souls fellows, and Sumner had been appointed at Balliol in 1925, to a position for which Namier might have been considered. Namier was third on Manchester's list, described as 'a former tutor at Balliol College, at present engaged in research and literary work in London'. Confidential opinions were then sought from leading historians.

Namier, of course, knew nothing of this. He was fortunate that, apart from Trevelyan and the former Manchester professor James Tait, who was probably asked for form's sake, all those consulted knew him personally: they included Howard Temperley, who had edited his chapter in the history of the peace conference; Alfred Zimmern, his former colleague in the PID, who was on record as considering him 'a man of quite outstanding ability';[170] Charles Webster, with whom he was also familiar from his time at the Foreign Office; and his old friend from Balliol, Kenneth Bell. The last person to whom Jacob wrote was A. F. Pollard, with whom Namier had crossed swords on Wedgwood's committee. His is the only reply to have survived. Their abrasive exchanges had left Pollard with a sour view of Namier's personality but he still wrote positively, after a fashion:

> With regard to your problem at Manchester, Sumner is a bit of porcelain and Namier is a brazen pot, a Jew of the Jews, and the worst bore I know. Still, he may be one of those intolerable bores who, as Leslie Stephen said of Robert Owen, are 'the salt of the earth'. He is extraordinarily able, hard-working, vigorous and original, and has certainly developed an area of historical investigation of his own. You would gain enormous *réclame* by his appointment, but I should not envy you the task of controlling him as a colleague, and I think he has had no experience of academic teaching.[171]

Strictly speaking, this last statement was untrue, although Namier's brief experience tutoring and lecturing in Oxford would not have stood comparison with any of his rivals.

When the senate committee reconvened on 2 December, the letters were read out. Sumner (whom Pollard had described as 'a delightful fellow, with a fine mind, and would undoubtedly be *persona grata*') was still the front runner, but Jacob regretfully informed the committee that Sumner 'would not be able to consider an invitation'. Discussion then revolved around the respective merits of Namier and Feiling (whose second major book, when it appeared eight years later, Namier would consign to the dustbin of historiography), and it was decided to invite Namier for an informal meeting with members of the committee.[172] This was the source of the 'astonishing' telegram Namier remembered receiving: 'Would you consider appointment chair modern history, Jacob'.[173] The meeting took place on 16 December 1930, resulting in Namier being offered the job.[174] It was an unusual occasion. According to Jacob, 'Lewis interviewed the committee', his principal concern being whether he would be afforded enough 'leisure' to conduct 'massive historical research'.[175]

The brief biography of Namier drawn up by the committee for the university senate indicates the reasoning behind his appointment, and probably also reflects some of the content of the letters written about him. As well as his 'specialist investigations … in the eighteenth century', much was made of his time at the Foreign Office, where he had 'acquired a knowledge of the structure of modern Europe invaluable to his historical studies'. He was being presented as someone who could teach nineteenth-century Europe as well as eighteenth-century England. The fact that Temperley, Zimmern and Webster had all been asked about candidates, and that Sumner had been the first choice, also suggests strongly that what Jacob was looking for was someone in this area, who could bring the young Taylor along in what was then a major teaching interest of the department, rather than a specialist in the political history of George III's reign. In case there were any doubts about Namier's experience, the committee reported (there must be echoes here of Kenneth Bell) that at Oxford 'he was regarded as an inspiring tutor whose appeal was by no means confined to the potential first-class student'.[176]

It is possible that Trevelyan's review confirmed what Jacob was being told about Namier, although if that was the case he cannot have read the review with complete attention. More likely, the general nature of the reception given to both Namier's books had paved the way. Certainly something had changed drastically since Neale's resignation in 1927, when Namier had not even been mentioned as a possible candidate.[177] The actual record of the process, however, leaves little room for doubt that Jacob's story was a rationalisation long after the event, one that he himself may even have come to believe, and which served the function of making him appear more far-sighted and decisive than was actually the case: something of an academic buccaneer, not a picture of him that others recognised.[178] It makes a better story than professorial appointments in civic universities usually provide. However, none of this alters the fact that to Namier himself, who had not applied for the post, and knew nothing of what was going on, the offer came as a bolt from the blue. It also came at a good time. He was impatient with the way the Zionists in general treated him, as 'labourer not worthy of his hire';[179] and the Wedgwood committee was about to report.

Namier's appointment was announced in *The Times* and the *Manchester Guardian* in mid-February 1931.[180] The *Guardian* actually published a short 'appreciation', from a 'special correspondent', which is interesting for the way in which Namier was publicly perceived. It probably also represented the way in which he saw himself. His appointment was described as 'of more than usual significance', since it marked 'not only the coming of a distinguished lecturer and teacher to Manchester' (which was certainly an exaggeration), but a recognition of the importance of 'parliamentary studies'.

> Mr Namier's special field has been the system of patronage and the influence of the crown in the parliaments of George III's reign. He has familiarised himself to a greater degree than any other scholar with the huge collections of the Newcastle papers. He has been indefatigable in examining private archives, and has an unrivalled knowledge of the whereabouts of eighteenth-century constitutional material.

Meanwhile, Namier was adjusting to his new, and very surprising, situation. He told Lady Sandwich in November 1931 that he was busy preparing for classes, adding in a genuinely self-deprecating aside that this was all the more necessary since 'as my friend Sedgwick once put it with delightful eighteenth-century ambiguity, my knowledge of history is "microscopic"'. He was also resuming the life he had enjoyed before his appointment with the Zionists. The frequency of his book reviewing increased again, doubtless because, in his own terms, he was 'broke', having received no income since resigning his Zionist post in April.[181] He was writing regularly for the *Observer*, as well as other weeklies, demonstrating his knowledge of a wide range of eighteenth- and nineteenth-century subjects, and his unfailing ability to get to the heart of what was important about each work that passed before him. As always, the tone was severe: errors were recorded and summary judgment passed. And he resumed his social life in London. In January 1932 Walter Elliot saw him 'at tea-time with one of his continental financier friends, L. N. booming away'.[182] Not long afterwards Elliot took Namier to lunch, reporting the outcome to Blanche Dugdale:

> Lewis is in London for another week working at the Record Office. He is also writing an article for the *Evening Standard* on the theme ... [that] countries are not growing more dependent on each other, they are growing less dependent, and very rapidly at that. He was full of abuse against the League of Nations and had corresponded against it in the *Manchester Guardian* ... He was also full of abuse ... against Fortescue whom he had discovered in an error upon an army correspondence of 1763 which Fortescue had ignorantly dated September 1762 'and this from the historian of the British Army' said Lewis, incredulously. Indeed, to cut a long story short (and this is a literal phrase), he was in excellent form.[183]

Notes

1 Namier to Lady Sandwich, 4 Mar. 1929 (Mapperton, Sandwich papers, GM/PERS/3).
2 *Amer. rev.*, 191–202.
3 *Nation and Athenaeum*, 22 Jan. 1927.
4 *The Times*, 15 Jan. 1929.
5 *Listener*, 15 May 1929.
6 *Manchester Guardian*, 20 Jan. 1929. In a back-handed compliment, Feiling lavished praise on 'the enormous range of printed matter which he [Namier] has rescued from oblivion', and used this as a warning against an idolatrous devotion to manuscripts, which were not invariably superior to printed evidence.
7 Fifteen are quoted in a publicity leaflet produced by Macmillan (Rylands, Namier papers, 1/19/5). Namier was spared one critical review, by the Cambridge historian Kenneth Pickthorn, who had been commissioned by the literary magazine *Criterion*. Pickthorn thought 'less well of the book … than apparently anyone else' but was 'sick of being denigratory'. T. S. Eliot, the magazine's editor, suggested that 'if the Namier (I believe he is a Jew) is too much against the grain, will you please dismiss him with a short snort', but this did not appeal and no review appeared (*The letters of T. S. Eliot*, ed. Valerie Eliot and John Haffenden (6 vols so far, 1988–2016), iv, 495).
8 P. H. Kerr to H. A. L. Fisher, 11 Feb. 1929 (Rylands, Namier papers, 1/1a/1/32).
9 *Observer*, 28 Sept. 1929.
10 *TLS*, 16 May 1929.
11 Namier to Lady Sandwich, 2 Feb. 1929 (Mapperton, GM/PERS/3). According to Rabbi Maurice Perlzweig, with whom he worked in the Jewish Agency, Namier boasted that Lord Beaverbrook had sat up all night reading the book (Columbia University, Butler Library, Columbia Centre for Oral History, 'Reminiscences of Dr Maurice Perlzweig' (transcript), 329, 387).
12 Namier to Lady Sandwich, 2 Feb. 1929 (Mapperton, GM/PERS/3).
13 Namier to Lady Sandwich, 11 Sept. 1929 (Mapperton, GM/PERS/3).
14 Namier to Lady Sandwich, 15 Mar. 1929 (Mapperton, GM/PERS/3).
15 Rosenwald to Namier, 12 Feb. 1929 (CZA, Namier papers, A312\53). Frankfurter was a committed Zionist, who had served as the Zionist delegate to the Paris peace conference.
16 'More lasting than bronze': a quotation from Horace.
17 Namier to Rosenwald, 4 Mar. 1929 (CZA, A312\53); *Namier*, 205–6.
18 Namier to Nagel, 22 Feb. 1929 (Yale UL, Nagel papers, 364/I/40/466).
19 Namier to Lady Sandwich, 2 Feb. 1929 (Mapperton, GM/PERS/3).
20 *TLS*, 31 Jan. 1929. The author was Basil Williams, professor of history at Edinburgh.
21 In his book *The second Tory party, 1714–1832* (1938), Feiling accepted Namier's conclusion that 'no Tory party existed, in the modern sense of party, for most, if not all, of the eighteenth century', but added that 'there was nonetheless a continuous tradition and some elementary framework of party, and a descent of political ideas' (v).
22 See, for example, Arthur L. Cross (University of Michigan), *Journal of Modern History*, i (1929), 473–7; and Theodore C. Pease (University of Illinois), *American Historical Review*, xxxiv (1929), 824–6.
23 Namier to Lady Sandwich, 26 Nov. 1928 (Mapperton, GM/PERS/3); *History*, xiv (1929–30), 270.
24 D. A. Winstanley, *Personal and party government: a chapter in the political history of the early years of the reign of George III, 1760–1766* (Cambridge, 1910); D. A. Winstanley,

Lord Chatham and the Whig opposition (Cambridge, 1912). By 1940, he was express-ing disapproval of Namier's influence on other historians of the eighteenth century: Winstanley to J. R. M. Butler, 10 July 1940 (Trinity College, Cambridge, Butler papers, A1/147).

25 *EHR*, xliv (1929), 657–60.

26 Namier to Kerr. 6 Feb. 1929 (Rylands, Namier papers, 1/1a/2).

27 Kerr to Fisher, 5 Feb. 1929 (Rylands, Namier papers, 1/1a/1/27).

28 Fisher to Kerr, 13 Feb. 1929 (Rylands, Namier papers, 1/1a/1/37).

29 Fisher to Kerr, 12 Feb. 1929 (Rylands, Namier papers, 1/1a/1/36). Some time previously Murray Wrong had written to Fisher to suggest that Namier might be given a Rhodes lectureship at Oxford, 'partly to help him, partly to let us hear his conclusions', but noth-ing had transpired (Wrong to Fisher, 12 Aug. 1927 (Bodl., MS Fisher 81, fo. 27)).

30 Rhodes Trust minute, 19 Feb. 1929 (Rylands, Namier papers, 1/1a/1/39).

31 Endorsements on wrappers which had originally enclosed text to be sent to Macmillan (Rylands, Namier papers, 1/1b/9).

32 *Amer. rev.*, 37.

33 *Amer. rev.*, 80–1, includes a reference to his time in the PID.

34 *Amer. rev.*, 224.

35 *Amer. rev.*, 53.

36 *Amer. rev.*, 62.

37 *Amer. rev.*, 113.

38 *Amer. rev.*, 90.

39 *Amer. rev.*, 83–4.

40 Colley, 93–4.

41 W. T. Laprade, 'The present state of the history of England in the eighteenth century', *The Journal of Modern History*, iv (1932), 589.

42 W. T. Laprade, 'William Pitt and Westminster elections', *American Historical Review*, xviii (1913), 253–74; W. T. Laprade, 'Public opinion and the general election of 1784', *EHR*, xxxi (1916), 224–37. Cf. Butterfield, *George III and the historians*, 198.

43 Laprade, 'Present state of the history of England', 589. Namier was aware of Laprade's work and considered it reliable (Namier to R. W. Chapman, 24 Dec. 1949 (Houghton Library, Harvard University, Chapman papers, ser. 1, folder 8)), but there are no letters from him in Laprade's archive in the David M. Rubinstein Rare Book and Manuscript Library at Duke University (I am grateful to Tom Harkin of the library staff for confirm-ing this point), and none from Laprade in the various deposits of Namier papers.

44 *Skyscrapers*, 36–8, 40–1. See also *Structure*, ix; and Namier's review of Dora Mae Clark, *British opinion and the American revolution*, *History*, xviii (1933–34), 271.

45 *The Times*, 28 Oct. 1930.

46 *Observer*, 12 Oct. 1930.

47 *The Times*, 28 Oct. 1930.

48 *Bookman*, Nov. 1930, 127.

49 *Nation and Athenaeum*, 15 Nov. 1930. Cf. Colley, 13.

50 G. M. Trevelyan, *Clio, a muse, and other essays literary and pedestrian* (1913), 14.

51 Pease again in *American Historical Review.*, xxxvi (1931), 583–5; and R. L. Schuyler (Columbia University) in *Political Science Quarterly*, xlvi (1931), 284–7.

52 *EHR*, xlvii (1932), 677–9.

53 *Economica*, xxxvi (1932), 260–2.

54 *History*, xvi (1931–32), 172–6.

55 Elliot to Dugdale, 15 Oct. 1930 (NLS, Elliot papers, Acc. 12267/12).

56 *Nation & Athenaeum*, 28 June 1930.

57 See p. 160.

58 See, for example, the careful reservations in John Cannon, 'Lewis Bernstein Namier', John Cannon (ed.), *The historian at work* (1980), 139–40; and Colley, 49. The frontal assault on Namier's originality in Butterfield, *George III and the historians* was of a different order and purpose. This is discussed pp. 370–1.

59 Butterfield, *George III and the historians*, 197.

60 Albert von Ruville, *William Pitt earl of Chatham*, trans. H. J. Chaytor and Mary Morrison (3 vols, 1907). See, for example, his references to the Grenville connection (iii, 25, 182). For von Ruville see Michael Bentley, *Modernizing England's past: English historiography in the age of modernism 1870–1970* (Cambridge, 2005), 147–8.

61 See, for example, Winstanley, *Chatham and the Whig opposition*, 59–60.

62 *Amer. rev.*, 208–9, 269, 273.

63 Clarence Walworth Alvord, *The Mississippi valley in British politics: a study of the trade, land speculation, and experiments in imperialism culminating in the American revolution* (2 vols, Cleveland, Ohio, 1917), i, 15. For Alvord, see Bentley, *Modernizing England's past*, 148–9.

64 For example in *Amer. rev.*, 209.

65 Von Ruville, *Chatham*, iii, 106.

66 Alvord, *Mississippi valley*, i, 15.

67 J. P. Kenyon, *The history men: the historical profession in England since the Renaissance* (1983), 258–9; J. M. Price, 'Party, purpose and pattern: Sir Lewis Namier and his critics', *Journal of British Studies*, i, no. 1 (1961), 75–6.

68 P. M. Blaas, *Continuity and anachronism: parliamentary and constitutional development in Whig historiography and in the anti-Whig reaction between 1890 and 1930* (The Hague, 1978), 4–5, quoting J. H. Plumb in *New Statesman*, 1 Aug. 1969.

69 Published as *Letters from George III to Lord Bute, 1756–1766*, ed. Romney Sedgwick (1939).

70 Brian Tunstall, *William Pitt earl of Chatham* (1938), 141, 187, 247, 261–3, 275–6, 486. See rev. by Richard Pares, *EHR*, liv (1939), 735–6.

71 W. T. Laprade, 'The Stamp Act in British politics', *American Historical Review*, xxxv (1930), 735–57; W. T. Laprade, *Public opinion and politics in eighteenth-century England* … (New York, 1935). Not all American historians of Laprade's generation were averse to 'Namierisation'. Donald G. Barnes, then teaching in the University of Oregon, embarked on a study of *George III and William Pitt*, eventually published by Stanford in 1939, which was heavily influenced by Namier, who reviewed it, on the whole favourably, in *Manchester Guardian*, 1 Sept. 1939. Barnes's sister Viola, also a historian, had been a pupil of Charles M. Andrews at Yale.

72 Anne Whiteman, 'Lucy Stuart Sutherland 1903–1980', *Proceedings of the British Academy*, lxix (1983), 616.

73 Sutherland to Namier, 26 Nov. 1931 (Rylands, Namier papers, 1/9/7).

74 L. S. Sutherland, 'Introduction', Richard Pares, *The historian's business and other essays*, ed. R. A. Humphreys and Janet Humphreys (Oxford, 1961), x–xi; Geoffrey Parker, 'Michael Roberts 1908–1996', *Proceedings of the British Academy*, cxv (2002), 335.

75 R. R. Walcott, *English politics in the early eighteenth century* (Oxford, 1956), v.

76 R. R. Walcott to [editorial board, History of Parliament], 29 July 1951, enclosed in Namier to J. H. Plumb, 1 Aug. 1951 (CUL, Plumb papers).

77 J. H. Hexter, 'The problem of the Presbyterian Independents', *American Historical Review.*, xliv (1938), 29.

78 *Skyscrapers*, 46.

79 Repr. in *Skyscrapers*, 44–53.

80 *Skyscrapers*, 8.

81 For Wedgwood, see C. V. Wedgwood, *The last of the radicals: Josiah Clement Wedgwood MP* (1951); Paul Mulvey, *The political life of Josiah C. Wedgwood: land, liberty and empire, 1872–1943* (Woodbridge, 2010); and *Oxf. DNB*. Namier's own character sketch of Wedgwood is in *Avenues*, 171–3.

82 Norman Rose, *The Gentile Zionists: a study in Anglo-Zionist diplomacy, 1929–1939* (1973), ch. 4, esp. 73–4.

83 Extract from a letter 'sent to a friend abroad' (CZA, A312\7). Cf. *Namier*, 88.

84 *Namier*, 201–2; Rose, *Zionism*, 33; Mulvey, *Wedgwood*, 182–4.

85 For a more detailed account of what follows, see D. W. Hayton, 'Colonel Wedgwood and the historians', *Historical Research*, lxxxiv (2011), 328–55; and for an alternative reading, more sympathetic to Wedgwood, David Cannadine, 'Josiah Wedgwood and the History of Parliament', *In Churchill's shadow; confronting the past in modern Britain* (2002), 134–58; David Cannadine, 'The History of Parliament: past, present – and future?', *Parliamentary History*, xxvi (2007), 366–86.

86 J. C. Wedgwood, *Staffordshire parliamentary history from the earliest times to the present day* (4 vols, William Salt Soc., Stafford, 1917–33).

87 Pollard to Wedgwood, 6 Mar. 1928 (University of London Library, Pollard papers, MS 890, box 6a).

88 *The Times*, 19, 24 May 1928.

89 *The Times*, 30 May 1928.

90 Namier to Wedgwood, 9 June 1928 (Rylands, Namier papers, 1/9/1).

91 In print this became 'a microcosmos of English social and political life' (*Skyscrapers*, 47).

92 John Venn and J. A. Venn, *Alumni Cantabrigienses: a biographical list of all known students, graduates and holders of office at the University of Cambridge, from the earliest times to 1900* (10 vols, Cambridge, 1922–54). John Venn had published the first two volumes of part I (which covered the period up to 1751) by the time of his death in 1922. His son continued the project, completing part I in 1927.

93 Quoted in *Namier*, 199.

94 Wedgwood to Pollard, 9 July 1928 (University of London Library, Pollard papers, MS 890, box 35).

95 Memo by Wedgwood entitled 'What is in my mind as our goal', n.d. (PA, HPT8/6).

96 *Hansard*, ser. 5, Commons, ccxxiii, col. 2805; *The Times*, 25 Mar. 1929.

97 Buchan to Baldwin, 7 Feb. 1929 (CUL, Baldwin papers, 164, fo. 244); Namier to Frederick Kisch, 8 May 1930 (CZA, A312\12). Cf. J. C. Wedgwood, *Memoirs of a fighting life* (1940), 215. Lady Sandwich also helped, by sending Baldwin a copy of *The structure of politics* (Namier to Lady Sandwich, 15 Mar 1929 (Mapperton, GM/PERS/3)).

98 Stencilled copies of Treasury committee minutes, 1929–31 (HPT, N–29).

99 *Namier*, 200.

100 Treasury committee minute, 14 June 1929 (HPT, N–29).

101 Namier to Wedgwood, 19 June 1929 (LWL, Namier papers (3)).

102 Pollard to Wedgwood, 20 June 1929 (University of London Library, Pollard papers, MS 890, box 35).

103 Treasury committee minute, 27 June 1929 (HPT, N–29); Neale to Wallace Notestein, 19 Nov. 1929 (Yale UL, Notestein papers, MS 544/6/536).

104 *The Times*, 18 Oct. 1929.

105 'Draft interim report ...' (HPT, A–44); Treasury committee minute, 1 Oct. 1929 (HPT, N–29). See also Wedgwood to R. S. Rait, 13 Nov. 1929 (NRS, Scottish Committee on the History of Parliament archives, SCHP/1/8/3–4).

106 Treasury committee minute, 2 Apr. 1930 (HPT, N–29).

107 Wedgwood to Notestein, 16 Apr., 12 May 1930 (Yale UL, Notestein papers, 544/8/786); Wedgwood to Bull, 1 May 1930 (Churchill, Bull papers, 5/24); treasury committee minute, 19 June 1930 (HPT, N–29).

108 *Interim report of the committee on House of Commons personal and politics 1264–1832* (Cmd. 4130), 49–51.

109 *Interim report*, 52–3.

110 *Interim report*, 53; A. F. Pollard, *The evolution of parliament* (1920).

111 *Interim report*, 54. Besides the ideas it contains, there are certain features of the organisation of this passage which suggest Namier's direct involvement in the composition: phrasing, spelling and even elements of punctuation.

112 *Who's who*, 1930, 2268.

113 Namier himself seems to have suggested that he might represent Oxford, where he had a 'close association' (Osmond D'Avigdor Goldsmid to J. M. Rich, 13 Nov. 1929, Rich to Namier, 19 Mar. 1930 (LMA, Board of Deputies of British Jews archive, Acc/3121/B/04/NA/003)).

114 *Amer. rev.*, 18.

115 Rose, *Zionism*, 40.

116 Rose, *Zionism*, 41.

117 *Amer. rev.*, 251.

118 Rose, *Zionism*, 44. He described the executive as a whole as 'that absurd group' ('Lewis's notes on his early connection with Zionism', sent by Julia Namier to Lucy Sutherland in 1961 (Bodl., Sutherland papers, box 9)).

119 Rose, *Zionism*, 44.

120 Namier to the members of the Jewish Agency Executive, the Zionist Executive and the Political Committee, 23 Feb. 1931 (CZA, A312\12); draft by Leonard Stein of a review of Lucy Sutherland's British Academy memoir of Namier (Bodl., Stein papers, box 121).

121 Namier to Jones, 30 Aug. 1929 (NLW, Jones papers, F/1/50).

122 Memorandum by Namier [Sept. 1929] (NLW, Jones papers, F/1/51/1–3).

123 Rose, *Zionism*, 43.

124 Rose, *Zionism*, 43.

125 Rose, *Zionism*, 42–3; 'Turbulent Zionist', 37.

126 'Turbulent Zionist', 37–8.

127 Rose, *Zionism*, 45.

128 Passfield to Philby, 3 Oct. 1928 (St Antony's College, Oxford, Middle East Centre archive, Philby papers, 1/6/5/1/2); Philby to Passfield, 21 Oct., 1 Nov. 1929 (ibid., 1/6/5/1/6–7); final draft of proposals, 1 Nov. 1929 (ibid., 1/6/5/1/8).

129 Namier to Lady Sandwich, 11 Sept. 1929 (Mapperton, GM/PERS/3).

130 Namier to Lady Sandwich, 20 Feb. 1930 (Mapperton, GM/PERS/3).

131 *Report of the commission on the Palestine disturbances of August, 1929* (Cmd. 3530).

132 'Turbulent Zionist', 39.

133 Norman Rose, *Chaim Weizmann: a biography* (1986), 178.

134 'Turbulent Zionist', 39.

135 *Weizmann A*, xv, 127.

136 Thomas Jones, *Whitehall diary*, ed. Keith Middlemas (3 vols, 1969–71), ii, 255.

137 Namier to MacDonald, 12 June 1930 (Durham UL, Malcolm MacDonald papers, 9/1/46–9); *Weizmann A*, xiv, 334.

138 *Aide-mémoire* by Viscount Cecil, 6 Sept. 1930 (BL, Cecil of Chelwood papers, Add. MS 51100, fo. 61).

139 Lawrence to Namier, 15 July 1930 (Imperial War Museum, Spec. Misc. MSS CC); Leonard Stein to Namier, 14 July 1954 (CZA, A312\54); Columbia Centre for Oral History, 'Reminiscences of Dr Maurice Perlzweig' (transcript), 376–8.

140 *Namier*, 213.

141 Rose, *Zionism*, 47–8; draft by Namier, 'The statistical bases of Sir John Hope Simpson's report' (CZA, A312\10).

142 Unless otherwise stated, what follows is based on Namier, 'A historical summary of discussions leading up to the prime minister's letter of February 13th 1931 to Dr Weizmann', 27 Apr. 1931 (copies in CZA, A312\11; ibid., Z4\30451; Durham UL, MacDonald papers, 9/8/3–57; Bodl., Stein papers, box 121). A further copy, originating in the papers of Orde Wingate, was sold with associated materials by Bonham's, 11 Nov. 2015.

143 *Weizmann A*, xv, 8; Namier to Amery, 4 Feb. 1951, Amery to Namier 6 Feb. 1951 (Churchill, Amery papers, 2/1/45); Leo Amery, *The empire at bay: the Leo Amery diaries 1929–1945*, ed. John Barnes and David Nicholson (1988), 85–6; *The Times*, 23 Oct. 1930.

144 *Amery diaries 1929–1945*, ed. Barnes and Nicholson, 89; *The Times*, 18 Nov. 1930.

145 *Weizmann A*, xiv, 334; xv, 78; Rose, *Gentile Zionists*, 24.

146 *The political diary of Hugh Dalton 1918–40, 1945–60*, ed. Ben Pimlott (1986), 128–9.

147 See, for example, Namier to MacDonald, 12, 16 Jan. 1931 (Durham UL, MacDonald papers, 9/5/2, 26–8).

148 Namier to Mrs Dugdale, 11 Jan. 1931 (CZA, A312\12); notes of interview between Ramsay MacDonald, Weizmann and Namier, 24 Dec. 1930 (Durham UL, MacDonald papers, 9/6/30).

149 Namier to Lady Sandwich, 7, 30 Sept. 1931 (Mapperton, GM/PERS/3).

150 Namier to Weizmann, 20 Jan. 1931 (Durham UL, MacDonald papers, 9/5/29–33).

151 Isaac Kramnick and Barry Sheerman, *Harold Laski: a life on the left* (1993), 281.

152 Julia Namier to Lucy Sutherland, 12 Oct. 1962 (Bodl., Sutherland papers, box 9).

153 Elliot to Blanche Dugdale, 29 Nov. 1930 (NLS, Acc. 12267/12).

154 'Turbulent Zionist', 43.

155 Rose, *Zionism*, 54–6.

156 See note 142.

157 'Turbulent Zionist', 45; Rose, *Gentile Zionists*, 51. The telegram had been drafted by Namier (Namier to Weizmann, 3 Nov. 1932 (CZA, A312\12)).

158 Rose, *Zionism*, 53–4.

159 Rose, *Weizmann*, 289–93.

160 *Namier*, 19; *Weizmann A*, xv, 174.

161 Namier to Dugdale, 2 Nov. 1931 (CZA, A312\44).

162 Shepardson to Kerr, 4 Jan. 1929 (Franklin D. Roosevelt Presidential Library, Shepardson papers, box 7); Namier to Gay, 22 Jan. 1929 (Huntington Library, Gay papers, GY 2263).

163 See Gay's presidential address to the American Economic Association in December 1929, published in *American Economic Review*, xx (1930), 4.

164 Peter Novick, *That noble dream: the 'objectivity question' and the American historical profession* (Cambridge, 1988), 172–3.

165 *Namier*, 213–14, 220–1. It is retold in A. J. P. Taylor, *A personal history* (1983), 104–5; John Cannon's entry on Namier in *Oxf. DNB*; Colley, 13; and Cannadine, *Trevelyan*, 52, 206–7.

166 Kathleen Burk, *Troublemaker: the life and history of A. J. P. Taylor* (2000), 88–9; Adam Sisman, *A. J. P. Taylor: a biography* (paperback edn, 1995), 81–2.

167 *Namier*, 220. The original letter to Lady Namier has not survived.

168 Norman Sykes to Claude Jenkins, 28 July 1930 (Lambeth Palace Library, Jenkins papers, MS 1634, fos 232–3).

169 Senate committee minute, 7 Nov. 1930 (Manchester UL, university archives, senate committee book, xxv, no. 50).

170 Zimmern to C. P. Scott, 13 June 1919 (*Guardian* arch., A/N2/4).

171 Pollard to Jacob, 25 Nov. 1930 (University of London Library, Pollard papers, MS 890, box 6b). Namier had evidently 'plagued' Pollard over a range of issues: Neale to Notestein, 25 Nov. 1931 (Yale UL, Notestein papers, 544/I/6/536).

172 Senate committee minute, 2 Dec. 1930 (Manchester UL, university archives, senate committee book, xxv, no. 57).

173 *Namier*, 214.

174 Senate committee minute, 16 Dec. 1930 (Manchester UL, university archives, senate committee book, xxv, no. 72).

175 *Namier*, 220.

176 Senate committee minute, 16 Dec. 1930 (Manchester UL, university archives, senate committee book, xxv, no. 72).

177 F. M. Powicke to T. F. Tout, 10, 17, 25, 28, 30 May, 14 June 1927 (Rylands, Tout papers, 1/962). Feiling had been considered.

178 The medievalist David Knowles described him some thirty years later as 'a slow mover … He always reminds me of the vanished type of family doctor at the bedside' (Knowles to Sir Charles Webster, 21 Feb. 1960 (LSE, Webster papers, 1/36/95)).

179 'Lady Namier's notes', quoted in Rose, *Zionism*, 50.

180 *The Times*, 14 Feb. 1931; *Manchester Guardian*, 14 Feb. 1931.

181 Namier to Lady Sandwich, 14 Nov. 1931 (Mapperton, GM/PERS/3).

182 Elliot to Blanche Dugdale, 12 Jan. 1932 (NLS, Elliot papers, Acc. 12198/13).

183 Elliot to Dugdale, 9 Apr. 1932 (NLS, Acc. 12198/13).

6

Europe in decay, 1932–38

Manchester

The physical appearance of Manchester in the early twentieth century, dominated by dark Victorian commercial buildings, and with an oppressive atmosphere of smoke, noise and a permeating damp, was captured by the post-impressionist painter Adolphe Vallette, L. S. Lowry's teacher at the Manchester Municipal Art College. Vallette's pictures show grey, fog-bound streets, in which the inhabitants go grimly about their business. Even to a north-countryman like Alan Taylor, coming from Oxford to take up his assistant lectureship, the city seemed 'irredeemably ugly'.[1] It was still

> very much the Manchester of the nineteenth century even though the cotton trade was now in decline. It was very dirty, the buildings begrimed, with large smuts coming into the room if you opened a window. Clanking trams from all over Lancashire converged on the centre of the city where they stood in long rows like patient elephants. There was a tripe shop on every corner and an oyster bar, complete with jolly red-faced women, in Oxford Street.[2]

Provincial loyalty doubtless imparted a streak of romanticised affection to Taylor's sketch. For a southerner like the journalist Malcolm Muggeridge, then working on the *Manchester Guardian*, dirt and poverty predominated over the local colour supplied by tripe shops and the oyster bar. What Muggeridge remembered was 'the screeching trams, the massive blackened public buildings … the slums and the shops; the warehouses besides the stagnant Ship Canal, the clatter of surviving clogs'.[3] Things were evidently no better twenty years later, when a lecturer sent a mournful despatch to a former comrade in arms, now back in Oxford: 'university life is normal … the common room windows are firmly closed; and the soot shows up particularly well in the sunlight'.[4] And of course, there was the notorious Manchester weather, a tired staple of music-hall jokes. 'The climate rounds off the gloom', wrote Taylor, whose childhood had been spent in the more bracing coastal air of Birkdale, near

Liverpool. Despite comedians' insistence, Manchester was 'not remarkably rainy ... but persistently moist, which is even more depressing'.[5]

All this made the city a very unattractive place for Namier once the early excitement of his appointment had worn off. The fumes and damp weather were bad for his breathing. But his revulsion was not merely on health grounds. In childhood he had moved amid the elegance of Vienna and the provincial capitals of imperial Austria-Hungary, and in comparison found pre-war Bloomsbury aesthetically dismal. Industrial Manchester was repulsive. Within three years he could state categorically that 'I am by now thoroughly sick of this town, in which I somehow never manage to settle down'.[6] Like almost every other member of the university staff, he found accommodation in the southern suburbs. He took lodgings in a small redbrick semi-detached in Victoria Road, Fallowfield. There was 'a spare bedroom for guests, whom their doctor does not forbid going to Manchester'. Soon he moved a little further out, to a slightly more substantial residence in Heaton Road, Withington.[7] In the Heaton Road house he could entertain, but it was still dreary. Moreover, with his large appetite and relatively sophisticated taste in food, Namier found the cooking provided by Manchester landladies inadequate to his needs and tastes.[8] After a couple of years he resolved to move out altogether. Having enjoyed pleasant days with friends on the borders of Cheshire and Derbyshire, he eventually found lodgings there, within commuting distance of the university.[9]

He had not, in any case, ever moved permanently to Manchester. The department's working week ran from Monday to Thursday, and he seldom stayed for even that length of time. Sometimes he would arrive on Wednesday and return to London on Friday.[10] He kept his rooms in Kensington, since he needed a base for researches in the British Museum and Public Record Office, and for the work he was still doing for the Jewish Agency in an unofficial capacity. His closest friends were in London, as now was Marie Beer. And in 1933 he was successfully put up for membership of the Athenaeum. Being able to 'foregather' (one of his favourite words) at his club was not only a pleasure, but became a necessary means of forwarding business, academic and political.

Weekends, when he was not in London, were often spent in Shropshire, where Baffy's younger sister, Alison, lived with her elderly husband Lieutenant-Colonel Arthur Dawson Milne, a retired army doctor who had been Principal Medical Officer in the East African Protectorate, and their daughter Elizabeth. 'The Cottage', to which Milne had retired, was in fact a substantial, six-bedroomed property, standing in an acre of its own grounds in Oldbury Wells on the outskirts of Bridgnorth. Namier had begun to visit even before he took up the Manchester chair. Now he became a regular guest, especially after Arthur's death in 1932 left Alison and her daughter on their own.[11] He was almost one of the family, taking the Milnes' sheepdog out for walks in the surrounding hills. He got on particularly well with Elizabeth, as he always did with children.[12] Observing his lack of coordination, exacerbated by his height, she called him 'Clumsy Boy', abbreviated to 'C.B.', a nickname which amused him sufficiently for him to use it himself and which became the privileged form of address for a few of his intimate friends, mostly women.[13]

Namier was spending much of his time in transit between London and Manchester, with frequent weekends in Bridgnorth, and trips to archives around the country.[14] Never having learned to drive, he travelled these long distances by train and bus. In the 1950s, after his second marriage, Lady Namier drove him about, but even then he sometimes had to avail himself of public transport. His correspondence affords the occasional vignette of laborious journeys, for example travelling by Green Line coach from Marble Arch to Hatfield to inspect Lord Salisbury's papers, and lugging about with him the 'portable', but decidedly heavy, typewriter on which he tapped out his notes.[15]

Although Namier never accustomed himself to living in Manchester, there was in fact much more to the city than manufacturing and business, smoke, dirt and the clank of trams. It was the city of Howard Spring's bohemians as well as of latter-day Gradgrinds and Bounderbys. According to Alan Taylor, Manchester's vibrant cultural and intellectual life meant that it was 'the only English city that can look London in the face, not merely as a regional capital, but as a rival version of how man should live in a community'.[16] Concerts at the Free Trade Hall, which meant a great deal to Taylor, left Namier cold, but there was an established local intelligentsia to welcome him. It was easy for migratory southerners to poke fun at these apparently pretentious provincials. Above Manchester's palaces of commerce and industry, wrote Malcolm Muggeridge, 'there perched a little cluster of the culturally elect'. The university, the orchestra, the repertory theatre, and the *Manchester Guardian* 'all provided their quota, along with the occasional museum or art gallery curator, librarian, local scribe or lady novelist from the West Riding, Jewish or Armenian *aficionado* from Cheetham Hill, [or] rumbustious magnate with a taste for Trollope and a son at Bedales'.[17]

Manchester's 'culturally elect' did, however, include such genuinely important figures as the Australian-born moral philosopher Samuel Alexander. Taylor thought him 'the greatest man I have known', and after Alexander's death in 1938 Namier published a generous appreciation.[18] Furthermore, the *Manchester Guardian* was by no means a provincial newspaper: it had a national reach and its distinctively liberal voice gave it influence in Westminster politics.

No sooner had Namier accepted the chair at Manchester than he contacted the *Guardian*'s editor, Ted Scott, son of 'C.P.', to offer his services 'on the foreign side'.[19]

Nothing came of this approach, probably because neither Scott nor his father (who was still a power behind the scenes) entirely trusted Namier's politics. But with the death of both Scotts in 1932 a new editor was appointed, W. P. Crozier, whose sympathy for the Zionist cause and hostility to the Nazi regime in Germany put him on Namier's side.[20] When Crozier died in 1944 Namier lamented the loss of 'a great figure': 'In W. P. Crozier, the Jews and especially the Zionists – in fact all people who suffer and strive for a human cause – have lost a sensitive friend and an effective champion.'[21] As early as April 1933 Crozier published a lengthy letter by Namier – so long in fact that Namier was able to reprint it as an essay in one of his collections – arguing against the notion that Hitler's rise to power was due to the harshness of the Versailles settlement, and comparing the Nazi revolution unfavourably with the Bolshevik.[22] Other letters and articles followed, and regular book reviews. Indeed, for a time Namier became the paper's reviewer of first resort on modern European and eighteenth-century English history.

The university itself was different from anything Namier had encountered. It was 'old fashioned, still proud of not being Oxford or Cambridge, and not called the Victoria University for nothing'.[23] The History Department continued to bask in the glory brought to it by Tout, and frequently sent younger staff on to Oxford and Cambridge chairs. Its organisation was strongly hierarchical, though Jacob had relaxed Tout's iron rule and attempted to govern on more 'democratic' lines, consulting colleagues rather than dictating to them. There were three broad divisions, ancient, medieval and modern, and correspondingly three professors, together with a reader in economic history, five lecturers and one assistant lecturer, Alan Taylor. By 1937 the number of lecturers increased to seven. Some of the staff were Manchester products and knew the system; the rest were mainly recruited from Oxford (occasionally Cambridge) and found the methods of teaching unfamiliar and unsatisfactory. The 'modern' end was covered by Namier, Edward Hughes and Taylor. Hughes, a Manchester graduate and a specialist in eighteenth-century English history, taught the outline courses in British (that is to say English) history, while Namier and Taylor dealt with modern Europe, primarily the nineteenth century, and in Namier's case, added a special subject (a final-year course studied through original sources, culminating in a dissertation), on 'The eve of the American revolution, with the early reign of George III, 1760–71'. Most of the European history was taught by Taylor, so Namier's workload was light, especially as the honours students, from whom he would draw his special subject class, were few in number, between ten and twenty.[24] At the same time his junior colleagues 'were ramming a mob of students through the general or pass course'.[25]

Working with Hughes and Taylor, Namier forged lasting friendships. They were very different characters: Hughes, a farmer's son from Staffordshire, was solid and dependable;[26] Taylor was amusing and mercurial, sharing Namier's European interests and some of his European experiences. Taylor and Namier became close: it was Alan and his wife who entertained Namier at their cottage in Disley on the fringes of the Peak District. An assistant lecturer at Manchester was literally the professor's assistant, and Namier seems to have considered it his duty to mentor Taylor.[27] He pushed him into writing (as he pushed all who ever worked with him), found him a publisher, and got him reviewing for the *Manchester Guardian*. At the same time, he treated Taylor as an equal. There was no condescension: with a childlike enthusiasm Namier joined heartily in everything that was going on at the Taylors' (including on one occasion naked bathing in the river), seemingly delighted to find himself in the company of young people and accepted on their terms. Taylor remembered the Namier of this period as 'great fun', which, he added, was not how Lady Namier's biography had depicted him. 'There was in Lewis', wrote Taylor, 'a strange mixture of greatness and helplessness.' In their Manchester days, he declared, 'I loved Lewis without reserve.'[28] Taylor even gave his son the middle name Lewis, to Namier's embarrassment. For his part, Namier regarded Taylor not only as a highly promising historian and an excellent colleague, but as 'a good, warm-hearted friend'.[29]

The story of Namier's friendship with Taylor would have a sad and bitter ending. In Namier's capacity for intense personal affection there was also a dark side, and some of his closest attachments ended in alienation. In the case of Taylor the boot was on the other foot: Taylor broke with Namier in 1957 and would not see or speak to him again, something which clouded the last years of Namier's life.[30] Until then Namier exerted an enormous influence over Taylor, as the prefaces to the latter's books acknowledged. Taylor adopted Namier's prejudices – his dislike of Marx, his virulent anti-Germanism[31] – and, even though leaning further to the left than Namier, Taylor seems also to have absorbed some of the older man's core beliefs about history and politics: Namier's habit of generalising about national characteristics, for example,[32] or his scepticism of the role of 'public opinion' in determining the actions of governments and relations between states.[33]

Much of what we know of Namier's early days as a member of the Manchester History Department comes from Taylor's autobiography. However, this was written in old age, when Taylor was anxious to dispel the belief that he had been Namier's protégé. An alternative history comes from Lady Namier's biography, but is equally unreliable, from the opposite point of view. She drew her information from Jacob, who was unfailingly complimentary, and from one of Namier's favourite students, Ninetta Jucker. Thus Lady Namier presented her husband as a conscientious and inspiring teacher, to whom his pupils (especially the better ones) were devoted. In Taylor's version Namier made no effort to understand administrative processes and

5 Blanche Dugdale ('Baffy')

6 Chaim Weizmann and David Ben-Gurion

teaching practices at Manchester, and had to be instructed by his nominal assistant. According to Taylor, Namier taught only what he was interested in; he failed to provide a comprehensive course of lectures on nineteenth-century Europe (leaving Taylor to plug the gaps), did not know how to mark examination scripts, in which Taylor led him by the hand, and generally avoided as many academic duties as he could.

Like many active researchers, Namier thought routine university administration a waste of his talents and time: he was happy to admit, when he came to perform his 'last bout of academic duties', that 'I have never drunk very deep of them'.[34] Examination marking in particular was a 'horrible job'.[35] His irritation was intensified by self-inflicted pressure. In September 1932 he complained that 'on Saturday I have to go to Manchester for a new term of almost eleven weeks (this sounds almost like gaol – but fortunately is not so bad – merely I feel so bitterly the separation from the British Museum and the [Public] Record Office)'.[36]

Nevertheless, the evidence of the university archives shows that he did not shirk his duties as a teacher and examiner, nor did he confine himself to courses covering his own research interests.[37] Certainly his philosophy of teaching was unusual, and could be construed as making undergraduates study what interested him rather than what might, or should, interest them. He disliked teaching to a set syllabus. The essay titles he proposed were eccentric: first years were asked to write on 'what is and what should be in a newspaper'.[38] His approach to examinations was equally unconventional. Doubtless it would be commended by the 'teaching and learning' industry in modern universities as innovative and 'student-led'. But in the 1930s and 1940s it must have seemed to colleagues to be idiosyncratic and self-indulgent: something only a senior professor with Namier's prestige could get away with. His purpose, as one student recalled, was 'to test the quality of minds and the students' understanding of their work'. To this end 'he would have been prepared to let the candidates use any books they wished'. This was not permissible, so instead he set a limited number of the same stock questions every year, from which students had to select two and write 'fully'. They were not invigilated and a student collected the scripts at the end of the examination. Then Namier would see each individually to comment on their work.[39] Obviously, this could only be done in a small class, with honours students. And Namier made it plain that he was primarily interested in those at the top of the ladder, the better-equipped students whom he could go on to train in the techniques of research.

Not surprisingly, it was in the supervision of research students that Namier made his most important and distinctive contribution. Technically his first was Alan Taylor, who wrote up his Viennese findings into a PhD thesis. But Taylor was an exceptional case: Manchester University Press had insisted on his registering for a doctorate as a condition for publishing his book. Namier himself had no time for the PhD, a title he stigmatised as 'foolish', perhaps because it suggested Germanic pretension, and Taylor, although satisfying his examiners, did not bother to take the degree.[40] With rare exceptions, Namier's own research pupils undertook MAs instead. There was a steady stream, the brighter products of his eighteenth-century special subject. This was the kind of work he liked, 'teaching researchers rather than passmen'.[41] He confessed to an American friend in 1935 that 'a professorial job in certain ways seems a very light burden; but it is highly distracting. In fact, I sometimes feel that I ought to have a different kind of professorial job – in a postgraduate school, only to train researchers'.[42]

At first he threw himself into university and civic life. Lady Namier found among his effects his 'early Manchester pocket-diaries' (since destroyed), which were 'packed with university activities and social engagements'.[43] He belonged to various clubs and circles, including an 'Economics Group' which invited MPs such as Harold Macmillan to speak;[44] lectured on historical matters to a multiplicity of audiences – university students, schoolteachers and local historical societies;[45] and was 'entertained to lunch and dinner' by Manchester's worthies. But gradually, as the international situation worsened, his speaking engagements came to concentrate on the worsening plight of European Jewry. During his visits to Manchester he could be found chairing meetings of the university students' Zionist Society, of which he became president, and addressing a host of other Jewish groups, including the members of the Manchester Union of Jewish Literary Societies, the Friends of the

Hebrew University in Jerusalem and the conference of the World Union of Jewish Students.[46] This was not so much evidence of Namier immersing himself in the life of the city and its university, as of his bringing to Manchester the preoccupations of his other, and to him more important, life in London. It was also an indication of the cacophony of competing demands which he was trying to answer, and which before long began to overpower him. Professorial duties and political activism meant that the space for research and writing was squeezed thin.[47]

A profusion of projects

In contemplating the possibility of appointment to the Manchester chair, Namier had looked forward more than anything else to the opportunity to take forward his work on the eighteenth century, which had come to a standstill during his time at the Jewish Agency. His original scheme for a series of volumes on 'England in the age of the American revolution' covered the period from the end of George II's reign up to 1784. At the conclusion of *England in the age of the American revolution*, which traced the narrative as far as 1763, he observed, 'My next book, if ever written, will be on "The rise of party"'. The first task would be to describe 'the seven years of confusion, 1763–70, when cabinets used themselves up very quickly and changed frequently till a new stabilisation was reached under Lord North'.[48] However, no further books appeared. Besides the various commitments – academic and political – which ate up his time, there were other distractions and difficulties which kept him from following the route he had mapped out, some inherent in his approach to research.

The first was the inaccessibility of certain key sources. Namier had been able to write the inner history of the ministries of 1760–63, headed by Newcastle and Bute, from the papers of the principals, available in the British Museum, backed up by material in other collections, and to a lesser extent by editions of letters and memoirs, even if incomplete and unscholarly. But the ensuing period, covering the premiership of George Grenville (1763–65) and Lord Rockingham's short-lived ministry of 1765–66, was a different proposition. The Grenville papers had been exported to California following their purchase by the Huntington Library in 1925, and library staff had not had time to sort and catalogue what turned out to be a massive collection: about 350,000 pieces, containing much more than had been published in the nineteenth-century edition of Grenville's correspondence.[49] Although postal inquiries elicited photostats of specific items, Namier could not write about Grenville's ministry while a mountain of unexplored papers remained out of reach.[50]

A similar situation obtained with Rockingham, whose descendant, the Canadian-born 7th Earl Fitzwilliam (then embroiled in an unpleasant family feud), was 'unwilling to allow scholars access to his papers'.[51] Here again there existed a set of printed extracts made in the nineteenth century, but these were even less useful than the Grenville edition: not only incomplete but 'full of misdatings and mistakes'.[52] It was impossible for Namier to embark upon the kind of study he had produced for 1760–63 while the bulk of the Rockingham papers remained hidden from his view.

But if the Grenville and Rockingham papers remained tantalisingly inaccessible, other sets of manuscripts were coming to light, and in remarkable quantities. In 1931 the marquess of Bute found a further important cache of his ancestor's papers in the family estate office in London, though being 'a cantankerous fellow', he then decided to cart them off to his Welsh seat, Cardiff Castle, and have them sorted and catalogued before allowing Namier and Romney Sedgwick access to them.[53] Other collections Namier discovered for himself, in a whirlwind of cross-country expeditions to landed estates (and occasionally local record offices) undertaken in great haste during university vacations.[54]

Occasionally a visit to a muniment room would be facilitated by a resident archivist, as at Woburn Abbey.[55] More often Namier was allowed to rummage around on his own.[56] It was important to him that he always entered through the front door rather than the tradesman's entrance, seemingly oblivious of the outlandish figure he cut in country houses wearing a city suit and bowler hat. Once inside, and accepted as a guest (of sorts), he was not at all offended if on occasion a servant was stationed at his elbow to ensure that this strange foreigner did not pilfer any of the family treasures (assuming that he realised what was going on).[57] Not every 'paper chase', as Namier called them, was successful, but there was more than enough gold-dust in the gravel to keep him occupied. At Holland House, Lord Ilchester's mansion in Kensington, he was encouraged to work through the papers of the Fox family, and quickly found material (on the American sojourn of Henry Fox's niece, Lady Susan O'Brien), that he thought he might make up into a book.[58]

These finds were exciting, but they were a distraction from Namier's plan of campaign. Not only did he have the labour of reading through and making notes on the new material, which took much time and energy even with the support of the secretary he had acquired in the Manchester History Department; each discovery sparked an idea for a new publication. To embrace such possibilities with an unrealistic belief that everything he envisaged doing could be done, was engrained in Namier's character. It was partly a product of the naive enthusiasm which so endeared him to his friends, and partly a symptom of his addiction to 'history work'. He described its magnetic force in a letter to Baffy's son-in-law 'Jimmie' Fergusson, who had himself begun a piece of eighteenth-century research: Fergusson would soon 'know what it means and what a slavery it is; how every moment of one's leisure is taken up by it'.[59]

Namier's new projects took the form of editions of documents, in the same way that he had once considered printing Samuel Garth's letters from the collection at Haines Hill (an idea still not abandoned), and was preparing an article which would reproduce and analyse sets of secret service accounts, beyond those included in *The structure of politics*.[60] Each of these edited works would have a full scholarly apparatus, and an introduction drawing out the significance of the text. They would be very different from the feeble compilations of Victorian editors; and from the more recent efforts of Sir John Fortescue and others, which he had lambasted in reviews. The Grafton papers were a case in point. Namier was given privileged access to the archive of the third duke, prime minister 1768–70, whose papers were placed on temporary deposit for him at the Public Record Office.[61] What he found encouraged him to propose an edition of Grafton's correspondence, since he could obviously do so much better than Sir William Anson, whose edition had appeared in 1892, and this was duly added to his list of forthcoming publications.[62] He wrote to a friend:

> You will perhaps wonder at my taking on so much at the same time … but I find that all these things dovetail to a marvellous degree, and work on each lot of manuscripts helps with all the rest. If things go well, I shall have a whole library ready in a few years' time. In a way this work is easier because it is editing and not independent writing. But I shall do some of that too in the introductions.[63]

Namier's enthusiasm for editing – or at least for proposing editions – became almost obsessional. Friends like Walter Elliot, with a sardonic turn of mind, regarded it as a symptom of his devotion to the cult of the private archive. Enemies dismissed it as another means of showing how much more he knew about his period than anyone else. Some might also have speculated that he had come to prize the act of excavating the documentary record more highly than the construction of historical explanation: hence G. M. Trevelyan's reported observation that Namier was a 'great research worker; no historian'.[64] This textual work – none of which was ever completed – would have been a logical extension of the technique of exposition that he had already adopted, and which he continued to recommend to others, namely to allow his subjects as far as possible to speak for themselves.[65] It is also visible in his style of note-taking, where he invariably transcribed rather than summarised, presumably in order to retain direct contact with the evidence rather than permitting any other mind to interpose – even his own. His two books had each contained an array of lengthy quotations, sometimes extending across whole pages, as well as substantial documentary appendices. In practice, these blocks of indented text served to slow the pace of his prose. They might also convey a misleading impression, since there was inevitably an element of authorial selection, however long the excerpt might be.

Presenting a full text, therefore, was the best way to enable the reader to hear the authentic voice of the period.

The sheer volume of hitherto unknown documentation that Namier was bringing to light confirmed him in the opinion that collaborative research was the best method of mastering these sources, and the publication of scholarly editions the best means of dealing with them. This was certainly his view of future Anglo-American cooperation: the only way for Americans to get to grips with the new materials being discovered in Britain, and for British historians to be able to make proper use of papers in American repositories, would be to collate them, something that could not be done unless documents were published, 'and published in full'.[66]

He encouraged friends and research pupils to follow his example. Romney Sedgwick's edition of George III's letters to Bute was praised to the skies by Namier as a model of careful, forensic scholarship.[67] Namier's students found their MA theses cast in the same mould. The first of them, Ninetta Jucker, produced between 1934 and 1936 an edition of the political papers of Bute's private secretary, Charles Jenkinson.[68] Another star pupil, Maurice Schofield, was handed a very similar subject, the correspondence of Treasury secretary John Robinson with King George III.[69] Of course, to a jaundiced eye the work of both students could be seen as serving Namier's personal scheme of research, something his critics would later pounce upon as evidence of academic imperialism, though in Namier's defence it should be pointed out that he regarded all of those working with him as colleagues in a great enterprise which would have been too much for a single individual. To produce a scholarly edition of a particular set of documents was an excellent apprenticeship in the techniques of research and in acquiring a 'period sense'. Ninetta Jucker's thesis was eventually published by Macmillan as a very substantial book,[70] and Namier thought that Schofield's too should go into print, though he added (perhaps with a backward glance at his own personal history) 'he is a poor boy who has to earn his living, and possibly even help his family a little'.[71]

Some of Namier's projected editions, such as the Grafton papers, remained no more than pious aspirations, but two at least he took seriously enough to work on. He had already made use in his books of the Sandwich papers at Hinchingbrooke, and was particularly interested in the life and career of the fourth earl, who headed the admiralty in both the Bute and Grenville administrations. There was also a connection with the East India Company, which piqued Namier's interest in the interplay of commerce and politics.[72] In the late 1920s Namier formed a friendship with the earl and countess of Sandwich. The earl was a highly cultivated man of wide interests: an art collector with a strong interest in modern painting –which Namier shared – a published poet and an amateur of naval history.[73] He was already promoting the preparation of an edition of the private papers of his ancestor, covering the period 1771–82, for the Navy Record Society.[74]

Namier soon agreed to edit the letters relating to 1760–71, and began collecting material.[75] The project excited him, and as usual he proceeded in great haste, not only writing to the Huntington but requesting Sandwich's help in contacting owners of manuscripts.[76] By October 1932 he was able to send some of his preliminary annotations and commentaries,[77] but thereafter progress slowed dramatically, since there was such competition for his time. He was still engaged in the work in the early months of 1935, and in October of that year reported that the Grenville letters constituted 'the one remaining serious gap' in the edition; evidently he could not bring himself to go to press until he was sure what was in the Stowe manuscripts.[78] In the autumn of 1938 Lord Sandwich inquired. Namier was contrite, and determined to 'return to the Sandwich papers' in the near future. He was even able to say that he had obtained more copies of relevant letters from American libraries.[79] As late as 1953 he wrote: 'I have not given up the idea of publishing the Sandwich papers, but when or how I do not know. I may attempt a kind of joint publication of the Grenville, Bedford and Sandwich papers.'[80] No such work would ever appear.

The second major project was even grander in scale. In 1931 Namier had been admitted to Chewton Priory by the dowager Lady Waldegrave, and had come upon papers of Horace Walpole, including an original manuscript of Walpole's 'memoirs of the reign of King George III'.[81] He was fascinated by the memoirs as a historical source, and could now see the manifold deficiencies in the published version. He immediately decided to produce a new edition himself. Inevitably, this brought him into contact with the wealthy American literary scholar and collector Wilmarth S. Lewis ('Lefty' to his friends), whose interest in Horace Walpole's life and works had an almost manic quality. Lewis was a member of the English faculty at Yale, and was amassing an unrivalled collection of Walpoliana. His ambition was to publish an edition of Walpole's letters to replace the seventeen-volume set produced by Mrs Paget Toynbee in 1903–5, a book Namier regarded as hopeless: the editing was 'poor … and vastly overrated', with 'absurd bowdlerisations'.[82] Beginning in 1937, 'Lefty' Lewis's monumental edition would eventually run to 48 volumes.

He and Namier were therefore not rivals and could work together. They began to exchange ideas and information, and to encourage each other's ambitions, though Namier, with his usual lack of tact, made no bones about his opinion that the memoirs, intended as a history, were far more reliable than the letters, in which Walpole had included anecdotes to amuse his friends without much concern for veracity.[83] Namier intended 'a critical edition' of the memoirs, elaborating on Walpole's text from other sources and checking it against other evidence. Since for many events and incidents in the first half of George's reign Walpole was 'our best, and sometimes our only, authority', the edition would serve as a master-narrative for the period. Though Macmillan were prepared at one point to advertise the edition as in preparation, it ended up as yet another castle in the air: a project much thought about, talked about and worried over, which never attained a concrete form.[84]

A final complication, though a welcome one, arrived with an invitation to deliver the Ford Lectures in English History in Oxford in 1934. Namier could not refuse, even though the task of preparation diverted him from other important work, and the logistics of fitting the lectures into his already complex travel arrangements proved exhausting.[85] But Oxford was Oxford. He agonised over what to speak about 'because lectures of that kind have to be on the highest possible level'.[86] He did not want to recap his 'past research', and offer it as a 'still life', preferring to present the unripe fruits of work on which he was currently engaged. This meant focusing on the years of the Grenville and Rockingham administrations, and laying the groundwork for the next stage of his great political narrative. It also meant moving away from anatomising the House of Commons. The history of the ministries of Newcastle and Bute had revolved around a single question, how Newcastle was 'so easily over-thrown in the parliament of 1761, of which he himself had largely had the choice'. So naturally the election of 1761, and the resulting disposition of parliamentary forces, had been at the heart of the solution Namier provided. By contrast, the events of the ensuing period – 'the seven years of confusion' – were determined by events at court and in cabinet rather than in the Commons. In order to explain them Namier needed first to explore in greater depth the nature of constitutional relationships, just as in *The structure of politics* he had established the nature of elections and the pattern of parliamentary allegiance.[87] He would therefore lecture on 'King, cabinet and parliament in the early years of George III', attempting to sketch in a position that he would fill out properly as soon as the Grenville and Rockingham papers became available. He would discuss the role of the monarch, the nature of the cabinet and of the prime ministerial office, the composition of the government party in parliament ('the king's friends') and the part played by 'men of business'.[88]

The lectures were a great success, especially with the younger generation of listeners;[89] a further enhancement to his reputation. But of course their publication became another book project. No sooner had Namier's election as Ford's lecturer been announced than a representative of the Clarendon Press wrote to inform him that the press expected to be sent the text.[90] Namier could not think of simply putting his lectures directly into print, since the arguments were still 'crystallising', so the task of preparing a full version joined the tribe of monkeys perching on his back.[91]

Wedgwood's History of Parliament

Although the ambition to make a full biographical analysis of the membership of the eighteenth-century House of Commons was no longer a priority for Namier it had not vanished altogether from his mind: nothing ever did. The problem was that the kind of collective biography he envisaged – vastly different in scale from the prosopographies made by classical or medieval historians, and undertaken with no prior explanatory structure in mind – required very substantial resources in manpower and money. The only hope seemed to be Wedgwood's proposed 'History of Parliament', which like so much else had become a casualty of the exigencies in public finance brought on by the world economic crisis.[92] When the report of the Treasury committee was eventually published it was warmly welcomed by the prime minister, Ramsay MacDonald. At the same time MacDonald emphasised that government could not fund the research, though HMSO would be on hand to publish the finished product. The only thing that Wedgwood could do was to search for private donors, and he established a parliamentary committee to solicit subscriptions. Namier was not keen on this approach. It would be much better, he thought, if 'one man (or woman)' could be persuaded to give the entire sum of £30,000: what would really attract a private benefactor would be to have 'all the credit which results from financing such an enterprise'. His motives were not, however, merely practical. He asked Lady Sandwich if she would approach Lady Beit (widow of the philanthropist Sir Otto Beit, a former chairman of the Rhodes Trust), adding,

> If you see any chance of it and wish to help please let it come through me because he who would be willing to find the money will in many ways be able to call the tune; and I have various ideas as to the way in which the thing should be done with which I am sure you would agree but which would not be shared by all my colleagues on the committee.[93]

In this he was absolutely right. Wedgwood entertained a vision which was more expansive than Namier's, in essence both celebratory and pedagogical, educating the world in the virtues of representative institutions. Namier, with his reverence for the heritage of the British empire, could sympathise with this point of view, and in playing his own version of the same tune in letters to Wedgwood he was being neither insincere nor opportunistic.[94] Nonetheless, the two men had a very different conception of what a cooperatively written parliamentary history should look like. When we add to this Wedgwood's unsinkable self-belief, buccaneering methods and proprietorial attitude to the project, and Namier's overweening self-confidence, enhanced by his recent appointment, the stage was set for conflict.

The struggle for the direction of the history, between Wedgwood and his former allies, whom he scorned as a 'trades union' of professors, was prolonged and bitter. It involved not only Namier but the other historians whom Wedgwood had brought on to the treasury committee: Pollard, Neale and the American seventeenth-century scholar Wallace Notestein. Neale and Notestein aligned themselves with Namier; in fact Neale may be said to have led the academic objections to the course that Wedgwood had adopted. Pollard, who disliked Namier, and always regarded his and Neale's ambitions for the history as grandiose, was tolerant of Wedgwood but unconvinced of his scholarship and disinclined to indulge him.

After establishing his parliamentary committee in 1933 Wedgwood began to look for other academic advisers. Apart from Pollard, the members of the treasury committee were simply told that their work was done. One reason for dropping Namier and Neale was that the project had expanded in directions that they had previously opposed: Wedgwood wanted it to encompass Lords as well as Commons, and the pre-union Scottish and Irish parliaments, in order to maximise donations from parliamentarians and the general public. Biographical research was also underplayed in favour of the didactic purpose. More weight would be given in the published volumes to interpreting the historical development of the institution, an approach Namier thought was jumping the gun. It took some time for Namier to realise what was going on: as late as October 1934, in a letter in the *Manchester Guardian*, Wedgwood was still brandishing his name as an editor of one of the proposed chronological sections, and Namier declared himself willing and eager to take up the work 'when the means are available and you give the signal'.[95]

Over the following winter the relationship froze. Namier had still not been approached officially to take responsibility for an eighteenth-century section, while Neale had been cut out completely, and had taken Notestein with him. At the same time Wedgwood's own position had deteriorated. His line-up of prospective editors was unimpressive, and the parliamentarians entrusted with the administration of the project became alarmed. In March 1935 they proposed the appointment of an editorial committee to take responsibility for planning the work. Effectively, this would hand over control of the history to the professionals ('the real experts in parliamentary history'). Among the section editors would be Pollard and Neale for the sixteenth century and Namier for the eighteenth. Editors would be able to organise their sections as they saw fit, with no overarching structure of conclusions such as Wedgwood envisaged. Namier was keen to participate and was in frequent correspondence with Neale and Notestein. They agreed that what was important was the biographies. 'I hope', wrote Namier, 'that our slogan should be "first things first"; I mean that we should do our biographical volumes, and the conclusions directly emerging from them, while leaving ambitious and more far-reaching schemes to the future.'[96] As Notestein explained to Wedgwood: 'We are all anxious to see the project limited in scope to the membership … and the generalisations about that membership.' Subjects like procedure, constituencies and elections could be dealt with at a later date, and in any case 'some of these other matters Neale, Namier and myself are planning to deal with in very long books covering short periods'.[97]

After squirming, Wedgwood agreed to meet 'the historians' in London in December 1935. Namier was bullish, telling Notestein: 'We shall … constitute ourselves as the only and final authority' for the history. He also saw more publication possibilities out of the research that would be generated; this time, 'a quarterly review on parliamentary history'.[98] But no sooner had a meeting been arranged than Wedgwood began to wriggle again. He sent an agenda of his own, declaring that any decisions taken at the meeting would be 'unofficial', which Namier thought had 'wash[ed] out everything which was arranged between us'.[99] Namier and his fellow academics were then subjected to a harangue from Wedgwood, who argued that the purpose of the history had changed from the original conception.[100] Wedgwood would not give way. The result was stalemate. The 'experts' would come into the work only if they could constitute 'a strong and authoritative committee' to take over direction from Wedgwood, who, for his part, would have none of it.[101]

Wedgwood was able to convince the parliamentary committee on the basis of having to honour commitments to subscribers. In doing so, he depicted the 'trades union' as a gang of self-interested professors trying to muscle in on a great parliamentary enterprise. He was also able to make great play of the fact that his own fifteenth-century section was almost ready for the press. But at this crucial stage he fell ill, which gave a last opportunity to members of the parliamentary committee who feared the history was becoming a shambles. In April 1936 they established a joint subcommittee, comprising 'six parliament and six trades union' as Wedgwood put it, to serve as an editorial executive.[102] Namier was included. When this subcommittee met in July the academics made it a condition of their continued involvement that plans to publish Wedgwood's first volume should be halted until the text could be scrutinised. Wedgwood was horrified. He was certainly not going to submit his work to the likes of 'Neale and Namier![sic]'. Having recovered his health, he rallied his forces, and at a meeting of the full committee in July secured a compromise: his text would be sent to Pollard and G. M. Trevelyan to be vetted. Neither of these elder statesmen was particularly happy with what they read, but both felt that the volume should go to press. The risk of thwarting Wedgwood was that 'the whole affair will break out'.[103] Wedgwood was jubilant – 'the trades union opposition has collapsed' – and he was back in charge.[104]

It was a Pyrrhic victory. Wedgwood's first volume, published in December 1936, received mixed reviews; the second, which appeared in October 1938, was savaged, and was even made the subject of a leading article in *The Times* deploring the 'estrangement' between Wedgwood and 'the original group of parliamentary historians'.[105] The project limped on, with no prospect of further publication, until in 1940 Wedgwood's organisation was wound up and the funds transferred to a parliamentary trust.

By 1942 Wedgwood would no longer rank Namier among the 'bitter historians' who were his greatest enemies.[106] For his part, Namier would write generously of Wedgwood's last book, *Testament to democracy*, published in January 1943, an account of the parallel traditions of liberty and representative government held by Britain and its American ally. In his review he described Wedgwood as 'imbued with the finest tradition of England … a knight-errant of Englishry'. Even if Wedgwood could be stubbornly 'wrong-headed', 'never could one who had his courage, his passion for freedom, and his flaming hatred of cruelty and injustice be insignificant or ignoble'.[107] Perceived by Wedgwood's family as an olive branch extended to an old friend, this was above all an act of gratitude for Wedgwood's unswerving and very vocal support for the Jewish homeland in Palestine, which had reached a zenith in his wartime speeches.[108] Privately, Namier admitted, 'I have an affection for him … although he is so angry with me that he will not speak to me. The reason is that I found it impossible to work with him in his history of parliament, and he saw in me the leader of the historians' revolt. Still, I truly love the man – a fine creature … with noble instincts and no sense whatever.'[109]

Namier remained implacably opposed to participation in a history of parliament that followed Wedgwood's vision.[110] By the late 1930s parliamentary prosopography had slipped even further down his list of priorities, though he was willing to participate, alongside Neale and others, in a subcommittee established by the British Committee of Historical Sciences to take forward the history of representative institutions, an organisation envisaged by its creators as a coordinating body that could in due course take over Wedgwood's project.[111] His main interests, however, lay elsewhere.

Nazism and the Jewish cause

Despite Namier's commitment to his 'history work' and his determination to carry through anything and everything that he had begun, the blackness of Hitler came to dominate his mind. He had read *Mein Kampf* when it was first published in 1925/26, and unlike many of his contemporaries always took the author and his party very seriously.[112] Deep-seated hatred of German nationalism prompted the belief that, far from being an unrepresentative type, Hitler gave voice to 'the deepest instincts of Germany'.[113] Namier was on record as believing the German nation to be the quintessence of brutality. 'Even the cruelty of a Tartar does not approach that of a German', he had written during the Great War, in a passage that sounds uncannily prophetic of the horrors to come: 'the German beats the Mongol in being dispassion-ate, systematic, and scientific'. In particular, he made the sweeping (and implausible) observation that 'in every Jewish pogrom in Russia the moving spirit has been a person of German extraction'.[114] Hitler's election as Reich Chancellor in January 1933 filled him with dread. What happened next – the brutal repression of opposition following the Reichstag fire, the Nazi triumph at the elections in March 1933, and Hitler's seizure of dictatorial powers – confirmed his expectations.

From the first Namier recognised the malignancy of the Nazi regime, and its expansionist intent. He always considered Hitler a mediocrity: the Foreign Office assessment of the Führer's 'intelligence [and] clearness of mind' was, he thought, laughable.[115] Hitler was a man whose word meant nothing and whose purposes were base. 'These people are not civilised – no, not even human.'[116] Alan Taylor remembered Namier arriving at Disley in 1934 brandishing a newspaper which car-ried news of the Night of the Long Knives. Namier was beside himself with glee, shouting out, 'The swine are killing each other!'[117] He was openly contemptuous of the idea that Nazi Germany could be treated as a normal European state, even if this was advocated by old friends such as Philip Kerr, now Lord Lothian. Namier told Crozier of the *Manchester Guardian* that 'to understand Lothian's views of Hitler you must remember all the time that Lothian is a most convinced and fervent Christian Scientist. He thinks that if he can construct a great international praying league to pray for Hitler, whatever evil there is in Hitler will speedily be dissipated.'[118]

At the same time Namier was himself not an infallible prophet on European affairs. He recognised that Hitler would move first against Austria but for a long time thought that neighbouring countries, such as Czechoslovakia or Hungary, would mount a successful resistance.[119] Oddly, he also endorsed an idea which was becoming increasingly popular in Austria, that the best hope for the country lay in a Habsburg restoration; and this despite the vehement opposition of his former Czechoslovak friends, who regarded any prospect of the return of the Habsburgs as a *casus belli*. For Namier, however, it would be 'the greatest blow which could be inflicted on the Nazis … re-establish[ing] a truly conservative principle' by 'raising [the] standard of old world conservatism against [the] Nazi Bolshevism of the *canaille*'.[120]

Those who sought to explain, and by implication to excuse, the violence and aggressiveness of the German government by reference to the harshness of the Versailles treaty, were given short shrift. Before the Great War ended Namier had argued against a peace settlement which went too far – 'It is absurd to hurt an enemy whom one cannot annihilate, and nothing adds more to the strength and military spirit of a nation than to have suffered real wrongs'[121] – and later he had opposed both 'excessive reparations' and the prohibition on Austro-German integration. But he differed sharply from other commentators, who, taking their cue from Keynes's economic critique, argued that 'the reparations problem' was the underlying cause of 'the Nazi outburst'. This he declared to be nonsense. It was a by-product of an intellectual trend which he found distasteful: the increasingly vocal 'revisionist' interpretation of the origins of the Great War which denied that German militarism had constituted the prime cause, and in a morally neutral fashion sought to distribute blame for the catastrophe among all European states and their muddling statesmen. Namier would have no truck with any such rewriting of what he saw as self-evident historical truth.[122] His explanation for the rise of Hitler was different: in his view, it was a law of history that national defeats, of the kind that Germany had suffered in 1918, issued in 'frantic, almost insane resentments' which produced outbreaks of revolutionary nationalism. Usually, these revolutions opened with 'humanitarian ideas' and 'generous impulses' and afterwards were inevitably degraded under the pressure of political insecurity. The Nazis, however, were an exception: they were bad from the very beginning. Their revolution was 'counterfeit', and the persecution of Jews 'their only original contribution'.[123]

The 'atrocious happenings' in Germany haunted Namier.[124] He informed 'Lefty' Lewis that 'for personal reasons, my work is now completely disorganised by extraneous events. I am a national Jew, and the present events in Germany naturally touch me most closely, even though I have neither relatives nor friends over there; and all my leisure, and more than my leisure, is now taken up with attempts to help my German co-racials.'[125] Although he had no family in Germany, he did have aunts, uncles and cousins in Austria, who would be affected by the first steps of German aggression. But his feelings were no less deep when they were not personal. As Lady Namier noted, he identified with all persecuted Jews, much as the eponymous hero of George Eliot's novel *Daniel Deronda* was accused of having 'a passion for people who are pelted'. Namier once told Julia that 'he was bound to every Jew with his gut, or rather an umbilical cord which … tautened agonisingly when one, or a group, fell into dire adversity'.[126] This brought involvement in a range of committees, groups and institutions devoted to working on behalf of Jewish refugees from Nazi tyranny.[127]

Namier was particularly busy in trying to assist scholars and scientists who were being hounded out of government and university posts in Germany. He used his own contacts, in the academic, political and business worlds, which involved him in endless meetings and correspondence, and occasionally travel to the continent.[128]

His cousins Theo and Paul Frankel (two sons of his favourite aunt, Therese), may have been among those he helped: both came to Britain in 1938, and Paul took a job in Manchester. Later, Namier would visit Theo and his family in Wimbledon, where the children had to be on their best behaviour for 'Uncle Ulu'.[129] But individual acts of philanthropy were inadequate and in May 1933 Manchester's vice-chancellor, Sir Walter Moberly, organised a series of meetings to set up a fund to offer openings for displaced academics. Over the next five years Namier became heavily involved in administering this initiative.[130]

The task of finding employment and financial support for an ever-increasing number of refugees proved difficult and frustrating, and involved Namier in a great deal of legwork, taking up time he could ill afford.[131] In some cases he was obliged to look elsewhere for support to finance permanent posts at Manchester, as for example, from the London-based Academic Assistance Council. For years he acted as an unofficial liaison between the Academic Assistance Council and the vice-chancellor's committee in Manchester.[132] He also joined the academic committee of the Central British Fund for World Jewish Relief and Rehabilitation, which provided financial and other support to individuals, and attended its meetings whenever he was in London.[133] In 1936 he was briefly a member of the Council for German Jewry, appointed at Weizmann's behest as a sop to make up for disappointments elsewhere, but differed from colleagues in insisting that the resources of wealthy refugees be used to help poorer Jews to escape from the 'place of torment'. He soon resigned, adding this experience to an accumulating store of disillusionments.[134]

In an informal capacity Namier also busied himself in work for the Jewish Agency for Palestine, so much that he had to ask colleagues at Manchester to reschedule his timetable to enable extended stays in London.[135] Although never elected a member of the Zionist executive, or even as a delegate to any Zionist congress, he operated close to the centre of events, as an intimate friend and adviser to Weizmann, a point of contact with British politicians and civil servants, up to, and including, the prime minister and, perhaps most important, as co-author and editor of letters and memoranda from the Jewish Agency.[136] In all this he worked closely with Blanche Dugdale, whose diaries detail frequent meetings in the Jewish Agency's offices at 77 Great Russell Street in Bloomsbury, interspersed with working lunches and dinners, and taxi-rides to Whitehall and Westminster to harry ministers and Colonial Office officials, or consult with sympathetic MPs like Walter Elliot and Victor Cazalet (another friend of Namier's from post-war Oxford).[137]

As always, Namier's energetic participation was a mixed blessing to the Zionist cause. His sharp mind could find and hone arguments better than anyone else, and he had a broad range of acquaintances among all political parties. He was as likely to be found having lunch with the Labour MP (and ex-Fabian) Hugh Dalton as with Conservatives such as Elliot, Cazalet or Bob Boothby.[138] But his angularities made him an awkward and sometimes unpopular ambassador for the cause, while his refusal to suffer fools, and deep-rooted suspicion of any form of theocracy, whether Roman Catholic, Orthodox or rabbinical, made him plenty of enemies within the Zionist executive.[139] His colleague Moshe Shertok (later, as Moshe Sharett, prime minister of Israel), remembered 'a proud Jew' with a penetrating intellect who yet showed a 'complete lack of understanding of internecine Jewish conflicts and strife, with all of which he was impatient'. This 'led members of all conflicting groups to detest and dread him: they wished he would leave them, felt him to be alien to them'.[140] Namier even managed to turn a public appeal in Manchester for donations to a fund established in honour of Samuel Alexander into a dispute with leading members of Manchester's Jewish community who resented the fact that they had not been consulted.[141] What made things worse was Namier's obtuseness in failing to recognise when he had given offence, and his angry response to any opposition.[142] Not every clash of personality was Namier's fault and, although he never willingly swallowed an insult or shirked a battle, he was capable of restraining his reactions when he could be made to understand that they would cause serious harm. But in an organisation which was not short of prima donnas, including Weizmann himself, Namier's involvement often proved counter-productive.

The most striking evidence of Namier's effect on other people comes from Isaiah Berlin, whose memoir of him is one of the most vivid and perceptive re-creations of his personality.[143] As an undergraduate Berlin had been profoundly impressed by reading an essay of Namier's on Zionism.[144] He saw Namier in the flesh for the first time in August 1937, at a Zionist congress, and described him to a friend as 'A frightful man, I thought, who ought certainly be put on to something. It will be far worse if he is frustrated.'[145] Not long afterwards Namier came to visit Berlin at All Souls, intrigued by his election as the first openly Jewish fellow of the college, and by what he had heard of Berlin's interest in Marx, about whom Namier was himself now brimming with contempt. Berlin remembered that Namier 'had some respect for the fellows of All Souls. He believed them, for the most part, with certain exceptions which he did not wish to mention, to be intellectually qualified to do genuine research work.'[146] Having dismissed Marx – 'a typical Jewish half-charlatan, who got hold of quite a good idea and then ran it to death just to spite the Gentiles' – and urged Berlin to study Freud instead, Namier embarked on an account of his own life. Berlin was spellbound:

> He stood in the middle of my room and spoke his words in a slow, somewhat hyp-
> notic voice, with great emphasis and in a continuous unbroken drone, with few intervals

between the sentences, a strongly central European accent and a frozen expression. He kept his eyes immovably upon me, frowning now and then, and producing (I realised later that this was how he drew breath without seeming to do so) a curious mooing sound which blocked the gaps between his sentences. Not that I dreamt of interrupting: the entire phenomenon was too strange, the intensity of the utterance too great; I felt that I was being eyed by a stern and heavy headmaster who knew precisely what I was at, disapproved, and was determined to set me right.[147]

The friendship blossomed, and Namier became a regular visitor to All Souls.[148] It was on one of these visits, having tea in the common room, that Namier overheard a guest defending Germany's right to the possession of colonies. Assuming, wrongly, that the speaker was himself German, Namier commented, loudly enough for all to hear, '*Wir Juden und die andere farbigen meinen anders* [We Jews and the other coloured peoples think differently]'. As Berlin observed, 'he savoured the effect of these startling words with great satisfaction'.[149]

Zionist politics

After Weizmann's departure from the presidency of the Zionist Organisation in 1931 Namier remained attached to 'the chief's' coat-tails.[150] Their relationship was not without strain. Namier's hero-worship was always tempered by an awareness of Weizmann's failings, and now he found his efforts on behalf of Jewish refugees undermined by Weizmann's disorganisation: letters went unanswered and promises to attend fund-raising events were forgotten. On one occasion Namier wrote angrily, 'Frankly I was sick of writing to you time and again about business matters on which I had to make decisions here without having received a reply.'[151] He complained to Weizmann of having been made to 'look a perfect fool', and although he understood that Weizmann was overworked, could not refrain from pointing out that 'some consideration is also due to me'.[152] But neither Weizmann's muddling dilatoriness nor his disregard for sound advice to distance himself for a time from Zionist politics, were enough to alienate Namier entirely. When Weizmann began to involve himself again in the affairs of the Jewish Agency in London, he inexorably drew Namier in behind him.

On returning from Palestine in January 1935 Weizmann was in a state of great agitation. He called on Namier's help, who replied that 'I am at your disposal, any time'.[153] Weizmann confessed that he was in despair at what he had observed of Jewish settlements. The sight of middle-class immigrants unused to manual labour and lacking the technical skills to build houses and grow crops made him fear that the entire enterprise of the national home would collapse.[154] Namier had repeatedly warned of this very risk, though it was not something he would ever admit publicly; indeed, in articles and letters to the press he bragged of the new prosperity that Jews were bringing to Palestine, a tactic designed to stave off any suggestion that immigration might be curtailed because of the incapacity of the economy to absorb the increase in population, which was a condition of the mandate.[155]

The issue for Weizmann was education, and it led to a remarkable proposal. If the Hebrew University could be 'set right', would Namier accept a professorial post there? Namier refused: it would be futile, since 'my work is on eighteenth-century British, and nineteenth-century diplomatic history'. Asking him to teach 'other branches of history' would be like requiring a chemist like Weizmann to teach aspects of his subject in which he had no expertise. Then came a second proposition: if Weizmann took on the presidency of the Zionist Organisation again, would Namier come into the executive? The answer is revealing. Namier said that he would do so, but only if 'the rich men' would set aside £10,000 for him as an endowment of £500 p.a. for life. To relinquish his chair would not only be to 'give up my chances [in Manchester] but any I may have at Oxford, a sacrifice sufficiently big for one man to make'. An endowment would enable him to take up his research again whenever he left the executive.[156] Moreover, if he were to resign his present post he would first need a sabbatical from the executive in order to complete the text of his Ford Lectures: 'I have an obligation in this matter, and it might be the one tangible result of my four years' teaching in Manchester', a nice comment, perhaps, on his priorities as professor.[157]

Weizmann's proposal was genuine but he was in no position to make promises to Namier. Even though David Ben-Gurion's Palestine Labour Party was now the most substantial element in the mainstream Zionist movement and Ben-Gurion was someone with whom Namier always remained on good terms,[158] the same could not be said of other prominent Zionists. So when Weizmann accepted re-election to the presidency in August 1935 it was on the explicit understanding that there would be no place for Namier on the executive.[159] Weizmann tried to fob off his friend with talk of a new committee, with Namier at its head, to coordinate political work in London. This too came to nothing.[160] Weizmann, who never found it easy to grasp a nettle, allowed Namier to find this out for himself. Immediately, Namier fired off a long letter full of bitter reproaches. He had been 'let down' again. Leadership of the coordinating committee would have 'given me a "locus standi" in the organisation'.

> It is one of the regular difficulties which your most devoted friends have in co-operating with you that you do not seem to care in what position you place them, or how you add, unnecessarily, to their work and troubles. This is wrong towards your friends, and wrong towards the cause; and it is high time someone told you that straight out.[161]

Weizmann informed Namier that two members of the executive in particular, Nahum Goldmann and Selig Brodetsky, were dead set against him. In the past, Namier had worked closely with both, and they had presumably had enough of his tongue. Weizmann thought Namier could continue to help in an unofficial capacity, a suggestion that went down poorly.[162] Weizmann explained to Baffy that Namier

> simply does not understand the position. The fact is that in spite of the services which he rendered to the movement at a critical time, in spite of his great abilities (which I deeply appreciate, as did everyone else with whom he came into contact), there still remained some fundamental lack in his relationship to the movement; he was out of harmony with them; he was given to scourging them with scorpions – and this they took ill from a man who was, in their view, a stranger in their midst … Namier's services and abilities would never have compensated for this fundamental lack of sympathy. It was difficult for me to explain all this to Namier without hurting his feelings, and I tried to deal with the matter as carefully as I could, but I am afraid his *amour propre* has got the better of him.[163]

Namier eventually recovered from what Weizmann termed a prolonged fit of 'the sulks' and allowed himself to be persuaded back into the fold. The Zionists needed someone 'to deal with the German-Jewish problem', and according to Weizmann 'we all agreed … that Namier is the only man who can deal with the Foreign Office in such a matter'.[164] An invitation came to join Weizmann in Palestine in December 1935 to discuss the position of Jewish immigrants from Germany[165] At first Namier thought this was a blind, to get him away from London while intricate political discussions were taking place. But finding that the offer was genuine he immediately booked his flight, so keen was he to be of use, and to have some kind of recognised position within the movement. The time spent in Palestine was informative, and personally useful, since it restored amicable relations with Weizmann, but there was no practical outcome, and Namier returned to London in January 1936 to find that a new political crisis had blown up.[166]

The Nazi menace in Europe meant that more Jews than ever were going to Palestine. Of the quarter of a million Jewish settlers between 1923 and 1935 over half had arrived since 1933.[167] Tensions between these newcomers and the Arab population once again put British ministers on the spot. The government's first response was to resurrect the idea of a legislative council accommodating both Arabs and Jews, as a first step towards the establishment of a self-governing state. Namier was concerned that Weizmann seemed to be taking this seriously.[168] Namier put his objections to Weizmann in typically trenchant style.[169] Establishing a council would 'prematurely crystallise the national home' and effectively put a stop to Jewish immigration, which would have additional negative consequences for those seeking to escape Nazi tyranny.[170] It would also sideline the Jewish Agency, since henceforth the mandatory power would negotiate only with Jews in Palestine. Weizmann's single reservation, that there should be equal representation in any council for Arabs and Jews, was misguided. Namier naturally agreed that there could be no election by universal suffrage, which would leave Jews in a minority. In any case, he considered the majority of Arabs – about whom he could be remarkably scornful and openly racist – unfit to exercise a vote.[171] Weizmann's alternative was equally unsatisfactory. As usual, the chief was not thinking ahead. If it could not be avoided, the scheme had to be significantly modified:

> Palestine belongs to two nations: the Arabs resident within its borders, and the Jews desirous of making it their national home. A legislative council … must be based on the two nations and not on individuals (that is, not on their numbers on the spot). It is impossible to construct a legislative assembly on an 'amphibious' basis – in part territorial (the local Arabs) and in part tribal (Jews wherever they may be). The solution therefore is in two separate chambers, one for Jews and the other for Arabs … the Jewish chamber should consist of representatives of the Jewish population of Palestine and the non-Palestinian branches of the Jewish Agency.[172]

Politically this was a case that Weizmann could not make, believing that at this critical time the Jewish Agency should not appear intransigent.[173]

However, the scheme could still be fought in parliament, and over the winter of 1935–36, aided and abetted by Baffy Dugdale, Namier worked his political connections tirelessly to thwart the efforts of the colonial secretary, the National Labour MP, J. H. Thomas, to push through the establishment of the legislative council. He and Baffy were closer than ever, with Baffy prepared to entrust him with her most intimate secrets as she asked his advice about her personal life (not something many of his friends would have done).[174] She even boasted to Walter Elliot that Namier was 'under [her] thumb'.[175] Together they were able to encourage a successful campaign of resistance from MPs sympathetic to the Zionist cause, mainly on the Conservative side, and including Winston Churchill, with whom Namier had been in correspondence on historical matters, and Bob Boothby.[176]

The positive outcome of the parliamentary session gave Namier a renewed confidence in himself and in his strategy.[177] Not only had he forestalled the implementation of the legislative council, he had also secured the appointment of his own preferred candidate, Sir Neill Malcolm, as League of Nations high commissioner for German refugees. When Weizmann wrote in a mood of desperation at the unsympathetic attitude of the British High Commissioner to Palestine, Sir Arthur Wauchope, and apprehension at what this might augur for British government policy, Namier counselled caution:

If it comes to a fight, we shall fight like blazes; and you know well that I never shun a
fight, and never feel better than in a fight. Nonetheless, I would think it over not ten, but
fifty, times before letting ourselves in for it now, if there is any chance of avoiding it …
here we may rally in the next month or two some considerable influences … But if we let
it come to an open break, it may be very difficult to go back on it.[178]

Namier was as good as his word, and spent the next few weeks in a blur of activity:
consultations with Weizmann and Baffy, meetings with MPs, the composition of
letters to ministers and newspapers.[179] He was also able to extend his elevated social
contacts when Weizmann organised a small dinner party – doubtless with a political as well as convivial purpose – which included a brother and sister-in-law of the
duchess of York.[180]

The pressure intensified in late April 1936, when riots broke out in Jaffa, followed
by a general strike declared by the Arab National Committee; the beginning of a cycle
of inter-communal violence. Namier's first concern was to ensure that the situation
was properly reported in the British press, which seemed to be trying to share blame
when he himself felt strongly that the prime (if not the only) responsibility lay with
Arabs. 'So far the morale of our people … has been admirable. There has been neither
flinching nor reprisals – and it is not an easy thing to try to live a normal life when
people are daily murdered on the high road, when houses and crops are burned, and
trees uprooted.'[181] The danger was that the government might see inter-communal
violence as a reason to suspend immigration. So he did what he could to publicise the
truth as he read it in Zionist despatches from Palestine, writing privately to friends
like Lord Lothian and Basil Liddell Hart, and publicly to newspapers.[182] Lothian
was particularly useful because of his connection with *The Times*, and at Namier's
prompting composed a leader which Namier considered 'excellent'.[183] Namier also
made sure that Crozier on the *Manchester Guardian* was kept informed, sending him
'extremely confidential stuff' which included accounts of interviews with ministers
and officials.[184]

The ratcheting up of tension which followed the Jaffa riots, and Hitler's march
into the Rhineland, made Namier think in terms of the use of force to defend the
Jewish homeland. Thus far the British government's response had not been encouraging: they had scrapped the idea of a legislative council, but produced yet another
royal commission, this time headed by Lord Peel, to go to Palestine and report on
the causes of the disturbances. To Baffy, Namier lamented that 'in the past most of
the Zionist leaders were so damned pacifist and high-minded, and the one who had
military inclinations – I mean Jabotinsky – was so damned literary and theoretical'.
From a radicalism of words, 'we shall have to pass to a most intense "radicalism of
deeds"'. He was convinced that there needed to be 'a real Jewish militarism', and

claimed to have 'taken steps to get in touch with the Committee of Imperial Defence', to propose the raising and training of a specifically 'Jewish regiment of territorials' in Britain, 'ready for the next great emergency'. 'A force of thirty to forty thousand men might impress the general staff and trembling Cabinet ministers.' If the British wouldn't play, he even considered (perhaps only half-seriously) going to the French to set up a Jewish regiment in the Foreign Legion.[185]

These arguments were taken further in a memorandum 'written for private circulation' in November 1936, which depicted the Arabs as intransigently anti-British and the troubles in Palestine as being fomented by Mussolini, while Jewish settlers were naturally loyal to the empire, and should be given military training in order to be able to defend their own, and British imperial, interests.[186] For all his bellicosity, Namier still clung to the notion of a Zionist state as a part of the British empire – the old 'dominion' scheme – even when other Zionists, including Weizmann, were disheartened by British policy and sensed that the Zionist movement might soon need to sever the British connection.[187] A year later Namier was discussing with Lord Eustace Percy the means by which 'English culture' might be spread among the Jews in Palestine, through education, at school and university level, and the foundation of a Jewish equivalent to the British Council.[188]

Meanwhile the Zionist executive was struggling to maintain unity. It seemed more and more likely that immigration would be halted, and at one point Weizmann suggested that the Jewish Agency take the initiative in offering to consent to a temporary suspension. This was strongly opposed by Ben-Gurion, with Namier's backing: it would split the movement and provoke a Jewish civil war in Palestine.[189] Namier felt that the Jewish Agency had to take its lead from Zionists in Palestine: there should be no wavering.[190] He was increasingly exasperated with Weizmann, but was dissuaded by Ben-Gurion from any thoughts of retiring from the fray.[191] 'I am well aware that you are not a man to be preached to', Ben-Gurion wrote, 'and that it is not your fault that you are not in a position to devote your whole time to our political work', but

> We are now confronted with a new political era … Our affairs in London must now be watched upon by alert and sensitive men who are imbued with initiative and who have freed themselves from obsolete political habits.[192]

Namier remained close to Ben-Gurion, and made a second visit to Palestine in December 1936, this time staying at the King David Hotel in Jerusalem.[193] His ostensible objective was to make peace between Ben-Gurion and Weizmann, but conciliation was scarcely his forte, and Baffy recorded in her diary with no pretence at surprise: 'It seems that L's presence is NOT oiling the wheels between Chaim and B-G!' Otherwise he seems to have enjoyed himself. He flew from London to

Alexandria with Wauchope's ADC, Henry Hovell-Thurlow-Cumming-Bruce, a second lieutenant in the Seaforth Highlanders, and, breaking their journey in Athens, the two men made a sightseeing trip to the Acropolis. Years later Namier was able to recall the experience as an opening gambit in an application to his former travelling companion, now Lord Thurlow, to see his family papers.[194]

By early 1937 it was rumoured that the Peel commission report would favour a partition of Palestine into a Jewish and an Arab state.[195] Like Weizmann and most of his colleagues, Namier was willing to accept partition, believing that the mandate was dead in the water. He drafted a memorandum advocating the establishment of a Jewish state for his parliamentary friends to forward to the commission.[196] When details of the report were leaked, in June 1937, he came out strongly in favour, even if the suggested frontiers were unsatisfactory. It would at least be a firm basis for negotiation. Not everyone agreed: Ben-Gurion vented his objections in a series of inflammatory speeches in Palestine, his outrage focused on the commission's accompanying recommendation of a short-term limit to immigration while the details of partition were worked out. Somehow he was brought round, almost certainly by Namier, who argued that this was not the time for 'Catastrophen-politik'.[197]

At the next Zionist congress in Zurich in August, a month after the official publication of the Peel report, and the British government's acceptance of the principle of partition, Ben-Gurion assisted Weizmann in persuading a majority to empower the agency to enter into negotiations with the British on this basis. Namier had flown over to Switzerland with Baffy, though he stayed in a different hotel, away from the members of the executive.[198] Although satisfied with the outcome, his pleasure was tinged with personal disappointment, for, despite Weizmann's best efforts, he again found himself excluded from the executive. The insurmountable problem was his unpopularity with a number of influential people, especially in the English Zionist Federation. After initial anger he accepted the outcome, but, as Baffy noted, it made his position 'very difficult'.[199] Election to an advisory committee established by the Jewish Agency to coordinate political work in London was a poor compensation, though he did manage to get it written up in the *Manchester Guardian*.[200]

By the end of 1937 Namier was enveloped in gloom about the prospects for European Jewry. While more Jews than ever were clamouring to leave for Palestine, the British government was backtracking on the recommendations of the Peel commission, and there were rumours that a halt would be put to Jewish immigration. The Arabs were intractable – the first pan-Arab congress, convened in September, had referred to the Zionist presence in Palestine as a 'cancer' which had to be cut out – and the Germans and Italians were bent on making trouble. Namier was well aware of pro-Arab sentiments in the Foreign Office and in parliament. With a few exceptions, such as Walter Elliot, his more reliable contacts stood outside the government. Partition, which he had come to see as the best solution, since it would establish a Jewish state (size did not matter at this stage), seemed further off than ever, and even Ben-Gurion was trying to devise a different plan.[201] Namier and Baffy spent New Year's Eve with the Milnes at Oldbury, and by the time the clock reached midnight they were the only people still up, after a long talk about Palestine which left both of them depressed.

Moving to the right

What he saw as betrayals over Palestine by successive governments in the 1930s, combined with the failure of ministers to comprehend the true nature of the European crisis and the absolute necessity of standing up to the dictators, stiffened Namier's political opinions and shifted their centre of gravity firmly to the right. In the 1920s he had continued writing for liberal or left-leaning periodicals, as well as for the *Manchester Guardian*, but the liberal element in his world-view was steadily dissolving. Since adolescence his mind had swung between a fiercely modernist progressivism and an exaggerated respect for social and political tradition. When he told Josiah Wedgwood in 1928 that a proper understanding of the history of parliament would be 'of … enormous importance for that type of conservatism which is common to all of us constitutionalists', he was being honest.[202] But it was 'conservatism' without a capital letter; he idealised the British constitution as something which had grown up organically, and therefore represented, and responded to, the deepest instincts of the British people.[203] It was different from the artificial political systems dreamt up by left-wing intellectuals, which had no roots in national history or national culture, and also from those right-wing European regimes such as the former Austrian and Russian empires which had imposed autocratic government on subject peoples.

He explained his changing political affiliation in a letter to Lady Sandwich written as early as 1934, in which he asked her 'whether you are not coming to agree with me about our "National Government"? The Conservatives in it are by far the best; our allies, the Labour and Liberal renegades, are the worst.'[204] By 'our allies' he presumably meant those who had been friendly towards the Zionist Organisation. He added:

> I do not like people who change either their party or their religion. In 'Alice in Wonderland' the ugly child of the duchess changes into a lovely little pig; in politics the most lovely little pigs change into very ugly children. How I would love Ramsay MacDonald and Thomas if they had remained conservative Labour men; and how I dislike them as obtuse Labour and sham Nationals[205] … The people with whom I pin my faith are the left wing of the Conservative party under the leadership of men like

Walter Elliot etc. I might myself go Labour if the Labour people were not so incalculably stupid. But if they come back into office they will do no better than they have done last time. I frankly told Malcolm MacDonald that to carry on as they do there is no need to overthrow either the Conservatives or Liberals. If, on the other hand, they try any of their socialist experiments they will come an even worse cropper. The only thing is to have people in office with the proper sense of tradition, sufficient experience to prevent them from naïve experiments, but at the same time people who have no undue regard for money bags. This I think we should still be able to get from the left wing of the Conservatives, and shall get nowhere else.

Dislike for political turncoats did not extend to Winston Churchill, for whom he conceived a very high regard. Their connection was brought about in December 1933 when Churchill sent Namier a signed copy of the first volume of his life of the first duke of Marlborough. The book was delivered by the hand of Churchill's research assistant, a young Oxford historian called Maurice Ashley, who had recently joined the staff of the *Manchester Guardian*.[206] Ashley venerated Namier from afar, and it may have been on his initiative that Churchill sought Namier's views on his own book.[207] Namier in his turn was highly flattered. He had met Churchill a decade earlier at lunches with Victor Cazalet, and told Churchill that 'I have always been an admirer and follower of yours and, in view of the European situation am more so now than before'.[208]

The critique he eventually sent Churchill was full of praise and encouragement: he was particularly keen that in future volumes, rather than 'try to write as other history-writers do', Churchill should allow himself to make full use of his 'understanding of the practical problems of statecraft', something that was outside the experience of 'don-bred dons'. There were of course criticisms and suggestions, but moderated by Namier's self-denying ordinance about periods he had not studied in detail: 'I speak as a layman in so far as your period is concerned'.[209] Churchill seems to have accepted these 'cogent comments', though in expanding on Namier's suggestion and declaring that 'one of the most misleading factors in history is the practice of historians to build a study exclusively out of the records which have come down to them', he may have been going a little far for Namier's taste.[210] Churchill's history and Namier's history were in fact further apart than the two men were prepared to admit to each other. They agreed in dismissing the Whig historians (in Churchill's case, Macaulay) but in other respects Churchill was far from swallowing Namier's revision of eighteenth-century politics. His *History of the English-speaking peoples*, published after the war, would speak slightingly of 'modern scholars' who denied there was a two-party system in eighteenth-century Britain.[211] For the time being, however, such differences were smothered. The correspondence over *Marlborough* was followed by a meeting, and although each was inclined to lecture the other on how to write history, a friendship of sorts developed.[212]

In Namier's increasing alignment with Conservative politics there may have been a form of snobbery. His researches now brought him to country houses as a guest, and on terms approaching social equality. He had outgrown dependence on introductions from friends, or the recollection of a previous acquaintance in Oxford or the Foreign Office. He stayed with Lord Derby at Knowsley, was invited to lunch by the duke of Bedford, and worked his way through the Ragley Hall muniments together with the marquess of Hertford's brother.[213] To judge by the way he flourished the names of his aristocratic acquaintances in his correspondence, this was a privilege he relished.[214]

A connection between Namier's evolving political opinions and his ideas about history is harder to draw. His stated belief that the whole history of eighteenth-century England could be written from the vantage point of the English country house stemmed as much from the fact that he was discovering so much material in private archives as from the pleasure derived from mingling with members of the peerage. In any case, from childhood he had always appreciated the special importance of the social and political role played by the aristocracy. Similarly, his distaste for aristocratic radicals like the Rockinghams and their descendants the Foxite Whigs did not arise from identifying himself with the more conservative elements of the twentieth-century landed class, but from different starting points further back in his own biography. His scepticism of the Rockinghamite argument of a reassertion of royal absolutism under George III can be traced to the influence of the 'nativist' historians he had met in America before the Great War, and distaste for the vulgar American revolutionary republicanism which blazoned the iniquities of British imperial government to justify rejecting America's British heritage. Undoubtedly, the events of the 1930s confirmed Namier's sensitivity to the irrational basis of much political discourse and the destructive power of ideas and ideologues, but it was not his disillusionment with the Liberal and Labour parties that prompted such thoughts; their mainsprings lay further afield, in Nazi Germany and Fascist Italy.

A decade of disappointment?

Social acceptance was important to Namier but it did not greatly mellow his personality. His book reviews continued to be severe, on occasion savage; and in private he was even more brutal in exposing second-rate work when presented to him for comment by publishers.[215] He could also be unnecessarily abrasive on public occasions, whether political meetings or academic conferences, and even in personal letters. Even those predisposed to think well of him found him frightening, like Siegfried Sassoon, whom he once visited and succeeded in intimidating without making any effort.[216] In consequence, his unpopularity extended beyond his exasperated Zionist colleagues, and beyond the politicians and civil servants whom he persecuted in offices and clubs, to fellow historians who saw him from a distance and perceived him as arrogant and driven by personal hatreds.[217] He continued to hunt after Sir John Fortescue, who had died in 1933 but whose reputation lived on, and in 1937 published an extraordinary little book with Manchester University Press, listing additions and corrections to Fortescue's first volume of the correspondence of George III.[218] He had been collecting these errors for years, and providing lists for his students. It seemed easier to get the university press to print them, and thereby benefit the academic world beyond Manchester. But to professors of an older generation, like Trevelyan, this was not the behaviour of a gentleman.[219]

Yet it would be misleading to over-emphasise the levels of personal hostility that Namier could arouse. When he was put up for the Athenaeum (by Edwyn Bevan and Denis Buxton) an unusually large number of members signed the ballot certificate to signify personal knowledge of him or his work: 136 then voted for him and only five against.[220] And in any case, pugnacity represented only one side of his character: he showed a different personality to his Manchester pupils, to those friends whose careers he helped to forward – Alan Taylor, Edward Hughes or his former Foreign Office colleague Ted Carr, whose first book Namier pushed through to publication – and to the younger historians whose work he read, like Lucy Sutherland and James Fergusson.[221] His loyalty to friends was most obviously marked by his continued devotion to Marie Beer, despite her increasing infirmity and the indications of mental instability which alarmed him so much. When she inherited some money and decided to return to Austria, he did his best to dissuade her from going; then, after the *Anschluss* he visited her in Vienna, ignoring the danger he was putting himself in from casual Nazi violence, and managed to arrange for her return to England, making himself responsible for her, both legally and financially.[222]

The great plans for books that Namier had envisaged after the publication of *England in the age of the American revolution* and the unexpected blessing of the Manchester chair, had come to very little by 1938. The series which his first two books were supposed to inaugurate had fizzled out. He had given the Ford Lectures as a means of kick-starting the next section, but they were nowhere near publication. Apart from his corrections to Fortescue, and a translation of the German historian Wolfgang Michael's history of the reign of George I (again only the first volume) his published historical writings since 1931 were all composed of book reviews, of which he wrote an unconscionable number, largely for the remuneration they brought, but also in order to keep his hand in. To some extent he had been held back by the continual unearthing of new material, and the persistent elusiveness of key sources in American libraries, which together proved an effective deterrent to the continuation of his narrative of the 1760s. The disintegration of Wedgwood's History of Parliament scheme had also frustrated his hopes of harnessing a cohort of researchers to work the ground thoroughly.

In other respects he only had himself to blame, since he was constantly inventing and pursuing new projects, always with enthusiasm. When Macmillan persuaded him to edit a series of 'Studies in Modern History' he told Fergusson that 'it will be a rattling good series, and I shall not admit any books which are not up to the standard'.[223] The series chugged along, and produced useful books, but it took up time that could have been spent on his own writing. He refused to abandon any project: there was no let-up in the search for eighteenth-century manuscripts, nor had he forgotten his long-planned history of nineteenth-century Europe, of which he was able to show Baffy the first few lines in June 1937.[224] He was like a circus performer spinning plates, and in the end there were simply too many for him to watch them all.

Even more important in his own mind was the gathering world crisis and the travails of Jewish migrants both in Europe and in Palestine, which absorbed his emotions and drained his energies.[225] Ever since his break with his family, and the separation from Clara, his private life had been chaotic and unhappy, but it had taken second place to his public life; now that too was falling to pieces. Time allowed him to do no more than a fraction of the things that needed to be done. To make matters worse, the 'writer's cramp' in his right hand had become considerably worse: 'I practically cannot write at all', he told Lady Sandwich in 1934.[226] Neither conventional medicine nor psychoanalysis could offer a solution, and a suggestion that the problem was psychosomatic did nothing to lift his frustrations. After his return from Vienna with Marie, Namier had visited Baffy to pour out his sorrows. 'Lewis dined alone with me', she wrote in her diary, 'and discussed the affairs of his life till 1 a.m. He is pushing alone into an arid desert. One can do nothing. His hand and mind alike refuse to help him. Poor Lewis.'[227]

Notes

1 A. J. P. Taylor, 'The world's cities (1): Manchester', *Encounter*, viii (1957), 4.
2 A. J. P. Taylor, *A personal history* (1983), 104.
3 Malcolm Muggeridge, *Chronicles of wasted time* (2 vols, 1972–73), i. 180.
4 Bob Osbourn to J. P. Cooper, 22 Apr. 1950 (Trinity College, Oxford, Cooper papers, DD 279/A/05. O2).
5 Taylor, 'Manchester', 4.

6 Namier to Lady Sandwich, 14 Feb. 1934 (HPT, N–52).

7 Index card entry for Namier (*Guardian* arch., A/N2/13); Namier to Blanche Dugdale, 31 Aug. 1931 (CZA, Namier papers, A312\12); *Manchester Guardian*, 16 Mar. 1932; Namier to Sir Christopher Needham, 13 Feb. 1933 (Rylands, Namier papers, 1/9/17); James Fergusson to Namier, 12 Oct. 1933 (HPT, N–54).

8 *Namier*, 225.

9 Namier to Lady Sandwich, 14 Feb. 1934 (HPT, N–52).

10 Namier to Basil Liddell Hart, 9 Nov. 1936 (LH, 1/539/13).

11 He seems to have spent every New Year with the Milnes throughout the 1930s (Dugdale diaries).

12 A friendship which was sustained throughout his life: Namier to Lady Maude Fetherstonhaugh, 14 Oct. 1954 (HPT, N–57).

13 *Namier*, 221–2. Among those who corresponded with him as 'C. B.' were his sometime Manchester pupil Betty Kemp (see their letters in St Hugh's College, Oxford, Kemp papers, box 1, fos 31–42, and HPT, N–54, N–63); and his friend Barbara Smythe (Smythe to Namier, 21 Sept. [1952] (HPT, N–71)).

14 Namier to Lady Sandwich, 14 Feb. 1934 (HPT, N–52).

15 Namier to R. L. Drage, 6 Dec. 1954 (HPT, N–59).

16 Taylor, 'Manchester', 3.

17 Muggeridge, *Chronicles of wasted time*, i, 180–1.

18 Taylor, *Personal history*, 102; *Manchester Guardian*, 4 Sept. 1938.

19 E. T. Scott to James Bone, 5 May 1931 (*Guardian* arch., A/N2/13).

20 For Namier's relations with Crozier see David Ayerst, '*Guardian': biography of a newspaper* (1971), 547. Taylor, *Personal history*, 111, asserted that Namier bungled this opportunity by insistently telling Crozier 'how things were done in London', and that Namier was also at daggers drawn with Crozier's successor, A. P. Wadsworth. However, Namier's correspondence with both men, preserved in *Guardian* arch., suggests no such antipathy.

21 *Manchester Guardian*, 18 Apr. 1944.

22 *Manchester Guardian*, 26 Apr. 1933, headlined 'Germany's so-called "revolution"' and reprinted as 'Pathological nationalisms', *In the margin*, 21–6.

23 Taylor, *Personal history*, 101.

24 Information from published university registers (available in Manchester UL), supplemented by a copy of the printed handbook for the honours school of history, July 1937 (St Hugh's, Oxford, Kemp papers, box 1, fos 3–12).

25 Taylor, *Personal history*, 103.

26 *The Times*, 6, 13 July 1965.

27 The fact that Taylor had been a pupil of G. N. Clark and 'Sligger' Urquhart at Oxford gave him another claim on Namier's attention (C. J. Wrigley, *A. J. P. Taylor: radical historian of Europe* (2006), 48–9).

28 Taylor, *Personal history*, 112; Taylor, *Letters to Eva 1969–1983*, ed. Eva Haraszti Taylor (1991), 251.

29 Reference for Taylor, sent by Namier to the secretary to the tutorial board at Magdalen (K. B. McFarlane), 9 May 1938 (Magdalen College, Oxford, college archives, FD/2).

30 See pp. 365–6.

31 For example, A. J. P. Taylor, *The course of German history: a survey of the development of Germany since 1815* (1945), 7, 13.

32 Taylor, *Course of German history*, 14.

33 A. J. P. Taylor, *The Italian problem in European diplomacy, 1847–1849* (Manchester, 1934), 8.

34 Namier to Asa Briggs, 6 Nov. 1952 (HPT, N–50); Namier to Sir Hughe Knatchbull-Hugessen, 12 Feb. 1953 (ibid., N–54).

35 Namier to W. S. Lewis, 21 June 1933 (LWL, Lewis corresp., Namier (1)).

36 Namier to Lady Sandwich, 25 Sept. 1932 (Mapperton, Sandwich papers, GM/PERS/3).

37 Manchester University archives, minutes of Faculty of Arts, vi (1933–).

38 *Namier*, 224 (quoting a reminiscence by Ninetta Jucker).

39 John Brooke, quoted in *Namier*, 279.

40 Adam Sisman, *A. J. P. Taylor: a biography* (paperback edn, 1995), 96; Kathleen Burk, *Troublemaker: the life and history of A. J. P. Taylor* (2000), 92–3.

41 Namier to Sir Hughe Knatchbull-Hugessen, 12 Feb. 1953 (HPT, N–54).

42 Namier to W. S. Lewis, 13 Feb. 1935 (LWL, Namier corresp. (1)). A few years later Namier suggested that Lewis might 'encourage the Yale history department' to send him 'for special training one or more of their best men' (Lewis to Namier, 25 July 1939 (ibid.)).

43 *Namier*, 225.

44 Namier to Sir Christopher Needham, 13 Feb. 1933 (Rylands, Namier papers, 1/9/17).

45 See, for example, *Jewish Chronicle*, 29 Jan. 1932; *Manchester Guardian*, 28 Oct. 1937.

46 Namier to Chaim Weizmann, 5 Oct. 1932 (CZA, A312\15); *Manchester Guardian*, 20 Nov. 1933, 5, 23 Mar. 1934, 21 June 1935, 30 Mar. 1936; *Jewish Chronicle*, 9 Mar., 15 June, 17 Aug. 1934, 6 Dec. 1935, 31 July 1936, 30 Apr., 23 July 1937; Namier to Nathan Laski, 11 Sept. 1938 (Rylands, Alexander papers, C/4/7); Namier to W. S. Lewis, 28 June 1933 (LWL, Namier corresp. (1)).

47 Namier to Lady Sandwich, 15 Oct. 1932 (HPT, N–70); same to Ld Sandwich, 3 Nov. 1934 (ibid., N–51).

48 *American rev.*, 418; *Crossroads*, 75.

49 *The Grenville papers …*, ed. W. J. Smith (4 vols, 1852–53). Namier considered Smith 'a far better editor than most of his contemporaries' but still capable of omitting passages from letters 'without marking such deletions', and expressed no confidence in his selections (Namier to W. S. Lewis, 15 Mar. 1933 (LWL, Lewis corresp., Namier (1)). So far as Namier was aware at this time, the Stowe collection included all of George Grenville's papers (*Crossroads*, 76). This was not in fact the case, and smaller bodies of Grenville documents were available in the British Museum and elsewhere (*Additional Grenville papers*, ed. John Tomlinson (Manchester, 1962)).

50 Namier to Godfrey Davies, 24 Sept. 1932 (Huntington Library, Davies papers, 43/51); Namier to W. S. Lewis, 15 Mar. 1933 (LWL, Lewis corresp., Namier (1)); Namier to Max Farrand, 13 Feb. 1933 (HPT, N–70).

51 *Crossroads*, 76; Namier to ——, n.d. (Rylands, Namier papers, 1/1b/3). The papers were subsequently deposited in Sheffield Public Library (now Sheffield City Archives).

52 *Memoirs of the marquess of Rockingham and his contemporaries…*, ed. earl of Albemarle (2 vols, 1852); Namier to ——, n.d. (Rylands, Namier papers, 1/1b/3); Paul Langford, *The first Rockingham administration* (Oxford, 1973), 294; R. J. S. Hoffman, *The marquis: a study of Lord Rockingham, 1730–1782* (New York, 1973), x–xi.

53 Namier to Blanche Dugdale, 2 Nov. 1931 (CZA, A312\44); Namier to W. S. Lewis, 23 May 1933 (LWL, Lewis corresp., Namier (1)); same to Visct Sandon, 24 Apr. 1951 (HPT, N–56).

54 Namier to James Fergusson, 10 Aug. 1932 (HPT, N–54).

55 Gladys Scott Thomson to Namier, 11 Jan. 1932 (HPT, N–71).

56 Namier to Gladys Scott Thomson, 8 Mar. 1933 (HPT, N–71); Granville Proby to Namier,

8 Dec. 1934 (University of Chicago Library, Special Collections Research Center, Misc. MSS Collection); Namier to Ld Crawford, 22 Dec. 1952 (HPT, N–53).

57 Private information.

58 Ilchester to Namier, 1, 22 Jan. 1932 (Rylands, Namier papers, 1/9/17); Namier to Ilchester, 19, 25 Jan., 7 June 1932 (ibid.); same to Sir Christopher Needham, 13 Feb. 1933 (ibid.).

59 Namier to James Fergusson, 1 Nov. 1932 (HPT, N–54).

60 Namier to ——, 7 Feb. 1927 (Rylands, Namier papers, 1/9/7); same to Godfrey Davies, 24 Sept. 1932 (Huntington Library, Davies papers, 43/51).

61 Namier to Joan Wake, 15 Apr. 1955 (HPT, N–62). For Wake, see *Oxf. DNB*.

62 Namier to W. S. Lewis, 13 Feb. 1935 (LWL, Lewis corresp., Namier (1)); *Autobiography and political correspondence of Augustus Henry, third duke of Grafton …*, ed. Sir William R. Anson (1898).

63 Namier to Lady Sandwich, 11 July 1932 (Mapperton, GM/PERS/3).

64 A. L. Rowse, *Memories of men and women* (1980), 131; J. H. Plumb, *The collected essays of J. H. Plumb*, i: *The making of an historian* (Hemel Hempstead, 1988), 8. It is quoted at the conclusion of John Cannon's entry on Namier in *Oxf. DNB*.

65 Information from Eveline Cruickshanks.

66 Namier to W. Reeve Wallace, 30 Apr. 1937 (Rylands, Namier papers, 1/9/7).

67 *Letters from George III to Lord Bute 1756-66*, ed. Romney Sedgwick (1939); *Personalities and powers*, 47.

68 Manchester University archives, minutes of Faculty of Arts, vi, 108, 130, 240, 244, 275.

69 Manchester University archives, minutes of Faculty of Arts, vi, 274. Another student, Violet Morewood, was set to produce 'A new edition of the Chatham correspondence, 1766-70'.

70 Charles Jenkinson, *The Jenkinson papers 1760-1766*, ed. Ninetta S. Jucker (1949).

71 Namier to W. S. Lewis, 15 June 1939 (LWL, Lewis corresp., Namier (1)). Schofield became a schoolteacher, and though he did not publish his MA thesis was a noted local historian: M. J. Power, 'Obituary: Maurice M. Schofield 1915–1989', *Transactions of the Historic Society of Lancashire and Cheshire*, cxxxix (1989), 203).

72 *Structure*, 286-7.

73 *The Times*, 18 June 1962.

74 *Private papers of John, earl of Sandwich, first lord of the Admiralty, 1771-1782*, ed. G. R. Barnes and J. H. Owen (4 vols, Navy Record Society, lxix, lxxi, lxxv, lxxviii, 1932–38).

75 Namier to W. S. Lewis, 15 Mar. 1933 (LWL, Lewis corresp., Namier (1)). He even envisaged extending his work to 1782 (Namier to Max Farrand, 13 Feb. 1933 (HPT, N–70)).

76 Namier to Ld Sandwich, 3 Sept. 1932 (HPT, N–70); same to Lady Sandwich, 31 Oct. 1932 (ibid.).

77 Namier to Ld Sandwich, 4 Oct. 1932 (HPT, N–70); Sandwich to Namier, 16 Nov. 1932 (ibid.).

78 Namier to W. S. Lewis, 22 Jan., 13 Feb. 1935 (LWL, Lewis corresp., Namier (1)); Namier to Godfrey Davies, 2 Oct. 1935 (Huntington Library, Davies papers, 43/53).

79 Sandwich to Namier, 5 Dec. 1938 (HPT, N–70); Namier to Sandwich, 6 Dec. 1938 (ibid.).

80 Namier to Frank Spencer, 31 Dec. 1953 (HPT, N–56).

81 Romney Sedgwick to W. S. Lewis, 17 Dec. 1967 (LWL, Lewis corresp., Sedgwick); Namier to same, 15 Mar. 1933 (ibid., Namier (1)); *Namier*, 225.

82 Namier to Lewis, 19 Apr. 1933 (LWL, Lewis corresp., Namier (1)).

83 Namier to Lewis, 19 Apr. 1933 (LWL, Lewis corresp., Namier (1)).

84 Cutting from *TLS*, n.d. (LWL, Lewis corresp., Namier (2)); Namier to Lewis, 19 Apr. 1933 (ibid., Namier (1)).

85 He was obliged to dictate the lectures to a temporary secretary at Manchester who made 'fantastical mistakes' (Julia Namier to Lucy Sutherland, 9 Apr. 1961 (Bodl., Sutherland papers, box 9)).

86 Namier to Chaim Weizmann, 21 Nov. 1932 (CZA, A312\12).

87 *Crossroads*, 74–6.

88 *Crossroads*, 73–123.

89 Including, for example, the future medievalist K. B. McFarlane: J. P. Cooper to McFarlane, 17 May [1948] (Trinity College, Oxford, Cooper papers, DD 279/I). Christopher Hill and John Owen also kept their notes of the lectures, which they made available to Lucy Sutherland when she edited what was available in *Crossroads*, 73–117 (Sutherland to Owen, 4 Jan. 1963 (Bodl., Sutherland papers, box 9); Balliol, Hill papers, 123).

90 *Namier*, 226.

91 Namier to W. S. Lewis, 2 Mar. 1934 (LWL, Lewis corresp., Namier (1)); Namier to W. Reeve Wallace, 30 Apr. 1937 (Rylands, Namier papers, 1/9/7).

92 For what follows, see D. W. Hayton, 'Colonel Wedgwood and the historians', *Historical Research*, lxxxiv (2011), 338–55; David Cannadine, 'Josiah Wedgwood and the History of Parliament', *In Churchill's shadow; confronting the past in modern Britain* (2002), 134–58; David Cannadine, 'The History of Parliament: past, present – and future?', *Parliamentary History*, xxvi (2007), 366–86; Paul Mulvey, *The political life of Josiah C. Wedgwood: land, liberty and empire, 1872–1943* (Woodbridge, 2010), ch. 13.

93 Namier to Lady Sandwich, 15 Oct. 1932 (HPT, N–70).

94 See p. 186.

95 *Manchester Guardian*, 17 Oct. 1934, Namier to Wedgwood, 17 Oct. 1934 (PA, History of Parliament Trust papers, HPT/5/10).

96 Namier to Notestein, 7 Nov. 1935 (Yale UL, Notestein papers, 544/6/534).

97 Notestein to Wedgwood, 14 Aug. 1935 (Yale UL, Notestein papers, 544/6/560).

98 Namier to Notestein, 7 Nov. 1935 (Yale UL, Notestein papers, 544/6/534).

99 Namier to Wedgwood, 8 Nov. 1935 (PA, HPT/5/10).

100 'Statement by Mr Wedgwood' (PA, HPT 8/23).

101 Powicke to Wedgwood, with report, 23 Jan. 1936 (PA, HPT/5/2).

102 Wedgwood to Pollard, 11 July 1936 (University of London Library, Pollard papers, MS 890, box 35).

103 Trevelyan to Pollard, 22, 23, 25 July 1936 (University of London Library, MS 890, box 35); Trevelyan to Salisbury, 24 July 1936 (PA, HPT/5/26).

104 Wedgwood to Pollard, 4 Oct. 1936 (PA, HPT/5/11); earl of Crawford to John Buchan (NLS, Buchan papers, Mf. MS 306, box 7).

105 *The Times*, 31 Oct. 1938.

106 Wedgwood to F. M. Stenton, 9 Mar. 1942 (Reading UL, Stenton papers, MS 1148/19/2/1).

107 *Avenues*, 171.

108 C. V. Wedgwood, *The last of the radicals: the life of Josiah Clement Wedgwood, MP* (1951), 178.

109 Namier to W. P. Crozier, 5 Nov. 1942 (*Guardian* arch., B/N8A/140).

110 Dermot Morrah to Wedgwood, 15 Nov., 10 Jan. 1939 (PA, HPT/8/30); Morrah to E. F. Jacob [Jan. 1939] (ibid.).

111 Morrah to Jacob, 24 Mar., 2 May 1939 (PA, HPT/8/30); 'Sub-commission on estates, Document, no. 1' (HPT, N–29); agenda for meeting of 'subcommission', 28 Apr. 1939

(ibid.); draft letter to parliamentary historians, [1939] (ibid.); F. M. Powicke to Helen Cam, 1 Aug. 1943 (Girton College, Cambridge, Cam papers, 4/1/1, file 5); Valerie Cromwell, 'Professor John Roskell, FBA, the re-birth of the British sub-committee of the commission and the History of Parliament, 1948–60', *Parliaments, Estates and Representation*, xix (1999), 191–203.

112 Namier to Robert Boothby, 3 Feb. 1932 (CZA, A312\44).

113 'Turbulent Zionist', 49; Rose, *Zionism*, 60. Namier read *Mein Kampf* in the original. Baffy's husband, Edgar Dugdale, produced an abridged English translation in 1933.

114 L. B. Namier, *Germany and eastern Europe* (1915), 17. See also *Conflicts*, 80.

115 W. P. Crozier, *Off the record: political interviews 1933–43*, ed. A. J. P. Taylor (1973), 45.

116 Namier to W. S. Lewis, 23 May 1933 (LWL, Namier corresp. (1)).

117 Crozier, *Off the record*, 45.

118 Crozier, *Off the record*, 45. This observation betrays at once Namier's dry assessment of the naïveté of the religious-minded politician and his residual disdain for the ineffectualness of the League of Nations.

119 *Manchester Guardian*, 28 June 1935; Crozier, *Off the record*, 44.

120 Notes by Blanche Dugdale on a conversation with Namier, Apr. 1933 (NLS, Elliot papers, Acc. 12267/13); Namier, 'Austria' [n.d.] (typescript in Rylands, Namier papers, 1/1b/9); Elizabeth Wiskemann, 'Catholic Austria and the Hapsburgs', *The Nineteenth Century and After*, June 1934, 651.

121 Namier, *Germany and eastern Europe*, 119.

122 Victor Feske, *From Belloc to Churchill: private scholars, public culture, and the crisis of British Liberalism, 1900–1935* (Chapel Hill, N.C., 1996), 208–10.

123 *Manchester Guardian*, 26 Apr., 9 May 1933; *In the margin*, 21–6. He rehearsed these arguments in another letter to the *Manchester Guardian* on 22 July 1935.

124 Namier to Lady Sandwich, 20 Apr. 1933 (Mapperton, GM/PERS/3).

125 Namier to Lewis, 6, 18, 23 May 1933 (LWL, Namier corresp. (1)).

126 'Turbulent Zionist', 6.

127 He was, for example, a member with Baffy of the Inter-Aid Committee for Children from Germany (C. R. Kotzin, 'Christian responses in Britain to Jewish refugees from Europe, 1933–1939' (Southampton University PhD thesis, 2000, 292)).

128 Bill Williams, *'Jews and other foreigners': Manchester and the rescue of the victims of European fascism, 1933–1940* (Manchester, 2011), 48; Namier to W. S. Lewis, 9 Oct. 1933 (LWL, Namier corresp. (1)); *Manchester Guardian*, 5, 23 Mar. 1934, 4 Sept. 1938; Namier to Michael Polyani, 7 July 1934 (Chicago UL, Polyani papers, box 2, folder 17); same to Basil Liddell Hart, 10 May 1938 (LH, 1/539/16).

129 Information from Hannah Selinger; obituary of Paul Frankel in *Independent*, 29 Oct. 1992.

130 Williams, *'Jews and other foreigners'*, 36–7, 43; Namier to Chaim Weizmann, 30 Jan., 3, 9 May 1934 (CZA, A312\15).

131 *Weizmann A*, xv, 438–9; xvi, 74, 113, 275, 310; xvii, 31; Rose, *Zionism*, 63–4.

132 See Namier's correspondence with the secretary to the Academic Assistance Council, and others, 1934–38 (Bodl., MS S.P.S.L. 165/3, fos 327–63).

133 See entries in the committee's minute book, 1933–4 (Wiener Library, MF 27/6/2, 18, 23, 37, 41, 111). 139.

134 *Weizmann A*, xvii, 123; *Jewish Chronicle*, 21 Aug. 1936; 'Turbulent Zionist', 70–72; Rose, *Zionism*, 72–4. He himself contributed £250 (the equivalent of nearly £17,000 today) (*Jewish Chronicle*, 10 July 1936).

135 'Turbulent Zionist', 72; Namier to Chaim Weizmann, 12 Feb. 1936 (CZA, A312\14).

136 Namier to Basil Liddell Hart, 13 Apr. 1951 (LH, 1/539/63). In October 1934, for example, he sent Baffy notes of a meeting with Ramsay MacDonald at Chequers (Namier to Dugdale, 31 Oct. 1934 (CZA, Z4\31206)).

137 *Baffy* covers the period after 1936. For Cazalet, see Namier to Ld Gage, 13 July 1953 (HPT, N–54), and p. 162.

138 Hugh Dalton, *The fateful years: memoirs 1931-1945* (1957), 426; *The political diary of Hugh Dalton, 1918-40, 1945-60*, ed. Ben Pimlott (1986), 206–7; Walter Elliot to Blanche Dugdale, 7 May 1936 (NLS, Elliot papers, Acc. 12198/6).

139 Minute by Ld Cranborne, 22 Apr. 1936, quoted in A. J. Sherman, *Island refuge: Britain and refugees from the 3rd Reich 1933-1939* (1974), 71; Walter Elliot to Blanche Dugdale, 7 May 1936 (NLS, Elliot papers, Acc. 12198/6); Columbia University, Butler Library, Columbia Centre for Oral History, 'Reminiscences of Dr Maurice Perlzweig' (transcript), 329–30, 381, 386; Rose, *Zionism*, 72.

140 Note by Lady Namier (CZA, A312\1).

141 Namier to the vice-chancellor, 5, 14 Sept. 1938, 31 Jan. 1939 (Rylands, Alexander papers, C/4/6); Nathan Laski to Namier, 9, 13 Sept. 1938 (ibid., C/47); Namier to Laski, 11 Sept. 1938 (ibid.); Laski to the vice-chancellor, 13 Sept. 1938 (ibid.).

142 Simon Kelly to Namier, 6 Sept. 1938 (CZA, A312\47); P. I. Wigoder to Chaim Weizmann, 14, 21 Sept. 1938 (ibid.).

143 Isaiah Berlin, *Personal impressions* (1980), 63–82.

144 Berlin, *Personal impressions*, 63.

145 Isaiah Berlin, *Flourishing: letters 1928-1946*, ed. Henry Hardy (2004), 248.

146 Berlin, *Personal impressions*, 64.

147 Berlin, *Personal impressions*, 64–5.

148 Namier to Berlin, 26 Nov. 1937 (telegram) (Bodl., MS Berlin 105, fo. 280).

149 Berlin, *Personal impressions*, 72.

150 *Weizmann A*, xv, 198, 200, 227, 262, 297, 408.

151 'Turbulent Zionist', 51–5; Namier to Weizmann, 15 May 1933 (CZA, A312\15).

152 Rose, *Zionism*, 64–5.

153 'Turbulent Zionist', 60.

154 *Weizmann A*, xvi, 419; Rose, *Zionism*, 67–8.

155 'Turbulent Zionist'', 61; Namier to Ld Lothian, 5 May 1936 (NRS, Lothian papers, GD 40/17/313/778–9); *The Times*, 20 May 1936; *In the margin*, 55–6.

156 Namier to Marie Beer, 30 Jan. 1935 (CZA, A312\15); 'Turbulent Zionist', 62.

157 Namier to Marie Beer, 30 Jan. 1935 (CZA, A312\15).

158 In 1942 Ben-Gurion declared that he 'did not attach any value to anybody's opinion [in the Jewish Agency or the Zionist Executive] except Namier's' (*Weizmann A*, xx, 318).

159 'Turbulent Zionist', 63.

160 Rose, *Zionism*, 69–70.

161 Namier to Weizmann, 18 Nov. 1935 (CZA, A312\15).

162 *Weizmann A*, xvii, 59, 70.

163 *Weizmann A*, xvii, 71–3.

164 *Weizmann A*, xvii, 96.

165 *Weizmann A*, xvii, 97.

166 *Palestine Post*, 9 Jan. 1936; *Weizmann A*, xvii, 118; Rose, *Zionism*, 72.

167 Rose, *Zionism*, 66, quoting figures from the report of the Peel Commission (1938).

168 Norman Rose, *Chaim Weizmann: a biography* (1986), 312.

169 Rose, *Zionism*, 66–7.

170 'Turbulent Zionist', 58–9.

171 He told Malcolm MacDonald that 'the most educated Arabs were our equals; but this was a mere fraction of the Arab population … if he had seen the fellahin, the Negroid types from Jericho and other parts, or the average labourers crouching in the bazaars as I saw them, walking through the miles of these bazaars on a Friday night, he would see how the very idea of equal and universal suffrage was ridiculous in such a country' (memo by Namier, [1936] (CZA, A312\44)).

172 Walter Elliot thought that this contained 'the germ of a brilliant idea' (Elliot to Blanche Dugdale [23 Sept. 1934] (NLS, Acc. 12198/4)).

173 Rose, *Zionism*, 66–7; Rose, *Weizmann*, 312–13.

174 Walter Elliot to Dugdale, 31 Dec. 1934 (NLS, Acc. 12198/4).

175 Elliot to Dugdale, 31 May 1943 (ibid., Acc. 12267/15).

176 *Baffy*, 1, 5–3, 5–6, 10–12; Blanche Dugdale to Visct Cecil, 17 Feb. 1936 (BL, Cecil of Chelwood papers, Add. MS 51157, fo. 243). M. N. Penkower, *Palestine in turmoil* (2 vols, New York, 2014), i, 234, 255.

177 *Weizmann A*, xvii, 197.

178 Namier to Weizmann, 27 Jan. 1936 (CZA, A312\14).

179 Rose, *Zionism*, 72; *Baffy*, 1–12.

180 *Weizmann A*, xvii, 227, 233.

181 Namier to Ld Lothian, 4 May 1936 (NRS, Lothian papers, GD 40/17/313/769–70).

182 Namier to Lothian, 4 May 1936 (NRS, GD 40/17/313/769–70); same to Basil Liddell Hart, 19 June 1936 (LH, 1/539/12); *Manchester Guardian*, 2 Sept. 1936.

183 Geoffrey Dawson to Lothian, 5 May 1936 (NRS, GD 40/17/313/777); Namier to same, 5 May 1936 (ibid., GD 40/17/313/778–9).

184 Rose, *Zionism*, 75.

185 Namier to Dugdale, 23 Aug. 1936 (CZA, A312\44).

186 Published subsequently in *In the margin*, 84–93. For a reiteration of the belief that the Italians had 'foster[ed] Arab rebellion' in 1936, see *Conflicts*, 147. It was the line being taken at the time by the Jewish Agency (*Baffy*, 20).

187 Rose, *Weizmann*, 313.

188 'Turbulent Zionist', 68–9.

189 Rose, *Weizmann*, 315; Rose, *Zionism*, 77.

190 'Turbulent Zionist', 75.

191 'Turbulent Zionist', 75–6; *Baffy*, 25.

192 Ben-Gurion to Namier, 4 Nov. 1936 (CZA, A312\19).

193 *Palestine Post*, 14 Dec. 1936.

194 Namier to Ld Thurlow, 10 Feb. 1953 (HPT, N–56).

195 For what follows, see Rose, *Zionism*, 79–84.

196 Notes of meeting of the London Political Advisory Committee of the Zionist Organisation, 20 Apr. 1937 (CZA, A312\20); Namier to Moshe Shertok, 9 July 1937 (CZA, A3122\21); *Dalton diary*, ed. Pimlott, 206–7; Norman Rose, *The Gentile Zionists: a study in Anglo-Zionist diplomacy, 1929–1939* (1973), 129.

197 'Lewis Namier's other Zionism', *Jewish Observer and Middle East Review*, 26 Aug. 1960 (cutting in LH, 1/569/156); note of meeting 7 July 1937 (CZA, A312\21).

198 *Baffy*, 55.

199 *Weizmann A*, xviii, 195; *Baffy*, 60; Rose, *Zionism*, 83–4.

200 *Palestine Post*, 18 Aug. 1937; *Manchester Guardian*, 23 Aug. 1937. He attended meetings regularly (CZA, A312\22–3, 25–6).

201 Ben-Gurion to Namier, 8 Dec. 1937 (CZA, A312\22).

202 Namier to Wedgwood, 9 June 1928 (Rylands, Namier papers, 1/9/1).

203 In a review in the *Observer* on 25 Aug. 1929, he had commented that 'British institutions are of a firm, organic texture'.

204 Namier to Lady Sandwich, 14 Feb. 1934 (HPT, N–51). He had confided to Baffy in 1932 his dissatisfaction with the National Government and preference for 'a straight, clean party issue', that is to say a purely Conservative administration (Namier to Dugdale, 27 Jan. 1932 (CZA, A312\44)).

205 In 1957 he told a friend that he had never trusted Ramsay MacDonald because MacDonald had been against going to war in 1914; he felt that at heart MacDonald was pro-German and anti-French (Namier to Sir Walford Selby, 4 Sept. 1957 (Bodl., Selby papers, MS Eng. 6600, fo. 234)).

206 Namier to Churchill, 15 Dec. 1933 (Churchill, Chartwell papers, CHAR8/326, fo. 83). See also Feske, *From Belloc to Churchill*, 204–5, 219; Charles-Édouard Levillain, 'Churchill historien de Marlborough', *Commentaire*, no. 139 (2012), 785.

207 Lucy Sutherland to Namier, 26 Nov. 1931 (Rylands, Namier papers, 1/9/7).

208 *Namier*, 228.

209 *Namier*, 228–30; Randolph Churchill and Martin Gilbert, *Winston S. Churchill* (8 vols, 1966–88), v, 501–2.

210 Churchill to Namier, 18 Feb. 1934 (Churchill, Churchill additional papers, WCHL1/14).

211 Maurice Ashley, *Churchill as historian* (1968), 144, 219; Peter Clarke, *Mr Churchill's profession: statesman, orator, writer* (2012), 172–4.

212 *Namier*, 231. Cf. J. P. Kenyon, *The history men: the historical profession in England since the Renaissance* (1983), 258, which suggests that Namier's tactlessness in offering 'a bleakly discouraging analysis' of the first volume of *Marlborough* cost him Churchill's patronage, an interpretation for which I could find no supporting evidence.

213 Berlin, *Personal impressions*, 71–2; Gladys Scott Thomson to Namier, 11 Jan. 1932 (HPT, N–71); Namier to W. S. Lewis, 2 May 1933 (LWL, Lewis corresp., Namier (1)).

214 For example, Namier to W. S. Lewis, 23 May, 21 June, 24 Sept. 1933 (LWL, Lewis corresp., Namier (1)); same to Lucy Sutherland, 27 Oct. 1937 (Bodl., Sutherland papers, box 9).

215 Namier to Ld Sandwich, 6 Dec. 1938 (HPT, N–70); same to P. P. Howe, 14 Mar. 1938 (Reading UL, Bodley Head archive, BH1/RR1/365).

216 Max Egremont, *Siegfried Sassoon: a biography* (2005), 416.

217 Michael Bentley, *The life and thought of Herbert Butterfield: history, science and God* (Cambridge, 2011), 115.

218 L. B. Namier, *Additions and corrections to Sir J. Fortescue's edition of the correspondence of George III, volume i* (Manchester, 1937).

219 Rowse, *Memories of men and women*, 131.

220 Information on Namier's election to the Athenaeum (on 8 Mar. 1933) supplied by the club archivist, Ms Jennie de Protani. This must cast at least a little doubt on the statement by Berlin (*Personal impressions*, 70) that 'London clubmen (whom [Namier] often naïvely pursued) viewed him with distaste'.

221 Carr to T. M. Farmiloe, 11 Apr. 1978 (Birmingham UL, Carr papers, box 26); same to Macmillan, 17 Aug. 1937 (ibid., box 27); Jonathan Haslam, *The vices of integrity: E. H. Carr, 1892–1982* (1999), 55; Sutherland to Namier, 26 Nov. 1931 (Rylands, Namier papers, 1/9/7);

Fergusson to same, 29 July 1932, 9 Dec. 1933, Namier to Fergusson, 10 Aug., 20, 27 Nov., 6 Dec. 1933 (HPT, N–54).

222 *Namier*, 233–4.

223 Namier to Fergusson, 9 Nov. 1933 (HPT, N–54).

224 Namier to Lucy Sutherland, 27 Oct. 1937 (Bodl., Sutherland papers, box 9); *Namier*, 235.

225 He confessed after the Second World War that in the 1930s 'Zionist work engrossed my time to the neglect of my own history work' (Namier to L. S. Amery, 2 Feb. 1951 (Churchill, Amery papers, 2/1/45)).

226 Namier to Lady Sandwich, 14 Feb. 1934 (HPT, N–51).

227 *Namier*, 228, 234.

7

In the Nazi era, 1938–47

Crisis in Palestine

In December 1937 Namier hoped to be awarded a period of sabbatical leave but told a friend, 'If that happens I must only pray that Palestine should not take up too much of my time.'[1] Given the world situation, such prayers were bound to be futile. In March 1938 Austria was absorbed into the German Reich, and during the damp and sometimes thundery summer of 1938, as Hitler's further demands over Czechoslovakia precipitated a crisis, Namier was preoccupied with the agony of the Jewish people. He devoted himself to their cause and to the work of the Jewish Agency in particular. This meant frequent attendance at the office in Great Russell Street, at weekends, on weekdays borrowed from his Manchester duties and throughout university vacations. He advised on strategy, drafted documents and letters to the press, lobbied friends and acquaintances in parliament and Whitehall, and accompanied Weizmann to meetings with ministers. He also attended endless relief committees, continued to help individual refugees, and in 1938 acted as vice-chairman of the organising committee for the Palestine Exhibition and Fair in Queen's Hall, which raised £10,000 for the Jewish National Fund.[2]

Although the Peel commission's report had been published in July 1937, the cabinet postponed acting on its recommendations to relinquish the mandate and partition Palestine into two states. Violent Arab opposition and divisions in the Zionist camp made prospects for partition uncertain. In deference to parliament, ministers took their proposals to the mandates commission of the League of Nations before presenting them formally at Westminster. In September 1937 the Foreign Secretary, Anthony Eden, announced that the British were again appointing a commission, this time headed by Sir John Woodhead, to go to Palestine and work out details of a partition plan. In Zionist circles, faith in the government's honesty was wearing thin. Malcolm MacDonald's return to the Colonial Office in May 1938, this time as colonial secretary, had at first seemed a harbinger of better things, but the honeymoon was short-lived.[3] In August 1938 Namier and another representative of the agency waited on MacDonald to press him about rumoured changes to policy over Palestine. His reassurances did not ring true.[4] Weizmann pressed for a radical change in policy, to turn away from Britain and appeal to American Jewry.[5] Namier was equally agitated, not least at what he saw as MacDonald's failure to stand up to Arab pressure, regarding this almost as a personal affront from a friend whom he had always trusted. MacDonald's assurances of continued commitment to partition were undermined by other comments about immigration under a renewed mandate, and by private warnings from sympathetic ministers.[6] Namier told a Zionist conference that 'We must not allow ourselves to be patted on the back and at the same time betrayed.' At the same time he warned against a change of direction: 'In our dangerous situation we could not afford to do it … to show a break today to the world would be to bring catastrophe upon the Jews even more quickly.'[7]

As the summer wore on, and the European crisis deepened, the Zionist executive realised that partition was a chimera. If it were ever to be offered, the dimensions of the new Jewish state would be so restricted as to make it not worth having.[8] Alternative solutions surfaced, including an idea pursued by David Ben-Gurion for an independent Palestinian state organised on a federal basis, with 'complete autonomy' for 'all peoples', and a cap on immigration when Jews came to constitute half the total population. This was a reworking of an idea Namier had floated a year before. Namier now revived his own scheme, and, consonant with his belief in operating wherever possible within a British imperial context, discussed it with various friends in London, including Orde Wingate, a cousin of his old Oxford friend, Ronald Wingate. Orde, an intelligence officer with the British army in Palestine, had become a committed Zionist. With official permission he organised joint British and Jewish 'special night squads', part-funded by the Jewish Agency, to combat the Arab revolt, sometimes by questionable methods. He and Namier grew close,[9] and Orde took up the federal idea, which became known as the 'Wingate plan'.

The Munich agreement in September 1938 threw everything over. Namier deplored appeasement as an act of cowardice which would only encourage Hitler and make a European war certain, and was particularly affronted by the betrayal of the Czechs.[10] Munich also intensified the threat to European Jewry, with immediate and disastrous results for the Jewish population of Czechoslovakia, so that the necessity to secure a refuge became even more urgent. At the same time Malcolm MacDonald was telling Weizmann and Namier that, having read the assurances given to the Hashemites during the Great War by the British high commissioner in Egypt, he believed that the Arabs had suffered an injustice. Such talk seemed to Namier to be preparing the way for a further betrayal, this time of the Jews.[11] After *Kristallnacht* in November,

Zionist energies were focused on saving thousands of Jewish children in Germany and Austria. The British government's refusal to bend its own rules on Palestinian immigration for this special case brought relations to breaking point.[12] The situation in Palestine itself was also much worse: in October the Old City of Jerusalem was occupied for five days by Arab insurgents. Attacks on Jews increased, and Namier found himself, alongside others in the Jewish Agency, struggling to prevent rash and counter-productive retaliation.[13]

Then came the publication of the Woodhead report in November 1938, which offered three partition plans, none of them attractive to the Jewish Agency. The British government took the same view, for different reasons, and in the Commons MacDonald declared the partition scheme impracticable and announced a conference of Jewish and Arab leaders in London on future policy for Palestine.[14] Namier thought that MacDonald was preparing 'A Palestine Munich', assisted by 'the professional pro-Arabs' in the Colonial and Foreign offices, and his personal relations with MacDonald became steadily more acrimonious.[15] Namier opposed Zionist participation in the conference unless German Jewish children were accepted into Palestine, but was overruled, and eventually attended proceedings, in St James's Palace in February and March 1939, as a member of the 'advisory panel' appointed by the Jewish Agency executive, having been given leave of absence by Manchester for the purpose.[16]

Predictably, the conference was a failure, serving only to intensify differences between the Zionists and the government.[17] MacDonald seemed to have been entirely converted to the Arab cause, and his proposals – a strict limit on Jewish immigration for a specified period, renewable only with Arab consent – were regarded by the Zionists as violating the Balfour declaration.[18] Namier was an ardent advocate of breaking off talks, and in private excoriated those Zionists who disagreed with him, using an epithet he had coined for Jews who lacked the courage to defend their own people: 'the "Order of Trembling Israelites"'.[19] Eventually, amid confusion and rancour, the conference broke down and, simultaneously, news came in of the occupation of northern Czechoslovakia by German forces.[20] Namier told Alan Taylor that the conference had been

> a downright torture to me; I have suffered as a Jew and felt ashamed as a British subject. It was worse than Munich – a Munich even without the excuse of danger. As for meanness in tactics, it could hardly have been exceeded. They tried to bully and frighten us into accepting their betrayal of promises. It was almost like the Nazis in a concentration camp: when they beat up someone they make him sign that he has been well treated and that nothing has happened to him ... I have never been so much disappointed in any human being as I am in Malcolm ... I don't want to see any more ministers, politicians, or anyone of that tribe. Their consciences and their smiles are all made of rubber.[21]

Recent events had sorely tested Namier's personal and political loyalties. Throughout the 1930s he had been steadily drawing closer to the Conservative Party, convinced that Labour politicians, besides being intellectually unimpressive, were at heart pacifist, unwilling to resist the dictators and not to be trusted over Palestine. In 1938 he involved himself in the activities of the Manchester students' Conservative Association, and lectured at the party's Ashridge College.[22] Fortunately, only one of his Conservative friends, Walter Elliot, could conceivably be described as a 'Municher', having opted to remain in government despite reservations over appeasement.[23] Neither Baffy – who was very close to Elliot – nor Namier seems to have borne any grudge over this, despite their hatred of appeasement in general. Their other contacts in the party – Churchill, Boothby, Cazalet, Paul Emrys Evans[24] and eventually Leo Amery and Harold Macmillan – all rebelled.

Some of these were men whom Namier thought of as being on the left of the Conservative Party, and this enabled him to sustain his self-identification alongside them as a 'Tory radical'.[25] It was a definition he had adopted in the late 1920s, enabling him to reconcile his residual progressive sympathies with an increasing aversion to the programmatic radicalism of the left. Psychologically, it also permitted him to retain an instinctive revulsion at the complacent 'old guard' while prizing the virtues of traditional institutions and elites. Doubtless he saw it less as an synthesis of opposites than an example of conflicting ideas coexisting in a state of unresolved tension within a single mind, a phenomenon to which he attached a great deal of importance in his understanding of human behaviour, having probably taken it first from his reading of Dostoyevsky and then developed it in discussions at Balliol with Charles Stone.[26]

Following the collapse of the St James's Palace talks the situation steadily deteriorated. For the British government the European crisis took precedence, and the affairs of Palestine were seen entirely through the lens of imperial strategy, which required friendly relations with Arab states in order to protect the route to India.[27] Never one to let concern for his audience's feelings get in the way of truth, Namier explained these facts of life to the Jewish Agency executive:

> they should not delude themselves. They did not count as a military force. The government regarded the Arabs as indispensable and the Jews not ... He did not think even Mr Churchill would worry very much about their affairs at the present moment. They must realise that in the present circumstances they were only a small problem, and that the most important thing was the action to be taken vis-à-vis the totalitarian states.[28]

When the government did eventually make a policy announcement on Palestine, in a White Paper in May 1939, Namier and his colleagues could scarcely claim to be surprised.[29] The key issue was immigration. The total number of Jews in Palestine was not to exceed one-third of the total population, so immigration would be restricted to a quota of 10,000 a year for the next five years, plus 25,000 refugees to be admitted as soon as the high commissioner was 'satisfied that adequate provision for their maintenance is ensured', a concession which was presented as a 'contribution' to the refugee problem. There would be no further immigration without Arab consent after 1944. This was not something the agency, and the entire Zionist movement, could do anything but reject out of hand and pledge to resist.[30]

Namier's resentment was principally directed at MacDonald, whom he lambasted not only in print[31] but in person. Isaiah Berlin repeated a story which Namier had told him, that on meeting MacDonald shortly after the publication of the White Paper,

> I said to him 'Malcolm' – he is, you know, still Malcolm to me – I know him quite well – 'I am writing a new book.' He said, 'What is it, Lewis?' I replied, 'I will tell you what it is. I have called it 'The two MacDonalds: a study in treachery'.[32]

For the time being there was little that Namier could do beyond flinging insults, and writing angry letters to *The Times* on the issue of immigration into Palestine, to expose ministers' disregard of their own White Paper in the way they were treating refugees.[33] When the contents of the White Paper had first leaked out his eyes had been fixed on the House of Commons, where the efforts of sympathetic MPs might, he thought, 'shake MacDonald's nerve'.[34] When this failed, he had little else to offer. During the summer he was not asked to attend the Zionist congress, despite Weizmann's efforts to get him an invitation;[35] instead, according to Moshe Shertok, in a private communication to Lady Namier, he spent his energies in 'transforming, from London, a system of Jewish escape channels on the continent into a network of paramilitary sabotage'.[36]

But the announcement in August of the Nazi-Soviet pact, which Namier understood to mean that war was imminent, lit a spark. He told Walter Elliot that he was prepared to fly to Geneva and attempt to bring back a pledge of 'world Jewry' to 'stand by Great Britain', though in the event neither the government nor the agency thought this wise. In Namier's view it was the only policy Zionists could adopt. Everything must be subordinated to the defeat of Germany. When Weizmann returned from the congress with a mandate to pledge the support of the Jewish Agency in any fight against Hitler, Namier helped him draft a letter to Chamberlain to this effect, and by the time war was declared he was back at Great Russell Street, without official status but doing the work of a member of the executive.[37]

Secondment

Namier's reaction to the declaration of war was a mixture of grave anxiety and a kind of exhilaration. He made his will, and through Vera Weizmann acquired a lethal dose of veronal as security against becoming a Nazi prisoner. In fact, he kept this safe throughout the war, only disposing of it after his marriage in 1947, something that speaks volumes about his state of mind.[38] In June 1940, after the fall of France, he took the further precaution of weeding his personal papers, presumably to protect refugees whom he had helped to relocate.[39] Yet at the same time he was also profoundly relieved that Britain had finally stood up to Hitler. This was no thanks to 'Chamberlain and his crew' but to 'the British nation': 'it was the pressure of public opinion which prevented the miserable crew of Munichers from ratting a second time'.[40] Clearly there were occasions when 'public opinion' did become a reality.[41]

In 1939 Manchester had finally granted him a sabbatical, but the war meant that it had to be postponed.[42] With so many teaching staff likely to be absent, all hands were called to the pump. However, Namier was also wanted in London; or so he thought. After Munich he had 'talked to a friend at the Foreign Office about rejoining the Intelligence Department or anything of that kind they may wish to employ me in', seemingly unaware of the hostility he had aroused in Whitehall by his aggressive advocacy of the Zionist cause. In May 1939, following the British guarantee to Poland, he made a second attempt, though this time he did express a fear that the Foreign Secretary, Halifax, and the under-secretary, R. A. Butler, might have taken against him 'after certain encounters we had in the Palestine conference'. Again, there was no response.[43] Just before the outbreak of war he told Manchester's vice-chancellor, Sir John Stopford, that he had made 'my application to the Foreign Office and sooner or later it is quite possible that they may have some use for my services'. He also warned Stopford that there would be a great deal of work for him at the Jewish Agency, especially if ministers decided to raise a force of Jewish volunteers.[44] When Stopford inquired whether Namier might help the university out in the autumn, he offered to give a course of lectures in the summer term of 1940: the timing would be better because 'during winter travelling at night will be very difficult and travelling during the day will mean loss of time'.[45]

In response to more insistent requests, the university eventually received a communication from Rear-Admiral Godfrey, director of naval intelligence, that Namier 'has recently been doing valuable work for this division, and unless his services are urgently required by the university, I should value his further co-operation'.[46] Godfrey was desperately short of intelligence information, and looking for help wherever he could find it.[47] He may have been pointed in Namier's direction by the

7 Clara Namier

8 Julia, Lady Namier

anonymous 'friend in the Foreign Office', or by Winston Churchill, now back as First Lord of the Admiralty. Whatever the source of the naval connection, Godfrey's letter lends some credence to a story told many years later by Alan Taylor, in a private letter, that Churchill 'took Namier on with him at the Admiralty as a political adviser', even though the suggestion was pooh-poohed by someone who had been a senior naval intelligence officer at the time.[48]

Taylor's addendum, that 'subsequently the Admiralty … got rid of Namier as soon as Churchill became prime minister', does not seem to be true. Correspondence in the Manchester university archives indicates a different course of events.[49] On the same date as Godfrey's letter, Weizmann also wrote to Stopford to beg that Namier be allowed to continue his work for the Jewish Agency, since this was 'of national importance'; in particular, Namier would have to take responsibility in Weizmann's absence for communicating with the Foreign Office and other government departments.[50] This plea was supported by R. A. Butler, swallowing any reservations about dealing with Namier on a personal level: 'We know Namier here, and would welcome this arrangement. It is of great importance that there should be suitable contact between this department and the Jewish Agency.'[51] After negotiation it was agreed to 'lend' Namier's services to the agency, which would provide him with a salary of £850 p.a.[52] The arrangement was not to Jacob's taste as head of department, but was renewed in August 1940 at the specific request of the colonial secretary.[53]

There was another way for Namier to make himself useful to the British government. Despite his unpopularity with nationalist elements in Poland, he had long-standing contacts with prominent figures in the Polish government in exile: Stanisław Kot, who was minister of internal affairs, August Zaleski minister for foreign affairs and Marian Kukiel deputy minister of war. In addition, one of Namier's parliamentary friends, Victor Cazalet, was the government minister responsible for liaison with the Poles.[54] It was inevitable that Namier should become involved, in an unofficial capacity, and equally certain that his involvement would cause friction. Privately, he considered that the Polish government in exile cut a 'pathetic' figure, and although he kept this particular opinion to himself, he was far from being a natural diplomat, and his inability to suppress disapproval of Polish territorial claims in Galicia (even while siding with the Poles against German demands in the north), constantly threatened detonations.[55]

Elements in the Foreign Office were also worried about his political sympathies. He seemed too close to the Polish left, and to Kot in particular.[56] And while Namier proved a useful conduit between Kot's Polish underground force and the Special Operations Executive, whose executive officer was none other than Gladwyn Jebb,[57] his opinions on strategy were deeply suspect, in particular his preference for cooperation with the Soviet Union. In October 1939 Namier prepared a memo-randum on Polish affairs for Butler, which praised Kot and Kukiel and warned against right-wing elements (the National Democrats were 'nationalists of a fascist or semi-fascist mentality').[58] A year later the head of the Polish government, General Sikorski, encouraged by Kot, concluded that it was necessary to work with the Soviets and encouraged Poles to enlist in the Red Army, provoking a political crisis among the exiles. Namier, who had been impressed by Sikorski, weighed in behind him.[59] Having been sent by Butler to brief an official, Namier urged the importance of supporting Sikorski against 'intriguers', including an ancient enemy of his own, the National Democrat Count Horodyski.[60] But while some listened with interest, others found Namier's recommendations unpalatable. Victor Cavendish-Bentinck, the chairman of the Joint Intelligence Committee, snorted:

> I knew and mistrusted Dr L. B. Namier 21 years ago. He is a fanatical Hebrew. His views on Poles are largely dictated by whether or not they are in his opinion friendly to Jews. I am not surprised to see Dr Namier's criticism of Count Horodyski, he has hated him like poison for a quarter of a century.[61]

Inevitably, it was not long before a government minister advised the Poles 'to dis-pense with Namier's services'.[62] Namier kept up his contacts with Polish friends, and with his old friend Edvard Beneš, now Czech president in exile, but largely for the benefit of the Jewish Agency.[63] What he called 'my work in connection with eastern Europe' had gone.[64]

Namier was restricted to the role he had come to occupy in the months preced-ing the war, as a link between the Jewish Agency and government, making use of personal as well as official channels.[65] Malcolm MacDonald remained a stumbling block, either in the matter of assistance to refugees, or permitting Jewish recruits to be raised and trained in Britain, or in Palestine. Nor was MacDonald willing to modify one iota of the policy enshrined in his White Paper.[66] Namier therefore attempted a flanking manoeuvre, raising issues of concern directly with Butler at the Foreign Office. He based these requests on an assumption that the White Paper was 'in abeyance' for the duration of the war, to which he hoped to secure a witting or unwitting concurrence. An embarrassed Butler reported to MacDonald, who was understandably cross, stating firmly that the White Paper was not in abeyance, and objecting to Namier's efforts to 'get in … by the back door'. The proper lines of com-munication must be followed.[67] Namier took no notice, and continued to plague the Foreign Office. He was particularly exercised on the subject of restrictions on Jewish immigration into Palestine, about which he wrote repeatedly to the press, scorning MacDonald's suggestion that Jewish children under Nazi rule were living with their _nts and 'not facing any special dislocation by not being allowed to emigrate'. 'What Jewish homes in Germany were like even before the war' was well known;

> what they are now most people shudder to think. Worst of all is the position of those Jews in Germany who as Polish citizens are allies of this country: most of the men have been taken to Buchenwald even before the war … and their children, even if they had promises of certificates, are now being told by the colonial secretary to enjoy the peace of their homes.[68]

Behind Namier's anguished commentary on the condition of Jewish families and children in Nazi-controlled territory lay a terrible uncertainty about his own family, immediate and extended. He told Baffy in August 1940 that the only disturbance to his sleeping patterns had been a 'bad night … due to a discussion about what I should do for my family which I had in the evening with Kot'.[69] For those Bernsteins who had kept their Jewish heritage, the outlook was indeed grim: Józef's youngest brother Salomon and sister Debora died in Treblinka in 1942, along with Salomon's wife, Debora's husband Szymon Rundstein, and the Rundsteins' children and grandchildren. Those who had abandoned their faith had a better chance of survival, although Namier was not to know it. His mother, widowed sister and two nieces (aged 14 and 10 at the outbreak of war) were residing in Lwów, which was under Soviet occupation from September 1939. When Hitler launched Operation Barbarossa in June 1941 Namier went with Baffy to the Foreign Office to ask for help in persuading the Soviet ambassador, Maisky, to have them evacuated 'to a place of greater safety'.[70] Nothing came of this. But after the Nazi take-over and Anna's death (probably in 1942), Teodora and the two girls moved to Warsaw, where their Jewish background was not common knowledge, and they could live in relative safety as Polish Catholics.

Driven by his fears, Namier found another avenue of attack, through Winston Churchill. Brendan Bracken, the Irish-born Conservative MP who was Churchill's confidant, was in close touch with Namier and Baffy.[71] Bracken took Namier seriously, but not reverently: in Namier's absence he referred to him, with a touch of derision, as 'Uncle Louie'.[72] Churchill, too, respected Namier, but was not blind to his shortcomings, not least Namier's tendency to exaggerate the goodwill and capacity of friends and allies. Churchill may even have played upon it, making promises that he knew he could not keep.[73] During the winter of 1939–40 Namier believed that Churchill would be able to accomplish what the Foreign Office could not.[74] At Bridgnorth for Christmas 1939, where he was joined by Baffy, he received a telephone call from Bracken telling him that MacDonald – 'the little rabbit' – was 'finished', after being given a thorough talking-to by Churchill. Then came the welcome news that Churchill 'had intervened vigorously' to countermand a despatch from the

Foreign Office to Lord Lothian, British ambassador to the United States, requiring Lothian to make no concessions to the Jews.[75]

It was a nasty shock, therefore, to hear from Bracken in February 1940 that MacDonald had defeated Churchill in cabinet and secured agreement to promulgate the restrictions on land sales proposed in the White Paper.[76] Namier took the disappointment very badly. He had got into the habit of sending confidential information and papers to the *Manchester Guardian*, as an essential element in his propaganda campaign on behalf of the agency,[77] and promptly despatched a copy of the 'secret' communication with this news. In the covering note, he could barely contain himself:

> Mr Malcolm MacDonald has won his great battle … The principle of the Nuremberg legislation has now been introduced into Palestine by H. M. G; there is to be discrimination against the Jews in the matter of land purchase, on grounds of race and religion. A marvellous example they set to the Arabs to whose government they mean to deliver us in future as a statutory minority! … This country fights for 'the rule of law' and demands that the rights of the weak should be as safe as those of the strong. And this is how H. M. G. applies these principles in the administration of their mandate![78]

Namier struck back in a long letter to the *Guardian*. MacDonald was praised for having 'achieved his Munich … the scene was dominated by Mr MacDonald, an artistic, a magnificent skater. With supreme skill he skimmed over the ice, rounding obstacles and drawing whatever figures he chose. The one thing which the figure-skater cannot do is to walk straight.'[79]

While all this was going on Namier became involved in what Norman Rose has called 'one of the more outlandish attempts to resolve the Palestine question, the so-called Philby scheme'.[80] St John Philby was then advising the king of Saudi Arabia, Ibn Saud. In September 1939 Namier ran into him at the Athenaeum, together with Philby's son 'Kim', a journalist connected with the Secret Intelligence Service and also, of course, a Soviet mole. Namier described Kim as 'a very nice, clever young fellow'. When Kim left the club, Namier and St John talked on their own. In a report to the Jewish Agency, Namier prided himself on his cleverness and perspicacity during the interview (unaware, of course, that, like everyone else, he had been hoodwinked by Philby *fils*), and clearly thought that he had made a catch. St John Philby alluded to the fact that the Agency had – or could raise – substantial funds, and obliquely suggested an arrangement with Ibn Saud. On Namier's recommendation Weizmann and Moshe Shertok met Philby to hear his proposals in greater detail: western Palestine would be given over entirely to the Jews, except for a 'Vatican city' in Jerusalem. In return the Jews would work for a unified Arab state, under Ibn Saud. Money would also change hands: some £20 million.[81]

Nothing came of these intrigues, over which there hangs an air of unreality, enhanced by the stage-set of London clubland, and the presence of Kim Philby, albeit in a walk-on part. Perhaps only Namier and St John Philby were in earnest. Even Weizmann, who was more inclined than colleagues to clutch at straws, eventually realised there was nothing to clutch at. Namier was the last to abandon hope in the scheme, which finally sank at the end of 1943.[82] Conversations with T. E. Lawrence may have predisposed Namier to look for a solution which could accommodate both Jews and Arabs.[83] At any rate, he maintained contact with Philby after others had given up. He admired Philby in rather the same way he had admired Lawrence, and, for that matter, Orde Wingate, describing him as 'a queer fellow – direct, wild, incalculable, and yet refreshingly reasonable', whose 'real passionate desire is for Arab independence', and was genuinely 'prepared for concessions to us in Palestine at the price of true Arab development all round'.[84] Philby's wife, Dora, was a near-neighbour in Gloucester Walk, and also a friend: at first she passed messages to Namier from Arabia. Later Philby and Namier corresponded directly.[85] At one point they even concocted an artificial quarrel in the letters pages of the *Manchester Guardian*, which enabled both of them to ventilate the idea of a 'middle eastern settlement' that would 'satisfy the aspirations both of Arabs and the Jews'.[86]

Working for the Jewish cause

Namier was delighted by Churchill's elevation to the premiership in May 1940. Malcolm MacDonald was promptly replaced, and his successor, the Conservative Lord Lloyd, although pro-Arab, was not perceived to be as virulently anti-Zionist as MacDonald had become by the end of his tenure. Namier had run across Lloyd years before, in the PID, and respected and liked him, partly because of Lloyd's opposition to appeasement, and partly because he was 'a British imperialist who loved all that was fine and great in the achievements of his race'.[87] Under Lloyd, the prospect of Jews in Palestine being permitted to contribute to the war effort seemed to have brightened.[88] Ever since the declaration of war, Weizmann had impressed on government the importance of recruiting 'a Jewish division' in Palestine. This was close to Namier's heart: it would identify Palestine with the cause of the empire, and he looked forward to being able to contrast Jewish enthusiasm for the British cause with Arab indifference, a point he was always making.[89]

He also had a strongly romantic, almost cavalier, streak, which occasionally rose to the surface and induced a fervent belief in the right of Jews to bear arms not merely in self-defence but in their struggle for justice.[90] According to Lady Namier, 'his heart went out' to members of the Jewish defence force, the Haganah, arrested by the British in Palestine in the autumn of 1939, in whom he recognised kindred spirits, boasting that he had himself been 'one of Piłsudski's marksmen' in Galicia in 1905.[91] More important, however, were the political implications of recruitment: embodying a Jewish force, under its own flag, would not only demonstrate Jewish loyalty but undermine the policy prescribed in the White Paper.

During the summer of 1940 Namier was hard at work arguing the case, to the Colonial Office directly, and to his other political contacts.[92] Some progress was made, and in October 1940 Lloyd announced government approval in principle for the raising of 10,000 Jewish recruits, of whom no more than 3,000 were to come from Palestine. There was still to be no separate Jewish Fighting Force. Undeterred, Namier kept talking – to Lloyd, to the designated commander of the Jewish force, to anyone in government who would listen.[93] It was what he was good at, repeating the same arguments with a remorseless rationality, in the hope that this would erode resistance. This time, however, the dripping water proved ineffective; and when Lloyd died unexpectedly in February 1941 things seemed to take a turn for the worse. The next colonial secretary, the Irish peer Lord Moyne, was more assertively pro-Arab than Lloyd. He had also been chairman of the Polish Relief Fund in 1939, where he had met Namier's enemies among the exiled Poles. Namier considered his appointment 'truly incredible' and 'a sore blow to us', though he was later to change his mind.[94] No sooner was Moyne settled in office than the Jewish Agency heard that the recruitment proposal had been put on ice for at least four months.

In the midst of this struggle, in May 1941, Anthony Eden dropped a bombshell, the reverberations of which not only shook Namier's confidence but increased his frustration with the British establishment and drove him to espouse Zionist self-reliance. In a speech at the Mansion House reviewing British foreign policy, Eden praised the Arab peoples and promised to support aspirations for Arab unity. On the Jewish question he said nothing.[95] His comments produced alarm and consternation among Zionists.[96] Namier and Berl Locker were deputed to put the Jewish case to Moyne. Namier stated bluntly that enough land must be made available for post-war immigrants to enable the creation of 'a sound Jewish commonwealth', self-governing but 'maintain[ing] a connection with the British empire'. There could be no question of settling Jewish refugees elsewhere.

> We do not hesitate to warn you and all those who mean honestly by the Jewish people against such manoeuvres; some vague vision of a bright future in an unnamed, undiscovered country will be painted to defeat our claim to the land of our fathers, fully acknowledged under the mandate, and to a return which for more than two thousand years has formed the essence of our existence.[97]

It was clear to Moyne that in practice this would mean giving all Palestine to the Jews, with local Arabs absorbed into neighbouring Arab states,[98] an idea which went down badly with Moyne himself, and even more so with the pro-Arab element in the Colonial and Foreign offices, and seems to have confirmed a determination that Zionist demands be resisted.[99]

In these negotiations Namier appeared as a zealot: severe, tireless and, in the words of one civil servant, 'utterly uncompromising'.[100] He gave the same impression in his public utterances. His articles in newspapers and magazines, whether urging the organisation of a separate Jewish regiment (a concession belatedly granted in 1944), pleading the case of refugees or demanding the establishment of an autonomous Jewish state, were invariably strident and acerbic. Even more combative were his letters to the press, contradicting what he saw as false statements about the situation in Palestine. Nor did he hesitate to write privately in the same voice to editors or contributors if spotting an example of anti-Zionist or anti-Jewish prejudice.[101] As in his academic writings and book reviews, he seemed to like nothing better than to get to grips with adversaries and correct them on points of fact or faulty reasoning.[102] A favourite target was the Palestine correspondent of *The Times*, Canon Thorley Bridgman, whom Namier considered blatantly pro-Arab, and harried relentlessly across the newspaper's correspondence columns.[103]

Of all the issues which moved him to write, the plight of Jewish refugees in Europe aroused the greatest passion. The tragedy of the *Struma*, a refugee boat sunk in the Black Sea near Istanbul in February 1942 with the loss of almost everyone on board, was a defining moment. The *Struma* had sailed from Rumania for Palestine, but Turkish authorities had refused the passengers permission to proceed or to disembark, following unsuccessful negotiations with the British, whose overriding concern was to maintain order in Palestine, and avoid antagonising Arab opinion at a crucial stage in the war. 'Jos' Wedgwood, driven to the highest pitch of indignation, promptly called for the British mandate to be transferred to the Americans, and in the House of Lords declared: 'I hope yet to live to see those who sent the *Struma*'s cargo back to the Nazis hanged as high as Haman,[104] cheek by jowl with their prototype and Führer, Adolf Hitler.'[105] Namier, who had appealed to Moyne in vain before the sinking, gave vent to his feelings in print, though it was not easy to get his views across when newspaper editors were wary of criticising government on this issue.[106] Namier dashed off a letter to *The Times* which pointed a finger in the direction of Whitehall,[107] and then wrote a detailed critical analysis of government policy over refugees which he intended for one of 'the weeklies'. After 'phoning round', he eventually secured a place for it in his friend Lady Rhondda's *Time & Tide*.[108]

This was the first of many efforts in which Namier felt that he was pushing against the current. The cumulative effect was to harden still further his belief in the necessity for an independent Jewish 'commonwealth' in Palestine. He argued the case in November 1941 in a lengthy article in *The Nineteenth Century and After*, returning to an image introduced in his first major essay on 'Zionism' in 1928, of world Jewry as a 'melting glacier'.[109] This time he did not present as alternatives 'evaporation', meaning complete assimilation, and the 'river' of the Zionist movement.[110] Assimilation was 'a confession of inferiority' and, in practice, did nothing to enable Jews to avoid prejudice and persecution. In a passage which may well reflect personal experience, he admitted that even in Britain – 'the country where the Jews are given the fairest deal' – they did not have equal opportunities, and that when the Jew 'errs, or merely incurs unpopularity, a resentment rises against him far more violent and venomous than were he a non-Jew'. The Zionist ideal was a form of 'national emancipation', essential to all Jews, since 'every man carries within him a communal memory and inheritance, the more distinctive the longer the conscious life of his race'. The Zionist Organisation considered this article so useful that it was twice reprinted as a separate pamphlet, in London and New York.[111] After reports began to emerge in 1942 of the mass murder of Polish Jews Namier repeated his message in a letter to *The Times*, in even more emotive terms: 'The blood of a million Jews murdered by the Nazis cries to heaven; the world-wide Jewish problem calls for a solution; it has its roots in Jewish homelessness; in Palestine, and through Palestine alone, can a solution be found.'[112]

By the spring of 1943 Namier's faith in British goodwill had dried up, and in a discussion with a 'very well-informed official' he could not stop himself blurting out that the Colonial Office and the high commissioner were 'obviously preparing to deliver us to the Arabs, and if we move, to shoot us down'.[113] He and his colleagues were given grounds for hope when Churchill set up a cabinet committee to consider the mandate, after which Namier redoubled his efforts to promote the idea of a Jewish state. He made no bones about his belief that the Arabs would have to be prepared to give up Palestine entirely for the sake of complete independence in their other territories. In an article in the *Manchester Guardian*, which was again reprinted and distributed as a pamphlet, he wrote: 'if it be accepted that the age-long tragedy of Jewry can be solved, and solved in Palestine alone, it would seem not unreasonable to demand from the Arabs the necessary renunciation'.[114] This had originally been drafted as a memorandum from the Jewish Agency to the cabinet committee but had wisely been rerouted along the way.[115] It would emphatically not have assisted Zionist sympathisers in government. Even after the cabinet committee reported, in December 1943, with a recommendation for partition which Weizmann and his friends, including Namier, were prepared to accept on the right terms, nothing was done. And when Churchill put the issue back on the agenda in the autumn of 1944 hope was quickly dashed again by the assassination of Lord Moyne, who had been transferred to the Middle East as minister resident. Action of any kind was postponed until the post-war peace conference.

Moyne's death at the hands of the Stern Gang was a bitter blow to Namier, who, like Weizmann, was appalled at the upsurge in terrorist action in Palestine by Jewish groups.[116] For all Namier's disillusionment with British policy, and professed admiration for men of action like Wingate, the murder of Moyne, who, despite his lack of sympathy for Zionism, nevertheless embodied the British imperial mission which Namier still idealised, was sickening.[117] The assassins were 'criminal lunatics'.[118] Self-defence was one thing; terrorism another. Besides, this latest turn of events threatened to undo all that Weizmann had achieved in trying to develop 'a sense of national responsibility' among Jews. Lady Namier's explanation of her husband's response, founded not only on close observation but presumably on Namier's conversation, was that

> Since his earliest involvement with the Jews, [he] had intensely resented any of them not living up to his highest demands on all men, including himself. Any disappointment in a Jew had triggered off a mood of self-hate. Disappointment in an Englishman – as member of the other nation he loved – was nothing like so intense.[119]

The turn of the tide in Europe

Hitler's invasion of Russia in June 1941, which Namier immediately recognised as a calamitous strategic error, attributable only to 'subconscious and irrational' motives, fundamentally changed the nature and the course of the European conflict.[120] When the United States also became a participant, after the attack on Pearl Harbor, the war at last conformed to what Namier had argued, ever since 1918, was the essential prescription for European stability: the containment of Germany by the great extra-European empires, comprising Britain and America in the west and Russia in the east.[121] He had long pinned his hopes on the 'peasant masses of eastern Europe' as Hitler's nemesis, and drew obvious lessons from the precedent of Napoleon's disastrous retreat from Moscow.[122] This led him to soft-pedal criticism of the Soviet regime: in November 1939 he insisted that life for Jews in Soviet-occupied Poland was relatively tolerable, with oppression confined to landowners, officials and priests, in contrast to Nazi-occupied Poland, where conditions were 'downright appalling'.[123]

In the first flowering of his conviction that Hitler's divisions would meet their doom on the steppes, Namier wrote two extraordinary pieces (extraordinary in the light of his subsequent political views) which recalled the youthful socialist, and the PID analyst whose kind words for Bolshevism scandalised his Foreign Office masters. A commission to review a book on the Russian peasantry gave him the chance to welcome the achievement of collective farming. 'In Soviet Russia', he wrote, 'excessive zeal and ruthlessness in certain officials, sometimes joined to insufficient technical knowledge, brought about, especially in distant regions, tragedies and losses on quite a serious scale. Yet taken as a whole the change seems to have been justified and successful.'[124] In another article, for the *Manchester Guardian*, he praised the achievements of the Soviet Union in 'industrial and city planning' as well as in agriculture, and detected in the regime 'deep Russian foundations'. He admitted that all this progress had been made

> at a terrible sacrifice; but the readiness of the peoples of the U.S.S.R. to make yet greater sacrifices in this war shows that they have found themselves in their new fatherland and that moral and educational progress has been achieved since 1917.[125]

That the Soviet Union was now an ally against Nazism meant an important change in Poland's position, and a sharpening of Namier's criticisms of Polish aspirations and policy. It was a fundamental principle with him that an accommodation with Russia was the best option for the Poles, and for Europe as a whole, since Russia was the vital counterpoise to Germany.[126] When the Ministry of Information advertised in July 1940 a pamphlet that depicted Hitler and Stalin gloating over their projected 'booty' in Poland, he was appalled: it would be 'rank folly ... at a time when Russia's attitude is of vital importance to us in the near and middle east and when the Poles themselves are coming to see that they must choose between Germany and Russia'.[127] After German tanks entered Soviet territory and the Russians and exiled Poles began talks, he was quick to blame the Polish government for any difficulties: they simply had to accept the unpalatable fact of their dependence.[128]

Festering anxieties on this score were discharged in a piece that Namier published anonymously in *The Times* in March 1943 entitled 'Britain, Russia and Europe'. As he reported gleefully to Crozier, it 'served as a peg' for a leading article in the same issue, by Ted Carr, calling for close cooperation between Britain and the Soviet Union and a recognition of Soviet interests in eastern Europe – in terms of territory and influence.[129] Namier used historical examples to argue that the future security of Europe depended on *Realpolitik* – cooperation between the British, Americans and Russians – rather than a revival, in any form, of the ineffectual League of Nations. 'Experience proves, most emphatically, that no western power, however great, can safely act on the eastern flank of Germany except in a genuine and close understanding with Russia.'[130]

The subliminal message was that the Poles must forgo some territorial claims: Walter Elliot certainly understood the article as being about the Polish question.[131] As far as the Allied cause was concerned, everything depended on maintaining good relations with the Soviet Union and Polish sacrifices were essential. Not even the German announcement in April 1943 of the discovery of the graves of 10,000 murdered Polish officers near Smolensk, which Goebbels proclaimed to be the work of the Soviets, could be allowed to disturb the waters. Baffy and Namier discussed this news together in a state of high alarm, but their only concern was the political fallout.[132] Namier took a similar line when he read news of the Warsaw uprising in the following year. He felt some natural sympathy for the Poles, and disapproved of the behaviour of the Red Army in waiting until the insurrection was defeated before crossing the Vistula to relieve the city, though his condemnation of the Soviets was tempered by a realisation that they had been provoked by the Poles' 'stupid broadcasts announcing that they will fight for Vilna and Lwów till annihilated'.

Unaware that his niece Anna had served in the underground forces as a nurse, and that Andrzej Ehrlich, the young son of his cousin Ludwik, had fought and been seriously wounded, Namier wrote to Baffy in a curiously detached way about the uprising: 'I am not astonished if the Poles feel bitter but they should remember how they always wished for a defeat of Russia. This being so, they have no right to expect much friendship on Russia's part.'[133]

In fact, Namier's relationship with the exiled Polish leaders had soured badly. In the early stages of the war he had been encouraged by Sikorski's attempts to secure an understanding with Stalin that would permit the re-establishment of an independent Polish state. A rapprochement between Poland and the Soviets was eventually agreed soon after the German invasion of Russia, through the efforts of Sikorski and Kot, but was never popular among their colleagues, and after Sikorski's death in a plane crash in July 1943 the more conservative elements regained sway. Namier observed with disgust that even 'representatives of the Polish Socialist party' had fallen into line, a miserable 'echo of the past'.[134] It was not long before he lobbed a few grenades of his own. Two more unsigned articles appeared in *The Times* in January 1944 insisting that the Curzon line of 1920 should form the frontier between a restored Polish republic and the Soviet Union. These arguments exuded a strong whiff of déjà vu, as Namier revisited the disputes surrounding the Paris peace conference, and repeated his demographic analyses, but he also concerned himself with the circumstances of the current war and the hard choice facing the Poles: the only way to secure their western border was to renounce unrealistic ambitions in the east.[135]

After the publication of the first of these articles Namier felt obliged to telephone Kot, now the Polish minister of information, to acknowledge authorship and explain himself. Having affirmed that 'I stand where I always stood in relation to the eastern frontier', he told Kot he was prepared to support Polish claims to east Prussia and other territories disputed with Germany, and to urge that the 'scattered' Polish 'minority' east of the Curzon line be given the opportunity to relocate in Poland.[136] Undoubtedly, this episode put a strain on his Polish friendships,[137] but the risk of losing friends was never a deterrent, and he did not retract an inch from the position he had staked out nearly thirty years before.[138]

He did, on the other hand, dip his head back below the parapet when it came to praising the Soviet Union. Discretion overcame the desire to shock when he declined an opportunity to help Alan Taylor out of a contretemps into which Taylor had embroiled himself by over-favourable comments about the Soviets in *Time & Tide*, including an endorsement of Soviet claims to sovereignty over the Baltic states. Somewhat disingenuously, considering that he was himself stamping once more on Polish sensitivities, Namier told Taylor that 'he had enough trouble over the borderlands after the First World War and did not want to be involved again' in a public controversy.[139] In this he may have been motivated by an unwillingness to jeopardise the goodwill of Lady Rhondda, who was always ready to publish his views on the Jewish question, and who disapproved of Taylor's comments. But there was another, equally important consideration, of a personal nature. He had met, and begun ardently to pursue, a woman who was not only Russian, but a survivor of Stalin's prisons with strong opinions about the Soviet regime.[140]

Julia

The stresses of life in wartime London increased the mental turmoil with which Namier had long been afflicted. He kept up his regular sessions with a psychoanalyst until at least 1942.[141] However, he was able to maintain an outward appearance of sang-froid. Air raids did not drive him to shelter. In October 1940 he went home from dinner at the Dugdales on foot during a heavy 'barrage'.[142] Despite protesting that 'I am overwhelmed with all kinds of war work, office work, etc.', he found time at night, while bombs were falling, to read the proofs of 'Lefty' Lewis's latest volume of Horace Walpole correspondence. 'Things on the spot', he told Lewis, 'are not nearly as bad as they probably appear to you at a distance.' 'It is a queer thing, but when one is in the midst of such events, somehow one does not feel them quite as much as one would have expected. We have settled down to this kind of life, and air raid alarms in the daytime no one minds any longer.'[143] To another correspondent he wrote: 'For my own part I have never gone to a shelter and sleep every night, more or less quietly, in my bed on the top floor of Gloucester Walk.'[144] This was despite a bomb-blast in the vicinity.[145] Lady Namier's biography contains several anecdotes illustrating his imperturbability during air raids, in one of which he continued working in his top-floor flat while the landlady and her niece cowered under the stairs.[146] In March 1942 he enrolled as Voluntary Fire Guard and spent nights fire-watching in Kensington.[147] We can only speculate at the impression he made on his fellow fire-watchers.

Gradually the strain of so much effort, prolonged tension, and his fears for European Jewry (including his own family), came to be reflected in his physical health. In particular, he seems to have developed a series of respiratory infections. The London atmosphere was never good for his breathing, and the Blitz made it very much worse. In the summer of 1942 he reported that he had been operated on, without specifying the problem, and would be out of action for a time.[148] In December 1942 he was suffering from bronchitis, and six months later was in hospital again, but whatever the problem was, it was not solved, and in December 1943 his secretary at the Jewish Agency reported yet another debilitating bout of flu.[149]

It was while recovering from the first operation that he met the woman who changed his life. Julia de Beausobre had come to England in 1934.[150] Born into a wealthy St Petersburg family, she had married a career diplomat, Nikolai de Beausobre, a Russian of Huguenot stock, and in 1917 was living with him in London, where they may well have run across Namier's first wife Clara – also employed at that time by the Kerensky government. Returning to Russia after the Bolshevik revolution Nikolai was arrested, imprisoned and finally executed. Julia, too, endured a spell in the Lubyanka and then in a labour camp, before being released without the papers necessary to qualify for food relief and accommodation. Her health was permanently damaged before her former nanny, who had returned to England, was able to raise the money (less than £500) to permit Julia to emigrate, a ransom which the Soviet government accepted because of its acute shortage of foreign currency. She made her way to London and a new life.

Julia – whose upbringing had been no more devout than Namier's – had by this time become a convinced Christian, with a deep attachment to the Orthodox faith, and a strong belief – like Dostoyevsky – in the redemptive power of suffering.[151] She also wrote poetry, unpublished but highly regarded by Russian literary friends and acquaintances, including Pasternak. In England she lectured and published on the nature of Orthodox Christianity, and made a reputation in the rarefied circles of those searching after spiritual enlightenment. Among her friends were the Swiss lawyer Gustav Kullmann and his Russian émigré wife Maria. In October 1942 the Kullmanns arranged a gathering at their house in Ladbroke Grove to which they invited a mixture of Christian and Jewish friends to explore a common experience of persecution. The guests included Julia de Beausobre and Lewis Namier. Gustav worked for the League of Nations as deputy high commissioner for refugees, in which capacity he had come to know Namier, who regarded him as 'a broad-minded, courageous, fine man'.[152] Julia remembered Namier's trenchant contribution to the discussion, 'attacking some Jews who sentimentally descanted on the contribution to mankind's spiritual regeneration bound to come from the Jewish mass-suffering in central Europe and further east'.[153] She was interested enough in this remarkable display of caustic candour to soften her own glacial demeanour a little.[154] What struck observers, however, was the effect she had on Namier; it was like a 'thunderclap'.[155]

There is no doubt that Julia was a striking personality, with a powerful moral integrity. Her experiences in prison and labour camp had not destroyed her looks – indeed, she dangled a string of male admirers[156] – and imparted a physical frailty which particularly enhanced her attractiveness to Namier. Like Clara before her, Julia needed to be taken care of. She was, however, a very different proposition from the fey and flighty young woman with whom Namier had fallen into bed and into marriage some thirty years earlier. Julia was very obviously aristocratic, in bearing and manner, and not a little snobbish:[157] 'the imperious, even scornful, tone of her voice … seemed forbidding to some'.[158] She was always impeccably turned out, self-confident and self-possessed, and much closer than Clara to being Namier's equal in intelligence. Her social superiority was an advantage in securing Namier's admiration, as was her saturation in Orthodox spirituality, affording an entrée into the 'soul of Russia', after which he had hankered since adolescence, without the contamination of peasant ignorance and superstition. He did not immediately jettison his scepticism of religion or hostility to priests of every stripe, but Julia's faith, and her discussion of it, fascinated him.

At this point Namier's emotional attachments were as restless, and indeed chaotic, as every other aspect of his life. Marie Beer's physical and mental decline had gone so far that in March 1939 she was committed to Friern Barnet mental hospital. As her only friend in England, Namier was the person required to give written consent. Despite a morbid horror of mental illness, he visited her every week that he was in London, until her death in 1954.[159] Around the same time that Marie was certified, he entered into another relationship, with a woman whom Julia would only refer to as 'Deirdre'. They were introduced late one evening after a chance encounter in the street, by a mutual male friend who asked Namier to see 'Deirdre' safely home to her flat. Although she was a married woman, her husband was permanently confined to a nursing home and their child was in boarding school. That same night she and Namier became lovers. It was an entirely physical relationship, with Namier giving her money in return for sex.[160] However, it lasted a long time; in fact, for several years after Namier had met Julia. There seems also to have been a Jewish girl who had a similar claim on him. Eventually Julia put her foot down, having found letters from 'Deirdre' and been 'badgered' by the other girl. Namier promptly gave both of them up.[161]

It evidently took some time for Namier and Julia to progress to this point. She herself describes their peculiar courtship in some detail in her biography. It seems clear from this account and from the reminiscences of her friends, that at first her attitude was cool, but Namier's persistence meant that, despite the alarm and distress caused by his recurrent emotional eruptions, she was eventually won over. By the summer of 1943, when he was to go into hospital, and anxiety dictated that he entrust someone with instructions about his papers, should he fail to survive his tonsillectomy, it was Julia that he chose.[162] He was soon taking her writing career in hand, advising on her prose style, arranging for her to review books for *Time & Tide* as 'an exercise in clear thinking expressed briefly'; acquiring Russian books from friends such as Isaiah Berlin for her to write about; and pushing her own work to publishers and newspaper editors.[163] In turn, she brought him into contact with a new crop of people, some very different from his usual acquaintance, and a few whom his older friends would have considered distinctly rum, such as the amateur philosopher John Bennett, a disciple of the Armenian mystic G. I. Gurdjieff and his 'fourth way', a combination of eastern and western religion and philosophy by means of which man and women could achieve their potential through attaining a higher state of consciousness. Bennett and his wife founded an 'institute for the comparative study of history, philosophy and the sciences', to which Julia gave lectures.[164] He was to be a witness at the Namiers' marriage.[165]

Namier seems to have proposed, after a fashion, early in 1945. At first Clara's continued existence was a stumbling block that could not be overcome. Namier was finally prepared to file for divorce but Julia would not hear of it.[166] By this time Clara was living with Alan Taylor and his wife in Oxford, and working as a maid at the Randolph Hotel. Early in 1945 she fell ill, and was taken into hospital, where Namier visited her. To his surprise – as one hypochondriac thinking of another, he assumed it was a melodramatic fantasy – she was in fact seriously ill, and on 11 February she died, intestate, leaving over £3,000, which all came to Namier. Most of this derived from the regular allowance he had given her since her return to England, and which she had hoarded unspent.[167] But in a final twist she had told him that she had become a Muslim, and wished to be buried as such. Namier had to sort out arrangements with the Shah Jahan mosque in Woking (the first mosque built in England), and make an appropriate donation, convinced that Clara had done this either on a whim or deliberately to annoy and embarrass him.[168] In Baffy's eyes he seemed 'relieved of a burden, but sad in a way. The big mistakes of life retain sadness.'[169]

Even then Julia would not consent. The insuperable problem was now Namier's religion, or rather his lack of it. Julia insisted that he had to be baptised before they could marry. The fact that she did not take up his offer to be received into the Orthodox church may indicate a suspicion – hidden in her biography – that he was acquiescing only to serve a turn, even though he seems always to have shown a dutiful lack of cynicism about spiritual matters when they were together. Baffy was confused: she could not believe that Lewis would have been baptised simply in order to marry Julia.[170] On the other hand, Namier certainly gave Malcolm Muggeridge an impression of belief when he and Julia came to dinner: Muggeridge (who had not yet come to faith himself) detected in his guests a 'sinister tendency to occultism' and noted how they remained 'rather obviously silent' when theosophy was discussed.[171] While old friends like Isaiah Berlin simply refused to believe that Namier had found God, John Brooke, who knew him better than anyone else in the last years of his life, apart from Lady Namier, suspected that he may have finally begun to turn to religion as a source of consolation in old age.[172]

As to where he might be baptised, the Roman Catholic church, the church of his parents, his sister and her family, was out of the question. Presbyterianism, which had once held a strong attraction for him, would not have chimed at all with Julia's religious practice. So he settled on the Church of England as the safest option, while well aware in his own mind that for other people a preference for Anglicanism over Dissent (and indeed for Roman Catholicism over Anglicanism) often reflected social snobbery.[173] Early in 1947 he received baptism at the hands of the dean of Westminster, his friend Alan Don, in St Faith's chapel in the abbey.[174] Then in June he and Julia were married, in a small Orthodox chapel off the Fulham Road, in the presence of 'a few friends'.[175] But these were for the most part new friends, not people like the Bevans and Buxtons, who had known Namier for most of his time in England. George Mitchell, yet another of Namier's Oxford pupils, who acted as best man, told Baffy all about it at lunch: he had been obliged to hold a gilt crown over Lewis's head 'for ten long minutes'. 'Had I been there', Baffy commented, 'I think we should have died of laughing.'[176]

The marriage was a tremendous success. Namier and his wife were able to be 'all in all' to each other, for Julia 'did not have "family" feelings ... of either blood connection or name'.[177] Those who had known Namier for many years, like Baffy's son-in-law 'Jimmie' Fergusson, felt that he mellowed and relaxed under Julia's influence. She was an accomplished hostess when they entertained, usually in the 'ladies' annexe' at his club, and as a couple they were much easier house guests than Namier on his own had ever been.[178] The exact nature of the relationship has been a subject of speculation. Some observers assumed that theirs was a *mariage blanc*.

At home they each had their own bedroom, and when booking hotels insisted on separate beds, if not separate rooms.[179] Julia was known to disapprove of what she considered to be 'the English obsession with sex'; nor did she ever use the word 'love' about her second husband, in contrast to her first, with whom she was said to have been 'wonderfully happy': instead she talked and wrote of her 'passionate concern' for Lewis. On the other hand, her friends were very cross at any suggestion that the marriage was not consummated, and regarded this kind of conjecture as ignorant nonsense.

It is clear that the Namiers were very happy, and, despite their very different backgrounds, and the rough edges of Namier's personality, were well suited and comfortable with each other. In fact, Julia's writings suggest something much deeper: that the marriage healed excruciating wounds in Namier's psyche. At least, she believed it had done so. The descriptions in her biography of his volcanic outbursts, and apparently suicidal urges (the retention of the veronal dose takes on sinister overtones), is of a piece with a poem that she wrote early in 1945, in which a lover (unnamed but without doubt Namier) confesses to 'the clawing horror that keeps me wide-eyed while you lie at rest'.[180]

Marriage also allowed Namier to find a permanent address in London after a period of enforced peregrination. After sustaining repeated collateral damage in air raids, Gloucester Walk was eventually deemed unsafe for human habitation in 1943. His landlady, Mrs Daybell, considered moving to another house with her lodgers – Namier and 'the Watkins family' – but dithered for too long, and in August Namier decamped to furnished rooms on the top floor of a house in Roland Gardens, off the Old Brompton Road, a few doors down from the Dugdales. This resulted in a further weeding of his papers.[181] He put his books in a cupboard in his office at the Jewish Agency, 'where certainly the greater part will rest till I go back to Manchester, or if fate is kind to me, till I move to Oxford or Cambridge, or *faute de mieux*, to London University'.[182] In the following spring he left Roland Gardens, but was unable to find permanent accommodation in London, and drifted from place to place, sometimes begging friends to take him in, and at other times staying at his club, while his letters were redirected to Great Russell Street.[183] At one point he was obliged to leave a trunk full of clothes for safe keeping with his cousin Theo Frankel.[184] Baffy was very concerned about him, since 'the lot of people today in cheap lodgings is hard'.[185] At least Namier's dreary routine was enlivened by country house weekends: in December 1946 he was spotted passing through London 'on his way to a Christmas party at one of the stately homes of Wales'.[186] After the wedding he moved into the small flat that Julia rented in The Grampians, an art-deco block near Shepherd's Bush Green, which became their home for the rest of his life.[187]

Meanwhile, in the spring term of 1945 he returned to his duties at Manchester (or as Baffy put it, resumed his exile), following a lengthy period of negotiation with the vice-chancellor, and took lodgings in a small redbrick house in the Cheshire village of Alderley Edge.[188] He was given a semi-formal farewell by his closest friends in the Zionist movement, at a dinner at the Dorchester, hosted by Weizmann, where Selig Brodetsky and David Ben-Gurion paid tribute. In reply Namier made 'a very moving little speech'.[189] Baffy refused to believe that he would withdraw completely from Zionist work, and for a while he continued to divide his time in London between historical research and attendance at the Zionist offices. After October 1945 he went to 77 Great Russell Street less and less, though he continued to contribute to the Zionist cause. In March 1946, for example, he produced an important two-part article for *Manchester Guardian* on 'The Jewish question', which reiterated his advocacy of a Jewish homeland, and emphasised the special responsibility of the 'English-speaking nations' to ensure that it came about.[190] Most of the arguments were familiar but it was indicative of a change in Namier's mood from the extreme bitterness that he had shown against British ministers and officials during the war that he now returned to the idea of a Jewish commonwealth within the British empire, 'or possibly of an even wider "Atlantic Union"'; a phrase which not only recognised the realities of postwar power relations but harked back to some of the preoccupations that imbued his thinking at the outset of his career.

To put it mildly, Namier's marriage came as a surprise to his Zionist colleagues. Baffy had reported the news in her diary with the addition of an exclamation mark, but noted that Namier was 'more Zionist than ever, convinced that Judaism and Christianity must in the end be reconciled', and that she herself had 'never felt so warm towards him'.[191] Some of his writings, including pieces written before he had met Julia, suggested that this kind of reconciliation between faiths was very much on his mind, and that from his own point of view he saw no fundamental division separating Christians and Jews. The 'Hebrew Nazarenes' who 'carried into the world our national faith coupled with their new tidings', and the remnant, 'a closed community' who 'preserved the old tradition', were equally 'a part of our' – that is to say the Jews' – 'national history'.[192] It was a viewpoint which is easy to understand given Namier's peculiar upbringing. And it was not unattractive to Baffy since she was herself a Christian.

Others were not so charitable. Weizmann in particular felt personally betrayed: he could not believe that Namier was sincere, and saw the baptism as 'some form of public renegadehood'. Namier's marrying in church he could stomach, but 'joining the Church of England on top of it, is something quite different'. He wrote bitterly to Baffy that it is difficult to imagine a greater breach than Namier's apostasy ... What he tells you about the integration of Christianity and Judaism, are meaningless phrases which do not make this act any better or more beautiful. It is a bad thing at all time, and particularly in the state of the Jewish people in which it finds itself now, it is unpardonable ... Well, he has gone; he has left the fold and there is nothing more I have to say about it. I trust that they will make no attempt to see me when I return to England.[193]

When the two men did meet, by accident, there was a highly unpleasant scene. It happened in what Namier called the 'ladies' annexe' of the Athenaeum (the ladies' drawing-room and dining room in Carlton Gardens), where Weizmann was meeting Baffy and Walter Elliot. The Namiers were dining separately with friends. At the drawing-room entrance Lewis and Julia came suddenly and unexpectedly face to face with Weizmann, who scowled and stalked off. Namier was in tears of rage, made more violent by the fact that Weizmann had, he felt, insulted Julia as well as himself. Henceforth he cut Weizmann entirely out of his life. According to Julia, 'he complained to me about it with extreme bitterness and sometimes on the verge of tears'.[194]

The break with Weizmann did not mean that Namier abandoned the Zionist Organisation. He must have been consulted on political matters up until the declaration of the State of Israel in 1948, since his private papers include copies of confidential communications between members of the executive.[195] But with regard to Weizmann, he remained obdurate. When the *Manchester Guardian* approached him in 1951 to review Weizmann's autobiography (in which he was himself conspicuously ignored), he refused on the grounds that 'any criticism ... would hurt Israeli interests', though 'I could, have destroyed' the book, 'to the joy of many Jews and still more numerous non-Jews'. He told the editor that he could not write about Weizmann

for personal reasons ... relations between us are completely broken off ... I have worked for him perhaps more disinterestedly than anyone except Mrs Dugdale. But now he is dead for me, above or below ground, and I shall not write a single word about him for publication, at least not in our time.[196]

Back to history

Amidst the whirlwind of his political activity, and the turbulence of his personal life, Namier still found time to publish works of history. In the summer of 1939 he brought out his first book in eight years (leaving aside the corrections to Fortescue, and the translation of Wolfgang Michael). *In the margin of history* was a collection of over thirty book reviews and periodical essays 'republished with a minimum of change'.[197] There were nine pieces on Hanoverian England but only four of these had appeared since his appointment at Manchester: three were book reviews, and the other, an article published in the *Manchester Guardian* in 1937, briefly traced the decline of the formal cabinet, presided over by the monarch, and its replacement by a smaller 'working cabinet' of chief ministers, from 1714 until 1921. This was a taste of his ongoing work on the eighteenth-century cabinet.[198]

There were also four pieces of 'Judaica', no less than three appreciations of T. E. Lawrence, whose death in 1935 had affected Namier deeply, and a clutch of essays on European history and politics, several dealing with the current crisis, one of which on 'German arms and aims', originally published in 1935, looked remarkably prophetic. He also reprinted several of his reviews of the memoirs of Hohenzollern and Habsburg statesmen, under the meaningful heading, 'Men who floundered into the war'.

The book was well received. *The Times* critic noted with pleasure that although 'Professor Namier is best known as a historian for historians … it is delightful to be reminded in his latest book that the erudition and neat turn of phrase which have always marked his work can be turned to lighter and sometimes to attractively polemical uses'.[199] Namier received such a good review from A. L. Rowse that he felt obliged to write a thank-you letter, while Alan Taylor was almost 'embarrassingly excessive' in praise lavished on the book in the *Manchester Guardian*.[200] Even Namier's parliamentary friend Walter Elliot, whose criticism could sometimes be uncomfortably candid, commended the book without reserve, though the bouquet he proffered was not without a thorn: these short pieces, he told Namier in a private letter, were better suited to their author's 'enormously intricate style'. 'In newspaper articles you have always in your mind's eye the desert of print in which your oasis is to appear, and temper the wind of your learning to the shorn convolutions of your readers' cerebral hemispheres'.[201]

The absence of anything more solid, especially on the eighteenth century, was as much a disappointment to Namier as to his admirers. He had been continuing to teach and supervise research on eighteenth-century subjects, and until the outbreak of war was continuing to collect materials; indeed, he was still in correspondence with likely owners of manuscripts as late as 1942.[202] His papers contain evidence that he was working towards the publication of his Ford Lectures, various editions of texts and further volumes of 'England in the age of the American revolution'. He managed to complete a draft of the first chapter of the next book in that series, on the Grenville ministry, in which he offered penetrating character sketches of Lord Bute and Henry Fox. The references indicate that it cannot have been written before 1939, and the first attempt contained a description, later removed, of Fox's dependants as representing 'the gangster element in the politics of his time', which has strong resonances of the Nazi era.[203] There are also notes on the making and unmaking of ministries, and fragments of a narrative relating to Lord Rockingham's ministry in 1765–66.[204] But the British Museum and Public Record Office were closed for the duration of the war, and in 1940, during the Battle of Britain, Namier decided to deposit his own transcripts and notebooks, and his annotated copy of Horace Walpole's memoirs, in the strong room of his Oxford bank.[205] He found sufficient time to help 'Lefty' Lewis over the Walpole letters, but without ready access to sources could not proceed with his own work.[206] Unfinished business always weighed on his mind, so he was continually promising to return to English parliamentary history.[207]

We can, however, get a glimpse of the way in which his ideas on the eighteenth century were developing from a book review that appeared shortly before war broke out. It suggests a toughening of his insistence on the fundamentally unprincipled nature of eighteenth-century politics, which in places now approached a caricature. This may well have been as much a reflection of his own contemporary frustrations over the behaviour of the Conservative government as the result of the distillation of his research. He reasserted his views on George III, and on party; and in the most important passage provided an abrasively phrased dismissal of the Rockingham Whigs and their claims to political principle. The Rockinghams themselves had no

> consistent, working 'political philosophy' but ... it was concocted for them by latter-day disciples from the king's fears, Burke's verbiage, and a certain 'sour grapes' virtue common to all oppositions. They pinned their hopes on the prince of Wales, and would have carried on under him as Pitt [the younger] did under George III. The system is the dog, the 'statesmen' the tail; if the tail wagged the dog this would indeed be 'news', but it does not happen.[208]

During the first three years of the war, Namier had time for nothing more serious than journalism: book reviews and articles in heavyweight newspapers and periodicals. He contemplated writing a book on 'German rule in Poland' but quickly abandoned the idea for lack of time.[209] There were essays in *The Times* and the *Manchester Guardian*, and slightly longer pieces in the *Spectator*, the *Nineteenth Century* and *Time & Tide*, which had always been a stalwart foe of Nazism. Aside from the *Zionist Review*, in which his name appeared for the first time in 1941, his choice of publisher was largely determined by past associations and personal contacts, though even now he had a tendency to lean towards liberal rather than conservative publications. When he took against an editor it was for personal rather than political reasons. In the most striking example, we find him breaking his long connection with the *New Statesman* after an incident in which both his moral sense and his *amour-propre* were outraged, something which happened more than once in his later career.

The story went like this: in August 1942 the *New Statesman* sent Namier a book for review by G. P. Gooch, the distinguished historian and former Liberal MP (and president of the National Peace Council 1933–36). *Studies in diplomacy and statecraft* was a collection of reprinted essays, mainly on twentieth-century diplomatic history. Namier had fixed Gooch in his sights for some time, as a friend of Germany who consistently pressed the case for a revision of the Versailles treaty and, until the invasion of Czechoslovakia, made sympathetic noises about the Nazi regime. The review contained faint praise – 'Dr Gooch's essays supply a useful record' – but errors were relentlessly, and sometimes painfully, exposed: 'his dismissing of Conrad von Hötzendorf's memoirs ... suggests that he has not read them'.[210] Namier took particular exception to the book's 'revisionist' thesis about the causes of the First World War, which Gooch located not in the natural bent of Germans and the German state towards military expansion but in the nature of 'the European system' of diplomacy.[211] When Germany was dragged into an east European quarrel, the *entente* obliged Britain to declare war. This was a red rag to Namier. Not only did it contradict his fundamental, and long-held, beliefs about European history; it was also the typical mindset of the 'Munichers'. '"Reconciliation with Berlin"', Namier wrote, 'was obviously to Dr Gooch the foremost aim which British statesmen ought to have pursued (and apparently reconciliation with "good Germans" remains so even now).' Gooch had wilfully ignored the threat posed by Germany to British interests before 1914, and had dismissed as bigotry the warnings of Sir Eyre Crowe, the Foreign Office's Cassandra, who according to Namier was 'a great and far-sighted civil servant'.[212]

This was too much for the *New Statesman*'s editor, Kingsley Martin, who in fact owed his job to Gooch's recommendation.[213] It seemed to Martin to be an ill-timed and unjustified assault on a distinguished public figure who had already made amends for any misplaced generosity to Hitler and now called for the Nazis' destruction. In this respect, of course, the review was only the latest instance of Namier's contemptuously iconoclastic treatment of established figures in the world of historical scholarship. Martin would not publish it, though he sent a cheque for the work. He questioned the premise behind Namier's arguments, that Britain and Germany were inevitable enemies, regarding it as 'purely nationalist', or, in a subsequent formulation, 'a racial view', which was simply untenable: 'we and at least *some* Germans have to live together eventually'. If things had gone differently at the beginning of the century the Nazi movement may never have arisen.[214] This only lifted Namier's hackles higher. 'I must say', he wrote, 'that never before in more than thirty years of reviewing have I had the experience of having a review returned to me by an editor.' Having observed that the magazine should have known his views on Germany in advance, he took specific exception to a 'personal remark' in Martin's letter suggesting that Namier was animated by 'the emotions of the moment'.

> It did not require either 1914, or 1933 or 1939 to teach me the truth about the Germans. Long before the last war I considered them a deadly menace to Europe and to civilisation. Anyone who knew me in those years will confirm it – ask, for instance, Kenneth Bell. When I went for the All Souls fellowship exam, in 1911, one of the reasons why I was turned down was that I then took what might now be described as the Eyre Crowe–Vansittart view of Germany.[215]

Later in the exchange Namier dilated further on the feebleness of 'Gooch, and Liberal pacifist critics, of his type', who 'would have favoured appeasement at any price before 1914'.[216]

Namier's newspaper and magazine articles always had a strong historical colouring, but, with a few exceptions, their subject-matter was contemporary. Many were pieces of straightforward political journalism which drew on historical parallels or were situated within a detailed and authoritative depiction of historical background. He wrote repeatedly about the 'German problem' in international relations, the German 'national character' and German nationalism, of which Hitler's regime was a natural culmination; and about the history and sufferings of the Jews, which demanded the establishment of a national home. But there were other articles on British domestic politics, whose purpose was not so obvious. Namier wrote about the party system and party organisation (the 'party machines'), on proportional representation, and on the unusual expedient of coalition government which had been adopted during the war. Some of these essays appear at first glance to be strictly historical, incorporating, for example, the author's research into and ruminations upon, cabinet government.[217] Nevertheless, there was an underlying thread. Namier was extolling the virtues of British constitutional practice, which had grown up 'organically', and was seeking to pre-empt interference by well-meaning but ill-informed critics who wished to extend the emergency arrangements of wartime beyond the exceptional circumstances that had called them into being.

These articles were gathered into another collection, *Conflicts*, which appeared in the summer of 1942. Namier subtitled the book 'studies in contemporary history', thereby signalling his arrival in a field of historical writing previously dominated by diplomatic historians and specialists in the discipline of 'international relations'. In Britain this centred on the institution founded by Lionel Curtis and presided over by Arnold Toynbee, the Royal Institute of International Affairs (Chatham House), for whose journal, *International Affairs*, Namier had reviewed. His irruption into this world was not to everyone's taste. A reviewer in *International Affairs* thought Namier's offering a mixed bag: there were 'flashes of … brilliancy', but the real value of the essays was often 'submerge[d] ... in trivialities of sparkling journalism'.[218] Happily, there were also more positive reviews in academic journals.[219]

Conflicts was well reviewed in the newspaper press, almost embarrassingly so. A full-page review in the *Times Literary Supplement*, for example, adorned with a photograph of Namier, marvelled at his 'deep and assured ... understanding of English history', and thoroughly endorsed his analysis of European history and of Nazism as a natural outflow of German militarism.[220] Alan Taylor, however, after discharging a torrent of praise for the book in the *Manchester Guardian*, permitted himself to be a little more critical in a second review in *Time & Tide*, where he identified three defects in the 'Namier way' of writing history: Namier's neglect of economic causation; his over-indulgence of the English governing class; and his weakness for English Toryism. In a passage that marks the first obvious political difference between the two men, or was possibly an attempt by Taylor to recall his friend to his radical past, Taylor wrote that Namier, in reacting against the liberal utopianism of the nineteenth century, had made the mistake of thinking that all Tories were as sensible as himself; if he, Taylor, were a Zionist he would rely as much on the Nonconformist conscience as on Tory imperialism. In fact, he added, Namier himself took this line in practical politics, thereby confirming that 'at bottom he is as idealistic as the rest of us'.[221]

In 1944 Namier was elected a fellow of the British Academy. The honour was overdue. Three years earlier G. N. Clark, himself a fellow since 1936 and regius professor at Cambridge, had canvassed his name to a potential seconder, the diplomatic historian Charles Webster, who had known Namier since the First World War and was, moreover, sympathetic to Zionism:

> It seems to me that he is by far the most important living British historian of periods subsequent to the middle ages who has not yet been elected ... He has written substantial books ... but he has done much more than this. He has opened up a new point of view. I do not think that in all respects he has fully appreciated the other possible points of view; but I do not see how anyone can question his outstanding originality ... He not only maintains the highest academic standards, but he has stood up for them repeatedly with complete disregard of the consequences to himself. When the history of recent British historiography is written, his work and his influence will be treated very seriously.[222]

Despite the care with which Clark phrased his encomium, Webster did not bite. Perhaps his nose had also wrinkled at the journalistic sparkle of *Conflicts*. By 1944, however, Namier could no longer be kept out. Clark put together a phalanx of highly distinguished historians to propose and support, headed by the economic historian Sir John Clapham and including R. W. Seton-Watson and A. F. Pollard. Webster was not included. The citation nodded briefly in the direction of Namier's work 'as a teacher and essayist and student of international affairs' but focused on 'the technical excellence of his scholarly contributions to the history of the party system in the eighteenth century which have had great influence on historical method'.[223] The election gratified Namier more than almost any of the honours he received later (his knighthood excepted). He insisted on putting 'FBA' on the title page of his books, 'as the only distinction fit to be included there'.[224]

1848

The academy honoured Namier further by inviting him to give the prestigious Raleigh Lecture in history in the year of his election. Namier told Manchester's vice-chancellor that preparing the lecture 'brought me back to my history work'.[225] He chose as his subject the European revolutions of 1848, which he regarded as the pivotal moment of the nineteenth century, a 'seed-plot of history'.[226] It might at first sight seem surprising that he did not return to his eighteenth-century stamping ground, but he had not developed enough new material on George III's reign to do justice to the occasion.[227] In any case the war had turned his mind in other directions. Ever since leaving the Foreign Office in 1920 he had intended to write a history of nineteenth-century Europe, to trace the origins and progress of the political movements which had wreaked such havoc in his own time: that task now seemed more urgent than ever.

Despite the 'doodle-bug' raids in London Namier's lecture drew a large audience. Baffy recorded in her diary that

> His friends turned up in force …The lecture was very Lewis-ish, tight-packed with original stuff. I gave a dinner party at the Carlton Grill, to celebrate his election to the British Academy, of a few of his and my oldest friends. Walter [Elliot], Bob Boothby, Jack Wheeler-Bennett … The evening was a tearing success, and I am sure Lewis was very happy. We all were.[228]

Even though few people considered Namier an outstanding lecturer, because of a declamatory and sometimes ponderous delivery, the lecture was not only memorable, but in print became the most important of his shorter works, republished several times, translated into various European languages, and still cited more than seventy years later.

In the lecture he called 1848 a 'revolution of the intellectuals'. His central thesis was that the upheavals across Europe, and especially the failed revolution in Germany, on which he concentrated, were the work of bourgeois liberals calling for 'a share in the government of states to be remodelled in accordance with the national principle', a definition of nationality based on language.[229] There was certainly 'an economic and social background' to the events of 1848, but the proletarian uprising in Paris was crushed, and the peasantry in the Austro-Hungarian empire were hurriedly emancipated – 'bought off' – in order to forestall a complete social revolution against the propertied. This left leadership in the hands of the bourgeois intelligentsia, self-appointed crusaders for 'human rights and national self-government'.[230]

Namier had grown up with a dislike of liberalism, as manifested in his father's politics, which he regarded as naive and wrong-headed. Namier thought that political economy elevated material interests into a governing human ethic, and failed to understand the power of religious or cultural instincts. Worse still, the liberals of mid-nineteenth-century Europe had unwittingly opened the way to the violence which characterised political life in his own time. But it was the 'national principle', and the dangers that came with it, which preoccupied him. Those who remodelled states and redrew borders on the basis of theories of their own devising did so without regard for history or for the feelings of the people whom they aspired to liberate. He drew a distinction between two principles of government that were in conflict in 1848: the 'dynastic' and the 'national'. The former was 'historic in its growth and survival, deeply rooted, but difficult to defend in argument'; the latter 'grounded in ideas, simple and convincing, but as unsuited to living organisms as chemically pure water'. The essential component of the dynastic principle was 'territorialism', and even though economic development created the conditions for a 'non-territorial ideology' it would never destroy the territorial principle: 'there is no escape from the interplay between groups of men and tracts of land, which forms the essence of history'. Britain was for Namier the exemplar of the territorial or proprietary principle in government, something European liberals who idealised the British constitution failed to appreciate.[231] The post-Enlightenment intellectuals who sought to make revolution in 1848 were transgressing a historical law.[232]

Namier also drew on twentieth-century experience to highlight the dangers inherent in the 'national principle', especially in central and eastern Europe, where populations were scattered by migration and colonisation. Linguistic nationalism posed a threat to peace and stability which became all the greater when 'proprietary claims' were made in the name of the people rather than a dynastic interest.[233] Such demands inevitably led to attempts to subject one national community to another.[234] It was in Germany that the true face of liberal nationalism was to be seen: aggressive and imperialist. In this respect, the liberal German academics who possessed the loudest voices in the Frankfurt Parliament, the institution that was to establish a liberal German state, were no better than Prussian reactionaries: 'the professorial lambs of Frankfurt, bitten by the pan-German dog, caught rabies'.[235] He supported this generalisation by a lengthy recapitulation of German nationalists' efforts to realise their ambitions in the east, which meant that the second half of his lecture dealt with central and eastern Europe, with Poland and Bohemia, and the Slavic congress held in Prague in 1848.

Here he was walking ground that he had previously laid out in his chapter in the official history of the Paris peace conference. As well as giving these long-standing obsessions another airing, he took a few swipes at Marx and Engels, whose attitudes towards the establishment of nation-states were no different from the liberal professors.[236] There were occasional glimpses, too, of distaste for politicians who played to the gallery and cynicism about the 'public opinion' to which they pandered.[237] But what is most striking is the present-mindedness of the argument, whether Namier was describing the conviction of German liberal nationalists in 1848 that 'a great inner transformation could not be achieved without war against Russia', or, more brutally, observed that 'German "liberals" [were] in reality forerunners of Hitler'.[238]

Doubtless there were listeners who felt uncomfortable with Namier's starker assertions. But the lecture made a powerful impact. No sooner had an extended version appeared in the Academy's *Proceedings* than it was reprinted separately as a short book, by Oxford University Press. Over the following decade the Academy authorised more reprints, without consulting Namier or paying him a royalty, which infuriated him.[239] The sweep of Namier's interpretation, the vigour of his arguments, and the sharpness of his prose fascinated and intoxicated readers. But the lecture was also, as Baffy Dugdale had written, 'packed with new stuff'; new to many in an English audience, at any rate. The analysis of events in eastern Europe brought a different dimension to the understanding of 1848, and when the lecture was published the variety of sources used – in French, German, Russian, Polish and Czech as well as English – underlined Namier's mastery of a range of languages and national histories.

Namier developed the case against the German liberals of 1848, and sought to fill it out with evidential detail, in his Waynflete Lectures at Magdalen College, Oxford, in 1947. These lectures were never published. Namier meant to finish them the following year, admitting that they required 'a good deal of additional research', and thought himself close to completing the work in the autumn of 1948. As ever, his best intentions were derailed.[240] Typescript drafts survive of four of the lectures as well as the notes he made in preparation. Although he had to confine himself to published sources, he ploughed through a remarkable number of books, mainly in the British Museum, in German, Italian, Polish and Dutch, and amassed what Alan Taylor called 'mountains of supplementary material'.[241] Most of the work was done between July and September 1947, in the Manchester long vacation, with another burst of activity around Christmas, and some final checking in February and March, as the lectures progressed.[242] He took as his subject the 'Frankfurt Parliament', though he was at pains to make clear at the outset that he had not chosen the subject because of the forthcoming centenary: 'that would be childish'. Instead, he wished to reflect on the historical period that had just come to an end with Germany's dismantling in the Second World War: an age in which Germany had made its 'bid for world dominion'.[243] And his objective was to show that (as he had persistently argued over the previous thirty years) the imperative to territorial expansion was inherent in German nationalism, even the supposedly liberal variety espoused by the Frankfurt constitutionalists.

The methods chosen to demonstrate this proposition, as revealed by his research notes, should come as no surprise. There was a certain amount of quotation, drawn from excerpts he had transcribed from the writings of the participants and a few reports of debates, similar to his reading in eighteenth-century pamphlets when preparing the Beit essay, with the addition in his notes of occasional pejorative comments: 'a confused … speech, full of claptrap'; 'a verbose, high-falutin' manifesto'.[244] But the bulk of his research was biographical, undertaken in a very different way from his work on the eighteenth-century English Parliament, and much closer to the kind of prosopography that Charles Beard pioneered: short, almost skeleton biographies, focusing on aspects of a member's life and career that he might tabulate – age, geographical and social origin, occupation and especially religion.[245] Comments on political affiliation were brief: 'clerical', 'radical' and so on. It was a reductionist approach that he would not have countenanced in his work on English history, and was driven by the need to come to conclusions quickly. Although the lectures were not intended as an exercise in structural analysis, the telling of the story had to be based on secure generalisations about the results of elections, the balance of forces within the parliament, and the social and political complexion of members. It was entirely new research and, especially for someone with a welter of other obligations, a remarkable achievement. As it was, Namier only had time to compile biographical data for 220 of the 831 members.

The work for the lectures differed from his English parliamentary history in another important respect. Instead of the empirical research he had practised and preached, in which one did not know the questions to ask until one had examined all the sources, this was an exercise in collecting detailed evidence to support predetermined conclusions. Germans, he argued, differed from other European nationalists in elevating the development of state power into a revolutionary ideal: in 1848 they had demanded *Macht* (might) alongside *Einheit* (unity) and *Freiheit* (liberty).[246] Their idealisation of *Macht* could be traced back to religion, always for Namier a key factor in determining racial character. He had little to say on south German Roman

Catholicism, the church which ever since childhood had been a bugbear to him. Instead, he concentrated on the Lutheranism of the north, which in his view differed from other non-hierarchical versions of Christianity by asserting the supremacy of the individual conscience and at the same time enjoining obedience to the territorial ruler, resulting in a kind of 'self-imposed inner discipline' which he considered 'the faith of the introvert'. Thus, while English Puritanism, and Dutch and Scottish Calvinism, were 'the nurseries of self-government and democracy', the notion of self-government had not entered into the German concept of freedom: Germans preferred to be ruled.[247] This elaborated a theme he had introduced repeatedly into essays published during and after the war, that Germans were predisposed to political subservience and the glorification of power and conquest: 'the individual German' lacked 'moral courage, self-assurance and independence' and sought 'safety, self-assertion and superlative power' through the nation and the nation-state.[248] He even reused quotations.[249]

'Diplomatic prelude'

Nineteenth-century Europe, and the distant origins of the twentieth-century cataclysms, had an uphill struggle to compete for Namier's attention with historical problems that were more recent and more urgent. There was no doubt in his mind that the immediate origin of the Second World War lay in Hitler's commitment to the aggrandisement of the Third Reich, the unwillingness of the French and British to face up to German threats, and the incapacity of the League of Nations to enforce an international world order. A series of articles, published in *The Nineteenth Century and After* in the early months of 1940, developed this argument within a historical perspective.[250] Namier showed first how Hitler had, 'with gangster-like skill, played on the consciences and fears of his opponents, and ... exploited the mental and moral exhaustion of his contemporaries'; second, how potential opposition within Germany had disintegrated – 'German aristocratic conservatism perished in the *débâcle* of 1918; German middle-class self-sufficiency in the *déroute* of inflation; while the organised working classes intent on rational progress were a creation, or fiction, of the radical intelligentsia'; third, how a fundamental misreading of the Versailles treaty had given Germans baseless grievances and some in the west a misplaced sense of guilt; and finally, how imposition of the vacuous pieties of the League of Nations had never been possible in the absence of a powerful military commitment from America and Britain and the involvement of the Soviet Union.[251]

The publication in 1939 of official collections of diplomatic documents by three of the four signatories to the Munich agreement, Britain, France and Germany, books known by the colour of their bindings – the British 'blue book', the French '*livre jaune*' and the German '*Weissbuch*' – gave him an opportunity to reconstruct the events leading up to war on a firm evidential basis. What was provided in these books was of course far from comprehensive, and was self-serving in terms of selection; nonetheless, its existence presented Namier with a fascinating historical challenge, and the possibility of elucidating, through documentary sources, the truth about matters bedevilled by special pleading in public discourse. After the Polish government in exile had followed suit, with its own 'white book', Namier wrote five long articles for the *Political Quarterly* which appeared between July 1941 and April 1945, using these 'coloured books' to trace a narrative of European diplomacy from Hitler's seizure of power until May 1939.[252] The idea of writing 'contemporary history' did not daunt him, and he vigorously defended the discipline in 1944 in a letter to the *Strand Magazine*.[253]

He found nothing in the documents to change his views; nor would readers acquainted with his writing have been surprised by the thrust of the arguments: 'the main facts and the broad outlines of recent events are known', he wrote, 'and hardly require re-stating'. On the other hand, the process of sifting and comparing different collections was fascinating, especially for someone enthralled by the technique of documentary research. He observed, privately, that

> Altogether, the writing of history from dated pronouncements is a funny job. I once told a class of mine, when a student argued from some well authenticated statements made by the people themselves, that I would undertake to write a most thoroughly documented history in which every single statement would be wrong. People will say, or even write, the most fantastical nonsense about their own thoughts and intentions, to say nothing of deliberate lies.[254]

Dealing with the 'coloured books', in particular,

> You must dig into them before you obtain enlightenment or amusement; first each must be read separately, then with its 'partner', and finally all of them together. This is a laborious proceeding; but by the time you have them all round you talking past each other – a bedlam – you begin to understand what they say, and, which is even more important, what each prefers to leave unsaid and unexplained.[255]

His articles told a story of premeditated Nazi aggression.[256] Predictably, Chamberlain and his colleagues were condemned, and not merely for the betrayal at Munich but for a failure to understand the meaning of Hitler's speeches and actions until too late. The 'clever explanations' of 'the Munichers' in the months leading up to the Nazi invasion of Czechoslovakia were no more than casuistry. Namier made great play with the thinness of the documentation in the British 'blue book', explaining absences with the observation that 'to the self-esteem of politicians, a record of drivel, fuddle and bungling is more painful than one of unprincipled but consistent action'.[257] He repeatedly contrasted the pusillanimous Chamberlain with Churchill, who 'alone, month after month and year after year, exposed the growing dangers of the international situation, pleaded for a consistent and active European policy, and pressed for rearmament on an adequate scale'.[258] But there were other 'guilty men', notably the spineless French foreign minister, Georges-Étienne Bonnet, and the conservative Polish politicians who had been misled by their own imperialist pretensions, and fear of Soviet Russia. Had the Polish government decided to stand up to Germany in 1938, he opined, there might well have been no Munich.[259]

Once the war was over, more evidence began to appear. In particular, Namier followed closely the reports of the Nuremberg trials, and picked out for the readers of the *Manchester Guardian* snippets of testimony which cast new light on German strategic planning.[260] He then produced three articles for the paper on the Czechoslovakian annexation.[261] Newspapers and magazines also sent him for review volumes of memoirs or the diaries of pre-war diplomats. At some point, probably in 1946, he recognised the possibility of turning these various articles and reviews into a book.

The articles on the 'coloured books' provided the foundation, and Namier spent much of his free time in 1946 and 1947 extending their narrative as far as the British declaration of war, using the newly available evidence, and extensive material gleaned from newspaper reports, mainly in the London and New York press. He was also able to supplement the written record by talking to participants. This was a great advantage to the contemporary historian – 'the careful and conversant reader will trace information perhaps not available elsewhere' – though it also meant that there would be unfootnoted, and unverifiable, statements.[262] Namier badgered the Foreign Office for information, until Ernest Passant, the civil servant designated to reply to these endless nit-picking queries, felt obliged to close the correspondence because of pressure of work.[263] Passant complained that Namier did not understand the constraints on office practices imposed by the European crisis: the professor was 'lacking in imagination'.[264] Thom Jones was also questioned about the Rhineland crisis in 1936, even though he had not been cabinet secretary at the time;[265] and to safeguard himself from error on the Polish side Namier sent his drafts for comment to Count Raczyński, the former Polish ambassador to Britain, and during the war a key member of the government in exile, even though he had previously regarded Raczyński's politics with distaste.[266]

Namier completed a text of *Diplomatic prelude 1938–1939* by the end of 1946,[267] but the publication process was slow, not least because of his concern over details, and endless fiddling with proofs. Macmillan published it in January 1948. Namier had appended to the narrative a second 'part', consisting of his Czechoslovakian articles in the *Manchester Guardian*, and three book reviews, which gave the later stages of the book an episodic feel reminiscent of his books on the eighteenth century. Moreover, as with *The structure of politics* or *England in the age of the American revolution* no general conclusions were offered. He did provide an 'Introduction and outline' at the beginning, which sketched in the broad lines of the narrative; otherwise, his arguments were embodied in the text, and he ended his story abruptly with the British and French declaring war. As some reviewers noted, the book presented a prosecutor's case against Chamberlain, and by extension a vindication of Churchill (who was sent a copy of the proofs).[268] Namier argued that not only had the policy of appeasement failed, but when Chamberlain did finally stir himself after the fall of Czechoslovakia, his efforts to stem the Nazi tide were doomed to failure. Neither Germany nor the rest of the world believed Britain would show any backbone, which encouraged Hitler to invade Poland.[269] Chamberlain then compounded matters by failing to secure an agreement with the Soviet Union in the summer of 1939 – 'the tragic core of diplomatic history during the half-year preceding the outbreak of war' – something for which the Poles could also be blamed, the British having allowed them to set conditions for cooperation which the Soviets regarded as humiliating.

The acclaim given to *Diplomatic prelude* eclipsed anything Namier had received before. With rare exceptions, reviews in the newspaper and periodical press were rapturous. Alan Taylor led the way in the *Manchester Guardian*, calling the book 'a showpiece of the historian's art', and followed this up with an enthusiastic radio commentary on the BBC Third Programme.[270] The very fact that the book had been chosen as the basis of a radio talk is evidence of the impression made on the reading public. It was in harmony with the temper of the time, and the power of the writing, the technical brilliance and the mastery of detail enhanced the moral authority which underpinned Namier's denunciation of the Chamberlain government. Reviews in academic journals, when they eventually came in, were for the most part just as categorical: Sir Llewellyn Woodward, professor of international relations at Oxford, writing in the *English Historical Review*, could not praise Namier's 'skill and judgment' highly enough; Humphrey Sumner, who had been Manchester's first choice for the chair of modern history in 1930, thought the book 'masterly'; and voices in America joined the chorus.[271]

There were one or two dissenters.[272] Perhaps the most roundly critical was the anonymous review in the *Economist*, later revealed as being by Max Beloff, who until 1946 had been a junior colleague of Namier's at Manchester, and a neighbour in Alderley Edge. Beloff declared that Namier was acting as both advocate and judge, and, moreover, had not made sufficient allowance for the complexities of the world situation.[273] Foreshadowing later denunciations of Namier as an enemy of 'ideas', the review went on, at a tangent, if not in absolute self-contradiction, to describe Namier as

> the most illustrious representative of the school of historians whose tacit assumption is that politics is only a matter of interest and power, and that ideals are merely the self-delusions by which statesmen obscure the unpleasant face of reality ... Within the limits of this sterile and dangerous philosophy, *Diplomatic prelude* is a masterpiece.

Beloff's criticism was not delivered from a pro-German standpoint, much less from any kind of sympathy with Nazism (he was Jewish himself), nor indeed from a liberal aversion to Namier's emphasis on *Realpolitik*. At bottom what outraged him was Namier's attitude to the Soviet Union, and Namier's assumption that the right policy for the Chamberlain government to have adopted from the start would have been an understanding with Stalin. Other sceptical reviewers made the same point: was the failure of negotiations with the Soviet Union in 1939 really such a missed opportunity? And could Stalin really have been trusted? The émigré German Raimund Pretzel, writing in the *Observer* under his pseudonym of 'Sebastian Haffner', paid tribute to Namier's consummate 'artistry', but argued that he entirely misread Russian ambitions.[274] For Namier to dismiss Pretzel's views, as he did, on the grounds that he 'is a German and I would have been astonished and disturbed had he praised me',[275] was a gross oversimplification. Pretzel was certainly a patriotic German, but he had been an opponent of Nazism in the 1930s, and had emigrated in order to marry his Jewish fiancée.[276]

The onset of the Cold War made Namier's positive appreciation of Russia's role in the world – a reflection of his lifelong view of the realities of European geopolitics – seem highly questionable, a point also made by an American reviewer, Raymond J. Sontag, a man with strong credentials as a Cold Warrior.[277] Over the next decade the analysis in *Diplomatic prelude* would come under increasingly hostile scrutiny. For all the garlands with which the book was bedecked on its debut, in the long run its publication would weaken rather than reinforce Namier's status as a historian. The passion that underlay his loathing for the 'men of Munich' worked on his *idées fixes* about European history to produce a philippic in which, in contradistinction to his more careful scholarship on eighteenth-century England, he had made mistakes, and occasionally strayed some way beyond the evidence to make statements for which there was no corroboration. Both Pretzel and Sontag made passing references in their reviews to the similarity between Namier in this incarnation and the great sages of English whiggery, like Lord Macaulay, whose histories of the eighteenth century he had so successfully debunked.

Acclaim and disappointment

As yet, however, these were small clouds in a dazzlingly blue sky. Even before the appearance of *Diplomatic prelude* Namier's reputation had reached a zenith. The fact that he had not published further instalments of his eighteenth-century series made no difference to the public perception that he was the great and unchallengeable authority on the reign of George III, while the recent collections of essays had demonstrated the remarkable range of his expertise, across the history of modern Britain and Europe. His authoritative judgments and epigrammatic style delighted reviewers. For many, within and beyond the academic world, he was in a league of his own: 'the principal mentor of the modern school of historiography in this country'.[278]

This adulation probably increased his dissatisfaction with Manchester, where his workload was, in his own words, 'exceptionally heavy', owing to the increasing number of students after the end of the war.[279] There was, however, a possibility, and a strong one given his present eminence in the historical profession, that he might be able to move back to Oxford. The regius professorship of history would become vacant in 1947 with the retirement of Sir Maurice Powicke. It was in this context that Alan Taylor obtained the invitation for Namier to deliver the Waynflete Lectures in the spring of that year. That Namier recognised the tactical opportunity he had been afforded is clear from the extraordinary efforts he made to give the lectures, despite encountering one problem after another in a kind of prolonged nightmare: appendicitis, requiring an emergency operation; gruelling cross-country train journeys made worse by the atrocious weather; rearrangements to his schedule which resulted in the last lectures clashing with university examinations.[280]

In fact, not one but two regius chairs in history were to be filled in 1947, in Cambridge as well as Oxford. For the Cambridge chair, the government consulted the outgoing holder, G. N. Clark, who was returning to Oxford as provost of Oriel, and Clark's Cambridge predecessor, G. M. Trevelyan. With Clark acting as intermediary, it was offered to another of Namier's Balliol contemporaries, Arnold Toynbee, who turned it down.[281] The eventual appointee was a pillar of the Cambridge establishment: J. R. M. Butler of Trinity College, son of a former master of the college, sometime 'independent Liberal' MP for Cambridge University, and one of George VI's university tutors. Attlee had recently nominated Butler as a general editor of the official history of the Second World War. However, Butler had no more than a single book to his name, and that had appeared before 1914. All he had published since 1928 was a fifty-page essay in the *Cambridge history of the British empire*.[282] A young Oxford historian, Charles Stuart, observed that Butler was 'not very distinguished':

'His appointment is, in fact, a straightforward Harrow job, via that old charlatan G. M. Trevelyan – another member of the "old school".'[283]

The outcome of the Oxford chair was even more painful. According to Alan Taylor, Attlee canvassed opinion in the university primarily through the provost of Worcester, J. C. Masterman, another 'quintessential establishment figure', though again Clark was also consulted and eventually came to exercise a polar influence over the process.[284] The appointment proved unexpectedly protracted.[285] There was a strong current of support for Namier: among others, Taylor 'lobbied hard' for him, which was probably a mixed blessing.[286] It was generally the older historians in the university who had reservations, while dons of a more recent vintage felt strongly that Namier 'must be right': Hugh Trevor-Roper, for example, who had been mightily impressed by *Diplomatic prelude*, considered him 'the best living English historian'.[287] There was also an element of Oxford faculty politics: medievalists, on the whole, seem to have been opposed to Namier, preferring one of their own.[288]

Unfortunately, the opposition proved more powerful. Taylor was told by Masterman: 'Those I have talked to fall into two groups: those like you who say Namier is the only man and those who say – anyone except Namier.' Taylor attributed this dislike in part to Namier's manner, in person and in print, especially his 'outspoken criticism of other historians'. He also thought that anti-Semitism may have been a factor. But he placed the greatest weight of blame on Namier's lack of social skills, alleging that while in Oxford for the Waynflete Lectures he had fully lived up to his reputation as a crashing bore.[289] The lectures themselves may also not have gone well. There had been insufficient time to prepare, and the strong anti-German tone may have been too much for some of his listeners. But the principal objection was on personal grounds. Over the years Namier had built up a capital of personal unpopularity by the indiscriminate use of his intellectual sledgehammer, and by being unnecessarily rude whenever he considered himself in the right.

By May 1947 the canvassing process had reached a kind of stasis, but a candidate had emerged whom Clark was likely to recommend: Vivian Galbraith, yet another Balliol contemporary of Namier's, and currently director of London University's Institute of Historical Research. If we are to believe the testimonials written years earlier by A. L. Smith and Kenneth Bell, Namier had outshone Galbraith (and indeed everyone else) as an undergraduate, yet Galbraith had been made a tutorial fellow at Balliol in the 1920s, when Namier was struggling without a regular income, and had been elected to the British Academy long before Namier. While Galbraith headed Clark's list for the regius chair, Namier was 'nowhere near the top': 'for personal reasons he would stimulate animosities in the faculty'.[290] And so Galbraith's appointment came to pass.

For Namier, this was a stunning blow, though he held no grudge against the victor. Soon afterwards came another disappointment, almost as acute. The Oxford chair in international relations occupied by Sir Llewellyn Woodward fell vacant; this carried with it a fellowship at Balliol. Julia's biography says nothing of it, and whether or not Namier put himself forward as a candidate is unknown, but he was certainly recommended by his old undergraduate friend Robin Barrington-Ward, editor of *The Times*, in a letter to the master of Balliol, and when the appointment went instead to someone else, Namier was observed by his Manchester colleagues to be in a particularly foul temper, cursing Woodward as the author of all his misfortunes.[291] His last chance of returning to Oxford had gone. There were consolations: in January 1948 he was invited to Rome to address the Accademia Nazionale dei Lincei, the Italian equivalent of the Royal Society and the British Academy combined.[292] More important to him, the governing body of Balliol made him an honorary fellow.[293] According to Julia, he was 'delighted'. But not even this relieved the pain of rejection.[294]

There seems to have been one other avenue of escape from Manchester, though Lady Namier's failure to mention it creates a mist of doubt. After the publication of *Diplomatic prelude* Namier informed his vice-chancellor that he had received the offer of a post in the Foreign Office, which he was considering seriously. On the face of it, this seems highly unlikely. His specialised knowledge would have been attractive, but it is inconceivable that any foreign secretary – let alone Ernest Bevin, whose middle-eastern policy made him a hate-figure to Namier[295] – would have wished to invite such an excitable and uncontrollable bull into his china shop. Perhaps what Namier was being offered was a temporary consultancy; or else he was manufacturing a pretext to resign so that he could spend all his time in London. However, he was 'not at all rich', and was anxious to make enough money to leave Julia comfortably off if she survived him (as he assumed she would).[296] In the end he wrote that he had decided after all 'to go on in the university', and would make the most of his forthcoming sabbatical year.[297] He let it be known in the senior common room in Manchester that he would stay until retirement age, which would arrive in 1953.[298] As always, he had 'an awful lot on my hands'. In November 1944, in a letter to 'Lefty' Lewis, he had recapitulated his priorities: 'I want to develop further my work on 1848; I must publish at last my Ford Lectures; I shall have to prepare new editions of the "Structure of politics" and of "England in the age of the American revolution" – both are by now completely out of print. And I feel that I am getting old! Fifty-six and a half with two world wars behind, is a good deal.'[299]

Notes

1 Namier to Ld Sandwich, 3 Dec. 1937 (Mapperton, Sandwich papers, GM/PERS/15).
2 'Turbulent Zionist', 82; Namier to Basil Liddell Hart, 10 May 1938 (LH, 1/539/16); *The Times*, 25 June 1938; *Jewish Chronicle*, 5 Nov. 1937, 28 Jan., 27 May, 4 Nov. 1938.
3 Norman Rose, *The Gentile Zionists: a study in Anglo-Zionist diplomacy, 1929–1939* (1973), 160–3.
4 Memo by Malcolm MacDonald, 21 Aug. 1938 (TNA, CAB 24/278/25).
5 Leo Amery, *The empire at bay: the Leo Amery diaries 1929–1945*, ed. John Barnes and David Nicholson (1988), 528; Norman Rose, *Chaim Weizmann: a biography* (1986), 338–9; Rose, *Zionism*, 86.
6 *Baffy*, 95–6.
7 Rose, *Zionism*, 86.
8 *Baffy*, 93.
9 So much is clear from Namier's panegyric in *Manchester Guardian*, 1 Apr. 1944, repr. in *Avenues*, 178–82.
10 Dugdale diaries, 1938, 62, 135.
11 Anita Shapira, *Ben-Gurion: father of modern Israel* (1985), 104.
12 Rose, *Zionism*, 87; Blanche Dugdale to Visct Cecil, 17 Nov. 1938 (BL, Cecil of Chelwood papers, Add. MS 51157, fo. 260).
13 'Turbulent Zionist', 82.
14 *Palestine. Statement by His Majesty's Government …* (Cmd. 5893).
15 *Avenues*, 181; Namier to W. P. Crozier, 16 June 1941 (*Guardian* arch., B/N8A/19); *Baffy*, 118; Shapira, *Ben-Gurion*, 113–14.
16 Rose, *Zionism*, 86–8; *Baffy*, 118; 'Turbulent Zionist', 85; memo on Palestine conference, 27 July 1946 (TNA, CAB 129/12/1).
17 Rose, *Zionism*, 89–91.
18 *Baffy*, 121–5.
19 *Baffy*, 124.
20 'Turbulent Zionist', 86; *Baffy*, 126.
21 Namier to Taylor, 15 Mar. 1939 (Babington Smith). For Namier's contemptuous view of MacDonald's performance in particular, see Namier, *Dip. prelude*, 3: 'Early in 1939 I sat through meetings of an official conference and listened to a minister who talked by the hour because he was uneasy in his conscience.'
22 Walter Elliot to Blanche Dugdale, 27 Jan. 1938 (NLS, Elliot papers, Acc. 12198/8); Sir Arthur Bryant to Namier, 3 June 1938 (KCL, Bryant papers, E2/2).
23 Colin Coote, *A Companion of Honour: the story of Walter Elliot* (1965), 155–6.
24 Namier to Emrys Evans, 12 June 1952 (BL, Emrys Evans papers, Add. MS 58255, fo. 61).
25 Walter Elliot referred in a private letter in 1943 to the Beveridge report as having given some animation to 'the Tory radicals of Namier's latest brew' (Elliot to Blanche Dugdale, 19 Mar. 1943 (NLS, Elliot papers, Acc. 12267/15)). Namier had himself described his friend Lord Eustace Percy in 1937 as 'distinctly radical in many social matters although Conservative, and even diehard, in general politics': [Namier,] 'Lord Eustace Percy' [in 'Our London Correspondence'], *Manchester Guardian*, 31 July 1937.
26 *Namier*, 246–7.
27 Bernard Wasserstein, *Britain and the Jews of Europe 1939–1945* (Oxford, 1979), 17.
28 Minutes of meeting, 13 Apr. 1939 (CZA, Namier papers, A312\29).
29 On the White Paper, see Rose, *Gentile Zionists*, ch. 9.

30 *Palestine: statement of policy* (Cmd 6019); S. C. Wendehorst, *British Jewry, Zionism, and the Jewish state, 1936–1956* (Oxford, 2012), 195–8.

31 As, for example, in letters to *The Times*, 28 July, 5 Aug. 1939.

32 Isaiah Berlin, *Personal impressions* (1980), 73.

33 *The Times*, 28 July, 5, 28 Aug. 1939.

34 *Baffy*, 137.

35 *Weizmann A*, xix, 140.

36 'Turbulent Zionist', 89.

37 *Namier*, 240–1; *Weizmann A*, xix, 149; 'Turbulent Zionist', 89; Rose, *Zionism*, 92–3.

38 Namier to the manager, Westminster Bank, Oxford, 22 Sept. 1939 (CZA, Zionist Organisation archive, Z4\31206); *Namier*, 241–2.

39 Namier to Lucy Sutherland, 14 June 1940 (Bodl., Sutherland papers, box 9).

40 Namier to Liddell Hart, 12 Sept. 1949 (LH, 1/539/26).

41 See also Namier to Lady Sandwich 1 Oct. 1940 (Mapperton, GM/PERS/7), agreeing with her that internment had been a blunder: 'Still, parliament, the press *and public opinion* have done their share in putting things right.' Emphasis added.

42 Namier to Ld Sandwich, 6 Dec. 1938 (HPT, N–70); same to Alan Taylor, 15 Mar. 1939 (Babington Smith); same to W. S. Lewis, 2 Aug. 1939 (LWL, Lewis corresp., Namier (1)).

43 Namier to Sir John Stopford, 1 May 1939 (Manchester UL, university archives, VCA/7/562, folder 8).

44 Namier to Stopford, 1 Sept. 1939 (Manchester UL, university archives, VCA/7/562, folder 8).

45 Stopford to Namier, 4 Sept. 1939 (CZA, A312\4); same to same, 28 Sept. 1939 (Manchester UL, university archives, VCA/7/562, folder 8); Namier to E. F. Jacob, 14 Sept. 1939 (ibid.).

46 Godfrey to Stopford, 5 Oct. 1939 (Manchester UL, university archives, VCA/7/562, folder 8).

47 Keith Jeffery, *MI6: the history of the Secret Intelligence Service, 1909–1949* (2010), 335–7.

48 George Freimarck to Patrick Beesly, 27 Feb. 1979, Beesly to Freimarck, 6 Mar. 1979 (Churchill, Beesly papers, 2/40).

49 David Edgerton, *Britain's war machine: weapons, resources and experts in the Second World War* (2011), 252–3.

50 *Weizmann A*, xix, 169–70.

51 Butler to Stopford, 9 Oct. 1939 (Manchester UL, university archives, VCA/7/562, folder 8).

52 Stopford to Namier (Manchester UL, university archives, VCA/7/562, folder 8).

53 *Weizmann A*, xx, 35.

54 Robert Rhodes James, *Victor Cazalet: a portrait* (1976), 232 *et seq.*

55 Dugdale diaries, 1940, 105; Namier to W. P. Crozier, 4 July 1941 (*Guardian* arch., B/N8A/23); *The Times*, 4 Jan. 1945.

56 J. M. Le Rougetel to Ld Halifax, 19 Aug. 1940 (FO 371/24474, fo. 360); 'Report on the situation in Poland' [1940]' (ibid., fo. 367).

57 E. D. R. Harrison, 'The British Special Operations Executive and Poland', *Historical Journal*, xliii (2000), 1076; Jeffrey Bines, 'The Polish country section of the Special Operations Executive 1940–1946: a British perspective' (Stirling University, PhD thesis, 2008), 21, 24.

58 John Coutouvidis, 'Lewis Namier and the Polish government-in-exile, 1939–40', *Slavonic and East European Review*, lxii (1984), 421–6.

ipqhash:9b8c7e2a4f6d1e3c

59 Dugdale diaries, 22 July 1940, quoted in Rose, *Zionism*, 116; Namier to Dugdale, 6 Aug. 1940 (CZA, A312\44).

60 Memo by F. K. Roberts, 19 July 1940 (FO 371/24474, fo. 280).

61 Note by Cavendish-Bentinck, 22 July 1940 (FO 371/24474, fo. 279); Coutouvidis, 'Namier and the Polish government-in-exile', 426–7; John Coutouvidis and Jaime Reynolds, *Poland 1939–1947* (Leicester, 1986), 45–50; Sarah Meiklejohn Terry, *Poland's place in Europe: General Sikorski and the origin of the Oder-Neisse line, 1939–1943* (Princeton, 1983), 195–6.

62 J. L. Talmon to Lucy Sutherland, 10 Dec. 1962 (Bodl., Sutherland papers, box 9).

63 List of Namier's meetings with Polish and Czech statesmen, 1941–4 (CZA, A312\59).

64 Namier to August Zaleski, 1 July 1940 (Hoover Institution Archives, Zaleski papers, box 1, folder 4); same to W. P. Crozier, 4 July 1941, 8 Jan. 1942 (*Guardian* arch., B/N8A/23, 67); Namier to Sir John Stopford, 24 June 1940 (Manchester UL, university archives, VCA/7/56).

65 See, for example, *Weizmann A*, xx, 8, 82; List of Namier's interviews with ministers and civil servants, 1939–41 (CZA, A312\59); Oliver Harvey, *The diplomatic diaries of Oliver Harvey 1937–1940*, ed. John Harvey (1970), 325.

66 Namier to Crozier, 21 Sept. 1939 (*Guardian* arch., B/N8A/4).

67 Butler to MacDonald, 6 Nov. 1939 (FO 371/23251, fos 114–16); MacDonald to Butler, 8 Nov. 1939 (ibid., fos 124–9).

68 Press clippings (CZA, A312\4); Namier to J. R. Downie, 21 Nov. 1939 (FO 371/24096, fos 248–50); R. A. Butler to Malcolm MacDonald, 9 Dec. 1939 (ibid., fo. 259); copies of Dugdale diaries, 19, 20 Jan. 1940 (CZA, S25\178). See also M. N. Penkower, *The Jews were expendable: free world diplomacy and the Holocaust* (Detroit, 1987), 7; Rose, *Zionism*, 96–7.

69 Namier to Dugdale, 30 Aug. 1940 (CZA, A312\44).

70 Dugdale diaries, 1941, 81.

71 *Weizmann A*, xix, 213; *Baffy*, 151–2, 160, 162, 164.

72 Alan Hodge, rev. of *Namier*, *Financial Times*, 24 June 1971.

73 The publisher Victor Gollancz, a friend of Namier, recalled that 'A famous professor, a very great teacher in his subject, walked into my office one morning … and said "Victor, I've just come from Downing Street: Winston has given me Palestine for the Jews." I nodded gravely, and jeered inside; for the things that prime ministers and presidents had said to or done for him were already as familiar to me as if I'd experienced these favours myself. But I soon became convinced that I was being unjust. I concluded, on reflection, that my professor had in fact been to Downing Street, and that Mr Churchill, during the course of their conversation, had mentioned his fidelity to Zionism, and his determination, when occasion arose, to assist in the creation of a Jewish state' (Victor Gollancz, *My dear Timothy: an autobiographical letter to his grandson* (1952), 190).

74 *Baffy*, 162.

75 Copy of extracts from Dugdale diaries, 25 Dec. 1939 (CZA, S25\178); *Baffy*, 157, 159; Namier to Dugdale, 2 Jan. 1940 (CZA, A312\44); Amery, *Empire at bay*, ed. Barnes and Nicholson, 580.

76 *Baffy*, 162.

77 This practice dated back at least to 1936: see CZA, A312\17–18.

78 Namier to Crozier, 26 Feb. 1940 (*Guardian* arch., B/N8A/5).

79 *Manchester Guardian*, 15 Mar. 1940. See also his letter to *The Times*, 6 Mar. 1940.

80 Rose, *Zionism*, 94.

81 Memoranda by Namier, 24 Sept., 6 Oct. 1939 (CZA, A312\27). Philby gave his own account in *Arabian jubilee* (1952), 212–13.

82 Namier to W. P. Crozier, 31 Mar. 1943 (*Guardian* arch., B/N8A/203).

83 Namier to Cecil, 2, 4 Apr. 1940 (BL, Add. MS 51157, fos 266, 268); Cecil to Blanche Dugdale, 5 Apr. 1940 (ibid., fo. 269); Dugdale to Cecil, 8 Apr. 1940 (ibid., fo. 270); draft letter to *The Times* (ibid., fos 272–3).

84 Namier to W. P. Crozier, 8 Oct. 1941 (*Guardian* arch., B/N8A/42). This was despite the fact that in 1939 Philby had stood at a parliamentary by-election on an anti-war platform, an example of Namier's sometimes remarkable selectivity in relation to the political opinions of his friends.

85 Dora Philby to Namier, 21 Feb., 16 Apr. 1940 (St Antony's College, Oxford, Middle East Centre archive Philby papers, 1/6/7/11, 12); Namier to Philby, 14 Nov. 1941, 6 Dec. 1943 (ibid., 1/6/7/15, 16); *Weizmann A*, xix, 224; Namier to W. P. Crozier, 19 May 1943 (*Guardian* arch., B/N8A/42); *Namier*, 254.

86 *Manchester Guardian*, 6, 10 Oct. 1941; Namier to W. P. Crozier, 8 Oct. 1941 (*Guardian* arch., B/N8A/42).

87 Comment by Namier appended to obituary of Lloyd, *Manchester Guardian*, 6 Feb. 1941.

88 Rose, *Zionism*, 105–7; Namier to Lady Sandwich, 1 Oct. 1940 (Mapperton, GM/PERS/7).

89 Namier to W. P. Crozier, 1 July 1941 (*Guardian* arch., B/N8/A/21).

90 Berlin, *Personal impressions*, 72.

91 'Turbulent Zionist', 91–2. The leader of the group detained was Moshe Dayan.

92 [Namier?], 'War effort and war potentialities of Palestinian Jewry' (CZA, Namier papers, A312\8); Namier to Visct Cecil, 20 Aug. 1940, enclosing a memo on 'Palestine Jewry and the war' (BL, Cecil of Chelwood papers, Add. MS 51180, fos 52–3).

93 See, for example, *Weizmann A*, xx, 101–2, 107, 190.

94 Namier to Blanche Dugdale, 3 Sept. 1942 (CZA, A312\44).

95 *The Times*, 30 May 1941.

96 *The Times*, 4 June 1941; Harvey, *The war diaries of Oliver Harvey*, ed. John Harvey (1978), 19.

97 Namier to Moyne, 10 June 1941 (FO 371/27044, E. 3101).

98 'Extract from note of conversation between Lord Moyne, Dr Namier, and Mr Locker', 3 June 1941 (FO 371/27044, E. 3101).

99 'View of Dr Namier on Mr Eden's Mansion House speech' (FO 371/27044, E. 3101); Ld Moyne to L. S. Amery, 2 July 1941 (Churchill, Amery papers, 1/5/47).

100 'View of Dr Namier on Mr Eden's Mansion House speech' (FO 371/27044, E. 3101).

101 Namier to H. Wilson Harris, 23 Mar. 1941, 12 Jan. 1943, 24 Apr. 1944 (Rylands, Namier papers, 1/2/12); Raymond Mortimer to Namier, 30 Oct. 1942 (ibid.).

102 See, for example, his exchanges with Lord Samuel in *The Times*, 15, 18 Dec. 1938, or his correction of Alan Graham, MP, in *Manchester Guardian*, 13 Apr. 1944. He was equally anxious to point out such slips as he had made himself, before anyone else could do so. (*Manchester Guardian*, 20 Mar. 1940).

103 See, for example, *The Times*, 11 May, 27 Nov. 1940, 3 Dec. 1941, 13 Feb. 1943, 13 Apr. 1944, 4 Apr. 1945; Namier to W. P. Crozier, 26 Feb. 1943 (*Guardian* arch., B/N8A/182).

104 In the book of Esther, Haman the Agagite was the vizier of the Persian king Asahuerus. His genocidal plot against the Jews was foiled by Esther, Asahuerus' Jewish wife, and he was hanged on the gallows he had built for his intended victims.

105 C. V. Wedgwood, *The last of the radicals: Josiah Wedgwood, MP* (1951), 196–201.

106 Martin Gilbert, *Auschwitz and the Allies* (2001), 23–4; *The Times*, 27 Feb. 1942;

W. P. Crozier to Namier, 11 Mar., 29 Apr., 10 June 1942 (*Guardian* arch., B/N8A/91, 106, 117); Namier to Crozier, 26 Mar. 1942 (ibid., B/N8A/96).

107 *The Times*, 5 Mar. 1942.

108 W. P. Crozier to Namier, 3 Mar. 1942 (*Guardian* arch., B/N8A/90); *Time & Tide*, 14 Mar. 1942.

109 Repr. in *Conflicts*, 121–36.

110 *Skyscrapers*, 129–30.

111 *The Jews* (New York, 1943; London [1944]).

112 *The Times*, 3 Dec. 1942. See also ibid., 6 Apr. 1943.

113 Namier to W. P. Crozier, 31 Mar. 1943 (*Guardian* arch., B/N8A/203). See also *Weizmann A*, xxi, 61–2.

114 'The Jewish problem reargued', *Manchester Guardian*, 16 Nov. 1943. See also *Manchester Guardian*, 22 Dec. 1943, 4 Jan. 1944; Rose, *Zionism*, 124–8.

115 W. P. Crozier to Namier, 3 Nov. 1943 (*Guardian* arch., B/N8A/271). See also *Weizmann A*, xxi, 84.

116 Arnold Lawrence to Namier, 12 Nov. 1944 (CZA, Z4\31387); information from Mary Port.

117 'Turbulent Zionist', 103–4, 111.

118 Gilbert, *Auschwitz and the Allies*, 187.

119 'Turbulent Zionist', 112.

120 Namier, 'Hitler's Russian adventure', *Time & Tide*, 26 July 1941.

121 He reiterated this analysis in 'Then and now', *Time & Tide*, 13 Dec. 1941.

122 Walter Elliot to Blanche Dugdale, 17 Aug. 1940 (NLS, Acc. 12198/10); *Conflicts*, 62–8.

123 Thomas Lane, *Victims of Stalin and Hitler: the exodus of Poles and Balts to Britain* (Basingstoke, 2004), 57.

124 *Facing east*, 128.

125 Namier, 'The Russian revolution: 1917–1942', *Manchester Guardian*, 7 Nov. 1942.

126 He was never even hopeful that such rational calculation would prevail: one of his most frequently quoted bon mots – 'It is a mistake to suppose that people think: they wobble with the brain, and sometimes the brain does not wobble' – was written (in 1941) in the context of a derisive assessment of Polish policy in the interwar period (*Conflicts*, 72).

127 Namier to H. Wilson Harris, 30 July 1940 (Rylands, Namier papers, 1/2/12).

128 *War diaries of Oliver Harvey*, ed. Harvey, 19.

129 *The Times*, 10 Mar. 1943; Namier to Crozier, 31 Mar. 1943 (*Guardian* arch., B/N8A/203); Iverach McDonald, *The history of* The Times, v: *Struggle in war and peace 1939–1966* (1984), 106–8. Namier may have repeated the trick on 3 Apr., contributing an unsigned article to *The Times* on Jewish refugees which was picked up in an editorial.

130 *Facing east*, 98–103. See also Namier to Basil Liddell Hart, 24 Mar. 1951 (LH, 1/539/58).

131 Walter Elliot to Blanche Dugdale, 10 Mar. 1943 (NLS, Acc. 12267/15).

132 *Baffy*, 203.

133 Namier to Dugdale, 24 Aug. 1944 (CZA, A312\44).

134 Namier to W. P. Crozier, 12 July 1943 (*Guardian* arch., B/N8A/254).

135 Reprinted in *Facing east*, 103–13.

136 Namier to W. P. Crozier, 13 Jan. 1944 (*Guardian* arch., B/N8A/301).

137 He did remain on good terms with Marian Kukiel, at least, to the end of the war and beyond: Namier to A. P. Wadsworth, 12 Nov. 1950 (*Guardian* arch., B/N8A/355); R. V. Machell to Namier, 15 July 1947, with comment by Namier (Bristol UL, Hamish

Hamilton archive, DM/352/Ii); Kukiel's obituary of Namier, *Teki Historyczne*, xi (1960–1), 259–61.

138 See, for example, *The Times*, 4 Jan. 1945; *Facing east*, 96–8; Namier to A. P. Wadsworth, 12 Nov. 1950 (*Guardian* arch., B/N8A/355).

139 Chris Wrigley, *A. J. P. Taylor: radical historian of Europe* (2006), 141–3.

140 In February Baffy recorded that Namier had been 'interesting about Soviet "decentralisation" of armies and foreign policy. He says he would take it more seriously if they decentralised the OGPU' (Dugdale diaries, 1944, 12).

141 Julia Namier to F. G. Steiner, 22 Feb. 1965, Dr Katherine Jones to same, 7 Jan. 1965 (Churchill, Steiner papers, 6/5/1).

142 Dugdale diaries, 1940, 143.

143 Namier to Lewis, 12 Sept., 28 Oct., 27 Nov. 1940 (LWL, Lewis corresp., Namier (1)).

144 Namier to Lady Sandwich, 1 Oct. 1940 (Mapperton, GM/PERS/7).

145 *Namier*, 251.

146 *Namier*, 253–4.

147 Imperial War Museum Sp. Misc. MS Z6; Namier to W. P. Crozier, 18 June 1943 (*Guardian* arch., B/N8A/244).

148 *Namier*, 246–8; Namier to Rebecca West, 12 Aug. 1942 (Yale University, Beinecke Library, West papers, Gen. MSS 105, ser. I, box 13, folder 592); Namier to Crozier, 17 Aug. 1942 (Rylands, *Manchester Guardian* arch., B/N8A/123).

149 *Namier*, 253; W. P. Crozier to Namier, 3 Dec. 1942, 22 June 1943 (*Guardian* arch., B/N8A/144, 245); Namier to Crozier, 12 Sept. 1943 (ibid., B/N8A/254); Walter Elliot to Blanche Dugdale, 25 June 1943 (NLS, Acc. 12267/16); Namier's secretary to Crozier, 10 Dec. 1943 (*Guardian* arch., B/N8A/287).

150 For what follows see Julia de Beausobre, *The woman who could not die* (1938); Constance Babington Smith, *Julia de Beausobre: a Russian Christian in the west* (1983).

151 See, for example, Iulia de Beausobre, *Creative suffering* (1940).

152 Namier to W. P. Crozier, 4 Nov. 1942 (*Guardian* arch., B/N8A/139); Dugdale diaries, 1943, 28.

153 *Namier*, 248.

154 Reminiscences of Irina and Eric Prehn, 8/10 Aug. 1978, Najedja Gorodetsky, 1980 (Babington Smith).

155 Reminiscences of Walter Zander, 12 Oct. 1979 (Babington Smith).

156 Constance Babington Smith's notes (Babington Smith); reminiscences of Renée Sweet, 23 Dec. 1977 (ibid.).

157 Information from Mary Port; reminiscences of Eric Mascall, 13 July 1977 (Babington Smith). According to the reminiscences of Irina and Eric Prehn, 8/10 Aug. 1978 (ibid.), Julia disliked Jane Austen because she was 'common, middle-class'.

158 *The Times*, 21 Dec. 1977.

159 *Namier*, 234–5; notice of death, 22 Aug. 1954 (LWL, Namier papers, folder 2).

160 *Namier*, 239.

161 Reminiscences of Eric Mascall, 13 July 1977 (Babington Smith). This episode is given a different turn in *Namier*, 256.

162 *Namier*, 253.

163 Constance Babington's Smith notes (Babington Smith); *Namier*, 252–3; *Time & Tide*, 30 Jan., 27 Feb., 14 Aug., 4, 25 Sept., 2 Oct., 20 Nov. 1943, 1 Jan., 1 Apr., 12 Aug., 16 Sept., 7, 28 Oct., 18, 25 Nov., 9, 16 Dec. 1944, 6 Jan., 17 Mar., 5, 12, 19 May, 25 Aug., 20 Oct. 1945; John Lehmann to Namier, 17 Feb. 1943 (University of Texas at Austin, Harry Ransom

Research Center, Lehmann letters); Namier to Berlin, 4 Sept. 1946 (Bodl., MS Berlin 114, fo. 60); Julia to same, 12 Nov. 1946 (ibid., fo. 178); Namier to W. P. Crozier, 3 Apr. 1944 (*Guardian* arch., B/N8A/320).

164 Babington Smith, *Julia de Beausobre*, 84.

165 Marriage certificate; Julia Namier to F. G. Steiner, 22 Feb. 1965 (Churchill, Steiner papers, 6/5/1)).

166 *Namier*, 256.

167 Compare the account in *Namier*, 257 with A. J. P. Taylor, *A personal history* (1983), 168. The probate record confirms Lady Namier's version.

168 She was buried on 20 Feb. 1945 in the 'Mohammedan Ground' in Brookwood cemetery, some five miles from the mosque. Namier paid the costs (totalling £8 14s. 6d.). I am grateful to Tharik Hussain for supplying me with a copy of the relevant entry in the cemetery register.

169 Dugdale diaries, 1945, 16.

170 Dugdale diaries, 1947, 23.

171 Malcolm Muggeridge, *Chronicles of wasted time* (2 vols, 1972–73), ii, 308.

172 Information from Mary Port.

173 Namier to Donald Pennington, 5 Mar. 1954 (HPT, N–59).

174 *Namier*, 272.

175 *Namier*, 273; Constance Babington Smith's notes (Babington Smith).

176 *Namier*, 156; Dugdale diaries, 1947, 42.

177 Irina Prehn to Constance Babington Smith, 2 Dec. 1980 (Babington Smith).

178 Sir James Fergusson to E. W. M. Balfour-Melville, 25 Aug. 1953 (NRS, Scottish Committee on the History of Parliament archive, SCHP 1/9/125). Hugh Trevor-Roper warned that, 'except in the presence of the very great', Namier could be 'overpowering', though Julia was always 'charming' (*Letters from Oxford: Hugh Trevor-Roper to Bernard Berenson*, ed. Richard Davenport-Hines (2006), 130).

179 Julia Namier to Marina Chavchavadze, 24 Sept. 1949 (Babington Smith); same to Constance Babington Smith 17 Apr. 1954 (ibid.); Mary Drummond to the manager, Boscawen Hotel, East Looe, 21 Apr. 1954 (HPT, N–58).

180 'New Year dialogue', published in *Time & Tide*, 6 Jan. 1945.

181 Namier to Blanche Dugdale, 15 Aug. 1943 (CZA, A312\44).

182 Namier to Dugdale, 31 Aug. 1943 (CZA, A312\44).

183 *Namier*, 254; change of address card (*Guardian* arch., B/N8A/316).

184 Information from Hannah Selinger.

185 Dugdale diaries, 1944, 17.

186 Namier to Donald Atkinson, 18 July 1946 (CZA, Z4\31206); —— to Arthur Ruppin, 18 Dec. 1946 (ibid.).

187 The block is now Grade II Listed. Constance Babington Smith described the neighbourhood as 'slummy' – which was an exaggeration – and the flat as poky. In fact, it is 600 square feet in size, and has two bedrooms, one of which was 'Lewis's room' but it must indeed have felt 'very cramped' with both inhabitants' belongings in it, especially given Namier's inability to throw away papers and organise properly what he did keep. (Babington Smith, *Julia de Beausobre*, 61, 84, 86; Julia Namier to Kathleen Liddell Hart, 8 July 1960 (LH, 1/539/146)).

188 E. F. Jacob to Sir John Stopford, 30 June 1944 (Manchester UL, university archives, VCA/7/562, folder 8); Stopford to Chaim Weizmann, 6 July 1944 (ibid.); Weizmann to Stopford, 6 July 1944 (ibid.); Namier to Stopford, 17 Sept. 1944 (ibid., VCA/7/56);

Dugdale diaries, 1945, 4; Namier to Rebecca West, 3 Feb. 1945 (Yale University, Beinecke Library, West papers, Gen. MSS 105, ser. I, box 13, folder 592).

189 Rose, *Zionism*, 140–1.

190 Namier, 'The Jewish question: I – Anglo-Saxon responsibility', *Manchester Guardian*, 7 Mar. 1946; Namier, 'The Jewish question: II – diaspora and return', ibid., 8 Mar. 1946. Weizmann thought it very useful: *Weizmann A*, xxii, 98–9.

191 *Baffy*, 249.

192 *Conflicts*, 134.

193 Isaiah Berlin to Lucy Sutherland, 18 Sept. [1961] (Bodl., Sutherland papers, box 9); *Weizmann A*, xxii, 344–5.

194 Julia to Lucy Sutherland, 12 Oct. 1962 (Bodl., Sutherland papers, box 9).

195 Folder of documents relating to Palestine (CZA, A312\8).

196 Chaim Weizmann, *Trial and error* (1949); Namier to A. P. Wadsworth, 17 Dec. 1951 (Rylands, *Manchester Guardian* arch., B/N8A/366).

197 *In the margin*, v.

198 Namier to W. Reeve Wallace, 30 Apr. 1937 (Rylands, Namier papers, 1/9/7).

199 *The Times*, 25 July 1939. See also *TLS*, 8 July 1939 (H. M. Stannard), and Keith Feiling's generous review in *Observer*, 29 Oct. 1939.

200 Namier to Rowse, 31 Jan. 1940 (Exeter UL, Rowse papers, MS 113/3/1/N); Wrigley, *Taylor*, 187.

201 Elliot to Namier, 6 July 1939 (NLS, Acc. 12198/9).

202 Namier to Lucy Sutherland, 27 Oct. 1937 (Bodl., Sutherland papers, box 9); same to J. H. Plumb, 2 Dec. 1953 (CUL, Plumb papers).

203 LWL, Namier papers (1).

204 Rylands, Namier papers, 1/1b/6, 8, 14.

205 Namier to Lady Sandwich, 1 Oct. 1940 (Mapperton, GM/PERS/7); same to W. S. Lewis, [Jan. 1941] (LWL, Lewis corresp., Namier (1)).

206 Namier to Lewis, 27 Nov. 1940 (LWL, Lewis corresp., Namier (1)).

207 Namier to Frank Hardie, 12 Nov. 1942 (Bodl., Hardie papers, MS Eng. lett. c. 459, fo. 119).

208 *Manchester Guardian*, 1 Sept. 1939.

209 Namier to Blanche Dugdale, 8 Jan. 1941 (CZA, A312\44).

210 Galley proof (E. Sussex RO, Kingsley Martin papers, box 14/1).

211 For a full discussion of Gooch's contribution to the debate on origins of the First World War, see Frank Eyck, *G. P. Gooch: a study in history and politics* (1982), ch. 10.

212 Galley proof (E. Sussex RO, Martin papers, box 14/1). Namier sharpened the tone of this passage even further in corrections to the galleys.

213 Eyck, *Gooch*, 335.

214 Martin to Namier, 27, 28 Aug. 1942 (Rylands, Namier papers, 1/2/12). Original emphasis.

215 Namier to Martin, 28 Aug. 1942 (E. Sussex RO, Martin papers, box 14/1).

216 Namier to Martin, 2 Sept. 1942 (E. Sussex RO, Martin papers, box 14/1). The review was eventually published in *The Nineteenth Century and After*, February 1943, tacked on to another extended notice of the same book, critical but considerably less severe. After the end of the war, Namier found another opportunity to lambast Gooch's views of Germany, in an anonymous review of another of his books in the *TLS*, reprinted in *Facing east*, 41–51.

217 Namier to W. P. Crozier, 19 Mar. 1941 (Rylands, *Guardian* arch., B/N8A/7).

218 *International Affairs [Review Supplement]*, xix (1942), 535.

219 As, for example, by W. N. Medlicott, *History*, xxxiv (1939–40), 288.

220 *TLS*, 8 Aug. 1942.
221 *Manchester Guardian*, 24 July 1942; Wrigley, *Taylor*, 187–8; *Time & Tide*, 25 July 1942.
222 Clark to Charles Webster, 15 Jan. 1941 (LSE, Webster papers, 1/21/15).
223 Information from P. W. H. Brown, Hon. Fellowship Archivist at the academy.
224 'Jamie' Hamilton to A. J. P. Taylor, 10 Aug. 1956 (Bristol UL, Hamish Hamilton archive, DM/1352/Ii).
225 Namier to Sir John Stopford, 17 Sept. 1944 (Manchester UL, university archives, VCA/7/56).
226 *Avenues*, 55.
227 Namier to W. S. Lewis, 29 Nov. 1944 (LWL, Lewis corresp., Namier (1)).
228 Dugdale diaries, 1944, 69.
229 *1848*, 23–4.
230 *1848*, 24.
231 *1848*, 24.
232 In this respect, Namier was adapting the argument of the French philosopher Julien Benda, who had argued that nineteenth-century intellectuals betrayed the cause of reason and become apologists for the grosser forms of nationalism (Stefan Collini, *Absent minds: intellectuals in Britain* (Oxford, 2006), 294–6).
233 *1848*, 27.
234 *1848*, 30.
235 *1848*, 50, 53, 57.
236 In particular, the writings of that 'hearty, honest Teuton' Engels were picked apart for evidence of 'a high degree of mental incoherence' (*1848*, 51–2).
237 Lamartine's 'Manifesto to the powers' was said to have contained just 'enough verbiage to satisfy the public at home' (*1848*, 36).
238 *1848*, 33, 43.
239 See p. 317.
240 Namier to Hugh Trevor-Roper, 1 May 1947 (Dacre, 1/2/5); Namier to A. B. Rodger, 26 Sept. 1949 (Bodl., MS Eng. hist. d. 342, fo. 196).
241 Bodl., MSS Eng. hist. d. 341–2; Taylor to Betty Kemp, 19 July 1962 (St Hugh's College, Oxford, Kemp papers, box 1, fo. 116). See also the fragment in Rylands, Namier papers, 1/1b/4)
242 Bodl., MS Eng. hist. d. 342, fos 197–259.
243 Bodl., MS Eng. hist. d. 341, fo. 1.
244 Bodl., MS Eng. hist. d. 341, fo. 187; MS Eng. hist. d. 342, fo. 60.
245 Bodl., MS Eng. hist. d. 341, fos 120–6, 129–38, 204.
246 Bodl., MS Eng. hist. d. 341, fos 7, 9–11.
247 Bodl., MS Eng. hist. d. 341, fos 79–81; Rylands, Namier papers, 1/1b/4. He developed this particular point in 'The German wars', *National Review*, May, 1949.
248 *Conflicts*, 78–93. See also *Facing east*, 25–51.
249 For example, a passage from the draft of the first lecture (Bodl., MS Eng. hist. d. 341, fos 10–11) recycles material from a review by Namier of Alan Taylor's *The course of German history* in September 1945 (*Facing east*, 25–40).
250 Repr. in *Conflicts*, 1–61. He may have been the author of another article which had appeared in the same magazine in April 1939 on 'The end of Czechoslovakia': the interpretation of Hitler's intentions, and the means by which they were carried out, is of a piece with Namier's other writings; the terminology echoes his own; and the opening phrase, referring to 'The ides of March' is one he would himself use subsequently, in two

articles in the *Manchester Guardian* in 1946 on the Nazi annexation of Czechoslovakia (repr. in *Dip. prelude*, 405–12).

251 *Conflicts*, 53, 59, 32.

252 'Coloured books: 1 – pre-Munich', *Political Quarterly*, xii (1941), 266–91; 'Coloured books: II – from Munich to Prague', ibid., xiii (1942), 14–43; 'Coloured books: realignments', ibid., xiv (1943), 308–21; 'Coloured books: realignments II', ibid., xv (1944), 33–49; 'Coloured books: hesitations and prelude', ibid., xvi (1945), 139–57.

253 Rylands, Namier papers, 1/9/20.

254 Namier to Basil Liddell Hart, 12 Sept. 1949 (LH, 1/539/26).

255 *Dip. prelude*, 4.

256 For Namier's belief that Hitler had always intended to wage war, see Namier to Basil Liddell Hart. 24 Sept. 1949 (LH, 1/539 /28).

257 *Dip. prelude*, 59.

258 *Dip. prelude*, 60.

259 *Dip. prelude*, 36.

260 *Manchester Guardian*, 20 Nov. 1945.

261 *Manchester Guardian*, 14–16 Mar. 1945.

262 *Dip. prelude*, v.

263 'Questions for Foreign Office', 10 Sept. 1946 (Rylands, Namier papers, 1/9/5); questions submitted by Namier to the Foreign Office, 13, 17 Sept. 1946, and replies (FO 370/1252); Namier to Passant, 15, 30 Oct., 4, 5, 6, 26 Nov. 1946 (ibid.); Namier to Harvey, 31 Oct. 1946 (FO 370/1252); Passant to Namier, 4, 11 Nov. 1946 (Rylands, Namier papers, 1/9/5); Passant to Namier, 29 Nov. 1946 (FO 370/1252).

264 Comment by Passant on an internal Foreign Office memo, 15 Nov. 1946 (FO 370/1252).

265 Namier to Jones, 14 Oct. 1947 (NLW, Jones papers, WW/22/2).

266 Raczyński to Namier, 4, 14 Nov. 1946 (Rylands, Namier papers 1/9/5).

267 The preface is dated 15 Dec. 1946.

268 Churchill, Churchill papers, 2/55.

269 'One wonders, looking back, in which character the Chamberlain government were a greater menace to their country and its friends – as travellers in appeasement or as insurance brokers? Bankrupt, they tried to re-start business: a procedure equally inadmissible in politics and in trade' (*Dip. prelude*, 117).

270 Wrigley, *Taylor*, 188. See also Elizabeth Wiskemann's rev., *Spectator*, 23 Jan. 1948, I. F. D. Morrow's, *TLS*, 24 Jan. 1948, and H. R. G. Greaves's, *Political Quarterly*, xix (1948), 290–4.

271 *EHR*, lxiv (1949), 117–18 (Woodward); *International Affairs*, xxiv (1948), 426–7 (Sumner); *American Historical Review*, liv (1949), 331–2 (J. S. Beddie).

272 Besides the two reviews discussed, see M[alcolm] M[uggeridge], *Daily Telegraph*, 30 Jan. 1948.

273 *Economist*, 31 Jan. 1948. Beloff identified himself as the reviewer in Max Beloff, 'Two historians: Arnold Toynbee and Lewis Namier', *Encounter*, no. 74 (Apr. 1990), 52.

274 *Observer*, 8 Feb. 1948. See also rev. in *History*, new ser., xxxv (1950), 146–7 (W. N. Medlicott).

275 Namier to Sir Walford Selby, 5 Dec. 1952 (Bodl., MS Eng. 6600, fo. 201); see also Namier to F. A. Spencer, 1 Nov. 1952 (HPT, N–71).

276 A hostile unsigned review of Sebastian Haffner, *Offensive against Germany* (1941), *The Nineteenth Century and After*, Aug. 1941 pointed out that Haffner's call for the British government to admit German refugees into its armed forces, and to make war on the

Nazis on behalf of the real German people, ignored the fact that most Germans had supported Hitler and shared his war guilt. Whoever wrote it, the review was a perfect expression of Namier's views.

277 In *Journal of Modern History*, xxii (1950), 173–5. Sontag had worked during the war for OSS (the forerunner of the CIA), and held strong anti-Marxist views: Ian Tyrrell, *Historians in public: the practice of American history, 1890–1970* (Chicago, 2005), 314.

278 Rev. (by 'A. H.') of *Avenues, History Today*, ii (1952), 505.

279 Namier to Sir John Stopford, 28 Jan. 1947 (Manchester UL, university archives, VCA/7/56); Donald Atkinson, 'Memorandum on the staff-student position in the department of history' [c.1946] (ibid.).

280 *Namier*, 268–9, 271; Dugdale diaries, 1947, 2, 4–6; Sir John Stopford to Namier, 20 Jan. 1947 (Manchester UL, university archives, VCA/7/56); Julia Namier to Lucy Sutherland, 8 Jan. 1968 (Bodl., Sutherland papers, box 9); Sutherland to Julia Namier, 12 Jan. 1968 (ibid.).

281 Anthony Bevin to Clark, 30 May 1947 (Bodl., Clark papers, 213); Toynbee to Clark, 26 May, 11 June 1947 (ibid.).

282 For Butler, see *Oxf. DNB*.

283 Stuart to Trevor-Roper, 11 Sept. 1947 (Dacre, 1/2/1).

284 Taylor, *Personal history*, 189; Noel Annan, *Our age: portrait of a generation* (1990), 5; Francis Graham-Harrison to Clark, 1, 9 June 1947 (Bodl., Clark papers, 213); R. W. Livingstone to same, 5, 9 June 1947 (ibid.); Charles Stuart to Hugh Trevor-Roper, 27 May [1947] (Dacre, 1/2/1).

285 R. W. Livingstone to G. N. Clark, 5, 9 June 1947 (Bodl., Clark papers, 213).

286 Taylor, *Personal history*, 189; Wrigley, *Taylor*, 188. As well as being unpopular with some elements in the university Taylor was scarcely the most astute of tacticians: he later conceded that persuading the Labour Party chairman Harold Laski to write directly to Attlee in support of Namier's credentials was a mistake, since Attlee loathed Laski (Taylor, *Personal history*, 189).

287 *Letters from Oxford*, ed. Davenport-Hines, 22–3; *One hundred letters from Hugh Trevor-Roper*, ed. Richard Davenport-Hines and Adam Sisman (Oxford, 2014), 58–9.

288 This opposition seems to have been organised by W. A. Pantin of Oriel College, who had briefly overlapped with Namier at Manchester (K. B. McFarlane, *Letters to friends, 1940–1966*, ed. Gerald Harriss (Oxford, 1997), 145.

289 Taylor, *Personal history*, 189–90.

290 Charles Stuart to Hugh Trevor-Roper, 27 May [1947] (Dacre, 1/2/1). I have found no evidence to support the notion purveyed in William Palmer, *Engagement with the past: the lives and work of the World War II generation of historians* (Lexington, Ky, 2001), 215–16, that the choice of Galbraith was essentially political; that Attlee wanted a regius professor sympathetic to the Labour government.

291 Donald McLachlan, *In the chair: Barrington-Ward of* The Times, *1927–48* (1971), 267; J. P. Cooper to K. B. McFarlane, 10 Feb. 1948 (Trinity College Oxford, Cooper papers, DDE 279/I).

292 *Namier*, 275.

293 College minutes 1942–50, *s.v.* 25 June, 9 July 1948 (Balliol).

294 *Namier*, 279–80.

295 Max Beloff, *An historian in the twentieth century: chapters in intellectual autobiography* (1992), 91; Muggeridge, *Chronicles of wasted time*, ii, 308, 319.

296 Irina Prehn to Constance Babington Smith, 11 May 1980 (Babington Smith).

297 Namier to Stopford, 30 Mar. 1948 (Manchester UL, university archives, VCA/7/56).

298 Cooper to K. B. McFarlane, 17 May [1948] (Trinity College, Oxford., DDE 279/I).

299 Namier to W. S. Lewis, 29 Nov. 1944 (LWL, Lewis corresp., Namier (1)). In August 1945 he had told Baffy of his 'great new idea for a book on Germany', yet another project which came to nothing (Dugdale diaries, 1945, 94).

8

Crossroads of power, 1947–56

Return to Manchester

Marriage, and the return to full-time teaching, required a new routine. As far as Julia was concerned everything was subordinated to the task of supporting her husband. One of her friends thought that each of Julia's husbands had 'dominated her, made her follow his intellectual interests and so on', though 'she was truly feminine and did not mind living for her husband in every way'.[1] She had her own interests, writing and giving occasional talks on the BBC, and engaging in religious and charitable work, including prison visits at Wormwood Scrubs, but Namier's material needs and intellectual preoccupations came first, and the convicts had to make do without her when her husband was in London.[2]

Namier's permanent home was now Julia's flat, and he went north for a few nights every week in term-time. The lodgings in Alderley Edge proved inconvenient, mainly because there was no telephone,[3] so he moved to Disley, the village where the Taylors had once lived. The air was bracing and the views breathtaking, and for a while he was able to walk the hills again. Within a few years, however, he found himself incapable of strenuous exercise. Moreover, Julia thought the climate in the Peak District rather too bracing for someone whose health had been giving both of them cause for concern; and public transport was poor. She learned to drive and bought a car – a second-hand and rather ancient Morris Eight[4] – to help her husband get about. On her advice he moved again in 1950, to the spa town of Buxton, where he found rooms in a former theatrical boarding house in Hartington Road, uphill from the station. It too had 'crisp air' and a view, and although far from luxurious it suited his needs. Julia still worried – how would he cope in winter? – but he settled in well enough.[5] He called it his 'hermitage', and professed to look forward to his time there, when he could read instead of having to surrender to the demands of sociable living.[6]

Letters written by one of the assistant lecturers in modern history, John Cooper, to his former tutor at Oxford, K. B. McFarlane, provide a vivid account of departmental life amid the drabness of post-war Manchester. Cooper, like other Oxford products who came north, found the experience depressing. 'My entire state of mind … is likely to be that of a person separated from a world full of purposeful beings'.[7] The organisation and ethos of the history department was very different from Oxford: 'austerely professorial', as another exile put it.[8] In Cooper's case the professor was Namier, whom he came to dread like a 'wicked uncle'.[9] Namier harangued junior staff about their research and the importance of completing a major book, and ruined their lunches in the university refectory with monologues about his own work, interspersed with bitter denunciations of the Oxford history school which had cast him out. Although the honorary fellowship at Balliol had rekindled his love for his college – no social event at Balliol was now complete without the Namiers – his comments on Oxford history professors had lost none of their acerbity,[10] and when a proposal came forward to elect to the British Academy an Oxford historian with no reputation for original research he immediately reached for the black ball.[11] At Manchester Cooper felt that Namier was carrying on a 'war of nerves', pushing him onto a treadmill of lecturing on new subjects that had to be mugged up hastily, and insisting that he develop a final-year special subject at short notice. By contrast, Namier himself was excused routine duties and did a minimal amount of teaching, entirely in his own specialist areas.[12]

This was, of course, the standard Oxford view of Namier: a tyrannical monomaniac who neglected undergraduates in pursuit of his own ambitions. It had been one argument against his being offered the regius chair in 1947. So to an extent Cooper was telling McFarlane what he expected to hear. At the same time, Namier was never known to spare advice to those who worked under him, a habit in which his supreme confidence in his own abilities and judgment could make him seem overbearing. He still did very little administration, taught none of the labour-intensive first-year courses, and in his second-year survey lectures and third-year special subject taught what he liked, and what he knew: nineteenth-century Europe to second years; the early years of George III to finalists. Even in the survey course his focus remained highly personal, occasionally idiosyncratic, tending to focus on individuals.[13] It was one thing to dwell on the 1848 revolutions, but one of his students remembers an entire lecture devoted to the brief French premiership of the liberal conservative banker Casimir Perier (1831–32), whose achievement in restoring financial stability under the Orléans monarchy presumably appealed to Namier's political prejudices.[14]

However, Namier's concern and support for younger colleagues was genuine. Just as he had helped Taylor, Hughes and others in the 1930s, he now spent precious time and energy in advancing the careers of those for whom he felt responsible, such as the Manchester graduate Eric Robson, who also worked on the eighteenth century and whose death at the age of 36 hit Namier very hard;[15] and the seventeenth-century specialist, Donald Pennington – despite the fact that Pennington's left-wing political convictions were the polar opposite of Namier's own.[16] Even Cooper came to appreciate Namier's advice, however bombastically delivered. After returning to Oxford, he became a staunch defender of Namier against common-room opinion.[17]

As always, Namier's pupils, at least the able and intellectually engaged, found him an immensely stimulating teacher.[18] Naturally, they had to apply themselves to their work, and woe betide anyone who failed to make an effort: Namier's temper could flash, and his sarcasm was scorching. For the brightest, his classes put them to the test in ways they had not previously experienced: Denis Gray, who became Namier's research student, described undergraduate tutorials as 'an unparalleled and unforgettable lesson in the art of non-violent demolition'.[19] But what students heard stayed with them forever. John Tomlinson, another high achiever, told Julia that

> Namier's mind automatically searched for the essential, human characteristic in every situation. To hear him in seminar or conversation (they were really the same thing) doing this fruitfully with an historical situation you thought you already understood was one way you became aware of his extraordinary empathy.[20]

As much as anything else it was Namier's *obiter dicta*, his off-the-cuff comments about other historians, or about eighteenth-century statesmen and politicians, that lingered in the minds of his listeners. So marinated was he in the sources that, according to Tomlinson, he always seemed to be remembering history as personal experience. 'One often felt one had been talking to someone who had heard Townshend's champagne speech and seen Pitt carried into the Commons.'[21] For those who went on to research, the relationship became even more intense. They found themselves treated as equals: their work was still subjected to a powerful scrutiny, but if they could prove the master wrong no one was more delighted than Namier himself.[22] And the interest Namier took in their careers was keen and generous.

Despite the enjoyment of the long-postponed sabbatical year, which he was finally able to take up in 1948–49, Namier was increasingly discontented at Manchester. For all his professed affection for the Buxton 'hermitage', in reality he yearned for London, where he was close to the raw materials of his research, and where Julia took care of his comforts, with the vital assistance of a daily domestic help.[23] But it looked increasingly as if he was going to have to stay at Manchester until he reached the statutory age of retirement in 1953. There was no prospect of the chair at Oxford or Cambridge, which he had once envisaged as his escape route. So he began to think of providing for himself in a different way: a research project to be carried out under his direction that might attract the sponsorship of charitable trusts, and pay him a salary. Eventually just such a grand enterprise would manifest itself – a revived, and publicly funded, history of parliament – but in the meantime he would have to carry the baggage of his university duties on top of the sackload of projects with which he had encumbered himself.

Post-war politics

However energetic Namier may have seemed to outside observers, including the friends whose proofs he somehow found time to read (with the customarily intimidating attention to detail) in the interstices of a hectic and peripatetic life,[24] he considered himself to be an old man, and like many old men, did not care much for the scenes that confronted him. Although he was an enthusiast for every kind of technical advance, especially air travel, he regarded other aspects of the changing post-war world with suspicion and distaste: his research was 'work we shall have to do to preserve the past for I do not know whom, to come'.[25] Sometimes his lamentations touched the borders of caricature: he deplored the decline of manners in the young,[26] and the post-war dereliction of the aristocratic society that had entranced him in Edwardian Oxford.[27] In an England run by Trimmers and Widmerpools, there were precious few MPs who resembled his *beau idéal*, the 'independent country gentleman' of the eighteenth century.[28]

In terms of party politics he shifted even further to the right. Influenced perhaps as much by Julia's personal experience of Stalinist terror as by the creeping fogs of the Cold War, he renounced even his former reluctant acceptance of the Soviet presence in eastern Europe.[29] At the same time, his contempt for Marx, Marxists and indeed anything smacking of Marxism, became even more pronounced, coagulating into a kind of reflex: when a correspondent in the *TLS* took issue with one of his reviews on an eighteenth-century subject, he told the editor that it was not worth his while replying to 'a … diatribe of the Communist type'.[30] Residual sympathies for the liberal, progressive, side of politics disappeared. In 1952 he still claimed to read the *Manchester Guardian* religiously, but thereafter fell thoroughly 'out of conceit' with the paper's opinions.[31] He now called himself 'a Conservative' *tout court*, even if he only fully approved of his old friends in the party, like Bob Boothby, Walter Elliot, Harold Macmillan, Lord Sandwich's son Viscount Hinchingbrooke ('Hinch'), and of course Churchill himself, whose politics and policies he admired uncritically.[32]

Having long castigated Labour for incompetence and a debilitatingly narrow vision in international affairs, he deplored the behaviour of Attlee's cabinet in abandoning empire, in carrying out what he saw as a flagrantly anti-Jewish policy in Palestine, and, above all for imposing punitive taxation, for there was always a tendency in Namier to judge governments on the basis of his own vested interests, understandable in someone who since at least 1920 had not been able to consider himself financially secure.[33] It was essential to get rid of Labour. This forms the background to a letter to *The Times* before the 1950 election in which he dismissed the Liberals' electoral case. He argued that a stronger third party would not, as claimed, create stability; quite the reverse, in fact, since it would interfere with the natural processes of politics. 'The pendulum in the British system should swing in the constituencies and not in the House'. If floating voters flocked to the Liberals they would empower a centrist bloc that could thwart change.[34] In other words, they might keep Labour in power.

Probably the starkest illustration of Namier's growing crustiness can be found in an exchange of letters with a Manchester colleague, the South African anthropologist Max Gluckman, who in March 1953 asked him to sign a letter to the press protesting against the establishment of the Central African Federation. Namier refused. Gluckman expressed surprise, given Namier's 'liberal, anti-racialistic views'. This was a misreading, based on Namier's hatred of Nazism. What Gluckman had not realised was the extent to which the issue raised implications for Palestine, and also tapped into Namier's enduring concern for the 'white empires', deriving from his early affinity with British imperialists and long-held belief that only the power of extra-European powers could guarantee global security. Typically, Namier did not mince his words.

> Liberal or not, it is a matter of survival for the white man and his civilisation. I can sympathise with the Africans, and if I were an African would take the view they do. But for white men it is a question of holding their position for as long as they can, or clearing out while the going is good. On your findings, we ought to be pro-Arabs in Palestine.[35]

The Palestinian question remained the closest to his heart. News of the proclamation of the state of Israel in May 1948, with Ben-Gurion its first prime minister and Weizmann its first president, reached Namier in Buxton, but his joy was mixed with profound sorrow, for the very same day he heard of the death of Blanche Dugdale. He went for a long walk with Julia to try to take it all in. There, 'striding along a precipitous ridge', he exclaimed, 'Thank God for Ben-Gurion!', and, momentarily forgetting his quarrel with Weizmann, 'Thank God for Chaim in Israel's prehistory!', but at the same time he found it hard to realise that he had lost of one of his oldest and closest friends: 'No Baffy, I can't believe it'.[36]

Despite his return to academic life, and the break with Weizmann, Namier had not entirely given up working for Zionism. He was still willing to milk his political contacts, and continued to write to newspapers to argue the Zionist case.[37] About the state of Israel, however, he was conflicted. Although resolute in supporting Israel against its Arab enemies,[38] he had been greatly upset by the terrorist tactics of Jewish extremists in the lead-up to independence, and was suspicious of the religious ethos of the new state. He told Basil Liddell Hart that he would never emigrate to Israel himself as he would not be able to integrate, given that he had never been 'a member of the Jewish religious community' and in any case was now a baptised Anglican. Talking to Isaiah Berlin he deplored what he regarded as Israel's 'clerical tyranny'. When Berlin 'made light of this … [Namier] turned to me sternly and said: "You do not know rabbis and priests as I do – they can ruin any country."'[39] (Presumably Julia was not present.) To another correspondent he wrote of too much rabbinics and oriental Jewry. It was not for them that we "Litwaki" did the work'.[40]

On the positive side, an 'old friend' from the Jewish Agency, Eliahu Eilath, came to London as Israeli ambassador in 1950, and through Eilath, and Moshe Sharett (formerly Shertok), who had become Israel's foreign minister, Namier's advice was sought on the setting up of the Israeli diplomatic service.[41] He was delighted to renew his friendship with Sharett, and in the course of a long letter sent his 'love to David [Ben-Gurion, prime minister of Israel] and all my other old friends'.[42] And after Weizmann's death, he even accepted an advisory role on the project to publish an edition of Weizmann's papers, joining the editorial board.

One thing that did not change at all was his animus against Germany and almost everything German. He regarded any talk of German rearmament as extremely dangerous and thought it impossible that even part of a divided Germany could be 'reintegrated into the west'.[43] For Namier, blood-guilt rested on the German people as a whole. He resolved never to go to Germany again. There were 'six million reasons',[44] including uncles, aunts and cousins, and although his surviving correspondence does not explicitly refer to family members, this should not be mistaken for unconcern; the fact that his will included a bequest to a young cousin Eva Schutz, whom he had helped to settle in England, suggests the persistence of family feeling despite his continuing emotional as well as physical distance from his sister. He would not agree to meet any German 'unless I know that he was anti-Nazi throughout the entire period both preceding 1933 and after. Even those who turned against Hitler after having helped his rise share the responsibility for what has happened.'[45]

A suggestion from Basil Liddell Hart that regular *Wehrmacht* officers had not manifested any notable anti-Semitic feelings led to a lengthy correspondence, with Namier eventually losing his temper.[46] He told Liddell Hart in a phone call that he preferred not 'to discuss the Germans any further' in person, but continued to do so by letter, in a tone of ever-increasing acidity. It was, he said 'of the completest indifference to me whether Germans view Jews with favour or disfavour' and he was similarly unconcerned at 'the fate of Jews who continue living among Germans after all that has happened', for these were the kind of 'Trembling Israelites' he had long despised, preoccupied with what anti-Semites, or Gentiles in general, thought of them instead of being determined that Jews should be 'like unto all nations'. He finally erupted in a brutal dismissal of Liddell Hart's arguments: 'I hardly think you would have written a letter like yours ... to a member of any other nation which had lost one third of its people, murdered, and most of them tortured to death, by another nation.'[47] It says much for Liddell Hart's affection for Namier, and his understanding nature, that he did not allow this outburst to poison their relationship.[48]

Nor was Namier inclined to modify to any significant degree his view of the Munich agreement and the course of pre-war diplomacy in the light of new evidence.[49] The one minor exception was that he was now somewhat more indulgent towards the Polish position. He still felt that Chamberlain had given the guarantee to Poland in 1939 'with a well-nigh frivolous light-heartedness', but did not think it had emboldened the Poles to an unreasonable resistance to German demands and thus precipitated war. Had the Polish government conceded, Hitler would only have asked for more. Indeed, he was convinced that after a Polish capitulation Hitler would have immediately turned against the west, so giving a guarantee had been right.[50] But on all other issues Namier remained immovable. Although acknowledging that Britain was poorly prepared for war in 1938, he insisted that Germany had been just as weak, and blamed Chamberlain for failing to put to better use the respite he had gained.[51] He was also prepared to accept that there had been some 'wobbling' on the German side as war approached, but did not consider it in any way important.[52]

His performance in a radio broadcast in October 1948 was typical, when he gave the last talk in a series on the BBC Third Programme which looked back at Munich 'Ten Years After'.[53] He reaffirmed the position he had set out in *Diplomatic prelude* and in various essays and reviews, and took issue with all those contributors who had begged to differ (most politely in the case of Professor Agnes Headlam-Morley, the daughter of his old boss at the Foreign Office).[54] This time, however, he was as sharply critical of those on the left of British politics as he was of Chamberlainite Conservatives. Liberal and Labour politicians who believed in treaty revision by agreement, and foreign policy by conference, were castigated for their unworldliness, and he was not slow to point out that he had made the same arguments long before Munich. In line with his increasingly pronounced scepticism of the role of ideas and logic in determining political action, he also explained that Munich had not been the product of a rational assessment by ministers of strategic opportunities and probabilities: 'You are dealing with psychological facts and factors. Men deeply averse to war and convinced of its folly, required time to familiarise themselves with its prospect and brace themselves for the idea.'

Namier was able to have his say about the new evidence coming into the public arena through reviewing a cluster of memoirs, diaries and edited collections of documents in the *Times Literary Supplement*. This gave him an opportunity not only to rehearse his own analysis of events but also to apply his forensic historical skill to the texts. He took great pleasure in testing the veracity of the assertions in memoirs, probing for evidence of each author's psychological state. Unsurprisingly, none emerged with much dignity. As Namier observed, 'unless the author is a man of exceptional stature, an apologia seldom makes pleasant reading'. All 'self-vindications' were 'distasteful' and these examples particularly nauseating.[55] One victim, the French radical politician and appeaser Georges-Étienne Bonnet, foreign minister in 1938, did try to fight back. He had suffered especially painful lacerations: Namier had impugned his character, judgment and policies, as well as the truth of his recollections.[56] But letters of protest to the *Times Literary Supplement* only gave Namier further opportunities.[57] There soon appeared a lengthy and fully documented demolition of Bonnet's account of efforts to persuade the Poles to stand by Czechoslovakia in the spring of 1938: 'a sheer farrago'. This time Bonnet took nearly three years to respond, but the result was the same: another mauling.[58]

Implacable hostility towards those he regarded as primarily responsible for appeasement contrasted with Namier's selective memory about the personal histories of some of his friends. Just as he had exempted Walter Elliot from the general condemnation of 'Munichers', he was happy to ignore, or forget, the pre-war posturings of some erstwhile fascist sympathisers. While preparing for the Palestine Exhibition and Fair in 1938, he had plagued literary acquaintances for signed copies of their books, including the historian Arthur Bryant. Namier admired Bryant's writing and, in a striking contrast to his feelings towards G. P. Gooch and others, was willing to overlook Bryant's sympathy for Nazi Germany and opposition to war.[59] After 1945 he preferred to remember Bryant's wartime patriotic histories rather than pre-war eulogies of the Führer and condemnation of the 'arrogant', 'vulgar' and 'vicious' German Jews.[60] A similar story can be told of Namier's friendship with his college contemporary Arnold Lunn, a zealous Catholic convert whose hatred of Communism made him a fervent supporter of Franco in the Spanish civil war, and who for a time had also opposed war with Germany. Lunn too became a fervent British patriot after 1939, which is what Namier associated with him.[61] When Lunn went out to visit Palestine in 1946 Namier reassured Weizmann that Lunn was far from being an anti-Semite, as some people alleged: such stories were 'complete rot'.[62]

With these few exceptions, Namier was wholly unforgiving about the 'Nazi era', and remained so even as the temper of the times began to change. He was aware that the dynamic of the Cold War was modifying attitudes towards Germany among politicians and intellectuals: the Soviet Union was now the principal enemy. But he would not modify his views on Germany, or concede to arguments in defence of Chamberlain's policy, whether advanced by old Foreign Office hands or by an emerging generation of diplomatic historians; indeed, on this subject he seemed to be consumed by 'rage'.[63] In 1947 he had hoped that his Waynflete Lectures would 'educate English and American readers – though considering the incurable pro-German sentimentalism which once more crops up in this country, I have my doubts'.[64] Subsequently, he encountered this 'sentimentalism' at first hand, when he gave a talk to the Conservative Political Centre and two members of the audience walked out: 'I said some home truths about the Germans … [and] they could not stick hearing the Germans criticised.'[65]

Attitudes were changing around him, however: the isolated reviewers who had previously complained about the moralising in Namier's writings on pre-war diplomacy were gathering into a chorus. Some of the notices of the collections of essays that Namier published after *Diplomatic prelude* questioned the balance of his judgment and deprecated the violence of his tone even as they praised his penetrating intelligence and vivid prose style.[66] Once again, the German émigré Raimund Pretzel was the most outspoken. Writing in the *Observer*, he described one of Namier's collections as a 'brilliant, harsh and strident book', which was essentially a polemic, 'peculiarly unpleasant' in character because of its 'lack of fairness, objectivity and humanity', and cruelly unjust both to those who carried out the policy of appeasement, and to those Germans conflicted between anti-Nazism and patriotism.[67] Namier was unmoved. The review reminded him of 'the plaintive wailing of dogs at the moon in an Ukrainian winter night'.[68] He dismissed other would-be detractors in the same way, writing off a detailed critique by a young scholar as an 'attack against me of the would-be clever type from one of the Cambridge pro-Germans'.[69]

Publications and projects

Now that Namier was no longer working for the Zionist Organisation he was free to meet the expectations of an admiring public. Alan Taylor, in particular, felt that Namier could devote himself to the really important business of writing European history. Taylor looked forward to a history of nineteenth-century Europe, a full-length account of the 1848 revolutions and a detailed study of the Munich agreement, of which Namier claimed to have written half.[70] Taylor, who had left Macmillan in disgust at poor sales, persuaded Namier to follow him to his new publisher, Hamish

Hamilton, though Namier was disinclined to burn all his boats and kept his old publisher alongside the new.[71] He had himself found little to complain of with Macmillan;
indeed, after they had taken his first three books and his series of 'Studies in Modern
History' he described them as 'from my own personal experience … downright generous to authors'.[72] Taylor probably persuaded him that he could make more money
with Hamilton: Namier always took a keen interest in the financial arrangements for
his publications. He was not wealthy, and was determined not to be short-changed.
Resentment at the cavalier way in which he felt the British Academy treated him in
arranging for the republication of his Raleigh Lecture without consultation or royalties had produced a succession of blistering letters.[73]

With Macmillan, Namier really did have little to complain of in terms of finance,
as he himself freely admitted. Approached to join the Society of Authors, he hemmed
and hawed, since he was 'on the best of terms' with his publisher and did not need
the society to represent him, but when he discovered that the subscription was tax
deductable, did allow his name to go forward, 'not so much in the hope of your fighting my battles against my publishers, as of your fighting our joint battle against the
Income Tax people'.[74] But just as important as the lure of improved royalties was the
fact that Hamilton was prepared to carry on publishing collections of his essays, a
genre of which Macmillan had grown tired and felt was no longer profitable, despite
the attraction of the Namier brand and the generally glowing reviews. Macmillan
took two more books of this kind, *Europe in decay* (1950) and *In the Nazi era* (1952),
both focusing on pre-war diplomacy and presented as a 'continuation' of the work
Diplomatic prelude had begun. But they would not take the kind of omnium gath-
erum that Namier had in mind.

For his part, Hamish Hamilton, or 'Jamie' as he was known, was prepared to
accept an unpromising haul of small fish in the hope of landing a much bigger catch,
one of the major works that Taylor talked about, or even perhaps Namier's memoirs, which he thought should make 'a fascinating book'. But he proceeded with a
heavy heart, warned by Taylor that Namier had been talking of these projects for
the previous ten years. Moreover, collections of essays were 'the very devil to sell'.[75]
And Hamilton was soon complaining of Namier's endless communications, over
the minutiae of the printing process, the timing of publication, the American and
European rights, where the book should be reviewed and how many complimentary
copies should be sent out. With the first volume, *Facing east*, going through the press
in January 1947 Hamilton wrote to Taylor:

> Most of Namier's attentions are, mercifully, concentrated on Roger Machell [his editor],
> whom he has known for a long time. However, I don't escape altogether and confess
> that I was relieved when I read in *The Times* a couple of days ago that he was laid up

and unable to deal with correspondence. Within two hours, however, he was on the telephone worrying us about proofs![76]

Taylor continued to press Namier for the kind of books that Hamilton really wanted, even using newspaper reviews and articles to try and embarrass his old friend into getting on with the job. He reviewed *Europe in decay* somewhat discontentedly in the *Manchester Guardian*, questioning whether this *réchauffé* of leftovers was really needed, and was not a distraction from the important works that Namier should be writing. In what was obviously an attempt to tease, he complained that

> however much we may admire Mr Namier as a journalist and contemporary historian we cannot forget that these activities distract him from the great works on the history of eighteenth-century England which he alone is qualified to write. So long as his Ford Lectures of fifteen years ago remain unpublished we shall resent his preoccupation with Stalin and Hitler and such small fry.[77]

Namier was unmoved, seeing this merely as further evidence that his friend was 'both incalculable and irrepressible'.[78] And besides, there were other, less carping, reviews, which did not accuse Namier of wasting his own and the reader's time, even if some did remark on the incidental' nature of the essays being reprinted.[79] Actually, this thought had crossed his own mind; that reviewing and essay-writing, and working up the results into books, might not be the best use of a limited lifespan: 'I often wonder whether I have not given too much time to those disconnected essays. But then my life has largely been disconnected.'[80]

To Jamie Hamilton's chagrin, reheated essays were all that Namier had to offer. The next two books, *Avenues of history*, which Hamilton published in 1952, and *Personalities and powers* in 1955, were each a mixture of lectures, short articles and extended book reviews. At other times Namier tried to get Hamilton interested in a manuscript of Julia's, and a book on Napoleon's Russian campaign by Marian Kukiel. He even proposed that Hamilton restart the series 'Studies in Modern History', fearing that Macmillan had given up on it. None of these prospects was to Hamilton's taste.[81]

Namier never formally abandoned any of his projects on European history. Although he refused to sign a contract 'for his big book on European diplomacy since 1815', he still promised Hamish Hamilton that they would have 'first offer'.[82] However, despite his anguished moral preoccupation with the malignant consequences of the disintegration of the European system in the twentieth century, as a historian his heart remained in the eighteenth. The main dividend he expected to draw from his return to Manchester was the opportunity to resume the projects he had begun in the 1920s and 1930s.[83] Deep down he felt that the commitments of conscience to work up the Waynflete Lectures and to complete his study of 1848 were diversions from his primary purpose.[84] He pulled out of a major international conference in Amsterdam in September 1950 on the history of the Second World War after having initially agreed to give a paper,[85] and determined to cut down on book reviewing in spite of the remuneration,[86] a decision made easier in 1951 when he severed 'diplomatic relations' with the *TLS*, following a quarrel over the editing of his prose.[87] His sabbatical year in 1948–49 would be devoted to the eighteenth century: he even turned down a tempting invitation to return to America in the spring of 1949, to be lionised at Princeton, fearing that it would distract him and obstruct 'serious work'.[88]

As before, cooperation was the key. Namier had long since proved that the range of archival sources for his period was far greater than any of his predecessors dared to imagine. Now, as aristocratic households were being dismantled under the pressure of wartime losses and post-war taxation, more collections of manuscripts were becoming available, though paradoxically the uncertainty of the times meant that their long-term survival was also at greater risk. There was a great opportunity but in all likelihood a fleeting one. To take full advantage would be far beyond a single researcher, even someone as determined as Namier, and equipped with his extraordinary capacity to work through original papers, and to master a mountain of detail. He was also more than ever aware of the insistent call of mortality. Not that he slowed the pace of his research; far from it. He continued ploughing through local and private archives, chauffeur-driven by Lady Namier on 'paper chases' to record offices and country houses. But he was under no illusions that he could undertake this kind of work on his own, and in June 1947 approached Lucy Sutherland with a proposal that 'the small group of historians who work on the eighteenth century should meet some time for an informal conference and discuss some plan of work and possibly of co-operation'.[89]

At first his focus was still on locating and editing eighteenth-century texts. He had not forgotten his commitment to Lord Sandwich, nor Horace Walpole's memoirs.[90] As if this were not enough, he also contemplated a new edition of the letters of George Selwyn at Castle Howard, a selection of which had been printed in the mid-nineteenth century.[91] Research students were an obvious and ready source of additional manpower. He told Sandwich that

> I ... have now gone through my papers, transcripts, notes, etc., and arranged them. I was myself impressed by the mass I have, and have reached the conclusion that even were I to live another twenty years fully fit for work, I could not get through it all. I therefore think that the best thing I could do would be to organise a team from among my assistants and students, and with their help to get through the work.[92]

As in the 1930s, some of those who studied his special subject and wrote theses under his direction were assigned collections of documents. Two in particular followed Namier's own interests very closely: his first research student after the war, Frank Spencer, worked on the Walpole memoirs, 'with special reference to Walpole's political ideas'; while John Tomlinson produced an edition of 'selected papers of George Grenville, 1763–6', which in due course went into print.[93] But the scale of Namier's ambitions required something grander: an organisation of researchers given an institutional form, and backed by a funding body with deep pockets; such as had once seemed possible through Wedgwood's History of Parliament.

While the History of Parliament Trust slumbered Namier hatched a scheme of his own: to produce a comprehensive edition of the letters and papers of King George III. The project seems to have originated with his close friend Sir Owen Morshead, the royal librarian, who had heard that the University of Michigan intended to publish sections of the king's correspondence of which it possessed transcripts, and was concerned 'at the known inaccuracy of many of these transcripts and at their incompleteness'.[94] He and Namier decided to apply to the Pilgrim Trust for a grant. First, Morshead drew the trust's attention to the desirability of a comprehensive and authoritative edition of the king's letters and papers, which would draw on material in a variety of public and private collections. Then Namier briefed one of the trustees, the former cabinet secretary Thom Jones, who proposed that 'a small advisory panel', including Morshead and Namier, be set up to discuss with the trust's secretary, Lord Kilmaine, what could be done.[95]

When Kilmaine met Namier it transpired that what the professor had in view was something that would far exceed the trust's ability to finance, even if, as Namier emphasised, supplementary sources of funding would be sought. The project would create 'a large organisation in this country of paid research workers and a corresponding organisation in the USA. A work of some twenty to twenty-five volumes was contemplated and it might take as much as ten years to complete.' More specifically, Namier envisaged 'the team, under himself as director and editor-in chief, developing into almost a school of historical research on the period in question, in which young students would be proud to work for a part of their research programme.'[96] Namier's detailed description of the project prefigured, in many respects, what would be his conception of the History of Parliament when it was revived not long afterwards. It also shows that at this point he was interested as much in the functioning of government – crown and cabinet – as in the House of Commons; a shift in emphasis reflecting his recent work in modern European history, where, apart from his brief foray into the prosopography of the Frankfurt Parliament, he had concentrated on politics at the centre and the disastrous consequences of government action (or inaction):

From such a concentration and collation of material, results can be expected for British constitutional, imperial, parliamentary, naval and military history, etc., such as could never be achieved so long as this material remains dispersed, not properly examined or annotated, and much of it unpublished and even unknown … This would be a new venture in collective historical work. Every branch of science has its laboratories staffed by specialists working closely together under central direction; but historians are still expected to work in isolation, each ploughing his own furrow with a plough of truly archaic design … The organisation would become school for training young historians such as hardly exists anywhere at present.

At the same time, Namier had not forsaken the biographical approach. It was not in his nature to remove irons from the fire. He remained a member of the subcommittee on estates established by the British Committee of Historical Sciences; a body originally constituted from the historians who had led the academic opposition to Wedgwood in the 1930s, and were viewed by the History of Parliament trustees as the experts who would have to be involved if the project was to get under way again.[97] In the summer of 1947, before the George III project took shape, Namier had raised at the Anglo-American Conference of Historians in London the possibility of 'resuming work and co-operation' on House of Commons membership.[98] Interest was stirring: one of his own students was working on 'mercantile interests in the House of Commons, c.1710–13'; Neale was supervising theses on the composition of Elizabethan parliaments; at Yale Wallace Notestein had someone researching the personnel of the Long Parliament of Charles I; and even Neale's London colleague R. H. Tawney, best known as an economic historian, was 'anxious to get some studies of the membership of parliament'.

The History of Parliament revived

Meanwhile the History of Parliament Trust was at last lumbering into action. After Wedgwood's death in 1942 the trustees sought the advice of the eminent Anglo-Saxonist, Sir Frank Stenton, who was untainted by involvement in the war between Wedgwood and 'the professors'. He recommended stopping work until such time as a proper, academically respectable, history could be launched, preferably with public funds.[99] Soon afterwards Stenton joined the trust himself, and in 1948 he was charged with preparing a scheme for a cooperative history to be put before the treasury.[100] He sounded opinion across the historical profession. Neale was naturally to the fore: his major work on *The Elizabethan House of Commons* was about to appear.[101] He contacted Stenton in the hope of securing bursaries for postgraduate students (which was 'the way I always thought that the parliamentary history should be compiled').[102] Neale saw himself as the pre-eminent exponent of parliamentary prosopography.[103]

However, the historical profession, and the public at large, still identified Namier as the progenitor of the structural analysis of political history;[104] indeed, his reputation was such that people now spoke of 'Namierising' a subject, a conceit that Namier greatly enjoyed.[105] In Namier's case the trustees were not satisfied with receiving second-hand accounts of Stenton's conversations, and summoned Namier for direct discussions. He was, as usual, full of ideas. The prospect of substantial government funding for collaborative research was mouth-watering. To do the job properly would cost at least £100,000, and it was essential to have 'a central organisation under the direction of an editor-in-chief' to 'co-ordinate research in parliamentary history, which was at present proceeding in many universities (and in America) without the necessary consultation and authoritative guidance'.[106]

Stenton's recommendations followed the broad outlines of the plan laid down by Wedgwood's treasury committee.[107] The work should be organised around biographies of members, beginning with the Commons, and be divided into chronological sections, each under the direction of an expert. Individual sections should have an analytical introduction. At the same time Stenton retained elements of Wedgwood's didactic purpose by emphasising relevance and readability, and arguing that the introductions should add up to 'a history of parliament of a type which can be read by all manner of interested persons'. From this report, however, the trustees picked out only a few salient points: the biographical method; the chronological division into sections; and the recruitment of editors. Memories of previous conflicts deterred them from a more detailed prescription.

The Attlee government did not seem to need further detail: Attlee himself had been involved with the Wedgwood scheme at an early stage, and he and his cabinet were much more favourable to the idea of an officially sponsored history than were the Conservatives under Churchill, a contrast that had no effect whatsoever on Namier's political preferences.[108] In February 1951 the chancellor of the exchequer, Hugh Gaitskell, announced to the Commons a Treasury grant-in-aid to fund the history over the next twenty years, at £17,000 a year, to cover the costs of staff and publication (which would be undertaken by Her Majesty's Stationery Office).[109] Although in private senior treasury civil servants were 'horrified' by the likely expense, the decision was welcomed in parliament and in the press.[110]

A 'special correspondent' in *The Times* gave the trustees' authorised version, which stated that the history's 'prime objective' was 'to preserve a picture of the continuity of parliament and to set it in correct perspective within the constitution', and expressed the hope that the various sectional introductions 'will themselves form a readable history of parliament'.[111] In reality, however, the trustees were in no position to make such claims, having relinquished editorial control to the academics. Namier confidently told 'Jimmie' Fergusson, now Sir James Fergusson, keeper of the records of Scotland, to ignore anything he might read in newspapers: 'Everything is perfectly open for the historians engaged to determine.'[112]

By this time the list of 'historians' whom Stenton had recruited had shrunk to four: Namier, Neale, the thirteenth-century specialist Goronwy Edwards, and another medievalist, the legal historian Theodore Plucknett. Edwards was the director of London University's Institute of Historical Research, and had promised the history house-room. Plucknett was there to represent the interests of constitutional historians, and did not take responsibility for any of the research work. At a meeting in May 1951, these four, together with Stenton, unilaterally organised themselves into an 'editorial board'. It quickly became clear that the dominant voices would belong to Namier and Neale. Stenton, who took the role of chairman, was anxious not to upset the apple cart; Plucknett had no real interest in the biographical work and did not exert himself, while Edwards, despite his stature in the historical profession, was self-effacing in such assertive company.

The first decision taken by the editorial board was to divide the history into three broad 'provinces', medieval, early modern and modern (1679–onwards), under the overall supervision, respectively, of Edwards, Neale and Namier. This avoided the difficulties which would invariably have followed the appointment of either of the two great mastodons of the project as editor-in-chief, for it gave both Neale and Namier the opportunity to direct huge tracts of the history in the way they saw fit.[113] Namier was not entirely satisfied, however, and made an issue of the terminal date. There had been an unspoken assumption on all sides that the history would end with the Great Reform Act, as had been the case in the project's first incarnation, but Namier pushed for 1900, 'because he finds that there is a great deal of work in progress on nineteenth-century parliamentary history, but it is largely unco-ordinated, and he therefore feels that if it were linked up with the parliamentary history a valuable measure of co-ordination would be secured'.[114] He continued for several years to urge this chronological extension, until it became clear that the grant-in-aid was not infinitely elastic, and the work of producing biographies much more arduous than he had envisaged. It was indicative of the ambition which characterised his attitude to the history. He had at last found a vehicle for collaborative history, and the fuel with which to run it, and was determined that it should be driven as far and as fast as possible. His other historical interests were now left behind. 'The rest of my life', he declared, 'will be spent on the history of parliament.'[115]

Starting up

Once the History of Parliament got under way the pace of Namier's life became even more hectic, and his workload even heavier, a situation he embraced despite the fact that his health was worsening. His responsibilities as an editor were not so generously remunerated as to permit him to retire early from Manchester. During term-time he came down to London for 'long week-ends' every three weeks or so, returning in effect to the same kind of schedule that had obtained when he had divided his time between the university and the Zionist Organisation.[116] The effort was exhausting. In November 1952, having been ordered by his doctor to return to London for 'rest and treatment', he confided to a friend that he had been 'thoroughly unwell for two months, and ill for the last fortnight', adding, with his habitual fatalism, 'I am a fool to take on so much work, but perhaps it is best to die in harness.'[117]

He set up camp in London and gathered a team around him. His research notes, including the famed card-index, were transferred from Manchester to the Institute. Two assistants were engaged, John Brooke and Valerie Baum, both products of his special subject class.[118] Mrs Baum was officially appointed as his secretary but in practice became involved in research as well as typing letters and arranging meetings.[119] Ian Christie, an assistant lecturer at University College, London, who had secured an introduction through his Oxford tutor, Alan Taylor, was in and out of the office,[120] as was a young New Zealander, John Owen, then completing his doctorate at Oxford on the political history of the 1740s. Owen would later describe this period as the 'halcyon days' of the project.[121] Like Neale, Namier also brought in current research students, getting them to write theses on particular sets of MPs or constituencies.

This relocation meant that as far as the eighteenth-century was concerned Namier had to 'pass into a state of hibernation when I have to go ... north', and he began to resent the demands of the university more and more.[122] In 1952 he was able to give notice, since he would be 65 in the following June. The replacement process had its frictions, which did nothing to diminish his pleasure at leaving a city which he had never liked. The vice-chancellor, Sir John Stopford, wrote out of courtesy to ask him about likely candidates, and received in return an extensive list, with a candid, but not unkind, assessment of their qualities. Namier casually mentioned that he had already made private inquiries of several individuals, including Lucy Sutherland, Alan Taylor and Edward Hughes, which might well have been regarded as jumping the gun.[123] Although the departmental head continued to consult Namier, Stopford went elsewhere for names of potential candidates,[124] and when, eventually, the university appointed Albert Goodwin, an Oxford historian of eighteenth-century France with comparatively few publications, Namier commented sourly:

I have no views on the choice of my successor. My own final recommendations were not taken, nor was I consulted about him. If, in the next few years, he does something remarkable, their choice will be justified; but if he does nothing he will be elected to an Oxford professorship.[125]

He wrote to one candidate whom he had canvassed: 'I hear you went up to Manchester and seemed not to have liked the looks of the place. I am not astonished. I should not exchange comfortable rooms in a Cambridge college for digs in Manchester.'[126]

The fact that neither trustees nor editorial board had prescribed in detail how the History of Parliament would be written encouraged Namier to take the broadest possible view of his task. By nature his approach to historical research was empirical: one went to the evidence to discover what questions needed to be asked. He told one of his research students to be open to 'the things which no one can foresee before going through the material': this 'applied to every bit of my *Structure of politics* when I first took it in hand, and this is true whenever you break new ground'.[127] And he was himself far from clear about what he intended to do with the information which the History would collect. His letters give the impression that he was driven by the desire to find out everything about everything in his chosen period.[128]

Namier talked much of the 'sociological' character of the work, but was no more precise about its meaning than he had been in the 1920s. On one occasion, when questioned by a potential contributor, 'the board explained that it was used, for want of a better word, to indicate that they expected the introductory portion of each section of the History to be intimately related to the accompanying biographies'.[129] Nonetheless, the term continued to appear in publicity material: the biographies would 'elicit facts of sociological interest' and 'contribute new knowledge to social history'.[130] But even this formulation was too prosaic for Namier: he heralded the History as in essence 'a demographic study', which would offer 'a new pattern of aggregate character'.[131]

This expansive vision was at odds with the approach adopted by other editors, especially Neale, whose conception of the History was more limited, and more rigorously political. Although he had tolerated the inclusion of jargon about 'sociology' in order to secure funds, Neale became apprehensive once the money was banked. Namier's ambition threatened to derail the project. Editorial board minutes reveal conflict between Neale and Namier over the form the History should take. Neale insisted on brief biographies, perhaps only 'skeleton' entries, to establish key facts about each member's background and career, information which could then be tabulated and analysed quantitatively; something closer to the traditional prosopography practised by the German classicists of the nineteenth century. Namier disdained such 'Who's who' biographies, arguing for a literary style that would enable the author to convey 'whatever is most interesting or important in the life of the Member'. He was equally dismissive about tables, of which, he declared, he neither knew, nor wanted to know, anything.

Undoubtedly, there were personal issues: observers detected an intense mutual dislike, which could break out over trivialities.[132] Neale was unhappy that Namier had quickly secured the appointment of assistants, and a block grant for expenses, which seemed like favouritism.[133] But there was a wider question, namely the consequences of Namier's unconstrained passion for research on the prospect of meeting deadlines. The timescale was already formidably tight, and in attempting to satisfy the scepticism of Treasury civil servants the trustees were tendering hostages to fortune. Their first report, in 1952, embodied a warning from the editorial board that producing such a quantity of biographies required time, and that all would have to be written before surveys could be attempted, but the Treasury were still told to expect four printed volumes by 1958.[134] The following year's report stated that Namier and Neale each had about 1,500 biographies (three-quarters of their quota) in 'outline form' ready to be written up.[135] While this was true, at least in Namier's case, it ignored – perhaps deliberately – the issue of how long the writing up would take.

Anxiety over progress and completion dates would come back to haunt Namier and blight the last years of his life, but once the History had been launched he moved ahead with full steam. It was important to think beyond the period 1754–90, which he had chosen for his 'home farm', and he quickly recruited his old friend Romney Sedgwick to start work on the 1715–54 section as soon as Sedgwick retired from the civil service, with Arthur Aspinall of Reading University to follow on from 1790 into the early nineteenth century. For 1689–1714 the obvious choice was the Cambridge historian J. H. Plumb, who as a research pupil of G. M. Trevelyan in the 1930s had been given responsibility for this period by Wedgwood. Namier wrote to him, recalling their only previous meeting, when Plumb was beginning his research, an occasion which Plumb told others had been marked on Namier's part by a brusqueness bordering on contempt, but of which Namier evidently had a very different recollection.[136] Plumb gave every indication of being keen to help, and Namier came to regard him not only as the designated editor for 1689–1714, but as an important ally whose advice was essential on a period about which Namier felt himself ignorant.[137] However, Plumb was unwilling to commit. He never signed a contract, and although attending editors' meetings always assured the secretary in advance that he would have nothing to report.[138]

Establishing a team and identifying editors for the other modern sections were only the first steps. Namier envisaged a structure of cooperation between scholars that would be much more far-reaching. He began by milking contacts on both sides of the Atlantic.[139] But this was to be more than a bringing together of friends, colleagues and students. Namier described it as 'an enormous enterprise of "collective research"', involving the development of 'quite a new technique'.[140] He hoped to organise a national network, which he would coordinate – if not direct – and in an echo of the Wedgwood scheme, sought to involve local archivists and record societies, as well as amateur historians of the right sort, including school-teachers who had received postgraduate training in research techniques.[141] It was just the kind of enterprise to raise the hackles of those who suspected him of harbouring a desire, even a psychological need, to dominate the English historical profession.

In the summer of 1951, after he had addressed the Anglo-American Conference of Historians in London on the necessity for 'collective research' to cope with the 'bewildering variety of sources' confronting political, economic and social historians, he hosted a 'private meeting' of the 'modern historians' attending.[142] 'What I want us all to do', he told those he invited,

> is to state what each of us, or our assistants and pupils, are doing, or propose to do, in the field of parliamentary history; and what help each of us can give to the others, and would like to receive from them. Thus everyone working on a collection of documents … knowing what others require, will be able to inform them whenever he comes across something of importance to them … such mutual information may enable us fruitfully to co-ordinate, instead of duplicating, our work.[143]

In the following summer he convened a 'conference of parliamentary historians' – around eighty in total – to take place alongside the Anglo-American.[144]

He was also keen to preach the word on his travels.[145] He turned an invitation to lecture in Dublin in 1953 into an expedition which combined scoping archives with eliciting help from Irish academics. He had been in Ireland before, staying with friends in country houses. This time he set himself up in Dublin, having obtained a recommendation of a temperance hotel, suitable for a teetotaller who abhorred 'the smell of stale beer'.[146] During his stay in the city he looked in at the manuscripts room of the National Library and talked to university staff. Then, after a brief social visit to the 2nd Lord Moyne at Knockmaroon House, just beyond the Phoenix Park, he travelled up to Belfast.[147] However, he made few useful contacts.[148] Indeed, in terms of historical research he concluded that Ireland was still 'a backwater, unless you wish to study Irish history'.[149]

Just as disappointing, and in the long run more significant in signalling what would prove to be the limits of academic interest in the History, were visits made in the autumn of 1951 to Cambridge and Oxford. The network of collaborators built up through pre-existing personal connections could take him only so far; it was of prime importance to engage the two great universities. At first, prospects seemed

good. Given the slender resources available for research in arts and humanities subjects the grant to the History was bound to excite interest, and unsolicited inquiries
poured in. Yet while the magnetic attraction of money persuaded some to swallow
their personal dislike for Namier and distaste at submitting to his direction, others
complained. The treasury announcement, and Namier's proprietorial declarations
about the way it would be used, had aroused hostility. Namier, some said, was hoard-
ing public funds for his own benefit.

His appearance in Cambridge had less impact than he had hoped largely because
the occasion was in effect hijacked by Plumb and the nineteenth-century specialist
George Kitson Clark (whose first book, twenty years earlier, Namier had savaged).
Only selected members of the history faculty were invited to hear the great man, and
there was no opportunity for a general evangelisation.[150] Kitson Clark wrote an awkward letter to Herbert Butterfield at Peterhouse, a historian who regarded Namier
as an enemy, to inform Butterfield of the meeting, which Kitson Clark assumed he
would not wish to attend.[151] In his anxiety Kitson Clark seemed almost to disassociate
himself from the project: he himself disliked the very idea of collaborative research,
and feared that it would lead to the exploitation of research students.[152]

The Oxford visit was a disaster. Namier was invited to address an 'eighteenth-
century group' at Keble, and insisted on banging his recruiting drum. He gave his
usual plea for 'collective research'. A distinction should be made in history between
'basic preparatory work', which was 'best done collectively and once and for all' and
the 'superstructure', the 'work that everyone has to do for himself'. He explained that
'individuals can deal with individuals and with individual transactions, anything
approaching demography can better be done by teams'. He then described the way
the History was shaping up and concluded with a challenge: 'What was Oxford going
to do about it?'[153] The response shook him. Several speakers, picking up the distinction between 'basic work' and 'superstructure', and assuming that research students
and assistants would merely be making bricks for senior scholars to lay, questioned
whether it was really appropriate for young researchers to be harnessed in teams –
one even used the phrase 'galley slaves'[154] – rather than choosing their own subjects
to follow in their own way: a much better intellectual training, even if the immediate
results might not be so useful to the academic world at large.

Namier reacted badly. He took the comments as a personal attack, and was outraged by the 'disgraceful insinuation' that he intended to profit from the sweat of
others, like some academic gang-master.[155] To some extent, he had laid himself
open to the charge by talking about 'basic preparatory work', and by an observation beforehand at dinner, likening his section of the History to 'the great teams of
German scientists, working together on vital problems', which allowed others to

infer that he was distinguishing between 'collaborators', who could make a real intellectual contribution, and 'assistants', labouring under instruction.[156] Even though Namier did not regard his assistants as laboratory technicians, or treat them as such, there is no doubt that he saw them as contributing to the work he had in view rather than striking out on their own. He had an almost paternal concern for the welfare and career prospects of his research pupils, but nonetheless regarded a good pupil as a valuable asset and a great help to the supervisor's own research.[157] Their theses bore the same relation to published history as tadpoles did to frogs, and 'in another way the theses written here are tadpoles; the subjects are selected to fit into the pattern of our work', although they did also 'serve a purpose for the student' who was in effect doing an apprenticeship.[158]

Lady Namier depicted the episode as an unprovoked assault by the unmannerly young on a vulnerable elderly man, the equivalent of the petty 'persecution' Namier had recently undergone at the hands of an officious ticket-collector in Manchester, which had driven him to take legal action. Overworked, ill, and increasingly deaf, her husband had been subjected to 'harsh abuse'. It was yet another indication of the decay of civilisation in the post-war world, and (though she did not say so explicitly) another example of Oxford's vindictive hostility to one of its most distinguished sons.[159]

Those who were present, including friends of Namier, remembered differently. There was no riot of abuse, but a series of observations from several people genuinely taking issue with Namier's ideas. And others had weighed in on Namier's behalf. Lucy Sutherland thought that Julia's description of her husband as 'vulnerable and perplexed', was some way from the truth. Another witness, J. S. Bromley, who had the unenviable task of acting as Namier's host at Keble, remembered Namier giving as good as he got in discussion, having already fired himself up in advance by the memory of past rejection: even before the seminar he had declared himself to be '*le doyen des refusés*'.[160]

After the event, three of Namier's critics wrote to apologise for any misunderstanding, including his old friend E. T. ('Bill') Williams of Balliol.[161] Namier accepted their explanations and attributed everything that had gone wrong to the increasing deafness in his right ear, which meant that 'in future … I must not address any meetings followed by discussion in which I cannot do full justice to myself, to others, or to the subject'. Nevertheless, he felt that he had 'completely failed' in the object of his visit.[162] To Williams, who admitted having set the ball rolling 'just to have an argument', Namier wrote more personally.[163] He felt that Williams of all people, as editor of the *Dictionary of National Biography*, should have understood the seriousness of what the History was trying to do.

I did not come to Oxford for argument and fun, but to enlist co-operation; and I was defeated by 'affection and wickedness' as much as by captious, sabotaging opposition. I admit frankly that I did not expect such a reception: I am old and tired, and have too much work on my hands and therefore invariably refuse invitations to address societies. On this occasion I made an exception.

There were other problems. Sections in the modern province were making little progress: Sedgwick did not begin work until 1954; Plumb did not start at all; and Aspinall was using up funds to finance the collection of research materials without producing biographies. Namier was also irritated by a quarrel which broke out between the History and its Scottish equivalent, the Committee on the History of Parliament, originally established in 1936 as an offshoot of Wedgwood's scheme.[164] It had then been agreed that the histories of the two parliaments would proceed in parallel until the union of 1707, after which the Scottish story merged into the English. However, Wedgwood had insisted on breaking the volumes of the Westminster history at 1714 rather than 1707, overriding the arguments of lawyers on the Scottish committee that the union was a voluntary arrangement producing a new constitutional entity, the kingdom of Great Britain. After the announcement of the Treasury grant the dispute was reopened. For the Scots it was a matter of recognising a simple legal truth, though they were also concerned at the potential political profit for Scottish nationalists from an example of casual English arrogance. By contrast, for the English editorial board parliamentary history was essentially political, or even 'sociological', rather than constitutional: as Namier put it, the period 1689–1714

> forms one region, with one political 'climate'. There are peaks within it, but it is one system. The death of Queen Anne and the accession of the Hanoverians are events which change the political climate of Great Britain … they form a dividing line.[165]

There was no resolution, partly thanks to Namier's unhelpful interventions, which were driven by a belief that members of the Scottish committee were acting from narrow nationalistic motives. When Stenton proposed a diplomatic visit to Edinburgh, Namier was enraged at what seemed to be a pandering to prejudice, melodramatically comparing Stenton's journey north to Chamberlain's flight to Berchtesgaden.[166] The two histories thus proceeded separately, and Namier was unable to get the cooperation from Scottish scholars that he recognised as essential.

Worse still, the quarrel took on a personal dimension for him, causing a rupture with 'Jimmie' Fergusson, whom he had nominated as one of his literary executors.[167] From the first, Namier had tried to involve Fergusson in his section of the History.[168] But their correspondence reflected the same differences of view that characterised relations between the editorial board and the Scottish committee, and quickly took on a very frosty air. In March 1953 Namier changed his will, in response to 'the sharp differences we are having with the Scots and I myself with Fergusson'. Lucy Sutherland took over the executor's role.[169] Namier did not give up his attempt to persuade Fergusson to participate in the History and in the following summer invited himself and Julia to weekend with the Fergussons at their country home, Kilkerran House in Ayrshire. Dreading another verbal assault, Fergusson was pleasantly surprised that the visit passed with no mention of parliamentary history:

> My wife, who of course has known him for years, said to me afterwards that she found him definitely 'mellowed' and much gentler than of yore, and ascribed this to (a) Lady Namier, who is a perfectly delightful person (b) advancing years, and (c) the recognition of his work, and worth … We agreed that we both saw signs of his ageing – he is actually only 65.[170]

On the Monday, however, Namier came to see Fergusson in Edinburgh, in his office in Register House, and spent three hours discussing their differences. Fergusson reported that 'we had it out fairly, but without heat (the old Namier would, I think, have lost his temper several times!)'.[171]

Down to work

Namier threw himself into the work of his own section, despite the fact that the writer's cramp from which he had been suffering for many years had now become crippling: 'I am practically unable to write with my own hand', he complained in 1951. 'I do my work on the typewriter with my left.'[172] Secretarial assistance was one way of coping, and when there was no secretary present, at home in the evenings or during archival expeditions, Julia stood in. Namier was also keen on securing photostats or microfilm copies of documents where possible, to avoid the difficulty of transcription. In archives without suitable photographic equipment, he relied on his extraordinary ability to commit stupendous quantities of material to memory.[173]

What he had embarked upon was effectively a campaign to 'comb out the entire country' for manuscripts. The scale of his ambition is clear from a scheme which he and 'Lefty' Lewis unsuccessfully put to the Ford Foundation in 1953: an application for funds (the astronomical sum of $100,000 a year for three years) to set up an organisation based in 'an office in Bloomsbury', which would track down materials for the 'intellectual, social [and] political history' of the second half of the eighteenth century, to benefit both the History of Parliament and Lewis's monumental edition of Horace Walpole's correspondence, which had just reached volume 16 of a projected 48. Had the scheme got off the ground, there would have been a staff of ten research assistants, supervised by a director (presumably Namier himself).[174]

In his researches for the History Namier continued to set a premium on material in private hands, collections which had rarely if ever been used by historians and were in danger of dispersal.[175] A wellspring of influence was available to the History as a publicly funded institution numbering peers and MPs among its trustees and well-wishers. In addition, Namier exploited every contact of his own. An obliging owner who had already welcomed him would be asked to approach another 'possible'.[176] He wrote out of the blue to aristocratic acquaintances, however remote the association,[177] and to the offspring of men he had known in Oxford or worked alongside in the Foreign Office.[178] In one case, the earl of Coventry, the connection was even more strained: "I know an aunt of the present Lord Coventry, a most charming and intelligent woman. She was then Lady Suffield; I believe she has since remarried, but I have not seen her for years.'[179] If the History of Parliament trustees and his own address book failed him, he relied on whomsoever he could find in his own and in Julia's circle to effect an introduction. If all else failed he would summon Sir Owen Morshead at Windsor Castle to bring the weight of his name, and his letterhead, to bear.[180]

Some papers were sent up to the History's offices, or deposited temporarily in the University of London Library or the Public Record Office for the exclusive use of Namier and his assistants, a privilege which aroused envious resentment among some outsiders. Most had to be viewed *in situ*. These expeditions around the country, with Julia driving and Namier plotting journeys with the aid of an eighteenth-century 'road book',[181] drained both their energies. Julia found the day trips from London to places in the home counties particularly exhausting,[182] but in fact the scale of the longer 'circuits', even if more leisurely in terms of travel, and punctuated by restorative weekend visits to friends, made heavier cumulative demands.

The elaborate itineraries can be pieced together from their letters. In 1951, they journeyed extensively in Buckinghamshire, Hampshire, East Anglia, the Midlands and the north. The following year they took another tour of record offices in midland counties, going on to north Wales, then spent time in the north of England, travelling over 1,000 miles in all. A month's rest, and they were off again to Warwick, followed by peregrinations in Buckinghamshire and Essex. In November 1952 Namier's health collapsed, but despite spending weeks in bed, and admitting that he was struggling under 'an avalanche of work', he soon set out again.[183] Having driven around East Anglia, he and Julia spent a further month on the road in Shropshire, Yorkshire and Scotland, venturing as far north as Dunvegan Castle on Skye, a journey of over two thousand miles in total, then in September made an extended 'western circuit' to

Hampshire, Sussex, Wiltshire, Gloucestershire and Somerset. Namier confessed that 'I can hardly catch breath'.[184] But he did not slow his pace.

The following year it was Lincoln in January, then Sussex in the spring, and westwards to Wiltshire, Somerset, Dorset, Devon and Cornwall. Although he and Julia agreed that they should 'cut down the amount of work and travel we undertake', in July 1954 they were in the east midlands, and in August Shropshire and the Welsh borders, whereupon Namier was struck down again, with fibrositis and attacks of sciatica.[185] He passed a difficult winter, and began to worry about his heart, but a restful holiday in Switzerland, the first he had taken for a long time, restored mind and body sufficiently for another long northern trek in the autumn, to Yorkshire and Northumberland, and on to the north-east of Scotland.[186]

Despite the fatigue, Namier thoroughly enjoyed these tours: indeed, he was in his element, doing what he enjoyed most and hobnobbing with the aristocracy. He was much better placed now than he had been as a freelance researcher in the 1920s and 1930s. A few doors remained closed: Badminton and Berkeley Castle were impregnable; at Boconnoc House in Cornwall he arrived at the appointed time only to be told that the manuscripts were unavailable.[187] But these were exceptions. Other muniment rooms, previously barred, disclosed their contents. Namier was able to investigate the archival riches held by the dukes of Rutland at Belvoir Castle, while at Chatsworth the duke of Devonshire gave him 'full permission to have anything I want … copied'.[188] The official standing of the History, his own reputation, and Julia's charm, meant that he was greeted by the owners as an honoured guest, and on terms of familiarity, even though he may still have arrived in a suit. Frequently, he stayed overnight, or even for the weekend, and often thanked his hosts with copies of his books.

In London he was tied to a strict office routine, broken up by lunches with Sedgwick at a nearby Italian restaurant, and by supervisions with a clutch of research students. Some were pupils from Manchester whom he had started off before retirement. Others came through friends in different universities, with Namier acting as external supervisor under special dispensation. His weekly seminar at the Institute of Historical Research, nominally on 'British parliamentary history in the second half of the eighteenth century', was in effect an extension of the work of the History, and brought collaborators and students together.[189] At last he was doing what he had always thought was his real *métier*, training young historians. However, it all seemed to have come rather late, what with age, infirmity and the unremitting demands being made upon him.

The Romanes and other lectures

Namier felt that he had been entirely taken over by the History of Parliament. Its demands were 'unceasing ... and all my life has now to be planned accordingly'.[190] At different times he declared himself to be 'overwhelmed' or 'confused and oppressed', and he routinely described the History as his very own 'Frankenstein's monster'.[191] 'I am harder worked than ever I was in my life', he told Morshead.[192] When an American wrote to him about Munich he replied wearily that he only had time for British parliamentary history, though he was unwilling to close the door entirely on his other interests: 'I hope I may some day be able to go back to pre-1939 diplomatic history, though I think with awe of the mountains of material which will have grown up by then. And I am now 65, and certainly shall not be able to leave parliamentary history before I am 70.'[193] Even this forecast would prove wildly over-optimistic.

However, the weight of the History did not stop him from assuming new responsibilities. Although rejecting invitations to visit universities in America,[194] he joined editorial boards which required him to travel long distances to meetings, including the Paris-based edition of the works of Alexis de Tocqueville. He turned down a stream of requests to review books, agreeing only to take on commissions that particularly interested him or gave him the chance to promote the work of friends, but rarely refused a request for a public lecture, as long as the occasion was sufficiently grand. It was equally impossible for him to renounce the habit of devising new projects. Editions of texts were still a high priority, even if they now devolved on assistants and students.[195] He was loath to relinquish completely the ambition of editing the Sandwich manuscripts, but did finally abandon his proposed Selwyn edition after a visit to Castle Howard to re-examine the papers. He would 'have to limit myself *more or less* to the political and parliamentary aspects of eighteenth-century history'.[196] The qualification 'more or less' speaks volumes.

Other eighteenth-century projects suffered. He could make no progress with the Ford Lectures, which weighed heavily on his conscience.[197] Biographical studies of Lord Shelburne and the duke of Devonshire were stillborn.[198] On the other hand, the establishment of the History of Parliament did breathe life into an enterprise of an even older vintage, the extended narrative of British politics for which *The structure of politics* had been an extended introduction, and *England in the age of the American revolution* the first instalment. This was now reconfigured as a collaborative enterprise, to run from 1754 to 1784, and to serve as a complement to the 'analytical survey' in the History of Parliament volumes.[199] Namier himself would take the story forward with volumes on the ministries of Grenville (which he claimed to have started)[200] and Rockingham; Brooke would pick up the baton in 1768, followed by Eric Robson and

Ian Christie.[201] There was a further complication in that Namier now felt that these volumes could not deal in detail with general elections (as he had done in *England in the age*), which would have to be covered separately. He himself would take the elections of 1754, 1761 and 1768.[202] Namier was able to set up the series with Macmillan, and in 1956 John Brooke's study of the Chatham administration appeared, explicitly 'a development and expansion' of Namier's ideas.[203] Two years later came Christie's account of 1780–82, but nothing further appeared in Namier's lifetime.[204]

Although he was producing no new books, other than compilations of essays and reviews, Namier's public lectures fed his reputation. The first was in many respects the most important and at the time the most successful: the Romanes Lecture, delivered in Oxford in May 1952. This was a great event in the university's calendar, a public lecture in the Sheldonian Theatre, which constituted an opportunity for Oxford to recognise a leading figure in any discipline. The first lecturer, in 1891, was Gladstone, and Namier's immediate predecessors were the former cabinet secretary, Lord Hankey and the Nobel prize-winning physicist Sir John Cockroft. Namier described it as 'the "blue ribbon" of Oxford', and was acutely conscious both of the honour, and the opportunity to show Oxford what it had missed by refusing him the regius chair.[205] In consequence, he was unusually nervous about his own capacity to supply what was expected.

The lecture marked a return to the structural analysis of the House of Commons that Namier had pioneered in his first books and now intended to take much further through the History of Parliament. But the chronological scope of the lecture was much broader. He was conscious that his early writings, for all their revolutionary intent and dramatic impact, had not succeeded in painting out the traditional interpretation of eighteenth-century politics. Elements of the old orthodoxy still held attractions for university teachers. So in his lecture Namier intended to meet unbelievers head-on; to explain the structure of the House of Commons across the entire eighteenth and early nineteenth centuries and provide a chronology for the 'rise of party'.

For Namier, the emergence of Liberal and Conservative parties in nineteenth-century Britain had created the modern version of parliamentary government, with the monarch 'placed above parties and politics' while the prime minister and government 'took rise from parliament'. The peculiar excellence of the British system derived from the fact that this arrangement had developed historically, as the outcome of 'concrete factors'.[206] In the eighteenth century, without organised parties, a 'mixed' constitution prevailed, in which the monarch enjoyed very considerable power, especially in choosing and replacing prime ministers. Britain was in transition from royal to parliamentary government, and although contemporaries eulogised the eighteenth-century constitution as uniquely effective in combining stable government with the preservation of liberty, they failed to appreciate the tensions and contradictions which only the appearance of a party system would resolve. Hence the confusion over George III's intentions and actions, and the mistaken belief among some commentators that he had begun his reign with an attempt to re-establish monarchical absolutism.[207]

Namier was stretching across the entire eighteenth century the picture he had drawn for the 1760s. The House of Commons, he argued, was divided into three broad groups: the 'king's friends', mainly placemen and pensioners, who supported every administration because it was the king's administration; the 'independent country gentlemen'; and 'the politicians', factions consisting of the associates and clients of ambitious aristocrats. Each ministry was a coalition of one or more set of 'politicians' with the 'king's friends'. Few if any of the factions acted like parties: they did not, for example, resign from office en bloc with their leaders or refuse to cooperate with men of different principles. The Grenvilles were a rare example of a 'party' in this sense, but the Rockinghams, about whose Whig principles so much had been said, were emphatically not (cue a further jab at Burke).[208]

Pronouncing on periods in which he did not feel at home was an unnerving experience for Namier, and his response to the challenge reveals a side of his character that most people did not see: the anxiety that lay behind his booming self-confidence.[209] He was fully aware of the perils of employing a broad brush,[210] and generalising over periods which he had neither researched nor taught. (At Manchester he had avoided lecturing on English history before 1754 or after 1784 since he would have had to depend on books that he found 'grievously wrong' for his own period.)[211] So he sought advice from all quarters, sending colleagues and friends drafts for comment and correction.[212] He even asked J. H. Plumb for a reading list, for 'my knowledge of whigs and tories before 1740, and certainly before 1741, is not sufficient'.[213] An American historian, Robert Walcott, had begun to question the reality of parties in Queen Anne's reign, but although Namier liked the sound of Walcott's work he still sent the draft of his lecture to Plumb for comment.[214]

In a detailed critique Plumb urged Namier to qualify categorical statements and to be careful not to dismiss party altogether: the whigs, Plumb thought, did have a strong identity and organisation before 1714, even if the Tory interest was amorphous. Moreover, up to a third of the House of Commons remained independent, so that the 'party' card was still worth playing by politicians in opposition. Namier duly modified his position, though not exactly along these lines. He accepted that 'Whig' and 'Tory' represented 'enduring types moulded by deeply ingrained differences in temperament and outlook' and that these entities corresponded to real divisions in the constituencies, based on religious differences, which endured long into the Hanoverian era; essentially conceding one of the points Trevelyan had made in his review of *The structure of politics*. But he denied that this party distinction meant much, if anything, in the House of Commons: 'hardly ever was there anything like strict party voting' (a point which in due course would be proved quite wrong). And after the Hanoverian succession, with Tories proscribed, all politicians had to call themselves Whigs. The opprobrious name of Tory, Namier wrote, was left to independent country gentlemen and urban radicals, until by mid-century the party labels, though still used for want of anything better, had become meaningless.[215]

Suppressing his doubts, Plumb reassured Namier that the lecture was a triumph, and had completely devastated the traditional landscape of eighteenth-century politics. It was 'a magnificent and authoritative statement which will become the basic theorem for eighteenth-century parliamentary politics'.[216] Namier's Oxford friends were also very impressed: John Owen in particular was amused at the effect of the lecture on history tutors and anxious undergraduates. Namier had 'very obviously shattered the ingrained pre-conceptions of the entire audience ... It reminded me of a very large and weighty rock being thrown into an extremely stagnant pool.'[217] Namier's performance seemed to have completed his conquest of the 'whig interpretation'.

Namier's other public lectures were less impressive, and made less of a splash, though he was on good form when discussing the personality of George III in the Academy of Arts Lecture in 1953. While the burden of the lecture was to repeat his vindication of the king from Burke's accusations that George had acted unconstitutionally in attempting to revive a dead royal absolutism, the character sketch offered on this occasion was subtler and more sympathetic than that given in Namier's early works, doubtless a consequence of his immersion in George's correspondence, as well as his prolonged study of human psychology from a patient's perspective.[218]

On European history Namier had much less to say that was novel. His Creighton Lecture at the University of London in November 1952, was entitled 'Basic factors in nineteenth-century European history', a somewhat old-fashioned formulation, recalling – perhaps deliberately – A. F. Pollard's *Factors in modern history* (1921).[219] It was an hour-long rumination on the political problems created by the emergence of linguistic nationalism ('developed ... by uprooted urban intellectuals and ... communicated by them to the semi-educated both below and above their social strata'),[220] focusing on the demographic complexities of central and eastern Europe, and on the policies of the Prussian, Russian and Austrian governments. In the case of the Habsburgs, it represented no real advance on the analysis contained in Namier's chapter on the history of the Paris peace conference thirty years earlier. The one distinctive element was his constant comparison of ruling minorities in eastern Europe with the Protestant ascendancy class in Ireland. He had made similar allusions before but the image now assumed a central place in his argument, a reflection of his view that the British empire was now one of the political ruins of the twentieth century, 'destined to merge … into an as yet unnamed and ill-defined working community of English-speaking nations, centring on Washington rather than London'.[221]

The lecture was not a success, as some of those attending observed gleefully.[222] Lady Namier put this down to circumstances: Namier's poor health, and the university's failure to provide him with maps, or a proper lectern.[223] In truth, the text itself lacked sparkle and freshness; inevitably, perhaps, given his absorption in the History of Parliament. Previously Namier could always be relied on to startle his listeners with novelty, but now he was predictable, right down to his sermonising peroration, which cantered several well-worn hobby horses. First, he dismissed German bitterness about post-war ethnic cleansing as the frustration of would-be ethnic cleansers who had failed to accomplish what their enemies were doing more effectively; then, in a rambling coda, he dismissed as unsustainable any prospect of a western European superstate, and insisted that Britain would not in any case belong in one: 'All the past and all the present assign to this country a place in the community of English-speaking nations, which is now taking shape and without Britain would literally be deprived of its roots.'[224]

A similar staleness pervaded Namier's Ardilaun Lectures, read at Alexandra College, a Dublin girls' school, during his Irish journey in 1953. Again he spoke about nineteenth-century Europe, this time concentrating on France, and carrying his audience from the fall of Napoleon in 1814 through to the establishment of the Third Republic. Despite their location, the lectures were not without academic prestige and were customarily given by leading historians, often from Britain. Neale had lectured as far back as 1938. Namier's text does not survive, but the college magazine includes brief synopses, from which it seems clear that he presented no discoveries or new insights; however, the college's pupils were pleased enough, since he was 'covering a period of history of interest … for examination purposes'.[225]

Recognition

Public lectures, though gratifying occasions, were no substitute for the books that the world expected. When the long-suffering Jamie Hamilton brought out his firm's second collection of Namier's reprinted essays in 1955, *Personalities and powers*, there were the usual laudatory reviews from Namier's friends. But there was also a sense of disappointment. Plumb declared in the *Spectator* that no one 'since Macaulay, has been such a master of the historical essay', though in a back-handed compliment he wondered whether Namier's 'desire for meticulously accurate scholarship is best satisfied by a restricted theme'.[226] Small voices were also beginning to ask whether the History of Parliament was stifling Namier's creativity, and even whether the great enterprise was worth the immense effort he was putting in. But for the time being Namier could enjoy his fame.[227]

He was now an important public figure. Scholars in Europe and America studied his work as an exemplar of the historian's craft;[228] and he was written about in newspapers and weekly magazines as a celebrity as well as an academic, described in one article as 'the Great Cham of history', a Johnsonian allusion which greatly amused friends and colleagues.[229] He was also in demand as a broadcaster on the Third Programme, though he could not always find time to prepare as thoroughly as he wished, and was coy about speaking 'extempore'.[230] It took some time for producers and controllers at the BBC to feel comfortable with him: when his name was first put forward, just after the war, his *idées fixes*, especially his Zionist loyalties, and the 'jarring quality' of his accent, counted against him.[231] Early attempts were not successful, and he had to be reminded of 'the necessity of a loose, conversational style in writing for broadcasting'.[232] But he was keen to continue, and eventually his producer, Anna Kallin, thought she had 'got the trick of putting over [his] voice'.[233]

He even made an appearance in fiction. In 1951 the detective-story writer Cyril Hare set his novel *An English murder* in a remote country house cut off by winter snows, in which one of the house-guests is a visiting historian, Dr Wenceslaus Bottwink, a central European Jew, closeted in the attic poring over 'confidential letters written … by Lord Bute during the first three years of the reign of George III'. In the book Bottwink is the subject of a certain amount of prejudice, and like Namier has the reputation of being a crashing bore, especially at the breakfast table, since he does not appreciate the nuances of English etiquette and insists on talking about his work. As one character observes, 'Once let this fellow start talking, there was no stopping him … It was more than one could stand at this hour of the day.' Hare also poked fun at the recherché nature of Bottwink's research: his great discovery that was 'destined to confound all the experts – to the number of at least half a dozen – who were capable of understanding its significance'.[234] But overall Bottwink is portrayed sympathetically, and ends up solving the case.

There were also more tangible forms of public recognition: honorary degrees in Cambridge, Durham, Oxford and Rome. But the greatest pleasure came from his knighthood in 1952. He and Julia had already gloried in attending garden parties at Buckingham Palace, where 'we gaily paddled about in scintillating company'.[235] The news of the honour came as a wonderful surprise, the culmination of the Namiers' social ambitions, and was further enhanced by an avalanche of congratulatory letters and telegrams. In reassuring one correspondent that he would not pull rank, Namier wrote: 'Surely you will not go on addressing me as "Dear Sir Lewis" but as you did hitherto, "Dear Namier"'.[236] Nonetheless, he greatly enjoyed his new status. At Buckingham Palace he was delighted to find himself standing in line next to Arnold Lunn, and after being dubbed went off with Julia to drink champagne at a small party which Bob Boothby gave for Namier and another recipient of knighthood, the author Compton Mackenzie: 'They could hardly have been a more incongruous couple', Boothby recalled, 'but they got on like a house on fire. At the end Lewis Namier said, "And now the knights must go home to wash the dishes."'[237]

A similar peak of gratification, this time a recognition by other historians of his achievements, came in April 1956, when Namier was presented with a volume of essays assembled in his honour – he did not approve of its being called a Festschrift, wanting an English rather than a German word.[238] It was edited by Alan Taylor and Richard Pares and published by Macmillan. The contributors were all historians whom he regarded as close friends, and would have considered his peers. There were pieces by Pares, Lucy Sutherland, and Romney Sedgwick (a short collection of edited letters from Pitt the elder to Bute, which was emblematic of the times they had spent working together). Jimmie Fergusson and Arthur Aspinall both submitted essays despite recent quarrels with Namier, and the others on the list included Hugh Trevor-Roper, Ted Carr and Sir John Wheeler-Bennett. Subjects ranged from Oliver Cromwell's parliaments (Trevor-Roper) to the First World War (Taylor and Wheeler-Bennett), and the brief preface paid a fulsome tribute to Namier's qualities as a historian. He was said to be the master of both the microscope and the telescope, and an artist in prose. There was even a reference to the notorious 'salutary stringency of his reviews', though qualified by the observation that he also 'judged himself ... rigorously, accepting correction as readily as he bestows it on others.'[239] To complete Namier's pleasure the book was presented at a reception in Balliol. Namier confessed that he was 'deeply moved', and in his reply recalled the formative influence of the college, and of A. L. Smith in particular, but even on this occasion he could not entirely suppress his anxieties, and ended on a valetudinarian note: 'Proud as I feel on this occasion, I also feel very humble because I realise that only part of the tribute is to work done and delivered. The rest is on credit, and it is not easy to play the part of a promising young man at the age of 68.'[240]

Notes

1 Irina Prehn to Constance Babington Smith, 19 Sept. 1980 (Babington Smith).
2 Julia to Constance Babington Smith, 7 Oct. 1955 (Babington Smith); reminiscence of Barbara Ellis 4 Nov. 1979 (ibid.).

3 In order to telephone he had to go to Max Beloff's house nearby (Namier to Berl Locker, 27 Sept. 1945 (CZA, Namier papers, A312\50)).

4 Julia Namier to Lucy Sutherland, 8 May 1951 (Bodl., Sutherland papers, box 9).

5 *Namier*, 274, 283.

6 Namier to Basil Liddell Hart, 4 Jan. 1951 (LH, 1/539/42).

7 Cooper to McFarlane, 18 Jan. 1948 (Trinity College, Oxford, Cooper papers, DD 279/I).

8 Eric Christiansen, obituary of P. H. Williams, *New College Record* (2013), 137–8.

9 Cooper to McFarlane, 10 July 1948 (Trinity College, Oxford, DD279/I).

10 Isaiah Berlin recorded a particularly fine example dating from Namier's visits to Oxford for the Waynflete Lectures (*Personal impressions* (1980), 77).

11 The candidate concerned was the theologian, and historian of eighteenth-century France, J. M. Thompson: B. H. Sumner to Charles Webster, 9 Feb. 1946 (LSE, Webster papers, 1/26/9).

12 Cooper to McFarlane 18 Jan., 10 Feb., 13 Mar., 17 May 1948 (Trinity College, Oxford, DD279/I). Cooper offered a more generous view in 'Recollections of Namier', *Oxford Magazine*, 3 Nov. 1960, and in a review of Lady Namier's biography, *Listener*, 1 July 1971.

13 Information from Kenneth Hardman.

14 Information from Alan Hardy.

15 Namier to Donald Pennington, 17 May 1954 (HPT, N–59); *Manchester Guardian*, 17 May 1954.

16 Namier to H. N. Fieldhouse, 28 Feb. 1955 (HPT, N–60).

17 Cooper, 'Recollections of Namier'; Betty Kemp to Cooper, 4 Nov. 1960 (Trinity College, Oxford, Cooper papers DD279/A/K209).

18 *Namier*, 280.

19 Denis Gray, *Spencer Perceval: the evangelical Prime Minister 1762–1812* (Manchester, 1963), xi.

20 Note by Tomlinson [aft. 1960] (Rylands, Namier papers, 1/9/8). See also the comments of 'a former student' appended to the obituary of Namier in the *Guardian*, 22 Aug. 1960.

21 Note by Tomlinson [aft. 1960] (Rylands, Namier papers, 1/9/8); *The Times*, 24 Aug. 1960; *Namier*, 280.

22 The testimony of Alan Hardy, Jean Spendlove and Peter Thomas is unanimous on this point.

23 Whenever the 'help' was ill and unable to come there immediately ensued what Julia called a 'crisis', or, as her still undomesticated husband put it, a 'rondeau of delightful preoccupations': Julia to Constance Babington Smith, 10 Jan. 1955 (Babington Smith); Namier to Basil Liddell Hart, 4 Jan. 1951 (LH, 1/539/42).

24 See for example, Arthur Bryant to Namier, 20 July, 24 Oct. 1950 (KCL, Bryant papers, E/2/2); Namier to Basil Liddell Hart, 8 Nov. 1950 (LH, 1/539/31, 43–4).

25 Namier to Sir James Fergusson, 6 Mar. 1951 (HPT, N–54).

26 For example, Namier to Edward Hughes, 23 July 1953 (HPT, N–54). See also Irina Prehn to Constance Babington Smith, 11 May 1980 (Babington Smith).

27 He told Blanche Dugdale after the 1945 election that 'as a governing class we are finished' (*Baffy*, 223).

28 Namier to Visct Thurso, 10 Dec. 1952 (HPT, N–71).

29 *TLS*, 17 Mar. 1950.

30 Namier to Alan Pryce-Jones, n.d. (Yale University, Beinecke Library, Pryce-Jones papers, Gen MSS 513, box 16, folder 854).

31 Namier to Barbara Smythe, 22 Aug. 1951 (HPT, N–71); same to Ninetta Jucker, Feb. 1957 (HPT, N–65).

32 *Europe in decay*, 150–70.

33 Later, he took sharply against the Conservative government headed by Sir Anthony Eden, after a proposal to relax rent controls, since this threatened to increase the rent paid on Julia's flat (information from Mary Port).

34 *The Times*, 18 Feb. 1950.

35 Gluckman to Namier, 4 Mar. 1953 (HPT, N–54); Namier to Gluckman, 26 Feb., 5 Mar. 1953 (ibid.).

36 'Turbulent Zionist', 120; *Namier*, 274–5.

37 Memo by Namier, 20 May 1948 (CZA, A312\58); *The Times*, 14 Feb. 1949. See also Namier to Joseph Linton, 3 Feb. 1948 (CZA, A312\51).

38 Isaiah Berlin offers a telling anecdote on this point, illustrating Namier's belief that Jews in Israel were engaged in a life-or-death struggle with an implacable enemy: Berlin, *Personal impressions* (1980), 72.

39 Berlin, *Personal impressions*, 78.

40 Namier to Berenson, 14 Jan. 1954 (Biblioteca Berenson, Villa I Tatti, Berenson papers).

41 'Turbulent Zionist', 121–2.

42 Namier to Berl Locker, 18 Mar 1952 (CZA, A312\45); Namier to Sharett, 5 Mar. 1952 (ibid., A312\42).

43 Namier to Basil Liddell Hart, 30 July 1951 (LH, 1/539/75–6); same to Vincent Massey, 25 July 1955 (HPT, N–61).

44 Information from Peter Thomas; *New Statesman*, 25 June 1955.

45 Namier to R. P. H. Davies, 26 Feb. 1954 (HPT, N–57).

46 Namier to Liddell Hart, 1, 8 Mar., 4, 13 Apr. 1951 (LH, 1/539/49, 56, 61, 63).

47 Namier to Liddell Hart, 4 Apr. 1951 (LH, 1/539/61).

48 Liddell Hart to Namier, 11 Apr. 1952 (LH, 1/539/62); *The Times*, 29 Aug. 1960.

49 Namier to Sir Walford Selby, 21 Dec. 1951 (Bodl., Selby papers, MS Eng. c. 6600, fo. 196).

50 Namier to Basil Liddell Hart, 24 Sept. 1949 (LH, 1/539/28).

51 Namier to Arthur Bryant, 20 Nov. 1950 (KCL, Bryant papers, E/2/2).

52 Namier to Basil Liddell Hart, 12 Sept. 1949 (LH, 1/539/26).

53 A copy of the script can be found in CUL, Templewood papers, XVII.4/1/viii.

54 She had pipped Namier to the chair of International Relations at Oxford in 1948.

55 *Europe in decay*, 1.

56 *Europe in decay*, 38–77.

57 *TLS*, 19, 26 Feb., 9 Apr. 1949.

58 *TLS*, 24 Mar. 1950, 30 Jan., 13 Feb., 17, 24 July 1953; Namier, *In the Nazi era*, 183–6; Derwent May, *Critical times: the history of the* Times Literary Supplement (London, 2001), 303.

59 Namier to Bryant, 2, 13, 17 June 1938 (KCL, Bryant papers, E2/2); Bryant to Namier, 3 June 1938 (ibid.). Bryant's writing could accurately be described as pro-German rather than pro-Nazi, though it was excoriated by a reviewer in the *Jewish Chronicle* (23 Feb. 1940) as 'an apologia for Nazism'.

60 Namier to Bryant, 23 Jan., 1 Feb., 19 July 1949, 21 June 1950 (KCL, Bryant papers, E/2/2).

61 Richard Griffiths, *Fellow-travellers of the right: British enthusiasts for Nazi Germany 1933–9* (1980), 262, 264; Patrick Allitt, *Catholic converts: British and American intellectuals turn to Rome* (1997), 224.

62 Namier to Weizmann, 20 Feb. 1946 (CZA, A312\47). See also Namier's review of Lunn's *And the floods came: a chapter of wartime autobiography*, *Zionist Review*, 18 Sept. 1942.

63 Sir John Murray to Sir Walford Selby, 11 Nov. 1952, 28 Jan. 1956 (Bodl., MS Eng. c. 6600, fos 25, 110).

64 Namier to Trevor-Roper, 1 May 1947 (Dacre, 10/29/3).

65 Namier to Sir Walford Selby, 8 July 1949 (Bodl., MS Eng. c. 6600, f. 145).

66 *Fortnightly Review*, Apr. 1950 (Max Beloff); *History*, new ser., xxxv (1950), 146–7 (W. N. Medlicott); *Daily Telegraph*, 31 Oct. 1952 (Colin Welch); *Encounter*, 1 Nov. 1952 (anon.); *Quarterly Review*, ccxci (1953), 131 (anon.); *International Affairs*, xxix (1953), 228 (T. H. Minshall).

67 *Observer*, 19 Oct. 1952. The book in question was *In the Nazi era*.

68 Namier to Hugh Trevor-Roper, 11 Nov. 1952 (HPT, N–71).

69 D. C. Watt, 'Sir Lewis Namier and contemporary European history', *Cambridge Review*, June 1954; Namier to Sir Walford Selby, 5 Nov. 1954 (Bodl., MS Eng. 6600, fo. 217).

70 Namier to Ld Vansittart, 12 May 1953 (HPT, N–56); same to R. A. C. Parker, 28 Feb. 1955 (ibid., N–61).

71 Adam Sisman, *A. J. P. Taylor: a biography* (paperback edn, 1995), 152–3, 178–9.

72 Namier to James Fergusson, 13 Dec. 1933 (HPT, N–54).

73 Namier to Sir George Clark, 26 Dec. 1957, 10, 21 Jan., 19 Feb. 1958 (Bodl., Clark papers, 181); same to Melvin Kransberg, 10 Jan. 1958 (ibid.).

74 Namier to Anne Munro-Kerr, 9 Aug., 11 Oct. 1950 (BL, Society of Authors archive, Add. MS 63311, fos 38, 40).

75 Taylor to Hamilton, 30 July [1946] (Bristol UL, Hamish Hamilton archive, DM/1352/Ii); Hamilton to Namier, 2, 23 Aug. 1946 (ibid.); same to Taylor, 10, 15 Jan. 1946 (ibid.).

76 Hamilton to Taylor, 8 Jan. 1947 (Bristol UL, DM/1352/Ii).

77 *Manchester Guardian*, 7 Mar. 1950.

78 Namier to Arthur Bryant, 7 Dec. 1950 (KCL, Bryant papers, E/2/2).

79 Harold Nicolson, *Observer*, 5 Mar. 1950.

80 Namier to Bernard Berenson, 14 Jan. 1954 (Biblioteca Berenson, Berenson papers).

81 Roger Machell to Namier, 15 July 1947, 17 Oct. 1955 (Bristol UL, DM/1352/Ii); Jamie Hamilton to same, 12 Sept. 1947 (ibid.).

82 Memo by Roger Machell, 9 Jan. 1951 (Bristol UL, DM/1352/Ii); Namier to Machell, 18 Jan. 1951 (ibid.); Machell to Namier, 15 Jan. 1951 (ibid.).

83 Namier to Ld Sandwich, 7 May 1946 (Mapperton, GM/PERS/15).

84 Namier to W. S. Lewis, 14 Feb. 1946, 9 Sept. 1948 (LWL, Lewis corresp., Namier (1)).

85 *Manchester Guardian*, 25 Sept. 1950.

86 Namier to Alan Pryce-Jones, 8 May 1950 (Yale University, Beinecke Library, Pryce-Jones papers, Gen MSS 513, box 16, folder 854).

87 A. J. P. Taylor to Roger Machell, 29 Mar. [1952] (Bristol UL, DM/1352/Ii); Namier to Lucy Sutherland, 18 Aug. 1952 (Bodl., Sutherland papers, box 9); Namier to Wiktor Weintraub, 19 Nov. 1957 (HPT, N–66); notes by Herbert Butterfield of a conversation with Alan Pryce-Jones, n.d. (CUL, Butterfield papers, 190a/2).

88 Namier to W. S. Lewis, 9 Sept. 1948 (LWL, Lewis corresp., Namier (1)); same to Elliott Perkins, 29 Oct. 1948 (Harvard UL, Perkins papers, HUGFP 147, box 3).

89 Namier to Sutherland, 29 June 1947 (Bodl., Sutherland papers, box 9).

90 Namier to 'Dykah' Bell, 22 Sept. 1950 (Reading UL, G. D. Bell & Sons archive, MS 1640/389).

91 Namier to W. S. Lewis, 5 June 1951 (LWL, Lewis corresp., Namier (1)).

92 Namier to Ld Sandwich, 7 May 1946 (Mapperton, GM/PERS/15).

93 *Additional Grenville papers 1763-1765*, ed. John Tomlinson (Manchester, 1962).

94 Pilgrim Trust minutes, 23 Feb. 1949 (LMA, Pilgrim Trust archives, 4450/A/01/014, p. 1481).

95 Namier to Jones, 30 Jan. 1949 (NLW, Jones papers, WW/22/4); Pilgrim Trust minutes, 23 Feb. 1949 (LMA, 4450/A/01/014, p. 1481).

96 Pilgrim Trust minutes, 10 May 1949 (LMA, 4450/A/01/014, pp. 1492-3); Namier to Thomas Jones, 14 Mar. 1949 (NLW, Jones papers, M/4/11); 'Correspondence of King George III' (LMA, Pilgrim Trust archives, 4450/A/03/008, paper S. 393(40)).

97 Namier to Helen Cam, 15 Nov. 1946 (Girton College, Cambridge, Cam papers 4/1/1, file 7); F. M. Stenton to same, 5 Jan. 1943 (ibid., file 5).

98 Namier to Wallace Notestein, 2 Feb. 1948 (Yale UL, Notestein papers, 544/I/6/534).

99 *The Times*, 21 Dec. 1943; D. W. Hayton, 'Colonel Wedgwood and the historians', *Historical Research*, lxxxiv (2011), 254.

100 The account given in this chapter of the progress of the History, 1948–56, is based on D. W. Hayton, 'Sir Lewis Namier, Sir John Neale and the shaping of the *History of Parliament*', *Parliamentary History*, xxxii (2013), 190–201.

101 J. E. Neale, *The Elizabethan House of Commons* (1949). The form of the work bore similarities to *The structure of politics*, and was reviewed by Namier in *TLS*, 21 Oct. 1949.

102 Neale to Stenton, 20 Oct. 1946 (Reading UL, Stenton papers, MS 1148/19/2/1).

103 Neale to Notestein, 23 Oct. 1947 (Yale UL, Notestein papers, 544/I/6/536).

104 David Willson to Godfrey Davies, 16 Nov. 1951 (Huntington Library, Davies papers, 53/11).

105 According to Namier himself, Richard Pares coined the term (Namier to Elliott Perkins, 29 Oct. 1948 (Harvard UL, HUGFP 147, box 3).

106 [J. G. Edwards] to Namier et al., 15 Feb. 1949 (HPT, N–22); minutes of trustees' meeting, 17 Mar. 1948 (Reading UL, MS 1148/19/1/1).

107 Stenton's report, 3 June 1948 (copy) (TNA, T 219/649).

108 J. A. Barlas to P. D. Proctor, 13 Apr. 1948 (TNA, T 219/649); memo to Sir Bernard Gilbert, 1 Nov. 1950 (ibid., T 219/650/13).

109 *H.C. deb.*, ser. 5, cdlxxxiv, col. 1067–70.

110 E. W. Playfair to William Armstrong, 31 Mar. 1952 (TNA, T 219/651/73).

111 *The Times*, 21 Feb. 1951.

112 Namier to Fergusson, 6 Mar. 1951 (NRS, Scottish Committee on the History of Parliament archive, SCHP/1/11).

113 Stenton's report, 3 June 1948 (copy) (TNA, T 219/649); draft minutes of trustees' meeting, 26 Jan. 1951 (ibid., STAT 14/1478); memo for E. W. Playfair, 26 Jan. 1951 (ibid., T 219/650/71).

114 R. D. Barlas to A. M. Wilkie, 25 Nov. 1953 (TNA, T 219/651/220); [Edwards] to Stenton, 23 Apr. 1951 (Reading UL, MS 1148/19/2/1); Namier to Lucy Sutherland, 26 Apr. 1951 (Bodl., Sutherland papers, box 9).

115 Namier to Sir Walford Selby, 7 Aug. 1951 (Bodl., MS Eng. hist. c. 6600, fo. 189); same to A. P. Wadsworth, 17 Sept. 1951 (Rylands, *Guardian* arch., B/N8A/360).

116 Namier to W. S. Lewis, 22 Jan. 1952 (LWL, Lewis Corresp., Namier (1)).

117 Namier to Walter Elliot, 6 Nov. 1952 (HPT, N–50); same to Selby, 20 Nov. 1952 (Bodl., MS Eng. c. 6600, fo. 200).

118 Brooke, who was christened Jack and always known as Jack to friends and colleagues, published as 'John Brooke'.

119 Namier to Lucy Sutherland, 3 Oct. 1951 (HPT, N–71).
120 J. H. Burns, 'Ian Ralph Christie, 1919–1998', *Proceedings of the British Academy*, cv (2000), 372–5; Namier to Robert Adeane, 23 July 1952 (HPT, N–50); Christie to Helen Cam, 24 July 1952 (Girton College, Cambridge, Cam papers, 4/1/1, file 16).
121 Owen to Namier, 30 Dec. 1958 (HPT, N–67).
122 Namier to Lucy Sutherland, 17 Jan. 1953 (Bodl., Sutherland papers, box 9); same to Sir James Fergusson, 18 June 1951 (NRS, SCHP/1/51).
123 Namier to Stopford, 6 Nov. 1952 (Manchester UL, university archives, VCA/7/486, file 'Chair of Modern History (Goodwin)').
124 Namier to Cheney, 18 Dec. 1952 (excerpts) (Manchester UL, university archives, VCA/7/486, file 'Chair of Modern History (Goodwin)'); Stopford to Herbert Butterfield, 30 Oct. 1952 (CUL, Butterfield papers, 531/W/529).
125 Namier to J. A. Hawgood, 26 May 1953 (HPT, N–54).
126 Namier to J. H. Plumb, 20 Apr. 1953 (CUL, Plumb papers).
127 Namier to Peter Thomas, 5 Aug. 1953 (MS in private possession).
128 Memorandum by Namier beginning 'My section, 1754–90 …' (Reading UL, MS 1148/19/2/1); John Brooke, 'Namier and Namierism', *History and Theory*, iii (1964), 335.
129 Editorial board minutes, 26 Oct. 1954 (HPT).
130 *The Times*, 19 Apr. 1952.
131 *Avenues*, 10.
132 David Knowles to Helen Cam, 21 Jan. 1951 (Girton College, Cambridge, Cam papers, 2/2/3); Neale to E. L. C. Mullins, 13 Oct. 1959 (UCL, Neale papers, MS 433/12/8); J. H. Plumb, *The making of an historian: the collected essays of J. H. Plumb* (Hemel Hempstead, 1988), 99–100.
133 Neale to Stenton, 4 Oct., 4 Nov. 1951 (Reading UL, MS 1148/19/2/1).
134 TNA, T 219/651/65–77.
135 TNA, T 219/652/32.
136 Plumb, *Making of an historian*, 4; Namier to Plumb, 9 June 1951 (CUL, Plumb papers).
137 Namier to Sir John Stopford, 6 Nov. 1952 (Manchester UL, university archives, VCA/7/486, file 'Chair of Modern History (Goodwin)').
138 Plumb to E. L. C. Mullins, 18 Feb. 1953, 26 May 1955 (HPT, N–24).
139 Namier to Elliott Perkins, 26 Apr. 1951 (Harvard UL, HUGFP 147, box 3); same to W. S. Lewis, 25 Apr. 1951 (LWL, Lewis corresp., Namier (1)); same to Lucy Sutherland, 14 Mar. 1951 (Bodl., Sutherland papers, box 9).
140 Namier to Berl Locker, 18 Mar. 1952 (CZA, A312\45).
141 Namier to E. Ingram, 14 Oct. 1953 (HPT, N–54); list of schoolteachers working with or approached by the History of Parliament (ibid.).
142 'The Anglo-American Conference of Historians', *Bulletin of the Institute of Historical Research*, xxv (1952), 1; Namier, 'Collective research' [1951] (Rylands, Namier papers, 1/1a/4); 'Parliamentary historians invited, July 1951' (HPT, N–50); 'Meeting on parliamentary history, Tuesday 10 July …' (two lists) (ibid.). About 30 historians were invited.
143 Namier to Sir James Fergusson, 18 June 1951 (NRS, SCHP/1/52); same to Lucy Sutherland, 27 June 1951 (Bodl., Sutherland papers, box 9); same to Norman Gash, 2 July 1951 (HPT, N–50).
144 Lists of those invited to the conference on 'History of Parliament, 1679–1901', 9 July 1952, are at HPT, N–50.
145 He also approached the BBC about a broadcast on the Third Programme about the

History, but in the end had to be satisfied with an interview on the 'European Service' (Barbara Crowther to Namier, 1, 6, 13 May 1952 (HPT, N–53)).

146 Namier to J. H. Plumb, 27 Mar. 1956 (HPT, N–64); same to T. W. Freeman, 4 May 1953 (HPT, N–54).

147 T. W. Moody to Namier, 8 Oct. 1953 (HPT, N–55); Namier to David Erskine, 24 Nov. 1953 (ibid., N–54); J. C. Beckett diary 16–26 Nov. 1953 (PRONI, Beckett papers, D/4126/A/1/4).

148 Namier to Sir Hughe Knatchbull-Hugessen, 15 Apr. 1953 (HPT, N–54); same to F. A. Spencer, 31 Dec. 1953 (ibid., N–56); Namier to T. W. Moody, 6 Oct. 1954 (ibid., N–58); correspondence with Kenneth Darwin, 1954–59 (PRONI, FIN/17/1/J/4/1–2).

149 Namier to Lucy Sutherland, 24 Nov. 1953 (Bodl., Sutherland papers, box 9); same to J. B. Owen, 26 Jan. 1956 (HPT, N–64); same to P. D. G. Thomas, 7 Oct. 1958 (ibid., N–67).

150 Namier to Plumb, 7 Nov. 1951 (CUL, Plumb papers); Kitson Clark to Namier, 12 Nov. 1951 (HPT, N–50); invitation to meeting with Namier, 14 Nov. 1951 (CUL, Plumb papers).

151 Namier's relations with Butterfield are discussed at length pp. 366–75.

152 Kitson Clark to Butterfield, 5 Oct. 1951 (CUL, Butterfield papers, C531/C/49).

153 *Namier*, 199; J. S. Bromley to Lucy Sutherland, 25 Oct. 1970 (Bodl., Sutherland papers, box 9).

154 A. F. Thompson to Namier, 12 June 1953 (HPT, N–56).

155 Namier to Thompson, 17 June 1953 (HPT, N–56).

156 Thompson to Namier, 12, 28 June 1953 (HPT, N–56).

157 Namier to J. H. Plumb, 21 Feb. 1952, 26 Feb. 1954 (CUL, Plumb papers).

158 Namier to Sir Owen Morshead, 17 June 1955 (Rylands, Namier papers, 1/1b/17).

159 *Namier*, 299–301.

160 Sutherland to Julia, 30 Oct. 1970 (Bodl., Sutherland papers, box 9); same to Bromley, 16 Oct., 13 Nov. 1970 (ibid.); Bromley to Sutherland, 25 Oct. 1970 (ibid.).

161 A. F. Thompson to Namier, 12, 28 June 1953 (HPT, N–56); J. Steven Watson to Namier, 1 July 1953 (ibid.); Williams to Namier, 24 June 1953 (HPT, N–56).

162 Namier to Thompson, 17, 30 June 1953 (HPT, N–56).

163 Namier to Williams, 30 June 1953 (HPT, N–56).

164 For what follows see D. W. Hayton, 'Official histories of parliament and the nature of the union of 1707: a forgotten episode in Anglo-Scottish academic relations', *Scottish Historical Review*, xciii (2014), 80–108.

165 Namier to Sir James Fergusson, 18 Oct. 1951 (NRS, SCHP/1/9/69–70).

166 Namier to J. G. Edwards, 29 Nov. 1952 (HPT, N–19).

167 The will was dated 1 June 1950.

168 Namier to Fergusson, 6 Mar. 1951 (NRS, SCHP/1/11).

169 Namier to Lucy Sutherland, 4 Dec. 1952 (Bodl., Sutherland papers, box 9).

170 Fergusson to E. W. M. Balfour-Melville, 25 Aug. 1953 (NRS, SCHP/1/125).

171 Fergusson to Balfour-Melville, 25 Aug. 1953 (NRS, SCHP/1/125).

172 Namier to W. S. Lewis, 10 July 1952 (LWL, Lewis corresp., Namier (1)); Namier to E. L. C. Mullins, 27 June 1951 (HPT, N–24).

173 *Namier*, 305.

174 'First draft' of proposal, n.d. (LWL, Lewis corresp., Namier (2)); Namier to Lewis, 15, 27 July 1953 (ibid., Namier (1)); Lewis to Namier, 21 Aug. 1953 (ibid.).

175 Namier to Mrs Elizabeth Fooks, 17 Mar. 1954 (HPT, N–57).

176 See, for example, Earl Fortescue to Namier, 7 Jan. 1954 (HPT, N–57); Namier to Mrs Fooks, 10 Feb. 1954 (ibid.).

177 Lord Leconfield, for example, whom he may have met through mutual friends in the

Conservative Party (Namier to Roger Senhouse, 11 Feb. 1953 (HPT, N–56)). He wrote to the Hon. Mrs Fairfax-Lucy on the basis of having 'occasionally visited' her parents in the distant past (Namier to Lady Fairfax-Lucy, 23 May 1952 (HPT, N–50)); and Mrs Anthony Henley (the former Hon. Sylvia Stanley) on the basis of an encounter in the 1930s at a party given by 'Baffy' Dugdale: Namier to Mrs Anthony Henley, 21, 27 Sept. 1955 (ibid., N–60).

178 Namier to Ld Shuttleworth, 24 Nov. 1952 (HPT, N–56).

179 Namier to Visct Sandon,. 13 Feb. 1953 (HPT, N–56). The Hon. Olwen Gwynne Barker (1905–98) had divorced the 7th Baron Suffield in 1937.

180 Namier to Morshead, 16, 26 Feb., 8, 12, 16 Mar. 1954 (Rylands, Namier papers, 1/1b/17).

181 The 'itinerary' of roads in England and Wales published by John Cary in 1798 (Namier to A. P. Wadsworth, 4 Nov. 1954 (Rylands, *Guardian* arch., 149/N1/1)).

182 Julia to Irina Prehn, 21 Apr. 1953 (Babington Smith).

183 *Namier*, 294–7; Namier to W. S. Lewis, 15 Jan. 1953 (LWL, Lewis corresp., Namier (1)).

184 Namier to Mrs Elizabeth Fooks, 2 Oct. 1953 (HPT, N–54).

185 Namier to Francis Thompson, 13 Apr. 1954 (HPT, N–59); Mary Drummond to R. L. Drage, 8 Nov. 1954 (ibid.); Namier to same, 6 Dec. 1954 (ibid.)

186 *Namier*, 306–7; Namier to W. S. Lewis, 5 June 1955 (LWL, Lewis corr., Namier (2)); same to Donald Atkinson, 27 June 1955 (HPT, N–60).

187 Namier to Sir Richard Proby, 9 Jan. 1953 (HPT, N–55); same to Ld Drogheda, 26 Feb. 1954 (ibid., N–57); same to Lucy Sutherland, 18 May 1954 (Bodl., Sutherland papers, box 9).

188 Namier to J. P. Cooper, 7 July 1954 (Trinity College, Oxford, Cooper papers, D279/A/ N1.02); same to Sir Frank Stenton, 10 Oct. 1951 (Reading UL, MS 1148/19/2/1).

189 List of seminars at IHR, 1953–54 (HPT, N–58).

190 Namier to Ld Moyne, 16 June 1955 (HPT, N–61).

191 Namier to Bernard Berenson, 22 Nov. 1951 (Biblioteca Berenson, Berenson papers); same to J. B. Owen, 9 Dec. 1955 (HPT, N–61); same to Ld Lansdowne, 25 Aug. 1954 (ibid., N–58); same to Francis Thompson, 25 May 1955 (ibid., N–60).

192 Namier to Morshead, 14 Mar. 1955 (Rylands, Namier papers, 1/1b/17).

193 Namier to Philip Friedman, 7 July 1954 (Center for Jewish History, New York, YIVO archives, Friedman papers, RG 1258, folder 164); same to J. H. E. Fried, 20 Jan. 1953 (SUNY, Albany, Fried papers, series 7, box 7, no. 20).

194 *Namier*, 303.

195 Namier to Lucy Sutherland, 3 Oct. 1951 (Bodl., Sutherland papers, box 9); same to Francis Thompson, 27 Oct. 1951 (HPT, N–71).

196 Namier to W. S. Lewis, 6 July 1951 (LWL, Lewis corresp., Namier (1)). Emphasis added.

197 Namier to L. S. Amery, 4 Feb. 1951 (Churchill, Amery papers, 2/1/45); Namier to Plumb, 26 Nov. 1951 (CUL, Plumb papers).

198 Namier to Ld Lansdowne, 25 Aug. 1954 (HPT, N–58); same to Francis Thompson, 25 May 1955 (HPT, N–60).

199 Namier's foreword to John Brooke, *The Chatham administration* (1956), v.

200 Namier to J. B. Owen, 20 Jan. 1956 (HPT, N–64).

201 Namier to George Kitson Clark, 11 Feb. 1954 (HPT, N–57).

202 Namier to Christie, 29 Jan. 1952 (HPT, N–50); same to Owen, 1 Oct. 1754 (ibid., N–58).

203 Brooke, *Chatham admin.*, vii.

204 I. R. Christie, *The end of North's ministry 1780–1782* (1958).

205 Namier to Berl Locker, 18 Mar. 1952 (CZA, A312\45).

206 *Personalities and powers*, 13.

207 *Personalities and powers*, 19.

208 In language stronger than he had ever used before, he noted that the idea of a 'double cabinet', in which a court cabal presided over by Bute worked against the official ministry was 'a product of Burke's fertile, disordered and malignant imagination' (*Personalities and powers*, 21).

209 He once told Isaiah Berlin that 'I seldom feel quite certain about my own productions' (Namier to Berlin, 11 May 1958 (Bodl., MS Berlin 154, fo. 277)).

210 Namier to Sir James Fergusson, 11 Nov. 1953 (HPT, N–54).

211 Namier to R. R. Walcott, 1 Nov. 1951 (HPT, N–71); same to Arthur Aspinall, 8 Nov. 1951 (HPT, N–50); I. R. Christie, *Myth and reality in late eighteenth-century British politics and other papers* (1970), 10.

212 Namier to Arthur Aspinall, 9 Apr. 1952 (HPT, N–50); same to J. H. Plumb, 6 May 1952 (CUL, Plumb papers); same to Lucy Sutherland, 5 Feb. 1953 (HPT, N–56); *Personalities and powers*, 15, 23.

213 Namier to Plumb, 11 Dec. 1951, 7 Apr., 9 May 1952 (CUL, Plumb papers).

214 *Personalities and powers*, 32; Plumb to Namier, 12 May 1952 (HPT, N–52).

215 *Personalities and powers*, 32–3: 'names there must be in a political dichotomy, even if their meaning is uncertain and their use misleading'. He was prepared to allow the persistence in the Commons of a distinctive body of Tories until mid-century, when they became synonymous with the independent country gentlemen. Thereafter Toryism, especially a Jacobite variety, was a mark of eccentricity: of one MP who did remain an active Jacobite into the 1750s, Namier wrote, 'this proves him to have been barmy' (Namier to Sir James Fergusson, 11 Nov. 1953 (HPT, N–54); same Sir Thomas Kendrick, 21 Sept. 1954 (HPT, N–57)).

216 Plumb to Namier, 12 May 1952 (HPT, N–52).

217 Owen to Namier, 16 May 1952 (HPT, N–52).

218 The lecture is reprinted in *Personalities and powers*, 39–58.

219 The lecture was taking place in the university's Senate House, Pollard's former domain. There are two copies in Rylands, Namier papers, 1/1b/1, a first and a final draft. Namier revised it again for publication (*Personalities and powers*, 105–17).

220 Final draft (Rylands, Namier papers, 1/1b/1), 2.

221 Final draft (Rylands, Namier papers, 1/1b/1), 6.

222 Including Neale (private information).

223 *Namier*, 294–5.

224 Final draft (Rylands, Namier papers, 1/1b/1), 17. Namier omitted his very last remarks from the published lecture.

225 *Alexandra College Magazine*, cxvii (Dec. 1953), 30–1 (courtesy of the college librarian, Ms Aileen Ivory).

226 *Spectator*, 13 May 1955.

227 John Cannon, 'Lewis Bernstein Namier', John Cannon (ed.), *The historian at work* (1980), 148.

228 Catherine S. Sims, 'L. B. Namier (1888–)', Herman Ausubel, J. B. Brebner and E. M. Hunt (eds), *Some modern historians of Britain: essays in honor of R. L. Schuyler* (New York, 1951), 341–57; Alex Natan, 'Sir Lewis Namier: Historiker mit Vorurteilen', *Vierteljahrshefte für Zeitgeschichte*, i (1953), 352–6; Franco Venturi, 'Un grande storico; Sir Lewis Namier', *Il Ponte*, xiii (1957), 1046–55. Not all continental historians were *au fait*. Eric Hobsbawm recollected, with relish, that when he had met Fernand Braudel in Paris in the 1950s Braudel 'took me aside to say, "Do tell me, who exactly is this Namier that my English

visitors keep telling me about?"' (Eric Hobsbawm, *Interesting times: a twentieth-century life* (2002), 285).

229 Walter Elliot to Namier, 5 June 1952 (HPT, N–50); Roger Machell to 'Jamie' Hamilton, 7 Jan. 1956 (Bristol UL, DM/352/Ii). Note also *Observer*, 25 Nov. 1952; *Listener*, 16 July 1953; *TLS*, 28 Aug. 1953.

230 Namier to Anna Kallin, 10 Apr. 1952, 19 Feb., 25 Nov. 1953 (HPT, N–53); same to Michael Stephens, 4 July 1952 (ibid.); Anna Kallin to Namier, 17 Feb. 1953 (ibid.); Namier to Basil Liddell Hart, 19 Feb. 1953 (LH, 1/539/113); same to Heather Summers, 23 Nov. 1953 (HPT, N–53); same to Roger Senhouse, 21 Oct. 1953 (ibid., N–56).

231 G. R. Barnes to John Salt, 12 Mar. 1946 (BBC Written Archives); Salt to Barnes, 15 Mar. 1946 (ibid.).

232 Peter Laslett to Namier, 11 Feb. 1948 (BBC Written Archives); memo by Laslett, 22 July 1948 (ibid.).

233 Kallin to Namier, 16 Jan. 1951 (BBC Written Archives).

234 Cyril Hare, *An English murder* (1951), 121, 132.

235 *Namier*, 282.

236 Namier to J. H. Plumb, 17 July 1952 (CUL, Plumb papers).

237 *Namier*, 288–9; Lord Boothby, *Boothby: recollections of a rebel* (1978), 194.

238 Namier to J. H. Plumb, 30 Jan. 1956 (CUL, Plumb papers).

239 Richard Pares and A. J. P. Taylor (eds), *Essays presented to Sir Lewis Namier* (1956), vi. The review in the *Sunday Times*, 29 Apr. 1956, by Raymond Mortimer, repeated this encomium: Namier was 'the most scientific of historians', who 'shapes his discoveries into literature'.

240 Namier to W. S. Lewis, 4 May 1956 (LWL, Lewis corresp., Namier (2)); *Namier*, 307; *Manchester Guardian*, 26 Apr. 1956.

9

Conflicts, 1956–60

The troubles of the History of Parliament

From the moment of its reincarnation in 1951 the History of Parliament enveloped itself in a cloud of super-optimism. With the benefit of hindsight, one can only smile on reading forecasts of likely completion dates, given that the first volumes, Namier's, eventually appeared in 1964, while Neale's Elizabethan section finally saw the light of day thirty years after the work was set in motion. But we have to remember that the shape the History was to take – in terms of research, structure and presentation – was not laid out clearly in advance, nor were any of those involved aware of the scale of the job they had taken on. It was as if they had set out to climb a high mountain dressed and equipped for a country walk. The trustees delegated responsibility for 'academic direction' to the editorial board, and the board in turn failed to decide whether the biographical research should take the form of a classical prosopography – closely focused and statistically driven – such as Neale preferred, or the open-ended approach advocated by Namier, disdaining brief factual entries in favour of articles which attempted to discover not only the key facts about a member's background and career, but also an insight into character and motivation.

When Stenton tried to issue firm guidelines, he could not bring Neale and Namier to agree. In 1954 the board solemnly decided on the desirability of varying practice according to period, and produced a formula that was a masterpiece of vacuity: 'as a general rule, biographies should be as complete as knowledge and the limitations of space will allow'.[1] Namier carried on as he pleased. But he did not grasp the problem that he was creating. At first he had no idea how much time would be involved in writing a mass of biographies – roughly two thousand in all – in the style that he wanted.[2] The eventual realisation that this would take much longer than planned was continually delayed by over-confidence in his own abilities and anxiety not to miss anything. The determination to track down every scrap of evidence was too deeply engrained. 'Most historians walk straight along the road', John Brooke observed. 'Sir Lewis never walked a step without looking in every direction.'[3]

Under pressure at the outset, Stenton agreed to a five-year limit on research and preparation of the volumes.[4] Thereafter, impaled on this promise, neither trustees nor editorial board seemed able to talk sensibly about publication dates. In 1954 Namier spoke of having his section 'in shape in two or three years' time', and the trustees' report stated confidently that both Namier's and Neale's sections would be published in 1958.[5] Given actual rates of progress, these estimates were unrealistic to the point of absurdity. They were repeated a year later without a blush.[6]

By this time, however, icy winds were beginning to blow from the Treasury.[7] The change in the political weather coincided with the appointment of a new chancellor of the exchequer: of all people, Namier's publisher and friend, Harold Macmillan, who took a dim view of spending government money on what he regarded as a parliamentary vanity project. Macmillan and Namier were still on the best of terms,[8] but Macmillan's priority as chancellor was a thorough-going review of public expenditure. Informed by his publisher's instincts and experience – he had warned his son in the strongest possible terms against taking on the publication of the History of Parliament[9] – Macmillan fastened on the History as a suitable case for retrenchment. In January 1956 he scribbled on a departmental memorandum: 'Among many rackets today is a thing called History of Parliament … Couldn't it be stopped now – or retarded?'[10] His civil servants offered little encouragement. Given the commitments already made, it would be impossible to shut down the History completely, although an effort might be made to review the 'later stages' and prevent new sections from being started. Macmillan noted wearily, 'Let's try this. It is all a great nonsense.'[11]

When asked to suggest economies, the trustees started to flap. Their opening gambit was to suggest a reduction in research, but this issue was not negotiable: no one 'would be prepared to say to Sir Lewis Namier … that the such and such papers need not be examined closely and staff need not in consequence be employed to examine them.'[12] Nonetheless, something had to be done. The chairman, the Liberal MP Clement Davies, tried to be firm: the five-year limit for work on each section would have to be adhered to; if the History fell behind schedule, there would be parliamentary questions.

The editorial board then tried to address the issue of progress in a series of increasingly acrimonious meetings, which exposed the nature and scale of the problem: not only had the two flagship sections fallen far behind schedule, each had different priorities and different methods of working. Neale's first concern was his survey, while Namier refused to begin the survey until his biographies were written. 'He could not tell what he would want for the survey until he came to write it.'[13] Neale subsequently proposed radical surgery on the biographies: they should be 'designed to present certain agreed vital and demographic facts, and from these facts editors should compile statistical tables for inclusion, or at least consideration, in their surveys'. Namier responded that 'what was most valuable in his biographies was not amenable to presentation in statistical or tabular form, and would have to be set out at length in his survey'. The board sought to prepare a list of topics on which information could be presented statistically, an exercise which produced more confusion than clarity, and ended with a retreat. Some tables would be necessary, and authors should use them 'where practicable', but 'they should not allow their readers to forget that behind all the tables lay the indefinable quality and diversity of human relationships'.[14]

By the end of the year the trustees decided they would have to brazen out Treasury recriminations while continuing to demand from the editorial board 'a considered statement on completion dates'. This request produced the worst-tempered board meeting yet, in December 1956, with Neale and Namier returning to entrenched positions. Neale asked the board to reconsider the scale of the biographies, which had become 'a real burden'. Namier was only too happy to agree that the work had become oppressive – this was, after all, a leitmotiv of his private correspondence – but he was heartened to be 'contributing to a work of historical scholarship unprecedented in size and character. He was confident that all future historical work on the eighteenth century would start from the History. The burden was worth bearing and he would carry on.' Passions ran so high that the minutes became a matter of contention. The secretary's draft was amended first by Namier, and then by Neale, anxious that he would not appear 'the less genuine of the two; the would-be saboteur'. In fact, he considered Namier the 'would-be destroyer'. If other editors followed Namier's example, the entire enterprise would collapse. But Neale could not persuade the board: Namier's section had achieved more than any other and represented the best hope of getting something into print.[15]

Namier may have seen off attempts to alter the shape of his volumes, but there was no abatement of the anxiety engendered by the sharpening of Macmillan's axe. Politicians and civil servants remained remorselessly critical. When Macmillan moved to 10 Downing Street, his successors at the Treasury, Peter Thorneycroft (1957–58) and Derick Heathcoat-Amory (1958–60), inherited his cynicism. Sir Charles McAndrew, the chairman of ways and means, was also making threatening noises. As a Scottish Unionist, McAndrew may have been influenced by the rumbling dispute between the History and the Scottish Committee on the History of Parliament. He pressed Thorneycroft to close the History, as 'a racket and a complete waste of £17,000 a year'.[16] To make matters worse, in January 1957 the editorial board had no option but to modify the publication schedule again: Namier's section would now appear 'not earlier' than March 1959. The trustees were appalled. And when Clement Davies met Stenton, Neale and Namier, he was told by Namier that he did not expect to finish before April 1960.[17] The board's recorded explanation, couched in phrases so close to Namier's customary arguments that they must have come directly from his mouth, was that

> The sections on which Sir Lewis and Sir John were engaged had grown, unavoidably and necessarily, far beyond their original concept. The biographies were not so many separate items like pebbles on the shore; they had developed into an interlocking study of the political nation such as had never before been attempted, a study requiring immense labour, long hours, painstaking research, in which the shortest biographies often required most time and effort.[18]

Neale continued to press the case that Namier's open-ended approach to research had to be curtailed. In a private letter he described 'a fundamental clash between the working of my mind and that of our friend in the eighteenth century. I see it more clearly every time we meet. The rest of the board really *must* take the reins.'[19] Ultimately, however, Neale was undone by his own inability to produce. Once the editorial board grasped 'the extent of Neale's failure' it had no option but to put its faith in Namier, who might at least have a volume of biographies ready by his agreed date, if he could be persuaded to modify his method of working.[20] In June 1958 the trustees had to be given the bad news that Namier's section could not be finished before the end of 1961.[21] After a feeble effort to promote the idea that biographies might be presented in 'telegraphic English', the trustees conceded that they could not insist that editors 'lower their standards to any great extent'.[22] They were only too well aware where the root of their problems lay but it was too late to impose a new structure. As their secretary observed, since his retirement Namier

> has devoted his entire working life to the trust to the exclusion of other writing. He directs the minutiae of research, writes many of the biographies personally and has a hand in composing all of the remainder. His standard is so high that progress on his section is necessarily slow. He makes no secret of the fact that his section is to be the culmination of a life's work in that period of history.[23]

It is to the credit of the trustees, and Clement Davies in particular, that they managed to keep the History afloat in these very choppy waters. Davies could not control Namier, but he did stave off the circling sharks. In the spring of 1958, prompted by a Conservative backbencher who was mounting a personal crusade to 'exorcise' the History from the estimates, the Treasury enforced a reduction in the History's budget, which provoked another mini-crisis.[24] Two trustees, the Conservative John Foster and a former Labour treasury minister, W. G. Glenvil Hall, questioned whether academic aspirations had been set too high. Glenvil Hall in particular was prepared to state that at least 'part of the trustees' difficulties arose from Sir Lewis Namier's rather strong-minded attitude of the high standards to be applied'.[25] To silence these doubts Stenton gave an assurance that Namier had agreed to a self-denying ordinance in relation to searching for new material. His section would now be finished and sent to the press in sections in 1961.[26] Furthermore, in March 1959 Davies managed to squeeze a further £20,000 from the estimates, despite Heathcote-Amory's finger-wagging – this would be absolutely the last increase.[27] Davies still had to explain to parliament why the History was now scheduling its first publications for 1961/2, but survived interrogation by the public accounts committee and criticism in *The Times*, where a leader writer, pointedly quoting a comment in Namier's *The structure of politics* that sometimes in human affairs 'forms acquire an independent life of their own', suggested that the research for the History was now an end in itself and that 'over-elaboration has become a point of honour in some academic circles'.[28]

This constant uncertainty increased the pressure on Namier, who felt keenly his responsibility to the project itself, and to his staff.[29] He could not be satisfied with work done under such constraints of time.[30] As well as resisting the temptation to hunt after new manuscripts, at least as far as his conscience would allow, he was forced to introduce strict guidelines about the length and scope of biographies. In a detailed memorandum for the trustees in the spring of 1959, designed to allay fears over incremental extensions to his deadline,[31] he divided his MPs into three groups: the 'rank and file', who would have brief notices; the 'second-rank' figures, about a score in total, with substantial entries running to about five thousand words; and the 'chief figures', no more than a handful. None of these 'chief figures' had yet been written, because the work on the less prominent members 'forms in a way the canvas for them'. The first-rank parliamentarians had to be written up differently, since the available material was enormous and most of it readily accessible. There was no point in a detailed recitation of well-known careers. Namier only intended to provide character sketches, and to analyse relations with the king, ministerial colleagues and the House of Commons. The entries would be no longer than for men in the second rank. He would start straight away with Grenville. (In fact he wrote only two of these, Grenville and Henry Fox, both of whom he had studied closely while preparing his first two books.)

So far so good. But matters were complicated by a further sub-category, those Namier called the 'near first-rank men'. He cited as an example Charles Townshend, chancellor of the exchequer and author of the colonial revenue acts which had provoked the Boston Tea Party. Here again there were vast quantities of source materials, but no published biography to fall back on. Such lives would have to be treated in depth; they might even be the longest entries. This was the point at which Namier was no longer able to maintain his vow of abstinence. Although his arguments were plausible, there was also an element of self-indulgence: he was particularly interested in Townshend and was contemplating a full-dress biography.

The introductory survey was also a looming presence in his mind. He gave it a great deal of thought, but does not seem to have come to any precise conclusions about the form it should take. It ought to represent the pinnacle of his work: that was what both friends and enemies would expect. It should also constitute the ultimate vindication of the time and energy (and public money) spent on the History. Perhaps for this very reason he shied away from defining what it would be. In exchanges with Neale he consistently placed the biographies at the heart of his work – almost as if they were to justify themselves – and postponed any talk of the survey until he had the full complement of biographical research to hand. This line of thought was certainly of a piece with the rigorously empirical method he had adopted from the start, but the suspicion remains that he flinched from confronting the task of building a framework of argument and thinking through his conclusions. According to Lady Namier, he established the purpose of the survey in his own mind during the summer of 1956, as 'his section's guide to readers of his MPs' "political birth", their biographies'.[32] This was certainly what he told the editorial board in July 1956 while doing battle with Neale over tables: 'the survey should be a guide to the reading of the biographies and must necessarily include much that could not be expressed in statistical form'.[33] In November 1959, when pushed by the trustees, he simply repeated that he would not know the form his survey would take until the research was done, because the biographies were 'interlocking'. This was his favourite word in describing the work of his section, but some trustees might also have regarded it as an excuse for postponing tough decisions.[34]

Slowing down

Even before the Treasury began turning the screw, Namier felt that he was trapped. According to Julia, one of the reasons that *Moby Dick* made such an impression on him when he came to read the book in the last years of his life was that he recognised a mirror of his own self-destructive obsession.[35] Using another metaphor, he told a correspondent that 'I am still deep in the tunnel of the History of Parliament without even seeing the light at the end'.[36] With pressure increasing he had no alternative but to give all his time to the work. From the director's office at the Institute of Historical Research Goronwy Edwards observed this at first hand: Namier's days at the Institute ran from ten in the morning till seven at night. 'He used to say', Edwards remembered, that 'he had never worked so hard'.[37] Asked by the literary editor of the *Sunday*

9 Lewis Namier, 1947, by Walter Stoneman

10 Receiving a DCL at Oxford, June 1955, Namier in procession alongside Dame Ninette de Valois

Times in December 1957 to contribute to a feature on 'Books of the Year', Namier confessed that 'I do not believe I have read six books outside the narrow range (and enormous field) of my History of Parliament work during the entire year'.[38] And he assured anyone who would listen that he was unlikely to write anything else: 'You will not see me in print again till my section of the History of Parliament is out of the way, and then I may be too old to do anything.'[39]

Namier's health was also getting worse, with 'more ailments than I can enumerate'.[40] He was increasingly deaf, so much so that he attended only his own seminar at the Institute.[41] His eyesight was beginning to weaken, a consequence, he thought, of 'too much reading'.[42] To the chronic disability in his right hand could be added osteoarthritis in the spine, which made walking painful, and sitting for long periods uncomfortable.[43] Ever since childhood he had been a prey to respiratory infections, and in the London smogs these returned with menacing regularity. His digestive system was increasingly troublesome, and in the summer of 1956 he survived a scare when for a time a growth was suspected in his bladder.[44] None of this was helped by his insomnia, or constant worrying about Julia, whose health was also giving cause for concern.[45] So fragile was the Namiers' domestic economy that when their home help, 'our Mrs Allen', went down with influenza in the winter of 1956–57, and Lewis and Julia were obliged to 'to undertake many more chores than usual', they were soon exhausted enough to require a period of recuperation.[46]

Despite his physical decline, and the palpable necessity of conserving his energies in order to bring his section of the History to a conclusion, Namier found it impossible to curtail all his outside activities. At the same time as reassuring Lucy Sutherland that he had more or less given up book reviewing or refereeing for publishers (only three reviews appeared after 1956 and none in the last eighteen months of his life), he admitted that he was still working on manuscripts submitted for his series with Macmillan and reading for friends who sought his advice.[47] His involvement with the de Tocqueville project took him to Paris occasionally, and membership of the advisory board for the edition of Weizmann's papers was even more demanding of his energy and time, requiring frequent consultations by letter and a visit to Israel in 1958.[48] And while he had reluctantly abandoned his great history of nineteenth-century Europe, and had 'more or less given up' diplomatic history,[49] he was continuing with other projects: second editions of *The structure of politics* and *England in the age of the American revolution*; the next volume in the series, on the Grenville administration, which he claimed to have restarted in January 1956 at the urging of friends;[50] and the biography of Charles Townshend.

Namier was fascinated by Townshend's 'protean personality', a case study in the way 'exceptional ability' was undermined by a flawed character, formed – or rather deformed – in childhood. Townshend's difficult relationship with his father was the focus of Namier's analysis: like Tolstoy, unhappy families always fascinated him.[51] According to Julia, he began to talk about writing a biography of Townshend at about the time the History of Parliament restarted, and was encouraged by choice discoveries in some of the earliest archives to be inspected.[52] He was soon collecting material in earnest, and writing it up.[53] He was able to give a brilliant short account of Townshend's life and career as his Leslie Stephen Lecture at Cambridge in 1959;[54] and composed a long entry on Townshend for the History.[55] By the time of his death he had written the first seven chapters of the book, the narrative stopping in 1767 just at Townshend's appointment to the exchequer.[56]

He did, however, manage to put a stop to the search for manuscripts. In the spring of 1956 he paid a visit to Bolton Hall in the north riding of Yorkshire, but although he left files unopened in the muniment room, promising to return later in the year, he stayed in London throughout the summer, explaining to Lord Bolton that he had an 'awful lot of work' to get through.[57] He was by no means incapacitated from travelling, and spent a month on the continent in May: receiving an honorary degree in Rome, where he and Julia were 'entertained and feted', paying a brief visit to Bernard Berenson at Settignano near Florence, and enjoying a fortnight's rest in Switzerland.[58] Later in the year the Namiers also took a brief holiday in Holland.[59] But he seemed ready to call time on the days of endless 'paper chases': 'The time has come to stay put and try to put things into shape.'[60] There was one last hurrah: in the summer of 1957, before implementing his self-denying ordinance, he dragged Julia back to Yorkshire and Northumberland, and followed with a southern circuit through Hampshire, Dorset and Sussex.[61] But the long car journeys were now proving too much for both of them, and Namier finally agreed to call a halt.[62]

Fallings out

Namier's last years were also disfigured by a succession of misunderstandings with friends and acquaintances, all resulting in unpleasantness, and one particularly sad episode ending in a permanent estrangement. He had always been quick to anger and slow to forgive. The list of those with whom he had quarrelled was long and distinguished. It began with his own family, and included former intimates such as Malcolm MacDonald and Chaim Weizmann, both of whom he cut out of his life completely. Even Arnold Toynbee felt the icy blast, on account of something he had written about Palestine: 'if we passed each other in the street he would march past in grim silence'. But eventually, as Toynbee recalled,

We collided with each other in Lower Regent Street and, forgetting his vow of non-intercourse, Lewis picked up a thread that he had dropped in my room at Chatham House twenty or thirty months back. 'Toynbee, that footnote of yours ...' But this tenacity of Lewis's was so comical that I cut him short by laughing. 'Look here, Lewis', I said, 'this is ridiculous. We were at Balliol together, and we have been friends for years. It is absurd that footnotes should come between us, or politics either.' To my surprise, he checked himself, and the smile of the lovable Lewis broke out on the militant Lewis's face. Lewis never broke off relations with me again, though our views on the Palestine question remained as far apart as ever.[63]

In what he considered to be his old age Namier's customary bluntness could still affront those who only encountered what Toynbee called 'the belligerent Lewis' and were unacquainted with 'the lovable Lewis'. An exchange of letters with the New Zealander H. J. Hanham, then teaching at Edinburgh University, surprised Namier by revealing that Hanham had nursed a grudge over some imagined slight, and had only realised his misapprehension on a careful re-reading of Namier's letters.[64] On another occasion Namier's brusque rejection of a publication proposal from a young American historian, Peter Gay, prompted Gay to observe, in what he presumably considered a crushing dismissal, that 'your reputation has preceded you'.[65]

Namier's dealings with Gay were an exception to the general tenor of his behaviour in the last decade of his life. The financial returns from his writings had always been a subject on which his temper was at its keenest. Otherwise, although heavy-footed in his dealings with the outside world, he had shed some elements of the personality once summed up by Toynbee as 'always vehement, sometimes vindictive, and occasionally even venomous'.[66] If not exactly mellow, he had become more measured. When the Weizmann project became embroiled in controversy, he took a firm but judicious line. The problems centred on the executive editor, Mayir Vereté, whose work had come under criticism. In the opinion of the external members of the advisory board – Namier, Leonard Stein, Isaiah Berlin and Sir Charles Webster – Vereté was 'a difficult man but a scholar'.[67] Namier at first took Vereté's part, but came to realise that the faults were very far from being all on one side, and recommended that Vereté be given a chance to prove himself, but with a firm ultimatum.[68] When Vereté was eventually dismissed Namier did not expostulate on a point of principle, as he would have done twenty years earlier, but accepted the outcome as a regrettable necessity, commenting sardonically to Julia, 'aren't we a troublesome lot'.[69]

But even if less irascible, he was still able to upset friends, sometimes without trying. Isaiah Berlin, who knew Namier well and made every allowance for him, had his patience tested by what Namier insisted was a misconstruction of a sentence in a private letter. Thanking Berlin for an offprint, Namier had written, 'In all sincerity I admire you: how intelligent you must be to understand all you write.'[70] In a memoir published after Namier's death Berlin claimed to have been 'delighted', as anyone would have been 'who knew Namier and took pleasure in his prejudices and absurdities'.[71] Nonetheless, the story found its way into the gossip column of the *Sunday Times*. Namier was mortified, and immediately put pen to paper:

> Obviously you did not believe me sincere: which I was. Julia, who is good at philosophy, had read your essay first, and told me it was first-rate stuff – and so I made myself read it and admired as much of it as I was able to follow. Why will people not believe me when I admit my limitations? My maternal grandfather was a Jewish peasant who changed into a squire; my father was a squire all through; I am an 'am-ha-arets',[72] but with enough Talmudist ancestry through the Gaon not to despise Talmudists in turn. You did me injustice in treating as ill-mannered irony and circulating as such a remark which expressed sincere admiration. I trust you will now accept my explanation.[73]

Although this was not quite an apology, and included clumsy phrasing ('You did me injustice', 'I made myself read it'), Berlin was happy to let the matter go.[74]

Another to bridle at what he considered rough handling by Namier was J. H. Plumb who, unlike Berlin, brooded over his resentment until Namier was dead and he was able to hit back without fear of reprisal. Plumb may already have been uncomfortable with the indignity of having to toady to Namier but in the spring of 1956 was given a genuine grievance. This was Namier's less than gushing review of the first volume of the work which Plumb intended as his *magnum opus*, his biography of Sir Robert Walpole.[75] Namier's astringent comments, which included pointing out a bad error, were written entirely in the spirit of straightforward dealing with someone he considered his equal: he was forthright about mistakes committed by other friends, as well as grateful to have his own mistakes identified. But in Plumb's case he touched a nerve, and made things worse by signalling the reproof in advance in a private letter which drew attention to a 'howler which I can hardly gloss over in my review'.[76] This was not the first schoolmasterly correction Plumb had been obliged to endure,[77] but it was the first public admonition, made the more galling by the fact that Namier had previously admitted his own ignorance of the period and sought Plumb's advice when lecturing and writing about it. Plumb's response was submissive, but did include a hint of his real feelings which Namier did not pick up: an observation that Plumb's mistake was not as bad as one committed by Edward Hughes in his most recent book, which Namier had missed (or chosen to ignore) in a review.[78]

Outwardly Plumb gave no indication of his feelings, and held a party for the Namiers when they came to Cambridge.[79] But Plumb complained to his Cambridge colleague – and Namier's enemy – Herbert Butterfield, contrasting Butterfield's 'warm and friendly review' with 'the ill-written and ill-digested précis which Namier thought fit to write. Then I suppose it is quite impossible of him to be generous to another eighteenth-century historian, and I must be grateful that he took, at least, a neutral attitude.'[80] In February 1957 Namier was asked by the faculty board at Cambridge to act as a referee for Plumb's application for a Litt.D. He replied that he was too busy with his History of Parliament work.[81] Had news of this reached Plumb – and given the indiscreet nature of academic conversations it might well have done – it would have increased his sense of betrayal. Certainly, references to Namier in his private correspondence were now bitter and scornful.[82] Plumb's hostility extended to Namier's friends and collaborators. He wrote to A. L. Rowse that he expected to have to defend himself against 'Sergeant Sedgwick and Corporal Cooper', though he was careful to remain on good terms with Sedgwick.[83] He was even more poisonous in private about John Brooke, although this came after another critical review which Brooke later admitted had probably been unfair.[84]

Namier had repaired the offence he thought he had given to Berlin; he would never know how much Plumb resented him; but he did suffer considerably on another account: the breaking of his long friendship with Alan Taylor. Of all things, the occasion was Taylor's disappointment at not being offered the regius professor-ship of history at Oxford in 1957. Ten years earlier Namier had himself been full of righteous indignation at being overlooked for the same appointment. Now he was a party to the snubbing of Taylor, who, like Namier, had an elevated opinion of his own merits.

Although Taylor retained a deep admiration for Namier and his achievements as a historian, he was becoming increasingly restless at the direction in which Namier seemed to be going. In consequence, his reviews of Namier's books, while still laudatory – sometimes excessively so – were also barbed. One cause of dissension was politics. Taylor stayed true to his pre-war radicalism as Namier drifted ever fur-ther to the right. In 1950 Taylor wrote a review of *Europe in decay* which criticised the 'atmosphere of romantic praise' in which Namier always wrote about Churchill.[85] Then in 1953 a long unsigned piece by Taylor in the *Times Literary Supplement*, writ-ten to celebrate the twenty-fifth anniversary of the publication of *The structure of politics*, concluded by taking issue with Namier's contempt for intellectuals in poli-tics, and what Taylor considered his wilful inability to understand the force and even the importance of ideas:

> Every modern historian of the younger generation must regard Sir Lewis as his master; and yet we must beware of the flaw. Sir Lewis has wielded every weapon except one. He has exploited Marx and Darwin and Freud; he has appreciated both tradition and revo-lution. He has ignored the liberal spirit.[86]

Darwin had been accused of 'taking mind out of the universe'. Namier, Taylor wrote, 'has been the Darwin of political history', thus originating the accusation, repeated ever since, that Namier had 'taken the mind out of history'.

As a historian, Taylor was also frustrated beyond endurance by what he saw as Namier's wilful absorption in the minutiae of eighteenth-century parliaments and refusal to write the great books which were his destiny. He thought that Namier, encouraged by the flattery of those around him, was wasting his time in adding superfluous detail to a picture he had already painted. The publication in November 1956 of John Brooke's study of *The Chatham Administration, 1766–1768* released Taylor's pent-up anger, which issued in a brief but bilious review in the *Manchester Guardian*. Seven years earlier Taylor had reviewed Ninetta Jucker's edition of *The Jenkinson papers* much more respectfully: it was 'not an exciting book, nor even an interesting one; but it is indispensable for understanding the political system in the great age of the classical constitution'.[87] By contrast Brooke received both barrels. Thirty years earlier Namier had accomplished his historiographical revolution, Taylor declared; 'now he returns as triumphant leader of an historical school to carry the process further'. This was pointless. 'Even the most loyal admirer of Sir Lewis must tremble at the interminable series of volumes now being projected.' As for Brooke, who followed his master in method and conclusions, all he had achieved was to 'narrate in agonising detail how a number of twaddling eighteenth-century noblemen squabbled over places of profit'.[88]

Despite Taylor's occasional provocations, he and Namier had not yet fallen out. Namier could not help but recognise that Taylor was 'incalculable, and often irresponsible', but admired his talent and counted him among his closest friends.[89] After having failed in an attempt to promote Taylor's candidature for election as a fellow of the British Academy in 1951, he tried again in 1955, and this time was successful. He argued that Taylor's 'serious work deserves it, and his lighter contributions should not be held up against him'.[90] In his turn, Taylor helped organise and edit Namier's Festschrift. Not even his review of Brooke, with its potentially damaging insinuations about the History of Parliament, could alter Namier's feelings. Though 'very much annoyed', Namier shrugged his shoulders: at heart Taylor was still an *enfant terrible*, and nothing could be done about it.[91]

The story of the regius chair was a nine days' wonder in academic circles, but for the principals the effects were lasting. The story, as we know it, comes largely from two sources: the correspondence of Hugh Trevor-Roper, in long letters sent to Bernard Berenson in Florence and Wallace Notestein at Yale;[92] and a self-serving passage in Taylor's autobiography.[93] Lady Namier has nothing to say, nor is there anything in Namier's papers to set against Taylor's recollections of their conversations on the subject, which form the basis of the accounts given in biographies of Taylor.[94] Ultimate responsibility for the choice of Trevor-Roper lay with the Prime Minister Harold Macmillan, and there is not so much as a hint in his archive as to why Taylor was disregarded.

The choice of a regius professor had Oxford common rooms buzzing with gossip.[95] At first Macmillan found himself the recipient of conflicting information from the university, and according to Isaiah Berlin was in a state of perplexity.[96] He turned to Namier, who, having retired, could not conceivably be a candidate himself, and, besides his incomparable stature in the English historical profession, was a trusted friend. Macmillan's efforts to put an end to the History of Parliament had not affected their relationship, and Namier was flattered to be asked for advice.[97] He recommended Lucy Sutherland, to whom Macmillan wrote with a preliminary inquiry to see if she would be prepared to accept the chair.[98] Macmillan thought it might be 'fun' to have a female regius, even though he misheard her name ('Miss Sullivan') and thought she was a pupil of Namier.[99] However, she would only take the chair if she could keep her college headship, which was unacceptable to the university. So the choice fell open again. Taylor alleged that Namier telephoned to say that he would recommend him, as the only person fit to occupy it, but that Taylor would have to give up appearing on television and writing for the *Sunday Express*. Otherwise Namier would recommend Trevor-Roper. Taylor refused to submit to an ultimatum and put the phone down. Trevor-Roper was appointed.[100]

Taylor's version of these events, engendered by the belief that his old friend had 'betrayed' him,[101] is of a piece with all his later recollections of Namier, which invariably set Taylor himself firmly on the moral high ground. His memory of what Namier said to him about the regius chair cannot be accepted without question. In truth, we will never know what happened. Some indication of Namier's thinking may be taken from his ruminations in 1952, when asked by the vice-chancellor of Manchester University about his own successor.[102] He had recommended Taylor, but only after Lucy Sutherland, 'by far the strongest candidate' had told him she was not interested. Taylor, he wrote, had 'the makings of a first-rate historian', though his work was 'sometimes adorned rather than illuminated by a shower of rockets'.[103] As for Taylor's journalism, Namier conceded in1952 that his 'output is too great to be scholarly', but emphasised that 'his scholarship must not be judged by it'. In fact, most of Namier's own writings had appeared first in newspapers and magazines rather than academic journals, admittedly in broadsheet newspapers and heavyweight weeklies (though he had written in the distant past for the *Evening Standard*), and he never gave the impression that he objected to reaching a wide audience. It may well have been the tone of Taylor's journalism and broadcasting that he disliked. Namier's journalism was always intensely serious, and he might have considered that Taylor was merely reaching for effect.

It is also possible that political differences played a part. The Suez crisis threw these into sharp relief. Namier, driven by anxiety over the preservation of Israel and its people, was in favour of British military intervention: 'I feel we have done the right thing.'[104] He deplored the subsequent decision to withdraw troops, and sympathised with the Suez rebels on the Tory side, who included his friend Lord Hinchingbrooke, though he did not blame Macmillan personally.[105] In contrast, Taylor was a fierce critic of the invasion: he claimed later that he would not have taken the regius chair had it been offered, so disgusted was he by the Conservative government,[106] and in a public speech in London at the height of the crisis he compared the Suez landing to Hitler's aggression against Poland, a comparison that might have been calculated to offend Namier.[107]

In his observations to the Manchester vice-chancellor in 1952 Namier had also mentioned Trevor-Roper, praising his contributions to 'recent diplomatic history'. He was not qualified, he said, to pass judgment on Trevor-Roper's seventeenth-century studies, though 'when Trevor-Roper gets into controversy over some problem of that period in the *Times Literary Supplement*, he wipes the floor with his opponents': in other words, Trevor-Roper was a kindred spirit. Namier had known Trevor-Roper for some time, since 1947 at least, and they had been on good enough terms for Namier to be invited to Trevor-Roper's wedding in 1954.[108] Trevor-Roper had contributed an essay to his Festschrift. In January 1957, with Macmillan's accession to the premiership and the regius election in prospect, Trevor-Roper had invited the Namiers to Oxford, using a lunch with the duke and duchess of Northumberland as bait.[109] Comments in his letter concerning Oxford common room politics raised painful memories, and Namier added an interesting paragraph to his acceptance: 'I am sorry that Oxford continues to run true to form. Snap your fingers at it; produce a magnum opus, as you can; and the world outside will set right the wrongs of a very small circle.'[110] Later, he sent Trevor-Roper a note of congratulation on his appointment.[111] Perhaps in the end Namier grew tired of Taylor's posturing, acknowledged that he was an impossible choice, and settled for Trevor-Roper as a historian who would be acceptable to the prime minister and credible to the public, and whose nomination would also cock a snook at the Oxford establishment.

Namier soon discovered just how much he had offended Taylor. When the appointment was announced, Taylor published in the *New Statesman* a bitter denunciation of Macmillan: the prime minister evidently imagined himself as some eighteenth-century patronage-broker, which explained why he had taken Sir Lewis Namier as his 'adviser in practically everything'.[112] Taylor could not bring himself to cast stones at Namier's scholarship, in public or in private, but he ostentatiously refused all contact and rebuffed all advances. He explained to a mutual friend that

> I wasn't bitter or resentful towards Lewis but *dead* – I towards him, and for all I cared he towards me ... I didn't want the regius chair ... but I wanted him to say that I and no other ought to have it; just as I said ten years before that Lewis and no other ought to have it. So there really was no point in my trying to see him or to make it up. It was dead, killed by him, not by me.[113]

After Namier's death, the *Observer* published a piece which suggested that it was Namier rather than Taylor who had avoided the other's company. Julia was quick to write to the editor: 'This is not so. About a year before his death my husband wrote to Mr Taylor giving him a date when he would be at Oxford, so that they might meet. He received no answer. And though he bore Mr Taylor no grudge whatever, the discourtesy did sadden his last months.'[114]

The Butterfield affair

For the most part, Namier's struggles over the History and his fallings-out with fellow historians remained hidden from the public gaze. The unpleasant press coverage of his note to Isaiah Berlin was a rare exception. But he was eventually to become embroiled in a much more public dispute, over his approach to history and the malign influence which he was supposed to be exerting over the historical profession in England. This was a quarrel he had not sought, and on which he himself spent little time. In fact, he regarded criticism of the way he organised his work as impertinence. The reason these particular attacks upset him was that they coincided with the political difficulties facing the History of Parliament. The trustees always resorted to Namier's reputation as a trump card in negotiations with the Treasury. This was what had most concerned him about Alan Taylor's sneering review of Brooke. It even prompted him to urge Plumb to soften critical notices of Robert Walcott's attempt at 'Namierising' Queen Anne's parliaments, while acknowledging the book's weaknesses.[115]

The author of Namier's problems was Herbert Butterfield, professor of modern history at Cambridge.[116] His historical interests intersected with Namier's at two points. For many years Butterfield had been committed to preparing a biography of Charles James Fox, and was squatting on Fox's papers, which had been handed over to him by G. M. Trevelyan.[117] His approach to the period was very different from Namier's. Despite being the author of a short attack on *The Whig interpretation of history* (1931), a brisk denunciation of teleological history writing, which praised methodical research 'through the microscope' without citing individuals, Butterfield was himself something of a Whig, or at least a liberal, in his understanding of eighteenth-century politics. He sympathised with the rhetoric of Burke, Fox and the Rockinghams, and wished to re-emphasise the importance of ideas and issues. Namier's psychological and materialist determinism offended his Christian ethics. In a different way, Butterfield was diametrically opposed to Namier's views of European politics. Butterfield was sympathetic to Germany, if not to Nazism, and had supported appeasement. He continued to visit Germany as late as 1938, although he must have been aware of the treatment of Jews under the Nazis, and after the war argued for a rapid resumption of academic exchange.[118] He was repelled by Namier's overbearing and unforgiving anti-Germanism and his moralising approach to international relations.

Butterfield seems also to have had a personal aversion to Namier, something which was easier to nurture if one knew Namier at a distance and primarily through his writings. The two men first came into contact in the mid-1930s, when Namier was appointed as external examiner for Butterfield's Cambridge special subject on George III. At a conference in Oxford soon afterwards Butterfield saw Namier in a sharp exchange with Charles Webster. 'I learn', Butterfield wrote to a confidante, 'that Namier has a way of letting controversy run to "personalities" and has quite a list of "unforgiveables" among contemporary historians.'[119] (These 'unforgiveables' did not actually include Webster, with whom Namier was always on good terms.) In later years, Butterfield would speak of Namier as 'an old enemy of mine in the academic field', but at least some of this was in Butterfield's own mind.[120] Their early contacts made little impression on Namier. 'I met him once', he wrote in 1948, 'but have no very clear opinion about him either from that interview or from his published work.'[121] When Butterfield stated in 1957 that 'I have assumed for twenty years that I would never get any concessions from Namier', for example in sharing discoveries or access to manuscripts, this was an assumption based on a superficial reading of Namier's character rather than deriving from anything that Namier had actually said or done.

Throughout the 1930s and 1940s Butterfield had been contemplating a rebuttal of Namier's interpretation of Georgian politics, and in 1949 he eventually produced one, or at least a sort of rebuttal. *George III, Lord North and the people* was an account of the political crisis of 1779–80, when the dilapidated ministry of Lord North was assailed on three fronts: in the House of Commons by Burke's campaign of 'economical reform', in the English constituencies by the organisation of popular opinion in petitions and addresses, and in Ireland by parliamentary 'patriots' and an extra-parliamentary movement spearheaded by a paramilitary body, the Volunteers.

The purpose of Butterfield's book was to imply the limitations of Namier's analysis of the eighteenth-century political system by reasserting the importance of public opinion. He dedicated the book to G. M. Trevelyan, and was happy to declare his 'love' for the cause which the Rockinghams had professed to stand.[122] But it was by no means a frontal attack, and the introduction seemed to accept Namier's analysis of English 'political structure' in the 1760s, while suggesting that the events of 1779–80 marked the beginning of a new world, in which there were real issues to fight over.

To some extent, the book bears out Hugh Trevor-Roper's harsh verdict on Butterfield, that he was 'essentially a timorous man, who shied away from real issues behind a parade of subtlety'.[123] J. H. Plumb was of the same opinion, believing that Butterfield 'was rather frightened of Namier' and, rather than rejecting his work directly, 'fenced' at him, throwing in a dart whenever he could' and dancing away before the riposte.[124] Although there were some elements in the introduction which dissented explicitly from the Namier version – a carefully phrased qualification of Namier's dismissal of Burke's *Causes of the present discontents*, for example – Butterfield seems to have been intent on provoking Namier without challenging him directly, most obviously by ignoring his work.[125] Namier was not mentioned in text or footnotes (though to be fair, hardly any secondary authority was), even when Butterfield was paraphrasing his arguments.

If Butterfield had intended to provoke, he succeeded only to a limited degree. Namier did not respond publicly. He was perfectly happy to deride Butterfield's work in private, pointing out to correspondents its 'characteristic defects', including the inadequacies of Butterfield's prose style, and in special subject classes at Manchester referred to Butterfield as a 'fool'.[126] Later, when canvassing universities for support for the History of Parliament, he ignored Butterfield. He would not waste his time in responding to Butterfield's book. In 1949, having originally accepted it for the *Times Literary Supplement*, he turned the review over to his junior, Eric Robson, who dismissed Butterfield's attempt to revive Burke's accusations against George III, and derided 'the incomprehensible language used to maintain the sensational impression of impending revolution'.[127] Other reviews were equally negative, including a piece by Alan Taylor in the *New Statesman* which one of Butterfield's friends thought 'nasty and spiteful'.[128] Namier could not be blamed for all of this even though Butterfield seems to have regarded him as the originator. The most comprehensive demolition, in fact, came from the pen of Richard Pares, who was on friendly terms with Butterfield: Pares admired Namier, and the feeling was mutual, but they did not always agree, and Pares was sufficiently independent-minded not to rank himself, or to be ranked by Butterfield, in the 'Namier school'.[129]

For the next few years Butterfield stayed away from Namier's home ground, but his humiliation deepened his dislike of the man and his methods. Butterfield repaid Namier for his exclusion from the conferences on parliamentary history by keeping Namier from participating in the annual Wiles Lectures at Queen's University, Belfast, in which Butterfield had a guiding hand. The lectures were (and still are) followed by formal discussions with staff and students of the university and visiting experts. Namier was never invited. He was put forward as a possible lecturer in 1954 by the professor of modern history, Michael Roberts, to talk on a subject relating to 'diplomacy and international relations', and while Butterfield did not openly reject the suggestion, and a letter of invitation was prepared, it was not sent, and Namier was never mentioned again.[130] A few years later, when Namier was to receive an honorary degree at Cambridge, Butterfield, who by this time had published his first tentative criticisms of Namier and his methods, wrote to the university vice-chancellor to forestall any embarrassment at being called upon in his capacity as regius professor to entertain the honorand:

> I have for decades followed with complete exactitude a principle which I learnt from the practice of G. M. Trevelyan: namely, all honour to Namier only I cannot be the one to entertain him. It happens that in any case Namier wouldn't consent to be entertained by me.[131]

It evidently took time for Butterfield to steel himself for direct action, but by the autumn of 1956 the time seemed right. There were signs that academic opinion was turning against 'Namierisation'. The omens were apparent even to Namier himself.[132] Dissatisfaction with his explanation of Munich and its aftermath, which had hitherto been confined to occasional book reviews, had grown sufficiently to encourage a young academic at the LSE to publish an article in 1954 denouncing Namier's moralistic approach to international relations. This article emboldened other would-be giant-killers, and in 1957 a lecturer at Nottingham published an article in the inaugural issue of a journal produced in his own university – too obscure to attract Namier's notice – in which he 'developed some … critical reflections' on Namier's 'treatment' of eighteenth-century politics.[133]

There was also increasing impatience with the extent to which Namier's method, and his conclusions, were being taken up by the next generation and imposed upon other periods. This was first articulated in print by Alan Taylor, for reasons of his own. Hugh Trevor-Roper, in an otherwise positive review of *Personalities and powers* had also worried that Namier's 'revolution' had become orthodoxy. Namier was in danger, 'like all founders, of being judged by his disciples, those armies of unimaginative students who, in many a western university, mechanically "Namierise" whatever slice of history their professor has assigned to them'.[134] The publication in 1956 of Walcott's ill-considered 'Namierisation' of Queen Anne's reign provoked other sceptics.[135] Even Plumb's watered-down reviews concluded that 'factional strife, as such, is a key to only a part of the politics of Anne's reign'.[136] An editorial in the *TLS* warned against applying Namier's methods uncritically.[137] And in the *Manchester Guardian* Maurice Ashley (formerly a great admirer of Namier) questioned whether 'the "Namier reaction"' had now gone too far', and wondered whether 'Sir Lewis's disciples are not inclined to copy his methods without his wit and gracefulness'.[138] A consensus was starting to form, that Namier was training a body of followers who slavishly asked the same questions as their leader and came up with the same answers. The publication in the autumn of 1956 of Brooke's volume on the Chatham administration seems to have crystallised this opinion.[139] Those with qualms about the establishment and organisation of the History of Parliament imagined their worst fears were being realised.

Butterfield first appeared in the lists in December 1956 with a negative review of Brooke in the *Cambridge Review*, which he used as a lever to prise open what he considered to be the closed box of historical writing on George III's reign.[140] He followed up with a notice of John Owen's first book, *The rise of the Pelhams*, in the same journal, less contemptuous in tone, but making similar criticisms. By going out of his way to compliment Owen's 'quiet methods', and 'absence of cliquish arrogance or vulgar contentiousness', he implied that this was unusual in the academic stable from whence Owen came.[141] Then there appeared a more direct assault: a short article in the magazine *Encounter* in April 1957, entitled 'George III and the Namier school', which warned against exaggerating the extent and completeness of the 'Namier revolution': it was, Butterfield asserted, neither as innovative, nor as satisfying, as its devotees assumed.[142] Older traditions in the 'higher regions of scholarship' still had much to offer, and had in fact anticipated some of Namier's discoveries. Butterfield called for a return to narrative, to supplement and even perhaps to supplant structural analysis as an explanatory tool of political history, and for a renewed appreciation of the importance of political ideas: he thought that Namier and the 'modern school' were 'over-contemptuous about the writers on politics' and 'too blind to the part which they may play in actual life'. These arguments were developed more fully in book form in *George III and the historians*, published the following autumn.[143]

Butterfield was careful not to attack the detail of Namier's work; instead, he used Brooke as a kind of proxy, repeating his criticisms of Brooke's book every time he took the field, to the extent that Brooke felt justifiably aggrieved: 'I can think of no young historian publishing a first book who has had to face such repeated criticisms from so distinguished a scholar.'[144] It was Butterfield's contention that Namier's work had been turned into a template: ostensibly his quarrel was with 'the Namier school' rather than with the master himself. But many of his arguments – for example his reservations about the value of structural analysis, and his questioning final chapter, headed 'Can history be too mechanically scientific?' – obviously applied to Namier personally. Moreover, it was Butterfield's avowed intention to promote an attitude of healthy criticism in place of what he considered to be the servile acceptance of Namier's views.

The results of Butterfield's intervention would be mixed. His attempt to reha-bilitate the older generation of constitutional historians was dismissed and is now forgotten, even though his analysis of the historiography of the early years George III's reign took up more than half of his book. Although not entirely new, his assess-ment of the weakness of structural analysis was more effective: his renewed emphasis on narrative and on the importance of ideas provided the foundations for, and may even be said to have set in motion, the critique of 'Namierism' that rapidly gathered momentum after Namier's death. In the short term, however, what attracted more publicity and offered more of a threat to Namier's reputation was Butterfield's warn-ing of the dangers presented by the ascendancy of the 'Namier school' in historical writing in Britain on the eighteenth century. 'The Namier school is a formidable one', he wrote, 'because, apart from the massiveness of its researches, it represents the most powerfully organised squadron in our historical world at the present time, the disciples relaying the ideas of the master with closer fidelity than I remember to have been the case in any other branch of historical study since it became a serious form of scholarship.'[145]

No matter that Butterfield failed to name any members of this 'squadron' beyond Brooke, Sedgwick and John Owen, the characterisation struck a chord with many in the historical profession who suspected Namier of having intended something of the sort with his grandiose History of Parliament project, disapproved of his supervis-ing research students only on subjects which related to his own interests, and were prepared to believe that he would only tolerate the company of flatterers. The term 'the Namier school' had been in currency for some time, denoting those students of the eighteenth century, and beyond, who took up Namier's way of doing history.[146] Butterfield had attacked Namier at his most vulnerable point, where refutation would prove particularly difficult, for if Namier chose to defend his colleagues from attack, or if they defended him, the response would appear to reinforce Butterfield's case.

Namier did not accept Butterfield's criticisms; nor could he understand the point of historiography.[147] What was important was to find out what had happened in George III's reign, rather than what subsequent generations of historians thought had happened. In any case, there could be little value in sifting the works of Whig historians to find instances in which some of them had got things right, or nearly right, when the prevailing nature of the Whig interpretation had been fundamentally wrong. The memory of the way in which latter-day Whig historians had dismissed his own early work still rankled.

In the event, Namier chose not to answer directly, but Owen and Sedgwick did, which in a way served Butterfield's purpose. Namier turned down the opportunity to review the book himself, but wanted to see his objections articulated, especially the notion of the existence of a 'Namier school'. He refused an invitation to reply to the *Encounter* article, on the grounds that 'I am approaching 70, have an enormous task on my hands which does not allow me to engage on other work (least of all on controversies), and if some day I shall explain once more my approach to history and its techniques, I would not link it up with a reply to any attacks against me.' Instead, he recommended Brooke as someone who could 'expose Butterfield's methods as historian and controversialist', a suggestion which was not to the magazine's liking.[148] Afterwards, Brooke was kept out of the firing line since he had been so obviously singled out by Butterfield. Sedgwick, who had already intervened over Butterfield's review of Owen, contributed a dismissive review in the *Listener*, giving a few examples of the 'misrepresentations and mistakes' which he said littered the book.[149] Owen then took the fight to the enemy's home ground by tackling the book in the *Cambridge Review*.[150] This more lengthy treatment was intended as a comprehensive demolition. While ostentatiously disdaining to revisit 'the rather generous quota of factual errors' listed by other reviewers, Owen argued that Butterfield's case consisted of unsubstantiated generalisations and selective quotations, and with reference to the argument that the 'Namier school' had ungenerously ignored their predecessors, noted how few references to other historians' work had appeared in *George III, Lord North and the people*: Butterfield was evidently disinclined to practise what he preached.

More importantly, as far as Namier was concerned, Owen also challenged Butterfield's allegations about the existence of a 'Namier school'. Only three 'disciples' had been named, and although other eighteenth-century scholars had long been associated with Namier and accepted the essential validity of both his method and his general conclusions about the period – Lucy Sutherland, for example, Richard Pares or Ian Christie – it would be absurd to consider such individuals as subservient. Indeed, Butterfield had cited Pares' Ford Lectures to help his case against Namier, while Christie's volume in the series 'England in the age of the American revolution', which appeared in 1958, and which Namier read in typescript, suggested that the political world of 1780 was different from that of 1760 and that issues of principle had by then become more important.[151] Besides, Namier prided himself on allowing his students and the contributors to the History of Parliament to find their own answers to historical questions. No one who worked closely with Namier ever complained at being forced to tailor their views to his, and indeed some of his closest collaborators came to differ with him on important points.[152] As Owen put it in his review, 'those who are even remotely acquainted with the character and work of Sir Lewis Namier must know that there are few people to whom the idea of any interference with the free play of criticism is more repugnant.'[153]

This was a difficult case to make to those who had already made up their minds about Namier and his 'disciples', and by defending the master Owen had given more ammunition to those who were predisposed to believe in Butterfield's 'squadron'. Butterfield had left one opening, however. In support of his contention about the organised and disciplined nature of the Namierites he had misconstrued Namier's foreword to Brooke's book, and wrongly applied its description of the History of Parliament as a 'collective effort' to the series of separately authored volumes – 'England in the age of the American revolution' – of which Brooke's formed a part. The first person to pick this up was John Carswell, writing anonymously in the *TLS*.[154] Butterfield excused himself, somewhat unconvincingly, in a letter to the editor, on the grounds that he had assumed a link between the series and the History and therefore thought that Namier's foreword 'authorised the view' that Brooke's work 'embodied co-operative ideas of the school'.[155] This was an admission of weakness and too good an opportunity to resist. Sedgwick pounced on it in the *Listener*, and the very next day a letter appeared in the *TLS* from Namier himself pushing in the arrowhead: Butterfield's garbled version 'fits admirably into the picture he draws of the "Namier school", and shows how emotions have unconsciously affected his thinking'.[156] Butterfield could only offer public penance for the mistake, though in a fashion that almost anticipated the twenty-first-century fashion for conditional apology: '*If I was wrong*, I hope [Professor Namier] will still consider this to have been due to "emotion" rather than to any conscious distortion.'[157]

Butterfield admitted that this contretemps had given him a metaphorical 'black eye'.[158] Owen's review had been particularly effective, and according to its author, had been greeted by many in Cambridge 'with a kind of malicious glee … Sir Ivor Jennings [master of Trinity Hall] was delighted and commented that if Butterfield had any conscience he would resign his chair'.[159] The fact that Namier had left to others the task of disposing of his work fed Butterfield's enmity, in a kind of psychological vicious circle.[160] Nor had the book's reception elsewhere provided much consolation.[161] Most press notices were lukewarm: the consensus was that Butterfield had made a few useful corrections but had spoiled his case by exaggeration, and was in danger of attempting to reinstate a discredited mythology.[162] Reviews in academic journals were equally guarded.[163] However, there were a few positive responses, from which Butterfield drew encouragement: the conservative philosopher Michael Oakeshott praised the book in the *Spectator* (a review which reportedly angered Namier) and in the *Manchester Guardian* Roger Fulford, a self-proclaimed Whig, welcomed Butterfield's reinstatement of ideals and principles into eighteenth-century politics.[164] Even more satisfying was the review in *Encounter* by the liberal American historian Arthur Schlesinger Jr, who endorsed the protest against 'the depreciation of human purposes, ideas and ideals' in the reduction of history to 'social structure', and expressed the hope that Butterfield would 'win his fight' to reinstate narrative.[165]

Butterfield had expected Americans to be sympathetic, given their ideological investment in libertarian ideals. He actively searched for allies there, with success.[166] His private correspondence shows how important he felt this mission to be: it was a 'campaign' against everything that Namier stood for in history. His principal intention had been to 'fork criticisms of Namier out of people who had never put them into print before', and he anxiously totted up expressions of solidarity.[167] Predictably, one of these came from G. P. Gooch, who had suffered at Namier's hands in the past.[168] More surprising, and even more gratifying, was a letter from R. B. McCallum, master of Pembroke College, Oxford, a former pupil of Namier's at Balliol. McCallum recalled that he had once tried to persuade Namier that quite a few of the things Namier claimed to have 'discovered' were to be found in Lecky. This was an unfortunate choice of authority on McCallum's part, provoking Namier into a monologue which, McCallum said, left him dizzy.[169]

Gradually battle lines were being drawn up, and Namier's reputation was coming under hostile scrutiny. Many academics still thought of him as standing at the head of the historical profession in England, and in September 1957 a special feature article in the *Sunday Times* paid tribute to his pre-eminence as a historian, in 'setting new fashions for historical understanding'.[170] But it was not long before casual disparagement of Namier's history – as mechanical in its methods and desiccated in its texture – became commonplace in the newspaper press.[171] American interest in the controversy resulted in a symposium on 'Namier and the eighteenth century' at the Midwestern Conference on British Studies in the autumn of 1958, with scholars ranging themselves for and against.[172] Even Richard Pares, when contemplating likely candidates to succeed him as editor of the *English Historical Review*, jibbed at the possibility of handing over to John Owen, despite the excellence of Owen's scholarship, since Owen was 'a devout member of the Namier school, and I feel some hesitation about handing over the *Review* to a member of any of the gangs'.[173] One of Plumb's friends, the journalist John Raymond, even turned it into a joke, with a satirical piece in the *New Statesman* purporting to record minutes of the AGM of

'Namier inc.', in terms which assumed the existence of just the kind of organised academic enterprise that Butterfield had described.[174]

Namier was usually able to shrug off professional criticism but was sensitive to ridicule and seems to have been nettled by Raymond's piece. He was also concerned at the possible impact on the History of Parliament, and on the careers of the young people for whom he felt responsible. In the past several of his Manchester students had secured university posts, but now his brightest pupils and assistants were struggling to advance their careers. John Owen's Oxford fellowship was an exception, and in any case Owen had powerful friends in the university. By contrast, John Tomlinson had quit the academic jobs market to become a schools inspector, Alan Hardy was working at Conservative Central Office, and Brian Hayes had joined the civil service. Another research student, Peter Thomas, eventually became a lecturer at Glasgow after a string of disappointments, while John Cannon, for whom Namier repeatedly wrote enthusiastic references, only succeeded in securing a lectureship (at Bristol) after Namier's death.

Anxiety over the potential impact on the History of Parliament probably explains why Namier invited Butterfield in December 1957 to come and see for himself what was being done at the History's offices.[175] This occurred so soon after their bitter exchange in the *TLS* that Butterfield was alarmed. Having agreed at first, he then wrote to postpone on the grounds that he was writing up another article, this time for the journal *History*, which would reiterate and develop the arguments in his book.[176] Namier proved surprisingly amenable, which Butterfield again thought sinister.[177] Eventually, Butterfield did visit, in the following winter, and Namier was able to show him the reality of his supposedly mighty empire. The niceties were observed on both sides, and a form of diplomatic relations was ostensibly established, but as far as Namier was concerned, the damage had been done.[178]

Recessional

Although Namier emphatically rejected Butterfield's criticisms, and considered his characterisation of the 'Namier school' as absurd, there is no doubt that he was shaken by the controversy. The niggling comments of reviewers seemed to indicate a turning of the tide against his kind of history, and indeed against him personally. The breakdown in his relations with Alan Taylor – one of the friendships he most cherished – and Taylor's persistent sniping at the History of Parliament, which Namier was struggling to bring to completion under unremitting pressure, added to the strain. It is no surprise, therefore, to find that his life was clouded by ever-deepening intimations of mortality. *Vanished supremacies*, which Hamish Hamilton published in 1958, was marketed as 'The collected essays of Sir Lewis Namier, volume I', as if it were intended as the opening verse in a recessional. In the preface Namier spoke melodramatically of 'the dark days of old age ... rapidly advancing', adding (doubtless to the chagrin of his publisher), 'I see the rest of my days under a heavy mortgage to the History of Parliament, and to further work on materials which I have been collecting for it most of my life.'[179] According to Toynbee, he felt himself to be running 'an anxious race against time'.[180] Grumbles about the pressure of work on the History continued, occasionally reaching a new pitch: he told Lucy Sutherland that 'the burden is becoming too much for me', and evidently confided in Neale, of all people, that he regretted ever having participated in the project.[181]

Those who could observe him at close quarters were struck by the extent of his physical decline. When John Tomlinson visited the Institute of Historical Research Namier greeted him, as always, with characteristic 'old world courtesy', but 'the act of rising to his feet ... seemed an unbearable effort'.[182] The state of Namier's health was openly discussed at meetings of the History of Parliament trustees, who were seriously concerned as to whether he was robust enough to be able to finish his volumes.[183] His closest collaborator, John Brooke, claimed to have 'noticed in the last years of Namier's life a diminution in his efficiency. His mind was as clear as ever but he was no longer able to take the same trouble over details.'[184]

The assertion in Julia's biography that Namier now saw himself as a hindrance rather than a help to everyone, including the 'team' at the History, and felt that he ought to leave the stage while he could do so with dignity, probably over-dramatises his disillusionment. It does not tally with his evident commitment to the writing of the biographies, to which he devoted long hours. Moreover, her suggestion that his unhappiness was exacerbated by 'dissatisfaction' and even 'acrimony' in his section, and that he was in effect being bullied by his assistants, sounds like fantasy.[185] Certainly, Brooke did not always agree with Namier on points of interpretation, and there may have been occasional expressions of impatience – inevitable given the pressure under which everyone was working – but Namier himself had always been willing to argue matters out; so it is far more likely that it was Julia rather than Namier himself who perceived and resented any apparent insubordination.

The glimpses we have of Namier outside the History also convey the impression of a marked slowing down in the tempo of his life. He still hoped to organise 'a scheme' of sorts 'for publications connected with our work'[186] – for in the vice of endlessly projecting new books he remained incorrigible to the very end – but now the time spent working in the evenings was devoted to the revision of *England in the age of the American revolution* for a second edition (following the second edition of *The structure of politics*, which Macmillan had brought out in 1957). Entertaining was now reduced in scale. When Julia invited her friend Constance Babington Smith to share a meal at The Grampians she had to admit that Lewis's dinner would offer 'nothing much for a young palate, it has to suit his ageing digestion'. The menu would be mushroom patties with broccoli, a mild cheese or yogurt, fruit, and finally a lime tisane.[187] At weekends they could do little more than potter: Julia reported in September 1958 that she and Lewis had gone to Kew Gardens for 'a gentle walk … We sat about, here and there.'[188] Aside from visits to Oxford and to old friends like the Buxtons, who were now living on the Norfolk coast, any time out of London was more likely to be spent abroad, in the Swiss Alps or in Tuscany.

In the spring of 1958 Namier did manage a more extensive trip, to Israel, primarily to give his personal attention to editorial issues over the publication of the Weizmann papers, and to offer the staff at the Weizmann Institute at Rehovot the benefit of his expertise. This included taking an informal seminar in which he explored the different contributions to historical understanding made by Marx and Freud. Needless to say, Freud came out well; Marx much less so. However, according to Julia, the point of the talk was to emphasise, despite Namier's professed detestation of economics, the importance of both economic and psychological factors in shaping 'the interlocking private, communal and political life of every man'. Once the work was done he and Julia did a little travelling, and enjoyed themselves in spite of a heatwave.[189] In Jerusalem Namier was looked after by Jacob Talmon, a young Israeli historian whom he had got to know in London. Namier gave another talk, at the Hebrew University, along the lines of his seminar at Rehovot. As described by Talmon, this was a memorable occasion:

> The reception hall of the Sherman building was packed with teachers and students … Namier rose to his feet. His voice trembled and tears rolled down his cheeks as he began with the Hebrew 'If I forget thee, O Jerusalem'. It was not a lecture in the ordinary sense. Without a scrap of paper in his hand he gave us his testament as a scholar, recalling his early beginnings, his later successes and failures, issuing warnings, giving advice and encouragement to the young. The words were simple, but the things he said came straight from his deepest personal experience.[190]

Namier's view of Israel had mellowed. His involvement in the Weizmann edition made him feel generally more at ease with his Zionist past. Before his journey to Israel he had resumed his correspondence with Ben-Gurion, encouraged by a letter from Talmon, who had been appointed as Ben-Gurion's official biographer. Talmon reported to Namier an interview with the prime minister in which 'your name cropped up very early in the conversation. I noticed that B.G.'s face lit up with animated and friendly interest … He was delighted to hear that you would be visiting Israel … and was very much looking forward to seeing you.'[191] Isaiah Berlin, who accompanied the Namiers on part of their journey, described Namier as 'walking on air'. Perhaps allowing himself some imaginative licence, Berlin wrote to a friend that Namier

> was in a state of unspeakable admiration: loved everybody and everything: and when I complained that Tel Aviv was hideously ugly, tawdry, noisy, tense, and that Jewish Jerusalem was … self-conscious, pedantic, sad, pretentious and snobbish in a *petit bourgeois* way, he waved all this aside furiously, and said that the people he met were simple, dignified, brave, constructive and life-enhancing, and were also kind, generous and unbroken as human beings, and he was sorry to be seventy and not to be able to emigrate … I asked him if there were not too many rabbis for him. At this point he did react a little, and said he wanted them *all* dead. When I went to Jerusalem with him … every time he saw an old Chassid with a fur hat and side curls and long black coat, he gnashed his teeth and clenched his fists and uttered threatening sounds.[192]

On returning to England Namier wrote two articles for the *Sunday Times*, recording the remarkable achievements of the new state, and ending on a defiant note:

> In Israel a new civilisation is being built under the constant threat of immediate obliteration … So much, however, is certain: whatever the threat, the Israelis will not allow themselves to be led up the Munich path of territorial concessions complete with guarantees, and followed by ignominious extinction. If they have to die, they will go down fighting, with their morale unbroken.[193]

The Namiers endured another domestic crisis during the winter of 1959–60. Their doctor had ordered that Namier's favourite reading chair be resprung to relieve the pain in his spine. When the upholsterers delivered it, Julia took it upon herself to drag it into its accustomed position before her husband returned home, since he was forbidden on medical advice to lift heavy objects. But in doing so she strained her own back, aggravating a chronic weakness which had originated in her maltreatment in Stalin's prison camps. For most of January and February 1960 she was confined to bed in considerable pain. The sight of her suffering, she wrote, had a devastating effect on Lewis, and in retrospect she interpreted his meaningful silences at her bedside as an outward sign of an unspoken determination that he would not outlive her.[194] The tangible effect on Namier was to trigger a minor breakdown in his own health, to the extent that he was forced to take time off work for 'congenial reading'.[195] Within a few weeks Julia was on the mend, and Namier could go to Oxford to cast his vote for Harold Macmillan as chancellor of the university, in a campaign successfully orchestrated by Trevor-Roper.[196] But he felt no better in himself.[197] So in June 1960 the Namiers took an Italian holiday, in the thermal spa at Montecatini. 'Mud-baths' as Sedgwick put it, interspersed with sightseeing, evidently helped Julia, but not her husband.[198] He returned in as much discomfort as ever.

Their time in Tuscany had been cut short because Namier was to be presented with his second honorary degree from Oxford – a doctorate of civil laws. It was Macmillan's first Encaenia as chancellor, and the dozen honorary graduands were very much the prime minister's personal choice. After Oxford's vice-chancellor came the archbishop of York and the earl of Home. Sir John Wheeler-Bennett was also included. Namier's citation, which made a point of stating that his genius had first been recognised by A. L. Smith, called him the 'creator of the science of modern history, who has never forgotten to treat history as an art', and in a nod to the History of Parliament, which Macmillan had tried to shut down, noted that Namier 'wishes to discover the character, motives and ambitions of everyone of the great number of politicians of the period'.[199]

At around this time he and Julia were surprised by a visit from his niece Anna, Teodora's younger daughter, a law graduate from the University of Warsaw, who was following family tradition in pursuing a profession which her grandfather had practised and Namier himself had once contemplated. Anna remembered Julia as very welcoming, but Namier himself as cold and distant.[200] This unemotional reaction on his part is surprising, given Julia's recollection that he was often to be seen gazing upon photographs of his two nieces as children.[201] It may perhaps be accounted for by his deafness, which made conversation difficult, and by the very suddenness of the visit, which caught him off guard, and presumably opened the door to a draught of unwelcome memories. Julia's biography in fact tells us nothing about Teodora after her marriage in 1924. Although Teodora lived on until 1969, her elder daughter Klara until 1973, and Anna until 2016, Julia made no attempt to contact them while researching her book. In turn, Anna's sons were told nothing of their great-uncle until one of them discovered the family history for himself. Namier's 'disinheritance' by his father cast a long shadow.

In July 1960, following the excitement of the Encaenia, the staff at the History felt that Namier had rallied, and was recovering his old vigour, even though he was painfully thin.[202] When the History of Parliament trustees tackled him again about his survey, he was at last able to give an answer of sorts, indicating that he had pondered the subject, even if the structure was still not clear in his mind:

> The problem of selection was infinite and his difficulty lay in choosing which particular themes to pursue since all the many possible ones could not conceivably be included in one comparatively short survey. One possible line … was the independence of members, in particular its effect upon the 'treasury group'; another was an analysis of the representative character of the tories; yet another the social and political composition of the army officers in parliament and the extent to which these varied during the period; a fourth could be the character of contested elections and the extent to which these were

local or national in character …The correlation of these central themes from two thousand interlocking biographies was the problem now facing him.[203]

The rambling nature of this answer, and the sense of fatigue and oppression conveyed, ought to have been a warning; and indeed a former assistant on the History, who had not seen Namier for a while and caught sight of him at the Institute of Historical Research, was struck by how very frail he appeared.[204] Julia's biography implies that both she and her husband sensed somehow that his death was imminent, and while this can easily be dismissed as *ex post facto* rationalisation, there is no doubt that she was seriously concerned, telling a friend that 'he is ailing the whole time in spite of all the efforts by two excellent physicians'.[205]

Death

The end came with relative suddenness.[206] On Friday 19 August, having struggled all day at the Institute with his survey, Namier was due to spend the evening working with Julia on the revised edition of *England in the age of the American revolution*. When he reached their flat, having been strap-hanging on the Central Line all the way to Shepherd's Bush because 'an extraordinary cramp in his lower bowel' made it agonising for him to sit, Julia sent for the doctor, who prescribed painkillers and sent the patient to bed. Towards midnight the pain eased and Namier fell asleep, only to awake early next morning with obvious signs of internal bleeding. He would not allow the doctor to be called again until eight, and was then rushed by ambulance to St Mary's Hospital, Paddington, where a baffled surgeon organised an emergency operation to find out what was wrong. Julia was sent home, to return again at three that afternoon. At about half past one, while 'speaking cheerfully to his nurse', who was preparing him for theatre, he collapsed. Julia received a telephone call to say that it was all over, 'probably a burst aorta'. She told one of her closest friends that Lewis had died 'with a speed and nicety of outstanding elegance'.[207]

The post mortem showed the cause of the haemorrhage to be a small malignant tumour in the pancreas. Julia was told that the cancer could not have been present for more than six months, though she herself felt that 'the disease was with him for about two years', even if not localised. She convinced herself that he had in some way willed his own death to avoid the insupportable misery of outliving her. Although shocked and disorientated – 'I am only beginning to realise how, through the years, everything here has been built up to serve and help Lewis to live and to work. There simply is nothing else' – she could not grieve. Instead, she was thankful that his had not been a lingering death: 'to his last breath his mind was clear and his will unimpaired'.[208]

He had been haunted by the fate of his fellow eighteenth-century specialist Richard Pares, who was disabled and ultimately paralysed by an incurable illness. Namier had never feared death, but 'slow dying with increasing decrepitude and immobilisation he dreaded. This he was spared.'[209]

'He will be an irreparable loss to his friends, like you and me, who have known him so long, not only as a great historian, but as a very lovable human being. One can only be grateful to have had the privilege of knowing and collaborating with him. I shall miss him deeply, more than I can say.' Thus Romney Sedgwick, who had worked closely with Namier for over thirty years, wrote to 'Lefty' Lewis two days after Namier's death.[210] This aspect of Namier's character, his ability to inspire deep affection, was largely absent from the newspaper obituaries. Every writer paid tribute to his forensic skill, scholarly integrity, immense knowledge, incisive judgments and commanding prose style, and all registered the mark he had made on the eighteenth century, while at the same acknowledging – in a way that recently had become more common – that his work had limitations. *The Times* obituary, written by the obituaries editor, Colin Watson,[211] paid more attention than most to its subject's supposed weaknesses: his inability to write a sustained narrative, or to 'capture the movement of history', his failure to write the big books which his admirers craved, and his bludgeoning style in argument, both in person and in print. The culmination was a remarkable sentence stating that Namier's 'crushing blows' were 'the more unexpected from being delivered with a special Jewish dexterity'.[212]

Even an editor at Hamish Hamilton, who had grown to dread phone calls from Namier about proofs, complimentary copies or some other occasion of annoyance, found this article unbalanced, and Ian Gilmour, owner and former editor of the *Spectator*, was sufficiently exercised to go into print to record Namier's generosity and defend him against accusations of being a bore: 'To those who dislike a conversation being educative, and who prefer it to be in sentences, not in paragraphs, Namier's company demanded too great an effort. To everybody else he was a most stimulating and engaging companion.'[213] Others of Namier's friends, like Toynbee and Liddell Hart, wrote to the press with personal reminiscences of his fundamental good nature.[214] One unnamed correspondent, from an Oxford family whose children had known Namier as 'Uncle Lewis' (either the Smiths or the Bells), commented that 'Like Dr Johnson, he was the kindest of men in time of need, but could not stand humbug. That was why the force of his argument sometimes concealed the warmth of his heart.'[215]

Perhaps the most interesting published commentary came from Alan Taylor, writing in the *Observer*.[216] He could not forget the friendship that had once existed, and his appreciation was generous, acknowledging Namier's originality while reiterating the criticism that he could not provide 'sustained narrative': 'his work lacked movement, which many find the stuff of history. It was ponderous and immobile, like the man himself. He was a heavyweight, who liked to stand his ground, not run after events.' It was an acute analysis, but not unfair, and not quite as detached and objective as Taylor may have intended, ending with a reference to Namier's greatest disappointment, which had also been his own: 'He loved England, particularly the traditional England of the governing classes. Most of all he loved the University of Oxford. The university repaid this great historian by according him recognition only after he had passed retiring age.'

Namier's funeral, at Golders Green crematorium, was a private affair. Sedgwick was told that 'Julia does not want anyone except herself and a few relations to be present'. There would have been few enough blood relations in Britain to be asked, and neither Namier's sister nor his nieces could be expected to come from Poland: it is unlikely that they were even invited. Julia was supported by one or two of her own friends.[217] A public memorial service was eventually held two months later, on 27 October, at St Paul's Church, Knightsbridge, whose Anglo-Catholic traditions reflected Julia's taste if not her husband's. (In fact, nothing is known of Namier's own religious preferences in his last years, or even if he went to church at all.) The congregation sang the hymn 'The strife is o'er, the battle done'; there was a prayer from the parish priest, Father Michael Barney, which gave thanks for Namier's 'great learning, and for the exactness by which he measured truth'; and the choir sang the Russian contakion of the departed. Bob Boothby delivered the address, praising Namier's moral courage and his insight. 'Of the man himself', he concluded,

> I would say only this. He gave affection, and needed it. He found it not only in the love of his wife, and of a close circle of friends, but in the deep admiration of a host of pupils now scattered all over the world. In greater measure, perhaps, than he himself ever realised.[218]

A week later a much shorter service was held in the college chapel at Balliol. Julia was present, alongside Lucy Sutherland, Hugh Trevor-Roper, Isaiah Berlin and others of Namier's Oxford friends. This time there was no address. Appropriately, the last words to be spoken were those of the college prayer.[219]

Notes

1 Editorial board minutes, 1951–6, fo. 108 (HPT).
2 Lucy Sutherland to Namier, 26 June 1952 (Bodl., Sutherland papers, box 9); Namier to Sutherland, 2 July 1952 (ibid.).

3   Quoted in Ved Mehta, *Fly and the fly-bottle: encounters with British intellectuals* (1963), 187–8.

4   Trustees' minutes, Apr. 1951 (TNA, STAT 14/1478).

5   Namier to G. S. Pryde, 31 Mar. 1954 (HPT, N–59); trustees' rep. 1954–5 (TNA, T 219/652/79–84).

6   Trustees' rep. 1955–6 (IHR archives, HS7).

7   For what follows, see D. W. Hayton, 'Sir Lewis Namier, Sir John Neale and the shaping of the *History of Parliament*', *Parliamentary History*, xxxii (2013), 202–7.

8   For example, Namier to Macmillan, 11 Jan. 1957 (HPT, N–66); Macmillan to Namier, 18 Jan. 1957 (ibid.).

9   Harold to Maurice Macmillan, 10 Jan. 1952, quoted in Adam Sisman, *A. J. P. Taylor: a biography* (paperback edn, 1995), 236.

10 Memo [Jan. 1956] (TNA, T 219/653).

11 A. H. M. Hillis to Sir Alexander Johnston, 1 Feb. 1956 (TNA, T 219/653).

12 'Summary note on the organisation of the History of Parliament ... 26 June 1958 (NLW, Clement Davies papers, P/4/52); Clement Davies to Macmillan, 1 May 1956 (TNA, T 219/653); R. D. Barlas to M. F. Clapp, 7 May 1956 (TNA, T 219/653).

13 Editorial board minutes, 1956–8, fo. 2 (HPT).

14 Editorial board minutes, 1956–8, fos 6–8, 10 (HPT).

15 Editorial board minutes, 1956–8, fo. 45 (HPT).

16 G. S. Downey to A. H. M. Hillis, 30 Jan. 1957 (TNA, T 219/653); note by McAndrew, n.d. (ibid., T 219/653).

17 R. D. Barlas to E. L. C. Mullins, 16 May 1958 (NLW, Davies papers, P/4/25).

18 Editorial board minutes, 1956–8, fo. 43 (HPT).

19 Neale to E. L. C. Mullins, 5 June 1957 ('confidential') (HPT, N–20). Original emphasis.

20 E. L. C. Mullins to Sir Frank Stenton, 14, 19 May 1958 (HPT, N–22); memo by Mullins, 22 May 1958 (Reading UL, Stenton papers, MS 1148/19/1/6).

21 Report of editorial board to trustees, 31 Mar. 1958 (Reading UL, MS 1148/19/1/6).

22 'Note of a meeting held on 4 June 1958' (NLW, Davies papers, P/4/33); 'Memorandum on future development', Oct. 1958 (ibid., P/4/66); trustees' minutes, 8 July 1958 (ibid., P/4/58); trustees' minutes, 5 Nov. 1958 (Reading UL, MS 1148/19/1/6).

23 R. D. Barlas to Clement Davies, 13 May 1958 (NLW, Davies papers, P/4/30).

24 Alan Green to J. E. S. Simon, 29 Jan. 1958 (TNA, T 219/653); E. L. C. Mullins to Clement Davies, 5 Feb. 1958 (Reading UL, MS 1148/19/1/6).

25 'Summary note ... 26 June 1958' (NLW, Davies papers, P/4/52); trustees' minutes, 19 June 1958 (ibid., P/4/54).

26 'Statement by the editorial board ... 19 June 1958' (NLW, Davies papers, P/4/55); *aide-mémoire* agreed by editorial board [1958] (UCL, Neale papers, MS Add. 433/1/1).

27 Heathcote-Amory to Davies, 25 May 1958 (TNA, T 219/654/ 74–5).

28 *The Times*, 30 July 1959.

29 Namier to Lucy Sutherland, 30 June 1958 (Bodl., Sutherland papers, box 9).

30 Namier to Betty Kemp, 19 Dec. 1956 (St Hugh's College, Oxford, Kemp papers, box 1, fo. 89).

31 NLW, Davies papers, D/4/98.

32 *Namier*, 311.

33 Editorial board minutes, 1956–8, fo. 7 (HPT).

34 Notes of joint meeting between trustees and editorial board, 11 Nov. 1959 (Reading UL, Stenton papers, MS 1148/19/1/6).

35 *Namier*, 310.

36 Namier to Francis Thompson, 13 Jan. 1956 (HPT, N–64).

37 Edwards to Lucy Sutherland, 15 Sept. 1962 (Bodl., Sutherland papers, box 9).

38 Namier to Leonard Russell, 10 Dec. 1957 (University of Texas at Austin, Harry Ransom Center, Leonard Russell letters: box 1.1).

39 Namier to Donald Pennington, 19 Feb. 1957 (HPT, N–66).

40 Namier to H. H. Liebling, 30 Sept. 1957 (HPT, N–65); same to Robin Mackworth-Young, 2 Dec. 1959 (Rylands, Namier papers, 1/1b/17).

41 Isaiah Berlin, *Enlightening: letters 1946–60*, ed. Henry Hardy and Jennifer Holmes (2009), 237; Namier to Lucy Sutherland, 9 July 1956 (HPT, N–64); same to same, 4 Dec. 1956 (Bodl., Sutherland papers, box 9); IHR seminar attendance register 1958–75 (IHR archives).

42 Namier to Liebling, 30 Sept. 1957 (HPT, N–65).

43 Julia Namier to Constance Babington Smith, 26 Jan. 1960 (Babington Smith).

44 Namier to Ld Bolton, 3 July 1956 (HPT, N–63).

45 Julia to Constance Babington Smith, 30 Dec. 1957 (Babington Smith); Namier to Ld Bolton, 13 Jan. 1958 (HPT, N–67).

46 Julia to Rebecca West, 8 Feb. 1957 (Yale University, Beinecke Library, Rebecca West papers, Gen MSS 105, ser. I, box 13, folder 600).

47 Namier to Lucy Sutherland, 5 July 1956 (Bodl., Sutherland papers, box 9).

48 Namier to Isaiah Berlin, 28 Jan. 1957 (Bodl., MS Berlin 151, fos 65–6); 'Turbulent Zionist', 125–6.

49 Namier to Margaret Lambert, 29 Jan. 1958 (HPT, N–67); same to R. G. Colodny, 27 Nov. 1957 (ibid., N–65).

50 Namier to J. B. Owen, 20 Jan. 1956 (HPT, N–64).

51 *Crossroads*, 195, 197–200, 211–12.

52 Sir Lewis Namier and John Brooke, *Charles Townshend* (1964), v.

53 Namier to J. H. Plumb, 15 Mar. 1957 (HPT, N–66); same to H. L. Bradfer-Lawrence, 11 June 1957 (ibid., N–65); same to Lucy Sutherland, 30 Oct. 1958 (Bodl., Sutherland papers, box 9).

54 *Crossroads*, 194–212.

55 Sir Lewis Namier and John Brooke, *The House of Commons 1754–1790* (3 vols, 1964), iii, 539–48.

56 Namier and John Brooke, *Townshend*, v–vi.

57 Namier to Ld Bolton, 17 Feb., 6 Mar., 27 Aug. 1956 (HPT, N–63).

58 *Namier*, 307–10; Namier to Hugh Trevor-Roper, 6 May 1956 (Dacre); same to Isaiah Berlin, 8 May, 4 June 1956 (Bodl., MS Berlin 148, fos 24, 113); Mary Drummond to Geoffrey Beard, 22 May 1956 (HPT, N–63); Julia Namier to Irina Prehn, 6 June 1956 (Babington Smith).

59 *Namier*, 311.

60 Namier to Tom Barnard, 26 Oct. 1956 (HPT, N–63); same to Peter Walne, 9 Dec. 1957 (ibid., N–65).

61 Julia to Constance Babington Smith, 13 May, 1 July, 29 Aug. 1957 (Babington Smith); Lady Hardinge to Julia, 2 Sept. 1957 (HPT, N–65).

62 *Namier*, 314.

63 Namier to Blanche Dugdale, 16 Nov. 1931, 2 Aug. 1940 (CZA, Namier papers, A312\44); A. J. Toynbee, *Acquaintances* (1967), 68–9, 73.

64 See the correspondence between the two men in HPT, N–58.

65 Gay to Namier, 18 July, 7 Aug. 1960 (Bristol UL, Hamish Hamilton archive, DM/352/Ii); Namier to Gay, 22 July 1960 (ibid.).

66 Toynbee, *Acquaintances*, 68.

67 Berlin to Webster, 13 Apr. 1960 (LSE, Webster papers, 1/38); same to same, 29 Apr. 1960 (ibid., 1/36/105).

68 'Turbulent Zionist', 125–6; Namier to Yigael Yadin, 8 May 1960 (LSE, Webster papers, 1/38); Stein to Webster, 30, 31 May 1960 (ibid.); Namier to Stein, 8 July 1960 (CZA, A312\48).

69 'Turbulent Zionist', 127.

70 Namier to Berlin, 10 Feb. 1955 (Bodl., MS Berlin 140, fo. 198).

71 Isaiah Berlin, *Personal impressions* (1980), 78–9.

72 *Am ha'aretz*: people of the earth. Thus, in Namier's case, an ignorant countryman.

73 Namier to Berlin, 8 May 1956 (Bodl., MS Berlin 148, fo. 24).

74 Berlin, *Enlightening*, 530–1; Namier to Berlin, 4 June 1956 (Bodl., MS Berlin 148, fo. 113).

75 *Spectator*, 6 Apr. 1956.

76 Namier to Plumb, 7 Mar. 1956 (CUL, Plumb papers).

77 Namier to Plumb, 15 Jan. 1953, 14 Oct. 1954 (HPT, N–58); Plumb to Namier, 18 Jan. 1953 (ibid.).

78 Plumb to Namier, 8 Mar. 1956 (CUL, Plumb papers); same to same, 9 Apr. 1956 (HPT, N–64).

79 Plumb to Namier, 9 Apr. 1956 (CUL, Plumb papers); Namier to Plumb, 30 Apr. 1956 (ibid.).

80 Plumb to Butterfield, 6 May 1956 (CUL, Butterfield papers, 531/P/72).

81 Namier to G. R. Elton, 15 Feb. 1957 (HPT, N–66).

82 See Plumb's correspondence with C. P. Snow in CUL, Plumb papers.

83 Plumb to A. L. Rowse, 8 Jan. 1960 (Exeter UL, Rowse papers, MS113/3/1/P); Plumb to Sedgwick, 5 May, 1 June 1966 (CUL, Plumb papers).

84 David Cannadine, 'John Harold Plumb 1911–2001', *Proceedings of the British Academy*, cxxiv (2004), 286; Brooke to W. S. Lewis, 20 Mar. 1979 (LWL, Lewis corresp., Brooke).

85 *Manchester Guardian*, 7 Mar. 1950.

86 'The Namier view of history', *TLS*, 28 Aug. 1953.

87 *Manchester Guardian*, 14 June 1949.

88 *Manchester Guardian*, 16 Nov. 1956.

89 Namier to J. B. Owen, 20 Nov. 1956 (HPT, N–64).

90 Namier to V. H. Galbraith, 20 Dec. 1951 (HPT, N–53); same to Norman Sykes, 7 Dec. 1951 (ibid.); same to Lucy Sutherland, 10 Jan. 1955 (Bodl., Sutherland papers, box 9); Sir John Neale to Wallace Notestein, 20 Nov. 1962 (Yale UL, Notestein papers, MS 544/I/6/536).

91 J. B. Owen to Namier, 17 Nov. 1956 (HPT, N–64); Namier to Owen, 20 Nov. 1956 (ibid.).

92 *Letters from Oxford: Hugh Trevor-Roper to Bernard Berenson*, ed. Richard Davenport-Hines (2006), 219–25, 229–34; Trevor-Roper to Notestein, 12 May, 25 July 1957 (Yale UL, 544/I/8/747).

93 A. J. P. Taylor, *A personal history* (1983), 214–16.

94 Sisman, *A. J. P. Taylor*, 246–9; Kathleen Burk, *Troublemaker: the life and history of A. J. P. Taylor* (2000), 207–11.

95 Isaiah Berlin to Sir Charles Webster, 2 Feb. 1957 (LSE, Webster papers, 1/35/8); same to Namier, 4 Feb. 1957 (CZA, A312\42).

96 Berlin to Namier, 23 Mar. 1957 (CZA, A312\42).

97   Namier to Macmillan, 11 Jan. 1957 (HPT, N–66).

98   Macmillan to Sutherland, 2 May 1957 (Bodl., MS Macmillan, dep. c. 320, fo. 746).

99   Macmillan's diary, 5 Mar. 1957 (Bodl., MS Macmillan dep. d. 28, fo. 60).

100 Taylor, *Personal history*, 216.

101 A. J. P. Taylor, *Letters to Eva 1969–1983*, ed. Eva Haraszti Taylor (1991), 159.

102 Namier to Sir John Stopford, 6 Nov. 1952 (Manchester UL, university archives, VCA/7/486, file 'Chair of Modern History (Goodwin)').

103 He also told his students that 'Alan must have fireworks, and one day it will be his undoing' (information from Alan Hardy).

104 Unpublished letter of Namier to *The Times*, 25 Nov. 1955 (CZA, A312\58); Namier to Sir Hughe Knatchbull-Hugessen, 1 Nov. 1956 (HPT, N–63).

105 Namier to A. L. Rowse, 8 Nov. 1956 (Exeter UL, MS113/3/1/N); same to Sir Walford Selby, 4 Dec. 1956 (Bodl., Selby papers, MS Eng. c. 6600, fo. 226); same to Ld Hinchingbrooke, 17 Dec. 1956 (HPT, N–63).

106 Taylor to Betty Kemp, [*c*.1962?] (St Hugh's College, Oxford, Kemp papers, box 1, fo.111). It may well have been this attitude, rather than anything Namier said, that dished Taylor's chances of getting the regius chair. Trevor-Roper had been advised to keep quiet about Suez so as not to spoil his chances (Robert Blake to Trevor-Roper, 10 Jan. 1957 (Dacre, 1/2/3)).

107 Sisman, *A. J. P. Taylor*, 238–9.

108 Namier to Trevor-Roper, 28 Apr. 1947 (Dacre, 1/2/5); same to same, 26 Sept. 1954 (ibid.).

109 Trevor-Roper to Namier, 19 Jan. 1957 (HPT, N–66).

110 Namier to Trevor-Roper, 25 Jan. 1957 (Dacre, 1/2/3).

111 Namier to Trevor-Roper, 6 June 1957 (HPT, N–66).

112 *New Statesman*, 6 July 1957; Berlin, *Enlightening*, 589.

113 Taylor to Betty Kemp [*c*.1962?] (St Hugh's College, Oxford, Kemp papers, box 1, fo. 111). Original emphasis.

114 *Observer*, 7 May 1961; Julia Namier to Constance Babington Smith, 2 Apr. 1961 (Babington Smith).

115 Namier to Plumb, 30 Jan., 14, 28 Feb. 1956 (HPT, N–64).

116 A great deal has been written on Butterfield's assault on Namier and the 'Namier school': see, *inter alia*, I. R. Christie, 'George III and the historians – thirty years on', *History*, lxxxi (1986), 205–21; C. T. McIntire, *Herbert Butterfield: historian as dissenter* (2004), 279–91; K. C. Sewell, *Herbert Butterfield and the interpretation of history* (Basingstoke, 2005), 181–97; Jim Smyth, '"An invigorating controversy": Herbert Butterfield and the Namier school', *Eighteenth-Century Thought*, iv (2009), 347–71; Michael Bentley, *Modernizing England's past: English historiography in the age of modernism 1870–1970* (Cambridge, 2005), 153–68; Michael Bentley, *The life and thought of Herbert Butterfield: history, science and God* (Cambridge, 2011), 253–5. As Michael Bentley has observed (*Butterfield*, 254), Butterfield's name is a striking omission in Lady Namier's biography.

117 Bentley, *Butterfield*, 105–6.

118 Bentley, *Butterfield*, 137–46, 154–8, 267–70 provides a precise delineation of Butterfield's complex attitude to Nazi Germany.

119 Bentley, *Butterfield*, 114–15.

120 Butterfield to B. W. Downs, 11 Apr. 1957 (CUL, Butterfield papers, 76/2).

121 Namier to 'Dykah' Bell, 19 Apr. 1948 (Reading UL, G. D. Bell & Sons archive, MS 1640/362118).

122 Herbert Butterfield, *George III, Lord North, and the people 1779–80* (1949), viii.

123 Trevor-Roper to J. H. Plumb, 16 Sept. 1989 (CUL, Plumb papers).

124 J. H. Plumb, *The making of an historian: the collected essays of J. H. Plumb* (Hemel Hempstead, 1988), 9. Butterfield warned one of his protégés to be very careful about crossing swords with Namier: 'I am sure that Namier (apart from being unfair wherever possible) would pounce on the slightest slip' (Butterfield to Desmond Williams, 23 Mar. 1955 (CUL, Butterfield papers, 531/W/241)).

125 Butterfield, *George III, Lord North, and the people*, 15.

126 Namier to Arthur Bryant, 21 Nov. 1950 (KCL, Bryant papers, E/2/2); same to Hugh Trevor-Roper, 24 Apr. 1951 (Dacre, 1/2/2); information from Alan Hardy.

127 Namier to A. P. Wadsworth, 11 Oct., 1 Dec. 1949 (*Guardian* arch., B/N8A/342, 346); same to James Fergusson, 3 Nov. 1949 (HPT, N–54); *TLS*, 6 Jan. 1950.

128 *New Statesman*, 12 Nov. 1949; Helen Cam to V. H. Galbraith [?1949] (Girton College, Cambridge, Cam papers, 2/9/20).

129 *EHR*, lxv (1950), 526–9; Romney Sedgwick to Namier, 13 Nov. 1950 (HPT, N–71); Namier to Sedgwick, 14 Nov. 1950 (ibid.); *Sunday Times*, 8 Feb. 1953; Namier to J. M. Prest, 5 May 1958 (HPT, N–67); *EHR*, lxxiii (1958), 580–2; Bentley, *Modernizing England's past*, 166.

130 Bentley, *Butterfield*, 271–2; Sir Eric Ashby to Butterfield, 13 Sept. 1954 (Queen's University Belfast Library, Wiles Trust archive, QUB/E/4/2/11, box 01), Butterfield to Ashby, 14 Sept. 1954 (ibid.); Ashby to Namier, 24 Sept. 1954, marked 'not sent' (ibid.). During a discussion in one of Butterfield's own set of lectures in 1954 a student had the temerity to raise his voice 'in praise of Namier but Butterfield rather disagreed with him' and the student relapsed into silence (G. O. Sayles to Ashby, 7 Dec. 1954 (ibid.)).

131 Butterfield to B. W. Downs, 11 Apr. 1957 (CUL, Butterfield papers, 76/2).

132 Namier to J. B. Owen, 14 Feb. 1956 (HPT, N–64); Namier to Betty Kemp, 13 June 1955 (HPT, N–60); J. Steven Watson to Namier, 16 Aug. 1956 (HPT, N–64).

133 D. C. Watt, 'Sir Lewis Namier and contemporary European history', *Cambridge Review*, June 1954; *Daily Telegraph*, 20 May 1955 (a review by the journalist Colin Welch of *Personalities and powers*); Jim Smyth, *Cold War culture: intellectuals, the media and the practice of history* (2016), 45–6, 128–30; W. R. Fryer, 'The study of British politics between the Revolution and the Reform Act', *Renaissance and Modern Studies*, i (1957), 91–114. Fryer wrote a second article against Namier in the following year, published as 'King George III: his political character 1760–1784: a new whig interpretation', ibid., vi (1962), 68–101. He described the chronology of the articles in 'Namier and the king's position in English politics, 1744–84', *Burke Newsletter*, v (1963), 246–58.

134 *Sunday Times*, 15 May 1955. See also *Economist*, 2 July 1955.

135 Owen to Namier, 10 Feb. 1956 (HPT, N–64).

136 *EHR*, lxxii (1957), 126–9; *Spectator*, 6 Apr. 1956.

137 *TLS*, 9 Mar. 1956 (the reviewer was John Carswell).

138 *Manchester Guardian*, 2 Mar 1956.

139 See, for example, *The Times*, 18 Oct. 1956.

140 *Cambridge Review*, 1 Dec. 1956.

141 *Cambridge Review*, 25 May 1957.

142 Herbert Butterfield, 'George III and the Namier school', *Encounter*, viii, no. 4 (Apr. 1957), 70–6.

143 Herbert Butterfield, *George III and the historians* (1957).

144 Bentley, *Modernizing England's past*, 161.

145 Butterfield, *George III and the historians*, 10.

146 *Manchester Guardian*, 28 Jan. 1954; Guy Ortolano, 'Human science or a human face?

Social history and the "two cultures controversy"', *Journal of British Studies*, xliii (2004), 490.

147 Namier to Wyndham Deedes, 13 Oct. 1952 (CZA, A312\46); J. P. Cooper, 'Recollections of Namier', *Oxford Magazine*, 3 Nov. 1960, 65.

148 Namier to Stephen Spender, 21 Nov. 1957 (Bodl., MS Spender 58); Irving Kristol to Brooke, 31 Dec. 1957 (HPT, N–68).

149 *Cambridge Review*, 15 June 1957; *Listener*, 5 Dec. 1957.

150 *Cambridge Review*, 10 May 1958.

151 Butterfield, *George III and the historians*, 254, 274; I. R. Christie, *The end of North's ministry 1780–1782* (1958).

152 John Brooke to W. S. Lewis, 7 Feb. 1968 (LWL, Lewis corresp., Brooke); Christie, 'George III and the historians'; information from Peter Thomas and Jean Spendlove.

153 *Cambridge Review*, 10 May 1958. See also Namier to Hon. Mrs Fitzroy Newdegate, 6 Apr. 1955 (HPT, N–60).

154 *TLS*, 22 Nov. 1957.

155 *TLS*, 29 Nov. 1957.

156 *Listener*, 5 Dec. 1957; *TLS*, 6 Dec. 1957.

157 *TLS*, 13 Dec. 1957. Emphasis added.

158 Butterfield to Desmond Williams, 19 May 1958 (CUL, Butterfield papers, 531/W/271)). Butterfield was sufficiently wounded to write privately to the editors of some magazines to explain himself against the criticisms of reviewers: see his letters to the editor of the *Economist*, 26 Nov. 1957, and the *Listener*, 6 Dec. 1957 (CUL, Butterfield papers, 190a/11).

159 Owen to Brooke, [8 June 1968] (HPT, N–68). See Butterfield to Desmond Williams, 30 May 1958 (CUL, Butterfield papers, 531/W/274).

160 See Butterfield's correspondence with Desmond Williams and Robin Dudley Edwards of University College, Dublin, and the American Ross Hoffman, in CUL, Butterfield papers.

161 Lucy Sutherland thought Butterfield had been 'pained' by the critical reception of the book, and thought the whole affair would prove 'a nine days' wonder' (Sutherland to Namier, 10 Dec. 1957 (HPT, N–66)).

162 For example, Hugh Trevor-Roper, *Sunday Times*, 17 Nov. 1957. Alan Taylor, in another Sunday newspaper, was even-handed in his treatment of the principals but considered that none of it really mattered (*Observer*, 17 Dec. 1957).

163 R. W. Greaves, *History*, xliii (1958), 247–8; W. T. Laprade, *American Historical Review*, lxiii (1957–8), 967–8; D. B. Horn, *EHR*, lxxiv (1959), 300–1; Michael Roberts, *Irish Historical Studies*, xi (1958–9), 355–9.

164 *Spectator*, 22 Nov. 1957; Desmond Williams to Butterfield, 28 Feb. 1958 (CUL, Butterfield papers, 531/W/268); *Manchester Guardian*, 29 Nov. 1957. Namier had recommended Oakeshott to the *Spectator*, after reading Oakeshott's 'sensible review' of Brooke (Namier to Ian Gilmour, 19 Nov. 1957 (HPT, N–66)).

165 *Encounter*, x, no. 3 (Mar. 1958), 73–7.

166 Butterfield to Desmond Williams, 30 May 1958 (CUL, Butterfield papers, 531/W/274); Williams to Butterfield, 2 June 1958 (ibid., 531/W/276); *Burke Newsletter*, i (Summer 1959), 198–200.

167 Butterfield to Desmond Williams, 28 Jan. 1958 (CUL, Butterfield papers, 531/W/267).

168 Gooch's letter, and a sheaf of others, can be found in CUL, Butterfield papers, 190a/1. For Namier's treatment of Gooch, see pp. 281–2.

169 McCallum to Butterfield, 17 Jan. 1958 (CUL, Butterfield papers, 531/W/529); *Manchester Guardian*, 29 June 1963.

170 Jonathan Steinberg to Namier, 5 Mar. 1958 (HPT, N–67); *Sunday Times*, 22 Sept. 1957.

171 *Observer*, 1 June 1958; *Daily Telegraph*, 13 Mar. 1959; *Financial Times*, 14 Apr. 1959.

172 D. G. Barnes to Namier, 21 Jan. 1958 (HPT, N–67); C. R. Ritchison to same, 12 Aug. 1958 (ibid.).

173 Pares to J. G. Edwards, 17 Dec. 1957 (NLW, Edwards papers, 213).

174 *New Statesman*, 26 Oct. 1957, repr. in Raymond, *The doge of Dover, and other essays* (1960), 62–6.

175 Namier to Butterfield, 16, 24 Dec. 1957 (CUL, Butterfield papers, 76/1).

176 Butterfield to Namier, 31 Dec. 1957 (HPT, N–65); same to same, 13 Jan. 1958 (ibid., N–67); Herbert Butterfield, 'George III and the constitution', *History*, xliii (1958), 14–33.

177 Namier to Butterfield, 21 Jan. 1958 (CUL, Butterfield papers, 76/1); Butterfield to Desmond Williams, 28 Jan., 4 Mar. 1958 (ibid., 531/W/267, 269).

178 Butterfield to Namier, 10 Dec. 1958 (CUL, Butterfield papers, 76/1); Namier to Butterfield, 11 Dec. 1958 (CUL, Butterfield papers, 76/1).

179 *Vanished Supremacies*, v.

180 Notes by Toynbee [1964] (Bodl., Toynbee papers, box 40). See also Toynbee, *Acquaintances*, 82.

181 Namier to Sutherland, 30 June 1958, 26 Jan., 26 Aug. 1959 (Bodl., Sutherland papers, box 9); Neale to Sir Goronwy Edwards, 18 Feb. 1974 (HPT, N–20).

182 *Namier*, 329.

183 Minutes of trustees' meeting, 26 May 1960 (NLW, Davies papers, P/4/121); E. L. C. Mullins to Clement Davies, 1 June 1960 (ibid., P/4/119).

184 Brooke to W. S. Lewis, 1 July 1971 (LWL, Lewis corresp., Brooke).

185 *Namier*, 327–8.

186 Namier to E. T. Williams, 9 Feb. 1958 (HPT, N–56).

187 Julia Namier to Constance Babington Smith, 15 Nov. 1959 (Babington Smith).

188 Julia Namier to Constance Babington Smith, 10 Sept. 1958 (Babington Smith).

189 *Namier*, 315–18; Namier to Lucy Sutherland, 15 Apr. 1958 (Bodl., Sutherland papers, box 9); same to W. S. Lewis, 10 Mar., 29 Apr. 1958 (LWL, Lewis corresp., Namier (2)); Julia Namier to Kathleen Liddell Hart, 30 Nov. 1958 (LH, 1/539/141).

190 J. L. Talmon, 'The ordeal of Sir Lewis Namier: the man, the historian, the Jew', *Commentary*, xxxiii, no. 3 (1963), 237–46.

191 Talmon to Namier, 17 July 1957 (CZA, A312\49); Namier to Talmon, 13 May 1957 (ibid.); Namier to Ben-Gurion, 29 July 1957 (ibid., A312\42).

192 Berlin, *Enlightening*, 618–19. Original emphasis.

193 *Sunday Times*, 27 Apr., 4 May 1958.

194 *Namier*, 326–7; Julia to W. S. Lewis, 29 Nov. 1960 (LWL, Lewis corresp., Namier (2)).

195 Namier to Lady Hardinge, 17 Feb. 1960 (HPT, N–68); same to Trevor-Roper, 7 Feb. 1960 (Dacre).

196 Namier to Lucy Sutherland, 9 Mar. 1960 (Bodl., Sutherland papers, box 9); same to Betty Kemp, 20 Apr. 1960 (HPT, N–68).

197 Namier to Lucy Sutherland, 26 Apr. 1960 (HPT, N–69); same to J. S. Roskell, 31 May 1960 (ibid.).

198 Sedgwick to W. S. Lewis, 28 June 1960 (LWL, Lewis corresp., Sedgwick); Julia Namier to Constance Babington Smith, 13 July 1960 (Babington Smith).

199 Booklet of Encaenia addresses, 22 June 1960, with translation from the Latin (Bodl., MS Macmillan dep. c. 67, fos 166, 213).

200 Information from Jarosław Kurski.

201 *Namier*, 182.

202 John Brooke to Margaret Wynter, 26 Aug. 1960 (HPT, N–69).

203 Minutes of joint meeting of trustees and editorial board, 21 July 1960 (Reading UL, MS 1148/19/1/6).

204 A. N. Newman to John Brooke, 12 Sept. 1960 (HPT, N–69).

205 Julia Namier to Irina Prehn, 1 Aug. 1960 (Babington Smith).

206 Unless otherwise stated, what follows is drawn from *Namier*, 331–2.

207 Julia to Elliott Perkins, 1 Dec. 1960 (Harvard UL, Perkins papers, HUGFP 147, box 3); same to Constance Babington Smith, 20 Aug. 1960 (Babington Smith).

208 Julia to E. L. C. Mullins, 3 Sept. 1960 (HPT, N–24); same to W. S. Lewis, 29 Nov. 1960 (LWL, Lewis corresp., Namier (2)); same to Elliott Perkins, 1 Dec. 1960 (Harvard UL, HUGFP 147, box 3).

209 Julia to Sir Charles and Lady Webster, 19 Sept. 1960 (LSE, Webster papers, 1/36/131). John Brooke made the same point in a letter to A. N. Newman, 12 Sept. 1960 (HPT, N–69).

210 Sedgwick to Lewis, 21 Aug. 1960 (LWL, Lewis corresp., Sedgwick).

211 Information from Ms Anne Jensen, News UK Archives.

212 *The Times*, 22 Aug. 1960. See also *Daily Telegraph*, 22 Aug. 1960; *Manchester Guardian*, 22 Aug. 1960.

213 Roger Machell to A. J. P. Taylor, 24 Aug. 1960 (Bristol UL, DM/352/Ii); *Spectator*, 26 Aug. 1960.

214 *The Times*, 29 Aug. 1960.

215 *The Times*, 24 Aug. 1960.

216 *Observer*, 28 Aug. 1960.

217 Sedgwick to W. S. Lewis, 21 Aug. 1960 (LWL, Lewis corresp., Sedgwick); reminiscence of Marina Chavchavadze, 5 Sept. 1978 (Babington Smith).

218 Programme for memorial service (Rylands, Namier papers, 1/2/8); copy of prayer (ibid., 1/9/19); Robert, Lord Boothby, *My yesterday, your tomorrow* (1962), 251–2; *The Times*, 28 Oct. 1960. Harold Macmillan was represented by his son Maurice, MP.

219 *The Times*, 7 Nov. 1960; programme in St Hugh's College, Oxford, Kemp papers, box 8, fos 76–9.

10

Vanished supremacies

Reputation in decline

Namier left an estate valued at around £25,000 (a little under £450,000 in current values) after death duties.[1] Together with his royalties, Julia had enough to live in relative comfort, at first in the London flat and then at an old people's home in Surrey. She endowed a junior research fellowship in his name at Balliol, and spent the first decade of her widowhood building a monument to him by writing his life. The fact that her biography said little or nothing about Namier's history writing made the book a classic case of *Hamlet* without the prince, or at least without the ghost. It was also highly unfortunate, since by the time it appeared in 1970 Namier's reputation as a historian stood in need of rehabilitation.

Namier's rapid dethroning from the ascendancy he had once enjoyed over the English historical profession was succinctly described by John Cannon: 'not so much repudiated as outflanked'.[2] This 'outflanking' was in effect a triple bypass. First, while Namier's destruction of the myth of the young George III as a would-be absolutist, and his analysis of the 'political structure' of the House of Commons in the 1760s, were not seriously challenged, his generalisations about the party system across the eighteenth century, as set out in his Romanes Lecture, were overthrown. His successors reinstated the importance of party in the first half of the eighteenth century and completed the task Namier had once set himself by studying its resurgence in the 1770s. The 'political structure' Namier had analysed appeared as a temporary aberration. Second, the subject-matter of political history widened far beyond the confines of 'high politics'. An increasing interest in ideas and their articulation reawakened the study of 'public opinion', going beyond a study of newspapers and pamphlets of the kind that Namier himself had undertaken at the beginning of his career. Political ideas and political culture came to be studied for their own sake, a shift in emphasis which subverted Namierite history still further. Finally, Namier's focus on elites was replaced by interest in 'the people at large'; to begin with, the rioting crowds about whom he thought nothing could be discovered, and in due course the experiences, dispositions, manners and mentalities of society as a whole. His definition of 'ordinary men' came to appear quaint. Long before history suffered the vicissitudes of post-modernism and took its 'linguistic' and 'cultural' turns, Namier's history seemed passé.

To some extent, Namier's position as the acknowledged leader of the historical profession in England was already problematic. In 1961 the *New Yorker* magazine commissioned a staff writer, the blind Indian journalist Ved Mehta, to survey the state of English intellectual life. Mehta was impressed by the reverence shown to Namier by academic historians. But amidst the praise were critical comments. Hugh Trevor-Roper was reported as saying that, while he admired Namier, he considered the Namier method of limited value. Arnold Toynbee thought 'the days of the microscopic historians were probably numbered', and the Dutch historian Pieter Geyl, following Butterfield's line, complained that Namier had no real respect for statesmen, policies or ideas.[3] At about the same time E. H. Carr, in his classic primer, *What is history?* (1961), acknowledged Namier as 'the greatest British historian' of the twentieth century, but pigeonholed him as a conservative whose aversion to ideology was induced by political prejudice. Carr also observed that the period Namier had chosen for his investigations into political structure was unusually well suited to a static view of the past.[4]

Meanwhile, the explosion that Butterfield had set off in the world of academic history continued to produce a chain reaction, initially stuttering but ultimately inexorable. Butterfield himself renewed his main charges against Namier in a radio talk in May 1961: Namier had merely supplied a description of politics in 1760–62; and in any case true political history should be 'the study of statesmanship and things that enlarge the mind'.[5] A succession of articles and essays soon followed, taking stock of Namier's contribution to history. Some were tributes from colleagues and admirers, though even these marmoreal expressions of confidence in the lasting quality of Namier's achievements betrayed a certain unease, in the consciousness of having to make the case, and in conceding some of the objections of Namier's critics. Others were happy to be wholly negative, including a young Oxford don, Norman Hunt, who gave a radio broadcast contradicting Namier's assertions about eighteenth-century parties, which a correspondent in *The Listener* denounced as 'singularly tasteless'.[6]

In the United States, where the importance of the libertarian tradition to the national self-image rendered opinion more sensitive to Namier's debunking of the Whig narrative, a political scientist, Harvey Mansfield, mounted a frontal assault. Scrutinising Namier's contentions about George III, he found flaws in the reasoning and a failure 'to test the appearance of eighteenth-century politics'. Mansfield's grasp of mid-eighteenth-century history was unconvincing, but he scored several hits, notably in observing how Namier's own political convictions had coloured his text. In particular, Namier's belief in the superiority of the constitutional monarchy and party system of the nineteenth century rendered the arch-revisionist as much of a Whig as those he denounced. But the most striking aspect of the article was its tone: irreverent and even dismissive, in a way that Butterfield had never been.[7]

Hitherto, criticism of the 'Namier revolution' had focused on work that Namier had published twenty years before. When his more recent writing on the eighteenth century began to see the light of day, in a series of posthumous publications, and especially in his section of the History of Parliament, his detractors grew louder. There was an obvious irony here, given the amount of effort that went into preparing the material for the press. From the first Julia had been anxious to ensure that half-finished projects be polished up. John Brooke was a willing helper, despite the fact that he had been left with the 'terrific task' of finishing the History of Parliament volumes.[8] Together they completed for Macmillan the revised edition of *England in the age of the American revolution*. Next came *Crossroads of power*, a collection of essays on eighteenth-century politics, including as much as could be recovered of the Ford Lectures of 1934.[9] And in 1964 Macmillan brought out Namier's biography of Charles Townshend, so heavily revised by Brooke that authorship was officially shared.[10] More important, in that same year the 1754–90 section of the History of Parliament was finally published, under the joint authorship of Namier and Brooke.

The appearance of the History of Parliament volumes marked a decisive moment. *Crossroads of power* had been well received, with mild reservations swamped by the customary praise.[11] *The House of Commons 1754–1790* was treated very differently. Tributes were paid to the 'meticulous, luminous, humane scholarship which has gone into these three volumes', but reviewers in newspapers and magazines were disappointed. This great biographical dictionary was not a 'history of parliament' in the proper sense of the word. Brooke's survey was condemned as hard going, and altogether too representative of what Peter Laslett in the *Guardian* called 'negative, Namierian preoccupations'.[12] Presaging the future directions of eighteenth-century scholarship, J. H. Plumb in the *Spectator* lamented Namier's

> obsessive preoccupation with elections, patronage and management to the exclusion of all else … He possessed little sense of proportion; he turned his attention too late to both radicals and the constituencies; he remained largely indifferent to the activity of parliament or to the reactions of men and women outside formal politics.[13]

Predictably, the most violent denunciation came from Alan Taylor. The volumes were 'unreadable', embodying all the weaknesses Taylor had discerned in Namier himself: fixation on detail, a preference for history that stood still and did not move, and for 'a political system with ideas and principles left out'.[14]

The appearance later in the year of *Charles Townshend* gave critics a second pitch at the coconut shy. It was far from vintage Namier, though by no means a negligible contribution to eighteenth-century history. Most reviewers were critical.[15] Two went for the jugular. Taylor, in a savage review in the *Observer* headlined 'Sad failure', a verdict which could have been intended to apply equally to Townshend or the biography, complained of the 'relentless catalogue of insignificant details', adding: 'Anyone coming fresh to the period would be astonished to learn that Namier was ever regarded as a historian, let alone a great one.'[16] Plumb, in the *New York Review of Books*, also carried on where he had left off in his review of the History of Parliament, with more purple in his prose. The biography was a prime example of Namier's 'obsessional nature':

> Like some gigantic caterpillar he moved into the wood, up the trunk, along the branches, down the twigs, until he found his leaf; slowly he explored every vein, every spore, every tiny hair with the thoroughness of a camera attached to an electron microscope.[17]

The barrage naturally upset Julia, to whom Lucy Sutherland counselled stoicism. There was no point in worrying about Laslett or Taylor, she wrote; they were both 'very unreliable people'.[18] Not all Namier's former colleagues could afford to be so phlegmatic, however, because of the potential damage to the History of Parliament. *The Times* had already referred to the project as a 'white elephant', and there was a real danger that a poor press would persuade MPs that public funding be withdrawn.[19] News that the BBC had engaged Butterfield to broadcast about the History, produced acute anxiety, but Butterfield praised the ambition of the project, and the wealth of valuable detail published. What he criticised – once again – was the static quality of the analysis.[20] The secretary to the editorial board thought the programme 'fair-minded, even magnanimous when one recalls Namier's strictures on Butterfield'.[21]

But while funding was retained the project suffered serious reputational damage. The notion that the History was a misnomer took a firm hold. The books were dismissed as a mere accumulation of detail whose only function was as a work of reference. And this meant reputational damage to Namier as well. Comfort could be taken from respectful reviews in academic journals, but it was opinions vented in the daily and weekly press that agitated Brooke, in particular the intemperate attacks on Namier, by Bernard Levin in the *Daily Mail*, and Michael Foot in the left-wing weekly *Tribune*. Levin's remark that Namier 'knew more and understood less than any other historian', signalled, Brooke thought, 'the nadir of Namier's reputation'.[22]

Butterfield, who had started the outcry against Namier and the 'Namier method', now stepped back. His recent contributions had been measured, and there was an unlikely rapprochement with Brooke, who visited him in Cambridge and had a long talk which resulted in an 'amicable understanding' of their differences.[23] Henceforth, Butterfield had little to say about Namier, preferring to make his point indirectly. In an address to the Royal Historical Society in December 1968, surveying 'trends in scholarship, in … modern history' in the century since the society's foundation, Butterfield contrived not to mention his arch-enemy, and said nothing about structural analysis or prosopography.[24]

But if Butterfield had retired from the lists, others kept their lances up. Alan Taylor, who according to Isaiah Berlin, continued to 'hate [Namier] more than anyone else in the world', let slip no opportunity to ridicule the History of Parliament.[25] Even so, the idea – current among some observers – that Taylor wrote his controversial revisionist account of *The origins of the Second World War* (1961) to spite Namier's ghost, even to 'spit on Namier's grave', did not convince Brooke, and has been questioned by others, who have pointed out that elements of Taylor's argument actually echoed Namier's views, notably the strong emphasis on the historical tendency of German nationalism towards armed expansion.[26]

Taylor's animosity was surpassed by that of Plumb, who acknowledged that Namier was an indefatigable researcher, but considered his focus hopelessly narrow and dismissed the so-called 'Namier revolution' as a minor tremor. In his review of *Charles Townshend*, Plumb mentioned Namier's 'neurotic quirks' and 'strong streak of intellectual cruelty'. He developed this personal element in later commentaries, notably in a character assassination in the *New Statesman* in 1969, which depicted Namier as charmless, obsessive and sadistic, susceptible to flattery and loyal to his disciples only if they gave him unswerving devotion.[27]

Rewriting the eighteenth century

Plumb also played a key role in a controversy which did more than anything else to discredit Namier's interpretation of eighteenth-century politics: the debate over the importance of party in the early eighteenth century. The prime target of this historical revisionism was Robert Walcott's misconceived attempt to 'Namierise' the period, which Plumb had always been unhappy about.[28] Despite his own reservations about the quality of the work, Namier indulged Walcott: he enjoyed his company and admired the quantity of biographical research he had completed.[29] Moreover, he was loath to dismiss Walcott's arguments entirely, since they supported his own portrayal of eighteenth-century politics and, despite Plumb's warnings, alluded to Walcott's work in the Romanes Lecture.[30]

Even before 1960, research students on the late Stuart period were starting to re-emphasise the importance of Whig and Tory divisions in English politics. In the decade following Namier's death the trickle of books and articles became a flood.[31] Exploiting a range of manuscript sources that Walcott had not consulted, many in private hands, and making particular use of division lists – classic Namier tradecraft –younger scholars were able to demonstrate that the most significant determinant of parliamentary allegiance in the period 1701–14 was party, not family based 'connections'. The process culminated in the publication of two major books in 1967: Plumb's Ford Lectures on *The growth of political stability in England 1675–1725* and Geoffrey Holmes's magisterial *British politics in the age of Anne*, which provided a detailed and convincing analysis of the structure of early eighteenth-century politics.[32]

Holmes and Plumb presented Walcott as their prime quarry but behind Walcott stood bigger game. One of Plumb's correspondents pointedly congratulated him on 'taking on Walcott *and friends*'.[33] Naturally, there were implications for the way in which historians would henceforth assess Namier's achievement.[34] Reviewers – especially newspaper reviewers – gobbled this up, mentioning Namier almost as much as Walcott himself.[35] Holmes, for his part, was generous in praise of Namier, acknowledging that the biographical method remained 'an indispensable aid to the study of politics';[36] indeed, a case could be advanced that Holmes's work was itself in the Namierite tradition, applying Namier's techniques more systematically and with more intelligence than Walcott. This point was appreciated by some of Namier's colleagues, but not all: his former pupil Betty Kemp mounted a rearguard defence of Namier from what she regarded as obsessive revisionism, and while she may have been mistaken about Holmes's intentions, her instinct, that the destruction of Walcott's work would have long-term consequences for Namier's standing as a historian, was correct.[37] The restoration of party to a central role in early eighteenth-century politics prompted a general process of revision which dismantled the framework of the Romanes Lecture and left the 1760s looking like a brief disjunction in an otherwise continuous history of party development.

The destruction of the Walcott model also furthered the rehabilitation of ideas and principles as motive forces in eighteenth-century politics. This was already gathering strength from a parallel movement, the emergence of the so-called 'Cambridge school' in the 1950s and 1960s, which took a firmly historicist approach to political philosophy. For Plumb and Holmes, as for Butterfield, the restoration of party meant a restoration of principle as a factor in eighteenth-century political life, and a rejection of Namier's cynically materialist, or psychologically determinist, inter-pretation of human behaviour. With greater emphasis on the ideologies defining eighteenth-century politics there also came a heightened interest in the way ideolo-gies were deployed. Namier's account of eighteenth-century elections as commerce between aristocratic borough-mongers was replaced by a political landscape in which a volatile electorate had to be persuaded and cajoled. An upsurge in research into electoral politics seemed to reveal a more 'open' and 'participatory' system.[38] Party propaganda was emphasised as a key constituent of eighteenth-century elec-tioneering, reviving interest in a public opinion which Namier had comprehensively disparaged.

Historians were also taking note of those who stood outside Namier's definition of the 'political nation'. In 1962 the Australian Marxist George Rudé published *Wilkes and liberty*, a pioneering book which drew together research into elections, riots and petitioning.[39] Rudé did not include Namier's works in his select bibliography. His work showed not merely the possibility but also the value of excavating the lives and experiences of those beneath the propertied elite.[40]

The torch would be eagerly taken up by others, and eventually, in 1970 by one of Plumb's pupils, John Brewer, whose detailed examination of 'an amorphous, incipi-ent, popular political culture … given shape and direction by the issues of John Wilkes and, to a lesser extent, of America', was given a title deliberately echoing Namier's first book: *Party ideology and popular politics at the accession of George III*.[41] Brewer accepted some aspects of the framework that Namier had constructed but argued that the political instability of the 1760s had its origins in the politicisation of the lower classes, through a proliferation of cheap print and the street theatre of politically charged and heavily ritualised crowd behaviour. This was all very far from Namier's world and encouraged a belief in some quarters that Brewer had 'destroyed the prevailing interpretation of English political culture' that Namier had erected.[42]

In the half-century following 1960 the discipline of history was transformed. Many of these changes began within a few years of Namier's death. As early as 1964 John Brooke had been convinced that Namier was no longer esteemed at all as a historian. Certainly, the years in which his work had seemed revolutionary, when students were galvanised by excitement on reading *The structure of politics*, were long gone.[43] By the 1950s he had become an establishment figure and himself a target for iconoclasts. Those who venerated his work after his death belonged to an older generation: schoolmasters who had been taught by devotees of Namier, and uni-versity teachers of a certain age who still regarded him as 'the man who had found the ultimate way of doing history'.[44] The pompous elderly historian in Penelope Lively's novel, *How it all began* (2011) is described as representing 'the last gasp of the

Namier school'. Namier's fascination with the way in which 'a number of twaddling eighteenth-century noblemen squabbled over places of profit', to use Alan Taylor's words, seemed irrelevant to the broader experiences of classes and individuals, while his relegation of the significance of ideas in political life was presented almost as an affront to human dignity. The term 'Namierite' became pejorative. Whereas in the 1950s and 1960s Namier was held up in Britain and continental Europe as an exemplar of the craft of history writing, and even as late as the 1990s no general account of historiography was complete without a chapter on Namier,[45] by 2008 an account of 'fifty key thinkers of history' could safely omit him.[46]

Today it is Namier's occasional pieces, reviews and essays which are more frequently read and quoted than the books to which he dedicated so much of his life. He is celebrated as a prose stylist and quoted as an aphorist, while his eighteenth-century work is relegated to a back shelf. This outcome might not have greatly surprised him. For one thing, he always thought that essays were 'very much my genre'.[47] For another, he fully expected that his work would come under fire from a younger generation.[48]

Nonetheless, Namier remains influential, albeit that the influence is not always explicitly recognised. His cynicism about human motivation has found echoes in studies of 'high politics', even if some of the exponents of this kind of history, like the Cambridge historians Maurice Cowling or John Vincent, have seen themselves as answering to a very different voice: Butterfield's call for the revival of narrative in contradistinction to Namier's emphasis on structural analysis. In the same way, contemporary political commentators might be seen as taking their cue from Namier as they interpret a political scene which – especially at cabinet level – continues to offer evidence of the ready sacrifice of principle for personal advancement, and the crucial importance of the kind of connections – family, friendship and patronage – which Namier dissected in *The structure of politics*. Namier's belief in Freudianism as a guide to understanding historical figures and their actions has also been reflected in a resurgence of interest by academic historians in psychology and psychoanalysis. And scholars seeking to understanding the 'structure' of institutions continue to make use of the technique of collective biography, so much so that explicit disagreement with Namier's conclusions does not preclude a belief that, at this basic level, as one eighteenth-century specialist remarked, 'we are all Namierites nowadays'.[49]

The real Namier?

The influence of hostile reminiscences and casual anecdotes has created a picture of Namier the man as an arrogant egoist, heavily conscious of his own importance – a man regarded by contemporaries as 'the greatest living bore'.[50] For good measure, he has also been portrayed as a stereotypical self-hating Jew and a monumental snob, whose history writing reflected a largely unrequited love affair with the English aristocracy. Some elements of this characterisation have been accepted by his admirers on the right, who celebrate Namier's hard-headed realism, and relish the outrage his ideas – and their forceful expression – arouse in their political enemies.[51] A growling pugnacity and an unforgiving nature are appropriate to the hammer of liberal idealism. The affection that Namier inspired among friends, colleagues and pupils, his generosity to them, and his sharp sense of humour, have been submerged by the testimony of contemporaries unfortunate enough to have encountered him at his most bearish. And as the number of those who can remember the real Namier steadily dwindles, this image seems likely to become established as canonical. The 'lovable Lewis', as Arnold Toynbee called him, is vanishing behind the ogre of legend.

Like all caricatures, the prevailing impression of Namier has been built up around some bones of truth. Friends like Isaiah Berlin and Ian Gilmour who denied the most frequently levelled charge – that Namier was a world-class bore – admitted that his obsession with his own work and his social ineptitude could transform conversations into ad hoc lectures. Even Julia is said to have considered her husband a monomaniac.[52] Stories abound of his detaining friends and acquaintances like the ancient mariner: Toynbee's wife, on a chilly staircase, subjected to a recitation of 'the original Slav names of the cities of Germany east of the Elbe'; Thom Jones, the former cabinet secretary, at breakfast with Namier in his club and forced to 'read pages of the typescript of the book he is writing'; or Malcolm Muggeridge, listening to Namier intone 'in a slow, deliberate voice' an entire article just completed for the *TLS*.[53] Walter Elliot, the Conservative MP who was one of Namier's closest political contacts, admired his prose style in print but disliked hearing Namier's cadences declaimed in person: 'there are worse things than sleeping on a sofa', he once told 'Baffy' Dugdale, 'particularly if Lewis is speaking'.[54]

That Namier evidently considered the workings of his own mind to be of paramount interest can be interpreted as yet another manifestation of his self-importance, even pomposity. It is true that he could not take a joke against himself, and that he never underestimated the scale of his own achievements. But his determination to tell the world about his work was also a manifestation of naive enthusiasm. As Alan Taylor observed, there was a childish side to Namier's nature: a sentimental streak which could be disarming. Others saw him as an innocent, despite the surface sophistication. At the same time, the peculiar circumstances of his upbringing, and a succession of disappointments at crucial stages in his career, each rebuff taken to heart, bred in him an underlying chronic anxiety, demanding reassurance.

E. H. Carr, who knew him for nearly fifty years, was quite clear that what appeared to be arrogance in Namier was in fact a protective carapace covering 'an inner core of tormenting doubts'.[55]

Of more concern to Namier's friends was his uncontrollable temper, and his capacity for what Arnold Toynbee called 'paranoiac hatred', whether for historical figures, ideologies or entire ethnic or national groups – and, at a personal level, those who had betrayed him. According to Toynbee, this was 'a much more serious blemish than sometimes being a bore to people who did not happen to be interested in the workings of his mind'.[56] It was something Namier recognised within himself, telling Blanche Dugdale that he was only too well aware of his own 'violent, bitter, ill-tempered' nature.[57] The capacity to nurture grudges receded as he aged and mellowed, but never departed entirely. It lost him a few long-standing and close friends, which he found very painful, for, having distanced himself from his immediate family, he cherished friendships. Others were able to forgive him: 'I suppose all human beings have their blemishes', Toynbee wrote, 'but the great are great in spite of them, and Namier was one of those.' He meant greatness in spirit as well as in intellect and achievement.

The criticism that as a historian Namier was only interested in elites relates most obviously to his major publications on mid-eighteenth-century England. Clearly, he did identify the Georgian 'political nation' with the landowning elite: 'I have always maintained that British history in the eighteenth century is primarily a history of country houses.'[58] This view emerged naturally from the purpose of his research and his method of working. He had set himself to explain how the great Anglo-Saxon transatlantic empire had been sundered, and the residents of country houses were, after all, the men who had made the crucial decisions, either individually, as ministers, or collectively, in cabinet and parliament. Moreover, it was the memoirs, diaries and correspondence discovered in country-house muniment rooms that enabled him to reconstruct the parliamentary context, as well as the primary narrative, of the loss of the American colonies. However, he always emphasised the variegated nature of the parliamentary elite and was more interested in relatively obscure MPs, especially merchants and financiers, than in the grand eminences of the peerage.[59] On reading parts of a biography of Edward VII, he told the author that the vision of '"property represented in parliament by a few patrician clans competing for office" bears no resemblance to the picture I have of parliament in the eighteenth or early nineteenth century'.[60]

Namier persisted in seeing his research into parliamentary history as 'sociological'. He had been taught by sociologists and anthropologists, Pareto at Lausanne and Westermarck at the LSE, and as an enthusiast for all things modern had imbibed the intellectual excitement of these disciplines. At Oxford he specialised in political economy, and his writings on the contemporary scene in Europe during and after the First World War always maintained a strong statistical emphasis, even if his conclusions about economic performance were founded on ideas about human nature which – if at all – could only be tested biographically. His preliminary investigations into the House of Commons also had a statistical imperative. The much-discussed technique of structural analysis was simply an attempt to reach some kind of satisfactory quantification of parliamentary interests. Inevitably, given Namier's determination to find out everything about each MP, the research soon became more elaborate, probing character and motivation. But even in the 1950s, when he ostentatiously disowned economics as a worthwhile discipline – advising one prospective undergraduate to give up that dreadful subject and read history instead[61] – and disputed the utility of tabulating the data that the History of Parliament was unearthing, he seems still to have appreciated the precision that social science could supply.

Namier's own brand of supposedly 'sociological' history, involving the aggregation of information about individuals, could only be done at the level of the parliamentary elite. His research concentrated on individuals, and moreover the kind of individuals who left sufficient trace in the historical record to enable their lives to be reconstructed and understood. There is no evidence that he was drawn to the study of elites by the persuasive influence of any particular theory. Practical considerations were the determining factor. Even in the 1950s, when his historical preoccupations became narrower and more rigid, he was encouraging rather than dismissive to those who asked his advice about the possibility of research into popular politics in George III's reign, although sceptical that there would be enough first-hand evidence to enable it to be done properly (mistakenly as things turned out).[62]

Namier took a particular pleasure in his country-house visits. Unlike his students and assistants on the History of Parliament, he never entered by the back door: he lunched with owners and sometimes stayed as a guest. Although in the early days of these 'paper chases' he did not always understand the social conventions, he was oblivious to embarrassment, and evidently relished the idea of being on terms of friendship with members of the aristocracy. His former assistant Mary Port recalled a glimpse of Namier's class-consciousness. He announced that he was to spend the weekend at Whittingehame, the Balfour estate in the Scottish borders. Without thinking, Mary blurted out that her mother used to go there. This was a mistake. While Namier treated his staff as equals in the office, they were not on the same social plane outside.

To that extent, Namier can be convicted of snobbery. But, as Isaiah Berlin observed, he was not a snob in the strict sense of the term, since he did not in principle look down on social inferiors.[63] Indeed, he prided himself on being able get on with ordinary people, and believed that he had a genuine empathy, since he had talked familiarly with the servants on his father's estate, had taught working men in WEA classes at Oxford and had messed with the common soldiery during his brief stint in uniform. His snobbery was of a different sort: an idealisation of aristocracy in general, and of the English landed classes in particular, whose offspring had been companions at Balliol. This sentiment even carried over into personal relationships. Julia's attractiveness was in part owing to her aristocratic background and comportment: she conveyed an aura of genuine Russian nobility. To native Englishmen of later generations, themselves the products of public school and Oxbridge, this roseate view of the English upper classes seemed at best unrealistic and at worst ludicrous; a dewy-eyed foreigner's misreading of the class system.

Namier had translated to an English context, and in the process distilled, sentiments he had brought from Galicia. His feelings towards the Polish landowning aristocracy were conflicted: he admired them as upholders of intellectual and artistic aspirations above the numbing coarseness of peasant existence, but recognised that they were an alien imposition on Ruthenian soil; nor could he and his family ever truly belong among them. The English aristocracy, by contrast, was rooted in the land it occupied and, unlike the nobilities of eastern Europe, was open to the upwardly mobile, even Jews. In England the young Namier looked to the aristocracy for the preservation of cultural values. They were a necessary bulwark against the advance of bourgeois philistinism. His fellow undergraduates at Oxford, the flower of English society, would also be the future rulers of empire, and they seemed to him to be very different from the servants of the empires he had known: men of intellect and social responsibility with a serious imperial mission that contrasted with the decaying polities of Austria-Hungary and Russia. He maintained this view, which involved a degree of selective memory, throughout his life. As he grew older and more conservative his youthful modernist prejudices receded. He grew less intolerant of the middle classes and more antipathetic to mass democracy – a process that may have begun in 1920s Vienna. And he was even more resolute in his idealisation of England's historical ruling elite, seeing his parliamentary friends, the 'Tory radicals', as modern representatives of the tradition of the eighteenth-century 'independent country gentleman'.

A second important charge on the indictment of Namier as a historian is that he was hostile to ideas, and that his reductionist explanations of human behaviour 'took the mind out of history'. Originally this was a delayed liberal reaction to the subversion of whig historical orthodoxy in his first two books. The accusation was first levelled by Alan Taylor, whose standpoint derived from a family heritage of Lancastrian liberalism, and who accused Namier of having 'ignored the liberal spirit'.

There is no doubt that Namier was particularly doubtful of the value of 'the liberal spirit'. His dislike of liberalism began in adolescence; imbibed, along with panSlavism, from listening to his tutors and reading Dostoyevsky. The great figures of the European liberal pantheon may have been his family's household gods, but he saw them and their ideology as gods who had failed the Slavs of central and eastern Europe, while German liberalism had proved unable to withstand the pathology of the German national character and had transmuted into the Prussianised nationalism that would reach its apogee under the Nazis. The First World War and its aftermath only confirmed his distrust of *bien-pensant* progressivism, exemplified in the League of Nations, which he despised in spite of the fact that 'Baffy' Dugdale worked for it. The League was the creation of political ingénues, insulated from the realities of European politics, who believed they could 'cure humanity and lead it into better ways. It was an expression of the morality and idealism of the Anglo-Saxons, and of their ignorance of what it means to suffer of neighbours and disputed borderlands.'[64] With his background, Namier understood that, as George Orwell observed, 'nationalism, religious bigotry and loyalty are far more powerful forces than … sanity'.[65]

Namier was also impatient with silver-tongued orators like Charles James Fox, who clouded their sordid intentions with rhetorical vapour. Fox 'talked in a grand manner' and ostentatiously displayed 'moral indignation … towards other people' while leading a life of debauchery.[66] And the harm done by twentieth-century demagogues scarcely needed stating: 'what shams and disasters political ideologies are apt to be, we surely have had opportunity to learn'.[67] At the same time, Namier readily admitted the power of ideas to sway a parliamentary audience. The 'independent country gentlemen' of the eighteenth century had to be convinced by argument, and Namier fully appreciated that some politicians, of whom Pitt the elder was a classic example, owed their influence to powers of persuasion rather than to battalions of parliamentary dependants.

Namier's own biography, especially his early life, was marked by a personal commitment to ideals and ideologies: socialism, panSlavism, the libertarian constitutionalism inherited by Americans from seventeenth-century England, and eventually, and most enduringly, the precepts and aspirations of Zionism. How could such a man come to believe that ideas did not matter in politics, however sceptical he might be of liberal beliefs, and however much he disliked mountebanks who duped the public and their elected representatives with bogus appeals to principle?

The first thing to note is that Namier differentiated between levels of argument; between debates over specific problems, and what he would have considered the airy rehearsal of generalities. Under this latter heading would come high-flown discussions about constitutional practice in terms of prevailing notions of good government. Such commonplaces were generally innocuous, though they could be dangerous when exploited by those wishing mischief. This was the context of his notorious use of the term 'flapdoodle'. Namier could not see the point of the historian spending time in examining closely the way such sentiments were expressed. They were merely the 'current cant' of politics; the only conceivable interest lay in examining their relationship to political reality.

In the same way that he was mystified by Butterfield's interest in historiography – historians should study what happened in the past, not their predecessors' generally mistaken notions of what happened – Namier was unable to see the point of what we now call 'the history of ideas'. Or rather, he did not consider it to be the realm of the historian proper: the story of the development of political philosophy was best left to political philosophers like his friend Isaiah Berlin. Namier's overly candid confession of his own inability to comprehend Berlin's work was by no means disingenuous politeness, and although he was not the boor he claimed to be, he did not regard himself as an intellectual: 'I am no good at abstract thought.'[68] When a BBC producer asked Namier to contribute to a series on the Third Programme and sent him a copy of one of the other talks, by the philosopher Stuart Hampshire on 'Reason in politics', he was nonplussed, describing Hampshire's discourse as being 'in the clouds'. He wondered whether, 'if there is to be much of that kind in this series … you will want me as a bull in the china shop'.[69] Namier fully recognised the importance of ideas, especially in political life, but in a curious way as abstracted from human consciousness. In one late-night conversation with Baffy Dugdale he talked of 'the curious separate life which an *Idea* develops'.

> It has to be born in the brain of a man, but when it begins to grow in the minds of others, it becomes invested with qualities of its own, derived, of course, from them, but beyond the control of any one of them. They become in a way its servants, not its masters – must watch for its reactions, and in away obey them.[70]

For Namier the subject-matter of history was 'human affairs, men in action, things which have happened and how they happened; concrete events fixed in time and space, and their grounding in the thoughts and feelings of men'.[71] It was a view which became more deeply embedded the older he got, and the more enmeshed he became in the work of the History of Parliament. In his own work Namier encountered eighteenth-century constitutional principles primarily in the context of private correspondence, diaries and memoirs, or parliamentary debates, as politicians justified their own actions, to themselves and each other, and sought to persuade MPs to follow them. The contemporary pamphlets which he had studied so intensively in his first attempts at research were rarely cited in his two great books, and figured even more fleetingly in his entries in the History of Parliament. When he considered the expression of these grand ideas he concerned himself not with the ideas themselves but with the way in which they were being used. In examining any historical statement it was vital to take account of 'context, emphasis and circumstances'.[72] Ideas were instrumental; they expressed and in some cases disguised motives rather than constituting motives in themselves.

Character and motivation were what primarily interested Namier. His rejection of principle was not, as it has often been described, mere cynicism. The analysis was deeper and more systematic. By the time of his maturity he had cast aside his juvenile belief in a crude economic determinism, whether advocated by Marx or Charles Beard. Reports that he had once been influenced by Marx could be guaranteed to infuriate him. Nonetheless, while he was able to recognise relatively early in life that human beings are perfectly capable of thinking and acting against their self-interest, he retained a vestigial deference towards calculations of motive based on economic circumstances.

The other great influence on the young Namier was Freud, and this he never discarded. When reading eighteenth-century letters he always paid close attention to uses of language that were 'psychologically' or 'psycho-analytically significant'.[73] His character sketches of the leading characters in the political conflicts of the 1760s were heavily informed by Freudian psychology, always focusing on the gravitational effect of family and childhood experience. The Freudianism was quite explicit: Namier thought that the duke of Newcastle suffered from 'obsessionist neurosis', and made a similar 'diagnosis' of George III.[74] These refreshingly modern commentaries doubtless formed part of the book's attractiveness when it first appeared. At the time, Namier was still being psychoanalysed himself, and although he stopped attending sessions when he married Julia, he did not relinquish his belief in the importance of the workings of the subconscious, and in particular on the powerful and enduring impact of a tortured upbringing, to which he gave full rein in his public lectures on George III and Charles Townshend. 'History has … a psycho-analytic function', he wrote in an essay in 1952, adding sharply that 'it further resembles psycho-analysis in being better able to diagnose than to cure'.[75]

There was also a slightly comical side to Namier's very serious search for psychological insights, in his sincere belief in the pseudo-science of graphology. His interest went back to the 1930s, at least, and he was familiar enough with the system to be able to make deductions for himself, though he preferred to use the expertise of a London-based practitioner, Maurice Mannheim. Having obtained from Mannheim some interesting reports on examples of eighteenth-century handwriting, he insisted on subjecting applicants for posts at the History of Parliament to the same test.[76] Of one candidate Namier inquired:

> I wonder what you will make of him? Will he quarrel with people? Is there any presumption or sharpness in the writing? Is he intelligent and reliable? Look in the letter of 8 May at the fake addition to the 's' in Sussex, and again, in the second line, in 'passed' – apparently he tries to reproduce the 's' as it appears lower down in 'research'. I myself should think him involved, difficult and changeable.[77]

It is a miracle that anyone was ever appointed.

Namier's belief in the power of the subconscious can be related back to his views on race and inherited historical experience, manifest in a tendency to make sweeping statements about national types. These often occur in his essays and reviews on European history, and occasionally protruded through the detail of his English history.[78] Like Freud, he was fascinated by the art and artefacts of primitive civilisations, an enthusiasm fired by the discoveries he and his sister had made at Koszylowce. Again, like Freud, the study of these objects brought Namier to an awareness that there were deeper urges in the mind of man than could be encompassed by the workings of reason. He was thus perfectly comfortable with the concept of an innate racial memory: he could write that 'even the remotest' of all the ages of British history were 'still with us, in the tumuli and monoliths, in the blood and language of Englishmen'.[79] Exposure to Freud's theories, through his own reading and through undergoing psychoanalysis, enabled him to articulate more authoritatively the conviction that human beings 'are never moved by reason alone', and provided a more sophisticated and 'scientific' framework upon which to build his reconstructions of the mental processes of historical figures.[80]

Explicit rejection of the power of reason in human affairs was the basis of Taylor's charge that Namier had 'taken the mind out of history'. Namier never retracted, and on occasion vigorously defended the value of irrationality in human affairs, despite the fact that his own interventions in politics, either as a Foreign Office analyst or a Zionist campaigner, depended heavily on rational argument. 'The irrational is not necessarily unreasonable' was one aphorism, and elsewhere he wrote that rationality itself was an unattractive quality, since it brought only a cold calculation of self-interest – 'the most warm-hearted people are not rational'.[81] But the accusation bothered him, and in a radio talk in 1953 on 'Human nature in history' he went out of his way to justify himself: he had not 'taken the mind out of history' so much as given a full consideration to the mind's complexities, while reducing 'reason' to its properly subordinate place.[82] Others were unconvinced, and considered that

Namier's approach placed the very survival of history in peril. Butterfield's concluding argument in *George III and the historians* was that Namier's work, taken to its
logical conclusion, would render the subject meaningless: 'we are denying that ... in
George III and other people there are profounder purposes, deeper continuities of
aim and endeavour'.[83] In a short piece written in reply to criticisms of Namier, John
Brooke even suggested that Namier himself had similar doubts, more precisely that
his method might result in a narrative without shape or point.[84] Namier had begun
his study of 'the age of the American revolution' in order to understand how the
break with the colonies had taken place. He now risked ending his quest without a
meaningful answer. But consciousness of that possibility did not make him modify
in any way the approach to research that he developed in the 1920s.

Commentators have sometimes contrasted Namier's English history with his
European history. His parliamentary studies were oppressively detailed depictions
of a closed political world which focused on the making and unmaking of ministries,
and at an individual level on the making and unmaking of careers. By contrast, his
books and essays on nineteenth- and twentieth-century Europe dealt with grand
themes – the rise of nationalism, the outbreak of wars, the fall of empires – in the
context of a global vision of geopolitical imperatives. What this contrast actually
illustrates is not a different approach to European and English history so much as
the presence of conflicting forces within Namier's character: on the one hand, he
was driven towards making broad and unequivocal statements about major events
in the past which could provide lessons for the future, explaining, for example, the
profound importance to European stability of containing German nationalism by
an alliance between Russia and the 'Anglo-Saxon empires'; on the other, the compulsion to establish exactitude pushed him deeper and deeper into a mire of detail.
He was able to combine these two elements once, in his Waynflete Lectures, which
were in effect a prolonged sermon on the essential malignity of German liberalism
based on a mass of prosopography, but he was uneasy at the inadequacy of the biographical research, and had he found the time to work up the lectures into a book it
is likely that he would have attempted a History-of-Parliament-style scrutiny of the
Frankfurt assembly.

Namier's character was in fact an assortment of contradictory impulses. He was
a panSlavist who idealised the integrity of the Russian and Ukrainian peasantry
while at the same time despising their philistinism and their inefficient agriculture. He denounced nationalism as a disruptive and dangerous force, especially in
Poland, yet consistently espoused the rights of the Czechs to self-determination.
He regarded religion as a prime marker of national identity, but, at least until his
marriage, had no faith himself. He disparaged ideologies from the standpoint of a

committed Zionist, and worked tirelessly for Jewish relief despite being critical of individual Jews or Jewish groups. His wife and her friends were struck by the extent to which his attitude to his 'co-racials' was conflicted: he seemed to feel 'sadness but not always sympathy towards them'.[85] Julia saw this as a typical instance of a problem that Namier and the philosopher C. G. Stone had often discussed in their rooms at Balliol: the capacity to hold simultaneously opposing positions with regard to ideas, circumstances or individuals. Namier was so obsessed with his need to resolve this internal conflict without an upsurge of 'emotional turbulence' that he and Stone devised an explanatory theory of their own based on geometrical concepts (this was before Namier's exposure to Freud).[86]

Namier's biography offers alternative explanations of the paradoxes in his personality. The peculiarity of his family background and upbringing left the most obvious mark, instilling a profound ambivalence about his identity. Bernard Berenson, having observed him at close quarters, considered him to be 'the most Jew-haunted person of my acquaintance'.[87] This obsession was the fruit of a deep frustration within Namier's personality; derived from uncertainty about his identity, which he translated into antipathies. Neither truly Jewish nor truly Gentile, he was uncomfortable with religious Jews of all kinds, hostile to 'assimilationists' like his parents, and scornful of Jews who were hypersensitive to their own separateness: 'the organisation of trembling Israelites' who hid their Jewishness and the 'ghetto Jew', always emphasising the exceptional qualities of his race because 'he felt he had to pay ransom to everybody for being suffered to exist'.[88] Namier's expressed wish was that Jews should simply be treated in the same way as anyone else.

At the same time his parents' and his own rather different efforts to assimilate to the Gentile society in which he grew up were equally futile: he could not integrate into Polish society, nor despite his professed attachment to the Slavic cause could he genuinely feel part of Ruthenian Galicia. So he sought a surrogate identity, and eventually found it in Edwardian Oxford – or thought he had found it. But this new identity was insecure as well, undermined by repeated rejection by the university community that he idealised. Namier's relationship with the English academic and social elite was in fact highly complex: the suggestion that he can be pigeonholed with other 'white émigrés' who sought refuge from the instabilities of central eastern Europe in a country 'built on tradition and custom' takes insufficient account of this complexity. Namier may have been 'infatuated' with England, but powerful figures in the English establishment made clear to him that the infatuation was by no means mutual.[89]

The first half of Namier's life seems to have followed the guiding principle attributed to the heroine of Muriel Spark's novel, *The Mandelbaum gate*, that 'the human mind was bound in duty to continuous acts of definition'. The young Namier defined and redefined himself in a succession of different ways, as a socialist, a panSlavist, a modernist, a British imperialist, a Round Table federalist, an advocate of self-determinism, a Bolshevist sympathiser, a fiscal conservative and, eventually, a Zionist and a 'Tory radical'. All these changing definitions ran counter to the tradition of his father's family, who aspired to a Polish Catholic identity, revered the civilisation of Enlightenment Germany (as represented by Goethe) over the religious obscurantism of Russia (as represented by Dostoyevsky), and in politics held to a liberal nationalism that Namier disdained. In swimming against this current Namier was unique among the Bernstein cousinhood, who between them achieved great distinction in various intellectual disciplines. Yet while he seemed constantly to be casting around for new and often contradictory ways to provoke his parents, at one moment expressing his wish to become a Presbyterian while they were baptised into the Church of Rome, then embracing the aspirations of Ukrainian nationalists, and finally adopting the creed of the Zionists, Namier was not simply changing hats.

In each case, as he travelled from one enthusiasm to another, Namier retained something of the character and beliefs that he was ostensibly leaving behind. His panSlavism imprinted an enduring belief in the importance of both religion and territoriality in the formation and maintenance of national identity, which transferred across from his analysis of European nationalisms to his understanding of, and commitment to, Zionism. Moreover, his embrace of the British libertarian political tradition while at Oxford did not mark a shift from a belief in a political ideology founded on organic communities to one based on individuals, from *Gemeinschaft* to *Gesellschaft*, for he identified British and American constitutional thought with the 'Anglo-Saxon' racial inheritance. And most strikingly the Germanophobia, or rather the phobia of German nationalism, which was the corollary of his support for Slavic cultural and political pretensions, was further informed by the understanding of European geopolitics inculcated by Mackinder at the LSE, developed through his own observations before and during the First World War, and ultimately copperfastened by the experience of the Nazi era. Unlike, for example, Hans Kohn, a fellow Jewish intellectual from central Europe who shared Namier's negative view of the historical impact of German nationalism, Namier did not modify his views of Germans one iota after 1945. While Kohn appreciated the emergence of a genuine liberalism in the new West Germany, Namier could not believe that Germans had learned any lessons from the war.[90]

Namier's critics routinely denounce him as a spokesman for an outlook which we can recognise in the contemporary world and is to that extent timeless: elitist, materialist and cynical. In fact, in his understanding of the world, and of the workings of the human mind and of human society, Namier was very much a child of his own time. This was the period in which his ideas were formed and modified, c.1905–25, rather than the 1950s, when his influence was briefly at its height and his ideas about politics were supposedly in tune with the fleeting Zeitgeist.

The same might be said of his social attitudes, despite the gusto with which he adopted the advances of modern technology. Statements that would today be readily stigmatised as racist constitute one obvious example. Another would be his attitude towards sex. His own sexual life was neither restrained nor conventional, at least until his second marriage, but his attitudes were those of *fin-de-siècle* Vienna, and there was a great deal about England, and the wider world, after 1918 that he neither understood nor welcomed. To bright young men in 1920s Oxford, of whose ambiguous sexuality he was ignorant, he seemed to belong to an older and stuffier generation: he was 'Uncle Lewis'. In the 1950s even Julia thought him 'puritanical'.[91]

Namier's history was also very much of its time: the notion of historical research as 'scientific', grounded in the scrutiny of documents; the attempt to provide a structural analysis of eighteenth-century social and political systems, akin to the achievements of social scientists; even the emphasis on prosopography. Despite his belief that his own work was revolutionary, none of this was original to Namier, or unique to him. His originality and influence lay not his methods so much as in the manner of their application. Indeed, when defined in the *Oxford English dictionary*, which has entries for 'Namierian' and 'Namierisation' (with the additional descriptor 'now rare'), the Namier method seems only a very modest revolution: 'distinguished from the technique of earlier historians by a meticulous attention to detail and an emphasis upon the close study of original sources to uncover social and family connections'. To his contemporaries Namier was first and foremost a historian who was making extraordinary discoveries in private archives, and although he was not by any means the first scholar to trumpet their importance, he was the first historian of eighteenth-century England to attempt systematically to locate all available manuscript materials. The vigour and determination he brought to the task was facilitated by his photographic memory and ability to master oceans of information. He was also highly sophisticated in the way he dealt with documentary evidence, weighing, interrogating and questioning individual sources, and more important, correlating all the evidence so as to provide, as far as possible, a 'true' picture of events.

Far from fetishising documents, he well knew their pitfalls. He was also aware that, at least in writing contemporary history, 'a great many profound secrets are somewhere in print' as long as one knew where to look.[92] The importance of examining all available sources, and reading into the period as thoroughly as possible, was that it brought intimacy with the past. His students were struck by the way in which

Namier 'always seemed to be remembering history as personal experience'.[93] Alan Taylor interpreted this as a form of weakness; it showed how fundamentally unhistorical Lewis was in his mind. The eighteenth-century politicians, like the German revolutionaries of 1848, were contemporary to him; just as, in reverse, he always expected his contemporaries to behave according to the historical pattern. Hence his shattering disillusionment over the British governing class and Zionism.[94]

Other critics detected the same fault: Namier's power of empathy was such that when writing about George III or the duke of Newcastle he saw the world through their eyes, which detracted from his objectivity.[95] When dealing with politicians whom he disliked, Rockingham or Charles James Fox, his empathy would dissolve and a different sort of subjectivity, negative rather than positive, would take its place. As far as Namier was concerned, however, he was acquiring what he prized most, a real historical sense, which in his definition was 'an intuitive understanding of how things do not happen'.[96]

Namier's first books also seemed revolutionary because they embodied the principle of structural analysis. This was new only in so far as it did not seem to have been applied before to political history, and marked a sharp change from the customary narrative form. But, as John Cannon (who worked with Namier) pointed out long ago, structural analysis is something of a red herring for anyone searching for a definition of 'Namierism'; a red herring drawn across the trail, intentionally or not, by Herbert Butterfield. Structural analysis was not intended as an end in itself, but as a means to an end. Namier needed to establish certain basic facts about parliament in the 1760s; what kind of people sought election, how were they returned, to which parties or factions they belonged, and what was the size of these groupings within the House of Commons. The aim was to provide the context for his history of 1759–84; a necessary adjunct to the narrative, not a replacement for it.[97] The process of counting heads would also have to accompany the narrative as it went on; further calculations would inform what Namier expected to write about 'the rise of party'. But he never progressed beyond 1762, nor did he write the survey to his History of Parliament volumes, so we cannot see how a narrative would have developed. It has thus become easy to say that structural analysis was all he could write, and that he was fortunate in picking a particularly static period to write about.

Unfortunately, he gave further ammunition to those who denied his ability to convey movement in history, by the arguments presented in his Romanes Lecture. Designed to complete his victory over whig history, the lecture generalised across the eighteenth century and made claims for the chronological extension of Namier's 'structure of politics' which could not be justified and, at least as far as the early eighteenth century was concerned, were soon rejected.

Namier's identification with prosopography rests primarily on his advocacy and practice of collective biography in the History of Parliament project. His own early research had a strong prosopographical element, though this was largely hidden in *The structure of politics* and its companion volume. He used prosopography as a research technique, principally in order to organise his material. When he came to write his books the prosopographical element was only visible in the occasional statistical calculation and in the detailed case studies through which he constructed his arguments. His microscopic attention to the detail of the British parliamentary system in the 1760s was different in style and form to the prosopography of German classical scholars who were the real pioneers. It is often said that Namier set an example in prosopography which others followed, particularly the classicist Ronald Syme, whose first major book, *The Roman revolution* (1939) has been compared to Namier's works.[98] But however much Syme admired Namier, the form of his work was influenced more by predecessors in his own field.[99]

When Namier did eventually attempt a collective biography of the Georgian House of Commons his passion for discovering everything about everything drew him into a very different form of prosopography than Syme or others working on periods before the seventeenth and eighteenth centuries would have been able to accomplish. Namier disliked the statistical analysis which his colleague J. E. Neale favoured for the History of Parliament, considering it to be inadequate for his purposes. Finding out 'who the chaps were' meant more than simply recording their family connections, where they went to school, which offices they held, and so on. Namier's version of 'collective biography' required investigation of each subject's character, where possible through their own writings. It was ideally suited to the eighteenth century, where suitable materials were available but not in such great abundance as to make such a biographical analysis of the House of Commons unfeasible. It could not work in the same way for the medieval period, or Neale's Tudor century, nor, in a different way, was it appropriate for the nineteenth century, when the published record of every parliamentary debate and the proliferation of local newspapers, to give only two examples, rendered the source-base impossibly rich. Namier was fortunate that his kind of prosopography was so well suited to his period, but it was not easily transferable.

One feature of the History of Parliament has, however, proved longer-lasting: the concept of collaborative research. The argument that historical research on a massive scale is too much for the lone scholar, and is best done in groups, has reappeared in the modern era of research councils and large grants. However much academics working in the humanities may protest at the imposition by university managers of a model of research practice based rigidly on what is customary in scientific and engineering laboratories, those wishing to further their careers are obliged to write grant applications and lead research teams. Namier's earlier insistence on collaboration lay at the root of the opposition to his influence voiced at Oxford and Cambridge in the early 1950s, which was given a focus by Butterfield's denunciation of the 'Namier school'. It was not an innovation either, so much as a natural concomitant of the movement towards 'scientific' history in the late nineteenth and early twentieth centuries, which had given rise to collaborative projects like the *Dictionary of national biography*.

The professionalisation of history writing required that historians pool their expertise. This was not always popular among those suspicious of 'synthetic history',[100] but was becoming ever more necessary – and this was Namier's point – when the resources available to the historian were expanding exponentially, as was happening in his own field in the 1920s and 1930s, with the establishment of local record offices and discoveries of private papers. As always, Namier's ambition went beyond what was practicable. The technological equipment which would have permitted the kind of research he envisaged did not exist in the 1950s, so that, as Arnold Toynbee put it, he was obliged to 'assault infinity with his bare fists'.[101] Since then, the arrival of computers, digital cameras and all the conveniences of modern technology – in which Namier would have delighted – has brought his aspirations out of the realm of Don Quixote and into the everyday.

Namier's originality, and his claim to fame, lies not in his methods, therefore, but in their application; 'in the systematic thoroughness' of his research,[102] the perceptiveness of his judgments, and the clarity and force of his exposition. Not all his writings have stood the test of time. But he can still be claimed as the greatest technical historian of his generation, as well as a brilliant and provocative essayist. Those who knew him recognised an extraordinarily formidable mind: 'an unremittingly active intellectual power' as Isaiah Berlin put it.[103] First-hand descriptions of Namier concentrating his mental powers convey the impression of being in the presence of a great machine whose wheels were spinning too rapidly for their motion to be detectable. The clouds which darkened his personality, and which have been magnified by some commentators, should not obscure these talents and his remarkable achievements. He was indefatigable in his pursuit of truth, and indefatigable in his devotion to his work, and to his people (a contribution that in comparison with others who worked for the establishment of the state of Israel is rarely acknowledged).

The power of 'Namierism' has not disappeared but its influence has faded and its original shattering impact is now hard to imagine. Its creator is too often written about as a representative figure, even a spokesman, for a particular set of ideas about the past which are out of fashion, rather than as a historian who left a corpus of work the brilliance of which still glitters. Namier's continuing significance is to be sought in his own writings rather than in the kind of history which was once called 'Namierism'. The man is, and always was, more important than the method.

Notes

1 *The Times*, 22 Dec. 1960.
2 Cannon's entry on Namier in *Oxf. DNB*.
3 Ved Mehta, *Fly and the fly-bottle: encounters with British intellectuals* (1963).
4 E. H. Carr, *What is history?* (2nd edn, 1986), 32–4.
5 *Listener*, 18 May 1961.
6 J. P. Kenyon, *Listener*, 8, 22 June 1961.
7 H. C. Mansfield Jr, 'Sir Lewis Namier considered', *Journal of British Studies*, ii (1962), 28–55; Robert Walcott, '"Sir Lewis Namier considered" considered', ibid., iii (1964), 84–108; H. C. Mansfield Jr, 'Sir Lewis Namier again considered', ibid., iii (1964), 109–19.
8 Julia to Basil Liddell Hart, 1 Sept. 1960 (LH, 1/539/165–6); same to Elliott Perkins, 1 Dec. 1960 (Harvard UL, Perkins papers, HUGFP 147, box 3); Brooke to W. S. Lewis, 3 Jan., 25 Sept. 1961 (LWL, Lewis corresp., Brooke (1)); Sir Lewis Namier and John Brooke, *The House of Commons 1754–1790* (3 vols, 1964), i, p. x.
9 Sutherland to Brooke, 7 Feb. 1961 (Bodl., Sutherland papers, box 9); *Crossroads*, 73–4.
10 Brooke to Lucy Sutherland, 21 Sept., 23 Nov. 1960 (HPT, N–69); Sir Lewis Namier and John Brooke, *Charles Townshend* (1964), v–vi.
11 See, for example, Hugh Trevor-Roper, *Sunday Times*, 1 July 1962; J. H. Plumb, *Spectator*, 6 July 1962; Peter Laslett, *Guardian*, 6 July 1962.
12 *Guardian*, 8 May 1964.
13 *Spectator*, 22 May 1964.
14 *Observer*, 3 May 1964.
15 For example, *Guardian*, 4 Sept. 1964 (John Roberts); *Listener*, 17 Sept. 1964 (Maurice Hutt); *Journal of Modern History*, xxxvii (1965), 485–6 (G. H. Guttridge).
16 *Observer*, 6 Sept. 1964.
17 *New York Review of Books*, 3 Dec. 1964.
18 Sutherland to Julia Namier, 15 May 1964 (Bodl., Sutherland papers, box 9). See also Julia to Constance Babington Smith, 8 May 1964 (Babington Smith).
19 *The Times*, 1 May 1964; W. S. Lewis to John Brooke, 21 Sept. 1964 (LWL, Lewis corresp., Brooke (1)).
20 *Listener*, 8 Oct. 1964.
21 E. L. C. Mullins to Sir Frank Stenton, 29 Sept. 1964 (Reading UL, Stenton papers, MS 1148/9/1/8).
22 Brooke, 'Namier and his critics', 47. For Foot's aversion to Namier's 'structural studies' see K. O. Morgan, *Michael Foot: a life* (2007), 198–9.
23 Brooke to Butterfield, 30 July, 26 Nov. 1965 (CUL, Butterfield papers 531/B/170–1).
24 Herbert Butterfield, 'Some trends in scholarship 1868–1968, in the field of modern history', *Transactions of the Royal Historical Society*, ser. 5, xix (1969), 159–84.
25 Isaiah Berlin, *Building: letters 1960–1975*, ed. Henry Hardy and Mark Pottle (2013), 253.
26 William Palmer, *Engagement with the past: the lives and works of the World War II generation of historians* (Lexington, Ky, 2001), 217; memo by A. L. Rowse, n.d. (Exeter UL,

Rowse papers, MS 113/3/1/R); Mehta, *Fly and the fly-bottle*, 180–1; Colley, *Namier*, 100;
Adam Sisman, *A. J. P. Taylor: a biography* (paperback edn, 1995), 99–100.

27 *New Statesman*, 1 July 1969; repr. with additional flourishes in J. H. Plumb, *The making of an historian: the collected essays of J. H. Plumb* (Hemel Hempstead, 1988), 10–19.

28 See pp. 336, 366.

29 *Namier*, 324–5.

30 *Crossroads*, 214, 229–30.

31 Henry Horwitz, 'The structure of parliamentary politics', Geoffrey Holmes (ed.), *Britain after the Glorious Revolution* (1969), 96–114; Geoffrey Holmes, *British politics in the age of Anne* (revised edn, 1987), xxx–xxxi, 5–6.

32 Holmes, *British politics* (1967); J. H. Plumb, *The growth of political stability in England 1675–1725* (1967).

33 Peter Gay to Plumb, 3 Apr. 1967 (CUL, Plumb papers). Emphasis added.

34 John Kenyon, *The history men: the historical profession in England since the Renaissance* (1983), 261.

35 D. W. Hayton, 'In no one's shadow: Geoffrey Holmes's *British politics in the age of Anne* and the writing of the history of the House of Commons', *Parliamentary History*, xxviii (2009), 4–5.

36 Holmes, *British politics* (1st edn), 6–7.

37 Hayton, 'In no one's shadow', 4–6.

38 *Structure*, 235–357.

39 George Rudé, *Wilkes and liberty: a social study of 1763 to 1774* (Oxford, 1962).

40 George Rudé, 'Collusion and convergence in eighteenth-century English political action', *Government and Opposition*, i (1966), 511–28.

41 John Brewer, *Party ideology and popular politics at the accession of George III* (Cambridge, 1976), quotation at p. 17.

42 Lawrence Stone in *New York Review of Books*, 15 Mar. 1990.

43 William Palmer, *Engagement with the past: the lives and work of the World War II generation of historians* (Lexington, Ky, 2001), 61; Richard Cobb, *A sense of place* (1975), 43–4.

44 Noel Annan, *Our age: portrait of a generation* (1970), 174–5; Alan Bennett, *The history boys* (2004), 93; Keith Thomas, *New York Review of Books*, 14 June 1990; Richard Evans, *In defence of history* (1997), 33–4.

45 For example, J. P. Kenyon, *The history men: the historical profession in England since the Renaissance* (1983), 251–69; John Vincent, *An intelligent person's guide to history* (1995), ch. ix.

46 Marnie Hughes-Warrington, *Fifty key thinkers of history* (2009).

47 Namier to Melvin Arnold, 23 May 1955 (Rylands, Namier papers, 1/9/7).

48 Namier to Romney Sedgwick, 14 Nov. 1950 (HPT, N–71).

49 W. A. Speck, *Parliamentary History*, i (1982), 249. See also Colley, 101.

50 *Letters from Oxford: Hugh Trevor-Roper to Bernard Berenson*, ed. Richard Davenport-Hines (2006), 66.

51 See, for example, G. R. Elton, *Return to essentials: some reflections on the present state of historical study* (Cambridge, 1991), 81.

52 Mana Sedgwick to W. S. Lewis, 7 Mar. 1962 (LWL, Lewis corresp., Sedgwick).

53 Arnold Toynbee, *Acquaintances* (1967), 63; *The Times*, 26 Aug. 1960; Thomas Jones, *A diary with letters 1931–1950* (Oxford, 1954), 343; Malcolm Muggeridge, *Chronicles of wasted time* (2 vols, 1972–73), i, 64, 128.

54 Elliot to Dugdale, 21 Dec. 1943 (NLS, Elliot papers, Acc. 12267/16).

55 E. H. Carr, 'Lewis Namier', *From Napoleon to Stalin and other essays* (1971), 184.

56 Toynbee to J. L. Talmon, 22 June 1962 (Bodl., Toynbee papers, box 84).

57 Namier to Dugdale, 16 Nov. 1931 (CZA, A312\44).

58 Namier to Sir Archibald James, 18 Nov. 1955 (HPT, N–60).

59 John Brooke, 'Namier and Namierism', *History and Theory*, iii (1964), 333.

60 Namier to Philip Magnus-Allcroft, 7 Sept. 1959 (HPT, N–69).

61 Information from Vittorio Jucker.

62 Namier to J. Steven Watson, 16 Dec. 1954 (HPT, N–59); Namier to George Rudé, 27 Nov. 1957 (ibid., N–66).

63 Isaiah Berlin, *Personal impressions* (1980), 71.

64 *Conflicts*, 29.

65 George Orwell, 'Wells, Hitler and the world state', *Horizon*, Aug. 1941.

66 Namier to Miss M. R. Robiston, 28 Sept. 1954 (HPT, N–58); same to Francis Thompson, 25 May 1955 (ibid., N–60).

67 *Personalities and powers*, 7.

68 Namier to Isaiah Berlin, 8 May 1956, 26 Jan. 1959 (Bodl., MSS Berlin 148, fo. 24; 156, fo. 57).

69 Namier to Anna Kallin, 24 July 1953 (HPT, N–53).

70 Dugdale diaries, 1937, 161.

71 *Avenues*, 1.

72 Quotation taken from a typescript draft of the first chapter of the proposed second volume of *England in the age of the American revolution* (LWL, Namier papers (1)).

73 Namier's typed comments on proofs of W. S. Lewis's edition of Horace Walpole's *Correspondence* [1944] (LWL, Lewis corresp., Namier (1)).

74 *Amer. rev.*, 72, 84, 90.

75 *Avenues*, 5.

76 Namier to Lady Sandwich, 14 Nov. 1931 (Mapperton, GM/PERS/3); same to J. G. Edwards, 30 Oct. 1952 (HPT, N–24); correspondence with M. J. Mannheim, 1956–60 (ibid., N–63, N–66, N–68).

77 Namier to Mannheim, 13 May 1957 (HPT, N–66).

78 See *Amer. rev.*, 6–8, 13–20, 22, 25–6, 30.

79 *Nation and Athenaeum*, 22 Dec. 1928.

80 *Avenues*, 1.

81 *Personalities and powers*, 5; E. H. Carr to Herbert Butterfield, 2 Feb. 1960 (CUL, Butterfield papers, 531/C/10); fragment of writing by Namier [c.1940–45] (Rylands, Namier papers, 1/1b/9).

82 *Listener*, 24 Dec. 1953.

83 Herbert Butterfield, *George III and the historians* (1957), 298.

84 John Brooke, 'Namier and his critics', *Encounter*, xxiv, no. 2 (Feb. 1965), 48–9.

85 'Turbulent Zionist', 5; Irina Prehn to Constance Babington Smith, 11 May 1980 (Babington Smith).

86 'Turbulent Zionist', 4–5.

87 Berenson to Isaiah Berlin, 27 Apr. 1958 (Bodl., MS Berlin 154, fo. 219).

88 Namier to Michael Selzer, 10 Apr. 1953 (CZA, Namier papers, A312\63).

89 Perry Anderson, *English questions* (1992), 61–4, 73–4. Anderson attributes Namier's criticism of European races and states to his love affair with England, but Namier's detestation of the German, Russian and Austro-Hungarian empires antedated his arrival in England.

90 Compare Hans Kohn, *The mind of Germany* (1965), with Namier's comments on the German national character in drafts of his introduction to his Waynflete Lectures (Rylands, Namier papers, 1/1b/4; Bodl., MS Eng. hist. d. 341, fos 79–81).

91 Irina Prehn to Constance Babington Smith, 11 May 1980 (Babington Smith).

92 *Dip. prelude*, v.

93 See p. 289.

94 Taylor to Betty Kemp, 19 July 1962 (St Hugh's College, Oxford, Kemp papers, box 1, fo. 116).

95 W. R. Fryer, 'Namier and the king's position in English politics, 1744–84', *Burke Newsletter*, v (1963), 246–58.

96 *Avenues*, 4; Isaiah Berlin, *The proper study of mankind ...*, ed. Henry Hardy and Roger Hausheer (1997), 56, 146.

97 J. A. Cannon, 'Lewis Bernstein Namier', J. A. Cannon (ed.), *The historian at work* (1980), 140–1.

98 See, for example, Hamish Scott, 'The early modern European nobility and its contested historiographies, c.1950–1980', *Contested spaces of nobility in early modern Europe*, ed. M. P. Romaniello and Charles Lipp (2016), 23.

99 *The Times*, 7 Nov. 1960; Bentley, *Modernizing England's past: English historiography in the age of modernism 1870–1970* (Cambridge, 2005), 207–8; Arnaldo Momigliano, *Studies on modern scholarship*, ed. G. W. Bowersock and T. J. Cornell (Berkeley and Los Angeles, 1994), 73.

100 See for example, F. M. Powicke, *Modern historians and the study of history: essays and papers* (1955), 205.

101 Toynbee, *Acquaintances*, 85.

102 Carr, 'Namier', 190.

103 Berlin, *Personal impressions*, 81.

Bibliography

Manuscript sources

Canada

Kingston, Ontario
Queen's University, Douglas Library
  John Buchan papers: box 7 (consulted at NLS, Acc. 7214, Mf MS 306)

Toronto, Ontario
University of Toronto Archives
  A67.0007/02: Office of the President, ser. 1, Correspondence and subject files 1911–12

Ireland

Dublin
Alexandra College
  College archives (information kindly supplied by the librarian, Ms Aileen Ivory)
National Library of Ireland
  Sir Horace Plunkett papers (MS 42,222/35)
University College, Dublin, Department of Archives
  R. W. Dudley Edwards papers: LA 22

Israel

Jerusalem
Central Zionist Archives
  Sir Lewis Namier papers: A312\1–63 (includes copies of material from the Weizmann
    Archive at Rehovot (A312\9, 12–15))
  Zionist Organisation archive: Z4\30451, 31077–8, 31180, 31206, 31387, 32015, 32041, 32332

Italy

Florence
Biblioteca Berenson, Villa I Tatti
  Bernard and Mary Berenson papers

Bibliography

UK

Aberystwyth
National Library of Wales
  Clement Davies papers: P/4/21–155
  Sir Goronwy Edwards papers: 201, 213
  Thomas Jones papers: F/1, H/21, M/4, WW/22

Belfast
Public Record Office of Northern Ireland
  J. C. Beckett papers: D/4126/A/1/4
  Marquess of Londonderry papers: D/3099/17/30
  Department of Finance papers: FIN/17/1J/4/1–2
Queen's University Belfast, McClay Library
  Wiles Trust archive: QUB/E/4/2/11, boxes 01, 05

Birmingham
University of Birmingham, Special Collections, Cadbury Research Library
  E. H. Carr papers: boxes 26–7

Brighton
East Sussex Record Office
  Kingsley Martin papers: SxMs11/3/1/155
  Leonard Woolf papers: SxMs13/1/L/2/2, SxMs13/2/D/13/A/106

Bristol
University of Bristol Library
  Hamish Hamilton archive: DM/1352/Ii

Cambridge
Cambridge University Library
  Earl Baldwin papers: 164, 166–8
  Sir Herbert Butterfield papers: BUTT 76/1–8, 77/13, 190a/1, 531
  Sir John Plumb papers
  Viscount Templewood papers: XVII, File 4/1
Churchill College, Churchill Archives Centre
  L. S. Amery papers: AMEL 1/5/47, 1/6/6, 1/7/86, 2/1/45
  Patrick Beesly papers: MLBE 2/40
  Sir William Bull papers: BULL 5/22, 24
  Chartwell papers: CHAR 8/326
  Sir Winston Churchill additional papers: WCHL 1/14
  Baron Gladwyn papers: GLAD 7/14, 8/3, 8/29
  Sir James Headlam-Morley papers: HDLM Acc 688, box 2
  A. W. A. Leeper papers: LEEP 3/35
  Sir Cecil Spring Rice papers: CASR I 1/61, 5/4
  F. G. Steiner papers: STNR 6/5/1
Girton College
  Helen M. Cam papers: GCPP Cam 2/2/3, 10, 13–17, 2/7/10, 12, 16, 23, 4/1/1

St John's College
    Max Newman papers: M/2/4/14
Trinity College
    J. R. M. Butler papers: JRMB/A1

Durham
Durham University Library
    Durham University records: UND/CJI/1952, UND/DB4/FC35
    Malcolm MacDonald papers: 2/3, 5; 9/1–8

Edinburgh
National Archives of Scotland
    Earl of Balfour papers: GD 433/2/277
    Marquess of Lothian papers: GD 40/17/216
    Scottish Committee on the History of Parliament archive: SCHP1/1–5, 8–9
National Library of Scotland
    Baron Boothby papers: Acc. 12929, box 7
    Walter Elliot papers: Acc. 12198/1–12, Acc. 12267/10–20

Exeter
Exeter University Library
    A. L. Rowse papers: EUL MSS 113/3/1/N, P, R, T

Glasgow
University of Glasgow, Archive Services
    J. D. Mackie papers: DC 32/3/5

Kew
The National Archives
    Cabinet Office papers: CAB 24/17–18, 21–2, 24–5, 28–9, 143, 278; 37/144, 103/416, 129/12, 67
    Foreign Office papers: FO 370/1252; 371/2450, 2750, 2862, 3001–2, 3016, 3019, 3054, 3135, 3277–81, 3894, 3896–901, 3903–14, 3921–32, 3934, 4357–69, 4371–87, 23153, 23251, 24096, 24474, 24482, 27044; 395/10, 25–6, 108; 608/59–64, 66–8, 70, 195; 668/1; 925/37096, 37106
    Home Office papers: HO 144/1250, 1284; 334/59, 112, 157
    Earl Kitchener papers: PRO 30/57/45
    Prime Minister's papers: PREM 11/3906
    Stationery Office papers: STAT 14/1478–9
    Treasury papers: T 219/649–55

Leeds
Yorkshire Archaeological Society
    H. L. Bradfer-Lawrence papers: MD 335/16/1/7

London
Athenaeum archives
    Ballot books (information kindly supplied by the archivist, Ms Jennie De Protani)
British Academy
    Academy archives (information kindly supplied by the Fellow Archivist, Dr Peter Brown)

Bibliography

British Library
Viscount Cecil of Chelwood papers: Add. MSS 51100, 51157, 51173, 51179, 51186
Paul Emrys Evans papers: Add. MS 58255
Macmillan archive: Add. MSS 55065, 56023
Petty papers: Add. MS 72907
Society of Authors archive: Add. MS 63311
History of Parliament archive
Editorial Board minutes 1951–60
Minute book of the Committee on the History of Parliament 1933–41
Editorial Board papers: N–24–6, 29–30
Trustees' correspondence: N–25
Sir Goronwy Edwards correspondence: N–19
Sir Lewis Namier papers: N–50–71
Sir John Neale correspondence: N–20
Sir Frank Stenton papers: N–22
J. C. Wedgwood papers: A–44, A–50
Imperial War Museum
Special Misc. MSS CC, Z6
Institute of Historical Research, University of London
History of Parliament papers: HS7
Seminar attendance books
King's College London, Liddell Hart Centre for Military Archives
Sir Arthur Bryant papers: E2/2
Basil Liddell Hart papers: LH1/539
Lambeth Palace Library
Claude Jenkins papers: MS 1634
London Metropolitan Archives
Board of Deputies of British Jews archive
Lee & Pembertons archive
Pilgrim Trust archive: LMA/4450/A/01/014, LMA/4450/A/03/008
London School of Economics
Fabian Society archive: C55/4, G1, G9, G13
Sir Charles Webster papers: 1/17, 1/21, 1/23–24, 1/26, 1/28, 1/33, 1/35, 1/36, 19/38
Parliamentary Archives
History of Parliament Trust (J. C. Wedgwood) papers: HPT/5, 8
Earl Lloyd-George papers: LG/F/201/1/14
Herbert Samuel papers: SAM/A/155, SAM/H/9
Baron Stow Hill papers: STH/FS/1
John St Loe Strachey papers: STR 13/18
University College, London
Sir John Neale papers: MS Add 433
University College, London, School of Slavonic and East European Studies
R. W. Seton-Watson papers: SEW 3/3, 17/18–19
University of London Library
A. F. Pollard papers: MS 890, boxes 6a, 6b, 390
Wiener Library
Central British Fund for World Jewish Relief archive: MF Doc 27/6

Bibliography

Manchester
John Rylands University Library
 Samuel Alexander papers: B/4/32, C/4/6, C/4/7
 Manchester Guardian archive: 149/N/1, A/N2, B/N8A, D/977, D/2530
 Sir Lewis Namier (and John Brooke) papers: 1/1a/1–4, 6, 14–15; 1/1b/1, 3–12, 14–17; 1/2/1–3,
  5–9, 11–12; 1/4a/1, 3; 1/4b/2, 6, 11–12; 1/5b/4, 6; 1/8/3; 1/9/1–3, 5, 7–8, 15, 17, 19–20; 1/10/2,
  6–7; 1/18/3; 1/19/5; 1/20/1
Manchester University Library, University Archive
 Faculty of Arts minutes, Senate Committee books
 Vice-Chancellor's archive: VCA/7/56, VCA/7/486, VCA/7/562

Norwich
Norfolk Record Office
 Hamond of Westacre papers: HMN 6/303
 R. W. Ketton-Cremer papers: WKC 7/29

Oxford
Balliol College
 College Archives: College minutes, 1942–50; 'English Register', 1908–24; History Club
  papers 1907–9
 A. W. A. Leeper papers: II A–E
 A. L. Smith papers
Bodleian Library
 Laurence Alma-Tadema papers: MS Eng. Lett. c. 528
 Sir Isaiah Berlin papers: MSS Berlin 105, 107, 114–15, 131, 140, 145–6, 148, 151, 154–6
 Sir George Clark papers: 40, 181, 213, 216, 268
 Lionel Curtis papers: MSS Eng. hist. c. 786, c. 804, c. 807
 E. S. De Beer papers: MS Eng. c. 3117
 Sir Herbert Fisher papers: MS Fisher 81
 Strickland Gibson papers: MS Eng. lett. c. 594
 Frank Hardie papers: MS Eng. lett. c. 459
 Sir Lewis Namier working papers: MS Eng. hist. d. 341–2
 Sir Walford Selby papers: MS Eng. c. 6600
 Society for the Protection of Science and Learning archive: MS S.P.S.L. 165/3
 Stephen Spender papers: MS Spender 58
 Leonard Stein papers: box 121
 Earl of Stockton papers: MSS Macmillan dep. c. 307, 320, 515, 673, d. 28, 39
 Dame Lucy Sutherland papers: box 9
 A. J. Toynbee papers: boxes 40, 84
 Sir Alfred Zimmern papers: MS Zimmern 25
Christ Church
 Lord Dacre papers
House of St Gregory and St Macrina
 Constance Babington Smith papers
Magdalen College
 College archives: FD/2
St Antony's College, Middle East Centre Archive
 H. St J. B. Philby papers: 1/6

Bibliography

St Hugh's College
  Betty Kemp papers: boxes 1, 8
Trinity College
  J. P. Cooper papers: DD 279/A, F, I, K

Reading
BBC Written Archives, Caversham Park
Reading University, Special Collections Service
  G. D. Bell and Sons archive: MS 1640/389, 3269, 362118
  Bodley Head archive: BH1 RR1/365
  Macmillan Archive: MAC JEW, MAC JUC, MAC NAM
  Sir Frank Stenton papers: MS 1148/19/1–4

Southampton
University of Southampton, Archives and Manuscripts Section
  Leonard Stein papers: MS 170

MSS in private possession
Blanche Dugdale diaries, typescript (Fergusson papers)
Fourth marquess of Salisbury papers: 4M/269 (marquess of Salisbury, Hatfield House, Herts.)
Ninth earl of Sandwich papers: GM/PERS/3, 6–7, 15 (earl of Sandwich, Mapperton House, Dorset)

USA

Albany, N.Y.
University at Albany, SUNY, M. E. Grenander Department of Special Collections and Archives
  John H. E. Fried papers: series 7, box 7

Austin, Texas
University of Texas at Austin, Harry Ransom Center
  T. E. Lawrence papers: series IV, box 10, folder 6
  John Lehmann letters
  Leonard Russell letters: box 1.1

Cambridge, Mass.
Harvard University, Houghton Library
  R. W. Chapman papers: MS Hyde 97 (8)
Harvard University, Pusey Library, University Archives
  Elliott Perkins papers: HUGFP 147, box 3

Chicago, Ill.
University of Chicago Library, Special Collections Research Center
  Misc. MSS: letter of Granville Proby 1934
  Michael Polyani papers: series 1, correspondence

Bibliography

Farmington, Conn.
Lewis Walpole Library
  W. S. Lewis correspondence
  Sir Lewis Namier papers

Hyde Park, N.Y.
Franklin D. Roosevelt Presidential Library
  W. H. Shepardson papers: boxes 1, 7

New Haven, Conn.
Yale University, Beinecke Library
  Alan Pryce-Jones papers: GEN MSS 513, box 16, folder 854
  James M. Osborn corresp.: OSB MSS 7, box 56, folder 1145
  Rebecca West papers: GEN MSS 105, box 13, folder 592
Yale University, Sterling Memorial Library
  C. H. Nagel papers: MSS 364/I, boxes 11–12, 40
  Wallace Notestein papers: MSS 544/I, boxes 4–9

New York, N.Y.
Center for Jewish History, YIVO Archives
  Philip Friedman papers: RG 1258, folder 164
The Morgan Library and Museum
  Misc. Ray: letter of Namier to Sir James Thorold, 1953

Palo Alto, Calif.
Stanford University, Hoover Institution Archives
  August Zaleski papers: box 1, folder 4

San Marino, Calif.
Huntington Library
  E. F. Gay papers
  Godfrey Davies papers

Washington, D.C.
Georgetown University Library, Special Collections Research Center
  Sir Arnold Lunn papers: box 3, folders 6, 8; box 4, folders 5–6; box 10, folders 2, 4

Oral history sources

Columbia University, Butler Library, Columbia Centre for Oral History
  Reminiscences of Dr Maurice Perlzweig (tapes and transcript)
Institute of Historical Research, University of London
  'Interviews with historians': Rosalind Mitchison with Christopher Smout (issued on DVD)

Bibliography

Printed primary sources

Official publications

Interim report of the committee on House of Commons personal and politics 1264–1832 (Parl. papers, 1930 [Cmd. 4130], x.

Newspapers and periodicals

Daily Telegraph
Economist
Everyman
Fabian News
Financial Times
Jewish Chronicle
Land and Water
Listener
Manchester Guardian
Manchester Guardian Commercial
Nation and Athenaeum
National Review
New Europe
New Statesman
New Statesman and Nation
New York Times
Nineteenth Century and After
Observer
Palestine Post
Political Quarterly
Spectator
Sunday Times
Time & Tide
The Times
Times Literary Supplement
Week-end Review
Zionist Review

Other printed primary sources (excluding Namier's own published work)

Amery, Leo, *The empire at bay: the Leo Amery diaries 1929–1945*, ed. John Barnes and David Nicholson (1988).
Berlin, Isaiah, *Flourishing: letters 1928–1946*, ed. Henry Hardy (2004).
——, *Enlightening: letters 1946–60*, ed. Henry Hardy and Jennifer Holmes (2009).
——, *Building: letters 1960–1975*, ed. Henry Hardy and Mark Pottle (2013).
——, *Affirming: letters 1975–1997*, ed. Henry Hardy and Mark Pottle (2015).
Boothby, Robert, Lord Boothby, *My yesterday, your tomorrow* (1962).
——, *Boothby: recollections of a rebel* (1978).

Cobb, Richard, *My dear Hugh: letters from Richard Cobb to Hugh Trevor-Roper and others*, ed. Tim Heald (2011).

Crozier, W. P., *Off the record: political interviews 1933–43*, ed. A. J. P. Taylor (1973).

Dalton, Hugh, *The fateful years: memoirs 1931–1945* (1957).

——, *The political diary of Hugh Dalton 1918–40, 1945–60*, ed. Ben Pimlott (1986).

——, *The Second World War diary of Hugh Dalton 1940–1945*, ed. Ben Pimlott (1986).

Dugdale, Blanche ['Baffy'], *Baffy: the diaries of Blanche Dugdale 1936–1947*, ed. Norman Rose (1973).

Elliott, Sir Ivo (ed.), *Balliol College register, 1900–1950* (Oxford, 1953).

Eliot, T. S., *The letters of T. S. Eliot*, ed. Valerie Eliot and John Haffenden (6 vols so far, 1988–2016).

Gollancz, Victor, *My dear Timothy: an autobiographical letter to his grandson* (1952).

Harvey, Oliver, *The diplomatic diaries of Oliver Harvey 1937–1940*, ed. John Harvey (1970).

——, *The war diaries of Oliver Harvey*, ed. John Harvey (1978).

Headlam-Morley, Sir James, *A memoir of the Paris Peace Conference 1919*, ed. Agnes Headlam-Morley et al. (1972).

Hilliard, Edward, *The Balliol College register 1832–1914* (Oxford, 1914).

Jebb, H. M. Gladwyn, *The memoirs of Lord Gladwyn* (1972).

Jenkinson, Charles, *The Jenkinson papers 1760–1766*, ed. Ninetta S. Jucker (1949).

Jones, Thomas, *A diary with letters 1931–1950* (Oxford, 1954).

——, *Whitehall diary*, ed. Keith Middlemas (3 vols, 1969–71).

Lindsay, David, *The Crawford papers: the journals of David Lindsay twenty-seventh earl of Crawford and tenth earl of Balcarres 1871–1940 during the years 1892 to 1940*, ed. John Vincent (Manchester, 1984).

Muggeridge, Malcolm, *Chronicles of wasted time* (2 vols, 1972–73).

——, *Like it was: the diaries of Malcolm Muggeridge*, ed. John Bright-Holmes (1981).

Namier, Julia, *Lewis Namier: a biography* (1971).

Nicolson, Harold, *Diaries and letters 1939–1945*, ed. Nigel Nicolson (1967).

Schutz, Eva, *My long journey to London* (privately printed, 1994).

[Smith, Mary L.,] *Arthur Lionel Smith, master of Balliol (1916–1924): a biography and some reminiscences* (1928).

Taylor, A. J. P., *A personal history* (1983).

——, *Letters to Eva 1969–1983*, ed. Eva Haraszti Taylor (1991).

Temperley, Harold, *An historian in peace and war: the diaries of Harold Temperley*, ed. T. G. Otte (Farnham, 2014).

Tree, Viola, *Castles in the air: the story of my singing days* (1926).

Trevor-Roper, Hugh, *Letters from Oxford: Hugh Trevor-Roper to Bernard Berenson*, ed. Richard Davenport-Hines (2006).

——, *One hundred letters from Hugh Trevor-Roper*, ed. Richard Davenport-Hines and Adam Sisman (Oxford, 2014).

Wedgwood, J. C., *Memoirs of a fighting life* (1940).

West, Rebecca, *Selected letters of Rebecca West*, ed. B. K. Scott (2000).

Weizmann, Chaim, *Trial and error* (1949).

——, *The letters and papers of Chaim Weizmann*, ser. A, ed. M. W. Weisgal et al. (23 vols, 1968–80).

——, *The letters and papers of Chaim Weizmann*, ser. B, ed. Barnet Litvinoff (2 vols, New Brunswick, 1983).

Bibliography

Woolf, Leonard, *The journey not the arrival matters: an autobiography of the years 1939–1969* (1970).

Woolf, Virginia, *The letters of Virginia Woolf*, ed. Nigel Nicolson (6 vols, 1975–80).

Secondary sources

Abbatista, Guido, 'Lo struzzo e la "formidabile lumaca": Sir Lewis B. Namier e l'Italia', *Rivista Storica Italiana*, cxxi (2009), 1124–31.

Aberbach, David, *The European Jews, patriotism and the liberal state 1789–1939* (2013).

Adamthwaite, Anthony, *France and the coming of the Second World War 1936–1939* (1977).

Albanis, Elizabeth, 'Jewish identity in the face of anti-Semitism', *Historical Journal*, xli (1998), 895–900.

Alderman, Geoffrey, *Modern British Jewry* (Oxford, 1992).

Anderson, Perry, *English questions* (1992).

Annan, Noel, *Our age: portrait of a generation* (1990).

Ashley, Maurice, *Churchill as historian* (1968).

Babington Smith, Constance, *Iulia de Beausobre: a Russian Christian in the west* (1983).

Baker, Mark, 'Sir Lewis Namier: an eastern European's historical outline', *Past Imperfect*, i (1992), 113–32.

——, 'Lewis Namier and the problem of Eastern Galicia', *Journal of Ukrainian Studies*, xxiii, no. 2 (1998), 59–104.

Ball, Simon, *The guardsmen: Harold Macmillan, three friends, and the world they made* (2004).

Beales, Derek, 'Sir Lewis Namier and the party system', *Cambridge Review*, 31 May 1958.

Beckerman-Boys, Carly, 'The reversal of the Passfield White Paper, 1930–31: a reassessment', *Journal of Contemporary History*, li (2016), 213–33.

Beloff, Max, 'Two historians: Arnold Toynbee and Lewis Namier', *Encounter*, no. 74 (Apr. 1990), 51–4.

——, *An historian in the twentieth century: chapters in intellectual autobiography* (1992).

Bentley, Michael, *Modern historiography: an introduction* (1999).

——, *Modernizing England's past: English historiography in the age of modernism 1870–1970* (Cambridge, 2005).

——, *The life and thought of Herbert Butterfield: history, science and God* (Cambridge, 2011).

——, 'Shape and pattern in British historical writing', Stuart Macintyre, Juan Maigushca and Attila Pók (eds), *The Oxford history of historical writing*, iv: *1800–1945* (Oxford, 2011), 204–24.

——, 'British historical writing', Stuart Macintyre, Juan Maiguashca and Attila Pók (eds), *The Oxford history of historical writing*, v: *Historical writing since 1945* (Oxford, 2012), 291–310.

Berlin, Isaiah, *Personal impressions* (1980), 63–82.

——, *The proper study of mankind ...*, ed. Henry Hardy and Roger Hausheer (1997).

Biskupski, M. B. B., *"The most dangerous German agent in America": the many lives of Louis N. Hammerling* (DeKalb, Ill., 2015).

Blaas, P. B. M., *Continuity and anachronism: parliamentary and constitutional development in Whig historiography and in the anti-Whig reaction between 1890 and 1930* (The Hague, 1978).

Bosworth, R. J. B., *Explaining Auschwitz and Hiroshima: history writing and the Second World War* (1993).

Brock, M. G., and M. C. Curthoys (eds), *The history of the university of Oxford*, vii: *Nineteenth-century Oxford, part 2* (Oxford, 2000).

Bibliography

Brogan, Sir Denis, 'Sir Herbert Butterfield as a historian; an interpretation', J. H. Elliott and H. G. Koenigsberger (eds), *The diversity of history: essays in honour of Sir Herbert Butterfield* (1970), 3–15.

Brooke, John, *The Chatham administration 1766–1768* (1956).

——, 'Namier and Namierism', *History and Theory*, iii (1964), 331–47.

——, 'Namier and his critics', *Encounter*, xxiv, no. 2 (Feb. 1965), 47–9.

——, 'Namier, Sir Lewis Bernstein (1888–1960)', E. T. Williams and H. M. Palmer (eds), *The Dictionary of National Biography: Twentieth Century, 1951–1960* (Oxford, 1971), 795–8.

Burk, Kathleen, *Troublemaker: the life and history of A. J. P. Taylor* (2000).

Burns, J. H., 'Ian Ralph Christie, 1919–1998', *Proceedings of the British Academy*, cv (2000), 365–85.

Burrow, John, *A history of histories …* (2007).

Butler, J. R. M., *Lord Lothian (Philip Kerr) 1882–1940* (1960).

Butterfield, Herbert, *George III, Lord North, and the people 1779–80* (1949).

——, *George III and the historians* (1957).

——, 'George III and the Namier school', *Encounter*, viii, no. 4 (Apr. 1957), 70–6.

——, 'George III and the constitution', *History*, xliii (1958), 14–33.

——, 'Sir Lewis Namier as historian', *Listener*, 18 May 1961.

Cairns, J. C., 'Sir Lewis Namier and the history of Europe', *Historical Reflections/Réflexions Historiques*, i (1974), 3–35.

Calder, K. J., *Britain and the origins of the new Europe 1914–1918* (Cambridge, 1976).

Cannadine, David, *G. M. Trevelyan: a life in history* (1993).

——, *History in our time* (1998).

——, *In Churchill's shadow: confronting the past in modern Britain* (2001).

——, 'John Harold Plumb 1911–2001' in *Proceedings of the British Academy*, cxxiv (2004), 268–309.

——, 'The History of Parliament: past, present – and future', *Parliamentary History*, xxvi (2007), 366–86.

——, *Making history now and then: discoveries, controversies and explorations* (Basingstoke, 2008).

Cannon, J. A., 'Lewis Bernstein Namier', J.A. Cannon (ed.), *The historian at work* (1980), 136–53.

Carr, E. H., *What is history?* (2nd edn, 1986).

——, 'Lewis Namier', *From Napoleon to Stalin and other essays* (1971), 184–91.

Carsten, F. L., *The first Austrian republic 1918–1938: a study based on British and Austrian documents* (Aldershot, 1986).

Charney, Maurice, 'Sir Lewis Namier and Auden's *Musée des beaux arts*', *Philological Quarterly*, xxxix (1960), 129–31.

Christie, I. R., *Myth and reality in late eighteenth-century British politics and other papers* (1970).

——, 'George III and the historians – thirty years on', *History*, lxxxi (1986), 205–21.

Churchill, Randolph and Martin Gilbert, *Winston S. Churchill* (8 vols, 1966–88).

Cienciala, A.M., 'Polityka brytyjska wobec odrodzenia Polski, 1914–1918' in *Zeszyty historyczne*, no. 16 (1969), 79–94.

—— and Titus Komarnicki, *From Versailles to Locarno: keys to Polish foreign policy, 1919–1925* (Lawrence, Ks., 1984).

Clark, J. C. D., *Revolution and rebellion: state and society in England in the seventeenth and eighteenth centuries* (Cambridge, 1986).

Bibliography

Clarke, Peter, *Mr Churchill's profession: statesman, orator, writer* (2012).

Cohen, M. J., *Churchill and the Jews* (1985).

Cole, Margaret, *The life of G. D. H. Cole* (1971).

Colley, Linda, *Namier* (1989).

Collini, Stefan, *English pasts: essays in history and culture* (Oxford, 1999).

——, *Absent minds: intellectuals in Britain* (Oxford, 2006).

——, *Common reading: critics, historians, publics* (Oxford, 2008).

Coote, Colin, *A Companion of Honour: the story of Walter Elliot* (1965).

Coutouvidis, John, 'Lewis Namier and the Polish government in exile, 1939–40', *Slavonic and East European Review*, lxii (1984), 421–8.

—— and Jaime Reynolds, *Poland 1939–1947* (Leicester, 1986).

Cowling, Maurice, *Religion and public doctrine in England*, iii: *Accommodations* (Cambridge, 2001).

Davies, Norman, 'The Poles in Great Britain, 1914–1919', *Slavonic and East European Review*, l (1972), 63–89.

——, *White eagle, red star: the Polish-Soviet war, 1919–1920* (1972).

——, 'Great Britain and the Polish Jews, 1918–20', *Journal of Contemporary History*, viii (1973), 119–42.

——, *God's playground: a history of Poland*, ii: *1795 to the present* (Oxford, 2005).

Davis, H. W. C., *A history of Balliol College*, rev. R. H. C. Davis and Richard Hunt (Oxford, 1963).

Dobrova, E. A., 'Lewis Namier – a person in history', A. P. Davidson (ed.), *In the world of English history* (Moscow, 2003), 260–8.

Eberhardt, Piotr, 'The Curzon Line as the eastern boundary of Poland: the origins and the political background', *Geographica Polonica*, lxxxv (2012), 5–21.

Egremont, Max, *Siegfried Sassoon: a biography* (2005).

Ellis, E. L., *T.J.: a life of Dr Thomas Jones, C.H.* (Cardiff, 1992).

Elton, G. R., *The practice of history* (paperback edn, 1969).

——, *Political History: Principles and Practice* (1970).

Endelman, T. M., *The Jews of Britain, 1656 to 2000* (Berkeley, Calif., 2002).

Evans, L. T., 'Sir Otto Herzberg Frankel ...', *Biographical Memoirs of Fellows of the Royal Society*, xlv (1999), 166–81.

Evans, Richard, *In defence of history* (1997).

Feske, Victor, *From Belloc to Churchill: private scholars, public culture, and the crisis of British Liberalism, 1900–1939* (Chapel Hill, N.C., 1996).

Fink, Carole, *Defending the rights of others: the Great Powers, the Jews, and international minority protection, 1878–1938* (Cambridge, 2006).

Fryer, W. R., 'The study of British politics between the Revolution and the Reform Act', *Renaissance and Modern Studies*, i (1957), 91–114.

——, 'King George III: his political character 1760–1784: a new whig interpretation', ibid., vi (1962), 68–101.

——, 'Namier and the king's position in English politics, 1744–84', *Burke Newsletter*, v (1963), 246–58.

Gaines, D. I., 'Namier on 18th century England', *The Historian*, xxv (1963), 213–25.

G[albraith], V. H.,' 'Sir Lewis Namier', *Balliol College Record*, 1961, 39–40.

Giua, Maria Antonietta, 'Ronald Syme e Lewis B. Namier: Nota su un rapporto intellettuale controverso', *Rivista Storica Italiana*, cxxi (2009), 1246–54.

Glendinning, Victoria, *Leonard Woolf: a life* (2007).

Bibliography

Goldstein, Erik, 'The Round Table and the New Europe', *The Round Table: the Commonwealth Journal of International Affairs*, lxxxvii (1998), 177–89.

Graziosi, Andrea, 'Il mondo in Europa. Namier e il "Medio oriente europeo", 1815–1948', *Contemporanea: Rivista di Storia dell' 800 e dell' 900*, x (2007), 193–228.

Green, S. J. D., and Peregrine Horden (eds), *All Souls and the wider world: statesmen, scholars and adventurers, c.1850–1950* (Oxford, 2011).

Hadaczek, K, *La colonie industrielle de Koszyłowce … de l'époque énéolithique: album des fouilles* (Lèopol, 1914).

Hall, Ian, 'The realist as moralist: Sir Lewis Namier's international thought', Lisa Hill (ed.), *British international thinkers from Hobbes to Namier* (Basingstoke, 2010), 227–46.

Harrison, E. D. R., 'The British Special Operations Executive and Poland', *Historical Journal*, xliii (2000), 1071–91.

Haslam, Jonathan, *The vices of integrity: E. H. Carr, 1892–1982* (1999).

Hayton, D. W., 'In no one's shadow: Geoffrey Holmes's *British politics in the age of Anne* and the writing of the history of the House of Commons', *Parliamentary History*, xxviii (2009), 1–14.

——, 'Colonel Wedgwood and the historians', *Historical Research*, lxxxiv (2011), 328–55.

——, 'Sir Lewis Namier, Sir John Neale and the shaping of the *History of Parliament*', *Parliamentary History*, xxxii (2013), 187–211.

——, 'Official histories of parliament and the nature of the union of 1707: a forgotten episode in Anglo-Scottish academic relations', *Scottish Historical Review*, xciii (2014), 80–108.

——, 'Lewis Namier: nationality, territory and Zionism', *International Journal of Politics, Culture and Society*, xxx (2017), 171–82.

Hexter, J. H., 'Doing history', *Commentary*, li, no. 6 (1971), 53–62.

Himmelfarb, Gertrude, *The new history and the old* (Cambridge, Mass., 1987).

Holmes, Colin, *Anti-Semitism in British society 1876–1939* (1979).

Holmes, Geoffrey, *British politics in the age of Anne* (1967).

Hooker, J. R., 'Lord Curzon and the "Curzon Line"', *Journal of Modern History*, xxx (1958), 137–8.

Horne, Alastair, *Macmillan* (2 vols, 1988–89).

Hunczak, Taras, 'Sir Lewis Namier and the struggle for Eastern Galicia, 1918–1920', *Harvard Ukrainian Studies*, i (1977), 198–210.

Ignatieff, Michael, *Isaiah Berlin: a life* (New York, 1998).

James, Clive, *Cultural amnesia: necessary memories from history and the arts* (corrected edn, 2012).

James, Robert Rhodes, *Victor Cazalet: a portrait* (1976).

Jebb, Miles (Lord Gladwyn), *Patrick Shaw-Stewart, an Edwardian meteor* (Wimborne Minster, 1910).

Johnston, Edith Mary, 'Managing an inheritance: Colonel J. C. Wedgwood, the *History of Parliament* and the lost History of the Irish Parliament', *Proceedings of the Royal Irish Academy*, lxxxix (1989), sect. C, 167–86.

Jones, John, *Balliol College: a history* (2nd edn, Oxford, 2005).

Kaindl, R. F., 'Neolithische Funde mit bemalter Keramik in Koszylowce Ostgalizien)', *Jahrbuch für Altertumskunde*, ii (1908), 144–50.

Kearney, Hugh, 'Historical achievement', *Studies*, xlv (1956), 467–70.

Kenyon, John, *The history men: the historical profession in England since the Renaissance* (1983), 251–69.

Kramnick, Isaac, and Barry Sheerman, *Harold Laski: a life on the left* (1993).

Bibliography

Kukiel, Marian, 'Sir Lewis Namier', *Teki Historyczne*, xi (1960–1), 259–61.

Latawski, Paul (ed.), *The reconstruction of Poland, 1914–23* (Basingstoke, 1992).

——, 'The Dmowski–Namier feud, 1915–1918', *Polin: studies in Polish Jewry, ii* (Oxford, 1987), 37–49.

Lavin, Deborah, 'History, morals and the politics of empire: Lionel Curtis and the Round Table', John Bossy and Peter Jupp (eds), *Essays presented to Michael Roberts ...* (Belfast, 1976), 117–32.

——, *From empire to international commonwealth: a biography of Lionel Curtis* (Oxford, 1995).

Levillain, Charles-Édouard, 'Churchill historien de Marlborough', *Commentaire*, no. 139 (2012), 781–7.

Lukowski, Jerzy and Herbert Zawadski, *A concise history of Poland* (Cambridge, 2001).

Lundgreen-Nielsen, Kay, *The Polish problem at the Paris Peace Conference: a study of the great powers and the Poles, 1918–1919* (Odense, 1979).

Macfie, A. L., 'Namier, Zionism and the Palestine question: a case study of objectivity, truth and balance in the writing of history', *Rethinking History*, xx (2016), 512–22.

MacMillan, Margaret, *Peacemakers: the Paris conference of 1919 and its attempt to end war* (2001).

Mansfield, H. C. Jr, 'Sir Lewis Namier considered', *Journal of British Studies*, ii (1962), 28–55.

——, 'Sir Lewis Namier again considered', *Journal of British Studies*, iii (1964), 109–19.

Marwick, Arthur, *The nature of history* (1970).

May, Derwent, *Critical times: the history of the* Times Literary Supplement (2001).

McDonald, Iverach, *The history of* The Times, v: *Struggle in war and peace 1939–1966* (1984).

McGregor, Arthur, *Summary catalogue of the continental archaeological collections in the Ashmolean Museum* (Oxford, 1997).

McIntire, C. T., *Herbert Butterfield: historian as dissenter* (2004).

Mehta, Ved, *Fly and the fly bottle: encounters with British intellectuals* (1963).

Miller, Karl, 'Teachers, writers' in Jeremy Treglown and Bridget Bennett (eds), *Grub Street and the ivory tower: literary journalism and literary scholarship from Fielding to the internet* (Oxford, 1998), 250–61.

Mulvey, Paul, *The political life of Josiah C. Wedgwood: land, liberty and empire, 1872–1943* (Woodbridge, 2010).

Natan, Alex, 'Sir Lewis Namier: Historiker mit Vorurteilen' In *Vierteljahrshefte Für Zeitgeschichte*, i (1953), 352–6.

Ng, Amy, *Nationalism and political liberty: Redlich, Namier and the crisis of empire* (Oxford, 2004).

——. 'A portrait of Sir Lewis Namier as a young socialist', *Journal of Contemporary History*, xl (2005), 621–36.

Ortolano, Guy, 'Human science or a human face? Social history and the "two cultures" controversy', *Journal of British Studies*, xliii (2004), 482–505.

Owen, J. B., 'The Namier way', *New Statesman*, 23 Jan. 1962.

Palmer, William, *Engagement with the past: the lives and works of the World War II generation of historians* (Lexington, Ky, 2001).

Parker, Christopher, *The English historical tradition since 1850* (Edinburgh, 1990).

Pavliuk, Oleksander, 'Ukrainian-Polish relations in Galicia in 1918–1919', *Journal of Ukrainian Studies*, xxiii, no. 1 (1998), 1–23.

Penkower, M. N., *Palestine in turmoil* (2 vols, New York, 2014).

Phillips, N. C., 'Namier and his method', *Political Science*, xiv (1962), 16–26.

Pisuliński, Jan, 'Nieznany list brytyjskiego historyka', *Zeszyty Historyczna*, 141 (2002), 225–32.

431

Bibliography

Plumb, J. H., 'The atomic historian', *New Statesman*, 1 July 1969.

——, *The making of an historian: the collected essays of J. H. Plumb* (Hemel Hempstead, 1988).

Prażmowska, Anita, *Poland: a modern history* (2010).

Price, J. M., 'Party, purpose and pattern: Sir Lewis Namier and his critics', *Journal of British Studies*, i, no. 1 (1961), 71–93.

Raymond, John, 'Namier, Inc.', *The doge of Dover, and other essays* (1960), 62–6.

Roorda, D. J., 'Sir Lewis Namier: een inspirerend en irriterend historicus', *Tijdschrift voor Geschiedenis*, lxxv (1962), 325–55.

Rose, Norman, *The Gentile Zionists: a study in Anglo-Zionist diplomacy, 1929–1939* (1973).

——, *Lewis Namier and Zionism* (Oxford, 1980).

——, *Chaim Weizmann: a biography* (1986).

Rousseau, G. S. *Perilous enlightenment: pre- and post-modern discourses, sexual, historical* (Manchester, 1991).

Rowse, A. L., *Historians I have known* (1955).

——, *Memories of men and women* (1980).

Royle, Trevor, *Orde Wingate: irregular soldier* (1995).

Rubinstein, W. D., *A history of Jews in the English-speaking world: Great Britain* (Basingstoke, 1996).

Rusin, Bartłomiej, 'Lewis Namier a kwestia "linii Curzona" i kształtowania się polskiej granicy wschodniej po I wojnie światowej', *Studia z Dziejów Rosji i Europy Srodkowo-Wschodniej*, xlviii (2010), 95–116.

Sanger, Clyde, *Malcolm MacDonald: bringing an end to empire* (Montreal and Kingston, Ont., 1995).

Schofield, Victoria, *Witness to history: the life of John Wheeler-Bennett* (2012).

Sedgwick, Romney, 'The Namier revolution: Sir Lewis Namier (1888–1960)', *History Today*, x (1960), 723–4.

Seton-Watson, Christopher, 'Czechs, Poles and Yugoslavs in London, 1914–1918', *L'émigration politique en Europe aux XIXe et XXe siècles; actes du colloque de Rome (3–5 Mars 1988)* (Rome, 1991), 277–93.

Seton-Watson, Hugh, and Christopher Seton-Watson, *The making of a new Europe: R. W. Seton-Watson and the last years of Austria-Hungary* (1981).

Shanes, Joshua, *Diaspora nationalism and Jewish identity in Habsburg Galicia* (Cambridge, 2012).

Shapira, Anita, *Ben-Gurion: father of modern Israel* (1971).

Sharp, Alan, 'Britain and the protection of minorities at the Paris peace conference, 1919', A. C. Hepburn (ed.), *Minorities in history: Historical Studies, xii* (1978), 170–88.

——, 'Some relevant historians – the Political Intelligence Department of the Foreign Office, 1918–1920', *Australian Journal of Politics and History*, xxxiv (1988–9), 358–68.

Sherman, A. J., *Island refuge: Britain and refugees from the Third Reich 1933–1939* (1974).

Sims, Catherine S., 'L. B. Namier (1888–)', Herman Ausubel, J. B. Brebner and E. M. Hunt (eds), *Some modern historians of Britain: essays in honor of R. L. Schuyler* (New York, 1951), 341–57.

Sisman, Adam, *A. J. P. Taylor: a biography* (paperback edn, 1995).

——, *Hugh Trevor-Roper: the biography* (2010).

Smith, Adrian, *The* New Statesman: *portrait of a political weekly, 1913–1931* (1996).

Smith, E. A., 'Sir Lewis Namier and British eighteenth-century history', *Parliamentary Affairs*, xvii (1964), 465–9.

Smyth, Jim, '"An invigorating controversy": Herbert Butterfield and the Namier school', *Eighteenth-Century Thought*, iv (2009), 347–71.

——, 'Lewis Namier, Herbert Butterfield and Edmund Burke', *Journal for Eighteenth-Century Studies*, xxxv (2011), 381–9.

——, *Cold War culture: intellectuals, the media and the practice of history* (2016).

Soffer, R. N., *Discipline and power: the university, history, and the making of an English elite, 1870–1930* (Stanford, Calif., 1994).

——, *History, historians and conservatism in Britain and America: the Great War to Thatcher and Reagan* (Oxford, 2009).

Stedman Jones, Gareth, 'History: the poverty of empiricism', Robin Blackburn (ed.), *Ideology in social science: readings in critical social* theory (1972), 96–115.

Steiner, George, 'The arts of memory', *New Yorker*, 1 Jan. 1972.

Stern, Eliyahu, *The genius: Elijah of Vilna and the making of modern Judaism* (2013).

Stone, Lawrence, *The past and the present revisited* (2005).

Sutherland, L. S., 'Sir Lewis Namier (1888–1960)', *Proceedings of the British Academy*, xlviii (1962), 371–85.

——, 'Lewis Namier and institutional history', *Annali della Fondazione Italiana per la Storia Amministriva*, iv (1967), 35–43.

Talmon, J. L., 'The ordeal of Sir Lewis Namier: the man, the historian, the Jew', *Commentary*, xxxiii (1963), 237–46.

——, 'Namier (Bernstein-Namierowski), Sir Lewis (1888–1960)', *Encyclopaedia Judica* (2nd ed., 22 vols, Farmington Hills, Md, 2007), xiv, 770–1.

Taylor, A. J. P., *A personal history* (1983).

Terry, Sarah Meiklejohn, *Poland's place in Europe: General Sikorski and the origin of the Oder-Neisse line, 1939–1943* (Princeton, 1983).

Toynbee, A. J., 'Lewis Namier, historian', *Encounter*, no. 16 (Jan. 1961), 39–43.

——, 'Sir Lewis Namier and history', *Harper's Magazine* (May 1967), 55–61.

——, *Acquaintances* (1967).

Venturi, Franco, 'Un grande storico; Sir Lewis Namier', *Il Ponte*, xiii (1957), 1046–55.

Vincent, John, *An intelligent person's guide to history* (1995).

Vital, David, *A people apart: the Jews in Europe 1789–1939* (Oxford, 1999).

Walcott, Robert, '"Sir Lewis Namier considered" considered', *Journal of British Studies*, iii (1964), 84–108.

Wasserstein, Bernard, *Britain and the Jews of Europe 1939–1945* (Oxford, 1979).

Watt, D. C., 'Sir Lewis Namier and contemporary European history', *Cambridge Review*, June 1954.

Weaver, J. R. H., *Henry William Carless Davis 1874–1928* (1933).

Weber, Thomas, *Our friend 'the enemy': elite education in Britain and Germany before World War I* (Stanford, Calif., 2007).

Wedgwood, C. V., *The last of the radicals: Josiah Wedgwood, MP* (1951).

Wendehorst, S. C., *British Jewry, Zionism, and the Jewish State, 1936–1956* (Oxford, 2012).

Whiteman, Anne, 'Lucy Stuart Sutherland 1903–1980', *Proceedings of the British Academy*, lxix (1983), 611–30.

Wierzbieniec, Wacław, 'The processes of Jewish emancipation and assimilation in the multi-ethnic city of Lviv during the nineteenth and twentieth centuries', John Czaplica (ed.), *Lviv: a city in the crosscurrents of culture* (Cambridge, Mass., 2005), 223–50.

Williams, Andrew, *Failed imagination? New world orders of the twentieth century* (Manchester, 1998).

Bibliography

Williams, Bill, *"Jews and other foreigners": Manchester and the rescue of the victims of European fascism, 1933–1940* (Manchester, 2011).

Winkler, H. R., 'Sir Lewis Namier', *Journal of Modern History*, xxxv (1963), 1–19.

Worden, Blair (ed.), *Hugh Trevor-Roper the historian* (2016).

Wrigley, Chris, *A. J. P. Taylor: radical historian of Europe* (2006).

Zięba, Andrzej, 'Historyk jako produkt historii, czyli o tym, jak Ludwik Bernstein przekształcał się w Lewisa Namiera', Adam Walaszek and Krzysztof Zamorski (eds) *Historyk i historia: studia dedykowane pamięci Prof. Mirosława Frančicia* (Cracow, 2005), 149–74.

Electronic sources

The Oxford Dictionary of National Biography (online edition: www.oxforddnb.com)

Index

There is no separate entry for Sir Lewis Namier himself, who appears in this index as LBN

Index

Austria, republic of 142, 227
  Anschluss 142, 164
  Social Democrats 142
  Socialists 97, 142
Avenues of history (1952) 9, 11, 318

Babington Smith, Constance, journalist and
  biographer 7, 302, 377
Badminton House, Gloucs. 333
Baldwin, Stanley, 1st Earl Baldwin 185–7,
  194
Balfour, Arthur, 1st earl of Balfour 158, 161,
  167, 186
  foreign secretary 91, 93, 104, 107, 116
Balfour declaration 1917 116–17, 151, 254
Balliol College *see* Oxford, University of
Bancroft, George, historian
  papers 64
Baranowska Klara (née Modzelewska), elder
  daughter of Teodora Modzelewska
  (q.v.) and niece of LBN 262, 379
Barnes, Donald G., historian 204
Barnes, Viola, historian 204
Barney, Fr Michael 382
Barrett, Rachel, suffragette 28
Barrington-Ward, R. M. ('Robin'),
  newspaper editor 295
Baum, Mrs Valerie 324
BBC
  talks about LBN 291, 392, 394
  talks by LBN 314–15, 339, 345–6, 404,
  406
Beard, Charles A., historian 64–5, 154, 156,
  183, 287, 405
Beausobre, Iulia de *see* Namier, Julia
Beausobre, Nikolai de, husband of Iulia
  (q.v.) 271
Beaverbrook, 1st Baron *see* Aitken, Max
Bedford, 11th duke of *see* Russell, Herbrand
Bedford papers
  projected edition 221
Bedford Place, Bloomsbury 27
Beer, George L., historian 63–4
Beer, Marie 23, 145, 152–3, 161
  affair with LBN 4, 141, 145
  death 273
  in England 152, 210, 273
  physical and mental decline 4, 152, 241,
  272
  in Vienna 23, 138–9, 241
Beit, Lilian (née Carter), Lady Beit 223
Beit Prize *see* Oxford, University of

Belarus *see* 'White Russia'
Belfast 327
  Queen's University 369
  Wiles Lectures 369, 387
Bell, Kenneth, historian 39, 50, 119, 134,
  199
  wife and children 134, 381
Bellot, H. H., historian 180
Beloff, Max, historian 291–2, 341
Belorussia *see* 'White Russia'
Belvoir Castle, Lincs. 333
Benda, Julien, philosopher 304
Beneš, Edvard 74, 139, 261
Ben-Gurion, David
  friendship 236, 277, 313, 377
  in Zionist movement 182, 232, 237–8, 248,
  253, 312
Bennett, John, philosopher 274
Ben Solomon, Elijah (Gaon of Vilna) 13, 19,
  46–7, 95, 361
Berenson, Bernard 359, 363, 408
Berkeley Castle, Gloucs. 333
Berlin, (Sir) Isaiah 274, 360–1, 382
  admiration for LBN 151, 413
  assessment of LBN 399, 401–2
  attitude to religion 5, 275, 313, 378
  and Julia Namier's biography 5
  reminiscences of LBN 230–1, 250, 341, 342,
  377–8
  and Weizmann Papers edition 360
Bernstein (Bernsztajn, later Niemirowska),
  Anna (née Sommerstein), mother of
  LBN 14–15, 21, 24, 40, 47, 113–14, 137,
  145, 262
Bernstein (Bernsztajn), Balbina (née
  Wilner), paternal grandmother of
  LBN 12–13
Bernstein (Bernsztajn), Debora *see*
  Rundstein, Debora
Bernstein (Bernsztajn) family 2, 12–13, 20,
  228, 262, 409
Bernstein (Bernsztajn), Jakob, paternal
  grandfather of LBN 12–13
Bernstein (Bernsztajn, later Niemirowski),
  Józef, father of LBN
  character 5, 14
  death 145–6
  education 13
  as landowner 23–4, 113–14, 137–8
  marriage 14
  occupation 14–15
  political views 15, 21, 110, 114, 117–18

436

Index

Index

Index

Index